P9-CEG-343

Clashing Views on

Global Issues

SIXTH EDITION, EXPANDED

TAKING SIDES

Clashing Views on
Global Issues

SIXTH EDITION, EXPANDED

Selected, Edited, and with Introductions by

James E. Harf
Maryville University

and

Mark Owen Lombardi
Maryville University

The McGraw-Hill Companies

Connect
Learn
Succeed™

TAKING SIDES: CLASHING VIEWS ON GLOBAL ISSUES, SIXTH EDITION, EXPANDED

Published by McGraw-Hill, a business unit of The McGraw-Hill Companies, Inc., 1221 Avenue of the Americas, New York, NY 10020. Copyright © 2010 by The McGraw-Hill Companies, Inc. All rights reserved. Previous edition(s) 2009, 2007, 2005. No part of this publication may be reproduced or distributed in any form or by any means, or stored in a database or retrieval system, without the prior written consent of The McGraw-Hill Companies, Inc., including, but not limited to, in any network or other electronic storage or transmission, or broadcast for distance learning.

Some ancillaries, including electronic and print components, may not be available to customers outside the United States.

Taking Sides® is a registered trademark of the McGraw-Hill Companies, Inc.
Taking Sides is published by the **Contemporary Learning Series** group within the McGraw-Hill Higher Education division.

1 2 3 4 5 6 7 8 9 0 DOC/DOC 1 0 9 8 7 6 5 4 3 2 1 0

MHID: 0-07-738192-0
ISBN: 978-0-07-738192-9
ISSN: 1536-3317

Managing Editor: *Larry Loeppke*
Director, Specialized Production: *Faye Schilling*
Senior Developmental Editor: *Jill Meloy*
Editorial Coordinator: *Mary Foust*
Permissions Coordinator: *Rita Hingtgen*
Senior Marketing Manager: *Julie Keck*
Senior Marketing Communications Specialist: *Mary Klein*
Marketing Coordinator: *Alice Link*
Project Manager: *Erin Melloy*
Design Specialist: *Brenda A. Rolwes*
Cover Graphics: *Rick D. Noel*

Compositor: MPS Limited, A Macmillan Company
Cover Image: © Corbis/Royalty Free

Library of Congress Cataloging-in-Publication Data

Main entry under title:
  Taking sides: clashing views on controversial global issues/selected, edited, and with
  introductions by James E. Harf and Mark Owen Lombardi.—6th ed., expanded.

Includes bibliographical references and index.
1. Globalization. 2. International relations, 3. Global environmental change. 4. Population.
5. Emigration and immigration. I. Harf, James E., *ed.* II. Lombardi Mark Owen, *ed.* III. Series.
303

Editors/Academic Advisory Board

Members of the Academic Advisory Board are instrumental in the final selection of articles for each edition of TAKING SIDES. Their review of articles for content, level, and appropriateness provides critical direction to the editors and staff. We think that you will find their careful consideration well reflected in this volume.

TAKING SIDES: Clashing Views on GLOBAL ISSUES

Sixth Edition, Expanded

EDITORS

James E. Harf
Maryville University
        and
Mark Owen Lombardi
Maryville University

ACADEMIC ADVISORY BOARD MEMBERS

Rafis Abazov
Columbia University

Robert Abu Shanab
University of Nevada - Las Vegas

Lisa Alfredson
University of Pittsburgh

David Allen
Temple University, Philadelphia

Lawrence Backlund
Philadelphia University

Alice Baldwin-Jones
CUNY/Sophie Davis School of Biomedical Education

Mary Ellen Batiuk
Wilmington College

Elson Boles
Saginaw Valley State University

Carl L. Boss
Hiram College

Gloria C. Cox
University of North Texas

Adriana Crocker
University of Illinois

Graciella Cruz-Taura
Florida Atlantic University

Ajit Daniel
Winona State University

Rick Davis
Brigham Young University

Nick Despo
Thiel College

Thomas P. Dolan
Columbus State University

Gary Donato
Mass Bay Community College

June Teufel Dreyer
University of Miami

Wilton Duncan
ASA Institute

Charles Ellenbaum
Wheaton College

Tahmineh Entessar
Webster University

Mohammed K. Farouk
Florida International University

Femi Ferreira
Hutchinson Community College

Erich Frankland
Casper College

Charles Fuller
Triton College

Steve Garvey
Muskegon Community College

Richard W. Griffin
Ferris State University

Nicholas Gurney
Muskegon Community College

Editors/Academic Advisory Board continued

Noreen Hannon
North Carolina A&T State University

Michael J. Harkins
William Rainey Harper College

Elizabeth Hegeman
John Jay College

Rolf Hemmerling
Webster University

Robert M. Hordon
Rutgers University

James Hufferd
Des Moines Area Community College

Maria Ilcheva
Florida International University

Kunihiko Imai
Elmira College

Jean-Gabriel Jolivet
Southwestern College

Sukanya Kemp
University of Akron

Vishnu Khade
Manchester Community College

Tadesse Kidane-Mariam
Edinboro University of Akron

Vani V. Kotcherlakota
University of Nebraska-Kearney

Lorri Krebs
Salem State College

Azzedine Layachi
Saint John's University

Howard Lehman
University of Utah

Carmela Lutmar
Princeton University

Richard M. Martin
Gustavus Adolphus College

Michael McCarthy
Keene State College

Linda McFarland
Saint Joseph's College

Silva Meybatyan
University of the District of Columbia

John Miller
Wheaton College

Kristine Mitchell
Dickinson College

Maggi M. Morehouse
University of South Carolina

Kay Murnan
Ozarks Technical Community College

Tim Muth
Florida Institute of Technology

Raphael Chijioke Njoku
University of Louisville

Mujahid Nyahuma
Rowan University

Nikitah Okembe-RA Imani
James Madison University

Charles Perabeau
Olivet Nazarene University

Ray Polchow
Zane State College

Margaret Power
Illinois Institute of Technology

Curt Robinson
California State University

Abdoulaye Saine
Miami University

James C. Saku
Frostburg State University

Cheryl J. Serrano
Lynn University

Barbara A. Sherry
Northeastern Illinois University

Samuel Stanton
Grove City College

Paul Tesch
Spokane Community College

Kishor Thanawala
Villanova University

Kumru Toktamis
Brooklyn College

Kenneth Wade
Champlain College

Christa Wallace
University of Alaska-Anchorage

Howard Warshawsky
Roanoke College

Julie Weinert
Southern Illinois University–Carbondale

Mark D. Woodhull
Schreiner University

Tetsuji Yamada
Rutgers University

Jeff Zuiderveen
Columbus State University

Preface

This volume reflects the changing nature of the contemporary world in which we live. Not only are we now witnessing a dramatic leap in the *scope* of global change, but we are also experiencing a *rate* of change in the world unparalleled in recorded history. Change in the international system is not a new phenomenon. Since the creation in the early 1500s of a Euro-centric world system of sovereign nation-states that dominated political, economic, and social events throughout the known world, global change has been with us. But earlier manifestations of change were characterized by infrequent bursts of system-changing episodes followed by long periods of "normalcy," where the processes and structures of the international system demonstrated regularity or consistency.

First, the Catholic church sought to recapture its European dominance and glory during the Middle Ages in a last gasp effort to withstand challenges against its rule from a newly developed secularized and urbanized mercantile class, only to be pushed aside in a devastating continental struggle known as the Thirty Years' War and relegated to irrelevant status by the resultant Treaty of Westphalia in 1648. A century and a half later, the global system was again challenged, this time by a French general turned emperor, Napoleon Bonaparte, who sought to export the newly created utopian vision of the French Revolution beyond the boundaries of France to the rest of the world. Napoleon was eventually repelled by a coalition of major powers intent on preserving the world as these countries knew it.

Soon nineteenth-century Europe was being transformed by the intrusion of the Industrial Revolution on the daily lives of average citizens and national leaders alike. Technological advances enhanced the capacity of countries to dramatically increase their military capability, achieving the ability to project such power far beyond their national borders in a short time. Other threats to the existing world order also emerged. Nationalism began to capture the hearts of various country leaders who sought to impart such loyalties to their subjects, while new ideologies competed with one another as well as with nationalism to create a thirst for alternative world models to the existing nation-state system. The result was another failed attempt by a European power, this time Germany, to expand its influence via a major war, later to be called World War I, throughout the continent. The postwar map of Europe reflected major consequences of the abortive German effort.

Almost immediately, the international system was threatened by a newly emergent virulent ideology of the left intent on taking over the world. Communism had gained a foothold in Russia, and soon its leaders were eager to transport it across the continent to the far corners of the globe, threatening to destroy the existing economic order and, by definition, its political counterpart. Shortly thereafter, a competing virulent ideology from the right, fascism, emerged. Under its manipulation by a new German leader, Adolph Hitler, the international system was once again greatly threatened. Six long years of war and unthinkable levels of devastation and destruction followed, until the fascist threat was turned back. The communist threat persisted, however, until late in the millennium, when it also virtually disappeared, felled by its own weaknesses and excesses.

In the interim, new challenges to global order appeared in the form of a set of issues like no other during the 500-year history of the nation-state system. The nature of these global issues and the pace at which they both landed on the global agenda and then expanded were to quickly affect the international system. This new agenda took root in the late 1960s, when astute observers began to identify disquieting trends: quickening population growth in the poorer sectors of the globe, growing disruptions in the world's ability to feed its population, increasing shortfalls in required resources, and expanding evidence of negative environmental impacts, such as a variety of pollution evils. Some of these issues—like decreasing levels of adequate supplies of food, energy, and water—emerged as a result of both increased population growth and increased per capita levels of consumption. Dramatic population increases, in turn, resulted in changes in global population dynamics—increasing aged population or massive new migration patterns. The emergence of this set of new issues was soon followed by another phenomenon, globalization, which emphasized increasing speedy flows of information through innovative technology and a resultant diffusion of regional cultures throughout the globe and the emergence of a global macro-culture. Globalization not only affected the nature of the international system in these general ways but also influenced both the manner in which these global issues impacted the system and how the latter addressed them.

The major consequence of the confluence of these events is the extent to which and the shortened time frame in which the change affects them. No longer is the change measured in centuries or even decades. It is now measured in years or even months. No longer are likely solutions to such problems simple, known, confined to a relatively small part of the globe, and capable of being achieved by the efforts of one or a few national governments. Instead, these global issues are characterized by increased rapidity of change, increased complexity, increased geographical impact, increased resistance to solution, and increased fluidity.

One only has to compare the world as it existed when these issues first appeared to the world of today to grasp the difference. When students first began to study these issues in the early 1960s, their written analysis was accomplished either by putting pen to pad or by engaging an unwieldy typewriter. Their experience with a computer was limited to watching a moon landing through the eyes of NASA Mission Control. The use of phones was relegated to a location where a cord could be plugged into a wall socket. Their written correspondence with someone beyond their immediate location had a stamp on it. Their reading of news, both serious and frivolous, occurred via a newspaper. Visual news invaded their space in 30-minute daily segments from three major TV networks. Being entertained required some effort, usually away from the confines of their homes or dorm rooms. Today, of course, the personal computer and its companion, the Internet, have transformed the way students learn, the way they communicate with one another, and the way they entertain themselves. Facebook and Twitter have joined our vocabulary.

The age of globalization has accelerated, affecting and transforming trends that began over three decades ago. No longer are nation-states the only actors on the global stage. Moreover, their position of dominance is increasingly challenged by an array of other actors—international governmental organizations, private international groups, multinational corporations, and important individuals—who might be better equipped to address newly emerging issues (or who might also serve as the source of yet other problems).

An even more recent phenomenon is the unleashing of ethnic pride, which manifests itself in both positive and negative ways. The history of post–Cold War conflict is a history of intrastate, ethnically driven violence that has torn apart those countries that have been unable to deal effectively with the changes brought on by the end of the Cold War. The most insidious manifestation of this emphasis on ethnicity is the emergence of terrorist groups who use religion and other aspects of ethnicity to justify bringing death and destruction on their perceived enemies. As national governments attempt to cope with this latest phenomenon, they too are changing the nature of war and violence. The global agenda's current transformation, brought about by globalization, demands that our attention turn toward the latter's consequences.

The recent economic collapse, or what some now call "the Great Recession," is evidence of this rapid globalization. Economic shifts were greatly accelerated throughout the global community by technology, interdependence, and connectivity such that governments, analysts, and the public at large were unable to comprehend the destabilizing events as they happened. Further, relations between states such as Russia, China, and the United States rapidly altered as a result.

The format of *Taking Sides: Clashing Views on Controversial Global Issues*, Sixth Edition, Expanded follows the successful formula of other books in the Taking Sides series. The book begins with an introduction to the emergence of global issues, the new age of globalization, and the effect that 9/11, the current global economic crisis, and a reemerging Russia—as well as the international community's response to these events—that characterizes the first decade of the twentieth century. It then addresses 22 current global issues grouped into four units. Population takes center stage in Unit 1 because it not only represents a global issue by itself, but it also affects the parameters of most other global issues. Population growth, aging, location, and policy making are considered. Unit 2 addresses a range of problems associated with global resources and their environmental impact. Units 3 and 4 feature issues borne out of the emerging agenda of the twenty-first century. The former unit examines widely disparate expanding forces and movements across national boundaries, such as global pandemics and human trafficking, as well as the contemporary global economic crisis. Unit 4 focuses on new security issues in the post-Cold War and post-September 11 eras, such as whether the world is headed for a nuclear 9/11 or whether China will become the next superpower.

Each issue has two readings, one pro and one con. The readings are preceded by an issue *Introduction* that sets the stage for the debate and briefly describes the two readings. Each issue concludes with a *Postscript* that summarizes the issues, suggests further avenues for thought, and provides suggestions for further reading. At the back of the book is a listing of all the *contributors to this volume,* with a brief biographical sketch of each of the prominent figures whose views are debated here.

Changes to this edition   This expanded sixth edition represents a significant revision. Four of the 22 issues are completely new: "Is the Global Economic Crisis a Failure of Capitalism?" (Issue 15); and "Are We in a New Cold War?" (Issue 16). One other issue is rephrased: "Should the International Community Refocus on Programs to Help Developing Countries Curb Population Growth?" (Issue 2). In 7 of the remaining 17 issues, one or both selections were replaced to bring the issues up to date.

A word to the instructor: An instructor's manual with test questions (multiple choice and essay) is available through the publisher for the instructor using Taking Sides in the classroom. A general guidebook, *Using Taking Sides in the Classroom,* which discusses methods and techniques for integrating the pro–con approach into any classroom setting, is also available. An online version of *Using Taking Sides in the Classroom* and a correspondence service for Taking Sides adopters can be found at http://www.mhcls.com/usingts/. *Taking Sides: Clashing Views on Global Issues* is only one title in the Taking Sides Series. If you are interested in seeing the table of contents for any of the other titles, please visit the Taking Sides Web site at http://www/mhcls.com/takingsides/.

James E. Harf
Maryville University

Mark Owen Lombardi
Maryville University

To my daughter, Marie: May your world conquer those global issues left unresolved by my generation. (J.E.H.)

For Betty and Marty, who instilled a love of education and a need to explore the world. (M.O.L.)

Contents In Brief

Contents

This *Business Week* cover story outlines the aging of the population in both the developed world and the newly emerging economies, suggesting that the time for action is now. This Rand Corporation study suggests that because of declining fertility, European populations are either growing more slowly or have actually begun to decline. Although these trends "portend difficult times ahead," European governments should be able to confront these challenges successfully.

Divya Abhat, editor of *E/The Environmental Magazine,* and colleagues suggest that the world's cities suffer from environmental ills, among them pollution, poverty, fresh water shortages, and disease. The UNFPA 2007 Report suggests that cities, in fact, facilitate a number of desirable conditions, such as gender-equitable change, more diverse employment possibilities, more economic well-being and security for women, women's empowerment, and access to better health care, among other positive changes.

Environmental journalist Ronald Bailey in his review of the Bjørn Lomborg controversial book, *The Skeptical Environmentalist: Measuring the Real State of the World* (Cambridge University Press, 2001), argues that "An environmentalist gets it right," suggesting that finally someone has taken the environmental doomsdayers to task for their shoddy use of science. Bioscientist David Pimentel takes to task Bjørn Lomborg's findings, accusing him of selective use of data to support his conclusions.

Nansen G. Saleri, president and CEO of Quantum Reservoir Input and the oil industry's preeminent authority on the issue, suggests that the world is "nowhere close to reaching a peak in global oil supplies." He argues that the future transition to oil alternatives will be the result of their superiority rather than the diminishing supply of oil. Lester R. Brown, founder and president of Earth Policy Institute, suggests that there has been a "pronounced loss of momentum" in the growth of oil production, a likely result of demand outpacing discoveries, leading to declining oil production prospects.

This 2007 report by the UN's Office on Drugs and Crime provides "robust evidence" that "drug control is working" and "the world drug problem is being contained." Ethan Nadelmann argues that prohibition has failed by not treating the "demand for drugs as a market, and addicts as patients," resulting in "boosting the profits of drug lords, and fostering narcostates that would frighten Al Capone."

The document from the World Health Organization lays out a comprehensive program of action for individual countries, the international community, and WHO to address the next influenza pandemic. H.T. Goranson, a former top national scientist with the U.S. government, describes the grave dangers posed by global pandemics and highlights flaws in the international community's ability to respond.

Janie Chuang, practitioner-in-residence at the America University Washington College of Law, suggests that governments have been finally motivated to take action against human traffickers as a consequence of the concern over national security implications of forced human labor movement and the involvement of transnational criminal syndicates. Dina Francesca Haynes, associate professor of law at the New England School of Law, argues that none of the models underlying domestic legislation to deal with human traffickers is "terribly effective" in addressing the issue effectively.

Meredith and Hoppough argue that the data supports the conclusion that globalization works for both rich and poor. They particularly point to the growing middle class in many countries throughout Asia, Africa, and Latin America, to support this conclusion. Weber et al. argue that globalization and the American predominance that drives it amplify a myriad of evils, including terrorism, global warming, and interethnic conflict, creating a less stable and less just world community.

Allan Brian Ssenyonga, a Ugandan freelance writer for *The New York Times*, suggests that America is now selling its culture to the rest of the world "as a new and improved product of what we (the world) have as a culture." He decries the negative effects of the global spread of many things American. Tyler Cowen, a George Mason University professor of economics, argues that the "complaint of '(American) cultural imperialism' is looking increasingly implausible" as the evidence suggests that (1) local culture commands loyalty, and (2) cultural influences come from many external cultures, not just from America.

Katsuhito Iwai, professor of economics at the University of Tokyo, argues that the current economic collapse is a sign of the inherent instability of global capitalism. He argues that capitalism's failure in this crisis is inherent because capitalism is based on speculation and therefore belief or faith in the strength of the system and its various parts. Dani Rodrik, professor of international political economy at Harvard University's John F. Kennedy School of Government, contends that the current economic downturn is not a sign of capitalism's failure but rather its need for reinvention and adaptation. Rodrik argues that this is precisely why capitalism will survive and thrive because it is so changeable based on new trends and conditions.

Stephen F. Cohen, professor of Russian studies at New York University, suggests that U.S.–Russian relations have "deteriorated so badly they should now be understood as a new cold war—or possibly a continuation of the old one." He argues that the origins of this circumstance can be found in the attitudes and policies of both the Clinton and Bush administrations. Stephen Kotkin, professor of history and director of the Program in Russian Studies at Princeton University, argues that Russia has not reverted to totalitarianism under Putin and his successor. Rather, it is a combination of a closed unstable political system and a growing economic power that poses a threat to the West for that reason, not because its poses a military threat.

Issue 17.   Are We Headed Toward a Nuclear 9/11?   321

YES: **Brian Michael Jenkins,** from "Terrorists Can Think Strategically: Lessons Learned from the Mumbai Attacks," Rand Corporation (January 2009)   *323*

NO: **Graham Allison,** from "Time to Bury a Dangerous Legacy—Part I," *Yale Global Online* (March 14, 2008)   *327*

Brian Michael Jenkins, senior advisor to the President of the Rand Corporation, in testimony before the U.S. Senate Committee on Homeland Security and Governmental Affairs, posited that a team of terrorists could be inserted into the United States and carry out a Mumbai-style attack as terrorism has "increasingly become an effective strategic weapon." Graham Allison, Harvard professor and director of the Belfer Center for Science and International Affairs, affirms that we are not likely to experience a nuclear 9/11 because "nuclear terrorism is preventable by a feasible, affordable agenda of actions that . . . would shrink the risk of nuclear terrorism to nearly zero."

Issue 18.   Is Religious and Cultural Extremism a Global Security Threat?   331

YES: **Hussein Solomon,** from "Global Security in the Age of Religious Extremism," *PRISM* (August 2006)   *333*

NO: **Shibley Telhami,** from "Testimony Before the House Armed Services Committee: Between Terrorism and Religious Extremism" (November 3, 2005)   *342*

Solomon argues that when religious extremism, which is a security threat in and of itself, is merged with state power, the threat to global security is potentially catastrophic and must be met with clear and uncompromising policies. He contends that this is present across all religions, and he uses both a born-again George Bush and a fundamentalist Mahmoud Ahmadinejad as his examples. Telhami, on the other hand, does not argue that religious extremism is the threat, but rather that global security threats are from political groups with political agendas and not extremism as such.

Issue 19.   Is a Nuclear Iran a Global Security Threat?   347

YES: **U.S. House of Representatives Permanent Select Committee on Intelligence, Subcommittee on Intelligence Policy,** from "Recognizing Iran as a Strategic Threat: An Intelligence Challenge for the United States" (August 23, 2006)   *349*

NO: **Office of Director of National Intelligence,** from "Iran: Nuclear Intentions and Capabilities," *National Intelligence Estimate* (November 2007)   *373*

The House Select Committee concludes that Iran's weapons program and missile development technology combined with the nature of fundamentalist regimes pose a grave security threat and thus must be addressed. The National Intelligence Estimate contends that Iran is not a global security threat because they have decided to suspend their nuclear weapons program and would not be able to develop the capacity for such weapons until at least 2015.

Yao analyzes the current state of the Chinese economy and policy and postulates several possible scenarios for development. Ultimately, Yao surmises that China will develop as the next superpower by the mid-twenty-first century. Bardhan argues that there are many variables and factors that can and will hinder China's development into a superpower, including vast poverty, weak infrastructure, and China's authoritarian government.

The International Strategy for Disaster Reduction Secretariat, a unit within the United Nations, suggests that countries are making "significant progress" in strengthening their capacities to address past deficiencies and gaps in their disaster preparedness and response. At the center of progress is the plan, *Hyogo Framework for Action 2005–2015*, which is aimed at reducing human and nonhuman disaster losses. David Rothkopf, president of Garten Rothkopf (an international consulting agency) and a member of former president Bill Clinton's international trade team, argues that the efforts of international organizations to prevent natural disasters from escalating into megadisasters "have fallen short of what is required."

Fareed Zakaria argues through the acts of moderate Muslims across the Islamic world, "We have turned the corner on the war between extremism and the West and . . . now we are in a new phase of clean up and rebuilding of relationships." His argument rests on the actions of Muslim regimes in Saudi Arabia, Pakistan, and Indonesia who are fighting back against jihadism, engaging in military and political policies that are marginalizing extremists and consequently winning the war. Scott Stewart contends that despite Western victories against al-Qaeda based in the Afghan–Pakistan border region, regional groups and cells have taken up the slack and the threat of extremism and jihad is still strong and ominous. He focuses on the work of these groups in Somalia, Yemen, and North Africa to illustrate this continued fight.

Correlation Guide

The *Taking Sides* series presents current issues in a debate-style format designed to stimulate student interest and develop critical thinking skills. Each issue is thoughtfully framed with an issue summary, an issue introduction, and a postscript. The pro and con essays—selected for their liveliness and substance—represent the arguments of leading scholars and commentators in their fields.

Taking Sides: Clashing Views on Global Issues, 6/e, Expanded, is an easy-to-use reader that presents issues on important topics such as *global population, global resources and the environment, expanding global forces and movements, and the new global security dilemma.* For more information on *Taking Sides* and other *McGraw-Hill Contemporary Learning Series* titles, visit www.mhhe.com/cls.

This convenient guide matches the issues in **Taking Sides: Global Issues, 6/e, Expanded**, with the corresponding chapters in one of our best-selling McGraw-Hill Political Science textbooks by Rourke/Boyer.

Taking Sides: Global Issues, 6/e, Expanded	International Politics on the World Stage, Brief, 8/e by Rourke/Boyer
Issue 1: Are Declining Growth Rates Rather Than Rapid Population Growth Today's Major Global Population Problem?	**Chapter 1:** Thinking and Caring about World Politics **Chapter 6:** Power and the National States: The Traditional Structure **Chapter 12:** Preserving and Enhancing the Global Commons
Issue 2: Should the International Community Refocus on Programs to Help Developing Countries Curb Population Growth?	**Chapter 12:** Preserving and Enhancing the Global Commons
Issue 3: Is Global Aging in the Developed World a Major Problem?	**Chapter 6:** Power and the National States: The Traditional Structure **Chapter 12:** Preserving and Enhancing the Global Commons
Issue 4: Does Global Urbanization Lead Primarily to Undesirable Consequences?	
Issue 5: Do Environmentalists Overstate Their Case?	**Chapter 12:** Preserving and Enhancing the Global Commons
Issue 6: Should the World Continue to Rely on Oil as a Major Source of Energy?	**Chapter 6:** Power and the National States: The Traditional Structure **Chapter 10:** Globalization in the World Economy **Chapter 11:** Global Economic Competition and Cooperation **Chapter 12:** Preserving and Enhancing the Global Commons
Issue 7: Will the World Be Able to Feed Itself in the Foreseeable Future?	**Chapter 8:** International Law and Human Rights: An Alternative Approach **Chapter 12:** Preserving and Enhancing the Global Commons

(Continued)

Taking Sides: Global Issues, 6/e, Expanded	International Politics on the World Stage, Brief, 8/e by Rourke/Boyer
Issue 8: Is the Threat of Global Warming Real?	**Chapter 1:** Thinking and Caring about World Politics **Chapter 12:** Preserving and Enhancing the Global Commons
Issue 9: Is the Threat of a Global Water Shortage Real?	**Chapter 12:** Preserving and Enhancing the Global Commons
Issue 10: Can the Global Community "Win" the Drug War?	
Issue 11: Is the International Community Adequately Prepared to Address Global Health Pandemics?	**Chapter 8:** International Law and Human Rights: An Alternative Approach **Chapter 10:** Globalization in the World Economy
Issue 12: Do Adequate Strategies Exist to Combat Human Trafficking?	**Chapter 8:** International Law and Human Rights: An Alternative Approach
Issue 13: Is Globalization a Positive Development for the World Community?	**Chapter 2:** The Evolution of World Politics **Chapter 5:** Globalization and Transnationalism: The Alternative Orientation **Chapter 7:** International Organization: An Alternative Structure **Chapter 10:** Globalization in the World Economy **Chapter 12:** Preserving and Enhancing the Global Commons
Issue 14: Is the World a Victim of American Cultural Imperialism?	**Chapter 8:** International Law and Human Rights: An Alternative Approach
Issue 15: Is the Global Economic Crisis a Failure of Capitalism?	
Issue 16: Are We in a New Cold War?	**Chapter 9:** Pursuing Security
Issue 17: Are We Headed Toward a Nuclear 9/11?	**Chapter 9:** Pursuing Security
Issue 18: Is Religious and Cultural Extremism a Global Security Threat?	**Chapter 4:** Nationalism: The Traditional Orientation **Chapter 5:** Globalization and Transnationalism: The Alternative Orientation **Chapter 9:** Pursuing Security
Issue 19: Is a Nuclear Iran a Global Security Threat?	**Chapter 3:** Level of Analysis **Chapter 6:** Power and the National States: The Traditional Structure **Chapter 9:** Pursuing Security
Issue 20: Will China Be the Next Superpower?	**Chapter 1:** Thinking and Caring about World Politics **Chapter 2:** The Evolution of World Politics
Issue 21: Is the International Community Making Progress in Addressing Natural Disasters?	**Chapter 8:** International Law and Human Rights: An Alternative Approach **Chapter 12:** Preserving and Enhancing the Global Commons
Issue 22: Has Al-Qaeda and Its Jihad against the United States Been Defeated?	**Chapter 9:** Pursuing Security

Introduction

Global Issues in the Twenty-First Century

James E. Harf

Mark Owen Lombardi

Threats of the New Millennium

As the new millennium dawned, the world witnessed two very different events whose impacts are far reaching, profound, and in many ways shape the discourse of global issues. One episode was the tragedy of 9/11, a series of incidents that ushered in a new era of terrorism. It burst upon the international scene with the force of a mega-catastrophe, occupying virtually every waking moment of national and global leaders throughout the world and seizing the attention of the rest of the planet's citizens who contemplated both the immediate implications and the long-term effects of a U.S. response. The focused interest of national policymakers was soon transformed into a war on terrorism, while average citizens sought to cope with changes brought on by both the tragic events of September 2001 and the global community's response to them. Both governmental leaders and citizens continue to address the consequences of this first intrusion of the new millennium on a world now far different in many ways since the pre-9/11 era. Unfortunately, as the world inches toward the end of the millennium's first decade, other challenges to global welfare and security have emerged. At the global level, a severe financial crisis has begun to force world leaders to question the major tenets of contemporary capitalism. At the national level, a reemerging Russian presence based on its flexing of its new economic muscles backed by a growing military might has brought back fears of a new Cold War.

The second event at the beginning of the millennium was less dramatic and certainly did not receive the same fanfare, but still has both short- and long-term ramifications for the global community in the twenty-first century. This was the creation of a set of ambitious millennium development goals by the United Nations. In September 2000, 189 national governments committed to eight major goals in an initiative known as the UN Millennium Development Goals (MDG): eradicate extreme poverty and hunger; achieve universal primary education; promote gender equality and empower women; reduce child mortality; improve maternal health; combat HIV/AIDS, malaria, and other diseases; ensure environmental sustainability; and develop a global partnership for development. This initiative was important not only because the UN was setting an actionable 15-year agenda against a relatively new set of global issues but also because it signified a major change in how the international community would henceforth address such problems confronting human-kind. The new initiative represented recognition of: (1) shared responsibility between rich and poor nations for solving such problems; (2) a link between goals; (3) the paramount role to be played by national governments in the process; and (4) the need for measurable outcome indicators of success. The UN Millennium Development Goals initiative went virtually unnoticed by much of the public, although governmental decision-makers involved with the United Nations understood its significance.

These two major events, although vastly different, symbolize the world in which we now find ourselves, a world far more complex and more violent than either the earlier one characterized by the Cold War struggle between the United States and the Soviet Union, or the post-Cold War era of the 1990s, where global and national leaders struggled to identify and then find their proper place in the post-Cold War world order. Consider the first event, the 9/11 tragedy. It reminds us all that the use and abuse of power in pursuit of political goals in earlier centuries is still a viable option for those throughout the world who believe themselves disadvantaged because of various political, economic, or social conditions and structures. The only difference is the perpetrators' choice of military hardware and strategy. Formally declared wars fought by regular national military forces committed (at least on paper) to the tenets of just war theory have now been replaced by a plethora of "quasi-military tactics" whose defining characteristics conjure up terrorism, perpetrated by individuals without attachments to a regular military and/or without allegiance to a national government and country, and who do not hesitate to put ordinary citizens in harm's way. At the same time, a few rogue states have opted for more bellicose approaches to inter-nation behavior, whether seeking nuclear weapons or choosing to use natural resources as a weapon.

On the other hand, the second event of the new century, the UN Millennium Goals initiative, symbolizes the other side of the global coin, the recognition that the international community is also beset with a number of problems unrelated to military actions or national security, at least in a direct sense. Rather, the past three or four decades have witnessed the emergence and thrust to prominence a number of new problems relating to social, economic, and environmental characteristics of the citizens that inhabit this planet. These problems impact the basic quality of life of global inhabitants in ways very different from the scourges of military violence. Yet they are just as dangerous and just as threatening. And they also unite us as global citizens in the same way that terrorism separates us. At the heart of this global change affecting the global system and its inhabitants for good or for ill is a phenomenon called globalization.

The Age of Globalization

The Cold War era, marked by the domination of two superpowers in the decades following the end of World War II, has given way to a new era called globalization. This new epoch is characterized by a dramatic shrinking of the globe in terms of travel and communication, increased participation in global policymaking by an expanding array of national and nonstate actors, and an exploding volume of problems with ever-growing consequences. While the tearing down of the

Berlin Wall almost two decades ago dramatically symbolized the end of the Cold War era, the creation of the Internet, with its ability to connect around the world, and the fallen World Trade Center, with its dramatic illustration of vulnerability, symbolize the new paradigm of integration and violence.

Globalization is a fluid and complex phenomenon that manifests itself in thousands of wondrous as well as disturbing ways. In the past couple of decades, national borders have shrunk or disappeared, with a resultant increase in the movement of ideas, products, resources, finances, and people throughout the globe. This reality has brought with it great advances and challenges. For example, the ease with which people and objects move throughout the globe has greatly magnified fears like the spread of disease. The term "epidemic" has been replaced by the phrase "global pandemic," as virulent scourges unleashed in one part of the globe now have greater potential to find their way to the far corners of the planet. The world has also come to fear an expanded potential for terrorism, as new technologies combined with increasing cultural friction and socioeconomic disparities have conspired to make the world far less safe than it had been. The pistol that killed the Austrian Archduke in Sarajevo in 1914, ushering in World War I, has been replaced by the jumbo jet used as a missile to bring down the World Trade Center, snuffing out the lives of thousands of innocent victims. We now live in an era of global reach for both good and ill, where a small group or an individual can touch the hearts of people around the world with acts of kindness or can shatter their dreams with acts of terror.

This increase in the movement of information and ideas has ushered in global concerns over cultural imperialism and religious/ethnic wars. The ability both to retrieve and to disseminate information in the contemporary era will have an impact in this century as great as, if not greater than, the telephone, radio, and television in the last century. The potential for global good or ill is mind-boggling. Finally, traditional notions of great-power security embodied in the Cold War rivalry have given way to concerns about terrorism, genocide, nuclear proliferation, cultural conflict, and the diminishing role of international law.

Globalization heightens our awareness of a vast array of global issues that will challenge individuals as well as governmental and nongovernmental actors. Everyone has become a global actor and so has policy impact. This text seeks to identify those issues that are central to the discourse on the impact of globalization. The issues in this volume provide a broad overview of the mosaic of global issues that will affect students' daily lives.

What Is a Global Issue?

We begin by addressing the basic characteristics of a *global issue*.[1] By definition, the word *issue* suggests disagreement along several related dimensions:

1. whether a problem exists and how it comes about;
2. the characteristics of the problem;

---

[1]The characteristics are extracted from James E. Harf and B. Thomas Trout, *The Politics of Global Resources,* Duke University Press, 1986. pp. 12–28.

3. the preferred future alternatives or solutions; and/or
4. how these preferred futures are to be obtained.

These problems are real, vexing, and controversial, because policymakers bring to their analyses different historical experiences, values, goals, and objectives. These differences impede and may even prevent successful problem solving. In short, the key ingredient of an issue is disagreement.

The word *global* in the phrase *global issue* is what makes the set of problems confronting the human race today far different from those that challenged earlier generations. Historically, problems were confined to a village, city, or region. The capacity of the human race to fulfill its daily needs was limited to a much smaller space: the immediate environment. In 1900, 90 percent of all humanity was born, lived, and died within a 50-mile radius. Today, a third of the world's population travel to one or more countries. In the United States, 75 percent of people move at least 100 miles away from their homes and most travel to places their grandparents could only dream about.

What does this mobility mean? It suggests that a vast array of issues are now no longer only local or national but global in scope, including but not limited to food resources, trade, energy, health care, the environment, disease, conflict, cultural rivalry, populism, and nuclear Armageddon.

The character of these issues is thus different from those of earlier eras. First, they transcend national boundaries and impact virtually every corner of the globe. In effect, these issues help make national borders increasingly meaningless. Environmental pollution or poisonous gases do not recognize or respect national borders. Birds carrying the avian flu have no knowledge of political boundaries.

Second, these new issues cannot be resolved by the autonomous action of a single actor, be it a national government, international organization, or multinational corporation. A country cannot guarantee its own energy or food security without participating in a global energy or food system.

Third, these issues are characterized by a wide array of value systems. To a family in the developing world, giving birth to a fifth or sixth child may contribute to the family's immediate economic well-being. But to a research scholar at the United Nations Population Fund, the consequence of such an action multiplied across the entire developing world leads to expanding poverty and resource depletion.

Fourth, these issues will not go away. They require specific policy action by a consortium of local, national, and international leaders. Simply ignoring the issue cannot eliminate the threat of chemical or biological terrorism, for example. If global warming does exist, it will not disappear unless specific policies are developed and implemented.

These issues are also characterized by their persistence over time. The human race has developed the capacity to manipulate its external environment and, in so doing, has created a host of opportunities and challenges. The accelerating pace of technological change suggests that global issues will proliferate and will continue to challenge human beings throughout the next millennium.

In the final analysis, however, a global issue is defined as such only through mutual agreement by a host of actors within the international community. Some may disagree about the nature, severity, or presence of a given issue. These concerns then become areas of focus after a significant number of actors (states, international organizations, the United Nations, and others) begin to focus systematic and organized attention on the issue itself.

Defining the Global Issues Agenda

The election of President Barak Obama has opened up opportunities for the United States to adopt differing policies to the new global agenda. Although it is still early in the new administration, already there are signs of differing approaches to issues such as terrorism, civil conflict, nuclear proliferation, and resource use. The long-term impacts of these changes have yet to be determined.

The Nexus of Global Issues and Globalization

Since 1989, the world has been caught in the maelstrom of globalization. Throughout the 1990s and into the twenty-first century, scholars and policy-makers have struggled to define this new era. As the early years of the new century ushered in a different and heightened level of violence, a sense of urgency emerged. At first, some analyzed the new era in terms of the victory of Western or American ideals, the dominance of global capitalism, and the spread of democracy versus the use of religious fanaticism by the have-nots of the world as a ploy to rearrange power within the international system. But recent events call into question assumptions about Western victory or the dominance of capitalism. Others have defined this new era simply in terms of the multiplicity of actors now performing on the world stage, noting how states and their sovereignty have declined in importance and impact vis-à-vis others such as multinational corporations and nongovernmental groups like Greenpeace and Amnesty International. Still others have focused on the vital element of technology and its impact on communications, information storage and retrieval, global exchange, and attitudes, culture, and values.

Whether globalization reflects one, two, or all of these characteristics is not as important as the fundamental realization that globalization is the dominant element of a new era in international politics. The globalization revolution now shapes and dictates the agenda. To argue otherwise is frankly akin to insisting on using a rotary phone in an iPhone world. This new period is characterized by several basic traits that greatly impact the definition, analysis, and solution of global issues. They include the following:

- an emphasis on information technology;
- the increasing speed of information and idea flows;
- the ability of global citizens to access information at rapidly growing rates and thus empower themselves for good or for ill;
- a need for greater sophistication and expertise to manage such flows;

- the control and dissemination of technology; and
- the cultural diffusion and interaction that come with information expansion and dissemination.

Each of these areas has helped shape a new emerging global issues agenda. Current issues remain important and, indeed, these factors help us to understand them on a much deeper level. Yet globalization created a new array of problems that is reshaping the global issues landscape and the dialogue, tools, strategies, and approaches that the next U.S. president and indeed all global actors will take.

For example, the spread of information technology has made ideas, attitudes, and information more available to people throughout the world. Americans in Columbus, Ohio, had the ability to log onto the Internet and speak with their counterparts in Kosovo to discover when NATO bombing had begun and to gauge the accuracy of later news reports on the bombing. Norwegian students can share values and customs directly with their counterparts in South Africa, thereby experiencing cultural attitudes firsthand without the filtering mechanisms of governments or even parents and teachers. Scientific information that is available through computer technology can now be used to build sophisticated biological and chemical weapons of immense destructive capability, or equally to promote the dissemination of drugs and medicines outside of "normal" national channels. Ethnic conflicts and genocide between groups of people are now global news, forcing millions to come to grips with issues of intervention, prevention, and punishment. And terrorists in different parts of the globe can communicate readily with one another, transferring plans and even money across national and continental boundaries with ease.

Globalization is an international system and it is also rapidly changing. Because of the fluid nature of this system and the fact that it is both relatively new and largely fueled by the amazing speed of technology, continuing issues are constantly being transformed and new issues are emerging regularly. The nexus of globalization and global issues has now become, in many ways, the defining dynamic of understanding global issues. Whether dealing with new forms of terrorism and new concepts of security, expanding international law, solving ethnic conflicts, dealing with mass migration, coping with individual freedom and access to information, or addressing cultural clash and cultural imperialism, the transition from a Cold War world to a globalized world helps us understand in part what these issues are and why they are important. But most importantly, this fundamental realization shapes how governments and people can and must respond.

Identifying the New Global Issues Agenda

The organization of this text reflects the centrality of globalization. Units 1 and 2 focus on the continuing global agenda of the post-Cold War era. The emphasis is on global population and environmental issues and the nexus between these two phenomena. Has the threat of uncontrolled world population growth subsided or will the built-in momentum of the past four decades override any recent strides in slowing birth rates in the developing world? Should the international community recommit to addressing this problem? Is global aging about to unleash a host of problems for governments of the developed world? Is rapid urbanization creating a whole new set of problems unique to such urban settings? Do environmentalists overstate their case or is the charge of "crying wolf" by environmental conservatives a misplaced attack? Is the world running out of natural resources or is the concern of many about resource availability, be it food, oil, water, air, and/or pristine land, simply misguided? Should the world continue to rely on oil or should the search for viable alternatives take on a new urgency? Will the world be able to feed itself or provide enough water in the foreseeable future? Is global warming for real?

Unit 3 addresses the consequences of the decline of national boundaries and the resultant increased international flow of information, ideas, money, and material things in this globalization age. Can the global community win the war on drugs? Is the international community prepared for the next global health pandemic? Has this community also designed an adequate strategy to address human trafficking? Is globalization a positive or negative development? Is the world a victim of American cultural imperialism? Does the global financial crisis represent a failure of modern capitalism?

Unit 4 addresses the new global security dilemma. Are we in a new Cold War as a consequence of a resurgent Russian foreign policy? Are we headed for a nuclear 9/11? Are cultural and ethnic violence and wars the defining dimensions of conflict in this century? Is this the China century?

The revolutionary changes of the last few decades present us with serious challenges unlike any others in human history. However, as in all periods of historic change, we possess significant opportunities to overcome problems. The task ahead is to define these issues, explore their context, and develop solutions that are comprehensive in scope and effect. The role of all researchers in this field, or any other, is to analyze objectively such problems and search for workable solutions. As students of global issues, your task is to educate yourselves about these issues and become part of the solution.

Internet References . . .

Population Reference Bureau

The Population Reference Bureau provides current information on international population trends and their implications from an objective viewpoint. The PopPov Research Network section of this Web site offers maps with regional and country-specific population information as well as information divided by selected topics.

http://www.prb.org

United Nations Population Fund (UNFPA)

The United Nations Population Fund (UNFPA) was established in 1969 and was originally called the United Nations Fund for Population Activities. This organization works with developing countries to educate people about reproductive and sexual health as well as about family planning. The UNFPA also supports population and development strategies that will benefit developing countries and advocates for the resources needed to accomplish these tasks.

http://www.unfpa.org

Population Connection

Population Connection (formerly Zero Population Growth) is a national, nonprofit organization working to slow population growth and to achieve a sustainable balance between Earth's people and its resources. The organization seeks to protect the environment and to ensure a high quality of life for present and future generations. More recently, it has focused on women's population issues.

http://www.populationconnection.org

The CSIS Global Aging Initiative

The Center for Strategic and International Studies (CSIS) is a public policy research institution that approaches the issue of the aging population in developed countries in a bipartisan manner. The CSIS is involved in a two-year project to explore the global implications of aging in developed nations and to seek strategies on dealing with this issue. This site includes a list of publications that were presented at previous events.

http://www.csis.org/gai/

The Population Council

The Population Council is an international, nonprofit organization that conducts research on population matters from biological, social science, and public health perspectives. It was established in 1952 by John D. Rockefeller, III.

http://www.popcouncil.org

The Population Institute

The Population Institute is an international, educational, nonprofit organization that seeks to voluntarily reduce excessive population growth. Established in 1989 and headquartered in Washington, D.C., it has members in 172 countries.

http://www.populationinstitute.org

Global Population

*I*t is not a coincidence that many of the global issues in this book emerged at about the same time as world population growth exploded. No matter what the issue, the presence of a large and fast-growing population alongside it exacerbates the issue and transforms its basic characteristics. In the new millennium, declining growth rates, which first appeared in the developed world but are now also evident in many parts of the developing world, pose a different set of problems. The emergence of a graying population throughout the globe, but particularly in the developed world, has the potential for significant impact. And the rapid growth within urban areas of the developing world continues to pose a different set of problems. The ability of the global community to respond to any given issue is diminished by certain population conditions, be it an extremely young consuming population in a poor country in need of producers, an expanding urban population whose local public officials are unable to provide an appropriate infrastructure, a large working-age group in a nation without sufficient jobs, or an ever-growing senior population for whom additional services are needed.*

Thus we begin this text with a series of issues directly related to various aspects of world population. It serves as both a separate global agenda and as a context within which other issues are examined.

- Are Declining Growth Rates Rather Than Rapid Population Growth Today's Major Global Population Problem?

- Should the International Community Refocus on Programs to Help Developing Countries Curb Population Growth?

- Is Global Aging in the Developed World a Major Problem?

- Does Global Urbanization Lead Primarily to Undesirable Consequences?

ISSUE 1

Are Declining Growth Rates Rather Than Rapid Population Growth Today's Major Global Population Problem?

YES: Michael Meyer, from "Birth Dearth," *Newsweek* (September 27, 2004)

NO: Danielle Nierenberg and Mia MacDonald, from "The Population Story . . . So Far," *World Watch Magazine* (September/October 2004)

ISSUE SUMMARY

YES: Michael Meyer, a writer for *Newsweek International,* argues that the new global population threat is not too many people as a consequence of continuing high growth rates. On the contrary, declining birth rates will ultimately lead to depopulation in many places on Earth, a virtual population implosion, in both the developed and developing worlds.

NO: Danielle Nierenberg, a research associate at the Worldwatch Institute, and Mia MacDonald, a policy analyst and Worldwatch Institute senior fellow, argue that the consequences of a still-rising population have worsened in some ways because of the simultaneous existence of fast-rising consumption patterns, creating a new set of concerns.

Beginning in the late 1960s, demographers began to observe dramatic increases in population growth, particularly in the developing world. As a consequence, both policymakers and scholars focused on projections of rising birth rates and declining death rates, the consequences of the resultant increased population levels, and strategies for combating such growth. By the mid-1970s, growth rates, particularly in the developing world, were such that the doubling of the world's population was predicted to occur in only a few decades. Consensus on both the resultant level of population growth and its implications was not immediately evident, however. And indeed, as the last millennium was coming to an end, a billion people were added to the world's population in just 12 short years. Contrast this time frame with the fact that it had taken all of recorded history until 1830 for the planet to reach a population of one billion and 100 years for the second billion.

In the last decade of the millennium, however, something unforeseen happened. Population growth slowed, not only in the developed sector of the globe but also in the developing world. The UN Population Fund lowered its short-term and long-term projections. With the turn of the century, individual demographers began to change their calculations as well, as the release of yearly figures suggested the need to do so.

More specifically, no longer could observers simply place all developing countries into a high-growth category and reserve the low-growth category for countries of the developed world. It had become clear that an increasing number of poorer countries had begun to experience a dramatic drop in fertility as well as growth rates.

These recent trends have been surprising, as most observers had long believed that the built-in momentum of population growth in the last third of the twentieth century would have major impacts well into the new century. The logic was understandable, as numbers do matter. They contain a potential built-in momentum that, if left unchecked, creates a geometric increase in births. For example, let us assume that a young third-world mother gives birth to three daughters before she reaches the age of 20. In turn, each of these three daughters has three daughters before she turns 20. The result of such fertility behavior is a nine-fold (900 percent) increase in the population (minus a much lower mortality-rate influence) within 40 years, or two generations. Contrast this pattern with that of a young mother in the developed world, who is currently reproducing at or slightly above/below replacement level. Add a third generation of fertility, and the developing-world family will have increased 27-fold within 60 years, while the developed-world family's size would remain virtually unchanged.

Thus, problems relating to population growth may, in fact, be at the heart of most global issues. If growth is a problem, control it and half the ecological battle is won. Fail to control it, and global problem solvers will be swimming upstream against an ever-increasing current. It is for this reason that the question of "out-of-control" population growth was selected to be the first issue in this volume.

Michael Meyer describes how families in both the developed and developing worlds are choosing to have fewer children and chronicles what he believes to be an array of negative consequences associated with this population transition. Danielle Nierenberg and Mia MacDonald argue that even though the rate of growth has declined, it is applied to a much larger base than at any time in history, including the last century.

YES

Michael Meyer

Birth Dearth

Everyone knows there are too many people in the world. Whether we live in Lahore or Los Angeles, Shanghai or Sao Paulo, our lives are daily proof. We endure traffic gridlock, urban sprawl and environmental depredation. The evening news brings variations on Ramallah or Darfur—images of Third World famine, poverty, pestilence, war, global competition for jobs, and increasingly scarce natural resources.

Just last week the United Nations warned that many of the world's cities are becoming hopelessly overcrowded. Lagos alone will grow from 6.5 million people in 1995 to 16 million by 2015, a miasma of slums and decay where a fifth of all children will die before they are 5. At a conference in London, the UN Population Fund weighed in with a similarly bleak report: unless something dramatically changes, the world's 50 poorest countries will triple in size by 2050, to 1.7 billion people.

Yet this is not the full story. To the contrary, in fact. Across the globe, people are having fewer and fewer children. Fertility rates have dropped by half since 1972, from six children per woman to 2.9. And demographers say they're still falling, faster than ever. The world's population will continue to grow—from today's 6.4 billion to around 9 billion in 2050. But after that, it will go sharply into decline. Indeed, a phenomenon that we're destined to learn much more about—depopulation—has already begun in a number of countries. Welcome to the New Demography. It will change everything about our world, from the absolute size and power of nations to global economic growth to the quality of our lives.

This revolutionary transformation will be led not so much by developed nations as by the developing ones. Most of us are familiar with demographic trends in Europe, where birthrates have been declining for years. To reproduce itself, a society's women must each bear 2.1 children. Europe's fertility rates fall far short of that, according to the 2002 UN population report. France and Ireland, at 1.8, top Europe's childbearing charts. Italy and Spain, at 1.2, bring up the rear. In between are countries such as Germany, whose fertility rate of 1.4 is exactly Europe's average. What does that mean? If the UN figures are right, Germany could shed nearly a fifth of its 82.5 million people over the next 40 years—roughly the equivalent of all of east Germany, a loss of population not seen in Europe since the Thirty Years' War.

From *Newsweek*, vol. 144, issue 13, September 27, 2004, pp. 54–61. Copyright © 2004 by Newsweek, Inc. All rights reserved. Used by permission and protected by the Copyright Laws of the United States. The printing, copying, redistribution, or retransmission of the Material without express written permission via PARS International is prohibited.

And so it is across the Continent. Bulgaria will shrink by 38 percent, Romania by 27 percent, Estonia by 25 percent. "Parts of Eastern Europe, already sparsely populated, will just empty out," predicts Reiner Klingholz, director of the Berlin Institute for Population and Development. Russia is already losing close to 750,000 people yearly. (President Vladimir Putin calls it a "national crisis.") So is Western Europe, and that figure could grow to as much as 3 million a year by midcentury, if not more.

The surprise is how closely the less-developed world is following the same trajectory. In Asia it's well known that Japan will soon tip into population loss, if it hasn't already. With a fertility rate of 1.3 children per woman, the country stands to shed a quarter of its 127 million people over the next four decades, according to UN projections. But while the graying of Japan (average age: 42.3 years) has long been a staple of news headlines, what to make of China, whose fertility rate has declined from 5.8 in 1970 to 1.8 today, according to the UN? Chinese census data put the figure even lower, at 1.3. Coupled with increasing life spans, that means China's population will age as quickly in one generation as Europe's has over the past 100 years, reports the Center for Strategic and International Studies in Washington. With an expected median age of 44 in 2015, China will be older on average than the United States. By 2019 or soon after, its population will peak at 1.5 billion, then enter a steep decline. By midcentury, China could well lose 20 to 30 percent of its population every generation.

The picture is similar elsewhere in Asia, where birthrates are declining even in the absence of such stringent birth-control programs as China's. Indeed, it's happening despite often generous official incentives to procreate. The industrialized nations of Singapore, Hong Kong, Taiwan and South Korea all report sub-replacement fertility, says Nicholas Eberstadt, a demographer at the American Enterprise Institute in Washington. To this list can be added Thailand, Burma, Australia and Sri Lanka, along with Cuba and many Caribbean nations, as well as Uruguay and Brazil. Mexico is aging so rapidly that within several decades it will not only stop growing but will have an older population than that of the United States. So much for the cliche of those Mexican youths swarming across the Rio Grande. "If these figures are accurate," says Eberstadt, "just about half of the world's population lives in subreplacement countries."

There are notable exceptions. In Europe, Albania and the outlier province of Kosovo are reproducing energetically. So are pockets of Asia: Mongolia, Pakistan and the Philippines. The United Nations projects that the Middle East will double in population over the next 20 years, growing from 326 million today to 649 million by 2050. Saudi Arabia has one of the highest fertility rates in the world, 5.7, after Palestinian territories at 5.9 and Yemen at 7.2. Yet there are surprises here, too. Tunisia has tipped below replacement. Lebanon and Iran are at the threshold. And though overall the region's population continues to grow, the increase is due mainly to lower infant mortality; fertility rates themselves are falling faster than in developed countries, indicating that over the coming decades the Middle East will age far more rapidly than other regions of the world. Birthrates in Africa remain high, and despite the AIDS epidemic its population is projected to keep growing. So is that of the United States.

We'll return to American exceptionalism, and what that might portend. But first, let's explore the causes of the birth dearth, as outlined in a pair of new books on the subject. "Never in the last 650 years, since the time of the Black Plague, have birth and fertility rates fallen so far, so fast, so low, for so long, in so many places," writes the sociologist Ben Wattenberg in "Fewer: How the New Demography of Depopulation Will Shape Our Future." Why? Wattenberg suggests that a variety of once independent trends have conjoined to produce a demographic tsunami. As the United Nations reported last week, people everywhere are leaving the countryside and moving to cities, which will be home to more than half the world's people by 2007. Once there, having a child becomes a cost rather than an asset. From 1970 to 2000, Nigeria's urban population climbed from 14 to 44 percent. South Korea went from 28 to 84 percent. So-called megacities, from Lagos to Mexico City, have exploded seemingly overnight. Birthrates have fallen in inverse correlation.

Other factors are at work. Increasing female literacy and enrollment in schools have tended to decrease fertility, as have divorce, abortion and the worldwide trend toward later marriage. Contraceptive use has risen dramatically over the past decade; according to UN data, 62 percent of married or "in union" women of reproductive age are now using some form of nonnatural birth control. In countries such as India, now the capital of global HIV, disease has become a factor. In Russia, the culprits include alcoholism, poor public health and industrial pollution that has whacked male sperm counts. Wealth discourages childbearing, as seen long ago in Europe and now in Asia. As Wattenberg puts it, "Capitalism is the best contraception."

The potential consequences of the population implosion are enormous. Consider the global economy, as Phillip Longman describes it in another recent book, "The Empty Cradle: How Falling Birthrates Threaten World Prosperity and What to Do About It." A population expert at the New America Foundation in Washington, he sees danger for global prosperity. Whether it's real estate or consumer spending, economic growth and population have always been closely linked. "There are people who cling to the hope that you can have a vibrant economy without a growing population, but mainstream economists are pessimistic," says Longman. You have only to look at Japan or Europe for a whiff of what the future might bring, he adds. In Italy, demographers forecast a 40 percent decline in the working-age population over the next four decades—accompanied by a commensurate drop in growth across the Continent, according to the European Commission. What happens when Europe's cohort of baby boomers begins to retire around 2020? Recent strikes and demonstrations in Germany, Italy, France and Austria over the most modest pension reforms are only the beginning of what promises to become a major sociological battle between Europe's older and younger generations.

That will be only a skirmish compared with the conflict brewing in China. There market reforms have removed the cradle-to-grave benefits of the planned economy, while the Communist Party hasn't constructed an adequate social safety net to take their place. Less than one-quarter of the population is covered by retirement pensions, according to CSIS. That puts the burden of elder care almost entirely on what is now a generation of only children. The one-child policy has led to the so-called 4-2-1 problem, in which each child will be potentially responsible for caring for two parents and four grandparents.

Incomes in China aren't rising fast enough to offset this burden. In some rural villages, so many young people have fled to the cities that there may be nobody left to look after the elders. And the aging population could soon start to dull China's competitive edge, which depends on a seemingly endless supply of cheap labor. After 2015, this labor pool will begin to dry up, says economist Hu Angang. China will have little choice but to adopt a very Western-sounding solution, he says: it will have to raise the education level of its work force and make it more productive. Whether it can is an open question. Either way, this much is certain: among Asia's emerging economic powers, China will be the first to grow old before it gets rich.

Equally deep dislocations are becoming apparent in Japan. Akihiko Matsutani, an economist and author of a recent best seller, "The Economy of a Shrinking Population," predicts that by 2009 Japan's economy will enter an era of "negative growth." By 2030, national income will have shrunk by 15 percent. Speculating about the future is always dicey, but economists pose troubling questions. Take the legendarily high savings that have long buoyed the Japanese economy and financed borrowing worldwide, especially by the United States. As an aging Japan draws down those assets in retirement, will U.S. and global interest rates rise? At home, will Japanese businesses find themselves competing for increasingly scarce investment capital? And just what will they be investing in, as the country's consumers grow older, and demand for the latest in hot new products cools off? What of the effect on national infrastructure? With less tax revenue in state coffers, Matsutani predicts, governments will increasingly be forced to skimp on or delay repairs to the nation's roads, bridges, rail lines and the like. "Life will become less convenient," he says. Spanking-clean Tokyo might come to look more like New York City in the 1970s, when many urban dwellers decamped for the suburbs (taking their taxes with them) and city fathers could no longer afford the municipal upkeep. Can Japanese cope? "They will have to," says Matsutani. "There's no alternative."

Demographic change magnifies all of a country's problems, social as well as economic. An overburdened welfare state? Aging makes it collapse. Tensions over immigration? Differing birthrates intensify anxieties, just as the need for imported labor rises—perhaps the critical issue for the Europe of tomorrow. A poor education system, with too many kids left behind? Better fix it, because a shrinking work force requires higher productivity and greater flexibility, reflected in a new need for continuing job training, career switches and the health care needed to keep workers working into old age.

In an ideal world, perhaps, the growing gulf between the world's wealthy but shrinking countries and its poor, growing ones would create an opportunity. Labor would flow from the overpopulated, resource-poor south to the depopulating north, where jobs would continue to be plentiful. Capital and remittance income from the rich nations would flow along the reverse path, benefiting all. Will it happen? Perhaps, but that presupposes considerable labor mobility. Considering the resistance Europeans display toward large-scale immigration from North Africa, or Japan's almost zero-immigration policy, it's hard to be optimistic. Yes, attitudes are changing. Only a decade ago, for instance, Europeans also spoke of zero immigration. Today they recognize the need and, in bits and pieces, are beginning to plan for it. But will it happen on the scale required?

A more probable scenario may be an intensification of existing tensions between peoples determined to preserve their beleaguered national identities on the one hand, and immigrant groups on the other seeking to escape overcrowding and lack of opportunity at home. For countries such as the Philippines—still growing, and whose educated work force looks likely to break out of low-status jobs as nannies and gardeners and move up the global professional ladder—this may be less of a problem. It will be vastly more serious for the tens of millions of Arab youths who make up a majority of the population in the Middle East and North Africa, at least half of whom are unemployed.

America is the wild card in this global equation. While Europe and much of Asia shrinks, the United States' indigenous population looks likely to stay relatively constant, with fertility rates hovering almost precisely at replacement levels. Add in heavy immigration, and you quickly see that America is the only modern nation that will continue to grow. Over the next 45 years the United States will gain 100 million people, Wattenberg estimates, while Europe loses roughly as many.

This does not mean that Americans will escape the coming demographic whammy. They, too, face the problems of an aging work force and its burdens. (The cost of Medicare and Social Security will rise from 4.3 percent of GDP in 2000 to 11.5 percent in 2030 and 21 percent in 2050, according to the Congressional Budget Office.) They, too, face the prospect of increasing ethnic tensions, as a flat white population and a dwindling black one become gradually smaller minorities in a growing multicultural sea. And in our interdependent era, the troubles of America's major trading partners—Europe and Japan—will quickly become its own. To cite one example, what becomes of the vaunted "China market," invested in so heavily by U.S. companies, if by 2050 China loses an estimated 35 percent of its workers and the aged consume an ever-greater share of income?

America's demographic "unipolarity" has profound security implications as well. Washington worries about terrorism and failing states. Yet the chaos of today's fragmented world is likely to prove small in comparison to what could come. For U.S. leaders, Longman in "The Empty Cradle" sketches an unsettling prospect. Though the United States may have few military competitors, the technologies by which it projects geopolitical power—from laser-guided missiles and stealth bombers to a huge military infrastructure—may gradually become too expensive for a country facing massively rising social entitlements in an era of slowing global economic growth. If the war on terrorism turns out to be the "generational struggle" that national security advisor Condoleezza Rice says it is, Longman concludes, then the United States might have difficulty paying for it.

None of this is writ, of course. Enlightened governments could help hold the line. France and the Netherlands have instituted family-friendly policies that help women combine work and motherhood, ranging from tax credits for kids to subsidized day care. Scandinavian countries have kept birthrates up with generous provisions for parental leave, health care and part-time employment. Still, similar programs offered by the shrinking city-state of Singapore—including a state-run dating service—have done little to reverse the birth dearth. Remember, too, that such prognoses have been wrong in the past. At the cusp of the postwar baby boom, demographers predicted a sharp fall in fertility and a global birth dearth. Yet even if this generation of seers turns out to be right, as seems likely, not all is bad. Environmentally, a smaller world is almost certainly a better world, whether in terms of cleaner air or, say, the return of wolves and rare flora to abandoned stretches of the East German countryside. And while people are living longer, they are also living healthier—at least in the developed world. That means they can (and probably should) work more years before retirement.

Yes, a younger generation will have to shoulder the burden of paying for their elders. But there will be compensations. As populations shrink, says economist Matsutani, national incomes may drop—but not necessarily per capita incomes. And in this realm of uncertainty, one mundane thing is probably sure: real-estate prices will fall. That will hurt seniors whose nest eggs are tied up in their homes, but it will be a boon to youngsters of the future. Who knows? Maybe the added space and cheap living will inspire them to, well, do whatever it takes to make more babies. Thus the cycle of life will restore its balance. . . .

**Danielle Nierenberg and
Mia MacDonald**

The Population Story . . . So Far

Forty years ago, the world's women bore an average of six children each. Today, that number is just below three. In 1960, 10–15 percent of married couples in developing countries used a modern method of contraception; now, 60 percent do.

To a considerable extent, these simple facts sum up the change in the Earth's human population prospects, then and now. In the mid-1960s, it was not uncommon to think about the human population as a time bomb. In 1971, population biologist Paul Ehrlich estimated that if human numbers kept increasing at the high rates of the time, by around 2900 the planet would be teeming with sixty million billion people (that's 60,000,000,000,000,000). But the rate of population rise actually peaked in the 1960s and demographers expect a leveling-off of human numbers this century.

Every couple of years the United Nations Population Division issues projections of human population growth to 2050. In 2002, UN demographers predicted a somewhat different picture of human population growth to mid-century than what the "population bombers" thought likely a generation ago. World population, growing by 76 million people every year (about 240,000 people per day), will pass 6.4 billion this year. The latest UN mid-range estimate says there will be about 8.9 billion people on Earth by 2050. And, according to this new scenario, total population will begin to shrink over the next hundred years.

These numbers are leading some people to say that the population bomb has been defused. A few nations, such as Italy and Japan, are even worried that birth rates are too low and that their graying populations will be a drain on the economy. (Some studies suggest that China, the world's most populous country, may also "need" more people to help support the hundreds of millions who will retire in coming decades.)

We're not out of the woods yet. While the annual rate of population growth has decreased since 1970—from about 2 percent to 1.3 percent today—*the rate is applied to a much larger population* than ever before, meaning that the added yearly increments to the population are also much larger. These numbers show that the largest generation in history has arrived: 1.2 billion people are between 10 and 19. In large measure, it will be their choices—those they have, and those they make—that determine where the global population meter rests by mid-century.

From *World Watch*, September/October 2004, pp. 14–17. Copyright © 2004 by Worldwatch Institute. Reprinted by permission. www.worldwatch.org

Population × Consumption

Potential for catastrophe persists. In many places, population growth is slowly smoldering but could turn into a fast burn. Countries as diverse as Ethiopia, the Democratic Republic of Congo, and Pakistan are poised to more than double their size by 2050 even as supplies of water, forests, and food crops are already showing signs of strain and other species are being squeezed into smaller and smaller ranges. Arid Yemen will likely see its population quadruple to 80 million by 2050. The UN estimates that populations in the world's 48 least-developed countries could triple by 2050. And if the world's women have, on average, a half a child more than the UN predicts, global population could grow to 10.6 billion by mid-century.

But it is a mistake to think that population growth is only a problem for developing countries. While consumption levels need to increase among the 2.8 billion people who now live on less than $2 a day, high rates of population growth combined with high levels of consumption in rich countries are taking a heavy toll on the Earth's natural resources:

- Carbon dioxide levels today are 18 percent higher than in 1960 and an estimated 31 percent higher than they were at the onset of the Industrial Revolution in 1750.
- Half the world's original forest cover is gone and another 30 percent is degraded or fragmented.
- Industrial fleets have fished out at least 90 percent of all large ocean predators—tuna, marlin, swordfish, cod, halibut, skate, and flounder—in just the past 50 years, according to a study in *Nature* in 2003.
- An estimated 10–20 percent of the world's cropland, and more than 70 percent of the world's rangelands, are degraded.

As global consumption of oil, meat, electricity, paper products, and a host of consumer goods rises, the impact of population numbers takes on a new relevance. Although each new person increases total demands on the Earth's resources, the size of each person's "ecological footprint"—the biologically productive area required to support that person—varies hugely from one to another. The largest ecofootprints belong to those in the industrialized world.

Further, new demographic trends can have significant impacts as well. Since 1970, the number of people living together in one household has declined worldwide, as incomes have risen, urbanization has accelerated and families have gotten smaller. With fewer people sharing energy, appliances, and furnishings, consumption actually rises. A one-person household in the United States uses about 17 percent *more* energy per person than a two-person home.

And while some nations are getting nervous about declining birth rates, for most of the world the end of population growth is anything but imminent. Although fertility rates are ratcheting down, this trajectory is not guaranteed. Projections of slower population growth assume that more couples will be able to choose to have smaller families, and that investment in reproductive health keeps pace with rising demand. But along the route to the eventual leveling-off of global population, plateaus are possible. And smaller families are not guaranteed in countries where government resources are strained or where health care, education, and women's rights are low on the list of priorities.

In the West African country of Niger, for example, the availability of family planning and reproductive health services has declined, while birth rates have increased. According to a recent report by the World Bank, the average woman in Niger will give birth to eight children in her lifetime, up from seven in 1998 and more than women in any other nation. Niger is already bulging with young people; 50 percent of the population is under age 15 and 70 percent is under 25.

Biology ≠ Destiny

A series of global conferences in the 1990s—spanning the Rio Earth Summit in 1992, the Cairo population conference (1994), the Beijing women's conference (1995), and the UN's Millennium Summit in 2000—put issues of environment, development, poverty, and women's rights on the global policy table. As a result, discussions of the relationship between growing human numbers and the Earth's ability to provide are increasingly framed by the realities of gender relations. It is now generally agreed that while enabling larger numbers of women and men to use modern methods of family planning is essential, it is not sufficient. Expanding the choices, capacities, and agency of women has become a central thread in the population story. Consumption—what we need and what we want—is, too.

Many studies have shown that women with more education have smaller, healthier families, and that their children have a better chance of making it out of poverty. Likewise, wealthier women and those with the right to make decisions about their lives and bodies also have fewer children. And women who have the choice to delay marriage and childbearing past their teens tend to have fewer children than those women—and there are millions of them still—who marry before they've completed the transition from adolescence. Equalizing relations between women and men is also a social good: not only is it just, but a recent World Bank report found that in developing countries where gender equality lags, efforts to combat poverty and increase economic growth lag, too.

Yet women's rights and voices remain suppressed or muted throughout the world. Over 100 million girls will be married before their 18th birthdays in the next decade, some as young as 8 or 9. Early childbearing is the leading cause of death and disability for women between the ages of 15 and 19 in developing countries. At least 350 million women still lack access to a full range of contraceptive methods, 10 years after the Cairo conference yielded a 20-year plan to balance the world's people with its resources. Demand for services will increase an estimated 40 percent by 2025.

The assault of HIV/AIDS is also increasingly hurting women: more than 18 million women are living with HIV/AIDS, and in 2003 women's rate of infection for the first time equaled men's. In the region hardest hit, sub-Saharan Africa, 60 percent of adults living with HIV are women. Two-thirds of the world's

876 million illiterates are women and a majority of the 115 million children not attending grade school are girls. In no country in the world are women judged to have political, economic, and social power equal to that of men.

Even in the United States, women's reproductive rights are increasingly constrained by the growing number of restrictions and conditions on choice imposed by state and federal laws. Like the U.S. lifestyle, the current Administration's blinkered view of sexuality has gone global. The United States has withheld $34 million from the UN Population Fund (UNFPA) every year of the Bush Administration due to a dispute over abortion. And the "global gag rule," a relic of the Reagan presidency reimposed by President Bush, binds U.S. population assistance by making taboo any discussion of abortion in reproductive health clinics, even in countries where it is legal.

The impacts reach more deeply than the rhetoric: due to the loss of U.S. population funds, reproductive health services have been scaled back or eliminated in some of the world's poorest countries, precisely where fertility rates are highest and women's access to family planning most tenuous. In Kenya, for instance, the two main providers of reproductive health services refused to sign a pledge to enforce the gag rule, with the result that they lost funds and closed five family planning clinics, eliminating women's access to maternal health care, contraception, and voluntary counseling and testing for HIV/AIDS. In Ethiopia, where only 6 percent of women use modern methods of contraception, the gag rule has cut a wide swath: clinics have reduced services, laid off staff and curtailed community health programs; many have suffered shortages of contraceptive supplies.

Need ↑ Funds ↓

A recent study by UNFPA and the Alan Guttmacher Institute estimated that meeting women's current unmet need for contraception would prevent each year:

- 23 million unplanned births;
- 22 million induced abortions;
- 1.4 million infant deaths;
- 142,000 pregnancy related-deaths (including 53,000 from unsafe abortions); and
- 505,000 children losing their mothers due to pregnancy-related causes.

The non-medical benefits are not quantified but are considerable: greater self-esteem and decision-making power for women; higher productivity and income; increased health, nutrition, and education expenditures on each child; higher savings and investment rates; and increased equality between women and men. We know this from experience: recent research in the United States, for example, ascribes the large numbers of women entering law, medical, and other professional training programs in the 1970s to the expanded choices afforded by the wide availability of the Pill.

Despite these benefits, vast needs go unmet as the Cairo action plan remains underfunded. The United States is not the only culprit. UNFPA reports that donor funds for a basic package of reproductive health services and population data and policy work totaled about $3.1 billion in 2003—$2.6 billion less than the level agreed to in the ICPD Program. Developing country domestic resources were estimated at $11.7 billion, a major portion of which is spent by just a handful of large countries. A number of countries, particularly the poorest, rely heavily on donor funds to provide services for family planning, reproductive health, and HIV/AIDS, and to build data sets and craft needed policies.

A year from now, donors will be expected to be contributing $6.1 billion annually, $3 billion more than what has already been spent. "A world that spends $800 billion to $1 trillion each year on the military can afford the equivalent of slightly more than one day's military spending to close Cairo's $3 billion external funding gap to save and improve the lives of millions of women and families in developing countries," says UNFPA's executive director, Thoraya Obaid. But as the world's priorities lie in other arenas, it is looking increasingly unlikely that the Cairo targets—despite their modest price tag in a world where the bill for a war can top $100 billion—will be met.

But it isn't only poor people in developing countries who will determine whether the more dire population scenarios pass from speculation to reality. Family size has declined in most wealthy nations, but the U.S. population grew by 32.7 million people (13.1 percent) during the 1990s, the largest number in any 10-year period in U.S. history. At about 280 million people, the United States is now the third most populous nation in the world and its population is expected to reach 400 million by 2050. A recent study suggests that if every person alive today consumed at the rate of an average person in the United States, three more planets would be required to fulfill these demands.

Whether or not birth rates continue to fall, consumption levels and patterns (affluence), coupled with technology, take on new importance. The global consumer class—around 1.7 billion people, or more than a quarter of humanity—is growing rapidly. These people are collectively responsible for the vast majority of meat-eating, paper use, car driving, and energy consumption on the planet, as well as the resulting impact of these activities on its natural resources. As populations surge in developing countries and the world becomes increasingly globalized, more and more people have access to, and the means to acquire, a greater diversity of products and services than ever before.

It is the combined effect of human numbers and human consumption that creates such potent flash-points. Decisions about sexuality and lifestyle are among the most deeply personal and political decisions societies and their citizens can make. The fate of the human presence on the Earth will be shaped in large part by those decisions and how their implications unfold in the coming years. This population story's ending still hasn't been written.

POSTSCRIPT

Are Declining Growth Rates Rather Than Rapid Population Growth Today's Major Global Population Problem?

The growth issue can be structured most simply as one of an insurmountable built-in momentum vs. dramatic change in fertility attitudes and behavior. Demographers are correct when they assert that the population explosion of the latter part of the twentieth century had the potential of future fertility disaster because of the high percentage of the population who are either in the middle of or about to enter their reproductive years. They are also correct when they assert that the last decade has witnessed major transitions away from high growth rates, even in many parts of the developing world.

The key word is "potential." Its relevance grows out of the built-in momentum that has caused the developing world's actual population to rise substantially in the last thirty-five years despite a decline in the growth rate. In its 2001 analysis of population patterns, the United Nations suggested that population growth in the first half of the twenty-first century would increase by over 50 percent, or by more than 3 billion (United Nations, *World Population: The 2000 Revision—Highlights,* 2001). This was higher than its projections of just two years earlier, due primarily to higher projected fertility levels in countries that are slow to show signs of fertility decline.

The entire growth of the first half of the twenty-first century would take place in the developing world, according to the study. It acknowledged that population would also grow in the developed world during the first 25 years of the new century, but then it would decline to levels approximating 2000 by mid-century. On the other hand, despite lowering birth rates in the less developed world, the built-in momentum would result in a 65 percent projected growth (from 4.9 billion in 2000 to 8.1 billion in 2050) during the first half of the century.

The United Nations revised its earlier predictions in 2002, tempering projections for future growth (*World Population Prospects: The 2002 Revision,* 2003). The executive director of the UN Population Fund explained it by suggesting that "men and women in larger numbers were making their own decisions on birth spacing and family size, contributing to slower population growth."

A perusal of the Population Reference Bureau's *2007 World Population Data Sheet* confirms, however, that while the developed world is growing slowly (1.6 million per year), the developing world is continuing

15

its rapid growth (80 million per year at current rates). Birth rates, while falling worldwide, are still high enough in the poorer sectors of the globe to ensure continued high growth for some time into the future.

It has become increasingly clear that today's youth will not produce at the same level as their parents and grandparents, based on the evidence of the last quarter-century. Two factors are at work here. The demographic transition is evident in those countries of the developing world that are experiencing economic growth. Birth rates have dropped significantly, leading to lowered growth rates. In over one-third of the world's countries, containing 43 percent of the globe's population, women are having no more than two children on average. But while the rates are higher than those for the newly industrializing countries of the third world, growth rates for the remaining developing countries have also dropped in a large number of cases. In the latter situation, policy intervention lies at the heart of such lowered rates. The latter effort has been spearheaded by the United Nations and includes the work of many nongovernmental organizations as well. In global conferences held every 10 years (1974, 1984, and 1994), the entire international community has systematically addressed the problem of third-world fertility, admittedly from different perspectives. Yet world population is still growing at a 1.2 percent rate, adding 80 million people annually.

Acknowledging declining birth rates still begs the question: Is there still a built-in momentum that will lead to negative consequences? William P. Butz addresses this question in *The Double Divide: Implosionists and Explosionists Endanger Progress Since Cairo* (Population Reference Bureau, September 2004). The Implosionists argue that falling birth rates throughout the world is the most important variable. They suggest that the biggest global population problem in the immediate future will be how to cope with the wide range of challenges confronting countries with declining fertility rates. The Explosionists counter that there will still be substantial population growth, even in those countries that have recently begun to experience low birth rates. To them, world leaders and organizations must not ignore those problems that emerge from populations whose percentage of young are still quite high. Three who share the implosionist position are David R. Francis ("Now, Dangers of a Population Implosion," *Christian Science Monitor,* October 7, 2004); Denis Dutton ("Now It's the Population Implosion," *New Zealand Herald,* July 23, 2003); and Kerry Howley ("Baby Bust!, *Reason,* July 2008). On the other hand, Werner Fornos advances the explosionists' position in "A Global Concern: A Population Crisis Still Looms" (*International Herald Tribune,* January 14, 2004).

A book that focuses on the demographic divide is Paul A. Laudicina's *World Out of Balance* (McGraw-Hill, 2004). Two important books advocating the implosionist position are Phillip Longman's *The Empty Cradle: How Falling Birthrates Threaten World Prosperity and What to Do About It* (Basic Books, 2004) and *The End of World Population Growth in the 21st Century: New Challenges for Human Capital Formation and Sustainable Development* (Wolfgang Lutz, Warren Sanderson, and Sergei Scherbov, eds., Earthscan Publishers, 2004). Two books advancing the explosionist thesis are *No*

Vacancy: Global Responses to the Human Population Explosion (Michael Tobias, Bob Gillespie, and Elizabeth Hughes, eds., Hope Publishing House, 2006) and K. Bruce Newbold's *Six Billion Plus: World Population in the Twenty-First Century* (Rowman & Littlefield Publishers, 2006).

In a sense, both viewpoints are correct as each acknowledges declining birth rates in the developing world and an eventual leveling-off of growth there. Their disagreement does point out dramatic implications of ever so slight variations in both the timing and the degree of fertility reduction among the poorer countries.

The United Nations (www.un.org/popin) serves as an authoritative source on various population data, whether historical, current, or future oriented. One of the UN agencies, the United Nations Population Fund, or UNFPA (www.unfpa.org), issues an annual *State of the World Population,* as well as other reports. See, for example, its *World Population Prospects: The 2008 Revision—Highlights* (2009).

Two Washington private organizations, the Population Reference Bureau (PRB) (www.prb.org) and The Population Institute (www.populationinstitute.org), publish a variety of booklets, newsletters, and reports yearly. Admittedly, these sources tend to emphasize the continued urgency rather than the seeds of progress, although recent articles have described the positive aspects of the current population transition. One particularly useful PRB publication is *World Population Beyond Six Billion* (*Population Bulletin,* March 1999). Four other important PRB publications are: *Global Demographic Divide* (Mary M. Kent and Carl Haub, 2005); *Transitions in World Population* (March 2004); *World Population Highlights: Key Findings from the PRB's 2007 World Population Data Sheet* (2007); and "World Population Highlights" (*Population Bulletin,* September 2008). A particularly succinct discussion of this "demographic divide" is found in PRB's *The Demographic Divide: What It Is and What It Means* (Mary Mederios and Carl Haub, 2008). Other sources focus on either success stories or the potential for success growing out of recent policy intervention. The Population Council of New York (www.popcouncil.org) falls into the latter category.

For over a decade, until the death of one of the participants, two individuals took center stage in the debate over population growth and its implications. Paul Ehrlich led the call for vigorous action to curb population growth. His coauthored works, *The Population Bomb* (1971) and *The Population Explosion* (1990), advanced the notion that the Earth's resource base could not keep pace with population growth, and thus the survival of the planet was brought into question. The late Julian Simon's *Population Matters: People, Resources, Environment, and Immigration* (1990) and *The Ultimate Resource 2* (1996) challenge Ehrlich's basic thesis. Simon's place in the debate appears to have been assumed by Ronald Bailey, science correspondent for *Reason* magazine. Two important publications by Bailey are *Global Warming and Other Eco-Myths* (Forum, 2002) and *Earth Report 2000* (McGraw-Hill, 2000).

A succinct, centrist, and easily understood analysis of the future of world population can be found in Leon F. Bouvier and Jane T. Bertrand,

World Population: Challenges for the 21st Century (1999). The annual *State of the World* volume from the Worldwatch Institute typically includes a timely analysis on some aspect of the world population problem. Two recent books describing declining global population rates are *Oh No, We Forgot to Have Children: How Declining Birth Rates Are Reshaping Our Society* (Deirdre Macken, Allen and Unwin, 2006) and *NO VACANCY: Global Responses to the Human Population Explosion* (Michael Tobias et al., Hope Publishing House, 2006). See also "Fewer Babies Pose Difficult Challenges for Europe" (Joseph Chamie, *YaleGlobal*, October 8, 2007).

Numerous Web sites can be found under world population on www .msn.com (type in "world population Web sites").

ISSUE 2

Should the International Community Refocus on Programs to Help Developing Countries Curb Population Growth?

YES: Terry M. Redding, from "The Population Challenge: Key to Global Survival," *The 21st Century Papers* (The Population Institute, 2007)

NO: Steven W. Mosher, from "McNamara's Folly: Bankrolling Family Planning," *PRI Review* (March–April 2003)

ISSUE SUMMARY

YES: Terry M. Redding, a communications consultant to The Population Institute, suggests that population *growth* is being unfortunately neglected in international development discussions, as the latter's focus has been on other aspects of population such as reproductive health and women's empowerment.

NO: Steven W. Mosher, president of the Population Research Institute, an organization devoted to debunking the idea that the world is overpopulated, argues that self-interest was the motivation for past efforts on the part of international funding agencies, including the World Bank, to curb population by pressuring developing countries to adopt fertility reduction programs.

The history of the international community's efforts to lower birth rates throughout the developing world goes back to the late 1960s, when the annual growth rate hovered around 2.35 percent. At that time, selected individuals in international governmental organizations, including the United Nations, were persuaded by a number of wealthy national governments as well as by international nongovernmental population agencies that a problem of potentially massive proportions had recently emerged. Quite simply, demographers had observed a pattern of population growth in the poorer regions of the world quite unlike that which had occurred in the richer countries during the previous 150–200 years.

Population growth in the developed countries of the globe had followed a rather persistent pattern during the last two centuries. Prior to the Industrial

Revolution, these countries typically experienced both high birth rates and death rates. As industrialization took hold and advances in the quality of life for citizens of these countries occurred, death rates fell, resulting in a period of time when the size of the population rose. Later, birth rates also began to decline, in large part because the newly industrialized societies were better suited to families with fewer children. After awhile, both birth and death rates leveled off at a much lower level than during preindustrial times.

This earlier transition throughout the developed world differed, however, from the newer growth pattern in the poorer regions of the globe observed by demographers in the late 1960s. First, the transition in the developed world occurred over a long period of time, allowing the population to deal more readily with such growth. On the other hand, post-1960s' growth in the developing world had taken off at a much faster pace, far outstripping the capacity of these societies to cope with the changes accompanying such growth. Second, the earlier growth in the developed world began with a much smaller population base and a much larger resource base than did the developing world, again allowing the richer societies to cope more easily with such growth. The developing world of the 1960s, however, found percentages of increase based on a much higher base. Coping under the latter scenario proved much more difficult. Finally, industrialization accompanied population change in the developed world, again allowing for those societies to address resultant problems more easily. Today's developing world has no such luxury. New jobs are not available, expanded educational facilities are nonexistent, unsatisfactory health services remain unchanged, and modern infrastructures have not been created.

The international community formally placed the population issue—defined primarily as excessive birth rates in the developing world—on the global agenda in 1974 with the first major global conference on population, held in Bucharest, Romania. There was much debate over the motives of both sides. Both rich and poor countries eventually pledged to work together. Finally, each side bought into the assumption that "the best contraceptive was economic development," but until development was achieved, national family planning programs would help lower growth rates. A decade later at the 1984 Mexico City global population conference, the international community and national governments had joined forces to combat high growth rates. By 1994, when nations of the world reconvened in Cairo to assess progress, considerable success had been achieved in getting developing countries to accept such programs. At Cairo, however, a major change occurred. Calls for population planning were replaced by cries for reproductive health and women's empowerment. For the past decade and a half, the focus and funds to accompany it have moved away from family planning to these other issues.

In the first selection, Terry M. Redding argues that ignoring "serious consideration of high fertility and family planning has been a mistake and suggests a return to the earlier emphases. In the second selection, Steven Mosher views the efforts of organizations such as the United Nations Population Fund much differently. In his view, these organizations have always sought to impose birth-control methods on the developing world in the misguided name of "virtuous and humanitarian motives," while attacking the motives of their opponents as self-serving or worse.

YES

Terry M. Redding

The Population Challenge: Key To Global Survival

Neglecting the Human Connection

Stabilizing the growth of the world's human population is a goal that must be achieved if we are to preserve our options for the future and improve the odds for the world's sustainability. Challenges such as climate change and global warming, fragile and failed states, migration and refugee crises, food and water insecurity, poverty, disease, debt, and illiteracy are caused or exacerbated by unchecked rapid population growth.

Discussions on addressing these challenges, however, often neglect serious consideration of high fertility and family planning. Former U.S. President Bill Clinton singled out population growth as the key issue that candidates in the 2008 presidential election were avoiding. This is puzzling and troubling, as population growth is the single world issue that binds all the others together; it is the root of many problems affecting the tree of humanity.

Indeed, trees provide an apt analogy to the current global reality: In countries with quality reproductive health services and policies serving as the roots, the branches—including economics, health, and education—are stable. As this paper will demonstrate, in countries with poor reproductive health services and policies for their roots, many branches are not healthy and cannot thrive; the tree may even fail. Just as the health and even the survival of a tree rely on strong roots, the health and viability of a country and indeed the planet can be traced to population.

Still, unlike many other global problems and crises, the technology to meet the population challenge is readily available and extremely cost effective, if we have the will to supply it to those in need.

By the year 2050, world population is projected to grow from its current 6.7 billion to 9.3 billion; less optimistic calculations, based on fertility not declining from 2006 rates, place the figure at nearly 12 billion. Practically all growth is estimated to occur in the developing countries, especially in the poorest of those countries, which already produce virtually all of the world's human numbers.

While many nations have reduced rapid population growth, more than 3 billion people currently under 25 years old will soon enter their prime reproductive years. Providing this largest youth generation in history with appropriate sexual and reproductive health services and education is essential

From *The 21st Century Papers*, Number 2, 2007, pp. 1–9, 11–13, 15, 16, 18, 21–22, 23–24 (excerpts). Copyright © 2007 by Population Institute. Reprinted by permission.

to ease poverty, increase educational opportunities, preserve the environment, improve health, and provide political security. Meeting this challenge will be especially important in developing countries considered "fragile states," wherein booming populations would further stress already limited resources.

For population growth to slow and birthrates decline, Christopher Flavin, President of the Worldwatch Institute, has said, "It is essential that women and men around the world have increased access to sound information, a range of contraceptive options, and related health services. Access to voluntary family planning allows women and couples to time their births and choose the size of their families."

But at this critical moment, international support for family planning services faces ongoing annual reductions as the political climate has chilled and funds from many sectors are diverted to HIV/AIDS programs. In many countries, contraceptive use has risen only slowly or has stalled.

Ironically, in many developing countries, sexual and reproductive health education and services, especially meeting family planning needs, presents a cost-effective component in mitigating any of the above-mentioned issues.

The Challenge of Unmet Need

At the core of addressing population growth is managing unmet need. There is well documented unmet need for family planning, especially among the 2 billion people living on less than $2 a day.

Slower population growth offers a demographic dividend, allowing a country to invest more in education and health, thus serving the broader agendas of social and economic development.

It is also recognized that women are at the center of reproductive health efforts and addressing unmet need. As demographer Ruth Dixon-Mueller explains:

> Population control policies and programs would probably be unnecessary if women could exercise their basic economic, political and social rights and genuine reproductive choice. In addition, programs need to address the widespread unmet need in many countries for reproductive health services that would enable women to regulate the timing of their childbearing and, in particular, help women to avoid unwanted and mistimed pregnancies and unsafe abortion.

The definition of unmet need has undergone refinements over 25 years of discussion, but the basic objective is to estimate the proportion of women not using contraception who either want to cease further childbearing or want to postpone the next birth at least two years. The greatest need is in sub-Saharan Africa, where an average of 26 percent of married women are in the unmet need category. Other reports estimate the need among never-married women at 9 percent.

One calculation shows 113.6 million women (both married and unmarried) have an unmet need for contraception in the developing world. The World

Health Organization (WHO) estimates that over 120 million couples worldwide do not use contraceptives, despite wishing to limit or space their children.

While unmet need has lessened globally in recent decades, there are many more women now, in absolute numbers, than in years past, and many more younger women. Today there are almost 3 billion people under the age of 25, the largest generation of young people in history, 87 percent of whom live in the developing world. Meeting their sexual and reproductive health needs is central to their well being, as well as to population stabilization, poverty reduction, and sustainable development. The decisions of this "critical cohort" in the timing, sizing and spacing of their families will be a key factor in whether world population growth will be stabilized.

Where the need is met, family planning services work. In the 28 most populous countries receiving U.S. family planning assistance, the average number of children per family has dropped from 6.1 in the 1960s to 4.2 in 2003. In Colombia, Indonesia, and Mexico, the family average is three children, and in Taiwan and Thailand, early recipients of U.S. assistance, the average is two children.

The West African country of Ghana made family planning a public health priority in the early 1980s, and since then modern contraceptive use among married women has risen from 5.2 percent in 1988 to 18.7 percent in 2003. Ghana's rate of 64 infant deaths per 1,000 live births stands out from the regional average of 100 deaths, and the rate of HIV infection (2.2 percent) is half the West African average.

Further, one estimate shows that family planning services are preventing three-quarters of the induced abortions that would otherwise occur in the developing world. In addition, if every woman in the developing world with unmet need for a modern method used one, 52 million unintended pregnancies could be avoided annually.

Of the 46 million pregnancies that are terminated every year, only 60 percent are carried out under safe conditions. Almost all unsafe abortions take place in the developing world, with South America having the highest ratio. Although age patterns differ regionally, two-thirds of unsafe abortions occur among women aged 15 to 30.

The Cost-Effective Alternative

Prevention would seem a better policy. The cost to provide the services and supplies is estimated at $3.9 billion annually, but the savings would be much greater.

One example cited is a typical low-fertility Latin American country where every dollar spent on family planning saves $12 in health and education costs. Unfortunately, inflation-adjusted family planning spending has fallen since the mid-1990s. In the United States, President Bush's requests for overseas family planning program funding have been reduced from $425 million during the tenure of Secretary of State Colin Powell to $357 million under Secretary Condoleezza Rice.

The $34 million appropriated by Congress annually to the United Nations Population Fund (UNFPA) but blocked by the Bush administration, by one estimate, could have prevented 2 million unintentional pregnancies, nearly 800,000 abortions, 4,700 maternal deaths, and 77,000 infant and child deaths.

The planet now carries more people of child-bearing age than ever before, and yet a desired and cost-effective component in addressing the world's booming population is largely ignored in most policy discussions. The funds invested now in population programs will prevent conflicts, benefit the planet, and yield higher returns than any other investments in humanity's future. A convergence of potential calamities looms; offering couples the freedom to determine their own fertility is perhaps the only practical, the only realistic, option.

Population and the Millennium Development Goals

One notable example of how population growth is being overlooked in international development discussions comes through the Millennium Development Goals (MDGs) of the United Nations (UN). Eight MDGs (with 18 individual targets), based on the Millennium Declaration adopted in September 2000 by all 189 member states of the UN General Assembly, outline critical areas to be addressed by 2015, but did not originally cite population growth. One population researcher efficiently sums up the oversight: "Although reproductive health was not specifically included as an independent goal or a measurable target in the MDGs, for years experts have provided evidence that investing in reproductive health services is integral to meeting them all."

A 2007 report from the All Party Parliamentary Group (APPG) on Population, Development and Reproductive Health in the United Kingdom explores the impact of population on the first seven goals, and concludes "The evidence is overwhelming: the MDGs are difficult or impossible to achieve with the current levels of population growth in the least developed countries and regions."

The last half of the twentieth century provides the foundation for this conclusion:

> On the whole, those countries and regions where information and contraceptives were made available saw a moderate to rapid decline in the birth rate. In addition, there was an improvement in the economy, the health of women and their families, and the autonomy, education and status of women. The countries where many pregnancies remained unwanted and the birth rate did not fall are now seeing an explosive growth of urban slums, a failure of the state to keep pace with educational demands and, in some cases, the continuing oppression of women.

On a positive note, the APPG report states that the UN has approved a new target of universal access to reproductive health care by 2015, to be placed under Goal 5, Improve Maternal Health.

Still, "It is clear that the MDGs are difficult or impossible to achieve without a renewed focus on, and investment in, family planning." The recommendations in the report include targeting 10 percent of international development aid to population and reproductive health, putting the availability of contraceptive supplies as a top priority, and eliminating barriers to family planning.

Rising from Poverty

One country claims to have already met the first MDG target. The People's Republic of China reported to the APPG that through a combination of lowered birth rates and economic reform, 150 million people have been lifted out of abject poverty, thus meeting the MDG for poverty reduction a decade earlier than the target date. Nonetheless, controversy surrounding China's "One Child" policy will make others uncertain of the means to achieve the end. In fact, China is one case cited by population experts as having created an unwarranted stigma among critics and commentators on the topic of reproductive health.

Economists acknowledge that the link between slower population growth and economic development is complex and does not always result in an escape from poverty. Still, a "demographic dividend" occurs when family sizes drop rapidly, leaving relatively more people of working age with fewer dependents, and the ability to invest more resources in those dependents in terms of health and education. In developing countries where the birth rate has fallen, between 25 and 40 percent of economic growth is attributable to the demographic change.

Population Growth Outpacing Education

The second MDG, achieving universal primary education, seems especially daunting in the face of rising population pressures. In Tanzania, literacy rates fell from 90 percent in 1986 to 68 percent in 1995, attributed to increased school fees as the government was unable to keep pace with public service costs for its growing population. The country's population during the period grew from just under 22 million to nearly 30 million.

Almost 30 percent of the world population is under age 15, and the United Nations Children's Fund (UNICEF) estimates there are 115 million children of primary school age who are not in school. In high growth countries, the number of school-aged children doubles every 20 years. Assuming a class size of 40, an extra 2 million school teachers per year are required just to meet existing needs.

According to one World Bank report, the annual cost of meeting the MDG education goal ranges from $10 to $30 billion. In another report, World Bank researchers estimate the annual costs in low-income countries would be $9.7 billion annually, of which $3.7 billion would be needed from international assistance, many times higher than actual aid flows. Africa, for example, would need 75 percent of their total from external support.

While hope comes from countries that have registered an improvement of 20 percent or more within a decade in the primary school completion rate (e.g., Brazil, Nicaragua, Cambodia, South Africa, The Gambia), progress is fragile, and other countries, even some with strong financial resources, have lost ground (e.g., Albania, Zambia, Qatar, Bahrain, United Arab Emirates, Kenya, and Venezuela).

Success in achieving universal primary education nonetheless raises an interesting series of questions. Should countries meet the goal, will they have follow-on capacity to meet the needs of the large numbers of students who would like to continue their education to various levels? Do they have the capacity to satisfy the employment options for newly educated students? Would a brain drain result as students go abroad seeking higher education? No doubt many students would not be satisfied to return to a simple or subsistence lifestyle, but it is doubtful that most countries would have the capacity to build yet more schools and train enough staff to accommodate the greater ambitions of their students.

A slowing of the exponential rate of increase in the population of young people would allow countries to more realistically over time create the infrastructures to accommodate their numbers and ambitions. Thus the attainment of access to education for all children presents a powerful argument for the immediate and urgent need to extend access to family planning.

Although there may be potential local obstacles, the curricula for these children should include health education, and reproductive health education should be considered as students enter reproductive age.

Gender Educational Parity Missing Mark

The second and third millennium goals are closely intertwined. The first part of the target for MDG 3 has already passed without being met: "Eliminate gender disparity in primary and secondary education preferably by 2005." While 125 countries, both developing and industrialized, were on course to eventually achieve gender parity, overall enrollment remains low.

Some 94 countries missed the 2005 target for gender parity, and 86 may not achieve this by 2015, according to the United Nations Educational, Scientific and Cultural Organization (UNESCO). By contrast, Iran (where family size has declined to replacement level fertility) has already achieved a 90 percent gender balance, and more women than men enter Iran's universities.

High Fertility and Child, Maternal Mortality

Reducing child mortality and improving maternal health, MDGs 4 and 5, respectively, are essential aspects in addressing population stability. High fertility is strongly associated with child mortality and greatly increases a woman's lifetime risk of dying from pregnancy-related causes. Women will never be empowered until they achieve full control over their reproductive health.

The data indicate that much progress is required. Since 1990, there has been less than a one percent annual decline in deaths of women from pregnancy and childbirth complications. In 2005, 536,000 women—one each minute—died of maternal causes. The world's poorest countries account for

99 percent of these, the vast majority of which are preventable with at least minimal prenatal care and the assistance of skilled birth attendants. According to estimates, access to voluntary family planning could reduce maternal deaths by 20 to 35 percent.

Population and Fragile/Failed States

The issues affected by population range well beyond those promoted by the MDGs. In recent years the term "fragile states" has been used by the World Bank and other prominent international organizations, not without some controversy, to describe countries at risk from a mix of internal and outside factors.

The World Bank publishes a list of low-income countries under stress (LICUS), or fragile states, from among the 82 International Development Agency (IDA) borrowing countries. In fiscal year 2007 there were 34 countries on the list, up from 25 in 2005. The designation refers to countries scoring 3.2 and below on the Country Policy and Institutional Assessment (CPIA), which is the primary tool to assess the quality of country policies and the main input to IDA's Performance-Based Allocation system. In general terms, they are states that lack either the capacity or the will to deliver on core state functions, and where international partners find it difficult to engage.

Although country contexts vary considerably, the fragile states are home to almost 500 million persons, with child mortality rates twice as high as other low income countries, life expectancy 12 years lower, maternal mortality rates some 20 percent higher, and gross domestic product (GDP) rates typically half that of the others. Additional challenges these fragile states must confront are extreme poverty, low levels of human and social development, weak institutional capacity, and slow growth. Three out of four are affected by ongoing armed conflicts.

In a policy and principle strategy document for dealing with fragile states, Europe's Organization for Economic Cooperation and Development expressed its intent to focus on state building as the central objective, including "ensuring security and justice, mobilizing revenue, establish an enabling environment for basic service delivery, strong economic performance, and employment generation." The document notes that efforts must recognize the interdependence of political, security, economic and social spheres, and that gender equity, social inclusion, and human rights must be consistently promoted.

However, a special focus on population stabilization is needed as well. A state's natural resources are usually known and finite: arable land, port access, available water and forest lands, as well as infrastructure: roads, bridges and major buildings, which take medium to long-term planning to develop. However, population growth may often be much more difficult to quantify. What is known is that if a state is having trouble delivering services to its existing citizens, rapid population growth will surely hamper development planning and strategies. And common among nearly all the fragile states is high population growth. . . .

Population and the Environment

Any modern consumer of mass media is familiar with climate change and interrelated topics such as global warming, greenhouse gases, environmental degradation, and pollution. Of the challenges discussed so far, expanding population is perhaps most closely intertwined with climate change, and yet population is routinely ignored in most discussions. As such, population growth should become a second front in the battle against climate change, as one of the easiest and least costly, yet most neglected, options available.

It is recognized that the industrialized world, especially the United States, is among the major contributors to global warming through the burning of fossil fuels. No real progress can be made until industrialized countries address their high consumption and resulting effects on the planet. Least developed countries produce only a fraction of the emissions of the industrialized world. Total emissions from the developing world are expected to exceed those from the industrialized world by 2015.

Nonetheless, programs addressing the various issues of climate change that neglect the incorporation of population growth strategies are seriously flawed. In March 2007 the Associated Press reported that the head of the U.S. National Oceanic and Atmospheric Administration (NOAA) said the biggest challenge facing the world is population growth and people's desire to live in coastal areas where they can be endangered by storms.

Although wealthier, industrialized countries with large populations account for much of the consumption and greenhouse gases, environmental degradation in many less-industrialized countries is increasing as their rising populations struggle to survive, and this will have serious, long-term consequences. Such activities as clearing forests for grazing, crops, and living space, chopping wood for fuel, over-fishing and abuse of local marine ecosystems, diversion and overuse of fresh water systems, illegal strip mining and forestry, and unchecked burning for agriculture will only increase as populations grow. The environments in resource-poor countries will be especially at risk.

Addressing population growth is not an issue of limiting numbers of specific groups of human beings. But it is clear that many regions will remain at risk until their populations are stabilized and the capacity to adequately support more people is created. One economic report notes the evidence shows that ignoring climate change will eventually damage economic growth, but that tackling it does not cap the aspirations for growth for rich or poor countries.

The Intergovernmental Panel on Climate Change reports that many human systems are sensitive to climate change, including water resources, agriculture and forestry, fisheries, human settlements, energy, industry, insurance and other financial systems, and human health. The IPCC projects adverse impacts such as a general reduction in potential crop yields in most tropical and subtropical regions; decreased water availability for populations in many water-scarce regions; an increase in the number of people exposed to vector-borne and water-borne diseases; an increase in heat stress mortality; and increased energy demand for space cooling.

Nonetheless, population seems to be missing from many environmental discussions. Of the few voices making the connection between population and global warming, perhaps the most well known is Chris Rapley, head of the Science Museum in London. Quoted in a July 2007 *Telegraph* newspaper article, Rapley said, "My position on population is that I am disturbed that no one will talk about it." Among other things, Rapley told the newspaper that saving a gigaton of carbon emissions through education for women and birth control programs would cost 1,000 times less than any of the other technical options available, such as nuclear power, renewables, or increased car efficiency.

A year earlier, Rapley opined on a British Broadcasting Corporation website that population was a "Cinderella" subject, rarely visible in public or even private, and noting that it is in fact ". . . A bombshell of a topic, with profound and emotive issues of ethics, morality, equity and practicability."

Along with the issues discussed in international global warming meetings, Rapley noted that attention is merited by a much broader range of human impacts contributing to global warming, such as land cover, the water cycle, the health of ecosystems, and biodiversity, as well as the release of other chemicals into the environment, the massive transport and mixing of biological material worldwide, and the unsustainable consumption of resources. All of these effects interconnect and add up to the collective footprint of humankind on the planet's life support systems:

> Although reducing human emissions to the atmosphere is undoubtedly of critical importance, as are any and all measures to reduce the human environmental "footprint," the truth is that the contribution of each individual cannot be reduced to zero. Only the lack of the individual can bring it down to nothing. So if we believe that the size of the human "footprint" is a serious problem (and there is much evidence for this) then a rational view would be that along with a raft of measures to reduce the footprint per person, the issue of population management must be addressed.

In describing how environmental writers are part of the problem for not mentioning population growth in their discussions, environmental writer and activist John Feeney notes that it is well known among scientists that the size and growth of the global population is a root cause of environmental degradation, including climate change. He comments on one author who avoids the subject because it is "political poison," stemming from negative reactions to news of coercive family planning policies in some countries, free market capitalism that stresses growth, and political wrangling by concerned groups.

In an online article about peak oil and carrying capacity, Canadian writer Paul Chefurka calls population the "elephant in the room:"

> At the root of all the converging crises of the World Problematique is the issue of human overpopulation. Each of the global problems we face today is the result of too many people using too much of our planet's finite, non-renewable resources . . . The true danger posed by our exploding population is not our absolute numbers but the inability of our environment to cope with so many of us doing what we do.

Population and Clean Water/Sanitation

Of the conflicts between population and resources, the one which will emerge the soonest and perhaps most dramatically will involve clean drinking water and a scarcity of water for sanitation, agriculture, and other uses. In the most tragic of circumstances, humans can survive in war zones and through natural disasters, they can bear disease and live marginally without shelter. Even a lack of adequate food does not mean a quick death. But humans can survive a lack of potable water for only a few days at most.

The United Nations has stated that more than 2.7 billion people will face severe water shortages by 2025 if world consumption of water continues at current rates, and another 2.5 billion will live in areas where it will be difficult to find sufficient fresh water to meet their needs. However, the UN also predicts consumption rates will increase by up to 12 percent per decade until 2025.

The head of the UN agency tasked with promoting socially and environmentally sustainable housing has warned that water will become the dominant issue of this century and its availability could threaten the world's social stability. Indeed, the UN Development Programme made the issue of water scarcity the subject of its 2006 Human Development Report. . . .

International development funding has not responded to this rising need and may not always reach those who need it most. The share of water as part of total official development assistance has remained at about 5 percent, while spending for education, health, and emergency aid has risen sharply. In addition, between 1990 and 2004, 60 percent of development assistance for water went to 20 countries and is still being distributed unequally between countries, according to a World Water Council report.

The implications of water needs and population growth are troubling. Of the top 20 recipient nations for water sector funding, 11 are in the top 20 overall in terms of world population rankings. However, only seven are rated by the UN as being least developed or other low income countries. According to the World Water Council, the three predominant factors when it comes to receiving aid are being demographically small, politically stable, and geopolitically "visible."

Populous and poor states not among the top 20 recipient will need to address their water risks without the bulk of international support. Family planning would be a very effective component in helping them manage the future. . . .

Population and Food Security

Food security is closely tied in many ways to climate change and water scarcity. Several additional factors affect the dynamic, however, including global food production (and the uncertainty over shifts from harvesting corn to producing more corn for ethanol), domestic subsidies, food aid, world prices for fertilizers and pesticides, and genetically modified crops.

In an interesting twist that clearly outlines the complex and troubling interrelationship between population growth, agriculture and climate change, while agriculture is a victim of climate change, it is also part of the problem. Livestock accounts for 18 percent of global greenhouse gas emissions, while forestry and deforestation is responsible for 18 percent of carbon dioxide emissions. Rice production is perhaps the main source of anthropogenic methane, emitting some 50 to 100 million metric tons per year.

Growing populations in states with at-risk agricultural production will only exacerbate the potential for both internal and cross-border conflicts. Lester R. Brown, president of the Earth Policy Institute, writes ". . . achieving an acceptable worldwide balance between food and people may now depend on stabilizing population as soon as possible, reducing the unhealthily high consumption of livestock products in industrial countries, and restricting the conversion of food crops to automotive fuels. . . ."

Population and Global Security

Population growth was an underlying if not a primary cause of the largest conflict in human history, the Second World War. In Germany, Adolf Hitler's principle of *lebensraum*, or "living space" for the growing German population, was a central component of his justification for the Nazi invasions into neighboring countries.

In Japan, an island nation with high population density in many areas, the need for resources for a growing population and economy was a part of the drive to invade Manchuria and other parts of China, as well as much of the rest of the Pacific region, beginning in the 1930s. Public policy researcher Jack Goldstone notes that population-related conflicts have been going on for centuries.

Growing populations in areas of dwindling resources have caused or intensified conflicts in many corners of the world. The situation in Sudan's Darfur region is one of the better-known of these. According to Kenyan environmentalist Wangari Maathai, 2004 Nobel Peace Prize recipient, "Darfur is an example of a situation where a dire scarcity of natural resources is manipulated by politicians . . . At its roots it is a struggle over controlling an environment that can no longer support all the people who must live on it."

Another key issue in conflict is rapid urbanization and the "youth bulge" in many countries. A spike in the numbers of young people can create strains on public services, such as education and health, and other resources, exacerbated by a lack of jobs, leading to increased poverty, overcrowding, frustration, alienation and unrest. Alternatively, as the proportion of young adults decreases, so does political instability, for example in Japan, South Korea, Thailand, and Sri Lanka.

Along these same lines, researchers have demonstrated that in countries with low birth rates and low infant mortality, the likelihood of civil conflict is less than in those with high birth rates and high infant mortality. As birth rates and infant mortality increase, the likelihood of civil conflict increases in a clear progression.

Population researcher Katherine Weiland has argued: "Family planning programs should be implemented as an essential component of national security for developing as well as developed countries. Achieving global security requires a worldwide commitment, through global cooperation, to attacking the social and economic problems that lead to insecurity." This cooperation and commitment is critical because,

> In today's interconnected world, conflict in less developed countries affects not only one country or region but has dangerous implications for global security. Globalization has created a world where stable countries are no longer isolated from their unstable neighbors and civil strife can easily move across borders and erupt into war.

Demographers and both social scientists and military experts have linked global security and population, which was regarded as a non-traditional security issue just a decade ago.

These include the promotion of a demographic transition of populations from high to low rates of birth and death; ensuring easily accessible reproductive health services for refugees, civilians in post-conflict environments, and all military personnel; and supporting improvements in the legal, educational and economic status of women to reach a "security demographic," a distinctive range of population structures and dynamics that make civil conflict less likely.

According to Goldstone, there are six major population trends that are likely to pose significant security challenges to developed nations by 2025, among them being the rapid growth and predominant role of urban populations in developing countries, shrinking populations in Europe, opposing age shifts between aging developed and youthful developing countries, and increasing migration from developing to developed countries. . . .

Population and Other Issues

The convergence of the concerns described through this paper will, of course, have a shock wave effect on several other associated issues, such as migration, refugees, poverty, health, and education.

To touch briefly on one of these, scientists are already issuing alarms related to increased risks from disease as populations rise. For example, countries with high population growth will experience the most severe increases in diarrheal and infectious diseases caused by climate change. WHO has tied rising global population to an unprecedented number (39 in all) of emerging new diseases, including AIDS, Ebola, SARS, and bird flu.

The many factors at the interface of human population growth and disease were explored in a 2007 paper in *Human Ecology,* and included health hazards such as poor vector control and sanitation, water and food contamination, air pollution, natural disasters, and chemical pollution.

Thus, the impact of population growth goes far beyond the issues covered here. But again, population is the root from which all issues and concerns are developed, and represents the obvious starting point in addressing realistic and practical resolutions.

Summary

The purpose of this paper has been to show the connections between population growth and several key, broad-ranging topical issues, whether meeting the Millennium Development Goals, resolving issues of climate change, addressing shortages of water and food, or examining aspects of global security. These connections are at times understood to various degrees by decision-makers, while at other times population has been overlooked or ignored.

A focus on population growth and international family planning programming, including commodities, distribution, and education, should be a part of any resolutions discussed for the myriad problems reviewed in this report. Family planning is one of the most proven and most cost-effective components for reaching real solutions to many of the world's more pressing problems.

It is recognized that reproductive health and family planning issues are complex and involve history, politics, local agendas, ethics, cultural norms and values, power relations, health, women's and human rights, economics, poverty, education and myriad other components and realities. All are urgent, and effective programs must include a comprehensive understanding of all issues.

Sexual and reproductive health, particularly family planning, is not a panacea in stabilizing global pressures. It also does not operate in a vacuum, any more than the other issues described. The potential solutions to each are also inextricably bound to each other. But as a component, population stability is a necessary and critical step in the effort to secure a positive future for all the earth's citizens; moreover, it is the key theme that binds them all.

There is reason for hope. Countries in which family planning is a routine part of health care have stabilized their populations, seen economic growth and political stability, and have provided education and health care for a greater share of their population. Tunisia, Egypt, Indonesia, and Mexico are just a few success stories for international family planning efforts.

Ultimately, the decisions of individual women will determine population growth. Given modern family planning knowledge, options, and access, women limit the size and spacing of their families. How well the world responds in providing information, education and supplies to those in need will be the key to managing the numerous, potential threats of the modern era.

Steven W. Mosher  **NO**

McNamara's Folly: Bankrolling Family Planning

At the same time that Reimert Ravenholt was setting up his "powerful population program," the nations of Western Europe, along with Japan, were being encouraged by the administration of President Lyndon B. Johnson to make family planning a priority of their own aid programs. International organizations, primarily the UN and its affiliated agencies, were also being leveraged on board. Together, they helped to create and maintain the illusion that the international community was solidly behind population control programs. (It wasn't, and isn't, as we shall see.) But it was the World Bank and its billions that was the real prize for the anti-natalists. And they captured it when one of their own, Robert McNamara, was appointed as President in 1968.[1]

McNamara Moves In

McNamara came to the World Bank from the post of Secretary of Defense, where he had unsuccessfully prosecuted the Vietnam War by focusing on "kill ratios" and the "pacification of the natives" instead of victory. A former automobile executive, he was prone to cost-cutting measures which sometimes proved to be false economies, as when he decreed that a new class of ship—the fleet frigate—should have only one screw instead of the customary two. This saved the expense of a second turbine and drive train, but the frigate—known to the Navy as McNamara's Folly—lacked speed, was hard to berth, and had to be retired early.[2] The population policies he was to advocate suffered from similar defects.

When the Boards of the World Bank and the International Monetary Fund convened on October 1 of that year, President Johnson made a surprise appearance.[3] Technology in the underdeveloped nations, he said, had "bought time for family planning policies to become effective. But the fate of development hinges on how vigorously that time is used."

No More People

The stage was now set for McNamara to get up and attack the "population explosion," saying that it was "one of the greatest barriers to the economic growth and social well-being of our member states." The World Bank

From *PRI Review*, March/April 2003. Copyright © 2003 by Population Research Institute. Reprinted by permission.

would no longer stand idly by in the face of this threat, McNamara said, but would:

> Let the developing nations know the extent to which rapid population growth slows down their potential development, and that, in consequence, the optimum employment of the world's scarce development funds requires attention to this problem. Seek opportunities to finance facilities required by our member countries to carry out family planning programs. Join with others in programs of research to determine the most effective methods of family planning and of national administration of population control programs.[4]

It quickly became evident that "the optimum employment of the world's scarce development funds" meant in practice that the World Bank, the International Monetary Fund (IMF), and its network of regional development banks would act as loan sharks for the anti-natalists, pressuring sovereign nations into accepting family planning programs on pain of forfeiting vital short-term, long-term, and soft loans.[5] This practice is well known in the developing world, as when a Dhaka daily, *The New Nation,* headline read, "WB [World Bank] Conditions Aid to Population Control."[6]

McNamara also began providing loans for population and family planning projects, including those which involved abortion (both surgical and through abortifacient chemicals). By 1976 the National Security Council (NSC) was able to praise the World Bank for being "the principal international financial institution providing population programs."[7] Details are hard to come by, however. The World Bank is one of the most secretive organizations in the world, besides being effectively accountable to no one. It is known that there is a carefully segregated population division, which reportedly employs approximately 500 people. But those who work on conventional development projects are not privy to what goes on in this division, which is off-limits to all but those who work there.[8]

Fewer People, More Money

A rare inside look at the organization's activities in this area is provided by a recent World Bank report, entitled *Improving Reproductive Health: The Role of the World Bank.* Written in a distinctly self-congratulatory tone, the document reveals that the Bank has spent over $2.5 billion over the last twenty-five years to support 130 reproductive health projects in over 70 countries. Indonesia and Lesotho, for example, have been the site of "'information, education and communication' campaigns about sex and reproductive health." India has been the beneficiary of several different programs, which the report claims have "helped bring India two-thirds of the way towards her goal of replacement level fertility." No mention is made of the fact that the Indian campaigns have been notorious for their coercive tactics. Or that McNamara visited India at the height of the compulsory sterilization campaign in 1976 to congratulate the government for its "political will and determination" in the campaign and, one would suspect, to offer new loans.[9]

The World Bank also promotes abortion. *Improving Reproductive Health* openly admits that, since the 1994 Cairo Conference on Population and Development, the first of the World Bank's goals in the area of reproductive health has been "providing access and *choice* in family planning." [italics added] Except for its candor, this promotion of abortion should come as no surprise. In Burkina Faso, for example, we are told that World Bank projects have included "mobilizing public awareness and political support" [that is, lobbying] for abortion and other reproductive health services.

The Bank has long been accused of pressuring nations, such as Nigeria, into legalizing abortion. In 1988, for example, abortion was virtually unthinkable as an official family planning practice in Nigeria. As recently as 1990, the Planned Parenthood Federation of Nigeria was forced to defend itself against allegations that it promoted the sale and use of "contraceptives" that were abortifacient in character. A year later—and two months after approval of a $78 million World Bank population loan—the government announced proposals for allowing abortion under certain circumstances.[10]

Population control loans skyrocketed after the Cairo conference. The Bank reported that, in the two years that followed, it had "lent almost $1 billion in support of population and reproductive health objectives."[11] And the numbers have been climbing since then. But even this is just the tip of the iceberg. As Jacqueline Kasun notes, "Given the conditions which the bank imposes on its lending, the entire $20 billion of its annual disbursements is properly regarded as part of the world population control effort."[12]

No More Reform

Despite his predilection for population control, McNamara never abandoned more conventional aid modalities, roads, dams, power plants, and the like. Not so James Wolfensohn, who became the head of the Bank in 1995. Asked at the 1996 World Food Summit in Rome how the World Bank understood its mission towards the developing world, Wolfensohn replied that there was a "new paradigm" at the Bank. "From now on," Wolfensohn said, "the business of the World Bank will not be primarily economic reform, or governmental reform. The business of the World Bank will primarily be social reform." The Bank has learned, he added, that attempting to reform a nation's economics or government without first reforming the society "usually means failure."

The benefits to nations who are willing to fall into line in the "civil society" will be immediate and intensely attractive. "The World Bank will be willing to look favorably on any reasonable plan for debt reduction—and even debt forgiveness," Wolfensohn told the assembled reporters, "provided that the nation in question is willing to follow a sensible social policy." Wolfensohn went on to tell reporters that population control activities are a *sine qua non* for any social policy to be considered "sensible."[13]

The World Bank is also, according to Wolfensohn, prepared to begin "directly funding—not through loans" certain NGOs in the countries involved, to further ensure that governments adopt "sensible social policies." Thus fueled with money from the World Bank, the heat these favored NGOs will be able to generate on their governments to adopt, say, population control programs, including legalized abortion, will be considerable.[14] Of course, other international organizations, not to mention USAID and European aid agencies, have been using this tactic for many years with great effect. Recalcitrant governments (who may innocently believe that they do not have a population "problem") are thus sandwiched between the demands of international lenders and aid givers on the one hand, and the demands of "local" NGOs—loud, persistent and extremely well-funded—on the other.

Rapid Spread of Programs

With the U.S., international organizations, and an increasing number of developed countries now working in tandem to strong-arm developing countries into compliance, anti-natalist programs spread with startling rapidity. Bernard Berelson, the head of the Population Council, happily reported in 1970 that:

> In 1960 only three countries had anti-natalist population policies (all on paper), only one government was offering assistance [that is, funding population control programs overseas], no international organizations was working on family planning. In 1970 nearly 25 countries on all three developing continents, with 67 percent of the total population, have policies and programs; and another 15 or so, with 12 percent of the population, provide support in the absence of an explicitly formulated policy . . . five to ten governments now offer external support (though only two in any magnitude); and the international assistance system is formally on board (the U.N. Population Division, the UNDP, WHO, UNESCO, FAO, ILO, OECD, the World Bank).[15]

The recklessness with which Ravenholt, McNamara and others forced crude anti-natal programs upon the developing world dismayed many even within the movement. Ronald Freedman, a leading sociologist/demographer, complained in 1975 that, "If reducing the birth rate is that important and urgent, then the results of the expanded research during the 1960s are still *pathetically inadequate. There are serious proposals for social programs on a vast scale to change reproductive institutions and values that have been central to human society for millennia.*"[16] [italics added] This was social engineering with a vengeance, Freedman was saying, and *we don't know what we are doing.*

With even committed controllers saying "Slow down!" one might think that the anti-natalists would hesitate. But their army had already been assembled and its generals had sounded the advance; it could not be halted now. Even Freedman, rhetorically throwing up his hands, conceded that "many people . . . are eager for knowledge that can be used in action programs aimed at accelerating fertility decline," and that the programs would have to proceed by "a process of trial and error." The *trials* of course would be funded by the developed world; while the *errors,* murderous and costly, would be borne by poor women and families in the developed world.

What justification was offered for this massive investment of U.S. prestige and capital in these programs? Stripped of its later accretions—protecting the environment, promoting economic development, advancing the rights of women—at the outset it was mostly blatant self-interest. McNamara, who headed an organization ostensibly devoted to the welfare of the developing countries, had told the World Bank's Board of Governors in 1968 that "population growth slows down their potential development." But he told the *Christian Science Monitor* some years later that continued population growth would lead to "poverty, hunger, stress, crowding, and frustration," which would threaten social, economic, and military stability. This would not be "a world that anyone wants," he declared.[17] It was certainly not the world that many in the security establishment wanted, as secret National Security Council deliberations would soon make starkly clear.

Cold War Against Population

As the populations of developing world countries began to grow after World War Two, the U.S. national security establishment—the Pentagon, the Central Intelligence Agency, the National Security Agency, and the National Security Council—became concerned. Population was an important element of national power, and countries with growing populations would almost inevitably increase in geopolitical weight. This was obviously a concern in the case of countries opposed to U.S. interests, such as the Soviet Union and China. But even allies might prove less pliable as their populations and economies grew. Most worrisome of all was the possibility that the rapidly multiplying peoples of Asia, Africa, and Latin America would turn to communism in their search for independence and economic advancement *unless their birth rate was reduced*. Thus did population control become a weapon in the Cold War. . . .

Earth First (People Last): Environmental Movement Signs On

Every sorcerer deserves an apprentice. Hugh Moore, grand wizard of the population explosion, got his in the person of a young Stanford University entomologist by the name of Paul Ehrlich. In the very first sentence of his very first book Ehrlich proved beyond all doubt that he had already mastered Moore's panic-driven style. "The battle to feed all of humanity is over," he wrote. "In the 1970s the world will undergo famines—hundreds of million of people will starve to death in spite of any crash programs embarked upon now."[18]

In fact, he had gone Moore one better, as overzealous acolytes are prone to do. His book should have been named *The Population Explosion,* instead of *The Population Bomb,* for according to Ehrlich the "bomb" had already gone off and there was nothing to do now but wait for the inevitable human die-back. "Too many people" were chasing "too little food."[19] The most optimistic of Ehrlich's "scenarios" involved the immediate imposition of a harsh regimen of population control and resource conservation around the world, with the goal of reducing the number of people to 1.5 billion (about a fourth of its current level) over the next century or two. Even so, about a fifth of the world's population would still starve to death in the immediate future.

Such a prediction took pluck, for when the book appeared in 1968 there was no hint of massive famine on the horizon. The days of Indian food shortages were past. (We wouldn't learn about China's man-made calamity until a decade later.) The Green Revolution was starting to pay off in increased crop yields. And experts like Dr. Karl Brandt, the Director of the Stanford Food Research Institute, rebuked Ehrlich, saying that "Many nations need more people, not less, to cultivate food products and build a sound agricultural economy . . . every country that makes the effort can produce all the food it needs."[20]

But it wasn't his forecast of a massive human die-off that catapulted Ehrlich into the front rank of environmental prophets. (In a motif that has since become familiar, the book left readers with the impression that this might not be such a bad thing.) Rather it was his startling claim that our reckless breeding had jeopardized earth's ability to support life. All life, not just human life. Our planet was literally dying. Not only were the Children of Earth killing ourselves, we were going to take Mother with us as well.

The Population Bomb

Heavily promoted by the Sierra Club, *The Population Bomb* sold over a million copies. Ehrlich became an instant celebrity, becoming as much of a fixture on the "Tonight Show" as Johnny Carson's sidekick Ed McMahon. He command[ed] hefty lecture fees wherever he went (and he went everywhere), and always drew a crowd. People found it entertaining to hear about the end of the world. Likening the earth to an overloaded spaceship or sinking lifeboat, issuing apocalyptic warnings about the imminent "standing room only" problem, he captured the popular imagination. His prescriptions were always the same: "Join the environmental movement, stop having children, and save the planet."[21]

While Ehrlich fiddled his apocalyptic tunes, Moore burned to commit the growing environmental movement firmly to a policy of population control. His ad campaign, still ongoing, began suggesting that the best kind of environmental protection was population control. "Whatever Your Cause, It's a Lost Cause Unless We Control Population," one ad read. "Warning: The Water You are Drinking May be Polluted," read another, whose text went on to equate more people with more pollution. A third, addressed to "Dear President Nixon," claimed that "We can't lick the environment problem without considering this little fellow." It featured a picture of a newborn baby.

Birth of Earth Day

Moore went all out for the first Earth Day in 1970, printing a third of a million leaflets, folders, and pamphlets for campus distribution. College newspapers received free cartoons highlighting the population crisis and college radio stations a free taped show (featuring Paul Ehrlich). With his genius for marketing, Moore even announced a contest with cash awards for the best slogans relating environmental problems to what he called "popullution" [population pollution]. Students on over 200 campuses participated. The winner, not surprisingly, was "People Pollute."[22]

By 1971 most of the leading environmental groups had signed on to the anti-natal agenda, having been convinced that reducing the human birth rate would greatly benefit the environment. Perhaps it was their interest in "managing" populations of other species—salmon, condors, whales, etc.—that predisposed them to impose technical solutions on their own species. In any event, many of them were population hawks, who believed that simply making abortion, sterilization and contraception widely available was not enough. "Voluntarism is a farce," wrote Richard Bowers of Zero Population Growth as early as 1969. "The private sector effort has failed . . . [even the expenditure] of billions of dollars will not limit growth." Coercive measures were required. He proposed enacting "criminal laws to limit population, if the earth is to survive."[23]

Those who held such views were not content to merely stop people from multiplying, they demanded radical reductions in human numbers. The group Negative Population Growth wanted to cut the then–U.S. population of 200 million by more than half, to 90 million.[24] Celebrated oceanographer Jacques Cousteau told the *UNESCO Courier* in 1991, "In order to stabilize world populations, we must eliminate 350,000 people per day." Garrett Hardin of "The Tragedy of the Commons" fame opined that the "carrying capacity" of the planet was 100 million and that our numbers should be reduced accordingly. (Do we pick the lucky 100 million by lottery?) To carry out these decimations, Malthusian solutions are proposed, as when novelist William T. Vollman stated that, "there are too many people in the world and maybe something like AIDS or something like war may be a good thing on that level."[25] And lest we have compunctions about resorting to such measures, we should bear in mind, as Earth First! Founder Dave Foreman wrote, "We humans have become a disease, the Humanpox."

The Feminist Dilemma

The most radical of the feminists had a different definition of disease. Why should women be "subject to the species gnawing at their vitals," as Simone de Beauvoir so memorably wrote in her feminist classic *The Second Sex?* Why endure pregnancy at all, if contraception, sterilization and, especially, abortion, could be made widely available? With the legalization of abortion in the U.S. in 1973, feminists increasingly looked overseas, eager to extend their newfound rights to "women of color" elsewhere in the world. They had read their Ehrlich as well as their Beauvior, and knew that the world had too many people, or soon would. But family planning, especially abortion, provided a way out. "Let us bestow upon all the women of the world the blessing that we women in the privileged West have received—freedom from fear of pregnancy," the feminists said to themselves. "We will, at the same time and by the same means, solve the problem of too many babies. For surely impoverished Third World women do not actually want all those children they are bearing. Patriarchy has made them into breeding machines, but we will set them free."

Abortion "Needs" Appear

At the time, the population control movement remained ambivalent over the question of abortion. Hugh Moore had long wanted it as a population control measure, but Frank Notestein was still arguing in the early 1970s that the Population Council should "consistently and firmly take the anti-abortion stance and use every occasion to point out that the need for abortions is the proof of program failure in the field of family planning and public health education."[26]

But the women's movement would not be put off with the promise of a perfect contraceptive. They knew, better than anyone (and often from painful personal experience) that contraception, because of the inevitable failures, *always* led to abortion. As Sharon Camp of the Population Crisis Committee wrote "both abortion and contraception are presently on the rise in most developing countries."[27]

Abortion was, in the end, accepted by most controllers because it came to be seen as a necessary part of the anti-natal arsenal. The Rockefeller Commission, established by President Nixon, wrote that "We are impressed that induced abortion has a demographic effect wherever legalized" and on these grounds went on to call for "abortion on demand."[28] The Population Council followed the Commission in endorsing abortion as a means of population control by 1975.

In the end, feminist advocacy of abortion had proven decisive. The feminists had given the population control movement an additional weapon, abortion, to use in its drive to reduce human fecundity, and encouraged its aggressive use.

Third World Women

At the same time, it was soon apparent to many feminists that birth control was not an unmixed blessing for Third World women, who continued to be targets of ever-more aggressive programs in places like Indonesia, India, and Bangladesh. They began to demand further changes in the way programs were carried out, starting with male contraceptives and more vasectomies. Frank Notestein wrote of the feminists that, "As second-generation suffragists they were not at all disposed to allow the brutish male to be in charge of contraception. Women must have their own methods!" But more recent feminists "complain violently that the men are trying to saddle the women with all the contraceptive work. You can't please them if you do, and can't please them if you don't."[29]

Although expressed somewhat crudely, Notestein's comment pointed out the dilemma faced by feminists. On the one hand, they sought to impose a radically pro-abortion agenda on population control programs, whose general purpose—fertility reduction—they applauded. On the other they tried to protect women from the abuses that invariably accompanied such programs. But with the exception of the condom, other methods of contraception all put the burden on women. Vasectomies could easily be performed on men, but it was usually the woman who went under the knife to have her tubes tied. And abortions could only be performed on women. So, as a practical matter, the burden of fertility reduction was placed disproportionately on women. And when programs took a turn towards the coercive, as they were invariably prone to do in the Third World, it was overwhelmingly women who paid the price.

Feminist complaints did lead to some changes, but these were mostly cosmetic. Population controllers did learn, over time, to speak a different language or, rather, several different languages, to disguise the true, anti-natal purpose of their efforts. When Western feminists need to be convinced of the importance of supporting the programs, reproductive rights rhetoric is the order of the day. Thus we hear Nafis Sadik telling Western reporters on the eve of the 1994 U.N. Conference on Population and Development that the heart of the discussion "is the recognition that the low status of women is a root cause of inadequate reproductive health care." Such language would ring strange in the ears of Third World women, who are instead the object of soothing lectures about "child-spacing" and "maternal health." Population control programs were originally unpopular in many Middle Eastern countries and sub-Sarahan countries until they were redesigned, with feminist input, as programs to "help" women. As Peter Donaldson, the head of the Population Reference Bureau, writes, "The idea of limiting the number of births was so culturally unacceptable [in the Middle East and sub-Saharan Africa] that family planning programs were introduced as a means for promoting better maternal and child health by helping women space their births."[30] James Grant of the U.N. Children's Fund (UNICEF), in an address to the World Bank, was even more blunt: "Children and women are to be the Trojan Horse for dramatically slowing population growth."[31]

Corrupted Feminist Movement

The feminists did not imagine, when they signed onto the population control movement, that they would merely be marketing consultants. It is telling that many Third World feminists have refused to endorse population control programs at all, arguing instead that these programs violate the rights of women while ignoring their real needs. It must be painful for Western feminists to contemplate, but their own movement has been used or, to use Betsy Hartmann's term, "co-opted," by another movement for whom humanity as a whole, and women in particular, remain a faceless mass of numbers to be contracepted, sterilized, and aborted. For, despite the feminist rhetoric, the basic character of the programs hasn't changed. They are a numbers-driven, technical solution to the "problem of overpopulation"—which is, in truth, a problem of poverty—and they overwhelmingly target women.

This is, in many respects, an inevitable outcome. To accept the premise that the world is overpopulated and then seek to make the resulting birth control programs "women-friendly," as many feminists have, is a fateful compromise. For it means that concern for the real needs of women is neither the starting point of these programs, nor their ultimate goal, but merely a consideration along the way. Typical of the views of feminists actively involved in the population movement are those of Sharon Camp, who writes, "There is still time to avoid another population doubling, but only if the world community acts very quickly to make family planning universally available and to invest in other social programs, like education for girls, which can help accelerate fertility declines."[32] Here we see the population crisis mentality in an uneasy alliance with programs for women which, however, are justified chiefly because they "help accelerate fertility declines."

The alliance between the feminists and population controllers has been an awkward affair. But the third of the three most anti-natalist movements in history gave the population controllers new resources, new constituencies, new political allies, a new rhetoric, and remains a staunch supporter even today.

Population Firm Funding

Over the past decade the Population Firm has become more powerful than ever. Like a highly organized cartel, working through an alphabet soup of United Nations agencies and "nongovernmental organizations," its tentacles reach into nearly every developing country. It receives sustenance from feeding tubes attached to the legislatures of most developed countries, and further support through the government-financed population research industry, with its hundreds of professors and thousand of students. But unlike any other firm in human history, its purpose is not to produce anything, but rather to destroy—to destroy fertility, to prevent babies from being conceived and born. It diminishes, one might say, the oversupply of people. It does this for the highest of motives—to protect all of us from "popullution." Those who do not subscribe to its ideology it bribes and browbeats, bringing the combined weight of the world's industrial powers to bear on those in countries which are poor.

In 1991, the U.N. estimated that a yearly sum of $4.5 to $5 billion was being directed to population programs in developing countries. This figure, which has grown tremendously in the last 10 years, includes contributions from bilateral donors such as the U.S., the European nations and Japan, from international agencies like those associated with the UN, and from multilateral lending institutions, including the World Bank and the various regional development banks. It includes grants from foundations, like Ted Turner's U.N. Foundation, and wealthy individuals like Warren Buffet.

Moreover, a vast amount of money not explicitly designated as "population" finance is used to further the family planning effort. As Elizabeth Liagin notes, "During the 1980s, the diversion of funds from government non-population budgets to fertility-reduction measures soared, especially in the U.S., where literally hundreds of millions from the Economic Support Funds program, regional development accounts, and other non-population budgets were redirected to "strengthen" population planning abroad."[33]

More Money Spent

An almost unlimited variety of other "development" efforts—health, education, energy, commodity imports, infrastructure, and debt relief, for example—are also used by governments and other international agencies such as the

World Bank, to promote population control policies, either through requiring recipient nations to incorporate family planning into another program or by holding funds or loans hostage to the development of a national commitment to tackle the "over-population" problem.

In its insatiable effort to locate additional funds for its insatiable population control programs, USAID has even attempted to redirect "blocked assets"— profits generated by international corporations operating in developing nations that prohibit the transfer of money outside the country—into population control efforts. In September 1992, USAID signed a $36.4 million contract and "statement of work" with the accounting firm Deloitte and Touche to act as a mediator with global corporations and to negotiate deals that would help turn the estimated $200 *billion* in blocked assets into "private" contributions for family planning in host countries. The corporations would in return get to claim a deduction on their U.S. tax return for this "charitable contribution." The Profit initiative, as it is fittingly called, is not limited to applying its funds directly to family planning "services," but is also encouraged to "work for the removal" of "trade barriers for contraceptive commodities" and "assist in the development of a regulatory framework that permits the expansion of private sector family planning services." This reads like a bureaucratic mandate to lobby for the elimination of local laws which in any way interfere with efforts to drive down the birth rate, such as laws restricting abortion or sterilization.[34]

U.S.'s Real Foreign Aid Policy

Throughout the nineties, the idea of the population controllers that people in their numbers were somehow the enemy of all that is good reigned supreme. J. Brian Atwood, who administered the U.S. Agency for International Development in the early days of the Clinton administration, put it this way: "If we aren't able to find and promote ways of curbing population growth, we are going to fail in *all* of our foreign policy initiatives." [italics added] (Atwood also went on to announce that the U.S. "also plans to resume funding in January [1994] to the U.N. Fund for Population Activities (UNFPA).")[35] Secretary of State Warren Christopher offered a similar but even more detailed defense of population programs the following year. "Population and sustainable development are back where they belong in the mainstream of American foreign policy and diplomacy." He went on to say, in a line that comes right out of U.S. National Security Study Memo 200, that population pressure "ultimately jeopardizes America's security interests." But that's just the beginning. Repeating the now familiar litany, he claimed of population growth that, "It strains resources. It stunts economic growth. It generates disease. It spawns huge refugee flows, and ultimately it threatens our stability. . . . We want to continue working with the other donors to meet the rather ambitious funding goals that were set up in Cairo."[36]

The movement was never more powerful than it was in 2000 in terms of money, other resources, and political clout.

Losing Momentum

Like a wave which crests only seconds before it crashes upon the shore, this appearance of strength may be deceiving. There are signs that the anti-natal movement has peaked, and may before long collapse of its own overreaching. U.S. spending on coercive population control and abortion overseas have long been banned. In 1998 the U.S. Congress, in response to a flood of reports about human rights abuses, for the first time set limits on what can be done to people in the name of "voluntary family planning."[37] Developing countries are regularly denouncing what they see as foreign interference into their domestic affairs, as the Peruvian Congress did in 2002. Despite strenuous efforts to co-opt them, the opposition of feminists to population control programs (which target women) seems to be growing.[38] Many other groups—libertarians, Catholics, Christians of other denominations, the majority of economists, and those who define themselves as pro-life—have long been opposed.

As population control falls into increasing disrepute worldwide, the controllers are attempting to reinvent themselves, much the same way that the Communists in the old Soviet Union reemerged as "social democrats" following its collapse. Organizations working in this area have found it wise to disguise their agenda by adopting less revealing names. Thus Zero Population Growth in June 2002 became Population Connection, and the Association for Voluntary Surgical Contraception the year before changed its name to Engender Health. Similarly, the U.N., in documents prepared for public consumption, has recently found it expedient to cloak its plans in language about the "empowerment of women," "sustainable development," "safe motherhood," and "reproductive health." Yet the old anti-natal zeal continues to come through in internal discussions, as when Thoraya Obaid affirmed to her new bosses on the U.N. Commission on Population and Development her commitment to "slow and eventually stabilize population growth." "And today I want to make one thing very clear," she went on to say. "The slowdown in population growth does not mean we can slow down efforts for population and reproductive health—quite the contrary. If we want real progress and if we want the projections to come true, we must step up efforts . . . while population growth is slowing, it is still growing by 77 million people every year."[39] And so on.

Such efforts to wear a more pleasing face for public consumption will in the end avail them nothing. For, as we will see, their central idea—the Malthusian notion that you can eliminate poverty, hunger, disease, and pollution by eliminating the poor—is increasingly bankrupt.

Reducing the numbers of babies born has not and will not solve political, societal and economic problems. It is like trying to kill a gnat with a sledgehammer, missing the gnat entirely, and ruining your furniture beyond repair. It is like trying to protect yourself from a hurricane with a bus ticket. Such programs come with massive costs, largely hidden from the view of well-meaning Westerners who have been propagandized into supporting them. And their "benefits" have proven ephemeral or worse. These programs, as in China, have done actual harm to real people in the areas of human rights, health care, democracy, and so forth. And, with falling birth rates everywhere, they are demographic nonsense. Where population control programs are concerned, these costs have been largely ignored (as the cost of doing business) while the benefits to people, the environment, and to the economy, have been greatly exaggerated, as we will see. Women in the developing world are the principal victims.

Notes

1. The World Bank is to a large degree under the control of the United States, which provides the largest amount of funding. This is why the head of the World Bank is always an American. The activities of the Bank are monitored by the National Advisory Council on International Monetary and Financial Policies—called the NAC for short, of the Treasury Department. The 1988 annual report of the NAC states that "the council [NAC] seeks to ensure that . . . the . . . operations [of the World Bank and other international financial institutions] are conducted in a manner consistent with U.S. policies and objectives . . ." International Finance: National Advisory Council on International Monetary and Financial Policies, Annual Report to the President and to the Congress for the Fiscal year 1988, (Wash., D.C., Department of the Treasury), Appendix A, p. 31. Quoted in Jean Guilfoyle, "World Bank Population Policy: Remote Control," *PRI Review* 1:4 (July/August 1991), p. 8.

2. I served on board a ship of this class, the USS Lockwood, from 1974–76. As the Main Propulsion Assistant—the officer in charge of the engine room—I can personally attest that this fleet frigate, as it was called, was anything but fleet. On picket duty, it could not keep up with the big flattops that it was intended to protect from submarine attacks.

3. The 1968 meeting was 23rd joint annual meeting of the Boards of Governors of the World Bank and the International Monetary Fund. The two organizations always hold their annual meetings in tandem, underscoring their collaboration on all matters of importance.

4. McNamara moderated his anti-natal rhetoric on this formal occasion. More often, he sounded like Hugh Moore, as when he wrote: "the greatest single obstacle to the economic and social advancement of the majority of the peoples in the underdeveloped world is rampant population growth. . . . The threat of unmanageable population pressures is very much like the threat of nuclear war. . . . Both threats can and will have catastrophic consequences unless they are dealt with rapidly." *One Hundred Countries, Two Billion People* (London: Pall Mall Press, 1973), pp. 45–46. Quoted in Michael Cromartie, ed., *The 9 Lives of Population Control,* (Washington: Ethics and Public Policy Center, 1995), p. 62. McNamara never expressed any public doubts about the importance of population control, although he did once confide in Bernard Berelson that "many of our friends see family planning as being 'too simple, too narrow, and too coercive.'" As indeed it was—and is. Quote is from Donald Crichtlow, *Intended Consequences: Birth Control, Abortion, and the Federal Government in Modern America,* (Oxford: Oxford University Press, 1999), p. 178.

5. See Fred T. Sai and Lauren A. Chester, "The Role of the World Bank in Shaping Third World Population Policy," in Godfrey Roberst, ed., *Population*

Policy: Contemporary Issues (New York: Praeger, 1990). Cited in Jacqueline Kasun, *The War Against Population,* Revised Ed. (San Fransisco: Ignatius Press, 1999), p. 104.

6. 7 September 1994, p. 1. Cited in Kasun, p. 104.

7. U.S. International Population Policy: First Annual Report, prepared by the Interagency Task Force on Population Policy, (Wash., D.C., U.S. National Archives, May 1976). Quoted in Jean Guilfoyle, "World Bank Population Policy: Remote Control," *PRI Review* 1:4 (July/August 1991), p. 8.

8. Personal Communication with the author from a retired World Bank executive who worries that, if his identity is revealed, his pension may be in jeopardy.

9. Peter T. Bauer and Basil S. Yamey, "The Third World and the West: An Economic Perspective," in W. Scott Thompson, ed., *The Third World: Premises of U.S. Policy* (San Francisco: Institute for Contemporary Studies, 1978), p. 302. Quoted in Kasun, p. 105.

10. See Elizabeth Liagin, "Money for Lies," *PRI Review,* July/October 1998, for the definitive history of the imposition of population control on Nigeria; The Nigerian case is also discussed by Barbara Akapo, "When family planning meets population control," *Gender Review,* June 1994, pp. 8–9.

11. Word Bank, 1995 Annual Report, p. 18. Quoted in *PRI Review* 5:6 (November/December 1995), p. 7.

12. Kasun, p. 277.

13. David Morrison, "Weaving a Wider Net: U.N. Move to Consolidate Its Anti-Natalist Gains," *PRI Review* 7:1 (January–February 1997), p. 7.

14. Ibid.

15. Bernard Berelson, "Where Do We Stand," paper prepared for Conference on Technological Change and Population Growth, California Institute of Technology, May 1970, p. 1. Quoted in Ronald Freedman, *The Sociology of Human Fertility: An Annotated Bibliography* (New York: Irvington Publishers, 1975), p. 3. It's worth noting that Freedman's book was a subsidized product of the institution Berelson then headed. As Freedman notes in his "Preface," the "staff at the Population Council were very helpful in reading proof, editorial review, and making detailed arrangements for publication. Financial support was provided by the Population Council." (p. 2.)

16. Freedman, p. 4.

17. *Christian Science Monitor,* 5 July 1977. He went on to say that, if present methods of population control "fail, and population pressures become too great, nations will be driven to more coercive methods."

18. Paul R. Ehrlich, *The Population Bomb* (New York: Ballantine books, 1968).

19. The first three sections of Ehrlich's book were called, "Too many people," "Too little Food," and "A Dying Planet."

20. *Is there a Population Explosion?,* Daniel Lyons, (Catholic Polls: New York, 1970), p. 5.

21. Ehrlich has continued on the present day, writing one book after another, each one chock full of predictions of imminent disasters that fail to materialize. People wonder why Ehrlich doesn't learn from his experiences? The answer, I think, is that he has learned very well. He has learned that writing about "overpopulation and environmental disaster" sells books,

lots of books. He has learned that there is no price to pay for being wrong, as long as he doesn't admit his mistakes *in print* and glibly moves on to the next disaster. In one sense, he has far outdone Hugh Moore in this regard. For unlike Moore, who had to spend his own money to publish the original *The Population Bomb,* Ehrlich was able to hype the population scare *and* make money by doing so. He is thus the archetype of a figure familiar to those who follow the anti-natal movement: the population hustler.

22. Lawrence Lader, *Breeding Ourselves to Death,* pp. 79–81.

23. Richard M. Bowers to ZPG members, 30 September 1969, Population Council (unprocessed), RZ. Quoted in Critchlow, p. 156.

24. In later years, as U.S. population continued to grow, NPG has gradually increased its estimate of a "sustainable" U.S. population to 150 million. See Donald Mann, "A No-Growth Steady-State Economy Must Be Our Goal," NPG Position Paper, June 2002.

25. Quoted in David Boaz, "Pro-Life," *Cato Policy Report* (July/August 2002), p. 2.

26. Frank Notestein to Bernard Berelson, 8 February 1971, Rockefeller Brother Fund Papers, Box 210, RA. Quoted in Critchlow, p. 177. These concerns, while real enough to Notestein, apparently did not cause him to reflect on the fact that he was a major player in a movement that "detracted from the value of human life" by suggesting that there was simply too much of that life, and working for its selective elimination.

27. Population Action International, "Expanding Access to Safe Abortion: Key Policy Issues," Population Policy Information Kit 8 (September 1993). Quoted in Sharon Camp, "The Politics of U.S. Population Assistance," in Mazur, *Beyond the Numbers,* p. 126.

28. Critchlow, p. 165.

29. Frank Notestein to Bernard Berelson, April 27, 1971, Notestein Papers, Box 8, Princeton University.

30. Peter Donaldson and Amy Ong Tsui, "The International Family Planning Movement," in Laurie Ann Mazur, ed., *Beyond the Numbers* (Island Press, Washington, D.C., 1994), p. 118. Donaldson was, at the time, president of the Population Reference Bureau, and Tsui was deputy director of the Carolina Population Center.

31. World Bank 1993 International Development Conference, Washington, D.C., 11 January 1993, p. 3. Also quoted in *PRI Review* (September–October 1994), p. 9.

32. Sharon Camp, "Politics of U.S. Population Assistance," in *Beyond the Numbers,* pp. 130–1. Camp for many years worked at the Population Crisis Committee, founded by Hugh Moore in the early sixties. It has recently, perhaps in recognition of falling fertility rates worldwide, renamed itself Population Action International.

33. Quoted from Elizabeth Liagin, "Profit or Loss: Cooking the Books at USAID," *PRI Review* 6:3 (November/December 1996), p. 1.

34. Ibid., p. 11.

35. John M. Goshko, "Planned Parenthood gets AID grant . . . ," *Washington Post,* 23 November 1993, A12–13.

36. Reuters, "Christopher defends U.S. population programs," Washington, D.C., 19 December 1994.

37. The Tiahrt Amendment.

38. See Betsy Hartmann, *Reproductive Rights and Wrongs* (Boston: South End Press, 1995).

39. Thoraya Ahmed Obaid, "Reproductive Health and Reproductive Rights With Special Reference to HIV/AIDS," Statement to the U.N. Commission on Population and Development, 1 April 2002.

POSTSCRIPT

Should the International Community Refocus on Programs to Help Developing Countries Curb Population Growth?

There are at least two basic dimensions to this issue. First, should the international community have involved itself in the first place in reducing fertility throughout the developing world? That is, is it a violation of either national sovereignty (a country should be free from extreme outside influence) or human rights (an individual has the right to make fertility decisions unencumbered by outside pressure, particularly those from another culture)? And what should its motives have been? To put it another way, was advocacy of population control really a form of ethnic or national genocide? And second, has the international community erred in moving away from emphasizing family planning and instead focusing on other population-related aspects such as reproductive health and women's empowerment?

The first question was answered succinctly by Robert McNamera in 1992 ("The Population Explosion," *The Futurist,* November/December). His belief that the international community has an obligation to get involved is based on his assessment of the resultant damage to both the developing world where such high levels of growth are found and the rest of the world that must compete with the poorer countries for increasingly scare resources. For McNamara, a 2.6-fold increase in population and an 8-fold increase in consumption per capita (by the end of the twenty-first century) would result in a 20-fold impact on nonrenewable and renewable resources. He cites the projected agricultural needs to demonstrate that the Earth cannot sustain such consumption levels. Additionally, McNamara suggests that other consequences include environmentally unsustainable development, worsening of poverty, and negative impacts on the welfare of women and children. They appear to make an overwhelming case for fertility reduction. And the cost of policy intervention is small, in his judgment, compared to both gross national products and overseas general development assistance. And finally, given the projections, the developing world ought to embrace such policy intervention for its own good.

Those who oppose such intervention point to several different reasons. The first, originally articulated at the 1974 Bucharest conference, argues that economic development is the best contraceptive. The demographic transition worked in the developed world and there was no reason to assume that it will not work in the developing world. This was the dominant view of the developing countries at Bucharest, who feared international policy intervention, and at the same time wanted and needed external capital to develop. They soon came to realize that characteristics particular to the developing world in the latter part of the twentieth century meant that foreign aid alone would not be enough. It had to be accompanied by fertility reduction programs, wherever the origin.

Second, some who oppose intervention do not see the extreme negative environmental consequences of expanding populations. For them, the pronatalists (those favoring fertility reduction programs) engage in inflammatory discourse, exaggerated arguments, and scare tactics devoid of much scientific evidence.

Mosher goes further in the second selection, accusing McNamara, who served as U.S. Secretary of Defense during the Vietnam era, of using his position as one of the most important leaders in the international financial lending world to help prevent continuing population growth in the developing world because of its potential threat to the national security of countries like the United States. He also concludes that the interventionists are engaged in social engineering, not economic development.

And finally, cultural constraints can counteract any attempt to impose fertility reduction values from the outside. Children are valued in most societies. They, particularly male heirs, serve as the social security system for most families. They become producers at an early age, contributing to the family income.

McNamara is correct if one assumes that no changes—technological, social, and organizational—accompany predicted population growth. But others would argue that society has always found a way to use technology to address newly emerging problems successfully. The question remains, though: Are the current problems and the world in which they function too complex to allow for a simple solution?

The bottom line is that each has a valid point. Environmental stress is a fact of life, and increased consumption does play a role. If the latter originates because of more people, then fertility reduction is a viable solution. Left to its own devices, the developing world is unable to provide both the rationale for such action and the resources to accomplish it. The barriers are too great. While the international community must guard against behavior that is or appears to be either genocidal in nature or violates human rights, it must nonetheless move forward.

In 1994 at the Cairo population conference, the debate over whether external intervention in family planning was a good idea was pushed aside. In the words of one author, "an almost complete reformation of global policies and strategies" occurred (see Robinson and Ross, 2007, later in this section). Calls for dropping demographic and family planning benchmarks were replaced by the broader set of issues that centered around women's empowerment. The change was clear and explicit. The previously central issue of population, high growth rates in the developing world, was barely mentioned at Cairo and was almost completely ignored after the conference. Funding priorities changed as well. Within a decade, only about 10 percent of 1994 expenditure levels were targeted for family planning. Now, however, voices are beginning to be heard once again calling for a return to the central question of yesteryear.

An excellent account of the 1994 Cairo population conference's answer to how the international community ought to respond is found in Lori S. Ashford's *New Perspectives on Population: Lessons from Cairo* (1995). Other sources that address the question of the need for international action include William Hollingworth's *Ending the Explosion: Population Policies and Ethics for a Humane Future* (1996), Elizabeth Liagin's *Excessive Force: Power, Politics, and Population* (1996), and Julian Simon's *The Ultimate Resource 2* (1996). In 2003, the UN Commission on Population and Development held a weeklong meeting on educating people to curb population growth. More recent calls for action include top Australian and British scientists, according to several Internet blogs.

There are both United Nations and external analyses of the Cairo conference and assessments of progress made in implementing its Plan of Action. The U.N. Population Fund's Web site (www.unfpa.org) has a section entitled *ICPD and Key Actions*. There you will find numerous in-house analyses of both the conference and post-1994 action. In the broader UN Web site (www.un.org/popin), one finds a major study, *Progress Made in Achieving the Goals and Objectives of the Program of Action of the International Conference on Population and Development.* An external assessment is the Population Institute's report entitled *The Hague Forum: Measuring ICPD Progress Since Cairo* (1999). See its Web site at www.populationinstitute.org.

Two important historical accounts of the history of global population planning and the paradigm shift after 1994 from curbing population to reproductive health and women's empowerment are Global Population Policy: From Population Control to Reproductive Rights (Paige Whaley Eager, Ashgate Publishing, 2004) and The Global Family Planning Revolution: Three Decades of Population Policies and Programs (Warren C. Robinson and John A. Ross, eds., World Bank Publications, 2007). See the UN's World Population Policies, 2007, for an overview of policies relating to population growth. Also see UNFPA's "Financing the ICPD Programme of Action: Data for 2005; Estimates for 2006/2007" for an overview of resource assistance for the major categories of population-related activities. The Population Reference Bureau's "The Unfinished Agenda: Meeting the Need for Family Planning in Less Developed Countries" (Policy Brief, 2004) focuses on the need for continued family planning.

ISSUE 3

Is Global Aging in the Developed World a Major Problem?

YES: Pete Engardio and Carol Matlack, from "Global Aging," *Business Week* (January 31, 2005)

NO: Rand Corporation, from "Population Implosion?" Research Brief, Rand Europe (2005)

ISSUE SUMMARY

YES: This *Business Week* cover story outlines the aging of the population in both the developed world and the newly emerging economies, suggesting that the time for action is now.

NO: This Rand Corporation study suggests that because of declining fertility, European populations are either growing more slowly or have actually begun to decline. Although these trends "portend difficult times ahead," European governments should be able to confront these challenges successfully.

The developd world is now faced with an aging population brought on by declining birth rates and an increasing life expectancy. The phenomenon first appeared during the last quarter of the previous century with the demographic transition from high birth and death rates to lower rates. The drop in death rates in these countries was a function of two basic factors: (1) the dramatic decline in both infant mortality (within the first year of birth) and child mortality (within the first five years) due to women being healthier during pregnancy and nursing periods, and to the virtually universal inoculation of children against principal childhood diseases; and (2) longer lifespans once people reach adulthood, in large part because of medical advances against key adult illnesses such as cancer and heart disease.

Declining mortality rates yield an aging population in need of a variety of services—heath care, housing, and guards against inflation, for example—provided, in large part, by the tax dollars of the younger, producing sector of society. As the "gray" numbers of society grow, the labor force is increasingly called upon to provide more help for this class.

Declining birth and death rates mean that significantly more services will be needed to provide for the aging populations of the industrialized world, while at the same time, fewer individuals will be joining the workforce to provide the resources to pay for these services. However, some experts say that the new work force will be able to take advantage of the skills of the more aged, unlike previous eras. In order for national economies to grow in the information age, an expanding workforce may not be as important a prerequisite as it once was. Expanding minds, not bodies, may be the key to expanding economies and increased abilities to provide public services.

However, the elderly and the young are not randomly distributed throughout society, which is likely to create a growing set of regional problems. In the United States, for example, the educated young are likely to leave the "gray belt" of the north for the Sun Belt of the south, southwest, and west. Who will be left in the older, established sectors of the country that were originally at the forefront of the industrial age to care for the disproportionately elderly population? What will happen 30 and 40 years from now, when the respective sizes of the young and the elderly populations throughout the developed world will yield a much larger population at the twilight of their existence? Although the trend is most evident in the richer part of the globe, people are also living longer in the developing world, primarily because of the diffusion of modern medical practices. But unless society can accommodate their skills of later years, they may become an even bigger burden in the future for their national governments.

A 2001 report, *Preparing for an Aging World: The Case for Cross-National Research* (National Academy of Sciences), identified a number of areas in which policymakers need a better understanding of the consequences of aging and resultant appropriate policy responses. Unless national governments of the developed world can effectively respond to these issues, the economic and social consequences can have a significant negative impact in both the aging population cohort as well as throughout the entire society. This theme was reiterated in a major report of the Population Reference Bureau in March 2005 (*Global Aging: The Challenge of Success*), suggesting three major challenges of an aging population: (1) economic development issues, (2) health and well-being issues, and (3) the challenge of enabling and supportive environments.

In the first selection, the *Business Week* international cover story suggests that "the graying of the baby boom generation" represents "one of the greatest sociological shifts in history," the inevitable changing demographics of a much higher percentage of the population falling into the elderly category. This, in turn, will create "significant challenges" to society to maintain and improve the quality of life for seniors as well as for the entire population of the developed world. In the second selection, the Rand Corporation study suggests that because of declining fertility, European populations are either growing more slowly or have actually begun to decline. Although these trends "portend difficult times ahead," European governments should be able to confront these challenges successfully.

YES

Pete Engardio and
Carol Matlack

Global Aging

Jenny François doesn't have the world's most glamorous job. For 20 years she has commuted 45 minutes to the office of insurer Macif in Agen, France, where she punches data from insurance forms into a computer. But in the not-too-distant future, François and hundreds of millions of people like her in the industrialized world could look back at the early 21st century as the beginning of the end of a wonderful era, when even average workers could retire in reasonable comfort in their still-vigorous 50s. Thanks to France's generous pension system, François, 58, is in "pre-retirement." For the past three years she has worked just two days a week and still collects $1,500 a month—more than 70% of her old full-time salary. Her pay will decline only slightly when she reaches 60. "The system is great for me," François says, "and I think it should be every worker's right."

Lower Living Standards

It's already clear that the system will be far less generous to future retirees in France and elsewhere. And the message isn't going down easy. To avert a looming fiscal crunch, President Jacques Chirac's government in 2003 enacted new rules requiring people to work longer to qualify for benefits. The government endured a national wave of strikes. Italy and Germany also witnessed massive protests after their governments proposed similar measures. Despite electoral setbacks, Japanese Prime Minister Junichiro Koizumi still vows to ram through proposals to hike pension taxes from around 14% of pay to 18% by 2017 and to slash benefits from 59% of average wages now to 50%. In the U.S., the political debate is just starting to heat up over President George W. Bush's proposal to let workers park some of their Social Security contributions in personal investment accounts. Finland, South Korea, Brazil, and Greece all have recently moved or proposed to trim benefits, extend retirement ages, and hike workers' pension contributions.

   The rollback of pension promises is just one symptom of one of the greatest sociological shifts in history: The graying of the baby-boom generation. The ranks of 60-year-olds and older are growing 1.9% a year—60% faster than the overall world population. In 1950 there were 12 people aged 15 to 64 to support each one of retirement age. Now the global average is nine. It will be only four-to-one by mid-century, predicts the U.N. Population Div. By then

From *BusinessWeek*, January 31, 2005. Copyright © 2005 by BusinessWeek. Reprinted by permission of the McGraw-Hill Companies.

the elderly will outnumber children for the first time. Some economists fear this will lead to bankrupt pensions and lower living standards.

That's why even more cutbacks in retirement benefits are likely. "I don't even want to think about my children's pensions," says Lina Iulita, 72, referring to Italy's hugely underfunded system. "There won't be enough money coming in." In Iulita's town of Dormeletto, on the shore of Lake Maggiore, coffee bars are jammed with seniors. The town's over-75 population has doubled since 1971, and there are one-third fewer children under 6. Local schools and gyms have closed, while senior citizens' clubs are flourishing.

The trend has drawn the most attention in Europe and in Japan, where the working-age population will decline by 0.6% this year. By 2025 the number of people aged 15 to 64 is projected to dwindle by 10.4% in Spain, 10.7% in Germany, 14.8% in Italy, and 15.7% in Japan. But aging is just as dramatic in such emerging markets as China—which is expected to have 265 million 65-year-olds by 2020—and Russia and Ukraine. Western European employers won't be able to count on the Czech Republic, Hungary, and Poland for big pools of low-cost workers forever: They're aging just as quickly. Within 20 years, East Asia's dynamic tigers will be youthful no longer. South Korea, Thailand, Taiwan, Singapore, and Hong Kong will have a median age of 40. Indonesia, India, Brazil, Mexico, the Philippines, Iran, and Egypt will still boast big, growing pools of workers for two decades. But they're on the same demographic curve and will show the effects of an aging population a generation or two later. "The aging workforce is the biggest economic challenge policymakers will face over the next 20 years," says Monika Queisser, a pension expert at the Organization for Economic Cooperation & Development.

The same basic factors are driving this shift: declining fertility and longer lifespans. Both are signs of enormous progress in the 20th century. With rare exceptions—such as impoverished Sub-Saharan Africa—birth control and better opportunities for women have lowered birth rates from five or six children per female in the 1950s to as few as one or two today. A fertility rate of 2.1 is seen as the population breakeven point. Over the same period, great advances in health care have added two full decades to the world's average life span, to age 66 now.

For most of the postwar era, the combination of baby booms, healthier populations, and smaller families amounted to what economists call the "demographic dividend," a tremendous, once-only chance to spur rapid development in nations with the right pro-growth policies. As boomers flooded into the workforce—first in the West and Japan, then Latin America and East Asia—they provided the labor for economic take-offs. Then, as they became parents, boomers had fewer children. So adults had more money to spend on goods and services and invest in their families' education.

But analysts and policymakers are starting to obsess over the flip side of the story: What happens when the baby boom becomes the geezer glut? How successfully this transition is managed around the world could determine the rise and fall of nations and reshape the global economy. Two key ingredients of growth are increases in the labor force and productivity. If countries can't maintain the size of their labor forces—say, by persuading older workers to retire later, getting stay-at-home wives to find jobs, or taking in more immigrants—they must boost productivity to maintain current growth levels. That will be a particular challenge in Europe, where productivity growth has averaged just 1.3% since 1995.

By these measures the U.S. is in relatively healthy shape despite the hand-wringing over Social Security and Medicare. Because of a slightly higher fertility rate and an annual intake of 900,000 legal immigrants, America's population should grow from 285 million now to 358 million in 2025. And the U.S. median age will rise just three years, to 39, over the next quarter-century, before the aging of America really starts to accelerate. The U.S. also has one of the world's most diversified retirement systems, including Social Security, company pensions, 401(k) savings plans that are largely invested in stocks, and private retirement insurance policies.

Nations with insolvent pension systems or insufficient private nest eggs, meanwhile, could face "an unprecedented societal crisis," warns OECD Secretary General Donald J. Johnston. Analysts say pension systems in Europe, Asia, and Latin America will start running into serious funding problems in a decade or two. Further down the road, some economists fear inadequate retiree savings will lead to lower consumption and asset values. The McKinsey Global Institute predicts that by 2024, growth in household financial wealth in the U.S., Europe, and Japan will slow from a combined 4.5% annual clip now to 1.3%. That will translate into $31 trillion less wealth than if the average age were to remain the same. Higher productivity would help, says McKinsey Global Director Diana Farrell. But without radical changes in labor and pensions, U.S. output per worker would have to be at least twice as high as the 2.6% McKinsey projects for the next decade, in part because workers will be a smaller portion of the population. "You would need numbers way north of what we can reasonably expect," says Farrell.

Wharton School finance professor Jeremy J. Siegel also contends that productivity won't be enough to offset the rise in number of retirees. Most pensions now index benefits to wages, rather than inflation, "and wages tend to rise with productivity," he notes. "As wages go up, people will demand higher benefits, so you essentially are chasing your tail." Siegel, famous for his bullishness on investing in blue-chip stocks for the long run, also worries about what will happen when future retirees try to liquidate their nest eggs en masse. To keep asset values from plummeting, Siegel predicts that heavy investments from newly affluent emerging markets such as India and China will have to flow into U.S. stocks, property, and bonds.

Whether such scenarios play out, of course, is anyone's guess. Aging's impact on financial markets isn't well understood, and predicting what the economy will be like in three years, much less three decades, is hard enough. Some argue that only modestly higher productivity will be able to offset demographic shifts and that worrymongers use overly pessimistic assumptions of medical costs. And, with enough political will, certainly governments can do plenty to ameliorate the social and economic fallout. "Most of the debate now is about benefits and taxes, but other levers can be pulled to make the problem more tractable," says Richard M. Samans, a managing director at the World Economic Forum.

The Future Is Now

From Stockholm to Seoul to Santiago, policymakers are seeking to boost private savings in stock and bond funds, lure young immigrant workers, find cheaper ways to provide elder care, and persuade companies to hire or retain older workers. On their own, none of these approaches is seen as a practical solution: Germany would have to more than double its annual intake of 185,000 foreigners to make up for fewer births, while immigration to Japan, now just 56,000 a year, would have to leap elevenfold. And slashing pensions enough to guarantee long-term solvency would mean political suicide. But a combination of sensible changes might make a big difference.

Developing nations with young and growing populations, meanwhile, face other issues. India is on pace to catch up and pass China's 1.4 billion population in three decades, for example. The trouble is, 40% of Indians drop out of school by age 10. Efforts to greatly expand education could determine whether India is a future economic superpower or if it will be burdened with the world's biggest population of poor illiterates. In Iran, an explosion of educated youth now joining the workforce could fuel a takeoff—or foment political strife if there are no jobs.

Why the sudden attention to a demographic trend that has been obvious for decades? In part, it's because the future is already dawning in many nations. In South Korea and Japan, which have strong cultural aversions to immigration, small factories, construction companies, and health clinics are relying more on "temporary" workers from the Philippines, Bangladesh, and Vietnam. In reality they are becoming permanent second-class citizens. In China's northern industrial belt, state industries are struggling over how to lay off unneeded middle-age workers when there is no social safety net to support them.

Across Europe, meanwhile, baby boomers such as Jenny François in France are retiring in droves—even though the first of this generation won't reach 65 until 2011. Most of Europe's state-funded pension systems encourage early retirement. Now, 85.5% of adults in France quit work by age 60, and only 1.3% work beyond 65. In Italy, 62% of adults call it quits by age 55. That compares with 47% of people who earn wages or salaries until they are 65 in the U.S. and 55% in Japan. With jobless rates still high, there's been little urgency to change. "I feel like I am in good enough shape to work, but there isn't enough work to go around," says Uwe Bohn, pouring a cup of coffee in his 12th-floor apartment in a drab Berlin high-rise. Bohn, 61, retired four years ago after losing his civil-engineering job and failing for years to find steady work.

Dire Math

But financial pressures and the prospect of future labor shortages are spurring action. In France, business groups, unions, and the government will begin talks in February aimed at changing early-retirement rules. "We must correct fundamental aspects of that system," says Ernest-Antoine Seillière, chairman of French industrial investment firm Wendel Investissement and head of French employer group MEDEF.

With smart policies, older workers can be a boon to the economy, contends gerontologist Françoise Forette, president of the International Longevity Center in Paris. Research shows that better health care means today's veteran workers can remain productive much longer, especially with training, Forette says. "And if people work longer, there is no pension bomb—even in Europe." A World Economic Forum study to be released at its annual meeting from Jan. 26–30 in Davos, Switzerland, suggests labor shortfalls are solvable. Europe and Japan could make up for the decline in workers by keeping workers from retiring before 65 as well as by raising participation rates of women and people in their mid-20s to U.S. levels.

Some European countries are making progress. In Finland, new government and corporate policies are boosting the average retirement age. No longer is Italian home-appliance maker Indesit Co. coaxing older workers to retire early to make room for younger recruits. Instead, it's teaching its over-50 staff in its seven Italian factories new skills, such as factory and supply-chain management. So far the program is going smoothly, says Indesit human-resource director Cesare Ranieri. Luxembourg-based steelmaker Arcelor, which until 1991 offered early retirement at 92% of pay at age 50, says it has more than doubled productivity since raising the age to 60. Among other things, it hiked salaries for veterans who agreed to extra training and made it easier for them to work part time. "The policy proved very successful," says Arcelor human-resources manager director Daniel Atlan.

What really has pushed aging to the top of the global agenda, though, are ballooning fiscal gaps in the U.S., Europe, Japan, and elsewhere that could worsen as boomers retire. While U.S. Social Security is projected to remain solvent until at least 2042, the picture is more dire in Europe. Unlike the U.S., where most citizens also have private savings plans, in much of Europe up to 90% of workers rely almost entirely on public pensions. Benefits also are generous. Austria guarantees 93% of pay at retirement, for example, and Spain offers 94.7%. Without radical change, pensions and elder-care costs will jump from 14% of industrial nations' gross domestic product to 18% in 35 years, warns Washington's Center for Strategic & International Studies.

Fortunately, the global public appears to be bracing itself for rollbacks. Polling agency Allensbach reports that 89% of Germans don't believe their pensions are safe, from 63% a decade ago. Surveys of workers 25 and over by Des Moines financial-services provider Principal Financial Group (PFG) found that just 26% of French and 18% of Japanese are confident that their old-age system will pay the same benefits in the future as today.

Japanese workers such as Yumiko Wada certainly aren't in denial. "Old people today get quite a good pension, so they don't have a problem," says Wada, 30, an office employee in Tochigi. "But I wonder who will support us when we get old." Shunichi Kudo, 35, a salesman at a Fukuoka map-publishing house, says he agrees with Koizumi's plan to raise premiums and lower retiree benefits. "It's going to be difficult, and I don't like it, but I understand why it's happening," Kudo says.

The basic math of Japan's demographic profile is dire. Already, 17 of every 100 of its people are over 65, and this ratio will near 30 in 15 years. From

2005 to 2012, Japan's workforce is projected to shrink by around 1% each year—a pace that will accelerate after that. Economists fear that, besides blowing an even bigger hole in Japan's underfunded pension system, the decline of workers and young families will make it harder for the nation to generate new wealth: Its potential annual growth rate will drop below 1%, estimates Japan Research Institute Ltd. chief economist Kenji Yumoto, unless productivity spikes.

Japan's fiscal mess is so serious that it's hard to see an alternative to drastic future cuts. In 1998, Prime Minister Ryutaro Hashimoto hiked pension and social security contributions and the value-added tax, cutting disposable income by about $88 billion, or 2.5%. Japan's economy hasn't been the same since. Shock therapy is a "recipe for recessions," says Jesper Koll, chief Japan economist at Merrill Lynch & Co. (MER). Now, Tokyo plans to raise workers' burden by a more modest 0.3% of gross domestic product each year until 2017. Will that be enough to enable to Japan to meet its obligations to retirees? Probably not, Koll predicts, but Japanese citizens will endure that as well. "At the end of the day, part of the solution is going to be reduced contractual obligations," he says.

Shoring up public pensions is hardly the only avenue nations are exploring. In developing countries, privately managed savings accounts have been the rage. Two decades ago, nearly every Latin American nation had pay-as-you-go systems like Social Security, but more generous. Some granted civil servants retiring in their 50s full salaries for life. Widening budget deficits changed that. In 1981, Chile replaced its public system with retirement accounts funded by worker contributions and managed by private firms. Urged to follow suit by the World Bank, 11 other Latin nations introduced similar features. The movement also spread through Eastern Europe. The upsides have been enormous: Chile helped plug a big fiscal budget deficit, has mobilized $49 billion of pension-fund assets that make it easier for companies and governments to fund investments in the local currency with bond offerings, and most workers have some retirement benefits. Mexico and other Latin nations have seen similar payoffs.

Privatization alone is no panacea, however. For starters, private managers charge fees that often devour one-quarter of workers' funds—prompting calls for fee limits and greater regulation. Also, private funds are leaving many workers virtually uncovered, either because they don't contribute much or work in the so-called informal sector of small, unregistered businesses. In Mexico, only 38% of the 32.6 million accounts are active, receiving monthly deposits from workers, employers, and the government. Of Brazil's 68 million workers, meanwhile, 56% are in the informal economy and get no pensions beyond their own savings. What's more, the pension system for private-sector workers already runs $9 billion in the red each year. As for Brazil's 1.2 million civil servants, they still collect generous benefits and retire early. Yet the public system runs $10 billion deficits, and civil servants have thwarted attempts to scale back.

Argentina's experience also shows that privatized systems can leave the elderly at the margin in a mismanaged economy. As part of its overhaul of the insolvent public pension system, Argentina in 1994 launched a scheme relying on funds managed by 11 private firms. Some 65% of Argentina's 14.5 million workers signed up for the new system. For many people, the 1990s were like "springtime—a time of great hope," says Maria Rosa Febrero, 49, a day-care center manager who is thankful she didn't invest in the private system. As a ceiling fan rustles piles of paperwork in her spartan, humid office, Febrero gazes at tourist posters of Patagonia's idyllic snow-capped peaks. "The funds were promising huge pensions and a perfect retirement. A lot of people bought into the dream." Unfortunately, the government obliged funds to invest two-thirds of their assets in government bonds. Their value plunged after the 2001 financial crisis, when Buenos Aires forced funds to swap the bonds for new, discounted paper and then defaulted altogether. The government also cut its contributions to pension plans.

Urgent Needs

Now, Argentina is trying to encourage higher contributions to private funds by offering another debt swap that would restore part of the funds' assets. Needless to say, Argentinians are dubious. "The whole system is poorly managed and totally corrupt," says Marina Amor, 79, who makes ends meet on the same monthly $104 stipend she has received since her late husband retired in 1989 after paying into the public pension for 40 years. "No one believes them anymore. I don't think there are many people left who believe they will ever be able to retire."

The challenge of providing for the elderly is especially urgent in the world's two biggest nations—India and China. Only 11% of Indians have pensions, and they tend to be civil servants and the affluent. With a young population and relatively big families, many of the elderly can still count on their children for support. That's not the case in China. By 2030, there will be only two working-age people to support every retiree. Yet only 20% of workers have government- or company-funded pensions or medical coverage.

Pension and medical reform. Later retirement. Higher productivity. More liberal immigration. Around the world, governments and businesses are searching for creative policies in each of these areas as they come to grips with one of the most profound social transformations in history. "Right now all of these issues are being dealt with piecemeal," says Ladan Manteghi, international affairs director for the Association for the Advancement of Retired Persons' global aging center. It all adds up to a big agenda—one that will determine whether the global economy that achieved such astounding progress in the youthful 20th century will continue to prosper as it matures in the 21st.

Population Implosion?

Across Europe, birth rates are falling and family sizes are shrinking. The total fertility rate is now less than two children per woman in every member nation in the European Union. As a result, European populations are either growing very slowly or beginning to decrease.

At the same time, low fertility is accelerating the ageing of European populations. As a region, Europe in 2000 had the highest percentage of people age 65 or older—15 percent. According to data from the U.S. Bureau of the Census, this percentage is expected to nearly double by 2050.[1]

These demographic trends portend difficult times ahead for European economies. For example, a shrinking workforce can reduce productivity. At the same time, the growing proportion of elderly individuals threatens the solvency of pension and social insurance systems. As household sizes decrease, the ability to care for the elderly diminishes. Meanwhile, elderly people face growing health care needs and costs. Taken together, these developments could pose significant barriers to achieving the European Union (EU) goals of full employment, economic growth, and social cohesion.

Concern over these trends has sparked intense debate over the most effective policies to reverse them or mitigate their impact. The policy debate has focused on three approaches: (1) promoting increased immigration of working-age people; (2) encouraging more childbearing, especially among younger couples; and (3) reforming social policy to manage the negative consequences of these trends—including measures that could raise the retirement age or encourage more women to join the workforce. To date, this debate has produced more heat than light, and solid research-based evidence to inform the debate remains sketchy. Many aspects of the relationship between national policies and demographic trends are either disputed or not well understood, and it remains difficult to disentangle the effects of specific policy initiatives from the effects of broader social, political, and economic conditions.

To help inform EU policy deliberations, analysts from RAND Europe and RAND U.S. examined the relationships between policy and demographic change. The RAND team analysed the interrelationships between European government policies and demographic trends and behaviour, and assessed which policies can prevent or mitigate the adverse consequences of current low fertility and population ageing. The monograph, *Low Fertility and*

From *Research Brief*, RB-9126-EC (2005), pp. 1–3. Copyright © 2005 by Rand Corporation. Reprinted by permission. This research brief describes work done by RAND Europe documented in *Low Fertility and Population Ageing: Causes, Consequences, and Policy Options* (MG-206-EC, 2004), 172. Reproduced with permission via Copyright Clearance Center.

Population Ageing: Causes, Consequences, and Policy Options, documents the study's findings.

The study carried out three tasks: It analysed European demographic trends; it examined the relationship between national-level policies on the one hand and demographic trends and household behaviours on the other hand; and it conducted case studies of five countries—France, Germany, Poland, Spain, and Sweden—which represent a mix of original and new member states, with varying levels of fertility and net immigration, and with different policy approaches.

The study found that:

- Immigration is not a feasible way of reversing population ageing or its consequences.
- National policies can slow fertility declines under the right circumstances.
- However, no single policy intervention necessarily works.
- And, what works in one country may not work in another. Social, economic, and political contexts influence the effect of policies.
- Policies designed to improve broader social and economic conditions may affect fertility, indirectly.
- Population policies take a long time to pay dividends—increases in fertility taking a generation to translate into an increased number of workers—making such policies politically unattractive.

Increased Immigration Will Not Reverse Population Ageing

Allowing large numbers of working-age immigrants to enter EU countries is not a feasible solution to the problem of population ageing. The sheer numbers of immigrants needed to offset population ageing in the EU states would be unacceptable in Europe's current sociopolitical climate. Furthermore, over the longer term, these immigrants would themselves age. The study concluded that the debate should focus on using immigration as a potential tool for slowing—as opposed to overcoming—population ageing.

Government Policies Can Slow Fertility Declines

Government policies can have an impact on fertility. For example, Spain and France present an instructive contrast. Currently, Spain has the second-lowest rate of fertility among the original 15 EU member states. However, a generation ago (in 1971), Spain's fertility was among the highest in Europe. The dramatic decline in fertility since then is associated with a shift from the pronatalist Franco regime—which banned contraception and encouraged large families—to a democratic regime that has no explicit population policy.

In contrast, France, which was the first European nation to experience a decline in its fertility rate and which has had an aggressive set of pronatalist policies in place for many decades, now has the second-highest fertility rate in

Europe (behind Ireland). The fertility rate in France has not declined as much as that in other countries, and it actually increased between 1993 and 2002.

Reversing Fertility Decline Has Involved a Mix of Policies

No single policy intervention has worked to reverse low fertility. Historically, governments have attempted to boost fertility through a mix of policies and programmes. For example, France in recent decades has employed a suite of policies intended to achieve two goals: reconciling family life with work and reversing declining fertility. To accomplish the first goal, for example, France instituted generous child-care subsidies. To accomplish the second, families have been rewarded for having at least three children.

Sweden, by contrast, reversed the fertility declines it experienced in the 1970s through a different mix of policies, none of which specifically had the objective of raising fertility. Its parental work policies during the 1980s allowed many women to raise children while remaining in the workforce. The mechanisms for doing so were flexible work schedules, quality child care, and extensive parental leave on reasonable economic terms.

Political, Economic, and Social Contexts Influence Policy Impacts

Designing successful interventions is complicated by the fact that policies that work in one country may not work in another. Different interventions have varying effects because of the diverse, complex, and shifting political, economic, and social contexts in which they are implemented. The impact of these contexts appears in some of the sweeping political transitions Europe has witnessed over the past two decades.

For example, fertility declines in the former East Germany after unification appear to owe more to a shifting social environment than to policy change. Women who faced the unification with concerns about their economic situations were less likely to have children in the following year or two. The contrast between the former East Germany and West Germany is instructive. After reunification, the former West Germany's fertility rate remained relatively stable, whereas the former East Germany saw a precipitous decline over the next three years. Similarly, the transition to a free-market economy in Poland changed the economic environment and incentives for childbearing. Since 1989, Poland has experienced a sharp decrease in fertility.

Sweden provides a different kind of example. Although Sweden did not undergo political or economic transformation, its economic conditions nonetheless have affected fertility. Unlike in most other countries, fertility rates in Sweden are positively related to the earnings of women—likely because women's earnings in Sweden constitute a substantial proportion of dual-earner household income. Since parental-leave benefits are proportional to earnings, improvements in economic conditions lead to higher parental benefits, which can help promote increased fertility. Part of the decrease in fertility in Sweden during the 1990s is likely related to the decline in economic conditions.

Population Change Is Slow

Government policies intended to reverse fertility declines typically have a long-term focus and require many years to bear fruit. A few population policies may have an immediate effect (for example, those restricting/allowing abortion), but they are exceptions, and their effects tend to be on the timing of births rather than on completed fertility. Population policies to increase fertility take at least one generation before they ultimately increase the number of new entrants to the labour force.

As a result, there is a disconnect between electoral cycles (typically, 4–5 years) and the longer cycle of population policy. Politicians have limited incentives to advocate such policies, especially when doing so might entail the expenditure of political capital in entering a contentious policy domain. Therefore, population policies tend to lack both political appeal and political champions.

Instead, politicians tend to focus on policies for mitigating the effects of population ageing which have shorter time horizons. One policy for doing so is encouraging participation in the workforce. This can mean promoting a longer working life and encouraging new entrants, such as women, into the workforce. Related to this are policies that seek to enhance the productivity of older workers.

Conclusion

This study showed that, under certain conditions, European governments can successfully confront the looming economic threats of declining fertility rates and ageing populations. Policies that remove workplace and career impediments to childrearing are a critical part of any solution. However, reversing long-term ageing and low fertility remains problematic, given that policies for doing so may not pay dividends until the next generation reaches working age. Prior to that time, millions of baby boomers will have retired. Hence, a solution will require long-term vision and political courage.

Note

1. Kevin Kinsella and Victoria A. Velkoff, *An Aging World: 2001*, Washington, D.C.: U.S. Census Bureau, Series P95/01-1, 2001, p. 9.

POSTSCRIPT

Is Global Aging in the Developed World a Major Problem?

The issue of the changing age composition in the developed world was foreseen a few decades ago, but its heightened visibility is relatively recent. This visibility culminated in a UN-sponsored conference on aging in Madrid in April 2002. Its plan of action commits governments to address the problem of aging and provided them with a set of 117 specific recommendations covering three basic areas: older individuals and development, advancing health and well-being into old age, and ensuring enabling and supportive environments.

With the successful demographic transition in the industrial world, the percentage of those above the age of 60 is on the rise, while the labor force percentage is decreasing. In 1998, 19 percent of the first world fell into the post-60 category (10 percent worldwide). Children under age 15 also make up 19 percent of the developed world's population while the labor force is at 62 percent. With birth rates hovering around 1 percent or less, and life expectancy increasing, the percentages will likely continue to grow toward the upper end of the scale.

Paul Peterson has argued that the costs of global aging will not only outweigh the benefits, the capacity of the developed world to pay for these costs is questionable at best. The economic burden on the labor force will be "unprecedented," he suggests, and he offers a number of solutions ("Gray Dawn: The Global Aging Crisis" in *Foreign Affairs,* January/February 1999).

A particularly outspoken opponent of the "gloom" viewpoint is Phil Mullan. His book *The Imaginary Time Bomb; Why an Ageing Population Is Not a Social Problem* (I. B. Tauris, New York, 2000), criticizes how the idea of an aging developed world has become "a kind of mantra for opponents of the welfare state and for a collection of alarmists." Mullan is joined by Phillip Longman, author of *The Empty Cradle* (Basic Books, 2004), who suggests in a *Foreign Affairs* article ("The Global Baby Bust," May/June 2004) that the coming "baby bust" will yield a variety of positive consequences as well as negative ones.

Four excellent overviews of the issues to be addressed in an era of global aging are *Global Aging: The Challenge of Success* by Kevin Kinsella and David R. Phillips (Population Reference Bureau, *Population Bulletin,* vol. 60, no. 1, 2005; *Rethinking Age and Aging,* by Warren Sanderson and Sergei Scherbov (Population Reference Bureau, *Population Bulletin,* vol. 63, no. 4, 2008); the UN's *World Population Ageing: 1950–2050*; and *World Population Ageing 2007* (United Nations). See also the Population Reference Bureau's March 2007 report, *Cross-National Research on Aging*.

A good introduction to global aging is found in "Aging of Population," by Leonid A. Gavrilov and Patrick Heuveline (*The Encyclopedia of Population*, Macmillan Reference, 2003). An excellent discussion of global aging is found in the U.S. Department of State's report "Why Population Aging Matters: A Global Perspective" (March 2007). See also Toshiko Kaneda's *A Critical Window for Policymaking on Population Aging in Developing Countries* (Population Reference Bureau, 2006) for an assessment of the problem in the world's poor sectors. The most succinct presentation of the effects of global aging can be found in John Hawksworth's "Seven Key Effects of Global Aging" (PricewaterhouseCoopers' Web site, www.pwcglobal.com). This is "must reading" for those who want a concise, objective description of the potential consequence of the changing demographics associated with age distribution. His presentation focuses on the effects on economic growth, pensions systems, working lives, equity and bond markets, international capital flows, migration, and business strategies. A good source for the effect of declining population in Europe is "Population Policy Dilemmas in Europe at the Dawn of the Twenty-First Century" (*Population and Development Review*, The Population Council, Inc., March 2003). See also Jacques Vallin's "The End of the Demographic Transition: Relief or Concern?" (*Population and Development Review*, March 2002).

For some, such as Leon F. Bouvier and Jane T. Bertrand (*World Population: Challenges for the 21st Century*, Seven Locks Press, 1999), there seems to be a potential silver lining on the horizon. Although future increases in immigration will counterbalance the decline of the indigenous population, they assert, the real advance will be the decoupling of productivity expansion and workforce increases. The information age is knowledge-intensive, and becoming more so, not labor-intensive.

One author who accepts Bouvier and Bertrand's thesis is the noted scholar of management, Peter Drucker. In "The Future That Has Already Happened," *The Futurist* (November 1998), Drucker predicts that retirement age in the developed world will soon rise to 75, primarily because the greatest skill of this age group—knowledge—will become even more of an asset. He maintains that knowledge resources will become the most important commodity.

An important book on the fiscal problems facing the developed world because of aging can be found in Robert Stowe England's *The Fiscal Challenge of an Aging Industrial World* (CSIS *Significant Issues* Series, November 2001). An earlier report from CSIS is *Global Aging: The Challenge of the New Millennium* (CSIS and Watson Wyatt Worldwide). This document's presentation of the raw data is particularly useful. See also Ronald D. Lee's *Global Population Aging and Its Economic Consequences* (AEI Press, 2007); *Aging, Globalization and Inequality: The New Critical Gerontology* (Jan Baars et al., eds., Baywood Publishing Co., 2006); *Issues in Global Aging* (Frederick L. Ahearn, ed., Haworth Press, 2002); and *Global Health and Global Aging* (Mary Robinson et al., eds., Jossey-Boss, 2007); *Ageing Labour Forces: Promises and Prospects* (Phillip Taylor, Edward Elgar Publishing, 2008); and *Population Ageing and Economic Growth: Education Policy and Family Policy in a Model of Endogenous Growth* (Sandra Greece, Physica-Verlag Heidelbergh, 2009). Analyses of specific geographic areas can be found in *Ageing and the Labour Market in Japan: Problems and Policies* (Koichi Hamada, Edward Elger Publishing, 2007);

From Red to Grey: The "Third Transition" of Aging Populations in Eastern Europe and the Former Soviet Union (Mukesh Chawai, World Bank Publications, 2007); *Ageing in East Asia: Challenges and Policies for the Twenty-First Century* (Tsung-his Fu, ed., Routledge, 2009); *The Economic and Financial Market Consequences of Global Ageing* (Kieran McMorrow, Springer, 2004); and *Global Population Ageing and Migration in Europe* (Bo Malmberg, Routledge, 2010, forthcoming). For a look at the relationship between global health and ageing, see *Global Health and Global Aging* (Mary Robinson et al., eds., Jossey-Bass, 2007).

The Center for Strategic and International Studies (CSIS) in Washington is at the forefront of research and policy advocacy on the issue of global aging in the developed world. Its Global Aging Initiative (GAI) explores the international economic, financial, political, and security implications of aging and depopulation. Its report *Meeting the Challenge of Global Aging: A Report to World Leaders from the CSIS Commission on Global Aging* (CSIS Press, 2002) suggests that the wide range of changes brought on by global aging poses significant challenges in the ability of countries to address problems associated with the elderly directly and with the national economy as a whole. Two other reports include *Meeting the Challenge of Global Aging*, by Walter F. Mondale et al. (2002), and *Macroeconomic Impact of Global Aging: A New Era of Economic Frailty?* (2002). See the CSIS Web site (www.csis.org).

Other Web sites include LinkAge 2000: Policy Implications of Global Aging (library.thinkquest.org/), The International Center on Global Aging (www.globalaging.org/resources), and The Environmental Literacy Council (www.enviroliteracy.org). See also the Web site of the Program on the Global Demography of Aging at Harvard University (http://www.hsph.harvard.edu/pgda/).

Finally, the Second World Assembly on Aging in Madrid in April 2002 produced a huge number of documents. Its Plan of Action and other reports can be found at www.un.org

ISSUE 4

Does Global Urbanization Lead Primarily to Undesirable Consequences?

YES: Divya Abhat, Shauna Dineen, Tamsyn Jones, Jim Motavilli, Rebecca Sanborn, and Kate Slomkowski, from "Today's 'Mega-Cities' Are Overcrowded and Environmentally Stressed," http://www.emagazine.com (September/October 2005)

NO: UNFPA, from *UNFPA State of the World 2007: Unleashing the Potential of Urban Growth* (2007)

ISSUE SUMMARY

YES: Divya Abhat, editor of *E/The Environmental Magazine,* and colleagues suggest that the world's cities suffer from environmental ills, among them pollution, poverty, fresh water shortages, and disease.

NO: The UNFPA 2007 Report suggests that cities, in fact, facilitate a number of desirable conditions, such as gender-equitable change, more diverse employment possibilities, more economic well-being and security for women, women's empowerment, and access to better health care, among other positive changes.

T he year 2007 witnessed a turning point in the history of the world's cities. For the first time, the world's urban and rural populations were equal. Percentages are different for the developed and developing worlds, however. In 1950, 55 percent of the population of the developed world resided in urban areas, compared to only 18 percent in the developing world. By 2000, 76 percent of those in the developed world were urbanized, and it is expected, according to UN projections, to reach 82 percent by 2025. But because there will be low population growth throughout the developed world in the coming decades, the impact will not be substantial.

The story is different in the developing world. In 2000, the level of urbanization had risen to almost 40 percent, and is projected to be 54 percent in 2025. The percentages tell only part of the story, however, as they are not based on a stable national population level, but will occur in the context of

69

substantial increases in the national population level. To illustrate the dual implication of urban growth as the consequence of both migration to the cities and increased births to those already living in urban areas, the United Nations projects that the urban population in the developing world will more than double in size between 2000 and 2030, from just under 2 billion to almost 5 billion or nearly two-thirds of the world's population (*State of the World's Cities 2006/07*, UN-Habitat, Earthscan, 2007). Asia and Africa will experience the largest urban populations, but small and intermediate cities will absorb most of the urban growth.

Tremendous inequality will exist in cities. One out of three city dwellers resides in an urban environment that qualifies as slum conditions, defined as a lack of durable housing, lack of sufficient living area, lack of access to improved water, lack of access to improved sanitation, and lack of secure land tenure.

There are two ways to examine rapid urbanization. One can study the ability of society to provide services to the urban population. A second approach is to examine the adverse impacts of the urbanized area on the environment. The best place to begin a discussion of urbanization's effects is found in "An Urbanizing World" (Martin P. Brockerhoff, *Population Bulletin,* Population Reference Bureau, 2000). To Brockerhoff, increasing urbanization in the poor countries can be seen "as a welcome or as an alarming trend." He suggests that cities have been the "engines of economic development and the centers of industry and commerce." The diffusion of ideas is best found in cities around the world. And Brockerhoff observes the governmental cost savings of delivering goods and services to those in more densely populated environments.

The current problem is not that cities of the developing world are growing, but that they are expanding at a rapid pace. This calls into question the ability of both government and the private sector to determine what is necessary for urbanites to not only survive but to thrive. Many researchers believe that poverty and health problems (both physical and mental) are consequences of urbanization. Brockerhoff also alludes to the potential for greater harm to residents of cities from natural disasters and environmental hazards.

There is a more recent concern emerging among researchers about urbanization's impact—this time on biodiversity. One source has coined the phrase "heavy ecological footprints" ("Impact on the Environment," *Population Reports,* 2002) to describe the adverse effects. One study concludes, for example, that urban sprawl in the United States endangers more species than any other human behavior (Michael L. McKinney, "Urbanization, Biodiversity, and Conservation," *Bioscience,* 2002).

The two selections for this issue address the question of the consequences of urbanization. In the first selection, Jim Motavalli and colleagues argue that most urban dwellers in the developing world are already confronted by severe environmental problems that will only increase in nature as population continues to grow. In the second selection, the United Nations (UNFPA) Report advances the point that cities represent a better place to achieve a variety of positive goals, many relating to women's issues.

YES

Divya Abhat et al.

Cities of the Future: Today's "Mega-Cities" Are Overcrowded and Environmentally Stressed

We take big cities for granted today, but they are a relatively recent phenomenon. Most of human history concerns rural people making a living from the land. But the world is rapidly urbanizing, and it's not at all clear that our planet has the resources to cope with this relentless trend. And, unfortunately, most of the growth is occurring in urban centers ill-equipped for the pace of change. You've heard of the "birth dearth"? It's bypassing Dhaka, Mumbai, Mexico City and Lagos, cities that are adding population as many of their western counterparts contract.

The world's first cities grew up in what is now Iraq, on the plains of Mesopotamia near the banks of the Tigris and Euphrates Rivers. The first city in the world to have more than one million people was Rome at the height of its Empire in 5 A.D. At that time, world population was only 170 million. But Rome was something new in the world. It had developed its own sophisticated sanitation and traffic management systems, as well as aqueducts, multi-story low-income housing and even suburbs, but after it fell in 410 A.D. it would be 17 centuries before any metropolitan area had that many people.

The first large city in the modern era was Beijing, which surpassed one million population around 1800, followed soon after by New York and London. But at that time city life was the exception; only three percent of the world's population lived in urban areas in 1800.

The rise of manufacturing spurred relocation to urban centers from the 19th through the early 20th century. The cities had the jobs, and new arrivals from the countryside provided the factories with cheap, plentiful labor. But the cities were also unhealthy places to live because of crowded conditions, poor sanitation and the rapid transmission of infectious disease. As the Population Reference Bureau reports, deaths exceeded births in many large European cities until the middle of the 19th century. Populations grew, then, by continuing waves of migration from the countryside and from abroad.

From *E/The Environmental Magazine*, Vol. XVI, No. 5, September/October 2005. Copyright © 2005 by E/The Environmental Magazine. Reprinted by permission of Featurewell.

From First World to Third

In the first half of the 20th century, the fastest urban growth was in western cities. New York, London and other First World capitals were magnets for immigration and job opportunity. In 1950, New York, London, Tokyo and Paris boasted of having the world's largest metropolitan populations. (Also in the top 10 were Moscow, Chicago, and the German city of Essen.) By then, New York had already become the first "mega-city," with more than 10 million people. It would not hold on to such exclusivity for long.

In the postwar period, many large American cities lost population as manufacturing fled overseas and returning soldiers taking advantage of the GI Bill fueled the process of suburbanization. Crime was also a factor. As an example, riot-torn Detroit lost 800,000 people between 1950 and 1996, and its population declined 33.9 percent between 1970 and 1996. Midwestern cities were particularly hard-hit. St. Louis, for instance, lost more than half its population in the same period, as did Pittsburgh. Cleveland precipitously declined, as did Buffalo, Cincinnati, Minneapolis and many other large cities, emerging as regional players rather than world leaders.

Meanwhile, while many American cities shrank, population around the world was growing dramatically. In the 20th century, world population increased from 1.65 billion to six billion. The highest rate of growth was in the late 1960s, when 80 million people were added every year.

According to the "World Population Data Sheet," global population will rise 46 percent between now and 2050 to about nine billion. While developed countries are losing population because of falling birth rates and carefully controlled immigration rates (only the U.S. reverses this trend, with 45 percent growth to 422 million predicted by 2050), population is exploding in the developing world.

India's population will likely grow 52 percent to 1.6 billion by 2050, when it will surpass China as the world's most populous country. The population in neighboring Pakistan will grow to 349 million, up 134 percent in 2050. Triple-digit growth rates also are forecast for Iraq, Afghanistan and Nepal.

Africa could double in population to 1.9 billion by 2050. These growth rates hold despite the world's highest rates of AIDS infection, and despite civil wars, famines and other factors. Despite strife in the Congo, it could triple to 181 million by 2050, while Nigeria doubles to 307 million.

Big Cities Get Bigger—and Poorer

According to a 1994 UN report, 1.7 billion of the world's 2.5 billion urban dwellers were then living in less-developed nations, which were also home to two-thirds of the world's mega-cities. The trend is rapidly accelerating. *People and the Planet* reports that by 2007, 3.2 billion people—a number larger than the entire global population of 1967—will live in cities. Developing countries will absorb nearly all of the world's population increases between today and 2030. The estimated urban growth rate of 1.8 percent for the period between 2000 and 2030 will double the number of city dwellers. Meanwhile, rural populations are growing scarcely at all.

Also by 2030, more than half of all Asians and Africans will live in urban areas. Latin America and the Caribbean will at that time be 84 percent urban, a level comparable to the U.S. As urban population grows, rural populations will shrink. Asia is projected to lose 26 million rural dwellers between 2000 and 2030.

For many internal migrants, cities offer more hope of a job and better health care and educational opportunities. In many cases, they are home to an overwhelming percentage of a country's wealth. (Mexico City, for example, produces about 30 percent of Mexico's total Gross Domestic Product.) Marina Lupina, a Manila, Philippines, resident, told *People and the Planet* that she and her two children endure the conditions of city living (inhabiting a shack made from discarded wood and cardboard next to a fetid, refuse-choked canal) because she can earn $2 to $3 a day selling recycled cloth, compared to 50 cents as a farm laborer in the rural areas. "My girls will have a better life than I had," she says. "That's the main reason I came to Manila. We will stay no matter what."

Movement like this will lead to rapidly changing population levels in the world's cities, and emerging giants whose future preeminence can now only be guessed. "By 2050, an estimated two-thirds of the world's population will live in urban areas, imposing even more pressure on the space infrastructure and resources of cities, leading to social disintegration and horrific urban poverty," says Werner Fornos, president of the Washington-based Population Institute.

Today, the most populous city is Tokyo (26.5 million people in 2001), followed by Sao Paulo (18.3 million), Mexico City (18.3 million), New York (16.8 million) and Bombay/Mumbai (16.5 million). But by 2015 this list will change, with Tokyo remaining the largest city (then with 27.2 million), followed by Dhaka (Bangladesh), Mumbai, Sao Paulo, New Delhi and Mexico City (each with more than 20 million). New York will have moved down to seventh place, followed by Jakarta, Calcutta, Karachi and Lagos (all with more than 16 million).

The speed by which some mega-cities are growing has slowed. Thirty years ago, for instance, the UN projected Mexico City's population would grow beyond 30 million by 2000, but the actual figures are much lower. Other cities not growing as much as earlier seen are Rio de Janeiro, Calcutta, Cairo, and Seoul, Korea. But against this development is the very rapid growth of many other cities (in some cases, tenfold in 40 years) such as Amman (Jordan), Dar es Salaam (Tanzania), Lagos, and Nairobi.

The rise of mega-cities, comments the *Washington Post,* "poses formidable challenges in health care and the environment, in both the developed and developing world. The urban poor in developing countries live in squalor unlike anything they left behind . . . In Caracas, more than half the total housing stock is squatter housing. In Bangkok, the regional economy is 2.1 percent smaller than it otherwise would be because of time lost in traffic jams. The mega-cities of the future pose huge problems for waste management, water use and climate change."

In Cairo, Egypt, the rooftops of countless buildings are crowded with makeshift tents, shacks and mud shelters. It's not uncommon to see a family cooking their breakfast over an open fire while businesspeople work in their cubicles below. The city's housing shortage is so severe that thousands of Egyptians have moved into the massive historic cemetery known as the City of the Dead, where they hang clotheslines between tombs and sleep in mausoleums.

By 2015, there will be 33 mega-cities, 27 of them in the developing world. Although cities themselves occupy only two percent of the world's land, they have a major environmental impact on a much wider area. London, for example, requires roughly 60 times its own area to supply its nine million inhabitants with food and forest products. Mega-cities are likely to be a drain on the Earth's dwindling resources, while contributing mightily to environmental degradation themselves.

The Mega-City Environment

Mega-cities suffer from a catalog of environmental ills. A World Health Organization (WHO)/United Nations Environment Programme (UNEP) study found that seven of the cities—Mexico City, Beijing, Cairo, Jakarta, Los Angeles, Sao Paulo and Moscow—had three or more pollutants that exceeded the WHO health protection guidelines. All 20 of the cities studied by WHO/UNEP had at least one major pollutant that exceeded established health limits.

According to the World Resources Institute, "Millions of children living in the world's largest cities, particularly in developing countries, are exposed to life-threatening air pollution two to eight times above the maximum WHO guidelines. Indeed, more than 80 percent of all deaths in developing countries attributable to air pollution-induced lung infections are among children under five." In the big Asian mega-cities such as New Delhi, Beijing and Jakarta, approximately 20 to 30 percent of all respiratory disease stems from air pollution.

Almost all of the mega-cities face major fresh water challenges. Johannesburg, South Africa, is forced to draw water from highlands 370 miles away. In Bangkok, saltwater is making incursions into aquifers. Mexico City has a serious sinking problem because of excessive groundwater withdrawal.

More than a billion people, 20 percent of the world's population, live without regular access to clean running water. While poor people are forced to pay exorbitant fees for private water, many cities squander their resources through leakages and illegal drainage. "With the population of cities expected to increase to five billion by 2025," says Klaus Toepfer, executive director of the UNEP, "the urban demand for water is set to increase exponentially. This means that any solution to the water crisis is closely linked to the governance of cities."

Mega-city residents, crowded into unsanitary slums, are also subject to serious disease outbreaks. Lima, Peru (with population estimated at 9.4 million by 2015) suffered a cholera outbreak in the late 1990s partly because, as the *New York Times* reported, "Rural people new to Lima . . . live in houses without running water and use the outhouses that dot the hillsides above." Consumption of unsafe food and water subjects these people to life-threatening diarrhea and dehydration.

It's worth looking at some of these emerging mega-cities in detail, because daily life there is likely to be the pattern for a majority of the world's population. Most are already experiencing severe environmental problems that will only be exacerbated by rapid population increases. Our space-compromised list leaves out the largest European and American cities. These urban centers obviously face different challenges, among them high immigration rates.

Jakarta, Indonesia

A Yale University graduate student, who served as a college intern at the U.S. Embassy in Jakarta, brought back this account: "Directly adjacent to the Embassy's high-rise office building was a muddy, trash-filled canal that children bathed in every morning. The view from the top floors was unforgettable: a layer of brown sky rising up to meet the blue—a veritable pollution horizon. In the distance the tips of skyscrapers stretched up out of the atmospheric cesspool below, like giant corporate snorkels. Without fresh air to breathe, my days were characterized by nausea and constant low-grade headaches. I went to Indonesia wanting a career in government, and left determined to start a career working with the environment."

Jakarta is one of the world's fastest-growing cities. United Nations estimates put the city's 1995 population at 11.5 million, a dramatic increase from only 530,000 in 1930. Mohammad Dannisworo of the Bandung Institute of Technology (ITB) says 8.5 million people live within the city's boundaries at night and an additional 5.5 million migrate via 2.5 million private cars, 3.8 million motorcycles and 255,000 public transportation vehicles into the city during the day. This daily parade of combustion engines clogs the city streets and thickens the air, making Jakarta the world's third-most-polluted city after Bangkok and Mexico City.

Rapid growth has become one of the capital city's greatest challenges, as migrants continue to pour into Jakarta from the surrounding countryside in search of higher-paying jobs. An estimated 200,000 people come to the city looking for employment every year. In the face of such growth, the city has been unable to provide adequate housing, despite repeated attempts to launch urban improvement programs. The Kampung Improvement Program (KIP), established in the 1980s, was initially highly successful in boosting living conditions for more than 3.5 million established migrants, but it has been unable to accommodate the persistent migrant influx. There is an acute housing shortage, with a demand for 200,000 new units a year unfulfilled.

As Encarta describes it, "In the 1970s, efforts failed to control growth by prohibiting the entry of unemployed migrants. The current strategy emphasizes family planning, dispersing the population throughout the greater [metropolitan] region, and promoting transmigration (the voluntary movement of families to Indonesia's less-populated islands). Jakarta is a magnet for migrants . . . [During the late 1980s] most were between the ages of 15 and 39 years, many with six years of education or less."

The UN reports that the city's drinking water system is ineffective, leading 80 percent of Jakarta inhabitants to use underground water, which has become steadily depleted. In lowlying North Jakarta, groundwater depletion has caused serious land subsidence, making the area more vulnerable to flooding and allowing seawater from the Java Sea to seep into the coastal aquifers. According to Suyono Dikun, Deputy Minister for Infrastructure at the National Development Planning Board, more than 100 million people in Indonesia are living without proper access to clean water.

Jakarta's environment has been deteriorating rapidly, with serious air pollution and the lack of a waterborne sewer. Jakarta officials have only recently begun to acknowledge the source of over half of the city's air pollution, and have begun to take action against automobile congestion. The Blue Skies Program, founded in 1996, is dedicated to updating the city's public and private transportation technology. The project's successes to date include an increase in the percentage of vehicles meeting pollution standards, a near-complete phasing out of leaded gasoline, and an increase in the number of natural gas-fueled vehicles to 3,000 taxis, 500 passenger cars and 50 public buses.

The Blue Skies Project is pushing Jakarta toward a complete natural gas conversion and is working toward the installation of dedicated filling stations, establishing a fleet of natural gas-fueled passenger buses, supplying conversion kits for gasoline-fueled cars, and creating adequate inspection and maintenance facilities.

Jakarta has acknowledged its traffic problems and undertaken both small and large scale projects to alleviate the stresses of pollution and congestion. The city has launched a "three-in-one" policy to encourage carpooling, demanding that every car on major thruways carry at least three passengers when passing through special zones from 4:30 p.m. to 7:30 p.m. The city has also undertaken the construction of a nearly 17-mile monorail system.

But if Jakarta really wants to alleviate its infrastructure problems, it has to work from within, says Gordon Feller of the California-based Urban Age Institute. "The mayor needs to create a partnership between the three sectors—the government, the local communities and the nongovernmental agencies. The job of the mayor is to empower the independent innovators, not to co-opt or block them."

Dhaka, Bangladesh

Dhaka had only 3.5 million people in 1951; now it has more than 13 million. The city has been gaining population at a rate of nearly seven percent a year since 1975, and it will be the world's second-largest city (after Tokyo) by 2015. According to a recent Japanese environmental report, "Dhaka city is beset with a number of socio-environmental problems. Traffic congestion, flooding, solid waste disposal, black smoke from vehicular and industrial emissions, air and noise pollution, and pollution of water bodies by industrial discharge. . . .

Black smoke coming out from the discharge is intolerable to breathe, burning eyes and throats. The city dwellers are being slowly poisoned by lead concentration in the city air 10 times higher than the government safety limit."

Because of a heavy concentration of cars burning leaded gasoline, Dhaka's children have one of the highest blood lead levels in the world. Almost 90 percent of primary school children tested had levels high enough to impair their developmental and learning abilities, according to a scientific study.

Water pollution is already rampant. According to the Japanese report, "The river Buriganga flows by the side of the densely populated area of the old city. Dumping of waste to the river by . . . industries is rather indiscriminate. . . . The indiscriminate discharge of domestic sewage, industrial effluents and open dumping of solid wastes are becoming a great concern from the point of water-environment degradation."

Nearly half of all Bangladeshis live below the poverty line, able only to glance at the gleaming new malls built in Dhaka. Urbanization and the pressures of poverty are severely stressing the country's once-abundant natural resources. According to U.S. Aid for International Development (USAID), "Pressures on Bangladesh's biological resources are intense and growing."

They include:

- Poor management of aquatic and terrestrial resources;
- Population growth;
- Overuse of resources;
- Unplanned building projects; and
- Expansion of agriculture onto less-productive lands, creating erosion and runoff, among other by-products.

Bangladesh's expanding population destroys critical habitats, reports USAID, causing a decrease in biodiversity. Most of Bangladesh's tropical forests and almost all of the freshwater floodplains have been negatively affected by human activities.

But despite all the negatives, there is a growing environmental movement in Bangladesh that is working to save Dhaka's natural resources. The Bangladesh Environmental Network (BEN), for instance, works on reducing the high level of arsenic in Bangladesh's water supply (more than 500 percent higher than World Health Organization standards), combats the country's severe flooding problem and tries to defeat India's River Linking Project, which could divert an estimated 10 to 20 percent of Bangladesh's water flow. Bangladesh Poribesh Andolon holds demonstrations and international action days to increase citizen awareness of endangered rivers.

International development projects are also addressing some of the country's environmental woes, including a $44 million arsenic mitigation project launched in 1998 and jointly financed by the World Bank and the Swiss Development and Cooperation Agency. The project is installing deep wells, installing hardware to capture rainwater, building sanitation plants, and expanding distribution systems. A $177 million World Bank project works with the government of Bangladesh to improve urban transportation in Dhaka. Private companies from Bangladesh and Pakistan recently announced a joint venture to construct a waste management plant that could handle 3,200 metric tons of solid waste per day, turning it into organic fertilizer.

Mexico City

Mexico City is like an anxious teenager, growing up faster than it probably should. That phenomenon manifests itself in awkward contrasts: Sports cars zipping down crowded streets, choked with air pollution; a Wal-Mart rising against a skyline of the ancient ruins of Teotihuacan; and trendy designer knock-off bags lining the walls of a grungy street stall.

The locale has long been a cultural hub—the ancient Aztec capital of Tenochtitlán, where Mexico City now stands, was the largest city in the Americas in the 14th century with a population of about 300,000. When the Spanish razed Tenochtitlán they erected Mexico City in its place, though a smallpox epidemic knocked the population back to 30,000. Mexico City served as the center of Spain's colonial empire during the 1500s, but the modern-day metropolis only began to materialize in the late 1930s when a combination of rapid economic growth, population growth, and a considerable rural migration filled the city with people.

The larger metropolitan area now engulfs once-distinct villages and population estimates range from 16 million to 30 million, depending on how the city's boundaries are drawn. Regardless, Mexico City is now widely considered the world's third-largest city, and still growing; birth rates are high and 1,100 new residents migrate to the capital each day.

With so many people crammed into a closed mountain valley, many environmental and social problems are bound to arise. Mexico City's air was ranked by WHO as the most contaminated in the world in 1992. By 1998, the Mexican capital had added the distinction of being "the world's most dangerous city for children." Twenty percent of the city's population lives in utter poverty, the Mega-Cities Project reports, 40 percent of the population lives in "informal settlements," and wealth is concentrated in very few hands.

A combination of population, geography and geology render air pollution one of the city's greatest problems. WHO studies have reported that it is unhealthy to breathe air with over 120 parts per billion of ozone contaminants more than one day a year, but residents breathe it more than 300 days a year. More than one million of the city's more than 18 million people suffer from permanent breathing problems.

According to the U.S. Energy Information Administration, "Exhaust fumes from Mexico City's approximately three million cars are the main source of air pollutants. Problems resulting from the high levels of exhaust are exacerbated by the fact that Mexico City is situated in a basin. The geography prevents winds from blowing away the pollution, trapping it above the city."

The International Development Research Center has observed that "despite more than a decade of stringent pollution control measures, a haze hangs over Mexico City most days, obscuring the surrounding snow-capped mountains and endangering the health of its inhabitants. Many factors have contributed to this situation: industrial growth, a population boom and the proliferation of vehicles." More than 30 percent of the city's vehicles are more than 20 years old.

Solid waste creates another major problem, and officials estimate that, of the 10,000 tons of waste generated each day, at least one-quarter is dumped illegally. The city also lacks an effective sanitation and water distribution system. According to the United Nations, "Urbanization has had a serious negative effect on the ecosystem of Mexico City. Although 80 percent of the population has piped inside plumbing, residents in the peripheral areas cannot access the sewage network and a great percentage of wastewater remains untreated as it passes to the north for use as irrigation water."

Perhaps three million residents at the edge of the city do not have access to sewers, says the Mega-Cities Project. Untreated waste from these locations is discharged directly into water bodies or into the ground, where it can contaminate ground water. Only 50 percent of residents in squatter settlements have access to plumbing, and these residents are more likely to suffer from health effects linked to inadequate sanitation. Furthermore, Mexico City is now relying on water pumped from lower elevations to quench an ever-deepening thirst; as the city continues to grow, the need for water and the politics surrounding that need are likely only to intensify.

Mexican industry is centered within the city and is primarily responsible for many of the city's environmental problems as well as for the prosperity that certain areas have achieved. Mexico City houses 80 percent of all the firms in the country, and 2.6 million cars and buses bring people to work and shop in them. Sandwiched in between slums and sewers are glitzy, luxurious neighborhoods and shopping centers, as chic as any in New York or Los Angeles.

The streets of the Zócalo, a central city plaza modeled after Spanish cities, serve as Mexico City's cultural hub. Unwittingly, the plaza has become one of the economic centers as well. Most job growth in Mexico occurs in the underground sector—in street stalls that cover every square inch of sidewalk space, women flipping tortillas curbside, and kids hawking phone cards or pirated CDs to passersby. Despite efforts to clean up activities that are illegal or considered eyesores, street vendors make up an enormous part of Mexico's job force and, according to the *Los Angeles Times,* are primarily responsible for keeping the official unemployment rate below that of the United States. . . .

People In Cities:
Hope Countering Desolation

The unprecedented urban growth taking place in developing countries reflects the hopes and aspirations of millions of new urbanites. Cities have enormous potential for improving people's lives, but inadequate urban management, often based on inaccurate perceptions and information, can turn opportunity into disaster.

Conscious of this gap, the Programme of Action of the International Conference on Population and Development recommended that: "Governments should increase the capacity and competence of city and municipal authorities to manage urban development, to safeguard the environment, to respond to the need of all citizens, including urban squatters, for personal safety, basic infrastructure and services, to eliminate health and social problems, including problems of drugs and criminality, and problems resulting from overcrowding and disasters, and to provide people with alternatives to living in areas prone to natural and man-made disasters.". . .

The Unseen Dramas of the Urban Poor

Until recently, rural settlements were the epicentre of poverty and human suffering. All measures of poverty, whether based on income, consumption or expenditure, showed that rural poverty was deeper and more widespread than in cities. Urban centres on the whole offered better access to health, education, basic infrastructure, information, knowledge and opportunity. Such findings were easy to understand in view of budgetary allocations, the concentration of services and the other intangible benefits of cities.

Poverty, however, is now increasing more rapidly in urban areas than in rural areas but has received far less attention. Aggregate statistics hide deep inequalities and gloss over concentrations of harsh poverty within cities. Most assessments actually underestimate the scale and depth of urban poverty. . . .

Urban mismanagement often squanders urban advantages and the urban potential for poverty reduction. Although urban poverty is growing faster than in rural areas, development agencies have only recently begun to appreciate that they need new interventions to attack its roots.

From *UNFPA State of the World,* 2007, pp. 15, 16–18, 19–23, 24–26, 27, 29 (excerpts). Copyright © 2007 by United Nations Publications. Reprinted by permission.

Slums: Unparalleled Concentration of Poverty . . .

Over 90 per cent of slum dwellers today are in the developing world. South Asia has the largest share, followed by Eastern Asia, sub-Saharan Africa and Latin America. China and India together have 37 per cent of the world's slums. In sub-Saharan Africa, urbanization has become virtually synonymous with slum growth; 72 per cent of the region's urban population lives under slum conditions, compared to 56 per cent in South Asia. The slum population of sub-Saharan Africa almost doubled in 15 years, reaching nearly 200 million in 2005.

The United Nations Millennium Declaration recognized the importance of addressing the situation of slum dwellers in reducing overall poverty and advancing human development. Despite the strength of this commitment, monitoring progress on the situation of slum dwellers has been a challenge. Proactive policy interventions are needed now if nations are to meet the spirit of Target 11 of the Millennium Development Goals and ameliorate the lives of millions of the urban poor.

The Persistent Disparities

Nowhere are the disadvantages of the urban poor compared with other city dwellers more marked than in the health area. Poor women are at a particular disadvantage. Although cash income is much more important in cities than in villages, income poverty is only one aspect of urban poverty. Others are poor-quality and overcrowded shelter, lack of public services and infrastructure such as piped water, sanitation facilities, garbage collection, drainage and roads, as well as insecure land tenure. . . . These disadvantages increase the health and work burdens of the urban poor and also increase their risks from environmental hazards and crime.

Poor people live in unhealthy environments. Health risks arise from poor sanitation, lack of clean water, overcrowded and poorly ventilated living and working environments and from air and industrial pollution. Inadequate diet reduces slum-dwellers' resistance to disease, especially because they live in the constant presence of pathogenic micro-organisms. . . .

The United Nations Development Programme's *Human Development Report* for 2006 provides an excellent overview and analysis of the relations between power, poverty and water. It highlights the fact that the stark realities of slum life defy statistical analysis. Frequently, many people live in compounds made up of several houses where one toilet serves all adults and children. Toilets may be reserved for adults, and children forced to go elsewhere in the compound or in the streets where they play. Sharing three toilets and one shower with 250 households in a community is not at all unusual in cities of sub-Saharan Africa. Conditions like these increase stress on all inhabitants, especially women who are also subject to greater risks of gender-based violence. In Latin America, only 33.6 per cent of the urban poor have access to flush toilets, compared to 63.7 per cent of their non-poor urban counterparts.

Water is a scarce and expensive resource for the urban poor, often obtained in small quantities from street vendors. Bought this way, unit costs can be much higher than for people who have running water in their homes. If there is a piped supply, obtaining it may involve long journeys to the neighbourhood water post, long waits, tiring trips back home with full jerry-cans, careful storage to minimize wastage and reusing the same water several times, increasing the risk of contamination.

Water chores take up a substantial part of women's and girls' time. A partial time-use study covering 10 sites in East Africa found that the waiting time for water increased from 28 minutes a day in 1967 to 92 minutes in 1997. The physical and time burdens come not so much from long distances from the source of supply, as in villages, but from the large numbers who have to use the same source. . . .

The association between poverty, environment and housing in urban areas is critical because it indicates a key area for intervention. Policies directed to improving shelter in urban areas can have huge impacts on poverty reduction and on environmental well-being. Advances in health and mortality indicators depend very much on urban water and sewage treatment. . . .

Women's Empowerment and Well-being: The Pillars of Sustainable Cities

As women are generally the poorest of the poor . . . eliminating social, cultural, political and economic discrimination against women is a prerequisite of eradicating poverty . . . in the context of sustainable development.

The social and physical amenities of cities facilitate gender-equitable change. Indeed, the concentration of population in urban areas opens many possibilities for women—whether migrants or natives—to meet, work, form social support networks, exchange information and organize around the things of greatest importance to them. Cities tend to favour greater cultural diversity and, as a corollary, more flexibility in the application of social norms that traditionally impinge on women's freedom of choice.

Compared with rural areas, cities offer women better educational facilities and more diverse employment options. They provide more opportunities for social and political participation, as well as access to media, information and technology. Cities offer many roads to decision-making power through community and political participation. Women can use urban space to project their voices, to participate in community politics and development and to influence social and political processes at all levels.

Women stand to benefit from the proximity and greater availability of urban services, such as water, sanitation, education, health and transportation facilities; all of these can reduce women's triple burden of reproductive, productive and community work and, in so doing, improve their health status and that of their children and families.

Education in Urban Settings: Closing the Gender Gap?

Urbanization increases girls' access to education and promotes cultural acceptance of their right to education. Primary, and especially secondary, education for girls has crucial multiplier effects that increase women's social and economic status and expand their freedom of choice. Educated women tend to marry later and have fewer and healthier children. In adulthood, they have greater employment potential, income-earning capacity and decision-making authority within the household. Other benefits include knowledge and capacities to maintain and protect their health, including preventing unwanted pregnancies and sexually transmitted infections (STIs), including HIV/AIDS. All of these are helpful in the fight against poverty. . . .

The Job Marketplace: A Way Out?

Employment possibilities are far more diverse in urban areas for both men and women. Urbanization has significantly boosted women's labour force participation. Paid employment for women not only increases household income but can trigger transformations in gender roles and elevate women's status in the family and society.

Worldwide, there has been a significant increase in women's non-agricultural wage employment during recent years. New opportunities have arisen, especially in tradable sectors and in home-based businesses linked to global production networks. For example, of the 50 million workers in export processing zones, 80 per cent are young women.

However, most growth of female employment is in the informal sector, which accounts for most new employment opportunities in the world, and where women are a large majority, especially in Africa and Asia. Informal employment is critical in enabling women to absorb the economic shocks that poor households experience. In this regard, women's employment, paid and unpaid, is of fundamental importance in keeping many households out of poverty. The downside is that much informal work is unstable, of poor quality and poorly paid.

The Long Road to Property Ownership for Women

Physical and financial assets offer women more than economic well-being and security. Legal property tenure increases women's opportunities to access credit, generate income and establish a cushion against poverty. It also empowers them in their relationships with their partners and their families, reduces vulnerability to gender-based violence and HIV/AIDS and provides a safety net for the elderly.

Women own less than 15 per cent of land world-wide. In some countries, women cannot legally own property separately from their husbands, particularly in parts of Asia and sub-Saharan Africa. Lacking legal title to land and property, women have virtually no collateral for obtaining loans and credit, thus limiting their economic options. In some settings, although women can legally own and inherit property, custom dictates that men control it and that it passes only to male heirs on a man's death. It is difficult or impossible in these circumstances for women to exercise their property rights in practice.

There is evidence that the difficulty of securing title to property in rural areas is prompting women to migrate to cities in hopes of securing property there, where prospects are assumed to be better. Women may also have better access to legal information and support in urban areas. Because of the greater social dynamism and range of economic possibilities open to women, cities are likely to offer more opportunities to acquire property in the long run.

Legal reforms are still necessary, however, to secure women's equal rights to own property. Where laws are in place, cities continue to need programmes and recourse mechanisms to tackle informal barriers such as customary practices, low awareness of rights, the high cost of land and housing and discriminatory lending and titling policies.

Property rights and access to credit are closely linked, so it is not surprising that women face difficulties in obtaining financial assets. Microcredit programmes have partially filled this need. Making its mark initially in rural settings, microcredit is also allowing poor urban women to leverage their capacities and improve their incomes.

Power Through Voice: Getting It Done Through Community Organizations

Decision-making power is one of the main indicators of women's empowerment. The prospects for women's formal participation in politics are improving, despite the many challenges they face, including gender discrimination and prejudice, multiple poorly-rewarded responsibilities and calls on their time and energy, lack of support in crucial areas such as reproductive health and lack of resources.

Some governments have enacted quotas or parity laws to address these barriers and ensure that women have a critical level of participation in city councils and local governments. Nevertheless, women make up only 16 per cent of members of national parliaments in Africa and Asia and 9 per cent in the Arab States. These percentages are well below what is believed to be a "critical mass" for women to influence policy and spending priorities.

Despite this bleak picture in the capitals of nations, women's participation in decentralized governance has increased. Local spheres of government offer greater opportunities for women's empowerment and political participation, a situation that reflects positively on women's prospects as urbanization increases. Moreover, countries with a higher percentage of women councillors are likely to have a higher number of women parliamentarians, which may, in turn, benefit women at the municipal level.

Urbanization can thus be a powerful factor in creating the conditions for women's empowerment. Turning this potential into reality is one of the most effective ways of promoting human rights, improving the living conditions of the poor and making the cities of developing countries better places in which to live.

Cities lend themselves to women's social and political participation at many levels. For poor women whose lives have been confined to home, family and work, the act of joining an organization immediately broadens their prospects. When women actively participate in an organization, or take on leadership roles, they gain self-confidence, new skills, knowledge and a greater understanding of the world. Organizing can address many of the limitations that poverty imposes on poor women; it can begin to counter the costs and risks of informal work. It can also help to reduce poor women's vulnerability, insecurity and dependence, including a lack of knowledge about the outside world and how it works.

Organizing also helps women who have few assets to pool resources, thereby increasing their economic power. Savings and credit groups may help the working poor access microfinance services, and producers with little capital may buy raw materials at wholesale prices by combining their resources.

Such advantages could be enhanced with more support. Poor women need a representative voice in the institutions and processes that establish social and economic policies in a global economy, in order to continue improving the living and working conditions of the poor. International, regional and national negotiations regarding free trade agreements, the Millennium Development Goals and poverty reduction strategies all need to include the voices and concerns of the urban poor and, in particular, informal workers, the majority of whom are women. Ensuring a voice for poor urban women at the highest level requires that government and international organizations support the growth of their organizations and build capacity for leadership.

Accessing Reproductive Health: It Should Be Much Better

Access to health care is particularly critical for women, because of their reproductive functions, because they are disproportionately burdened with providing care for the elderly and the sick and because they do more to relieve poverty at the community level. Better access to education and employment for women contributes to their overall empowerment, their capacity to exercise their right to health, including reproductive health, and, overall, improves their life chances.

These services and opportunities tend to be more readily available to women in urban than in rural areas. But for poor women, lack of time and money, as well as the lack of freedom to make household decisions, or even to move about the city, can negate these advantages. In urban areas, inclusive health policies and programmes, accompanied by better targeting of services and resources, could rapidly improve women's health, in particular their reproductive health.

Gender relations and poverty condition how couples and families approach sexual and reproductive behaviour. Poor urban women are exposed to higher levels of reproductive health risks than other urban women. They are also less likely to obtain good-quality services. They are more likely to face gender-based violence in the home and on the streets and continue to be subject to harmful traditional practices.

Total fertility rates are lower in urban than in rural areas throughout the world. But this does not mean that all urban women have the same access to reproductive health care, or even that they can all meet their needs for contraception. Poor women within cities are significantly less likely to use contraception and have higher fertility rates than their more affluent counterparts.

At times their reproductive health situation more closely resembles that of rural women. . . .

Unmet need for contraception among women predictably varies according to relative poverty. Surveys covering Asia, Latin America, North Africa and sub-Saharan Africa show generally higher levels of unmet need among the rural population when compared to the urban population, with poor urbanites midway between the rural and the urban population as a whole. In South-East Asia, for example, estimated unmet need is 23 per cent among the urban poor, compared to only 16 per cent among the urban non-poor.

Overall, poverty may be a better indicator of fertility patterns than rural or urban residence. For policymakers concerned with the rate of urban growth, it will thus be especially important to look at the interactions between population and poverty, and increasingly within urban settings. Prioritizing women's empowerment, augmenting their access to education and employment and providing good quality sexual and reproductive health information and services to both women and men leverages their choices and is conducive to smaller, healthier families. This helps meet the needs and rights of individuals, while simultaneously improving prospects for economic growth and human well-being. . . .

Maternal and Infant Mortality

Maternal mortality remains astoundingly high, at about 529,000 a year, more than 99 per cent in developing countries, and much of it readily preventable. Four out of five deaths are the direct result of obstetric complications, most of which could be averted through delivery with a skilled birth attendant and access to emergency obstetric services.

Skilled attendance and access to emergency care explain why maternal mortality is generally lower in urban areas, where women are three times more likely to deliver with skilled health personnel than women in rural areas. However, poor urban women are less likely to deliver with a skilled birth attendant. For example, only 10-20 per cent of women deliver with skilled health personnel in the slums of Kenya, Mali, Rwanda and Uganda, compared to between 68 and 86 per cent in non-slum urban areas.

There are a number of reasons why poor urban women do not seek maternal care. These include poverty and the more pressing demands of other household expenses, other demands on their time given their many other responsibilities and the absence of supporting infrastructure such as transport and childcare.

Shelter deprivation increases mortality rates for children under five. In Ethiopia, the mortality rate in slums (180 per 1,000 live births) is almost double that in non-slum housing (95). Similar differentials prevail in Guinea, Nigeria, Rwanda and the United Republic of Tanzania. Countries such as the Philippines and Uzbekistan, with much lower levels of child mortality, also show a relationship between shelter deprivation and child survival.

Although poor children born in cities are closer to hospitals and clinics, and their parents are generally better informed, they still die at rates comparable to rural children. Overcrowded and unhealthy living conditions, without adequate water and sanitation, provide a rich breeding ground for respiratory and intestinal diseases and increase mortality among malnourished urban children. . . .

HIV/AIDS in an Urban Context: New Risks, New Opportunities

In urban settings, the risk and prevalence of HIV/AIDS increases, but the longer-term possibilities of reducing the epidemic appear to be better there. Currently, the situation is bleak. Rural-to-urban migrants leave behind not only partners and family but often customary restrictions on sexual behaviour as well. Cash dependency, coupled with poverty and gender discrimination, may increase transactional sex; at the same time, it reduces opportunities for negotiating safe sex, especially for women and girls but also for younger men and boys. Injecting drug use tends to be higher in urban settings. Sexually transmitted infections and tuberculosis, which increase the acquisition and transmission of HIV, are also more common in urban areas.

Some rural people living with HIV migrate to cities for better treatment and care, including antiretroviral drugs. As a result, HIV prevalence is generally higher in urban than rural populations in sub-Saharan Africa, the epicentre of the AIDS epidemic. Botswana and South Africa both have high urbanization levels and extremely high HIV prevalence.

Urban poverty is linked to HIV transmission and reduces the likelihood of treatment. Street children, orphans, sex workers and poor women in urban areas are particularly vulnerable to HIV infection. Poor urban women are more likely to become victims of sexual violence or human trafficking, increasing their risk; moreover, they are less likely to know how to protect themselves. Women threatened with violence cannot negotiate safe sex.

There is, however, some good news. Recent evidence of a downturn in HIV prevalence in urban areas of some countries suggests that urbanization may have the potential to reduce the epidemic. Condoms—key for HIV prevention—and information about HIV transmission may be more readily available in urban areas. Stigma and discrimination may also be lower in urban areas, because of better education and more exposure to people living with HIV/AIDS.

Social Contradictions in Growing Cities: Dialogue and Discord

The Increasing Speed of Cultural Change

Since the 1950s, rapid urbanization has been a catalyst of cultural change. As globalization proceeds, the urban transition is having an enormous impact on ideas, values and beliefs. Such transformations have not been as uniform or seamless as social scientists predicted. The widening gaps between social groups make inequality more visible. In this atmosphere, large cities can generate creativity and solidarity, but also make conflicts more acute.

Rapidly growing cities, especially the larger ones, include various generations of migrants, each with a diversity of social and cultural backgrounds. Urban life thus exposes new arrivals to an assortment of cultural stimuli and presents them with new choices on a variety of issues, ranging from how their families are organized to what they do with their leisure time. In this sense, urbanization provides opportunities for broad cultural enrichment and is a prime mover of modernization. Through interaction of new urbanites with rural areas, it also accelerates social change across different regions.

At the same time, urbanites may lose contact with traditional norms and values. They may develop new aspirations, but not always the means to realize them. This, in turn, may lead to a sense of deracination and marginalization, accompanied by crises of identity, feelings of frustration and aggressive behaviour. Many people in developing countries also associate the processes of modernization and globalization with the imposition of Western values on their own cultures and resent them accordingly.

Urbanization and Religious Revival

The revival of religious adherence in its varied forms is one of the more noticeable cultural transformations accompanying urbanization. Rapid urbanization was expected to mean the triumph of rationality, secular values and the demystification of the world, as well as the relegation of religion to a secondary role. Instead, there has been a renewal in religious interest in many countries.

The growth of new religious movements is primarily an urban phenomenon, for example, radical Islam in the Arab region, Pentecostal Christianity in Latin America and parts of Africa and the cult of Shivaji in parts of India. In China, where cities are growing at a breakneck pace, religious movements are fast gaining adherents.

Increased urbanization, coupled with slow economic development and globalization, has helped to increase religious diversity as part of the multiplication of subcultures in cities. Rather than revivals of a tradition, the new religious movements can be seen as adaptations of religion to new circumstances.

Research has tended to focus on extreme religious responses—which have indeed gained numerous followers—hence the tendency to lump them all under the rubric of "fundamentalism". Yet religious revivalism has varied forms with different impacts, ranging from detached "new age" philosophy to immersion in the political process. Along this continuum, there are many manifestations of religious adherence. Together, they are rapidly changing political dynamics and the social identities of today's global citizens. . . .

The Changing Demographics of Growing Cities
Young People in Young Cities

A clear youth bulge marks the demographic profile of cities in developing countries; this bulge is particularly large in slum populations. The individual successes and failures of young people as they ride the wave of urban growth will be decisive for future development since these drastic demographic changes, combined with persistent poverty and unemployment, are a source of conflict in cities across developing countries. Yet political processes rarely reflect the priorities of youth, especially the hundreds of millions of urban children who live in poverty and in conditions that threaten their health, safety, education and prospects.

Young people are typically dynamic, resourceful and receptive to change: But if they are uncared for, unschooled, unguided and unemployed, their energy can turn in destructive, often self-destructive, directions. Investing in urban children and youth, helping them to integrate themselves fully into society, is a matter of human rights and social justice. It is also the key to releasing potential economic benefits and ensuring urban security.

It is estimated that as many as 60 per cent of all urban dwellers will be under the age of 18 by 2030. If urgent measures are not taken in terms of basic services, employment and housing, the youth bulge will grow up in poverty. The number of children born into slums in the developing world is increasing rapidly. . . . Slums generally have a much higher proportion of children. The health problems associated with such environments have already been described. . . .

Ageing and Urbanization

The number and proportion of older persons is increasing throughout the world. Urbanization in developing countries will concentrate an increasing proportion of the older population in urban areas. In Africa and Asia, older persons still live predominantly in rural areas, but it is expected that this situation will be reversed before 2020.

Given the context of limited access to social services, high incidence of poverty and low coverage of social security in many countries, this increase in the numbers of older people will challenge the capacity of national and local governments. In principle, urban areas offer more favourable conditions: better health facilities, home-nursing services and recreational facilities, as well as greater access to information and new technologies. Urban areas also favour the rise of associations of older persons, as well as the development of community-based services to support the sick and the frail. . . .

POSTSCRIPT

Does Global Urbanization Lead Primarily to Undesirable Consequences?

It appears self-evident that rapidly growing urbanized areas, particularly in the developing world, create special circumstances. Our visual image of such places accents this fact. First-world travelers, particularly to the developing world, are likely to take away from that experience a litany of pictures that paint a bleak image of life there. The critical question, though, is whether such environments really do create major problems for those who live within such areas and policymakers who must provide goods and services. Conventional wisdom that such problems must exist is found everywhere throughout the urbanization literature. We easily could have selected any one of a dozen or more articles that asserted this situation with much conviction.

Perhaps, however, those problems observed by urban visitors might, in fact, be a consequence of some other situation unrelated to urbanization. Moreover, others allude to the advantages of urbanization for modernization. These individuals tend to bring a historical perspective to their analysis, but therein lies a potential fatal flaw. Urbanization occurred first in the current developed world, where cities grew more slowly and where governments had the capacity and the inclination to provide a better quality of life for urban dwellers.

The most definite source of information about urbanization is UN-Habitat's *State of the World's Cities 2006/07* (Earthscan, 2007). UN-Habitat had sponsored a global conference called the Third World Urban Forum (WUF3) in Vancouver in Summer 2006. Among the 2007 publication's major findings is that 95 percent of urban growth in the next two decades will occur in the developing world, which will house 4 billion people or 80 percent of the world's urban population by 2030 (others indicate a figure closer to 5 billion). This report focuses on urban problems in the context of the UN Millennium goals for development.

George Martine's *The State of World Population 2007: Unleashing the Potential of Urban Growth* (United Nations, UNFPA, 2007) analyzes why such growth is occurring and what preparations need to take place to address the dramatic increases in urban growth forecasted for the first third of the twenty-first century. Robert M. McDonald in "A World of a City" (ZNet/Activism, www.zmag.org, December 20, 2005) argues that urbanization presents a great opportunity for the world to achieve international peace through democracy and a sharing of common interests.

Another important source of information about urbanization is found in the United Nations' *2005 Revision of World Urbanization Prospects* (UN, 2006). Another important work is the National Research Council's *Cities Transformed: Demographic Change and Its Implications in the Developing World* (National Academies Press, 2003). The Population Reference Bureau has produced a comprehensive monogram called "An Urbanizing World" by Martin P. Brockerhoff (*Population Bulletin,* September 2004). An interesting approach to the subject is found in Mike Davis' "Planet of Slums" (*Harper's,* June 2004). A sophisticated analysis is found in a 2003 article in *Sociological Perspectives* by John M. Shandra, Bruce London, and John B. Williamson ("Environmental Degradation, Environmental Sustainability, and Overurbanization in the Developing World: A Quantitative, Cross-National Analysis," 2003). Klaus Toepler, Executive Director of the United Nations Environment Programme at the time, provides a thoughtful discussion of challenges facing megacities of the world. See also Mark R. Montgomery's "Urban Poverty and Health in Developing Countries" (Population Reference Bureau, Population Bulletin, vol. 64, no.2).

Two sources that present a balanced view on the effects of urbanization are *Urbanization and Growth* (Robert Buckley, Patyricia Annez, and Michael Spence, eds., World Bank Publications, 2008) and *The New Global Frontier: Urbanization, Poverty and Environment in the 21st Century* (George Martine et al., eds., Earthscan Publications, 2008).

Two articles with differing viewpoints are useful sources. Barbara Boyle Torrey, a member of the Population Reference Bureau's Board of Trustees and a writer/consultant, argues that extremely high urban growth rates are resulting in the developing world and will continue to create a range of negative environmental problems ("Urbanization: An Environmental Force to Be Reckoned With," Population Reference Bureau, April 2004). Gordon McGranahan and David Satterthwaite, members of London's International Institute for Environment and Development, suggest that there is little research about urban centers and their ability to provide sustainable development ("Urban Centers: An Assessment of Sustainability," *Annual Review of Energy and the Environment,* vol. 28, 2003). McGranahan and Satterthwaite do acknowledge that ecologically more sustainable patterns of urban development are needed. While they admit the existence of certain environmental impacts of urbanization, they are more concerned about how cities will handle these impacts in the future rather than concentrating on present deficiencies. Two books that present alternative assessments of the conditions in urban areas around the globe are the positively oriented *Urban Environmentalism Global Change and the Mediation of Local Conflict* (Peter Brand, Routledge, 2005) and the negatively slanted *Urbanization, Policing, and Security: Global Perspectives* (Gary Cordner, CRC, 2009). The negative view is also found in *Dispossessed: Life in Our World's Urban Slums* (Mark Kramer, Orbis Books, 2006).

An article that focuses on megacities is Frauke Kraas' "Megacities and Global Change: Key Priorities" (*Geographical Journal,* March 2007).

A number of books address contemporary challenges posed by urbanization throughout the world: *Global Urbanization* by Albert J. Dauray (in HTML and PDF format); *Third World Cities in Global Perspective: The Political*

Economy of Uneven Urbanization by David Smith (Westview Press, 1996); *Urban Environmentalism: Global Change and the Mediation of Local Conflict* by Peter Brand (Routledge, 2005); and *Financing Urban Shelter: Global Report on Human Settlements 2005* by the UN Human Settlements Program (Earthscan Publications, 2005); and *Scaling Urban Environmental Challenges: From Local to Global and Back* (Peter J. Marcotullio and Gordon McGranahan, eds., Earthscan Publications, 2007).

Internet References . . .

UNEP World Conservation Monitoring Centre

The United Nations Environment Programme's World Conservation Monitoring Centre Web site contains information on conservation and sustainable use of the globe's natural resources. The center provides information to policymakers concerning global trends in conservation, biodiversity, loss of species and habitats, and more. This site includes a list of publications and environmental links.

http://www.unep-wcmc.org

The International Institute for Sustainable Development

This nonprofit organization based in Canada provides a number of reporting services on a range of environmental issues, with special emphasis on policy initiatives associated with sustainable development.

http://www.iisd.ca

The Hunger Project

The Hunger Project is a nonprofit organization that is committed to the sustainable end of global hunger. This organization asserts that society-wide actions are needed to eliminate hunger and that global security depends on ensuring that everyone's basic needs are fulfilled. Included on this site is an outline of principles that guide the organization, information on why ending hunger is so important, and a list of programs sponsored by the Hunger Project in developing countries across South Asia, Latin America, and Africa.

http://www.thp.org

International Association for Environmental Hydrology

The International Association for Environmental Hydrology (IAEH) is a worldwide association of environmental hydrologists dedicated to the protection and cleanup of freshwater resources. The IAEH's mission is to provide a place to share technical information and exchange ideas and to provide a source of inexpensive tools for the environmental hydrologist, especially hydrologists and water resource engineers in developing countries.

http://www.hydroweb.com

United Nations Environment Programme (UNEP)

UNEP's general Web site provides a variety of information and links to other sources.

http://www.ourplanet.com

Global Resources
and the Environment

*T*he availability of resources and the manner in which the planet's inhabitants use them characterize another major component of the global agenda. Many believe that environmentalists overstate their case because of ideology, not science. Many others state that renewable resources are being consumed at a pace that is too fast to allow for replenishment, while nonrenewable resources are being consumed at a pace that is faster than our ability to find suitable replacements.

The production, distribution, and consumption of these resources also leave their marks on the planet. A basic set of issues relates to whether these impacts are permanent, too degrading to the planet, too damaging to one's quality of life, or simply beyond a threshold of acceptability.

- Do Environmentalists Overstate Their Case?
- Should the World Continue to Rely on Oil as the Major Source of Energy?
- Will the World Be Able to Feed Itself in the Foreseeable Future?
- Is the Threat of Global Warming Real?
- Is the Threat of a Global Water Shortage Real?

ISSUE 5

Do Environmentalists Overstate Their Case?

YES: Ronald Bailey, from "Debunking Green Myths," *Reason* (February 2002)

NO: David Pimentel, from "Skeptical of the Skeptical Environmentalist," *Skeptic* (vol. 9, no. 2, 2002)

ISSUE SUMMARY

YES: Environmental journalist Ronald Bailey in his review of the Bjørn Lomborg controversial book, *The Skeptical Environmentalist: Measuring the Real State of the World* (Cambridge University Press, 2001), argues that "An environmentalist gets it right," suggesting that finally someone has taken the environmental doomsdayers to task for their shoddy use of science.

NO: Bioscientist David Pimentel takes to task Bjørn Lomborg's findings, accusing him of selective use of data to support his conclusions.

In January 2007, the *Bulletin of Atomic Scientists* added to their "doomsday clock," originally created to forecast nuclear annihilation, the new threat of environmental catastrophe to its predictions. This was the latest in the war of words between the doomsdayers and the environmental skeptics. For a few decades, those skeptics of the claims of many environmentalists that the world was in danger of ecological collapse and in the not so distant future looked to Julian Simon for guidance. And Simon did not disappoint, as he constantly questioned these researchers' motives and methodology—their models, data, and data analysis techniques. Two seminal works, *The Ultimate Resource* and *The Ultimate Resource 2,* in particular, attempted to demonstrate that much research was really bad science. Simon's popularity reached its height when he took on the leading spokesperson of pending environmental catastrophe, Paul Ehrlich, in the late 1970s. Ehrlich, a professor at Stanford, along with his wife Anne (also a Stanford professor), had been echoing "the sky is falling message" since the late 1960s. Simon challenged Ehrlich to a "forecasting duel," betting him $10,000 that the cost of five nongovernment raw materials (to be selected by Ehrlich) would fall by the end of the next decade (1990). Ehrlich lost the bet. With Simons's death in 1998, the critics of environmental doomsdayers lost their most effective voice and their central rallying cry.

Bjørn Lomborg, a young Danish political scientist, changed all of that with the 2001 publication of his *The Skeptical Environmentalist: Measuring the Real State of the World* (a take-off on the annual State of the World Series produced by Lester Brown and the Worldwatch Institute). Lomborg's central thesis is that statistical analyses of principal environmental indicators reveal that environmental problems have been overstated by most leading figures in the environmental movement.

What distinguished Lomborg's book from the body of work that had earned Simon the unofficial title of "doomslayer" was that Lomborg received much greater and more widespread attention, both by the popular media and by those in academic and scientific circles. In effect, it has become the most popular anti-environmental book ever, prompting a huge backlash by those vested in the scientific community. Because the popular press appeared to accept Lomberg's assertions with an uncritical eye, the scientific community began a comprehensive counter-attack against *The Skeptical Environmentalist*. *Scientific American,* in January 2002, published almost a dozen pages of critiques of the book by four experts and concluded that the book's purpose of showing the real state of the world was a failure.

The attention paid Lomborg's book by *Scientific American* was typical of the responses found in every far corner of the scientific community. Not only were Lomberg's analyses attacked, but his credentials were as well. Researchers scurried to discredit both him and his work, with a passion unseen heretofore in the debate over the potential for global environmental catastrophe. The Danish Committees on Scientific Dishonesty was called upon to investigate the work. The Danish Ministry of Science, Technology and Innovation found serious flaws in Lomborg's critique. One reviewer concluded by observing that he wished he could find that the book had some scientific merit but he could not. The British Broadcasting Company (BBC) devoted a three-part series to Lomborg's claims. One critique was titled "No Friend of the Earth."

These examples illustrate the debate put forth in this issue, namely, do environmentalists overstate the case for environmental decay and potential catastrophe? Ronald Bailey, provides one of the few positive critiques of *The Skeptical Environmentalist*. His initial statement places the genesis of modern environmentalism in the radical movements of the 1960s, suggesting that their aim is to demonstrate that "the world is going to hell in a handbasket." Calling environmentalism an ideology, Bailey argues that like Marxists, environmentalists "have had to force the facts to fit their ideology." David Pimentel, a professor of insect ecology and agricultural sciences, argues that those who contend that the environment is not threatened are using data selectively while ignoring much evidence to the contrary.

YES

Ronald Bailey

Debunking Green Myths: An Environmentalist Gets It Right

Modern environmentalism, born of the radical movements of the 1960s, has often made recourse to science to press its claims that the world is going to hell in a handbasket. But this environmentalism has never really been a matter of objectively describing the world and calling for the particular social policies that the description implies.

Environmentalism is an ideology, very much like Marxism, which pretended to base its social critique on a "scientific" theory of economic relations. Like Marxists, environmentalists have had to force the facts to fit their theory. Environmentalism is an ideology in crisis: The massive, accumulating contradictions between its pretensions and the actual state of the world can no longer be easily explained away.

The publication of *The Skeptical Environmentalist,* a magnificent and important book by a former member of Greenpeace, deals a major blow to that ideology by superbly documenting a response to environmental doomsaying. The author, Bjorn Lomborg, is an associate professor of statistics at the University of Aarhus in Denmark. On a trip to the United States a few years ago, Lomborg picked up a copy of *Wired* that included an article about the late "doomslayer" Julian Simon.

Simon, a professor of business administration at the University of Maryland, claimed that by most measures, the lot of humanity is improving and the world's natural environment was not critically imperiled. Lomborg, thinking it would be an amusing and instructive exercise to debunk a "right-wing" anti-environmentalist American, assigned his students the project of finding the "real" data that would contradict Simon's outrageous claims.

Lomborg and his students discovered that Simon was essentially right, and that the most famous environmental alarmists (Stanford biologist Paul Ehrlich, Worldwatch Institute founder Lester Brown, former Vice President Al Gore, *Silent Spring* author Rachel Carson) and the leading environmentalist lobbying groups (Greenpeace, the World Wildlife Fund, Friends of the Earth) were wrong. It turns out that the natural environment is in good shape, and the prospects of humanity are actually quite good.

From *Reason* Magazine, February 2002, pp. 396–403, 406–409, 416–420. Copyright © 2002 by Reason Foundation, 3415 S. Sepulveda Blvd., Suite 400, Los Angeles, CA 90034. www.reason .com

Lomborg begins with "the Litany" of environmentalist doom, writing: "We are all familiar with the Litany. . . . Our resources are running out. The population is ever growing, leaving less and less to eat. The air and water are becoming ever more polluted. The planet's species are becoming extinct in vast numbers. . . . The world's ecosystem is breaking down. . . . We all know the Litany and have heard it so often that yet another repetition is, well, almost reassuring." Lomborg notes that there is just one problem with the Litany: "It does not seem to be backed up by the available evidence."

Lomborg then proceeds to demolish the Litany. He shows how, time and again, ideological environmentalists misuse, distort, and ignore the vast reams of data that contradict their dour visions. In the course of The Skeptical Environmentalist, Lomborg demonstrates that the environmentalist lobby is just that, a collection of interest groups that must hype doom in order to survive monetarily and politically.

Lomborg notes, "As the industry and farming organizations have an obvious interest in portraying the environment as just-fine and no-need-to-do-anything, the environmental organizations also have a clear interest in telling us that the environment is in a bad state, and that we need to act now. And the worse they can make this state appear, the easier it is for them to convince us we need to spend more money on the environment rather than on hospitals, kindergartens, etc. Of course, if we were equally skeptical of both sorts of organization there would be less of a problem. But since we tend to treat environmental organizations with much less skepticism, this might cause a grave bias in our understanding of the state of the world." Lomborg's book amply shows that our understanding of the state of the world is indeed biased.

So what is the real state of humanity and the planet?

Human life expectancy in the developing world has more than doubled in the past century, from 31 years to 65. Since 1960, the average amount of food per person in the developing countries has increased by 38 percent, and although world population has doubled, the percentage of malnourished poor people has fallen globally from 35 percent to 18 percent, and will likely fall further over the next decade, to 12 percent. In real terms, food costs a third of what it did in the 1960s. Lomborg points out that increasing food production trends show no sign of slackening in the future.

What about air pollution? Completely uncontroversial data show that concentrations of sulfur dioxide are down 80 percent in the U.S. since 1962, carbon monoxide levels are down 75 percent since 1970, nitrogen oxides are down 38 percent since 1975, and ground level ozone is down 30 percent since 1977. These trends are mirrored in all developed countries.

Lomborg shows that claims of rapid deforestation are vastly exaggerated. One United Nations Food and Agriculture survey found that globally, forest cover has been reduced by a minuscule 0.44 percent since 1961. The World Wildlife Fund claims that two-thirds of the world's forests have been lost since the dawn of agriculture; the reality is that the world still has 80 percent of its forests. What about the Brazilian rainforests? Eighty-six percent remain uncut, and the rate of clearing is falling. Lomborg also debunks the widely circulated claim that the world will soon lose up to half of its species. In fact, the best evidence indicates that 0.7 percent of species might be lost in the next 50 years if nothing is done. And of course, it is unlikely that nothing will be done.

Finally, Lomborg shows that global warming caused by burning fossil fuels is unlikely to be a catastrophe. Why? First, because actual measured temperatures aren't increasing nearly as fast as the computer climate models say they should be—in fact, any increase is likely to be at the low end of the predictions, and no one thinks that would be a disaster. Second, even in the unlikely event that temperatures were to increase substantially, it will be far less costly and more environmentally sound to adapt to the changes rather than institute draconian cuts in fossil fuel use.

The best calculations show that adapting to global warming would cost $5 trillion over the next century. By comparison, substantially cutting back on fossil fuel emissions in the manner suggested by the Kyoto Protocol would cost between $107 and $274 trillion over the same period. (Keep in mind that the current yearly U.S. gross domestic product is $10 trillion.) Such costs would mean that people living in developing countries would lose over 75 percent of their expected increases in income over the next century. That would be not only a human tragedy, but an environmental one as well, since poor people generally have little time for environmental concerns.

Where does Lomborg fall short? He clearly understands that increasing prosperity is the key to improving human and environmental health, but he often takes for granted the institutions of property and markets that make progress and prosperity possible. His analysis, as good as it is, fails to identify the chief cause of most environmental problems. In most cases, imperiled resources such as fisheries and airsheds are in open-access commons where the incentive is for people to take as much as possible of the resource before someone else beats them to it. Since they don't own the resource, they have no incentive to protect and conserve it.

Clearly, regulation has worked to improve the state of many open-access commons in developed countries such as the U.S. Our air and streams are much cleaner than they were 30 years ago, in large part due to things like installing catalytic converters on automobiles and building more municipal sewage treatment plants. Yet there is good evidence that assigning private property rights to these resources would have resulted in a faster and cheaper cleanup. Lomborg's analysis would have been even stronger had he more directly taken on ideological environmentalism's bias against markets. But perhaps that is asking for too much in an already superb book.

"Things are better now," writes Lomborg, "but they are still not good enough." He's right. Only continued economic growth will enable the 800 million people who are still malnourished to get the food they need; only continued economic growth will let the 1.2 billion who don't have access to clean water and sanitation obtain those amenities. It turns out that ideological environmentalism, with its hostility to economic growth and technological progress, is the biggest threat to the natural environment and to the hopes of the poorest people in the world for achieving better lives.

"The very message of the book," Lomborg concludes, is that "children born today—in both the industrialized world and the developing countries—will live longer and be healthier, they will get more food, a better education, a higher standard of living, more leisure time and far more possibilities—without the global environment being destroyed. And that is a beautiful world."

David Pimentel

 **NO**

Skeptical of the Skeptical Environmentalist

Bjørn Lomborg discusses a wide range of topics in his book and implies, through his title, that he will inform readers exactly what the real state of world is. In this effort, he criticizes countless world economists, agriculturists, water specialists, and environmentalists, and furthermore, accuses them of misquoting and/or organizing published data to mislead the public concerning the status of world population, food supplies, malnutrition, disease, and pollution. Lomborg bases his optimistic opinion on his selective use of data. Some of Lomborg's assertions will be examined in this review, and where differing information is presented, extensive documentation will be provided.

Lomborg reports that "we now have more food per person than we used to."[1] In contrast, the Food and Agricultural Organization (FAO) of the United Nations reports that food per capita has been declining since 1984, based on available cereal grains.[2] Cereal grains make up about 80% of the world's food. Although grain yields per hectare (abbreviated ha) in both developed and developing countries are still increasing, these increases are slowing while the world population continues to escalate.[3] Specifically from 1950 to 1980, U.S. grains yields increased at about 3% per year, but after 1980 the rate of increase for corn and other grains has declined to only about 1%.

Obviously fertile cropland is an essential resource for the production of foods but Lomborg has chosen not to address this subject directly. Currently, the U.S. has available nearly 0.5 ha of prime cropland per capita, but it will not have this much land if the population continues to grow at its current rapid rate.[4] Worldwide the average cropland available for food production is only 0.25 ha per person.[5] Each person added to the U.S. population requires nearly 0.4 ha (1 acre) of land for urbanization and transportation.[6] One example of the impact of population growth and development is occurring in California where an average of 156,000 ha of agricultural land is being lost each year.[7] At this rate it will not be long before California ceases to be the number one state in U.S. agricultural production.

In addition to the quantity of agricultural land, soil quality and fertility is vital for food production. The productivity of the soil is reduced when it is eroded by rainfall and wind.[8] Soil erosion is not a problem, according to Lomborg, especially in the U.S. where soil erosion has declined during the past

From *Skeptic* by David Pimentel, vol. 9 no. 2, 2002, pp. 90–93. Copyright © 2002 by David Pimentel. Reprinted by permission of the author.

decade. Yes, as Lomborg states, instead of losing an average of 17 metric tons per hectare per year on cropland, the U.S. cropland is now losing an average of 13 t/ha/yr.[9] However, this average loss is 13 times the sustainability rate of soil replacement.[10] Exceptions occur, as during the 1995–96 winter in Kansas, when it was relatively dry and windy, and some agricultural lands lost as much as 65 t/ha of productive soil. This loss is 65 times the natural soil replacement in agriculture.[11]

Worldwide soil erosion is more damaging than in the United States. For instance, in India soil is being lost at 30 to 40 times its sustainability.[12] Rate of soil loss in Africa is increasing not only because of livestock overgrazing but also because of the burning of crop residues due to the shortages of wood fuel.[13] During the summer of 2000, NASA published a satellite image of a cloud of soil from Africa being blown across the Atlantic Ocean, further attesting to the massive soil erosion problem in Africa. Worldwide evidence concerning soil loss is substantiated and it is difficult to ignore its effect on sustainable agricultural production.

Contrary to Lomborg's belief, crop yields cannot continue to increase in response to the increased applications of more fertilizers and pesticides. In fact, field tests have demonstrated that applying excessive amounts of nitrogen fertilizer stresses the crop plants, resulting in declining yields.[14] The optimum amount of nitrogen for corn, one of the crops that require heavy use of nitrogen, is approximately 120 kg/ha.[15]

Although U.S. farmers frequently apply significantly more nitrogen fertilizer than 120 kg/ha, the extra is a waste and pollutant. The corn crop can only utilize about one-third of the nitrogen applied, while the remainder leaches either into the ground or surface waters.[16] This pollution of aquatic ecosystems in agricultural areas results in the high levels of nitrogen and pesticides occurring in many U.S. water bodies.[17] For example, nitrogen fertilizer has found its way into 97% of the well-water supplies in some regions, like North Carolina.[18] The concentrations of nitrate are above the U.S. Environmental Protection Agency drinking-water standard of 10 milligrams per liter (nitrogen) and are a toxic threat to young children and young livestock.[19] In the last 30 years, the nitrate content has tripled in the Gulf of Mexico,[20] where it is reducing the Gulf fishery.[21]

In an undocumented statement Lomborg reports that pesticides cause very little cancer.[22] Further, he provides no explanation as to why human and other nontarget species are not exposed to pesticides when crops are treated. There is abundant medical and scientific evidence that confirms that pesticides cause significant numbers of cancers in the U.S. and throughout the world.[23] Lomborg also neglects to report that some herbicides stimulate the production of toxic chemicals in some plants, and that these toxicants can cause cancer.[24]

In keeping with Lomborg's view that agriculture and the food supply are improving, he states that "fewer people are starving."[25] Lomborg criticizes the validity of the two World Health Organization reports that confirm more than 3 billion people are malnourished.[26] This is the largest number and proportion of malnourished people ever in history! Apparently Lomborg rejects the WHO data because they do not support his basic thesis. Instead, Lomborg argues that only people who suffer from calorie shortages are malnourished, and ignores the fact that humans die from deficiencies of protein, iron, iodine, and vitamin A, B, C, and D.[27]

Further confirming a decline in food supply, the FAO reports that there has been a three-fold decline in the consumption of fish in the human diet during the past seven years.[28] This decline in fish per capita is caused by overfishing, pollution, and the impact of a rapidly growing world population that must share the diminishing fish supply.

In discussing the status of water supply and sanitation services, Lomborg is correct in stating that these services were improved in the developed world during the 19th century, but he ignores the available scientific data when he suggests that these trends have been "replicated in the developing world" during the 20th century. Countless reports confirm that developing countries discharge most of their untreated urban sewage directly into surface waters.[29] For example, of India's 3,119 towns and cities, only eight have full waste water treatment facilities.[30] Further-more, 114 Indian cities dump untreated sewage and partially cremated bodies directly into the sacred Ganges River. Downstream the untreated water is used for drinking, bathing, and washing.[31] In view of the poor sanitation, it is no wonder that water borne infectious diseases account for 80% of all infections worldwide and 90% of all infections in developing countries.[32]

Contrary to Lomborg's view, most infectious diseases are increasing worldwide.[33] The increase is due not only to population growth but also because of increasing environmental pollution.[34] Food-borne infections are increasing rapidly worldwide and in the United States. For example, during 2000 in the U.S. there were 76 million human food-borne infections with 5,000 associated deaths.[35] Many of these infections are associated with the increasing contamination of food and water by livestock wastes in the United States.[36]

In addition, a large number of malnourished people are highly susceptible to infectious diseases, like tuberculosis (TB), malaria, schistosomiasis, and AIDS.[37] For example, the number of people infected with tuberculosis in the U.S. and the world is escalating, in part because medicine has not kept up with the new forms of TB. Currently, according to the World Health Organization,[38] more than 2 billion people in the world are infected with TB,[39] with nearly 2 million people dying each year from it.[40]

Consistent with Lomborg's thesis that world natural resources are abundant, he reports that the U.S. Energy Information Agency for the period 2000 to 2020 projects an almost steady oil price over the next two decades at about $22 per barrel. This optimistic projection was crossed late in 2000 when oil rose to $30 or more per barrel in the United States and the world.[41] The best estimates today project that world oil reserves will last approximately 50 years, based on current production rates.[42]

Lomborg takes the World Wildlife Fund (WWF) to task for their estimates on the loss of world forests during the past decade and their emphasis on resulting ecological impacts and loss of biodiversity. Whether the loss of forests is slow, as Lomborg suggests, or rapid as WWF reports, there is no question that forests are disappearing worldwide. Forests not only provide valuable products but they harbor a vast diversity of species of plants, animals and microbes. Progress in medicine, agriculture, genetic engineering, and environmental quality depend on maintaining the species diversity in the world.[43]

This reviewer takes issue with Lomborg's underlying thesis that the size and growth of the human population is not a major problem. The difference between Lomborg's figure that 76 million humans were added to the world population in 2000, or the 80 million reported by the Population Reference Bureau,[44] is not the issue, though the magnitude of both projections is of serious concern. Lomborg neglects to explain that the major problem with world population growth is the young age structure that now exists. Even if the world adopted a policy of only two children per couple tomorrow, the world population would continue to increase for more than 70 years before stabilizing at more than 12 billion people.[45] As an agricultural scientist and ecologist, I wish I could share Lomborg's optimistic views, but my investigations and those of countless scientists lead me to a more conservative outlook. The supply of basic resources, like fertile cropland, water, energy, and an unpolluted atmosphere that support human life is declining rapidly, as nearly a quarter million people are daily added to the Earth. We all desire a high standard of living for each person on Earth, but with every person added, the supply of resources must be divided and shared. Current losses and degradation of natural resources suggest concern and a need for planning for future generations of humans. Based on our current understanding of the real state of the world and environment, there is need for conservation and protection of vital world resources.

References

1. Lomborg, B. 2001. *The Skeptical Environmentalist.* Cambridge University Press, 61.

2. FAO, 1961–1999. *Quarterly Bulletin of Statistics.* Food and Agriculture Organization of the United Nations.

3. Ibid.; PRB 2000. *World Population Data Sheet.* Washington, DC: Population Reference Bureau.

4. USBC, 2000. *Statistical Abstract of the United States 2000.* Washington, DC: U.S. Bureau of the Census, U.S. Government Printing Office.

5. PRB, 2000; WRI 1994. *World Resources 1994–95.* Washington, DC: World Resources Institute.

6. Helmlich, R. 2001. Economic Research Service, USDA, Washington, DC, personal communication.

7. UCBC, 2000, op. cit.

8. Lal, R., and Stewart, B. A. 1990. *Soil Degradation.* New York: Springer-Verlag: Troeh, F. R., Hobbs, J. A., & Donahue, R. L. 1991. *Soil and Water Conservation* (2nd ed.). Englewood Cliffs, NJ: Prentice Hall.

9. USDA, 1994. *Summary Report 1992 National Resources Inventory.* Washington, DC: Soil Conservation Service, U.S. Department of Agriculture.

10. Pimentel, D., and Kounang, N. 1998. "Ecology of Soil Erosion in Ecosystems," *Ecosystems,* 1, 416–426.

11. Lal and Stewart, 1990; Troeh et al., 1991, op. cit.

12. Khoshoo, T. N. & Tejwani, K. G. 1993. "Soil Erosion and Conservation in India (status and policies)." In Pimentel, D. (Ed.) *World Soil Erosion and Conservation.* pp. 109–146. Cambridge: Cambridge University Press.

13. Tolba, M. K. 1989. "Our Biological Heritage Under Siege." *BioScience,* 39: 725–728.

14. Romanova, A. K., Kuznetsova, L. G., Golovina, E. V., Novichkova, N. S., Karpilova, I. F., & Ivanov, B. N. 1987. *Proceedings of the Indian National Science Academy, B (Biological Sciences),* 53(5–6): 505–512.

15. Troeh, F. R., & Thompson, L. M. 1993. *Soils and Soil Fertility* (5th ed.). New York: Oxford University Press.

16. Robertson, G. P. 2000. "Dinitrification." In *Handbook of Soil Science.* M. E. Summer (Ed.), pp. C181–190. Boca Raton, FL: CRC Press.

17. Ibid.; Mapp, H. P. 1999. "Impact of Production Changes on Income and Environmental Risk in the Southern High Plains." *Journal of Agricultural and Applied Economics,* 31(2): 263–273; Gentry, L. E., David, M. B., Smith-Starks, K. M., and Kovacics, D. A. 2000. "Nitrogen Fertilizer and Herbicide Transport from Tile Drained Fields." *Journal of Environmental Quality,* 29(1): 232–240.

18. Smith, V. H., Tilman, G. D. and Nekola, J. C. 1999. "Eutrophication: Impacts of Excess Nutrient Inputs on Freshwater, Marine, and Terrestrial Ecosystems." *Environment and Pollution,* 100(1/3): 179–196.

19. Ibid.

20. Goolsby, D. A., Battaglin, W. A., Aulenbach, B. T. and Hooper, R. P. 2000. "Nitrogen Flux and Sources in the Mississippi River Basin." *Science and the Total Environment,* 248(2–3): 75–86.

21. NAS, 2000. *Clean Coastal Waters: Understanding and Reducing the Effects of Nutrient Pollution.* Washington, DC: National Academy of Sciences Press.

22. Lomborg, 2001, op. cit., 10.

23. WHO, 1992. *Our Planet, Our Health: Report of the WHO Commission on Health and Environment.* Geneva: World Health Organization: Ferguson, L. R. 1999. "Natural and Man-Made Mutagens and Carcinogens in the Human Diet." *Mutation Research, Genetic Toxicology and Environmental Mutagenesis,* 443(1/2): 1–10; NAS, 2000. *The Future Role of Pesticides in Agriculture.* Washington, DC: National Academy of Sciences Press.

24. Culliney, T. W., Pimentel, D., & Pimentel, M. H. 1992. "Pesticides and Natural Toxicants in Foods." *Agriculture, Eco-systems and Environment,* 41, 297–320.

25. Lomborg, 2001, op. cit., 328.

26. WHO, 1996. *Micronutrient Malnutrition—Half of the World's Population Affected* (Pages 1–4 No. Press Release WHO No. 78). World Health Organization; WHO, 2000a. *Malnutrition Worldwide. . . .*

27. Sommer, A. and K. P. West, 1996. *Vitamin A Deficiency: Health, Survival and Vision.* New York: Oxford University Press; Tomashek, K. M., Woodruff,

B. A., Gotway, C. A., Bloand, P. & Mbaruku, G. 2001. "Randomized Intervention Study Comparing Several Regimens for the Treatment of Moderate Anemia Refugee Children in Kigoma Region, Tanzania." *American Journal of Tropical Medicine and Hygiene,* 64(3/4): 164–171.

28. FAO, 1991. *Food Balance Sheets.* Rome: Food and Agriculture Organization of the United Nations; FAO, 1998. *Food Balance Sheets. . . .*

29. WHO, 1993. "Global Health Situation." *Weekly Epidemiological Record,* World Health Organization 68 (12 February): 43–44; Wouters, A. V. 1993. "Health Care Utilization Patterns in Developing Countries: Role of the Technology Environment in 'Deriving' the Demand for Health Care." *Boletin de la Oficina Sanitaria Panamericana,* 115(2): 128–139; Biswas, M. R. 1999. "Nutrition, Food, and Water Security." *Food and Nutrition Bulletin,* 20(4): 454–457.

30. WHO, 1992, op. cit.

31. NGS, 1995, *Water: A Story of Hope.* Washington, DC: National Geographic Society.

32. WHO, 1992, op. cit.

33. Ibid.

34. Pimentel, D., Tort, M., D'Anna, L., Krawic, A., Berger, J., Rossman, J., Mugo, F., Doon, N., Shriberg, M., Howard, E. S., Lee, S., & Talbot, J. 1998. "Ecology of Increasing Disease: Population Growth and Environmental Degradation." *BioScience,* 48, 817–826.

35. Taylor, M. R. & Hoffman, S. A. 2001. "Redesigning Food Safety: Using Risk Analysis to Build a Better Food Safety System." *Resources.* Summer, 144: 13–16.

36. DeWaal, C. S., Alderton, L., and Jacobson, M. J. 2000. *Outbreak Alert! Closing the Gaps in Our Federal Food-Safety Net.* Washington, DC: Center for Science in the Public Interest.

37. Chandra, R. K. 1979. "Nutritional Deficiency and Susceptibility to Infection." *Bulletin of the World Health Organization,* 57(2): 167–177; Stephenson, L. S., Latham, M. C. & Ottesen, E. A. 2000a. "Global Malnutrition." *Parasitology.* 121: S5–S22; Stephenson, L. S., Latham, M. C. & Ottesen, E. A. 2000b. "Malnutrition and Parasitic Helminth Infections." *Parastiology.* S23–S38.

38. WHO, 2001. "World Health Organization. Global Tuberculosis Control." *WHO Report 2001.* Geneva, Switzerland, WHO/CDS/TB/2001. 287 (May 30, 2001).

39. WHO, 2000b. "World Health Organization. Tuberculosis." *WHO Fact Sheet 2000 No104.* Geneva, Switzerland. . . .

40. WHO, 2001, op. cit

41. BP, 2000. *British Petroleum Statistical Review of World Energy.* London: British Petroleum Corporate Communications Services; Duncan, R. C. 2001. "World Energy Production, Population Growth, and the Road to the Olduvai Gorge." *Population and Environment,* 22(5), 503–522.

42. Youngquist, W. 1997. *Geodestinies: The Inevitable Control of Earth Resources Over Nations and Individuals.* Portland, OR: National Book Company; Duncan, 2001, op. cit.

43. Myers, N. 1996. "The World's Forests and Their Ecosystem Services." In G. C. Dailey (Ed.), *Ecosystem Services: Their Nature and Value* (pp. 1–19 in press). Washington, DC: Island Press.

44. PRB, 2000, op. cit.

45. Population Action International, 1993. *Challenging the Planet: Connections Between Population and the Environment.* Washington, DC: Population Action International.

POSTSCRIPT

Do Environmentalists Overstate Their Case?

The issue of whether science or ideology is at the heart of the environmental debate is a vexing one. The issue is framed by the juxtaposition of three groups. The first are those individuals, commonly called political or environmental activists, who emerged in the late 1960s and early 1970s following the success of the early civil rights movement. Taking its inspiration from the 1962 publication of Rachel Carson's *The Silent Spring,* which exposed the dangers of the pesticide DDT, many politically active individuals found a new cause. When the book received legitimacy because of President John Kennedy's order that his Science Advisory Committee address the issues raised therein, the environmental movement was under way. The second group, government policy makers were then a part of the mix and the third group, scientists, were soon to come on board. The first global environmental conference sponsored by the United Nations was held in Stockholm in 1972 to address atmospheric pollution on Scandinavian lakes. Emerging from the conference was a commitment of the international policymaking community to put environmental issues on the new global agenda. Environmentalism was now globalized.

Since the early 1970s, through a variety of forums and arenas, the issue has been on the forefront of this global agenda. As with any issue where debates focus not only on how to address problems but whether, in fact, the problems really exist in the first place, many disparate formal and informal interest groups have become involved in all aspects of the debate—from trying to make the case that a problem exists and will ultimately have dire consequences if left unsolved, to specific prescriptions for solving the issue. The intersection of science, public policy, and political activism then becomes like the center ring at a boxing match, where contenders vie for success. Objectivity clashes with passion as well-intentioned and not so well-intentioned individuals attempt to influence the debate and the ultimate outcome. In many cases, the doomsdayers gain the upper hand as their commitment to change seems greater than those who urge caution until all the scientific evidence is in.

The reaction to Lomborg illustrates this point perfectly. He has become the arch villain to environmentalists. One such Web site proclaims in headline, "Something is Rotten in Denmark" and then proceeds to "fight fire with fire" in attacking him (www.gristmagazine.com). *Grist Magazine* devoted a special issue (December 12, 2001) to the debate where experts in specific environmental fields took issue with Lomborg's conclusions.

There are a variety of links to the debate fueled by *The Skeptical Scientist.* The journal *Scientific American* launched an extreme attack against Lomborg, while *The Economist* came to his defense. Google.com shows 247,000 references to the young Danish political scientist at last count. Amazon.com provides an array of related books.

In sum, one is struck by both the forcefulness with which Lomborg makes his case and the even greater passion with which the scientific community responds. Although the latter may be more accurate with respect to the true state of the world, Lomborg provides a valuable service by reminding us that at the heart of any meaningful prescription for effective public policy is an accurate assessment of the nature of the problem. Science, not ideology, provides the instruments for such an assessment.

One principal source consistently sounding the alarm on environment issues is the Worldwatch Institute. Its Web site, www.worldwatch.org, yields an extraordinary amount of resources on environmental issues.

In the first few decades after environment was placed on the global agenda, Julian Simon was one of the few, and certainly the most read, critics of environmentalists for their ideological approach to environmental problems, causing them, in Simon's view, to ignore science when science yielded an answer different from the one sought by the environmentalists. His *The Ultimate Resource* and *The Ultimate Resource 2* represented two harshly critical books that sought to show how science had taken a back seat to ideology. Since his death in 1998, his role as principal vocal critic of extremists in the environmental movement has been assumed by Ronald Bailey, science correspondent for the monthly magazine *Reason*. His *Global Warming and Other Eco-Myths* (Forum, 2002) charges the environmentalists with using "False Science to Scare Us to Death" (part of the book's subtitle). The titles of earlier books also suggest his basic message: *Earth Report 2000: Revisiting the True State of the Planet* (McGraw-Hill, 1999); *ECOSCAM: The False Prophets of Ecological Apocalypse* (St. Martin's Press, 1993); and *The True State of the Planet* (The Free Press, 1995).

Another early critic of the environmental "eco-extremists" is John Berlau, author of *Eco-Freaks: Environmentalism Is Hazardous to Your Health!* (Thomas Nelson, 2006). An especially intriguing book is *The Really Inconvenient Truths: Seven Environmental Catastrophes Liberals Don't Want You to Know About—Because They Helped Cause Them* (Iain Murray, Regnery Publishing, 2008).

A number of additional sources attack the majority view that global warming is real: *An Appeal to Reason: A Cool Look at Global Warming* (Nigel Lawson, Gerald Duckworth & Co., 2009); *The Politically Incorrect Guide to Global Warming (and Environmentalism)* (Christopher C. Horner, Regnery Publishing, 2007); *Cool It: The Skeptical Environmentalist's Guide to Global Warming* (Bjorn Lomborg, Vintage, 2008); *Climate Confusion: How Global Warming Hysteria Leads to Bad Science, Pandering Politicians and Misguided Policies that Hurt the Poor* (Roy Spencer, Encounter Books, 2008); and *Red Hot Lies: How Global Warming Alarmists Use Threats, Fraud, and Deception to Keep You Misinformed* (Christopher C. Horner, Regnery Publishing, 2008).

Perhaps the most helpful Web site for gathering information about the debate as it relates to Lomborg is www.anti-lomborg.com. The Web site's name is misleading as it provides a list of pro-Lomborg sources in addition to those that attack him.

ISSUE 6

Should the World Continue to Rely on Oil as the Major Source of Energy?

YES: Nansen G. Saleri, from "The World Has Plenty of Oil," *Wall Street Journal* (March 4, 2008)

NO: Lester R. Brown, from "Is World Oil Peaking?" Earth Policy Institute (November 15, 2007)

ISSUE SUMMARY

YES: Nansen G. Saleri, president and CEO of Quantum Reservoir Input and the oil industry's preeminent authority on the issue, suggests that the world is "nowhere close to reaching a peak in global oil supplies." He argues that the future transition to oil alternatives will be the result of their superiority rather than the diminishing supply of oil.

NO: Lester R. Brown, founder and president of Earth Policy Institute, suggests that there has been a "pronounced loss of momentum" in the growth of oil production, a likely result of demand outpacing discoveries, leading to declining oil production prospects.

$\mathbf{A}$s 2008 arrived, gas prices passed the $3-a-gallon level, with no end in sight. Although the price of oil dropped to around $2.50 per gallon by the summer of 2009, a new era had arrived. This was not the first crisis in recent times, however, as the beginning of the new millennium had witnessed an oil crisis almost immediately, the third major crisis in the last 30 years (1972–1973 and 1979 were the dates of earlier problems). The crisis of 2000 manifested itself in the United States via much higher gasoline prices and in Europe via both rising prices and shortages at the pump. Both were caused by the inability of national distribution systems to adjust to the Organization of Petroleum Exporting Countries' (OPEC's) changing production levels. The 2000 panic eventually subsided but reappeared in 2005 in the wake of the uncertainty surrounding the Iraq war and the war of terrorism. Four major crises in 34 years thus characterize the oil issue.

These four major fuel crises are discrete episodes in a much larger problem facing the human race, particularly the industrial world. That is, oil, the earth's current principal source of energy, is a finite resource that ultimately will be totally exhausted. And unlike earlier energy transitions, where a more attractive source invited a change (such as from wood to coal and from coal to oil), the next energy transition is being forced upon the human race in the absence of an attractive alternative. In short, we are being pushed out of our almost total reliance on oil toward a new system with a host of unknowns. What will the new fuel be? Will it be from a single source or some combination? Will it be a more attractive source? Will the source be readily available at a reasonable price, or will a new cartel emerge that controls much of the supply? Will its production and consumption lead to major new environmental consequences? Will it require major changes to our lifestyles and standards of living? When will we be forced to jump into using this new source?

Before considering new sources of fuel, other questions need to be asked. Are the calls for a viable alternative to oil premature? Are we simply running scared without cause? Did we learn the wrong lessons from the earlier energy crises? More specifically, were these crises artificially created or a consequence of the actual physical unavailability of the energy source? Have these crises really been about running out of oil globally, or were they due to other phenomena at work, such as poor distribution planning by oil companies or the use of oil as a political weapon by oil-exporting countries?

For well over half a century now, Western oil-consuming countries have been predicting the end of oil. Using a model known as Hubbert's Curve (named after a U.S. geologist who designed it in the 1930s), policy-makers have predicted that the world would run out of oil at various times; the most recent prediction is that oil will run out a couple of decades from now. Simply put, the model visualizes all known available resources and the patterns of consumption on a time line until the wells run dry. Despite such prognostication, it was not until the crisis of the early 1970s that national governments began to consider ways of both prolonging the oil system and finding a suitable replacement. Prior to that time, governments, as well as the private sector, encouraged energy consumption. "The more, the merrier" was an oft-heard refrain. Increases in energy consumption were associated with economic growth. After Europe recovered from the devastation of World War II, for example, every 1 percent increase in energy consumption brought a similar growth in economic output. To the extent that governments engaged in energy policymaking, it was designed solely to encourage increased production and consumption. Prices were kept low, and the energy was readily available. Policies making energy distribution systems more efficient and consumption patterns both more efficient and lowered were almost nonexistent.

But today the search for an alternative to oil still continues. Nuclear energy, once thought to be the answer, may play a future role, but at a reduced level. Both water power and wind power remain possibilities, as do biomass, geothermal, and solar energy. Many also believe that the developed world is about to enter the hydrogen age in order to meet future energy needs. The question before us, therefore, is whether the international community has the luxury of some time before all deposits of oil are exhausted. The two selections for this issue suggest different answers to this last question. Nansen G. Saleri, the oil industry's preeminent authority on the issue, suggests that the world is not even close to reaching a peak in supplies. Lester R. Brown, no less an authority on the public interest side of the issue, argues that the world is already experiencing a loss of momentum in oil production growth, with future prospects declining.

YES

Nansen G. Saleri

The World Has Plenty of Oil

Many energy analysts view the ongoing waltz of crude prices with the mystical $100 mark—notwithstanding the dollar's anemia—as another sign of the beginning of the end for the oil era. "[A]t the furthest out, it will be a crisis in 2008 to 2012," declares Matthew Simmons, the most vocal voice among the "neo-peak-oil" club. Tempering this pessimism only slightly is the viewpoint gaining ground among many industry leaders, who argue that daily production by 2030 of 100 million barrels will be difficult.

In fact, we are nowhere close to reaching a peak in global oil supplies.

Given a set of assumptions, forecasting the peak-oil-point—defined as the onset of global production decline—is a relatively trivial problem. Four primary factors will pinpoint its exact timing. The trivial becomes far more complex because the four factors—resources in place (how many barrels initially underground), recovery efficiency (what percentage is ultimately recoverable), rate of consumption, and state of depletion at peak (how empty is the global tank when decline kicks in)—are inherently uncertain.

What Are the Global Resources in Place?

Estimates vary. But approximately six to eight trillion barrels each for conventional and unconventional oil resources (shale oil, tar sands, extra heavy oil) represent probable figures—inclusive of future discoveries. As a matter of context, the globe has consumed only one out of a grand total of 12 to 16 trillion barrels underground.

What Percentage of Global Resources Is Ultimately Recoverable?

The industry recovers an average of only one out of three barrels of conventional resources underground and considerably less for the unconventional.

This benchmark, established over the past century, is poised to change upward. Modern science and unfolding technologies will, in all likelihood, double recovery efficiencies. Even a 10% gain in extraction efficiency on a global scale will unlock 1.2 to 1.6 trillion barrels of extra resources—an additional 50-year supply at current consumption rates.

From *Wall Street Journal Sunday,* March 4, 2008. Copyright © 2008 by Nansen G. Saleri. Reprinted by permission of the author.

The impact of modern oil extraction techniques is already evident across the globe. Abqaiq and Ghawar, two of the flagship oil fields of Saudi Arabia, are well on their way to recover at least two out of three barrels underground—in the process raising recovery expectations for the remainder of the Kingdom's oil assets, which account for one-quarter of world reserves.

Are the lessons and successes of Ghawar transferable to the countless struggling fields around the world—most conspicuously in Venezuela, Mexico, Iran or the former Soviet Union—where irreversible declines in production are mistakenly accepted as the norm and in fact fuel the "neo-peak-oil" alarmism? The answer is a definitive yes.

Hundred-dollar oil will provide a clear incentive for reinvigorating fields and unlocking extra barrels through the use of new technologies. The consequences for emerging oil-rich regions such as Iraq can be far more rewarding. By 2040 the country's production and reserves might potentially rival those of Saudi Arabia.

Paradoxically, high crude prices may temporarily mask the inefficiencies of others, which may still remain profitable despite continuing to use 1960-vintage production methods. But modernism will inevitably prevail: The national oil companies that hold over 90% of the earth's conventional oil endowment will be pressed to adopt new and better technologies.

What Will Be the Average Rate of Crude Consumption Between Now and Peak Oil?

Current daily global consumption stands around 86 million barrels, with projected annual increases ranging from 0% to 2% depending on various economic outlooks. Thus average consumption levels ranging from 90 to 110 million barrels represent a reasonable bracket. Any economic slowdown—as intimated by the recent tremors in the global equity markets—will favor the lower end of this spectrum.

This is not to suggest that global supply capacity will grow steadily unimpeded by bottlenecks—manpower, access, resource nationalism, legacy issues, logistical constraints, etc.—within the energy equation. However, near-term obstacles do not determine the global supply ceiling at 2030 or 2050. Market forces, given the benefit of time and the burgeoning mobility of technology and innovation across borders, will tame transitional obstacles.

When Will Peak Oil Arrive?

This widely accepted tipping point—50% of ultimately recoverable resources consumed—is largely a tribute to King Hubbert, a distinguished Shell geologist who predicted the peak oil point for the U.S. lower 48 states. While his timing was very good (he forecast 1968 versus 1970 in fact), he underestimated peak daily production (9.5 million barrels actual versus 8 million estimated).

But modern extraction methods will undoubtedly stretch Hubbert's "50% assumption," which was based on Sputnik-era technologies. Even a modest shift—to 55% of recoverable resources consumed—will delay the onset by 20–25 years.

Where do reasonable assumptions surrounding peak oil lead us? My view, subjective and imprecise, points to a period between 2045 and 2067 as the most likely outcome.

Cambridge Energy Associates forecasts the global daily liquids production to rise to 115 million barrels by 2017 versus 86 million at present. Instead of a sharp peak per Hubbert's model, an undulating, multi-decade long plateau production era sets in—i.e., no sudden-death ending.

The world is not running out of oil anytime soon. A gradual transitioning on the global scale away from a fossil-based energy system may in fact happen during the 21st century. The root causes, however, will most likely have less to do with lack of supplies and far more with superior alternatives. The overused observation that "the Stone Age did not end due to a lack of stones" may in fact find its match.

The solutions to global energy needs require an intelligent integration of environmental, geopolitical and technical perspectives each with its own subsets of complexity. On one of these—the oil supply component—the news is positive. Sufficient liquid crude supplies do exist to sustain production rates at or near 100 million barrels per day almost to the end of this century.

Technology matters. The benefits of scientific advancement observable in the production of better mobile phones, TVs and life-extending pharmaceuticals will not, somehow, bypass the extraction of usable oil resources. To argue otherwise distracts from a focused debate on what the correct energy-policy priorities should be, both for the United States and the world community at large.

Lester R. Brown  **NO**

Is World Oil Production Peaking?

Is world oil production peaking? Quite possibly. Data from the International Energy Agency (IEA) show a pronounced loss of momentum in the growth of oil production during the last few years. After climbing from 82.90 million barrels per day (mb/d) in 2004 to 84.15 mb/d in 2005, output only increased to 84.80 mb/d in 2006 and then declined to 84.62 mb/d during the first 10 months of 2007.

The combination of world production slowing down or starting to decline while demand continues to rise rapidly is putting strong upward pressure on prices. Over the past two years, oil prices have climbed from $50 to nearly $100 a barrel. If production growth continues to lag behind the increase in demand, how high will prices go?

There are many ways of assessing the oil production prospect. One is to look at the relationship between oil discoveries and production, a technique pioneered by the legendary U.S. geologist M. King Hubbert. Given the nature of oil production, Hubbert theorized that the time lag between the peaking of new discoveries and that of production was predictable. Noting that the discovery of new reserves in the United States peaked around 1930, he predicted in 1956 that U.S. oil output would peak in 1970. He hit it right on the head.

Globally, oil discoveries peaked in the 1960s. Each year since 1984, world oil production has exceeded new oil discoveries, and by a widening gap. In 2006, the 31 billion barrels of oil extracted far exceeded the discovery of 9 billion barrels.

The aging of oil fields also tells us something about the oil prospect. The world's 20 largest oil fields were all discovered between 1917 and 1979. . . . Sadad al-Husseini, former senior Saudi oil official, reports that the annual output from the world's aging fields is falling by 4 mb/d. Offsetting this decline with new discoveries or with more-advanced extraction technologies is becoming increasingly difficult.

Yet another way of assessing the oil prospect is to look separately at the leading oil-producing countries where production is falling, the ones where production is still rising, and those that appear to be on the verge of a downturn. Among the leading oil producers, output appears to have peaked and turned downward in a dozen or so and to still be rising in nine.

From *Eco-Economy Update*, No. 5, November 15, 2007. Copyright © 2007 by Earth Policy Institute. Reprinted by permission.

Among the post-peak countries are the United States, which peaked at 9.6 mb/d in 1970, dropping to 5.1 mb/d in 2006; Venezuela, where output also peaked in 1970; and the two North Sea oil producers, the United Kingdom and Norway, which peaked in 1999 and 2000.

The pre-peak countries are dominated by Russia, now the world's leading oil producer, having eclipsed Saudi Arabia in 2006. Two other countries with substantial potential for increasing output are Canada, largely because of its tar sands, and Kazakhstan, which is developing the Kashagan oil field in the Caspian Sea, the only large find in recent decades. Other pre-peak countries include Algeria, Angola, Brazil, Nigeria, Qatar, and the United Arab Emirates.

Among the countries where production may be peaking are Saudi Arabia, Mexico, and China. The big question is Saudi Arabia. Saudi officials claim they can produce far more oil, but the giant Ghawar oil field—the world's largest by far and the one that has supplied half of Saudi oil output for decades—is 56 years old and in its declining years. Saudi oil production data for the first eight months of 2007 show output of 8.62 mb/d, a drop of 6 percent from the 9.15 mb/d of 2006. If Saudi Arabia cannot restore growth in its oil production, then peak oil is on our doorstep.

In Mexico, the second-ranking supplier to the United States after Canada, output apparently peaked in 2004 at 3.4 mb/d. U.S. geologist Walter Youngquist notes that Cantarell, the country's dominant oil field, is now in steep decline, and that Mexico could be an oil importer by 2015. Production in China, slightly higher than in Mexico, may also be about to peak.

A number of prominent geologists are convinced that global oil production has peaked or is about to do so. "The whole world has now been seismically searched and picked over," says independent geologist Colin Campbell. "Geological knowledge has improved enormously in the past 30 years and it is almost inconceivable now that major fields remain to be found."

Kenneth Deffeyes, a highly respected geologist, said in his 2005 book, *Beyond Oil,* "It is my opinion that the peak will occur in late 2005 or in the first few months of 2006." Youngquist and A. M. Samsam Bakhtiari of the Iranian National Oil Company each projected that production would peak in 2007.

The Energy Watch Group in Germany, which recently analyzed oil production data country by country, also concluded that world oil production has peaked. They project it will decline by 7 percent a year, falling to 58 mb/d in 2020. Bakhtiari projects a decline in oil production to 55 mb/d in 2020, slightly lower than the German group. In stark contrast, the IEA and the U.S. Department of Energy are each projecting world oil output in 2020 at 104 mb/d.

The peaking of world oil production will be a seismic event, marking one of the great fault lines in world economic history. When oil output is no longer expanding, no country can get more oil unless another gets less.

Oil-intensive industries will be hit hard. Cheap airfares will become history, for instance. The airline industry's projected growth of 5 percent a year over the next decade will evaporate. The food industry will be severely affected by rising oil prices, since both modern agriculture and food transport are oil-intensive. The automobile industry will suffer as well when demand for cars plummets. Pressures will intensify on the three or more major auto companies that are developing plug-in hybrid cars that run largely on electricity to bring them to market quickly.

Higher oil prices have long been needed both to more accurately reflect the indirect costs of burning oil, such as climate change, and to encourage more-efficient use of a resource that is fast being depleted. While higher prices are desirable, the rise should not be so abrupt that it leads to severe economic disruptions.

Some countries are much more vulnerable to an oil decline than others. For example, the United States—which has long neglected public transportation—is particularly vulnerable because 88 percent of the U.S. workforce travels to work by car.

Since options for expanding supply are limited, efforts to prevent oil prices from rising well beyond $100 per barrel in the years ahead depend on reducing demand, largely within the transportation sector. And since the United States consumes more gasoline than the next 20 countries combined, it must play a lead role in cutting oil use.

A campaign to reduce oil use rapidly might best be launched at an emergency meeting of the G-8, since its members dominate world oil consumption. If governments fail to act quickly and decisively to reduce oil use, oil prices could soar as demand outruns supply, leading to a global recession or—in a worst-case scenario—a 1930s-type global depression.

POSTSCRIPT

Should the World Continue to Rely on Oil as the Major Source of Energy?

The twenty-first century ushered in another in a series of energy crises that have plagued the developed world since 1972. Gas prices jumped to record heights, and then rose even higher in 2006–2008, and the prospects of a return to levels of even a decade ago.

Yet when one reads the UN assessment of foreseeable world energy supplies (Hisham Khatib et al., *World Energy Assessment: Energy and the Challenge of Sustainability,* United Nations Development Programme, 2002), a sobering message appears. Don't panic just yet. The study reveals no serious energy shortage during the first half of the twenty-first century. In fact, the report suggests that oil supply conditions have actually improved since the crises of the 1970s and early 1980s. The report goes further in its assessment, concluding that fossil fuel reserves are "sufficient to cover global requirements throughout this century, even with a high-growth scenario." Another source suggesting no shortages for some time is *The Myth of the Oil Crisis: Overcoming the Challenges of Depletion, Geopolitics, and Global Warming* (Robin M. Mills, Praeger, 2008). Francis R. Stabler argues in "The Pump Will Never Run Dry," (*The Futurist,* November 1998) that technology and free enterprise will combine to allow the human race to continue its reliance on oil far into the future. For Stabler, the title of his article tells the reader everything. The pump will not run dry!

To be sure, his view of the future availability of gas is a minority one. One supporter is Julian L. Simon who argues in his *The Ultimate Resource 2* (1996) that even God may not know exactly how much oil and gas are "out there." Chapter 11 of Simon's book is entitled "When Will We Run Out of Oil? Never!" Another Stabler supporter is Bjørn Lomborg in *The Skeptical Environment: Measuring the Real State of the World* (Cambridge University Press, 2001). Arguing that the world seems to find more fossil energy than it consumes, he concludes that "we have oil for at least 40 years at present consumption, at least 60 years' worth of gas, and 230 years' worth of coal." Simon and Lomborg are joined by Michael C. Lynch in a published article on the Web under global oil supply (msn.com) entitled "Crying Wolf: Warnings about Oil Supply."

Seth Dunn and Christopher Flavin argue ("Reinventing the Energy System," State of the World 1999, Worldwatch Institute, 1999) that the global economy has been built on the rapid depletion of nonrenewable resources, and such consumption levels cannot possibly be maintained throughout the twenty-first century, as they were the previous century. Although Flavin and Dunn's arguments probably have received a receptive audience among most scholars who are concerned with the increasing scarcity of nonrenewable resources, they require the reader to accept a set of assumptions about the acceleration of future energy consumption. But one can easily be seduced by the logic of their argument, because it "just seems to make sense."

An excellent report is the Worldwatch Institute's "Energy for Development: The Potential Role of Renewable Energy in Meeting the Millennium Goals" (September 15, 2005). The report identifies those renewable energy options currently in wide use somewhere in the world. Another World-watch Institute report, "Biofuels for Transportation: Global Potential and Implications for Sustainable Agriculture and Energy in the 21st Century" (June 7, 2006), addresses one particular alternative to oil. See also *The Politics of the Global Oil Industry: An Introduction* (Toyin Falola, Praeger, 2008) and *Oil Panic and Oil Crisis* (Steven Gorelick, Wiley-Blackwell, 2009).

Lester R. Brown et al. in *Beyond Malthus* (1999) suggest that most writers point to between the years 2010 and 2025 as the time when world oil production will peak. The consequence, if that is accurate, is a need for alternative sources. The student of energy politics, however, must be careful not to ignore how advances in energy source exploration and extraction have tended to expand known reserves. Is the future lesson that the tide has finally turned and no significant reserves remain to be discovered? Or is the lesson that history will repeat itself and modern science will yield more oil and gas deposits, as well as make their extraction cost effective?

James J. MacKensie has provided a comprehensive yet succinct article on the peaking of oil in "Oil as a Finite Resource: When Is Global Production Likely to Peak?" (World Resources Institute, March 2000). Seth Dunn of the Worldwatch Institute in *State of the World 2001* suggests that a new energy system is fast approaching because of a series of revolutionary new technologies and approaches. David R. Francis provides a balanced assessment of the peaking debate in "Has Global Oil Production Peaked?" (*Christian Science Monitor*, January 29, 2004).

A number of books present a dire picture of the oil crisis: *Oil Addiction: The World in Peril* (Pierre Chomat, Universal Publishers, 2004); *The Collapsing Bubble: Growth and Fossil Energy* (Lindsay Grant, Seven Locks Press, 2005); *The Future of Global Oil Production: Facts, Figures, Trends and Projections, by Region* (Roger D. Blanchard, McFarland & Company, 2005); *The Long Emergency* (James Howard Kunster, Grove/Atlantic, 2006); and two books by C. J. Campbell (*The Coming Oil Crisis*, Multi-Science Publishing Co., 2004; *Oil Crisis*, Multi-Science Publishing Co., 2005). Finally, the most recent book to address the end of the oil-based economy is *Profit from the Peak: The End of Oil and the Greatest Investment Event of the Century* (Brian Hicks, Wiley, 2008).

A much more optimistic picture of the future energy situation is Bill Paul's *Future Energy: How the New Oil Industry Will Change People, Politics and Portfolios* (Wiley, 2007). A book that charts a path to renewable energy is Hermann Scheer's *The Solar Economy: Renewable Energy for a Sustainable Global Future* (Earthscan Publications, 2004). Finally, a September 2006 special issue of *Scientific American* presented nine articles addressing various alternatives to oil.

The msn.com Web site provides numerous citations of articles on both sides of the issue.

ISSUE 7

Will the World Be Able to Feed Itself in the Foreseeable Future?

YES: Stephen Lendman, from "Global Food Crisis: Hunger Plagues Haiti and the World," *Global Research* (April 21, 2008)

NO: Bee Wilson, from "The Last Bite: Is the World's Food System Collapsing?" *The New Yorker* (May 19, 2008)

ISSUE SUMMARY

YES: Stephen Lendman, a research associate of the Centre for Research on Globalization in Montreal, argues that the global food crisis is related to rising prices in an economically troubled time rather than to a lack of food production.

NO: Bee Wilson, a critic for *The New Yorker,* argues that the global food system is in need of radical change if the world is going to be able to feed itself in the future but that such prospects are unlikely to happen, as the "global manufacturers and wholesalers have an interest in continuing . . . stroking our colossal hunger."

T he lead editorial in *The New York Times* on March 3, 2008, began with the sentence: "The world's food situation is bleak. . . ." The primary culprit, according to the editorial, is the rising cost of wheat. The blame, in turn, was placed on the growing impact of biofuels. Others echoed the same message, adding climate change and the rising cost of shipping to the list of culprits. The UN Food and Agricultural Organization also issued a series of warnings in late 2007 and early 2008 about the growing food crisis.

Visualize two pictures. A group of people in Africa, including a significant number of small children, who show dramatic signs of advanced malnutrition and even starvation. The second picture shows an apparently wealthy couple finishing a meal at a rather expensive restaurant. The waiter removes their plates still half-full of food, and deposits them in the kitchen garbage can. The implication is quite clear. If only the wealthy would share their food with the poor, no one would go hungry. Today the simplicity of this image is obvious.

This issue addresses the question of whether or not the world will be able to feed itself by the middle of the twenty-first century. A prior question, of course, is whether or not enough food is grown throughout the world today to handle the needs of all the planet's citizens. News accounts of chronic food shortages somewhere in the world seem to have been appearing with regular consistency for about 30 years. This time has witnessed graphic accounts in news specials about the consequences of insufficient food, usually somewhere in sub-Saharan Africa. Also, several national and international studies have been commissioned to address world hunger. An American study organized by President Carter, for example, concluded that the root cause of hunger was poverty.

One might deduce from all of this activity that population growth had outpaced food production and that the planet's agricultural capabilities are no longer sufficient, or that the poor have been priced out of the marketplace. Yet, the ability of most countries to grow enough food has not yet been challenged. During the 1970–2000 period, only one region of the globe, sub-Saharan Africa, was unable to have its own food production keep pace with population growth.

This is instructive because, beginning in the early 1970s, a number of factors conspired to lessen the likelihood that all humans would go to bed each night adequately nourished. Weather in major food-producing countries turned bad; a number of countries, most notably Japan and the Soviet Union, entered the world grain importing business with a vengeance; the cost of energy used to enhance agricultural output rose dramatically; and less capital was available to poorer countries as loans or grants for purchasing agricultural inputs or the finished product (food) itself. Yet the world has had little difficulty growing sufficient food, enough to provide every person with two loaves of bread per day as well as other commodities.

Why then did famine and other food-related maladies appear with increasing frequency? The simple answer is that food is treated as a commodity, not a nutrient. Those who can afford to buy food or grow their own do not go hungry. However, the world's poor became increasingly unable to afford either to create their own successful agricultural ventures or to buy enough food.

The problem for the next half-century, then, has several facets to it. First, can the planet physically sustain increases in food production equal to or greater than the ability of the human race to reproduce itself? This question can only be answered by examining both factors in the comparison—likely future food production levels and future fertility scenarios. A second question relates to the economic dimension—will those poorer countries of the globe that are unable to grow their own food have sufficient assets to purchase it, or will the international community create a global distribution network that ignores a country's ability to pay? And third, will countries that want to grow their own food be given the opportunity to do so?

The selections for this issue address the specific question of the planet's continuing ability to grow sufficient food for its growing population. Stephen Lendman argues that the world will only be able to feed itself, but only if the global food system is radically changed, which is highly unlikely. Bee Wilson suggests that rising prices in an economically troubled time, rather than a lack of food production, make it extremely difficult for the world to be adequately fed.

YES

Stephen Lendman

Global Food Crisis: Hunger Plagues Haiti and the World

Consumers in rich countries feel it in supermarkets but in the world's poorest ones people are starving. The reason—soaring food prices, and it's triggered riots around the world in places like Mexico, Indonesia, Yemen, the Philippines, Cambodia, Morocco, Senegal, Uzbekistan, Guinea, Mauritania, Egypt, Cameroon, Bangladesh, Burkina Faso, Ivory Coast, Peru, Bolivia and Haiti that was once nearly food self-sufficient but now relies on imports for most of its supply and (like other food-importing countries) is at the mercy of agribusiness.

Wheat shortages in Peru are acute enough to have the military make bread with potato flour (a native crop). In Pakistan, thousands of troops guard trucks carrying wheat and flour. In Thailand, rice farmers take shifts staying awake nights guarding their fields from thieves. The crop's price has about doubled in recent months; it's the staple for half or more of the world's population, but rising prices and fearing scarcity have prompted some of the world's largest producers to export less—Thailand (the world's largest exporter), Vietnam, India, Egypt, Cambodia with others likely to follow as world output lags demand. Producers of other grains are doing the same like Argentina, Kazakhstan and China. The less they export, the higher prices go.

Other factors are high oil prices and transportation costs, growing demand, commodity speculation, pests in southeast Asia, a 10-year Australian drought, floods in Bangladesh and elsewhere, a 45-day cold snap in China, and other natural but mostly manipulated factors like crop diversion for biofuels; these have combined to create a growing world crisis, with more on this below. It's at the same time millions of Chinese and Indians have higher incomes, are changing their eating habits, and are consuming more meat, chicken and other animal products that place huge demands on grains to produce.

Here's a UK April 8 *Times* online snapshot of the situation in parts of Asia:

— Filipino farmers caught hoarding rice risk a life in jail sentence for "economic sabotage;"
— thousands of (Jakarta) Indonesian soya bean cake makers are striking against the destruction of their livelihood;
— once food self-sufficient countries like Japan and South Korea are reacting "bitterly (as) the world's food stocks-to-consumption ratio plunges to an all-time low;"

From GlobalResearch.ca, April 21, 2008. Copyright © 2008 by Center for Research on Globalization (CRG). Reprinted by permission.

- India no longer can export millions of tons of rice; instead it's forced to have a "special strategic food reserve on top of its existing wheat and rice stockpiles;"
- Thailand is the world's largest rice producer; its price rose 50% in the past month;
- countries like the Philippines and Sri Lanka are scrambling for secure rice supplies; they and other Asian countries are struggling to cope with soaring prices and insufficient supply;
- overall, rice is the staple food for three billion people; one-third of them survive on less than $1 a day and are "food insecure;" it means they may starve to death without aid.

The UN Food and Agricultural Organization (FAO) reported that world-wide food costs rose almost 40% in 2007 while grains spiked 42% and dairy prices nearly 80%. The World Bank said food prices are up 83% since 2005. As of December, this caused 37 countries to face food crises and 20 to impose price controls in response.

It also affected aid agencies like the UN's World Food Program (WFP). Because of soaring food and energy costs, the WFP sent an urgent appeal to donors on March 20 to help fill a $500 million resource gap for its work. Since then, food prices increased another 20% and show no signs of abating. For the world's poor, like the people of Haiti, things are desperate, people can't afford food, they scratch by any way they can, but many are starving and don't make it. . . .

World Hunger—A Growing Problem for All Nations

The situation is so dire, protests may erupt anywhere, any time, and rich countries aren't immune, including America. Poverty in the world's richest country is growing, and organizations like the Center for Economic Policy Research (CEPR) and Economic Policy Institute (EPI) document it. They report on a permanent (and growing) underclass of over 37 million people earning poverty-level wages and say that official statistics understate the problem. They note an unprecedented wealth gap between rich and poor, a dying middle class, and growing millions in extreme poverty.

It affects the unemployed as well in times of economic distress, but official government data conceals to what extent. If employment calculations were made as originally mandated, the true rate would be around 13% instead of the Department of Labor's 5.1%. The same is true for inflation that's around 12% at the retail level instead of the official 4% that's hooey.

Under conditions of duress, hunger is the clearest symptom, it's rising, and current food inflation threatens to spiral it out of control if nothing is done to address it. It's the highest in decades with 2007 signaling what's ahead—eggs up 25% last year; milk 17%; rice, bread and pasta 12%, and look at prices on the Chicago Board of Trade (CBOT):

- grains and soy prices are at multi-year highs;
- wheat hit an all-time high above $12 a bushel with little relief ahead in spite of a temporary pullback in price; the US Department of

Agriculture forecasts that global wheat stocks this year will fall to a 30 year low of 109.7 million metric tons; USDA also projected US wheat stocks by year end 2008 at 272 million bushels—the lowest level since 1948;

— corn and soybeans are also at record levels; soybeans are at over $15 a bushel; corn prices shot above $6 a bushel as demand for this and other crops soar in spite of US farmers planting as much of them as possible to cash in on high prices.

Growing demand, a weak dollar, but mostly another factor to be discussed below is responsible—the increased use of corn for ethanol production with farmers diverting more of their acreage from other crops to plant more of what's most in demand. Forty-three per cent of corn production is for livestock feed, but around one-fifth is for biofuels according to the National Corn Growers Association (NCGA). Other estimates are as high as 25–30% compared to 14% two years ago, and NCGA estimates one-third of the crop in 2009 will be for ethanol, not food. It's fueling US and world food inflation with five year forecasts of it rising even faster.

In the world's poorest countries, people starve. Here, they go on food stamps with a projected unprecedented 28 million Americans getting them this year as joblessness increases in a weak economy. However, many millions in need aren't eligible as social services are cut to finance foreign wars and tax cuts for the rich, with poor folks at home losing out as a result. A family of four only qualifies now if its net monthly income is at or below $1721 or $20,652 a year. Even then, it gets the same $542 monthly amount recipients received in 1996 to cover today's much higher prices or around $1 dollar a meal per person and falling.

This is the UN's World Food Program (WFP)'s dilemma worldwide at a time donations coming in are inadequate. Its Executive Director, Josette Sheeran, said "Our ability to reach people is going down just as needs go up. . . . We are seeing a new face of hunger in which people (can't afford to buy food). . . . Situations that were previously not urgent" are now desperate. WFP's funding needs keep rising. It estimates them at $3.5 billion, they'll likely go higher, and they're for approved projects to feed 73 million people in 78 counties worldwide. WFP foresees much greater potential needs for unseen emergencies and for far greater numbers of people in need.

People (who aren't poor) in rich countries can manage with food accounting for about 10% of consumption. In ones like China, it's around 30%, but in sub-Saharan Africa and the poor in Latin America and Asia it's about 60% (or even 80%) and rising. It means food aid is vital, and without it people will starve. But as food prices rise, the amount forthcoming (when it's most needed) falls because not enough money is available and too few donors offer help.

Agencies that can are doing less with ones like USAID saying it's cutting the amount of food aid it provides but won't say why. It's mission is to help the rich, not the poor, or as it states on its web site: as a US government agency, it "receives (its) overall foreign policy guidance from the Secretary of State (and its mission is to) further America's foreign policy interests (in the areas of) economic growth, agriculture and trade. . . ." That leaves out the poor.

Oxfam worries about what USAID ignores. It called for immediate action by donors and governments to protect the world's poor against rising food prices. One spokesperson said: "Global economic uncertainty, high food prices, drought (and other factors) all pose a serious threat to (the) vulnerable." Another added: "More and more people are going to be facing food shortages in the future. (Because of) rising food prices we need to think (of its) impact on (the world's poor) who are spending up to 80% of their incomes on food."

The UN Special Rapporteur on the Right to Food, Jean Ziegler, also expressed alarm. In comments to the French daily Liberation he said: "We are heading for a very long period of rioting, conflicts (and) waves of uncontrollable regional instability marked by the despair of the most vulnerable populations." He noted that even under normal circumstances hunger plagues the world and claims the life of a child under age 10 every five seconds. Because of the present crisis, we now face "an imminent massacre."

Besides the usual factors cited, it's vital to ask why, but don't expect Brazil's Lula to explain. Biofuel production is the main culprit, but not according to him. Brazil is a major biofuels producer. Last year it signed an R&D "Ethanol Pact" with Washington to develop "next generation" technologies for even more production.

In an April 16 Reuters report, the former union leader was dismissive about the current crisis and rejected criticisms that biofuels are at fault. In spite of protests at home and around the world, he told reporters: "Don't tell me. . . . that food is expensive because of biodiesel. (It's) expensive because" peoples' economic situation has improved and they're eating more. It's true in parts of China and India, but not in most other countries where incomes haven't kept pace with inflation.

Biofuels—A Scourge of Our Times

The idea of combustible fuels from organic material has been around since the early auto age, but only recently took off. Because they're from plant-based or animal byproduct (renewable) sources, bio or agrofuels are (falsely) touted as a solution to a growing world energy shortage with a huge claimed added benefit—the nonsensical notion that they're clean and green without all the troublesome issues connected to fossil fuels.

Biofuel is a general term to describe all fuels from organic matter. The two most common kinds are bioethanol as a substitute for gasoline, and biodiesel that serves the same purpose for that type fuel.

Bioethanol is produced from sugar-rich crops like corn, wheat and sugar cane. Most cars can burn a petroleum fuel blend with up to 10% bioethanol without any engine modifications. Some newer cars can run on pure bioethanol.

Biodiesel is produced from a variety of vegetable oils, including soybean, palm and rapeseed (canola), plus animal fats. This fuel can replace regular diesel with no engine modifications required.

Cellulosic ethanol is another variety and is made by breaking down fiber from grasses or most other kinds of plants. Biofuels of all types are renewable since crops are grown in season, harvested, then replanted for more output repeatedly.

In George Bush's 2007 State of the Union address, he announced, "It's in our vital interest to diversify America's energy supply (and we) must continue investing in new methods of producing ethanol (to) reduce gasoline usage in the United States by 20% in the next 10 years. (To do it) we must (set) a mandatory fuels (target of) 35 billion gallons of renewable and alternative fuels in 2017 (to) reduce our dependence on foreign oil."

Congress earlier passed the Energy Policy Act of 2005 that mandated ethanol fuel production rise to 4 billion gallons in 2006 and 7.5 billion by 2012. It already reached 6.5 billion barrels last year and is heading for 9 billion this year.

The 2007 Energy Independence and Security Act gave added impetus to the Bush administration scheme with plenty of agribusiness subsidies backing it. Its final version sailed through both Houses in December, and George Bush made it official on December 19. It upped the stakes over 2005 with one of its provisions calling for 36 billion gallons of renewable fuels by 2022 to replace 15% of their equivalent in oil. It represents a nearly fivefold increase from current levels, and new goals ahead may set it higher as rising oil prices (topping $117 a barrel April 21) make a case for cheaper alternatives, and some in the environmental community claim biofuels are eco-friendly.

Hold the applause, and look at the facts. In a nutshell, organic fuels trash rainforests, deplete water reserves, kill off species, and increase greenhouse emissions when the full effects of producing them are included. At least that's what *Science* magazine says on the latter point. It reviewed studies that examined how destruction of natural ecosystems (such as tropical rain forests and South American grasslands) not only releases greenhouse gases when they're burned and plowed but also deprives the planet of natural sponges to absorb carbon emissions. Cropland also absorbs less carbon than rain forests or even the scrubland it replaces.

Nature Conservancy scientist Joseph Fargione (lead author of one study) concluded that grassland clearance releases 93 times the greenhouse gases that would be saved by fuel made annually on that land. For scientists and others concerned about global warming, the research indicated that biofuel production exacerbates the problem and thus should be reconsidered. Others disagree and so far the trend continues with Europe and America both setting ambitious goals that pay little attention to the consequences they ignore.

Eric Holt-Gimenez, executive director of the Food First/Institute for Food and Development Policy, pays close attention and wrote about it in an article published last June by Agencia Latinoamericana de Informacion (ALAI) and thereafter widely distributed. It's headlined "Biofuels: The Five Myths of the Agro-fuels Transition." As he puts it: "The mythic baggage of the agro-fuels transition needs to be publicly unpacked."

1. Agrofuels aren't clean and green. As cited above, they produce far greater greenhouse gas emissions than they save and also require large amounts of oil-based fertilizers that contribute even more.
2. Agrofuel production will be hugely destructive to forests in countries like Brazil where vast Amazon devastation is well documented and is currently increasing at nearly 325,000 hectares a year. By 2020 in Indonesia, "palm oil plantations for bio-diesel (will continue to be) the primary cause of forest loss (in a) country with one of the highest deforestation rates in the world."
3. Agrofuels will destroy rural development. Small farmers will be forced off their land and so will many thousands of others in communities to make way for Big Oil, Agribusiness, and Agribiotech to move in and take over for the huge profits to be extracted in the multi-billions.
4. Agrofuels increase hunger. The poor are always hurt most, the topic is covered above, and Holt-Gimenez quotes another forecast. It's the International Food Policy Research Institute's estimate that basic food staple prices will rise 30–33% by 2010, but that figure already undershoots based on current data. FPRI also sees the rise continuing to 2020 by another 26 to 135% that will be catastrophic for the world's poor who can't afford today's prices and are ill-equipped to raise their incomes more than marginally if at all.
5. Better "second-generation" argofuels aren't around the corner. Examples touted are eco-friendly fast-growing trees and switchgrass (a dominant warm season central North American tallgrass prairie species). Holt-Gimenez calls the argument a "bait and switch-grass shell game" to make the case for first generation production now ongoing. The same environmental problems exists, and they'll be hugely exacerbated by more extensive GMO crop plantings.

Holt-Gimenez sees agrofuels as a "genetic Trojan horse" that's letting agribusiness giants like Monsanto "colonize both our fuel and food system," do little to offset a growing demand for oil, reap huge profits from the scheme, get them at taxpayers' expense, and that's exactly what's happening with Big Oil in on it, too, as a way to diversify through large biofuel investments. More on this below.

The Ghost of Henry Kissinger

Kissinger made a chilling 1970 comment that explains a lot about what's happening now—"Control oil and you control nations; control food and you control the people." Combine it with unchallengeable military power and you control everything, and Kissinger likely said that, too.

He said plenty more in his classified 1974 memo on a secret project called National Security Study Memorandum 200 (NSSM 200) for a "world population plan of action" for drastic global population control. He meant reducing it by hundreds of millions, using food as a weapon, and overall reorganizing the global food market to destroy family farms and replace them with (agribusiness-run) factory ones. It's been ongoing for decades, backed since January 1995 by WTO muscle, and characterized now by huge agribusiness giants with monstrous vertically integrated powers over the food we eat—from research labs to plantings to processing to the supermarket and other food outlet shelves around the world.

But it's even worse than that. Today, five agribusiness behemoths, with little fanfare and enormous government backing, plan big at our expense—to control the world's food supply by making it all genetically engineered with biofuels one part of a larger scheme.

By diverting crops for fuel, prices have exploded, and five "Ag biotech" giants are exploiting it—Monsanto, DuPont, Dow Agrisciences, Syngenta and Bayer CropScience AG. Their solution—make all crops GMO, tout it as a way to increase output and reduce costs, and claim it's the solution to today's soaring prices and world hunger.

In fact, agribusiness power raises prices, controls output to keep them high, and the main factor behind today's situation is the conversion of US farmland to biofuel factories. With less crop output for food and world demand for it growing, prices are rising, and rampant commodity speculation exacerbates the problem with traders profiting hugely and loving it. It's another part of the multi-decade wealth transfer scheme from the world's majority to the elite few. While the trend continues, its momentum is self-sustaining, and it works because governments back it. They subsidize the problem, keep regulations loose, give business free reign, and maintain that markets work best so let them.

As mentioned above, about 43% of US corn output goes for animal feed, but growing amounts are for biofuels—now possibly 25–30% of production compared to around 14% two years ago, up 300% since 2001, and today the total exceeds what's earmarked for export, with no slowing down of this trend in sight. The result, of course, is world grain reserves are falling, prices soaring, millions starving, governments permitting it, and it's only the early innings of a long-term horrifying trend—radically transforming agriculture in humanly destructive ways:

— letting agribusiness and Big Oil giants control it for profit at the expense of consumer health and well-being;
— making it all genetically engineered and inflicting great potential harm to human health; and
— producing reduced crop amounts for food, diverting greater quantities for fuel, allowing prices to soar, making food as dear as oil, ending government's responsibility for food security, and tolerating the unthinkable—putting hundreds of millions of poor around the world in jeopardy and letting them starve to death for profit.

This is the brave new world neoliberal schemers have in mind. They're well along with their plans, marginally diverted by today's economic distress, well aware that growing world protests could prove hugely disruptive, but very focused, nonetheless, on finding clever ways to push ahead with what's worked pretty well for them so far, so they're not about to let human misery jeopardize big profits.

If they won't reform, people have to do it for them, and throughout history that's how it's always worked. Over time, the stakes keep rising as the threats become greater, and today they may be as great as they've ever been.

What better time for a new social movement like those in the past that were pivotal forces for change. Famed community organizer Saul Alinsky knew the way to beat organized money is with organized people. In combination, they've succeeded by taking to the streets, striking, boycotting, challenging authority, disrupting business, paying with their lives and ultimately prevailing by knowing change never comes from the top down. It's always from the grassroots, from the bottom up, and what better time for it than now. It's high time democracy worked for everyone, [so] that destructive GMO and biofuels schemes won't be tolerated, and "America the Beautiful" won't any longer just be for elites and no one else.

Bee Wilson  **NO**

The Last Bite: Is the World's Food System Collapsing?

In his "Essay on the Principle of Population," of 1798, the English parson Thomas Malthus insisted that human populations would always be "checked" (a polite word for mass starvation) by the failure of food supplies to keep pace with population growth. For a long time, it looked as if what Malthus called the "dark tints" of his argument were unduly, even absurdly, pessimistic. As Paul Roberts writes in *The End of Food* (Houghton Mifflin; $26), "Until late in the twentieth century, the modern food system was celebrated as a monument to humanity's greatest triumph. We were producing more food—more grain, more meat, more fruits and vegetables—than ever before, more cheaply than ever before, and with a degree of variety, safety, quality and convenience that preceding generations would have found bewildering." The world seemed to have been liberated from a Malthusian "long night of hunger and drudgery."

Now the "dark tints" have returned. The World Bank recently announced that thirty-three countries are confronting food crises, as the prices of various staples have soared. From January to April of this year, the cost of rice on the international market went up a hundred and forty-one per cent. Pakistan has reintroduced ration cards. In Egypt, the Army has started baking bread for the general population. The Haitian Prime Minister was ousted after hunger riots. The current crisis could push another hundred million people deeper into poverty. Is the world's population about to be "checked" by its failure to produce enough food?

Paul Roberts is the second author in the past couple of years to publish a book entitled *The End of Food*—the first, by Thomas F. Pawlick, appeared in 2006. Pawlick, an investigative journalist from Ontario, was concerned with such predicaments as the end of the tasty tomato and its replacement by "red tennis balls" lacking in both flavor and nutrients. (The modern tomato, he reported, contains far less calcium and Vitamin A than its 1963 counterpart.) These worries seem rather tame compared with Roberts's; his book grapples with the possible termination of food itself, and its replacement by—what? Cormac McCarthy's novel *The Road* contains a vision of a future in which just about the only food left is canned, from happier times; when the cans run out, the humans eat one another. Roberts lacks McCarthy's Biblical cadences, but his narrative is intended to be no less terrifying.

From *The New Yorker*, May 19, 2008. Copyright © 2008 by Bee Wilson. Reprinted by permission of Bee Wilson.

131

Roberts's work is part of a second wave of food-politics books, which has taken the genre to a new level of apocalyptic foreboding. The first wave was led by Eric Schlosser's *Fast Food Nation* (2001), and focussed on the perils of junk food. *Fast Food Nation* painted an alarming picture—one learned about the additives in a strawberry milkshake, the traces of excrement in hamburger meat—but it also left some readers with a feeling of mild complacency, as they closed the book and turned to a wholesome supper of spinach and ricotta tortellini. There is no such reassurance to be had from the new wave, in which Roberts's book is joined by *Stuffed and Starved: The Hidden Battle for the World Food System* by Raj Patel (Melville House; $19.95); *Bottomfeeder: How to Eat Ethically in a World of Vanishing Seafood,* by Taras Grescoe (Bloomsbury; $24.99); and *In Defense of Food: An Eater's Manifesto* by Michael Pollan, the poet of the group (Penguin Press; $21.95).

All of these authors agree that the entire system of Western food production is in need of radical change, right down to the spinach. Roberts opens with a description of E.-coli-infected spinach from California, which killed three people in 2006 and sickened two hundred others. The E. coli was traced to the guts of a wild boar that may have tracked the bug in from a nearby cattle ranch. Industrial farming means that even those on a vegan diet may reap the nastier effects of intensive meat production. It is no longer enough for individuals to switch to healthier choices in the supermarket. Schlosser asked his readers to consider the chain of consequences they set in motion every time they sit down to eat in a fast-food outlet. Roberts wants us to consider the chain of transactions and reactions represented by each of our food purchases—"by each ripe melon or freshly baked bagel, by each box of cereal or tray of boneless skinless chicken breasts." This time, we are all implicated.

Like Malthus, Roberts sees humanity increasingly struggling to meet its food needs. He predicts that in the next forty years, as agriculture is threatened by climate change, "demand for food will rise precipitously," outstripping supply. The reasons for this, however, are not strictly Malthusian. For Malthus, famine was inevitable because the math of human existence did not add up: the means of subsistence grew only arithmetically (1, 2, 3), whereas population grew geometrically (2, 4, 8). By this analysis, food production could never catch up with fertility. Malthus was wrong, on both counts. In his treatise, Malthus couldn't envisage any innovations for increasing yield beyond "dressing" the soil with cattle manure. In the decades after he wrote, farmers in England took advantage of new machinery, powerful fertilizers, and higher-yield seeds, and supply rose faster than demand. As the availability of food increased, and people became more prosperous, fertility fell.

Malthus could not have imagined that demand might increase catastrophically even where populations were static or falling. The problem is not just the number of mouths to feed; it's the quantity of food that each mouth consumes when there are no natural constraints. As the world becomes richer, people eat too much, and too much of the wrong things—above all, meat. Since it takes on average four pounds of grain to make a single pound of meat, Roberts writes, "meatier diets also geometrically increase overall food demands" even in those parts of Europe and North America where fertility rates are low. Malthus knew that some people were more "frugal" than others, but he hugely underestimated the capacity of ordinary human beings to keep eating. Even now, there is no over-all food shortage when measured by global subsistence needs. Despite the current food crisis, last year's worldwide grain harvest was colossal, five per cent above the previous year's. We are not yet living on Cormac McCarthy's scorched earth. Yet demand is increasing ever faster. As of 2006, there were eight hundred million people on the planet who were hungry, but they were outnumbered by the billion who were overweight. Our current food predicament resembles a Malthusian scenario—misery and famine—but one largely created by overproduction rather than underproduction. Our ability to produce vastly too many calories for our basic needs has skewed the concept of demand, and generated a wildly dysfunctional market.

Michael Pollan writes that the food business once lamented what it called the problem of the "fixed stomach"—it appeared that demand for food, unlike other products, was inelastic, the amount fixed by the dimensions of the stomach itself, the variety constrained by tradition and habit. In the past few decades, however, American and European stomachs have become as elastic as balloons, and, with the newly prosperous Chinese and Indians switching to Western diets, much of the rest of the world is following suit. "Today, Mexicans drink more Coca-Cola than milk," Patel reports. Roberts tells us that in India "obesity is now growing faster than either the government or traditional culture can respond," and the demand for gastric bypasses is soaring.

Driven by our bottomless stomachs, Roberts argues, the modern economy has reduced food to a "commodity" like any other, which must be generated in ever greater units at an ever lower cost, year by year, like sneakers or DVDs. But food isn't like sneakers or DVDs. If we max out our credit cards buying Nikes, we can simply push them to the back of a closet. By contrast, our insatiable demand for food must be worn on our bodies, often in the form of diabetes as well as obesity. Overeating makes us miserable, and ill, but medical advances mean that it takes a long time to kill us, so we keep on eating. Roberts, whose impulse to connect everything up is both his strength and his weakness, concludes, grandly, that "food is fundamentally not an economic phenomenon." On the contrary, food has always been an economic phenomenon, but in its current form it is one struggling to meet our uncurbed appetites. What we are witnessing is not the end of food but a market on the brink of failure. Those bearing the brunt are, as in Malthus's day, the people at the bottom.

Cheap food, in these books, is the enemy. Roberts complains that "the attributes of food that our economic system tends to value and to encourage"— like cheapness—"aren't necessarily the attributes that work best for the people eating the food, or the culture in which that food is consumed, or the environment in which it is produced." Cheap food distresses Raj Patel, too. Patel, a former U.N. consultant and a current anti-globalization activist, is an excitable fan of peasant coöperatives and Slow Food. He lacks Roberts's cool scope but shares his ambition to connect all the dots. Patel would like us to take lessons in "culinary sensuousness" from his "dear friend" Marco Flavio Marinucci, a San Francisco-based artist and, apparently, a master of the art of "gastronomical foreplay." Patel regrets that most of us are nothing like dear Mr. Marinucci.

We are all too busy being screwed over by the giant corporations to take the time to appreciate "the deeper and subtler pleasures of food." For Patel, it is a short step from Western consumers "engorged and intoxicated" with cheap processed food to Mexican and Indian farmers committing suicide because they can't make a living. The "food industry's pabulum" makes us all cogs in an evil machine.

It's easy to see what Roberts and Patel have against cheap food. For one thing, it's often disgusting. Roberts has a powerful passage on industrial chicken, showing how its vile flesh is a direct consequence of its status as economic commodity. In the nineteen-seventies, it took ten weeks to raise a broiler; now it takes forty days in a dark and crowded shed, because farmers are under constant pressure to cut costs and increase productivity. Every cook knows that chicken breast is no longer what it once was—it's now remarkably flabby and yielding. Roberts reveals that poultry experts have a term for this: P.S.E., or "pale, soft, exudative" meat. Today's birds, Roberts shows, are bred to be top-heavy, in order to satisfy consumers' desire for "healthy" white meat at affordable prices. In these Sumo-breasted monsters, a vast volume of lactic acid is released upon death, damaging the proteins—hence the crumbly meat. Poultry firms deal with P.S.E. after the fact, pumping the flaccid breast with salts and phosphates to keep it artificially juicier. What they don't do is try particularly hard to prevent P.S.E. They can't afford to. The average U.S. consumer eats eighty-seven pounds of chicken a year—twice as much as in 1980—but this generates a profit of only two cents per pound for the farmer.

So, yes, cheap food can be nasty, not to mention bad for farmers and the environment. Yet it has one great advantage that neither Patel nor Roberts fully grapples with: people can afford to buy it. According to the World Bank, four hundred million fewer people were living in extreme poverty in 2004 than was the case in 1981, in large part owing to the affordability of basic foodstuffs. The current food crises are the result of food being too expensive to buy, rather than too cheap. The rioters of Haiti would kill for a plate of affordable chicken, no matter how pale, soft, and exudative. The battle against cheap food involves harder tradeoffs than Patel and Roberts allow. No one has yet discovered how to raise prices for the overfed rich without squeezing the underfed poor.

If Roberts's overarching thesis is simplistic, he is nevertheless right in his scathing analysis of some of the market alternatives. The conventional view against which Roberts is arguing is that the food economy is "more or less self-correcting." When the economy gets out of kilter—through rapidly increased demand or sudden shortages and price rises—the market should provide the solution in the form of new technologies that "push the Malthusian monster back into its box." This is precisely what Malthus is thought to have missed—the capacity of a market economy to turn pressures on supply into innovations that can meet future demands. But endless innovation has now generated a series of demands that are starting to overwhelm the market.

Roberts depicts the global food market as a lumbering beast, organized on such a monolithic scale that it cannot adapt to the consequences of its own distortions. In a flexible, responsive market, producers ought to be able to react to a surplus of one thing by switching to making another thing. Industrial agriculture doesn't work like this. Too many years—and, in the West, too many subsidies—are invested in the setup of big single-crop farms to let producers abandon them when the going gets tough. Defenders of industrial agriculture point to its efficiency, but Roberts sees instead a system full to bursting with waste, often literally. American consumers demand huge amounts of cheese and meat. One consequence is the giant "poop lagoons" of Northern California. In traditional forms of mixed agriculture, animal manure is not a waste product but a valuable fertilizer. By contrast, the mainstream food economy is now dominated by monocultures in which crops and animals are kept apart. This system of farming has little use for poop, despite churning it out in ever-increasing volumes. The San Joaquin Valley has air quality as poor as Los Angeles, the result of twenty-seven million tons of manure produced every year by California's cows. "And cows are relatively benign crappers," Roberts points out; hogs—mass-produced to meet the demand for bacon on everything—are more prolific. On June 21, 1995, Roberts tells us, a hog lagoon burst into a river in North Carolina, destroying aquatic life for seventeen miles.

Repulsed by the sordid details of meat production, some consumers turn to fish instead. Yet the piscine world is subject to the same market paradoxes as meat. In *Bottomfeeder,* Taras Grescoe confirms that there are still plenty of fish in the sea. Unfortunately, these are not the ones that people want to eat. Aside from pollution, the oceans would be in quite a healthy state if consumers were less reluctant to eat fish near the middle or bottom of the food chain, such as herring, sardines, and mackerel. We would be healthier, too, since these oily fish are rich in omega-3, the fatty acid in which the Western diet is markedly deficient. Instead, we clamor to eat top-of-the-food-chain fish such as cod and bluefin tuna, many of whose stocks have collapsed; they will soon disappear from the seas altogether unless demand drops. So far, as with meat, the opposite is happening. With increasing affluence, the Chinese are developing a taste for sushi, which could soon see every last piece of glistening toro disappear.

Fish "farming," with its overtones of pastoral care, sounds like a better option, but Grescoe—who has travelled around the world in search of delicious and rare seafood—shows that it can be more damaging still. As with chicken, out-of-control demand for once premium foods has translated into grotesque and unsustainable forms of production. A taste for "popcorn shrimp in the strip malls of America" translates into the cutting down of tropical mangrove forests in Ecuador and the destruction of wild-shrimp stocks in Southeast Asia. Grescoe quotes Duong Van Ni, a hydrologist from Vietnam, where warm-water shrimp farms feed the insatiable Western appetite for all-you-can-eat seafood-shack specials and prawn curries. "Shrimp farming is so damaging to the environment and so polluting to the soil, trees, and water that it will be the last form of agriculture," Ni says. "After it, you can do nothing." Our thirst for cheap salmon is similarly destructive, and the results are as bad for us as they are for the fish. The nutrition expert Marion Nestle warns that you should broil or grill farmed salmon until it is well done and remove the skin, to get rid of much of the toxin-laden grease. As Grescoe remarks, if this is the only safe way to eat this fish, wouldn't it be better to eat something else?

The one thing farmed salmon has going for it is that the fish are, as Roberts says, "efficient feed converters": salmon require only a little more than a pound of feed for every pound of weight that they gain. The trouble is that the feed in this case isn't grain but other fish, because salmon are carnivores. Fishermen are granted large quotas to catch fish like sardines and anchovies—which are delicious and could be eaten by humans—only to have them turned into fish meal and oil. Thirty million tons, or a third of the world's wild catch, goes into the manufacture of fish meal and oil, much of which is used to raise farmed salmon. Farming salmon, Grescoe says, is "akin to nourishing tigers and lions with beef and pork," and then butchering them to make ground beef. The farming of herbivorous fish such as carp and tilapia, by contrast, actually increases the net amount of seafood in the world.

The great mystery of the world's insatiable appetite for farmed salmon is that it doesn't taste good. Grescoe, a Canadian who was reared on "well-muscled" chinook, gives a lurid description of the farmed variety, with its "herringbone-pattern flesh, barely held together by creamy, saliva-gooey fat." A flabby farmed-salmon dinner—no matter how much you dress it up with teriyaki or ginger—cannot compare with the pleasures of canned sardines spread on hot buttered toast or a delicate white-pollock fillet, spritzed with lemon. Pollock is cheaper than salmon, too. Yet in the United States there is little demand for it, or, indeed, for the small, wild, affordable (and sustainable) Northern shrimp, which taste sweeter than the watery jumbo creatures that the market prefers.

Given that the current food economy is so strongly driven by appetite, it does seem odd that so much of the desire is for such squalid and unsatisfying things. If we are going to squander the world's resources, shouldn't it at least be for the sake of rare and splendid edibles? Yet much of what is now eaten in the West is not food so much as, in Michael Pollan's terms, stuff that's merely "foodish." From the nineteen-eighties onward, many traditional foods were removed from the shelves and in their place came packages of quasi-edible substances whose selling point was nutritional properties (No cholesterol! Vitamin enriched!) rather than taste. Pollan writes:

There are in fact hundreds of foodish products in the supermarket that your ancestors simply wouldn't recognize as food: breakfast cereal bars transected by bright white veins representing, but in reality having nothing to do with, milk; "protein waters" and "nondairy creamer"; cheeselike foodstuffs equally innocent of any bovine contribution; cakelike cylinders (with creamlike fillings) called Twinkies that never grow stale.

Pollan shows that much of the apparent abundance of choice available to the affluent Western consumer is an illusion. You may spend hours in the supermarket, keenly scrutinizing the labels, but, when it comes down to it, most of what you eat is derived from the high-yield, low-maintenance crops that the food industry prefers to grow, and sells to you in myriad foodish forms.

"You may not think you eat a lot of corn and soybeans," Pollan writes, "but you do: 75 percent of the vegetable oils in your diet come from soy (representing 20 percent of your daily calories) and more than half of the sweeteners you consume come from corn (representing around 10 percent of daily calories)." You may never consciously allow soy to pass your lips. You shun soy milk and despise tofu. Yet soy will get you in the end, whether as soy-oil mayo and soy-oil fries; ice cream and chocolate emulsified with soy; or chicken fed on soy ("soy with feathers," as one activist described it to Patel).

Our insatiable appetites are not simply our own; they have, in no small part, been created for us. This explains, to a certain degree, how the world can be "stuffed and starved" at the same time, as Patel has it. The food economy has created a system in which some have no food options at all and some have too many options, albeit of a somewhat spurious kind. In the middle is a bottleneck—a relatively small number of wholesalers and buyers who largely determine what the starving farmers produce and what the stuffed consumers eat. In the Netherlands, Germany, France, Austria, Belgium, and the United Kingdom, there are a hundred and sixty million consumers, fed by approximately 3.2 million farmers. But the farmers and the consumers are connected to one another by a mere hundred and ten wholesale "buying desks."

It would be futile, therefore, to look to the food system for radical change. The global manufacturers and wholesalers have an interest in continuing to manipulate our desires, feeding our illusions of choice, stoking our colossal hunger. On the other hand, if desires can be manipulated in one direction, why shouldn't they be manipulated in another, more benign direction? Pollan offers a model of how individual consumers might adjust their appetites: "Eat food. Not too much. Mostly plants." As a solution, this is charmingly modest, but it is unlikely to be enough to meet the urgency of the situation. How do you get the whole of America—the whole of the world—to eat more like Michael Pollan?

The good news is that one developing country has, in the past two decades, conducted a national experiment in a more sustainable food system, proving that it is possible to feed a population less destructively. Farmers gave up synthetic fertilizers and pesticides and replaced them with old-fashioned crop rotations and mixed livestock-crop operations. Big industrial farms were split into smaller coöperatives. The bad news is that the country is Cuba, which was forced to make the switch after the fall of the Soviet Union left it without supplies of agrochemicals. Cuba's experiment depended on its authoritarian state, which commanded the "reallocation" of labor from cities to farms. Even on Cuba's own terms, the experiment hasn't been perfect. On May Day, Raúl Castro announced further radical changes to the farm system in order to reduce reliance on imports. Paul Roberts notes that there is no chance that Americans and Europeans will voluntarily adopt a Cuban model of food production. (You don't say.) He adds, however, that "the real question is no longer what a rich country would do *voluntarily* but what it might do if its other options were worse."

POSTSCRIPT

Will the World Be Able to Feed Itself in the Foreseeable Future?

Presumably, economist Thomas Robert Malthus was not the first to address the question of the planet's ability to feed its population. But his 1789 *Essay on the Principle of Population* is the most quoted of early writings on the subject. Malthus' basic proposition was that population, if left unchecked, would grow geometrically, while subsistence resources could grow only arithmetically. Malthus, who wrote his essay in response to an argument with his father about the ability of the human race to produce sufficient resources vital for life, created a stir back in the late eighteenth century. The same debate holds the public's attention today as the momentum of recent high population growth rates yields human increases unparalleled at any other time in human history.

A 2006 FAO report ("The State of Food Security in the World 2006," United Nations) lays out an argument for a more optimistic scenario for the twenty-first century. It predicts that the growth in global demand for food will rise only 1.5 percent a year for the next 30 years, a drop from the 1.5 percent of the previous 30 years. And the growth in global demand for cereals will be cut in half, from 2.5 percent per year to 1.2 percent. The report suggests that future demand will be met in three ways: (1) tapping into adequate potential farmland; (2) increasing the rate of irrigation; and (3) acquiring higher yield levels due to improved technology. This optimistic view is shared by Sylvie Brunel in *The Geopolitics of Hunger, 2000–2001: Hunger and Power* (Lynne Rienner, 2001).

Janet Raloff, a writer for *Science News*, looks at a number of factors—declining per capita grain harvests, the world's growing appetite for meat, the declining availability of fish for the developing world, and continuing individual poverty ("Global Food Trends, *Science News Online,* May 31, 2003). Lester R. Brown adds another dimension to the problem in *State of the World 2001* (W.W. Norton & Company, 2001). His pessimism about future food supplies arises from the belief that world leaders have not come forward with a comprehensive master plan to address the problem and are extremely unlikely to do so in the foreseeable future.

A balanced look at the planet's capacity to feed the UN's projected 2050 population is L.T. Evans' *Feeding the Ten Billion* (Cambridge University Press, 1998). In it, the author takes the reader through the ages, showing how the human race has addressed the agricultural needs of each succeeding billion people. The biggest challenge during the next half century, according to Evans, is to solve two problems: producing enough food for a 67 percent increase in the population, and eliminating the chronic undernutrition afflicting so many people. Solving the first problem requires a focus on the main components of increased food supply. For Evans, these include: "(1) increase in land under cultivation; (2) increase in yield per hectare per crop; (3) increase in the number of crops per hectare per year; (4) displacement of lower yielding crops by higher yielding ones; (5) reduction of post-harvest losses; and (6) reduced use as feed for animals."

The second problem brings into play many socioeconomic factors beyond those that are typically associated with agricultural production. Many studies have observed that the root cause of hunger is poverty. Addressing poverty, therefore, is a prerequisite for ensuring that the world's food supply is distributed such that the challenge of global hunger is met.

Three other sources are reports by the UN's Food and Agricultural Organization: *World Agriculture: Towards 2000; The State of Food and Agriculture 2002;* and *World Agriculture: Towards 2015/2030.* The central message of these studies is that the planet will be able to feed a growing population in the foreseeable future, if certain conditions are met. Another FAO report, *The State of Food Insecurity in the World 2005,* analyses the latest data on hunger in the context of the Millennium Development Goals. See also *Hunger 2009: Global Development Charting a New Course,* 19th Annual Report on the State of the World (Bread for the World Institute, 2009).

Another optimistic viewpoint about future food prospects is *The World Food Outlook* by Donald Mitchell, Merlinda D. Ingco, and Ronald C. Duncan (Cambridge University Press, 1997). Their basic conclusion is that the world food situation has improved dramatically for most of the regions of the globe and will continue to do so. The only exception is sub-Saharan Africa. See also *Feeding People Is Easy* (Colin Tudge, Pari Publishing, 2007).

For Julian L. Simon in "What Are the Limits on Food Production," *The Ultimate Resource 2* (Princeton University Press, 1996) the answer is simple. The world can produce vastly more food than it currently does, even in those places that rely on conventional methods. The essence of his argument is this: More people with higher incomes cause scarcity problems in the short run, which, in turn, results in raised prices. Into the picture then come inventors and entrepreneurs, some of whom will be successful in finding appropriate solutions.

David Pimentel et al., "Impact of Population Growth on Food Supplies and Environment," *Population and Environment* (1997) allude to the warnings of a number of impressive groups concerning the world's future food situation. They cite the Royal Society, the U.S. National Academy of Sciences, the UN Food and Agricultural Organization, and numerous other international organizations, as well as scientific research to support their view of the pending danger. For them, two issues are significant. The first is the existence of enough agricultural inputs: water, land, energy, and the like. The second is the global economic system that treats food as a commodity rather than a nutrient. For these authors, the bottom line is that population must be curtailed.

Two other sources are worth mentioning. *Halving Global Hunger* (Sara Scherr, Background Paper of the Millennium Project's Task Force 2 on Hunger,

April 18, 2003) provides an overview of existing knowledge relating to the reduction of hunger. Joachim von Braun and associates analyze two future policy scenarios for ensuring food security by 2050 (*New Risks and Opportunities for Food Security: Scenario Analyses for 2015 and 2050,* International Food Policy Research Institute, February 2005). See also von Braun's *The World Food Situation: New Driving Forces and Required Actions* (IFPRI, December 2007) and FAO's *The State of Food Insecurity in the World 2005; Seasons of Hunger: Fighting Cycles of Starvation Among the World's Rural Poor* (Stephen Devereux, Pluto Press, 2008); and *Hunger: A Modern History* (James Vernon, Belknap Press of Harvard University, 2007). Three works that examine the food issue in the context of other issues are *Global Warming and Agriculture: Impact Estimates by Country* (William R. Cline, Peterson Institute, 2007); *Eating Fossil Fuels: Oil, Food and the Coming Crisis in Agriculture* (Dale Allen Pfeiffer, New Society Publishers, 2006); and *Climate Change and Food Security: Adapting Agriculture to a Warmer World* (David Lobell and Marshall Burke, eds., Springer, 2009). A comprehensive look at the world food future is Richard Heinberg's "What Will We Eat as the Oil Runs Out?" (Global Public Media, December 2007). Finally, see *Global Food and Agricultural Institutions* (D. John Shaw, Routledge, 2008) and *The Fight over Food: Producers, Consumers, and Activists Challenge the Global Food System* (Wynne Wright and Gerad Middendorf, eds., Pennsylvania State University Press, 2008).

ISSUE 8

Is the Threat of Global Warming Real?

YES: David Biello, from "State of the Science: Beyond the Worst Case Climate Change Scenario," *Scientific American* (November 26, 2007)

NO: Richard S. Lindzen, from "No Global Warming," *Environment News,* The Heartland Institute (August 2006)

ISSUE SUMMARY

YES: David Biello summarizes the 2007 report of the United Nations Intergovernmental Panel on Climate Change (IPCC), which concludes that climate change is unequivocal, almost certain to be caused by human activity.

NO: Richard S. Lindzen takes issue with those who suggest that "the debate in the scientific community is over" regarding the existence of global warming, and argues that to believe in such warming requires one to "ignore the truly inconvenient facts."

In December 2007, the Intergovernmental Panel on Climate Change (IPCC) and former U.S. Vice President Al Gore, were jointly awarded the Nobel Peace Prize for their work "to build up and disseminate greater knowledge about man-made climate change, and to lay the foundations for measures" to counteract such change. This was the culmination of a story that began 15 years earlier at the UN-sponsored Earth Summit in Rio de Janeiro in 1992, when a Global Climate Treaty was signed. According to S. Fred Singer in *Hot Talks, Cold Science: Global Warming's Unfinished Debate* (Independent Institute, 1998), the treaty rested on three basic assumptions. First, global warming has been detected in the records of climate of the last 100 years. Second, a substantial warming in the future will produce catastrophic consequences—droughts, floods, storms, a rapid and significant rise in sea level, agricultural collapse, and the spread of tropical disease. And third, the scientific and policymaking communities know: (1) which atmospheric concentrations of greenhouse gases are dangerous and which ones are not, (2) that drastic reductions of carbon dioxide (CO_2) emissions as well as energy use in general by industrialized countries will stabilize CO_2 concentrations at close to current levels, and (3) that such economically damaging measures can be justified politically despite no significant scientific support for global warming as a threat.

Since the Earth Summit, it appears that scientists have opted for placement into one of three camps. The first camp buys into the three assumptions outlined above. In late 1995, 2,500 leading climate scientists announced in the first Intergovernmental Panel on Climatic Change (IPCC) report that the planet was warming due to coal and gas emissions.

Scientists in a second camp suggest that although global warming has occurred and continues at the present, the source of such temperature rise cannot be ascertained yet. The conclusions of the Earth Summit were misunderstood by many in the scientific community, the second camp would suggest. For these scientists, computer models, the basis of much evidence for the first group, have not yet linked global warming to human activities.

A third group of scientists, representing a minority, argues that we cannot be certain that global warming is taking place, let alone determine its cause. They present a number of arguments in support of their position. Among them is the contention that pre-satellite data (pre-1979) showing a century-long pattern of warming is an illusion because satellite data (post-1979) reveal no such warming. Scientists in the third camp are also skeptical of studying global warming in the laboratory. They suggest, moreover, that most of the scientists who have opted for one of the first two camps have done so as a consequence of laboratory experiments, rather than of evidence from the real world.

Despite what appear to be wide differences in scientific thinking about the existence of global warming and its origins, the global community has moved forward with attempts to achieve consensus among the nations of the world for taking appropriate action to curtail human activities thought to affect warming. A 1997 international meeting in Kyoto, Japan, concluded with an agreement for reaching goals established at the earlier Earth Summit. Thirty-eight industrialized countries, including the United States, agreed to reduction levels outlined in the treaty. However, the U.S. Senate never ratified the treaty, and the Bush administration decided not to support it. Nonetheless, the two basic criteria for going into effect—the required number of countries (55) with the required levels of carbon dioxide's emissions (55 percent of carbon dioxide emissions from developed countries) must sign the treaty—were met when Russia ratified the treaty on November 18, 2004. The treaty went into effect on February 19, 2005.

In the 2007 ICPP report (fourth in the series of IPCC reports), more than 2,500 scientists reaffirmed the existence of global warming. The first selection summarizes this most recent IPCC report. It suggests that among the risks are warming temperatures, heat waves, heavy rains, drought, stronger storms, decreased biodiversity, and sea-level rise. The second selection by Richard Lindzen, an MIT science professor, is one of the many writings by the author that attacks the basic thesis of the global warming advocates and the science on which it is based.

YES

David Biello

State of the Science: Beyond the Worst Case Climate Change Scenario

Climate change is "unequivocal" and it is 90 percent certain that the "net effect of human activities since 1750 has been one of warming," the Intergovernmental Panel on Climate Change (IPCC)—a panel of more than 2,500 scientists and other experts—wrote in its first report on the physical science of global warming earlier this year. In its second assessment, the IPCC stated that human-induced warming is having a discernible influence on the planet, from species migration to thawing permafrost. Despite these findings, emissions of the greenhouse gases driving this process continue to rise thanks to increased burning of fossil fuels while cost-effective options for decreasing them have not been adopted, the panel found in its third report.

The IPCC's fourth and final assessment of the climate change problem—known as the Synthesis Report—combines all of these reports and adds that "warming could lead to some impacts that are abrupt or irreversible, depending upon the rate and magnitude of the climate change." Although countries continue to debate the best way to address this finding, 130 nations, including the U.S., China, Australia, Canada, and even Saudi Arabia, have concurred with it.

"The governments now require, in fact, that the authors report on risks that are high and 'key' because of their potentially very high consequence," says economist Gary Yohe, a lead author on the IPCC Synthesis Report. "They have, perhaps, given the planet a chance to save itself."

Among those risks:

Warming temperatures. Continued global warming is virtually certain (or more than 99 percent likely to occur) at this point, leading to both good and bad impacts. On the positive side, fewer people will die from freezing temperatures and agricultural yield will increase in colder areas. The negatives include reduced crop production in the tropics and subtropics, increased insect outbreaks, diminished water supply caused by dwindling snowpack, and increasingly poor air quality in cities.

From *Scientific American*, November 26, 2007. Copyright © 2007 by Scientific American. Reprinted by permission. www.sciam.com

143

Heat waves. Scientists are more than 90 percent certain that episodes of extreme heat will increase worldwide, leading to increased danger of wildfires, human deaths and water quality issues such as algal blooms.

Heavy rains. Scientific estimates suggest that extreme precipitation events— from downpours to whiteouts—are more than 90 percent likely to become more common, resulting in diminished water quality and increased flooding, crop damage, soil erosion and disease risk.

Drought. Scientists estimate that there is a more than 66 percent chance that droughts will become more frequent and widespread, making water scarcer, upping the risk of starvation through failed crops and further increasing the risk of wildfires.

Stronger storms. Warming ocean waters will likely increase the power of tropical cyclones (variously known as hurricanes and typhoons), raising the risk of human death, injury, and disease as well as destroying coral reefs and property.

Biodiversity. As many as a third of the species known to science may be at risk of extinction if average temperatures rise by more than 1.5 degrees Celsius.

Sea level rise. The level of the world's oceans will rise, likely inundating low-lying land, turning freshwater brackish and potentially triggering widespread migration of human populations from affected areas.

"As temperatures rise, thermal expansion will lead to sea-level rise, independent of melting ice," says chemical engineer Lenny Bernstein, another lead author of the recent IPCC report. "The indications are that this factor alone could cause serious problems [and] ice-sheet melting would greatly accelerate [it]."

Such ice-sheet melting, which the IPCC explicitly did not include in its predictions of sea-level rise, has already been observed and may be speeding up, according to recent research that determined that the melting of Greenland's ice cap has accelerated to six times the average flow of the Colorado River. Research has also shown that the world has consistently emitted greenhouse gases at the highest projected levels examined and sea-level rise has also outpaced projections from the IPCC's last assessment in 2001.

"We are above the high scenario now," says climatologist Stephen Schneider of Stanford University, an IPCC lead author. "This is not a safe world."

Other recent findings include:

Carbon intensity increasing. The amount of carbon dioxide per car built, burger served or widget sold had been consistently declining until the turn of the century. But since 2000, CO_2 emissions have grown by more than 3 percent annually. This is largely due to the economic booms in China and India, which rely on polluting coal to power production. But emissions in the developed world have started to rise as well, increasing by 2.6 percent since 2000, according to reports made by those countries to the United Nations Framework Convention on Climate Change. Researchers at the Massachusetts Institute of Technology also recently argued that U.S. emissions may continue to increase as a result of growing energy demand.

Carbon sinks slowing.   The world's oceans and forests are absorbing less of the CO_2 released by human activity, resulting in a faster rise in atmospheric levels of greenhouse gases. All told, humanity released 9.9 billion metric tons (2.18×10^{13} pounds) of carbon in 2006 at the same time that the ability of the North Atlantic to take in such emissions, for example, dropped by 50 percent.

Impacts accelerating.   Warming temperatures have prompted earlier springs in the far north and have caused plant species to spread farther into formerly icy terrain. Meanwhile, sea ice in the Arctic reached a record low this year, covering just 1.59 million square miles and thus shattering the previous 2005 minimum of 2.05 million square miles.

"The observed rate of loss is faster than anything predicted," says senior research scientist Mark Serreze of the U.S. National Snow and Ice Data Center in Boulder, Colo. "We're already set up for another big loss next year. We've got so much open water in the Arctic now that has absorbed so much energy over the summer that the ocean has warmed. The ice that grows back this autumn will be thin."

The negative consequences of such reinforcing, positive feedbacks (white ice is replaced by dark water, which absorbs more energy and prevents the formation of more white ice) remain even when they seemingly work in our favor.

For example, scientists at the Leibniz Institute of Marine Sciences at the University of Kiel in Germany recently discovered that plankton consumes more carbon at higher atmospheric concentrations of CO_2. "The plankton were carbon-enriched," says marine biologist Ulf Riebesell, who conducted the study. "There weren't more of them, but each cell had more carbon."

This could mean that microscopic ocean plants may potentially absorb more of the carbon emitted into the atmosphere. Unfortunately, other research (from the Woods Hole Oceanographic Institution) has shown that such plankton does not make it to the seafloor in large enough amounts to sequester the carbon in the long term.

Further, such carbon-heavy plankton do not begin to appear until CO_2 concentrations reach twice present values—750 parts per million (ppm) in the atmosphere compared with roughly 380 ppm presently (a level at which catastrophic change may be a certainty)—and they are less nutritious to all the animals that rely on them for food. "This mechanism is both too small and too late," Riebesell says. "By becoming more carbon-rich, zooplankton have to eat more phytoplankton to achieve the same nutrition" and, therefore, "they grow and reproduce more slowly."

The IPCC notes that there are cost-effective solutions, such as retrofitting buildings for energy efficiency, but says they must be implemented in short order to stem further damage. "We are 25 years too late," Schneider says. "If the object is to avoid dangerous change, we've already had it. The object now is to avoid really dangerous change."

Richard S. Lindzen

No Global Warming

According to Al Gore's new film "An Inconvenient Truth," we're in for "a planetary emergency": melting ice sheets, huge increases in sea levels, more and stronger hurricanes, and invasions of tropical disease, among other cataclysms—unless we change the way we live now.

Bill Clinton has become the latest evangelist for Mr. Gore's proposal, proclaiming that current weather events show that he and Mr. Gore were right about global warming, and we are all suffering the consequences of President Bush's obtuseness on the matter. And why not? Mr. Gore assures us that "the debate in the scientific community is over."

That statement, which Mr. Gore made in an interview with George Stephanopoulos on ABC, ought to have been followed by an asterisk. What exactly is this debate that Mr. Gore is referring to? Is there really a scientific community that is debating all these issues and then somehow agreeing in unison? Far from such a thing being over, it has never been clear to me what this "debate" actually is in the first place.

The media rarely help, of course. When *Newsweek* featured global warming in a 1988 issue, it was claimed that all scientists agreed. Periodically thereafter it was revealed that although there had been lingering doubts beforehand, now all scientists did indeed agree. Even Mr. Gore qualified his statement on ABC only a few minutes after he made it, clarifying things in an important way. When Mr. Stephanopoulos confronted Mr. Gore with the fact that the best estimates of rising sea levels are far less dire than he suggests in his movie, Mr. Gore defended his claims by noting that scientists "don't have any models that give them a high level of confidence" one way or the other and went on to claim—*in his defense*—that scientists "don't know. . . . They just don't know."

So, presumably, those scientists do not belong to the "consensus." Yet their research is forced, whether the evidence supports it or not, into Mr. Gore's preferred global warming template—namely, shrill alarmism. To believe it requires that one ignore the truly inconvenient facts. To take the issue of rising sea levels, these include: that the Arctic was as warm or warmer in 1940; that icebergs have been known since time immemorial; that the evidence so far suggests that the Greenland ice sheet is actually growing on average. A likely result of all this is increased pressure pushing ice off the coastal perimeter of that country, which is depicted so ominously in

From *Environmental News*, August 2006; originally appeared in *The Wall Street Journal*, July 2, 2006. Copyright © 2006 by Richard S. Lindzen. Reprinted by permission of the author.

Mr. Gore's movie. In the absence of factual context, these images are perhaps dire or alarming.

They are less so otherwise. Alpine glaciers have been retreating since the early 19th century, and were advancing for several centuries before that. Since about 1970, many of the glaciers have stopped retreating and some are now advancing again. And, frankly, we don't know why.

The other elements of the global-warming scare scenario are predicated on similar oversights. Malaria, claimed as a byproduct of warming, was once common in Michigan and Siberia and remains common in Siberia—mosquitoes don't require tropical warmth. Hurricanes, too, vary on multidecadal time scales; sea-surface temperature is likely to be an important factor. This temperature, itself, varies on multidecadal time scales. However, questions concerning the origin of the relevant sea-surface temperatures and the nature of trends in hurricane intensity are being hotly argued within the profession. Even among those arguing, there is general agreement that we can't attribute any particular hurricane to global warming. To be sure, there is one exception, Greg Holland of the National Center for Atmospheric Research in Boulder, Colo., who argues that it must be global warming because he can't think of anything else. While arguments like these, based on lassitude, are becoming rather common in climate assessments, such claims, given the primitive state of weather and climate science, are hardly compelling.

A general characteristic of Mr. Gore's approach is to assiduously ignore the fact that the Earth and its climate are dynamic; they are always changing even without any external forcing. To treat all change as something to fear is bad enough; to do so in order to exploit that fear is much worse. Regardless, these items are clearly not issues over which debate is ended—at least not in terms of the actual science.

A clearer claim as to what debate has ended is provided by the environmental journalist Gregg Easterbrook. He concludes that the scientific community now agrees that significant warming is occurring, and that there is clear evidence of human influences on the climate system. This is still a most peculiar claim. At some level, it has never been widely contested. Most of the climate community has agreed since 1988 that global mean temperatures have increased on the order of one degree Fahrenheit over the past century, having risen significantly from about 1919 to 1940, decreased between 1940 and the early '70s, increased again until the '90s, and remaining essentially flat since 1998.

There is also little disagreement that levels of carbon dioxide in the atmosphere have risen from about 280 parts per million by volume in the 19th century to about 387 ppmv today. Finally, there has been no question whatever that carbon dioxide is an infrared absorber (i.e., a greenhouse gas—albeit a minor one), and its increase should theoretically contribute to warming. Indeed, if all else were kept equal, the increase in carbon dioxide should have led to somewhat more warming than has been observed, assuming that the small observed increase was in fact due to increasing carbon dioxide rather than a natural fluctuation in the climate system. Although no cause for alarm rests on this issue, there has been an intense effort to claim that the theoretically expected contribution from additional carbon dioxide has actually been detected.

Given that we do not understand the natural internal variability of climate change, this task is currently impossible. Nevertheless there has been a persistent effort to suggest otherwise, and with surprising impact. Thus, although the conflicted state of the affair was accurately presented in the 1996 text of the Intergovernmental Panel on Climate Change, the infamous "summary for policy makers" reported ambiguously that "The balance of evidence suggests a discernible human influence on global climate." This sufficed as the smoking gun for Kyoto.

The next IPCC report again described the problems surrounding what has become known as the attribution issue: that is, to explain what mechanisms are responsible for observed changes in climate. Some deployed the lassitude argument—e.g., we can't think of an alternative—to support human attribution. But the "summary for policy makers" claimed in a manner largely unrelated to the actual text of the report that "In the light of new evidence and taking into account the remaining uncertainties, most of the observed warming over the last 50 years is likely to have been due to the increase in greenhouse gas concentrations."

In a similar vein, the National Academy of Sciences issued a brief (15-page) report responding to questions from the White House. It again enumerated the difficulties with attribution, but again the report was preceded by a front end that ambiguously claimed that "The changes observed over the last several decades are likely mostly due to human activities, but we cannot rule out that some significant part of these changes is also a reflection of natural variability." This was sufficient for CNN's Michelle Mitchell to presciently declare that the report represented a "unanimous decision that global warming is real, is getting worse and is due to man. There is no wiggle room." Well, no.

More recently, a study in the journal *Science* by the social scientist Nancy Oreskes claimed that a search of the ISI Web of Knowledge Database for the years 1993 to 2003 under the key words "global climate change" produced 928 articles, all of whose abstracts supported what she referred to as the consensus view. A British social scientist, Benny Peiser, checked her procedure and found that only 913 of the 928 articles had abstracts at all, and that only 13 of the remaining 913 explicitly endorsed the so-called consensus view. Several actually opposed it.

Even more recently, the Climate Change Science Program, the Bush administration's coordinating agency for global-warming research, declared it had found "clear evidence of human influences on the climate system." This, for Mr. Easterbrook, meant: "Case closed." What exactly was this evidence? The models imply that greenhouse warming should impact atmospheric temperatures more than surface temperatures, and yet satellite data showed no warming in the atmosphere since 1979. The report showed that selective corrections to the atmospheric data could lead to some warming, thus reducing the conflict between observations and models descriptions of what greenhouse warming should look like. That, to me, means the case is still very much open.

So what, then, is one to make of this alleged debate? I would suggest at least three points.

First, nonscientists generally do not want to bother with understanding the science. Claims of consensus relieve policy types, environmental advocates, and politicians of any need to do so. Such claims also serve to intimidate the public and even scientists—especially those outside the area of climate dynamics.

Secondly, given that the question of human attribution largely cannot be resolved, its use in promoting visions of disaster constitutes nothing so much as a bait-and-switch scam. That is an inauspicious beginning to what Mr. Gore claims is not a political issue but a "moral" crusade.

Lastly, there is a clear attempt to establish truth not by scientific methods but by perpetual repetition. An earlier attempt at this was accompanied by tragedy. Perhaps Marx was right. This time around we may have farce—if we're lucky.

POSTSCRIPT

Is the Threat of Global Warming Real?

The issue of global warming is to the current era what acid rain was to the 1970s. Just as the blighted trees and polluted lakes of Scandinavia captured the hearts of the then newly emerging group of environmentalists, the issue of global warming has been front page news for over a decade and fodder for environmentalists and policymakers everywhere. Library citations abound, making it the most often written about global issue today. Web sites pop up, public interest groups emerge, and scientists and nonscientists pick up the rallying cry for one side or another. "Googling" the words "global warming" on the Internet yields over 44 million responses.

In a sense, the issue of global warming is a prototype of the contemporary issue making its way onto the global agenda. Recall that a global issue is characterized by disagreement over the extent of the condition, disagreement over the causes of the condition, disagreement over desirable future alternatives to the present condition, and disagreement over appropriate policies to reach desired end states.

All of these characteristics are present in global warming. Both sides of the issue can find a substantial number of scientists, measured in the thousands, to support their case that the Earth is or is not warming. Both sides can find hundreds of experts who will attest that the warming is either a cyclical phenomenon or the consequence of human behavior. Both sides can find a substantial number of policymakers and policy observers who will say that the Kyoto Treaty is humankind's best hope to reverse the global warming trend or that the treaty is seriously flawed with substantial negative consequences for the United States. It is an issue whose debate heats up on occasion as the international community grapples with answers to the various disagreements summarized earlier. Finally, it is an issue whose potential solutions will impact different sectors of the economy and different countries differently.

The IPCC 2001 report concludes the following. First, the global average surface temperature has risen over the twentieth century by about 0.6°C. Two, temperatures have risen during the past four decades in the lowest 8 kilometers of the atmosphere. Third, snow cover and ice extent have decreased. Fourth, global average sea level has risen, and ocean heat has increased. Fifth, changes have occurred in other important aspects of climate. Sixth, concentrations of atmospheric greenhouse gases have continued to increase as a result of human activity. Seventh, there is new and stronger evidence that most of the warming observed over the last 50 years is attributable to human activities. Eighth, human influences will continue to change atmospheric composition through-out the twenty-first century. Ninth, global average temperature and sea level are projected to rise under all IPCC scenarios. And tenth, climate change will persist for many centuries. The list is impressive.

The 2007 IPCC report suggested the following conclusions: First, "warm-ing of the climate system is unequivocal." Second, many natural systems around the world "are being affected by regional climate changes." Third, glo-bal greenhouse gases have grown 70 percent between 1970 and 2004. Fourth, global emissions of greenhouse gases "will continue to grow over the next few decades." And fifth, the consequences of these four conclusions will lead to the set of risks mentioned earlier. A number of books published since the 2007 Report echo and elaborate on its findings. Two such are *Dire Predictions: Understanding Global Warming* (DK ADULT, 2008) and *The Global Deal: Climate Change and the Creation of a New Era of Progress and Prosperity* (Nicholas Stern, Public Affairs, 2009).

Yet others argue the opposite position. In their comprehensive book on the subject (*Taken by Storm: The Troubled Science, Policy and Politics of Global Warming,* Key Porter Books, 2002), Christopher Essex and Ross McKitrick lay out a series of nine statements that comprise the "Doctrine" of global warm-ing. In their analysis of these components, they conclude that the evidence simply does not warrant the global community's undertaking policy making at this time to address a problem that may not exist or may have been caused by some other phenomena. Others sources include *A Question of Balance: Weigh-ing the Options on Global Warming Policies* (William D. Nordhaus, Yale Univer-sity Press, 2008) and *An Appeal to Reason: A Cool Look at Global Warming* (Nigel Lawson, Gerald Duckworth & Co., 2009).

Richard Lindzen has been an active critic of global warming advocates, testifying before the American Congress from time to time as well as publish-ing in the more popular media (see, for example, "Climate of Fear," *The Wall Street Journal,* April 12, 2006).

This view is a shared one. Brian Tucker's 1997 article in *The National Interest* ("Science Fiction: The Politics of Global Warming") suggests that science "does not support the conclusion that calamitous effects from global warming are nigh upon us." He continues: "There is no scientific justification for such a view." Tucker raises the stakes by asserting that the global warming controversy is much more than a debate about the causes and extent of the phenomenon. It is also about global development, power, and morality in the struggle between the rich and poor countries, with population "control" a central issue. This view is echoed by John R. Christy in "The Global Warm-ing Fiasco" (*Global Warming and Other Eco-Myths,* Ronald Bailey, Forum, 2002). He accuses those who suggest global warming is a major problem of adhering to the science of "calamitology" rather than the science of "climatology." His bottom line assessment is that "No global climate disaster is looming." Other sources include *Climate of Extremes: Global Warming Science They Don't Want You to Know* (Patrick J. Michaels, Cato Institute, 2009); *Climate Confusion: How Global Warming Hysteria Leads to Bad Science, Pandering Politicians and Misguided Policies That Hurt the Poor* (Roy Spencer, Encounter Books, 2008); and *The Deniers: The*

World Renowned Scientists Who Stood Up Against Global Warming Hysteria, Political Persecution, and Fraud (Richard Vigilante Books, 2008).

The Heartland Institute (www.heartland.org/studies/ieguide.htm) suggests "seven facts" to counteract observations such as those of the recent and earlier IPCC studies. First, "most scientists do not believe human activities threaten to disrupt the earth's climate." Second, "the most reliable temperature data show no global warming trend." Third, "global computer models are too crude to predict future climate changes." Fourth, "the IPCC did not prove that human activities are causing global warming" (a reference to the 1995 study). Fifth, "a modest amount of global warming, should it occur, would be beneficial to the natural world and to human civilization." Sixth, "reducing our greenhouse gas emissions would be costly and would not stop global warming." And seventh, "the best strategy to pursue is one of 'no regrets.'" The latter refers to the idea that it is not better to be safe than sorry (suggested by the other side), as immediate action will not make us safer, just poorer. Another sharp critique of the 2001 IPCC report is a Web-based book by Vincent Gray, *The Greenhouse Delusion: Critique of "Climate Change 2001": The Scientific Basis* (http://www.john-daly.com/tar-2000/summary.htm). Another oft-published critic is Bill McKibben (see, for example, "The Real News About Global Warming," *The New York Review of Books,* March 15, 2007).

The above references capture the extreme distance between the two sides in the debate. Other sources are equally certain of their position. Ross Gelbson in *The Heat Is On: The High Stakes Battle Over Earth's Threatened Climate* (Addison-Wesley, 1997) examines "the campaign of deception by big coal and big oil" that is keeping the global warming issue off the public policy agenda.

Three other studies make valuable reading, each one of which takes a different position (one each at the extreme ends of the debate and a third one that suggests moderate climate change.) S. Fred Singer's *Hot Talk; Cold Science: Global Warming's Unfinished Debate* (Independent Institute, 1998) enhances the author's reputation as one of the leading opponents of global warming's adverse consequences. At the other extreme, John Houghton, in *Global Warming: The Complete Briefing,* 2d ed. (Cambridge University Press, 1997), accepts global warming as a significant concern and describes how it can be reversed in the future. S. George Philander, in *Is the Temperature Rising?* (1998), concludes that the global temperatures will rise 2°C over several decades, creating the prospect of some regional climate changes, with major consequences. Roy W. Spencer's "How Do We Know the Temperature of the Earth?" (Ronald Bailey, ed., *Earth Report 2000,* 2000), presents a basic argument with evidence that the popular perception of global warming as an environmental catastrophe cannot be supported with evidence. Finally, an objective analysis of the issue can be found in Chapter 5 ("Is the Earth Warming?") of Jack M. Hollander's *The Real Environmental Crisis* (University of California Press, 2003).

For an official U.S. government Web site on global warming, see www.epa.gov/climatechange/index.html. Another U.S. government site is www.usgcrp.gov. A relevant Web site for a worldwide network of over 430 nongovernmental organizations, termed the Climate Action Network (CAN), is http://www.climatenetwork.org. Another site is http://earthsave.org/globalwarming.htm (EarthSave).

A book that presents in layman's terms the story of global warming is *Time Magazine's Global Warming* (2007). Al Gore's documentary, *An Inconvenient Truth* (both in DVD and in print, 2006), has become the poster source for those who support the link between human behavior and rises in global temperature. A source arguing that global warming is a recurring phenomenon and is caused by the sun is *Unstoppable Global Warming: Every 1,500 Years* by Dennis T. Avery and S. Fred Singer (Roman & Littlefield, 2007). Other anti-global warming books are Christopher C. Horner's *The Politically Incorrect Guide to Global Warming and Environmentalism* (Regnery Publishers, 2007); *Shattered Consensus: The True State of Global Warming* by Patrick J. Michaels (Rowan & Littlefield, 2005); and *Meltdown: The Predictable Distortion of Global Warming by Scientists, Politicians and the Media* (CATO Institute, 2005). A much more balanced book that lays out the conflicting claims in the debate is *The Science and Politics of Global Climate Change: A Guide to the Debate* by Andrew E. Dessler and Edward A. Parson (Cambridge University Press, 2006). An earlier readable and balanced account is Frances Drake's *Global Warming: The Science of Climate Change* (Hodder Arnold Publication, 2000).

Four recent overviews of the global warming issues are *Global Warming: A Very Short Introduction* (Mark Maslin, Oxford University Press, 2009); *Global Warming: The Complete Briefing* (John Houghton, Cambridge University Press, 2009); *A–Z of Global Warming* (Simon Rosser, Schmall World Publishing, 2008); and *The Global Warming Debate: Science, Economics, and Policy* (Kerry A. Lynch, American Institute for Economic Research, 2008).

What are we to make of all of this? Simply put, whether or not global warming exists and is caused by human behavior, the issue will remain on the front page until agreement can be reached on these two fundamental questions.

ISSUE 9

Is the Threat of a Global Water Shortage Real?

YES: Mark Clayton, from "Is Water Becoming 'the New Oil'?" *Christian Science Monitor* (May 29, 2008)

NO: Bjørn Lomborg, from *The Skeptical Environment: Measuring the Real State of the World* (Cambridge University Press, 2001)

ISSUE SUMMARY

YES: Mark Clayton, staff writer for *The Christian Science Monitor*, suggests that changes in population, pollution, and climate are creating water shortages around the globe, leading private companies to take advantage of the increased demand for clean water while governments are slow to act.

NO: Lomborg contends that water is not only plentiful but is a renewable resource that, if properly treated as valuable, should not pose a future problem.

Water shortages and other water problems are occurring with greater frequency, particularly in large cities. Some observers have speculated that the situation is reminiscent of the fate that befell ancient glorious cities like Rome. Recognition that the supply of water is a growing problem is not new. As early as 1964, the United Nations Environmental Programme (UNEP) revealed that close to a billion people were at risk from desertification. At the Earth Summit in Rio in 1992, world leaders reaffirmed that desertification was of serious concern.

Moreover, in conference after conference and study after study, increasing population growth and declining water supplies and quality are being linked together, as is the relationship between the planet's ability to meet its growing food needs and available water. Lester R. Brown, in "Water Deficits Growing in Many Countries: Water Shortages May Cause Food Shortages," *Eco-Economy Update 2002–11* (August 6, 2002), sums up the problem this way: "The world is incurring a vast water deficit. It is largely invisible, historically recent, and growing fast." The World Water Council's study "World Water Actions Report, Third Draft" (October 31, 2002) describes the problem in much the same way:

"Water is no longer taken for granted as a plentiful resource that will always be available when we need it." Some scholars are now arguing that water shortage is likely to become the twenty-first century's analog to the oil crisis of the last half of the previous century. The one major difference, as scholars are quick to point out, is that water is not like oil; there is no substitute.

Proclamations of impending water problems abound. Peter Gleick, in *The World's Water 1998–99: The Biennial Report on Freshwater Resources* (Island Press, 1998), reports that the demand for freshwater increased sixfold between 1900 and 1995, twice the rate of population growth. The UN study "United Nations Comprehensive Assessment of Freshwater Resources of the World" (1997) suggested that one-third of the world's population live in countries having medium to high water stress. One 2001 headline reporting the release of a new study proclaimed that "Global thirst 'will turn millions into water refugees'" (The Millennium Environment Debate, 1999). News reports released by the UN Food and Agricultural Organization in conjunction with World Food Day 2002 asserted that water scarcity could result in millions of people having inadequate access to clean water or sufficient food. And the World Meteorological Organization predicts that two out of every three people will live in water-stressed conditions by 2050 if consumption patterns remain the same.

Sandra Postel, in *Pillar of Sand: Can the Irrigation Miracle Last?* (W.W. Norton, 1999), suggests another variant of the water problem. For her, the time-tested method of maximizing water usage in the past, irrigation, may not be feasible as world population marches toward 7 billion. She points to the inadequacy of surface water supplies, increasing depletion of groundwater supplies, the salinization of the land, and the conversion of traditional agricultural land to other uses as reasons for the likely inability of irrigation to be a continuing panacea. Yet the 1997 UN study concluded that annual irrigation use would need to increase 30 percent for annual food production to double, necessary for meeting food demands of 2025.

The issue of water quality is also in the news. The World Health Organization reports that in some parts of the world, up to 80 percent of all transmittable diseases are attributable to the consumption of contaminated water. Also, a UNEP-sponsored study, *Global Environment Outlook 2000*, reported that 200 scientists from 50 countries pointed to the shortage of clean water as one of the most pressing global issues.

In the following selection, Mark Clayton argues that the changing human and physical environment is producing water shortages but that governments are slow to respond, while private companies exploit the situation. In the second selection, Bjørn Lomborg takes issue with the prevailing opinion in the global water debate. His argument can be summed up in his simple quote: "Basically, we have sufficient water." Lomborg maintains that water supplies rose during the twentieth century and that we have gained access to more water through technology.

YES

Mark Clayton

Is Water Becoming the New Oil?

Public fountains are dry in Barcelona, Spain, a city so parched there's a (9,000 ($13,000) fine if you're caught watering your flowers. A tanker ship docked there this month carrying 5 million gallons of precious fresh water—and officials are scrambling to line up more such shipments to slake public thirst.

Barcelona is not alone. Cyprus will ferry water from Greece this summer. Australian cities are buying water from that nation's farmers and building desalination plants. Thirsty China plans to divert Himalayan water. And 18 million southern Californians are bracing for their first water-rationing in years.

"Water," Dow Chemical Chairman Andrew Liveris told the World Economic Forum in February, "is the oil of this century." Developed nations have taken cheap, abundant fresh water largely for granted. Now global population growth, pollution, and climate change are shaping a new view of water as "blue gold."

Water's hot-commodity status has snared the attention of big equipment suppliers like General Electric as well as big private water companies that buy or manage municipal supplies—notably France-based Suez and Aqua America, the largest US-based private water company.

Global water markets, including drinking water distribution, management, waste treatment, and agriculture, are a nearly $500 billion market and growing fast, says a 2007 global investment report.

But governments pushing to privatize costly-to-maintain public water systems are colliding with a global "water is a human right" movement. Because water is essential for human life, its distribution is best left to more publicly accountable government authorities to distribute at prices the poorest can afford, those water warriors say.

"We're at a transition point where fundamental decisions need to be made by societies about how this basic human need—water—is going to be provided," says Christopher Kilian, clean-water program director for the Boston-based Conservation Law Foundation. "The profit motive and basic human need [for water] are just inherently in conflict."

Will "peak water" displace "peak oil" as the central resource question? Some see such a scenario rising.

"What's different now is that it's increasingly obvious that we're running up against limits to new [fresh water] supplies," says Peter Gleick, a water

From *The Christian Science Monitor*, May 29, 2008. Copyright © 2008 by Christian Science Monitor. Reprinted by permission. www.CSMonitor.com

expert and president of the Pacific Institute for Studies in Development, Environment, and Security, a nonpartisan think tank in Oakland, Calif. "It's no longer cheap and easy to drill another well or dam another river."

The idea of "peak water" is an imperfect analogy, he says. Unlike oil, water is not used up but only changes forms. The world still has the same 326 quintillion gallons, NASA estimates.

But some 97 percent of it is salty. The world's remaining accessible fresh-water supplies are divided among industry (20 percent), agriculture (70 percent), and domestic use (10 percent), according to the United Nations.

Meanwhile, fresh-water consumption worldwide has more than doubled since World War II, to nearly 4,000 cubic kilometers annually, and set to rise another 25 percent by 2030, says a 2007 report by the Zurich-based Sustainable Asset Management (SAM) group investment firm.

Up to triple that is available for human use, so there should be plenty, the report says. But waste, climate change, and pollution have left clean water supplies running short.

"We have ignored demand for decades, just assuming supplies of water would be there," Dr. Gleick says. "Now we have to learn to manage water demand and—on top of that—deal with climate change, too."

Population and economic growth across Asia and the rest of the developing world is a major factor driving fresh-water scarcity. The earth's human population is predicted to rise from 6 billion to about 9 billion by 2050, the UN reports. Feeding them will mean more irrigation for crops.

Increasing attention is also being paid to the global "virtual water" trade. It appears in food or other products that require water to produce, products that are then exported to another nation. The US may consume even more water—virtual water—by importing goods that require lots of water to make. At the same time, the US exports virtual water through goods it sells abroad.

As scarcity drives up the cost of fresh water, more efficient use of water will play a huge role, experts say, including:

- Superefficient drip irrigation is far more frugal than "flood" irrigation. But water's low cost in the US provides little incentive to build new irrigation systems.
- Aging, leaking water pipes waste billions of gallons daily. The cost to fix them could be $500 billion over the next 30 years, the federal government estimates.
- Desalination. Dozens of plants are in planning stages or under construction in the US and abroad, reports say.
- Privatization. When private for-profit companies sell at a price based on what it costs to produce water, that higher price curbs water waste and water consumption, economists say.

In the US today, about 33.5 million Americans get their drinking water from privately owned utilities that make up about 16 percent of the nation's community water systems, according to the National Association of Water Companies, a trade association.

"While water is essential to life, and we believe everyone deserves the right of access to water, that doesn't mean water is free or should be provided free," says Peter Cook, executive director of the NAWC. "Water should be priced at the cost to provide it—and subsidized for those who can't afford it."

But private companies' promises of efficient, cost-effective water delivery have not always come true. Bolivia ejected giant engineering firm Bechtel in 2000, unhappy over the spiking cost of water for the city of Cochabamba. Last year Bolivia's president publicly celebrated the departure of French water company Suez, which had held a 30-year contract to supply La Paz.

In her book *Blue Covenant,* Maude Barlow—one of the leaders of the fledgling "water justice" movement—sees a dark future if private monopolies control access to fresh water. She sees this happening when, instead of curbing pollution and increasing conservation, governments throw up their hands and sell public water companies to the private sector or contract with private desalination companies.

"Water is a public resource and a human right that should be available to all," she says. "All these companies are doing is recycling dirty water, selling it back to utilities and us at a huge price. But they haven't been as successful as they want to be. People are concerned about their drinking water and they've met resistance."

Private-water industry officials say those pushing to make water a "human right" are ideologues struggling to preserve inefficient public water authorities that sell water below the cost to produce it and so cheaply it is wasted—doing little to extend service to the poor.

"There are three basic things in life: food, water, and air," says Paul Marin, who three years ago led a successful door-to-door campaign to keep the town council of Emmaus, Pa., from selling its local water company. "In this country, we have privatized our food. Now there's a lot of interest in water on Wall Street. . . . But I can tell you it's putting the fox in charge of the henhouse to privatize water. It's a mistake."

Water and War: Will Scarcity Lead to Conflict?

Cherrapunjee, a town in eastern India, once held bragging rights as the "wettest place on earth," and still gets nearly 40 feet of rain a year. Ironically, officials recently brought in Israeli water-management experts to help manage and retain water that today sluices off the area's deforested landscape so that the area can get by in months when no rain falls.

"Global warming isn't going to change the amount of water, but some places used to getting it won't, and others that don't, will get more," says Dan Nees, a water-trading analyst with the World Resources Institute. "Water scarcity may be one of the most underappreciated global political and environmental challenges of our time." Water woes could have an impact on global peace and stability.

In January, United Nations Secretary-General Ban Ki Moon cited a report by International Alert, a self-described peacebuilding organization based in

London. The report identified 46 countries with a combined population of 2.7 billion people where contention over water has created "a high risk of violent conflict" by 2025.

In the developing world—particularly in China, India, and other parts of Asia—rising economic success means a rising demand for clean water and an increased potential for conflict. China is one of the world's fastest-growing nations, but its lakes, rivers, and groundwater are badly polluted because of the widespread dumping of industrial wastes. Tibet has huge fresh water reserves.

While news reports have generally cited Tibetans' concerns over exploitation of their natural resources by China, little has been reported about China's keen interest in Tibet's Himalayan water supplies, locked up in rapidly melting glaciers.

"It's clear that one of the key reasons that China is interested in Tibet is its water," Dr. Gleick says. "They don't want to risk any loss of control over these water resources."

The Times (London) reported in 2006 that China is proceeding with plans for nearly 200 miles of canals to divert water from the Himalayan plateau to China's parched Yellow River. China's water plans are a major problem for the Dalai Lama's government in exile, says a report released this month by Circle of Blue, a branch of the Pacific Institute, a nonpartisan think tank.

Himalayan water is particularly sensitive because it supplies the rivers that bring water to more than half a dozen Asian countries. Plans to divert water could cause intense debate.

"Once this issue of water resources comes up," wrote Elizabeth Economy, director of Asia Studies at the Council on Foreign Affairs, to Circle of Blue researchers in a report earlier this month, "and it seems inevitable at this point that it will—it also raises emerging conflicts with India and Southeast Asia."

Tibet is not the only water-rich country wary of a water-poor neighbor. Canada, which has immense fresh-water resources, is wary of its water-thirsty superpower neighbor to the south, observers say. With Lake Mead low in the US Southwest, and now Florida and Georgia squabbling over water, the US could certainly use a sip (or gulp) of Canada's supplies. (Canada has 20 percent of the world's fresh water.)

But don't look for a water pipeline from Canada's northern reaches to the US southwest anytime soon. Water raises national fervor in Canada, and Canadians are reluctant to share their birthright with a United States that has mismanaged—in Canada's eyes—its own supplies. Indeed, the prospect of losing control of its water under free-trade or other agreements is something Canadians seem to worry about constantly.

A year ago, Canada's House of Commons voted 134 to 108 in favor of a motion to recommend that its federal government "begin talks with its American and Mexican counterparts to exclude water from the scope of NAFTA." . . .

Water

There is a resource which we often take for granted but which increasingly has been touted as a harbinger of future trouble. Water.

Ever more people live on Earth and they use ever more water. Our water consumption has almost quadrupled since 1940. The obvious argument runs that "this cannot go on." This has caused government agencies to worry that "a threatening water crisis awaits just around the corner." The UN environmental report *GEO 2000* claims that the water shortage constitutes a "full-scale emergency," where "the world water cycle seems unlikely to be able to cope with the demands that will be made of it in the coming decades. Severe water shortages already hamper development in many parts of the world, and the situation is deteriorating."

The same basic argument is invoked when WWF [World Wildlife Fund] states that "freshwater is essential to human health, agriculture, industry, and natural ecosystems, but is now running scarce in many regions of the world." *Population Reports* states unequivocally that "freshwater is emerging as one of the most critical natural resource issues facing humanity." Environmental discussions are replete with buzz words like "water crisis" and "time bomb: water shortages," and *Time* magazine summarizes the global water outlook with the title "Wells running dry." The UN organizations for meteorology and education simply refer to the problem as "a world running out of water."

The water shortages are also supposed to increase the likelihood of conflicts over the last drops—and scores of articles are written about the coming "water wars." Worldwatch Institute sums up the worries nicely, claiming that "water scarcity may be to the nineties what the oil price shocks were to the seventies—a source of international conflicts and major shifts in national economies."

But these headlines are misleading. True, there may be *regional* and *logistic* problems with water. We will need to get better at using it. But basically we have sufficient water.

How Much Water in the World?

Water is absolutely decisive for human survival, and the Earth is called the Blue Planet precisely because most of it is covered by water: 71 percent of the Earth's surface is covered by water, and the total amount is estimated at

Excerpt from Chapter 13 of *The Skeptical Environmentalist: Measuring the Real State of the World* by Bjørn Lomborg, (Cambridge University Press, 2001) pp. 149–156. Copyright © 2001 by Bjørn Lomborg and David Pimentel. Reprinted by permission of Cambridge University Press and David Pimentel.

the unfathomably large 13.6 billion cubic kilometers. Of all this water, oceans make up 97.2 percent and the polar ice contains 2.15 percent. Unfortunately sea water is too saline for direct human consumption, and while polar ice contains potable water it is hardly within easy reach. Consequently, humans are primarily dependent on the last 0.65 percent water, of which 0.62 percent is groundwater.

Fresh water in the groundwater often takes centuries or millennia to build up—it has been estimated that it would require 150 years to recharge all of the groundwater in the United States totally to a depth of 750 meters if it were all removed. Thus, thoughtlessly exploiting the groundwater could be compared to mining any other non-renewable natural resource. But groundwater is continuously replenished by the constant movement of water through oceans, air, soil, rivers, and lakes in the so-called hydrological cycle. The sun makes water from the oceans evaporate, the wind moves parts of the vapor as clouds over land, where the water is released as rain and snow. The precipitated water then either evaporates again, flows back into the sea through rivers and lakes, or finds its way into the groundwater.

The total amount of precipitation on land is about 113,000 km^3, and taking into account an evaporation of 72,000 km^3 we are left with a net fresh water influx of 41,000 km^3 each year or the equivalent of 30 cm (1 foot) of water across the entire land mass. Since part of this water falls in rather remote areas, such as the basins of the Amazon, the Congo, and the remote North American and Eurasian rivers, a more reasonable, geographically accessible estimate of water is 32,900 km^3. Moreover, a large part of this water comes within short periods of time. In Asia, typically 80 percent of the runoff occurs from May to October, and globally the flood runoff is estimated at about three-quarters of the total runoff. This leaves about 9,000 km^3 to be captured. Dams capture an additional 3,500 km^3 from floods, bringing the total accessible runoff to 12,500 km^3. This is equivalent to about 5,700 liters of water for every single person on Earth *every single day*. For comparison, the average citizen in the EU uses about 566 liters of water per day. This is about 10 percent of the global level of available water and some 5 percent of the available EU water. An American, however, uses about three times as much water, or 1,442 liters every day.

Looking at global water consumption, as seen in Figure 1, it is important to distinguish between water withdrawal and water use. Water withdrawal is the amount of water physically removed, but this concept is less useful in a discussion of limits on the total amount of water, since much of the withdrawn water is later returned to the water cycle. In the EU and the US, about 46 percent of the withdrawn water is used merely as cooling water for power generation and is immediately released for further use downstream. Likewise, most industrial uses return 80–90 percent of the water, and even in irrigation 30–70 percent of the water runs back into lakes and rivers or percolates into aquifers, whence it can be reused. Thus, a more useful measure of water consumption is the amount of water this consumption causes to be irretrievably lost through evaporation or transpiration from plants. This is called water use.

Figure 1

Global, Annual Water Withdrawal and Use, in Thousand km³, and Percentage of Accessible Runoff, 1900–95, and Predictions for 2025

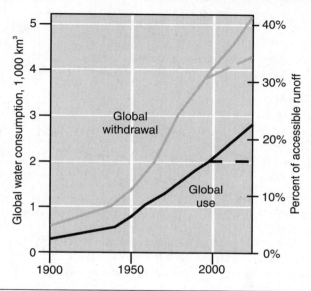

Source: Shiklomanov 2000:22 (high prediction), World Water Council 2006:26 (low prediction).

Over the twentieth century, Earth's water use has grown from about 330 km³ to about 2,100 km³. As can be seen from Figure 1 there is some uncertainty about the future use and withdrawal (mainly depending on the development of irrigation), but until now most predictions have tended to overestimate the actual water consumption by up to 100 percent. Nevertheless, total use is still less than 17 percent of the accessible water and even with the high prediction it will require just 22 percent of the readily accessible, annually renewed water in 2025.

At the same time, we have gained access to more and more water, as indicated in Figure 2. Per person we have gone from using about 1,000 liters per day to almost 2,000 liters over the past 100 years. Particularly, this is due to an approximately 50 percent increase in water use in agriculture, allowing irrigated farms to feed us better and to decrease the number of starving people. Agricultural water usage seems, however, to have stabilized below 2,000 liters per capita, mainly owing to higher efficiency and less water consumption in agriculture since 1980. This pattern is also found in the EU and the US, where consumption has increased dramatically over the twentieth century, but is now leveling off. At the same time, personal consumption (approximated by the municipal withdrawal) has more than quadrupled over the century, reflecting an increase in welfare with more easily accessible water. In developing countries, this is in large part a question of health—avoiding sickness through

Figure 2

Global Withdrawal of Water for Agriculture, Industry and Municipal Use, and Total Use, in Liters and Gallons Per Capita Per Day, 1900–95

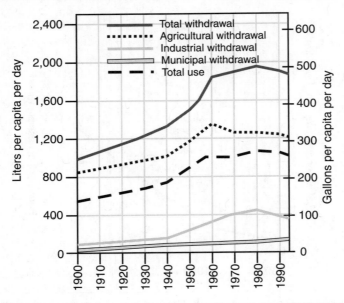

Source: Shiklomanov 2000:24.

better access to clean drinking water and sanitation, whereas in developed countries higher water use is an indication of an increased number of domestic amenities such as dishwashers and better-looking lawns.

So, if the global use is less than 17 percent of the readily accessible and renewable water and the increased use has brought us more food, less starvation, more health and increased wealth, why do we worry?

The Three Central Problems

There are three decisive problems. First, precipitation is by no means equally distributed all over the globe. This means that not all have equal access to water resources and that some countries have much less accessible water than the global average would seem to indicate. The question is whether water shortages are already severe in some places today. Second, there will be more and more people on Earth. Since precipitation levels will remain more or less constant this will mean fewer water resources for each person. The question is whether we will see more severe shortages in the future. Third, many countries receive a large part of their water resources from rivers; 261 river systems, draining just less than half of the planet's land area, are shared by two or more countries, and at least ten rivers flow through half a dozen or more countries. Most Middle Eastern countries share aquifers. This means that the water question also has an international perspective and—if cooperation breaks down—an international conflict potential.

Beyond these three problems there are two other issues, which are often articulated in connection with the water shortage problem, but which are really conceptually quite separate. One is the worry about water pollution, particularly of potable water. While it is of course important to avoid water pollution, in part because pollution restricts the presently available amount of freshwater, it is not related to the problem of water shortage *per se.* . . .

The second issue is about the shortage of *access* to water in the Third World. . . . This problem, while getting smaller, is still a major obstacle for global welfare. In discussing water shortage, reference to the lack of universal access to drinking water and sanitation is often thrown in for good measure, but of course this issue is entirely separate from the question of shortages. First, the cause is *not* lack of water (since human requirements constitute just 50–100 liters a day, which any country but Kuwait can deliver, cf. Table 1) but rather a lack of investment in infrastructure. Second, the solution lies not in cutting back on existing consumption but actually in increasing future consumption.

Finally, we should just mention global warming . . . and its connection to water use. Intuitively, we might be tempted to think that a warmer world would mean more evaporation, less water, more problems. But more evaporation also means more precipitation. Essentially, global climate models seem to change *where* water shortages appear (pushing some countries above or below the threshold) but the total changes are small (1–5 percent) and go both ways.

Not Enough Water?

Precipitation is not distributed equally. Some countries such as Iceland have almost 2 million liters of water for each inhabitant every day, whereas Kuwait must make do with just 30 liters. The question, of course, is when does a country not have *enough* water.

It is estimated that a human being needs about 2 liters of water a day, so clearly this is not the restrictive requirement. The most common approach is to use the so-called *water stress index* proposed by the hydrologist Malin Falkenmark. This index tries to establish an approximate minimum level of water per capita to maintain an adequate quality of life in a moderately developed country in an arid zone. This approach has been used by many organizations, including the World Bank, in the standard literature on environmental science, and in the water scarcity discussion in *World Resources*. With this index, human beings are assessed to need about 100 liters per day for drinking, household needs and personal hygiene, and an additional 500–2,000 liters for agriculture, industry and energy production. Since water is often most needed in the dry season, the water stress level is then set even higher—if a country has less than 4,660 liters per person available it is expected to experience periodic or regular water stress. Should the accessible runoff drop to less than

2,740 liters the country is said to experience chronic water scarcity. Below 1,370 liters, the country experiences absolute water scarcity, outright shortages and acute scarcity.

Table 1 shows the 15 countries comprising 3.7 percent of humanity in 2000 suffering chronic water scarcity according to the above definition. Many of these countries probably come as no surprise. But the question is whether we are facing a serious problem.

How does Kuwait actually get by with just 30 liters per day? The point is, it doesn't. Kuwait, Libya and Saudi Arabia all cover a large part of their water demand by exploiting the largest water resource of all—through desalination of sea water. Kuwait in fact covers more than half its total use through desalination. Desalting requires a large amount of energy (through either freezing or evaporating water), but all of these countries also have great energy resources. The price today to desalt sea water is down to 50–80¢/m^3 and just 20–35¢/m^3 for brackish water, which makes desalted water a more expensive resource than fresh water, but definitely not out of reach.

This shows two things. First, we can have sufficient water, if we can pay for it. Once again, this underscores that *poverty* and not the environment is the primary limitation for solutions to our problems. Second, desalination puts an upper boundary on the degree of water problems in the world. In principle, we could produce the Earth's entire present water consumption with a single desalination facility in the Sahara, powered by solar cells. The total area needed for the solar cells would take up less than 0.3 percent of the Sahara.

Today, desalted water makes up just 0.2 percent of all water or 2.4 percent of municipal water. Making desalination cover the total municipal water withdrawal would cost about 0.5 percent of the global GDP. This would definitely be a waste of resources, since most areas have abundant water supplies and all areas have some access to water, but it underscores the upper boundary of the water problem.

Also, there's a fundamental problem when you only look at the total water resources and yet try to answer whether there are sufficient supplies of water. The trouble is that we do not necessarily know *how* and *how wisely* the water is used. Many countries get by just fine with very limited water resources because these resources are exploited very effectively. Israel is a prime example of efficient water use. It achieves a high degree of efficiency in its agriculture, partly because it uses the very efficient drip irrigation system to green the desert, and partly because it recycles household wastewater for irrigation. Nevertheless, with just 969 liters per person per day, Israel should according to the classification be experiencing absolute water scarcity. Consequently, one of the authors in a background report for the 1997 UN document on water points out that the 2,740 liters water bench-mark is "misguidedly considered by some authorities as a critical minimum amount of water for the survival of a modern society."

Of course, the problem of faulty classification increases, the higher the limit is set. The European Environmental Agency (EEA) in its 1998 assessment somewhat incredibly suggested that countries below 13,690 liters per person per day should be classified as "low availability," making not only more than half

Table 1

Countries With Chronic Water Scarcity (Below 2,740 Liters Per Capita Per Day) in 2000, 2025, and 2050, Compared to a Number of Other Countries

Available water, liters per capita per day	2000	2025	2050
Kuwait	30	20	17
United Arab Emirates	174	129	116
Libya	275	136	92
Saudi Arabia	325	166	118
Jordan	381	203	145
Singapore	471	401	403
Yemen	665	304	197
Israel	969	738	644
Oman	1,077	448	268
Tunisia	1,147	834	709
Algeria	1,239	827	664
Burundi	1,496	845	616
Egypt	2,343	1,667	1,382
Rwanda	2,642	1,562	1,197
Kenya	2,725	1,647	1,252
Morocco	2,932	2,129	1,798
South Africa	2,959	1,911	1,497
Somalia	3,206	1,562	1,015
Lebanon	3,996	2,971	2,533
Haiti	3,997	2,497	1,783
Burkina Faso	4,202	2,160	1,430
Zimbabwe	4,408	2,830	2,199
Peru	4,416	3,191	2,680
Malawi	4,656	2,508	1,715
Ethiopia	4,849	2,354	1,508
Iran, Islamic Rep.	4,926	2,935	2,211
Nigeria	5,952	3,216	2,265
Eritrea	6,325	3,704	2,735
Lesotho	6,556	3,731	2,665
Togo	7,026	3,750	2,596
Uganda	8,046	4,017	2,725
Niger	8,235	3,975	2,573
Percent people with chronic scarcity	3.7%	8.6%	17.8%
United Kingdom	3,337	3,270	3,315
India	5,670	4,291	3,724
China	6,108	5,266	5,140
Italy	7,994	8,836	10,862
United States	24,420	20,405	19,521
Botswana	24,859	15,624	12,122
Indonesia	33,540	25,902	22,401
Bangladesh	50,293	35,855	29,576
Australia	50,913	40,077	37,930
Russian Federation	84,235	93,724	107,725
Iceland	1,660,502	1,393,635	1,289,976

Source: WRI 1998a.

the EU low on water but indeed more than 70 percent of the globe. Denmark receives 6,750 liters of fresh water per day and is one of the many countries well below this suggested limit and actually close to EEA's "very low" limit. Nevertheless, national withdrawal is just 11 percent of the available water, and it is estimated that the consumption could be almost doubled without negative environmental consequences. The director of the Danish EPA has stated that, "from the hand of nature, Denmark has access to good and clean groundwater far in excess of what we actually use."

By far the largest part of all water is used for agriculture—globally, agriculture uses 69 percent, compared to 23 percent for industry and 8 percent for households. Consequently, the greatest gains in water use come from cutting down on agricultural use. Many of the countries with low water availability therefore compensate by importing a large amount of their grain. Since a ton of grain uses about 1,000 tons of water, this is in effect a very efficient way of importing water. Israel imports about 87 percent of its grain consumption, Jordan 91 percent, Saudi Arabia 50 percent.

Summing up, more than 96 percent of all nations have at present sufficient water resources. On all continents, water accessibility has *increased* per person, and at the same time an ever higher proportion of people have gained access to clean drinking water and sanitation. While water accessibility has been getting *better* this is not to deny that there are still widespread shortages and limitations of basic services, such as access to clean drinking water, and that local and regional scarcities occur. But these problems are primarily related not to physical water scarcity but to a lack of proper water management and in the end often to lack of money—money to desalt sea water or to increase cereal imports, thereby freeing up domestic water resources.

Will It Get Worse in the Future?

The concerns for the water supply are very much concerns that the current problems will become worse over time. As world population grows, and as precipitation remains constant, there will be less water per person, and using Falkenmark's water stress criterion, there will be more nations experiencing water scarcity. In Figure 3 it is clear that the proportion of people in water-stressed nations will increase from 3.7 percent in 2000 to 8.6 percent in 2025 and 17.8 percent in 2050.

It is typically pointed out that although more people by definition means more water stress, such "projections are neither forecasts nor predictions." Indeed, the projections merely mean that if we do not improve our handling of water resources, water will become more scarce. But it is unlikely that we will not become better at utilizing and distributing water. Since agriculture takes up the largest part of water consumption, it is also here that the largest opportunities for improving efficiency are to be found. It is estimated that many irrigation systems waste 60–80 percent of all water. Following the example of Israel, drip irrigation in countries as diverse as India, Jordan, Spain and the US has consistently been shown to cut water use by 30–70 percent while increasing yields by 20–90 percent. Several studies have also indicated that

Figure 3

Share of Humanity With Maximum Water Availability in the Year 2000, 2025, and 2050, Using UN Medium Variant Population Data

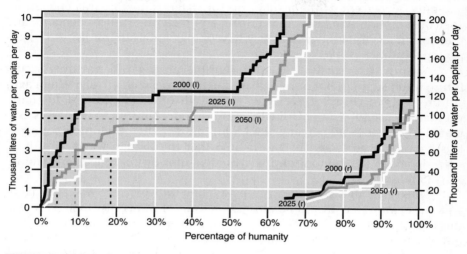

The left side uses the left axis, the right side the right axis.
Source: WRI 1998a.

industry almost without additional costs could save anywhere from 30 to 90 percent of its water consumption. Even in domestic distribution there is great potential for water savings. EEA estimates that the leakage rates in Europe vary from 10 percent in Austria and Denmark up to 28 percent in the UK and 33 percent in the Czech Republic.

The problem of water waste occurs because water in many places is not well priced. The great majority of the world's irrigation systems are based on an annual flat rate, and not on charges according to the amount of water consumed. The obvious effect is that participants are not forced to consider whether all in all it pays to use the last liter of water—when you have first paid to be in, water is free. So even if there is only very little private utility from the last liter of water, it is still used because it is free. . . .

This is particularly a problem for the poor countries. The poorest countries use 90 percent of their water for irrigation compared to just 37 percent in the rich countries. Consequently, it will be necessary to redistribute water from agriculture to industry and households, and this will probably involve a minor decline in the potential agricultural production (i.e., a diminished increase in the actual production). The World Bank estimates that this reduction will be very limited and that water redistribution definitely will be profitable for the countries involved. Of course, this will mean increased imports of grain by the most water-stressed countries, but a study from the International Water Management Institute indicates that it should be possible to cover these extra imports by extra production in the water-abundant countries, particularly the US.

At the same time there are also large advantages to be reaped by focusing on more efficient household water consumption. In Manila 58 percent of all water disappears (lost in distribution or stolen), and in Latin America the figure is about 40 percent. And on average households in the Third World pay only 35 percent of the actual price of water. Naturally, this encourages overconsumption. We know that pricing and metering reduces demand, and that consumers use less water if they have to pay for each unit instead of just paying a flat rate.

Actually, it is likely that more sensible pricing will not only secure future water supplies but also increase the total social efficiency. When agriculture is given cheap or even free water, this often implies a hidden and very large subsidy—in the United States the water subsidy to farmers is estimated to be above 90 percent or $3.5 billion. For the developing countries this figure is even larger: it is estimated that the hidden water subsidy to cities is about $22 billion, and the hidden subsidy to agriculture around $20–25 billion.

Thus, although an increasing population will increase water demands and put extra water stress on almost 20 percent of humanity, it is likely that this scarcity can be solved. Part of the solution will come from higher water prices, which will cut down on inefficient water use. Increased cereal imports will form another part of the solution, freeing up agricultural water to be used in more valuable areas of industry or domestic consumption. Finally, desalting will again constitute a backstop process which can produce virtually unlimited amounts of drinking water given sufficient financial backing.

POSTSCRIPT

Is the Threat of a Global Water Shortage Real?

Authors of the two selections agree that something must be done, that is, major public policymaking must occur, if the water future is going to be acceptable. They disagree, however, on the urgency of the task and the level of optimism (or pessimism) that they bring to their analyses of likely success. Clayton argues that for the first time in history, the world is coming up against limits to new water, creating the term "peak water". Population and economic growth is the culprit. As a consequence, private companies are rushing to control the available water, causing prices to rise. Unless the profit motive is replaced by viewing water as a basic human need (and right), the problem will only become greater.

Lomborg argues that our ability to find more water has resulted in a global usage rate of 17 percent of the readily accessible and renewable water. The consequence, according to Lomborg, is that the world has "more food, less starvation, more health and increased wealth [so] why do we worry?" He does suggest that there are significant problems and identifies three: (1) the unequal distribution of precipitation throughout the globe, (2) increasing global population, and (3) the fact that many countries receive their water through shared river systems. Additionally, water pollution and the shortage of access to water in the developing world are issues, but of a different sort.

Both readings point out the need for aggressive policy action on the part of governments and other actors in the global water regime. This is not to suggest, however, that the world's leaders have been idle. At least 10 major international conferences since 1977 have addressed water issues, resulting in significant action-oriented proposals. For example, the 1992 International Conference on Water and Environment in Dublin established four basic ideas (known as the Dublin Principles). The 1992 Earth Summit highlighted water as an integral part of the ecosystem.

The current cry is for aggressive global water management. Every major study related to water concludes with the observation that governments need to do much more if future water crises are to be avoided. The Web is replete with public (and private) interest groups urging more global action. The Third World Traveler site titles one such plea from the International Forum on Globalization "The Failure of Governments" in a discussion of the crisis. The World Water Council's recent draft of its *World Water Actions Report* presents an overview of global actions to improve water management and to spell out priorities for future efforts. The report centers on a new paradigm for looking at water. No longer to be viewed as a physical product, the paradigm calls for water to be seen as an ecological process "that connects the glass of water on the table with the upper reaches of the watershed." The key ideas are "scarcity, conservation, and awareness of water's life cycle from rain to capture, consumption, and disposal."

The good news for the World Water Council is that the international community has broad consensus, forged at the 10 conferences mentioned above, about the need for policy action. The creation of the World Water Council itself in 1996 and of the Global Water Partnership the same year is an example of such institutional action. But it was the Second World Water Forum, held at The Hague in The Netherlands in March 2000, that was a landmark event in raising global water consciousness. Among the many research reports and documents that emerged from the conference, two stand out: *Vision for Water, Life, and the Environment in the 21st Century* and *Towards Water Security: Framework for Action.*

Vision proposed five key actions: "Involve all stakeholders in integrated management, move towards full-cost pricing of all water services, increase public funding for research and innovation in the public interest, increase cooperation in international water basins, (and) massively increase investments in water." The *Framework for Action* document addresses the question of where do we go from here, suggesting four basic steps: "generating water wisdom . . . , expanding and deepening dialogue among diverse stakeholders, strengthening the capabilities of the organizations involved in water management, and ensuring adequate financial resources to pay for the many actions required."

A number of recent books echo the call for governmental action: *Troubled Water: Saints, Sinners, Truth and Lies About the Global Water Crisis* (Anita Roddick et al., Chelsea Green Publishing Company, 2004); *Water: Global Common and Global Problems* (Velma I. Grover, ed., Science Publishers, 2006); *Integrated Assessment of Water Resources and Global Change: A North–South Analysis* (Springer, 2007); and *Blue Covenant: The Global Water Crisis and the Coming Battle for the Right to Water* (New Press, 2008). See also *Water: A Shared Responsibility* (The United Nations World Water Development Report 2, 2006). Chris Wood argues in *Dry Spring: The Coming Water Crisis of North America* (Raincoast Books, 2008) that North America is ignoring the water crisis. Two sources that present a dire picture of the global water situation are *Water: A Shared Responsibility* (U.N. World Water Development Report, 2006) and *Water: The Causes, Costs, and Future of a Global Crisis* (Julian Caldecott, Virgin Books, 2008).

An important source for understanding the global water problem, particularly its relationship to food and the environment, is *Dialogue on Water, Food and Environment* (2002), published by 10 important actors in the field (FAO, GWP, ICID, IFAP, IWMI, IUCN, UNEP, WHO, WWC, and WWF). Perhaps it is fitting to end this discussion with the quote from UN Secretary General Kofi Annan on the cover of this report: "We need a blue revolution in agriculture that focuses on increasing productivity per unit of water—more crop per drop." Another work that lays out the basic parameters of global water is *Water: Global Common and Global Problems* (Velma I. Grover, Science Publishers, 2006). An easily readable discussion of the global water situation is found in *The Water Crisis* (Weigl Publishers, 2008). Finally, Mark W. Rosegrant,

Ximing Cai, and Sarah A. Cline ("Global Water Outlook to 2025: Averting an Impending Crisis," A Report of the International Food Policy Research Institute and the International Water Management Institute, September 2002) conclude that if current water policies continue, farmers will find it difficult to grow sufficient food to meet the planet's needs.

The fourth volume in a series by Peter H. Gleick and his research team analyzes current worldwide water trends and also addresses a variety of related world water issues (*The World's Water 2004–2005: The Biennial Report on Freshwater Resources,* Island Press, 2004). A source that examines the issues from the perspective of religion and rituals is *Troubled Waters: Religion, Ethics, and the Global Water Crisis* (Rowman & Littlefield Publishers, 2007).

Corruption in the water governance sector is discussed in *Global Corruption Report 2008: Corruption in the Water Sector* (Transparency International, Cambridge University Press, 2008).

A critic of the premise that the planet is about to experience a major water crisis is *Water Crisis: Myth or Reality?* (Peter P. Rogers, Taylor & Francis, 2006).

Internet References . . .

United Nations Office on Drugs and Crime

Established in 1997, this UN organization assists members in their struggle against illicit drugs and human trafficking. It focuses on research, assistance with treaties, and field-based technical assistance. It is headquartered in Vienna with 21 field offices.

http://www.unodc.org

Beckley Foundation Drug Policy Programme (BFDPP)

This British foundation aims to promote objective debate about national and international drug policies. It lists many other Web sites as well.

http://www.internationaldrugpolicy.net

World Health Organization

This international organization's Web site provides substantial information about current and potential pandemics as well as other Web site links. See also http://www.globalhealthreporting.org and http://www.globalhealthfacts.org for additional information.

http://www.who.int/en/

Council of Europe

The Council of Europe established a campaign in 2006 to combat trafficking of human beings. It focuses on creating awareness among governments, NGOs, and civil society about the problem, as well as promoting global public policy to combat the problem.

http://www.coe.int

Globalization Guide.Org

This Web site lists around 40 pro- and anti-globalization Web sites as well as other sources on both globalization and cultural imperialism.

http://globalizationguide.org

Globalization: Threat or Opportunity?

This Web site contains the article "Globalization: Threat or Opportunity?" by the staff of the International Monetary Fund (IMF). This article discusses such aspects of globalization as current trends, positive and negative outcomes, and the role of institutions and organizations. "The Challenge of Globalization in Africa," by IMF acting managing director Stanley Fischer, and "Factors Driving Global Economic Integration," by Michael Mussa, IMF's director of research, are also included on this site.

http://www.imf.org/external/np/exr/ib/2000/041200.htm

Expanding Global Forces and Movements

*O*ur ability to travel from one part of the globe to another in a short amount of time has expanded dramatically since the Wright brothers first lifted an airplane off the sand dunes of North Carolina's Outer Banks. The decline of national borders has also been made possible by the explosion of global technology. This technological explosion has not only increased the speed of information dissemination but has also expanded its reach and impact, making any individual with Internet access a global actor in every sense of the term.

Many consequences flow from this realization, including the expansion of the drug war and the global spread of health pandemics along with the trafficking in human beings against their will. In addition, flow of money, information, and ideas that connect people around the world also creates fissures of conflict that heighten anxieties and cause increased tensions between rich and poor, connected and disconnected, cultures and regimes. The impact of these new and emerging patterns of access has yet to be fully calculated or realized, but we do know that billions are feeling their impact, and the result is both exhilarating and frightening.

- Can the Global Community "Win" the Drug War?
- Is the International Community Adequately Prepared to Address Global Health Pandemics?
- Do Adequate Strategies Exist to Combat Human Trafficking?
- Is Globalization a Positive Development for the World Community?
- Is the World a Victim of American Cultural Imperialism?
- Is the Global Economic Crisis a Failure of Capitalism?

ISSUE 10

Can the Global Community "Win" the Drug War?

YES: United Nations Office on Drugs and Crime, from "2007 World Drug Report" (2007)

NO: Ethan Nadelmann, from "Drugs," *Foreign Policy* (September/October 2007)

ISSUE SUMMARY

YES: This 2007 report by the UN's Office on Drugs and Crime provides "robust evidence" that "drug control is working" and "the world drug problem is being contained."

NO: Ethan Nadelmann argues that prohibition has failed by not treating the "demand for drugs as a market, and addicts as patients," resulting in "boosting the profits of drug lords, and fostering narcostates that would frighten Al Capone."

In 1999, the United Nations pegged the world illicit drug trade at $400 billion, about the size of the Spanish economy. Such activity takes place as part of a global supply chain that "uses everything from passenger jets that can carry shipments of cocaine worth $500 million in a single trip to custom-built submarines that ply the waters between Colombia and Puerto Rico." *The UN 2007 World Drug Report* suggested the global drug problem was being contained, as there appeared to be "a leveling of growth in all of the main illegal drug markets." Opium production increased but was still much lower than any peak year. Cocaine and ATS (amphetamine-type stimulants) production remained stable, while cannabis production declined.

The report revealed that 5 percent of the world's population between the ages of 15 and 64 have used drugs at least once in the year under study (2005), compared to global tobacco use of 28 percent. Approximately 200 million people use drugs each year. At the global level, the opiates, particularly heroin, rank first in usage, followed by cocaine. Opiates remain the principal problem drug in Europe and Asia, while cocaine tops the list in South America and cannabis in Africa. Estimates suggest that in 2005, 42 percent of global cocaine production and 26 percent of global heroin production were intercepted by authorities. There were 1.5 million drug seizure cases, and large quantities of drugs were seized.

The report followed good news relating to government action in the 2004 report. Especially important was the emergence of a consensus among governments and global public opinion that the current levels of illegal drug use are unacceptable. In two drug-producing regions, declines in production actually occurred. In Southeast Asia, opium poppy cultivation continues to drop in Myanmar and Laos. In the Andean region, coca cultivation has declined for four straight years in the three leading producing countries (Colombia, Peru, and Bolivia).

The illegal movement of drugs across national borders is accompanied by the same kind of movement for illegal weapons; they go hand in hand with one another. It was estimated by the United Nations in its 2004 report that only 3 percent of such weapons (18 million of a total of 550 million in circulation) are used by government, the military, or police.

This increase in drug use has occurred despite a rather long history of government attempts to control the illegal international drug trade. Beginning in 1961, such efforts have been part of the social policies of governments worldwide. Precisely because drug policy crosses over into social policy, policymakers and scholars have been at odds over how best to deal with this ever-growing problem, whether talking about national policy or international policy. Simply stated, the debate has centered on legalization vs. prohibition, and treatment vs. prevention.

Policies of the United States have always had the goal of drug use reduction and punishment for abusers, resulting in less attention to treatment. This includes a number of important elements, as outlined in a Congressional Research Service Brief for Congress (2003): "(1) eradication of narcotic crops, (2) interdiction and law enforcement activities in drug-producing and drug-transmitting countries, (3) international cooperation, (4) sanctions/economic assistance, and (5) institution development." Many have charged the United States and those other countries that share its fundamental philosophy of drug wars of using the issue to expand its national power in other domains. On the other hand, other countries, particularly those in Western Europe, have been shifting attention for some time away from "repressive policies" and toward those associated with harm reduction and treatment.

The two selections in this section contribute to the debate over the proper approach to "winning" the drug war. The United Nation's 2007 report presents an optimistic picture of the effects of governmental action in the war on drugs, with strong language used to paint the picture. The second selection by Ethan Nadelmann suggests that, on the contrary, drug lords and narcostates are flourishing.

YES

2007 World Drug Report

1. Trends in World Drug Markets

1.1 Overview

1.1.1 Evolution of the World Drug Problem

Continued containment of the drug problem

The global drug problem is being contained. The production and consumption of cannabis, cocaine, amphetamines and ecstasy have stabilized at the global level—with one exception. The exception is the continuing expansion of opium production in Afghanistan. This expansion continues to pose a threat—to the security of the country and to the global containment of opiates abuse. Even in Afghanistan, however, the large scale production of opium is concentrated and expanding in a few southern provinces where the authority of the central government is currently limited and insurgents continue to exploit the profits of the opium trade.

On the whole, most indications point to a levelling of growth in all of the main illegal drug markets. This is good news and may indicate an important juncture in long-term drug control. A stable and contained problem is easier to address than one which is expanding chaotically, provided it is seen as an opportunity for renewed commitment rather than an excuse to decrease vigilance.

Most indications are, however, that Member States do have the will to re-commit to drug control. Although it is outside of the scope of this Report to assess policy, the estimates and trends which are provided in the following pages contain several examples of progress forged on the back of international collaboration. The extent of international collaboration, the sharing of intelligence, knowledge and experience, as well as the conviction that the global drug problem must be tackled on the basis of a 'shared responsibility' seem to be growing and bearing fruit.

**Following stabilization in 2005, opium production
increased in 2006 . . .**

The total area under opium cultivation was 201,000 ha in 2006. This is clearly higher than a year earlier (+33%) though still below the level in 1998 (238,000 ha) and some 29 percent lower than at the peak in 1991 (282,000 ha).

From *World Drug Report*, (2007) UNODC Series No. E. 07.XI.5, pp. 25–27, 29–31. Copyright ©
2007 by United Nations Publications. Reprinted by permission.

Given higher opium yields in Afghanistan than in South-East Asia, global opium production is, however, higher than in the 1990s.

Following a small decline of global opium production in 2005 (−5%), global opium production increased again strongly in 2006 (+43%) to reach 6610 mt, basically reflecting the massive expansion of opium production in Afghanistan (+49%). Afghanistan accounted for 92 percent of global illicit opium production in 2006. As a result global heroin production is estimated to have increased to 606 mt in 2006. The bad news from Afghanistan also overshadows the good news from South-East Asia. Opium production in the Golden Triangle (mainly Myanmar and Laos) declined by 77 percent between 1998 and 2006 and by 84 percent since the peak in 1991.

. . . while cocaine production remained stable

If only the area under coca cultivation is considered, a small decline by 2 percent to 157,000 ha was reported for the year 2006. As compared to the year 2000, the area under coca cultivation in the Andean region declined by 29 percent; in Colombia, it fell by as much as 52 percent. This progress was, however, not translated into a decline of global cocaine production, due to improved yields and production techniques. Global cocaine production is estimated to have remained basically unchanged in 2006 as compared to a year earlier or two years earlier. Following a revision of yield estimates, global production is now estimated at 984 mt. A decline in Colombia (−5 %) was compensated by increases reported from Bolivia (+18%) and Peru (+8%).

Cannabis production declined in 2005 . . .

Estimates for both cannabis herb and cannabis resin showed a decline for the year 2005. This decline follows several years of sustained growth. Global cannabis herb production is now estimated at 42,000 mt, down from 45,000 mt in 2004. Global cannabis resin production declined from 7,500 mt in 2004 to 6,600 mt in 2005, reflecting mainly the decline of cannabis resin production in Morocco.

. . . and ATS production stabilized

Global production of amphetamine-type stimulants seems to have stabilized at around 480 mt in 2005, slightly down from 500 mt in 2000. There has been a decline in ecstasy production (from 126 mt in 2004 to 113 mt in 2005), and a small decline in methampheta-mine production (from 291 to 278 mt) which was offset by an increase in global amphetamine production (from 63 to 88 mt).

Member States reported 1.5 million drug seizure cases to UNODC

Member States reported 1.5 million drug seizure cases to UNODC for the year 2005, 21 percent more than a year earlier. Some of the increase was due to improved reporting. One hundred and twelve countries provided detailed statistics on seizure cases in 2005, up from 95 countries in 2004. If only the data of those countries that reported in both 2004 and 2005 is considered, the increase amounts to 10 percent.

Figure 1

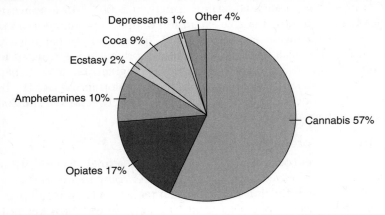

Breakdown of Seizure Cases in 2005 by Substance (N = 1.51 Million)

Depressants 1%   Other 4%

Coca 9%

Ecstasy 2%

Amphetamines 10%

Cannabis 57%

Opiates 17%

Source: UNODC, Government reports.

More than half (57%) of all seizure cases involved cannabis (herb, resin, oil, plants and seeds). Opiates (opium, morphine, heroin, synthetic opiates and poppy seeds), accounted for 17 percent, with heroin alone accounting for 14 percent of the total. This is followed by seizures of the amphetamine-type stimulants (12%). About half of these seizures (or 5.5% of the total) is accounted for by methamphetamine, followed by amphetamine (2.5%) and ecstasy (2%); the rest (2%) includes 'Captagon' tablets (Near East) and 'Maxiton Forte' (Egypt), 'ephedrone' (methcathinone) and various undefined amphetamines. Coca products account for 9 percent of global seizure cases; the bulk of coca related seizure cases concern cocaine (8% of total).

Depressants account for 1 percent of global seizure cases and other drugs for 4 percent. This includes substances such as methaqualone, khat, various synthetic narcotics, LSD, ketamine, various non-specified psychotropic substances, and inhalants. Some of these substances (such as khat, ketamine and some of the psychotropic substances) are not under international control, but are under national control in several Member States.

Largest quantities of drugs seized are cannabis, cocaine and opiates

Information on the quantities of drugs seized was provided by 118 countries for the year 2005 in reply to UNODC's Annual Reports Questionnaire. Supplementing ARQ data with information obtained from other sources,[1] UNODC has compiled data and information from 165 countries and territories. This forms the basis for the analysis which follows.

The largest seizures worldwide are for cannabis (herb and then resin), followed by cocaine, the opiates and ATS. All cannabis-related seizures amounted to more than 9,700 mt in 2005, including 5,947 mt for cannabis end products (herb, resin and oil). Cocaine seizures amounted to 752 mt, opiate seizures, expressed in heroin equivalents, amounted to 125 mt and ATS seizures (methamphetamine, amphetamine, non-defined amphetamines and ecstasy) amounted to 43 mt.

Increases in 2005 were reported for coca leaf, cocaine, the amphetamines as well as GHB and LSD. As global cocaine production remained unchanged, the strong increase in cocaine seizures is likely to have been the exclusive result of effective and successful law enforcement. Though amphetamines seizures increased in 2005 they are still below the peak levels of 2000 and 2001. Global trafficking in amphetamines over the last five years has remained basically stable.

Opiates seizures as a whole remained stable in 2005—reflecting stable global opium production in that year. Rising seizures of opium offset declines in heroin and morphine seizures. For 2006, however, preliminary data indicate a strong increase in opiates seizures, in line with growing levels of opium production in Afghanistan.

In 2005, global seizures of cannabis herb, resin and oil declined. The decline in cannabis herb seizures seems to be linked to intensified eradication efforts in a number of countries across the globe. The decline in cannabis resin seizures can be linked to the decline of cannabis resin production in Morocco.

Drug seizures in unit terms decline in 2005

As the quantities of drugs seized are not directly comparable, it is difficult to draw general conclusions on overall drug trafficking patterns from them. Since the ratio of weight to psychoactive effects varies greatly from one drug to another (the use of one gram of heroin is not equivalent to the use of one gram of cannabis herb), the comparability of the data is improved if the weight of a seizure is converted into typical consumption units, or doses, taken by drug users. Typical doses tend, however, to vary across countries (and sometime across regions within the same country), across substances aggregated under one drug category (e.g. commercial cannabis herb and high-grade cannabis herb), across user groups and across time. There are no conversion rates which take all of these factors into account. Comparisons made here are based on global conversion rates, of milligrams per dose,[2] found in scientific literature or used among law enforcement agencies as basic rules of thumb. The resulting estimates should be interpreted with some caution.

Based on such calculations, global seizures were equivalent to 32.5 billion units in 2005, down from 35.8 billion units a year earlier (−9%). As the number of drug seizure cases increased in 2005, the decline of seizures in unit equivalents cannot be attributed to reduced law enforcement activity. It most likely reflects the first signs of stabilization in global drug trafficking flows parallel to the stabilization in global drug production and drug consumption.

In units terms, more than half of all seizures (59%) are cannabis, followed by coca-related substances (24%), opiates (12%) and amphetamine-type stimulants (4%). While cannabis leads the table, irrespective of the measurement used, it may be interesting to note that in terms of drug units seized, cocaine ranks second. In terms of reported drug seizure cases, cocaine ranked fourth, behind the opiates and behind the ATS. This reflects the fact that, while there are many multi-ton seizures of cocaine every year, other drugs are usually trafficked in far smaller quantities.

A regional breakdown shows that 44 percent of all drugs, expressed in unit equivalents, were seized in the Americas, 29 percent in Europe, 18 percent in Asia, 9 percent in Africa and 0.2 percent in the Oceania region. Seizures declined in 2005 in Africa, in the Oceania region, in Europe and in North America but increased in South America and in Asia.

On a per capita basis, drug trafficking is most widespread in North America, reflecting higher abuse levels and/or the fact that law enforcement in North America is the most active in fighting drug trafficking. The largest amounts of drugs per inhabitant are seized in North America (19 doses per inhabitant), followed by South America (13 doses) and Europe (11 doses). The global average is 5 doses per inhabitant per year. Africa, Oceania and Asia are all below the global average. Within Asia, however, data differ among the various subregions. For the Near & Middle East/South-West Asia region, seizures amount to 11 doses per inhabitant, which is almost the same level as reported from Europe.

Overall stabilization in global drug use

The estimated level of drug use in the world has remained more or less unchanged for the third year in a row. Approximately 200 million people or 5 percent of the world's population aged between 15 and 64 years have used drugs at least once in the previous 12 months.

This continues to be a far lower level than tobacco use (28%). UNODC's estimate of the global number of problem drug users also remains unchanged at around 25 million people or 0.6% of the global population age 15–64.

With the exception of a small increase in cocaine use (based on prevalence estimates), use of all illicit drugs was either stable or declined slightly in 2005/6. The increases in cannabis and ecstasy use which were recorded in 2004/5 were not carried over into the 2005/6 period.

Consumed by almost 4 percent of the population or close to 160 million persons, cannabis continues to account for the vast majority of illegal drug use. Global cannabis use estimates are slightly lower than last year's estimates, due to ongoing declines in North America and—for the first time—some declines in the largest cannabis markets of Western Europe. Cannabis use in the Oceana region also continued to decline. In addition, a number of new household surveys found lower prevalence rates than UNODC had previously estimated for the countries concerned. Growth in cannabis use occurred in Africa, several parts of South America, some parts of Asia (South-West Asia, Central Asia and South Asia) and parts of Eastern and South-eastern Europe. Although it is too early to speak of general decline, signs of a stabilization of cannabis use at the global level are apparent.

Amphetamine-type stimulants (ATS), including amphetamines, methamphetamine and ecstasy, remain the second most widely consumed group of substances. Over the 2005/6 period 25 million people are estimated to have used amphetamines (including methamphetamine) at least once in the previous

Figure 2

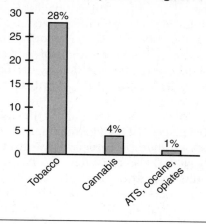

Use of Illicit Drugs Compared to the Use of Tobacco (in % of World Population Age 15–64)

Source: UNODC, WHO.

Figure 3

Illegal Drug Use at the Global Level (2005/2006)

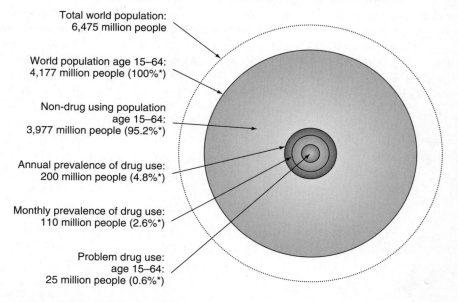

Total world population:
6,475 million people

World population age 15–64:
4,177 million people (100%*)

Non-drug using population
age 15–64:
3,977 million people (95.2%*)

Annual prevalence of drug use:
200 million people (4.8%*)

Monthly prevalence of drug use:
110 million people (2.6%*)

Problem drug use:
age 15–64:
25 million people (0.6%*)

* in per cent of population age 15–64

*in percent of population age 15–64.

12 months, about the same as a year earlier. An estimated 9 million people used ecstasy over the 2005/6 period, down from 10 million in 2004/5. Declines in ecstasy use occurred primarily in North America.

The number of opiates users remained stable at 2004/5 levels. As in that period, 16 million persons or 0.4 percent of the global population aged 15 to 64 consumed opiates. Out of these 16 million persons, 11 million or 0.3 percent of the population abuse heroin. Overall, consumption declined or stabilized in established markets, including those of Western Europe and North America, but increased in countries in the vicinity of Afghanistan as well as in new markets, such as Africa. In most of the countries of East and South-East Asia opiate abuse stabilized or declined.

UNODC's estimate of the global level of cocaine use increased slightly to 14 million persons or 0.3 percent of the global population. Continued increases in South America, Africa and Europe were partially offset by decreases reported from North America. UNODC also compiles data based on use trends as perceived by experts. Results from these data are not always identical to actual reported information.[3] Trend estimates provided by Member States to UNODC differ slightly, and indicate that global cocaine use declined slightly in 2005.

Notes

1. Government reports, HONLEA reports, UNODC Field Offices, Drug Abuse Information Network for Asia and the Pacific (DAINAP), ICPO/Interpol, World Customs Organisation (WCO), CICAD, EMCDDA, United States Department of State, *International Narcotics Control Strategy Report,* etc.

2. For the purposes of this calculation, the following typical consumption units (at street purity) were assumed: cannabis herb: 0.5 grams per joint; cannabis resin: 0.135 grams per joint; cocaine: 0.1 grams per line; ecstasy: 0.1 grams per pill; heroin: 0.03 grams per dose; amphetamines: 0.03 grams per pill; LSD: 0.00005 grams (50 micrograms).

3. A detailed explanation of this can be found in the Methodology section of this Report.

Drugs

Prohibition has failed—again. Instead of treating the demand for illegal drugs as a market, and addicts as patients, policymakers the world over have boosted the profits of drug lords and fostered narcostates that would frighten Al Capone. Finally, a smarter drug control regime that values reality over rhetoric is rising to replace the "war" on drugs.

"The Global War on Drugs Can Be Won"

No, it can't. A "drug-free world," which the United Nations describes as a realistic goal, is no more attainable than an "alcohol-free world"—and no one has talked about that with a straight face since the repeal of Prohibition in the United States in 1933. Yet futile rhetoric about winning a "war on drugs" persists, despite mountains of evidence documenting its moral and ideological bankruptcy. When the U.N. General Assembly Special Session on drugs convened in 1998, it committed to "eliminating or significantly reducing the illicit cultivation of the coca bush, the cannabis plant and the opium poppy by the year 2008" and to "achieving significant and measurable results in the field of demand reduction." But today, global production and consumption of those drugs are roughly the same as they were a decade ago; meanwhile, many producers have become more efficient, and cocaine and heroin have become purer and cheaper.

It's always dangerous when rhetoric drives policy—and especially so when "war on drugs" rhetoric leads the public to accept collateral casualties that would never be permissible in civilian law enforcement, much less public health. Politicians still talk of eliminating drugs from the Earth as though their use is a plague on humanity. But drug control is not like disease control, for the simple reason that there's no popular demand for smallpox or polio. Cannabis and opium have been grown throughout much of the world for millennia. The same is true for coca in Latin America. Methamphetamine and other synthetic drugs can be produced anywhere. Demand for particular illicit drugs waxes and wanes, depending not just on availability but also fads, fashion, culture, and competition from alternative means of stimulation and distraction. The relative harshness of drug laws and the intensity of enforcement matter surprisingly little, except in totalitarian states. After all, rates of illegal drug use in the United States are the same as, or higher than, Europe, despite America's much more punitive policies.

Reprinted in entirety by McGraw-Hill with permission from *FOREIGN POLICY,* September/October 2007, pp. 24–26, 28–29. www.foreignpolicy.com. © 2007 Washingtonpost. Newsweek Interactive, LLC.

"We Can Reduce the Demand for Drugs"

Good luck.   Reducing the demand for illegal drugs seems to make sense. But the desire to alter one's state of consciousness, and to use psychoactive drugs to do so, is nearly universal—and mostly not a problem. There's virtually never been a drug-free society, and more drugs are discovered and devised every year. Demand-reduction efforts that rely on honest education and positive alternatives to drug use are helpful, but not when they devolve into unrealistic, "zero tolerance" policies.

As with sex, abstinence from drugs is the best way to avoid trouble, but one always needs a fallback strategy for those who can't or won't refrain. "Zero tolerance" policies deter some people, but they also dramatically increase the harms and costs for those who don't resist. Drugs become more potent, drug use becomes more hazardous, and people who use drugs are marginalized in ways that serve no one.

The better approach is not demand reduction but "harm reduction." Reducing drug use is fine, but it's not nearly as important as reducing the death, disease, crime, and suffering associated with both drug misuse and failed prohibitionist policies. With respect to legal drugs, such as alcohol and cigarettes, harm reduction means promoting responsible drinking and designated drivers, or persuading people to switch to nicotine patches, chewing gums, and smokeless tobacco. With respect to illegal drugs, it means reducing the transmission of infectious disease through syringe-exchange programs, reducing overdose fatalities by making antidotes readily available, and allowing people addicted to heroin and other illegal opiates to obtain methadone from doctors and even pharmaceutical heroin from clinics. Britain, Canada, Germany, the Netherlands, and Switzerland have already embraced this last option. There's no longer any question that these strategies decrease drug-related harms without increasing drug use. What blocks expansion of such programs is not cost; they typically save taxpayers' money that would otherwise go to criminal justice and healthcare. No, the roadblocks are abstinence-only ideologues and a cruel indifference to the lives and well-being of people who use drugs.

"Reducing the Supply of Drugs Is the Answer"

Not if history is any guide.   Reducing supply makes as much sense as reducing demand; after all, if no one were planting cannabis, coca, and opium, there wouldn't be any heroin, cocaine, or marijuana to sell or consume. But the carrot and stick of crop eradication and substitution have been tried and failed, with rare exceptions, for half a century. These methods may succeed in targeted locales, but they usually simply shift production from one region to another: Opium production moves from Pakistan to Afghanistan; coca from Peru to Colombia; and cannabis from Mexico to the United States, while overall global production remains relatively constant or even increases.

The carrot, in the form of economic development and assistance in switching to legal crops, is typically both late and inadequate. The stick, often in the form of forced eradication, including aerial spraying, wipes out illegal and legal crops alike and can be hazardous to both people and local environ-ments. The best thing to be said for emphasizing supply reduction is that it provides a rationale for wealthier nations to spend a little money on economic development in poorer countries. But, for the most part, crop eradication and substitution wreak havoc among impoverished farmers without diminishing overall global supply.

The global markets in cannabis, coca, and opium products operate essen-tially the same way that other global commodity markets do: If one source is compromised due to bad weather, rising production costs, or political difficul-ties, another emerges. If international drug control circles wanted to think stra-tegically, the key question would no longer be how to reduce global supply, but rather: Where does illicit production cause the fewest problems (and the great-est benefits)? Think of it as a global vice control challenge. No one expects to eradicate vice, but it must be effectively zoned and regulated—even if it's illegal.

"U.S. Drug Policy Is the World's Drug Policy"

Sad, but true. Looking to the United States as a role model for drug control is like looking to apartheid-era South Africa for how to deal with race. The United States ranks first in the world in per capita incarceration—with less than 5 percent of the world's population, but almost 25 percent of the world's prisoners. The number of people locked up for U.S. drug-law violations has increased from roughly 50,000 in 1980 to almost 500,000 today; that's more than the number of people Western Europe locks up for everything. Even more deadly is U.S. resistance to syringe-exchange programs to reduce HIV/AIDS both at home and abroad. Who knows how many people might not have contracted HIV if the United States had implemented at home, and supported abroad, the sorts of syringe-exchange and other harm-reduction programs that have kept HIV/AIDS rates so low in Australia, Britain, the Netherlands, and elsewhere. Perhaps millions.

And yet, despite this dismal record, the United States has succeeded in constructing an international drug prohibition regime modeled after its own highly punitive and moralistic approach. It has dominated the drug control agencies of the United Nations and other international organizations, and its federal drug enforcement agency was the first national police organization to go global. Rarely has one nation so successfully promoted its own failed poli-cies to the rest of the world.

But now, for the first time, U.S. hegemony in drug control is being chal-lenged. The European Union is demanding rigorous assessment of drug control strategies. Exhausted by decades of service to the U.S.-led war on drugs, Latin Americans are far less inclined to collaborate closely with U.S. drug enforce-ment efforts. Finally waking up to the deadly threat of HIV/AIDS, China, Indonesia, Vietnam, and even Malaysia and Iran are increasingly accepting of syringe-exchange and other harm-reduction programs. In 2005, the ayatollah in charge of Iran's Ministry of Justice issued a *fatwa* declaring methadone main-tenance and syringe-exchange programs compatible with *sharia* (Islamic) law. One only wishes his American counterpart were comparably enlightened.

"Afghan Opium Production Must Be Curbed"

Be careful what you wish for.   It's easy to believe that eliminating record-high opium production in Afghanistan—which today accounts for roughly 90 percent of global supply, up from 50 percent 10 years ago—would solve everything from heroin abuse in Europe and Asia to the resurgence of the Taliban.

But assume for a moment that the United States, NATO, and Hamid Karzai's government were somehow able to cut opium production in Afghanistan. Who would benefit? Only the Taliban, warlords, and other black-market entrepreneurs whose stockpiles of opium would skyrocket in value. Hundreds of thousands of Afghan peasants would flock to cities, ill-prepared to find work. And many Afghans would return to their farms the following year to plant another illegal harvest, utilizing guerrilla farming methods to escape intensified eradication efforts. Except now, they'd soon be competing with poor farmers elsewhere in Central Asia, Latin America, or even Africa. This is, after all, a global commodities market.

And outside Afghanistan? Higher heroin prices typically translate into higher crime rates by addicts. They also invite cheaper but more dangerous means of consumption, such as switching from smoking to injecting heroin, which results in higher HIV and hepatitis C rates. All things considered, wiping out opium in Afghanistan would yield far fewer benefits than is commonly assumed.

So what's the solution? Some recommend buying up all the opium in Afghanistan, which would cost a lot less than is now being spent trying to eradicate it. But, given that farmers somewhere will produce opium so long as the demand for heroin persists, maybe the world is better off, all things considered, with 90 percent of it coming from just one country. And if that heresy becomes the new gospel, it opens up all sorts of possibilities for pursuing a new policy in Afghanistan that reconciles the interests of the United States, NATO, and millions of Afghan citizens.

"Legalization Is the Best Approach"

It might be.   Global drug prohibition is clearly a costly disaster. The United Nations has estimated the value of the global market in illicit drugs at $400 billion, or 6 percent of global trade. The extraordinary profits available to those willing to assume the risks enrich criminals, terrorists, violent political insurgents, and corrupt politicians and governments. Many cities, states, and even countries in Latin America, the Caribbean, and Asia are reminiscent of Chicago under Al Capone—times 50. By bringing the market for drugs out into the open, legalization would radically change all that for the better.

More importantly, legalization would strip addiction down to what it really is: a health issue. Most people who use drugs are like the responsible alcohol consumer, causing no harm to themselves or anyone else. They would no longer be the state's business. But legalization would also benefit those who struggle with drugs by reducing the risks of overdose and disease associated with unregulated products, eliminating the need to obtain drugs from dangerous criminal markets, and allowing addiction problems to be treated as medical rather than criminal problems.

No one knows how much governments spend collectively on failing drug war policies, but it's probably at least $100 billion a year, with federal, state, and local governments in the United States accounting for almost half the total. Add to that the tens of billions of dollars to be gained annually in tax revenues from the sale of legalized drugs. Now imagine if just a third of that total were committed to reducing drug-related disease and addiction. Virtually everyone, except those who profit or gain politically from the current system, would benefit.

Some say legalization is immoral. That's nonsense, unless one believes there is some principled basis for discriminating against people based solely on what they put into their bodies, absent harm to others. Others say legalization would open the floodgates to huge increases in drug abuse. They forget that we already live in a world in which psychoactive drugs of all sorts are readily available—and in which people too poor to buy drugs resort to sniffing gasoline, glue, and other industrial products, which can be more harmful than any drug. No, the greatest downside to legalization may well be the fact that the legal markets would fall into the hands of the powerful alcohol, tobacco, and pharmaceutical companies. Still, legalization is a far more pragmatic option than living with the corruption, violence, and organized crime of the current system.

"Legalization Will Never Happen"

Never say never. Wholesale legalization may be a long way off—but partial legalization is not. If any drug stands a chance of being legalized, it's cannabis. Hundreds of millions of people have used it, the vast majority without suffering any harm or going on to use "harder" drugs. In Switzerland, for example, cannabis legalization was twice approved by one chamber of its parliament, but narrowly rejected by the other.

Elsewhere in Europe, support for the criminalization of cannabis is waning. In the United States, where roughly 40 percent of the country's 1.8 million annual drug arrests are for cannabis possession, typically of tiny amounts, 40 percent of Americans say that the drug should be taxed, controlled, and regulated like alcohol. Encouraged by Bolivian President Evo Morales, support is also growing in Latin America and Europe for removing coca from international antidrug conventions, given the absence of any credible health reason for keeping it there. Traditional growers would benefit economically, and there's some possibility that such products might compete favorably with more problematic substances, including alcohol.

The global war on drugs persists in part because so many people fail to distinguish between the harms of drug abuse and the harms of prohibition. Legalization forces that distinction to the forefront. The opium problem in Afghanistan is primarily a prohibition problem, not a drug problem. The same is true of the narcoviolence and corruption that has afflicted Latin America and the Caribbean for almost three decades—and that now threatens Africa. Governments can arrest and kill drug lord after drug lord, but the ultimate solution is a structural one, not a prosecutorial one. Few people doubt any longer that the war on drugs is lost, but courage and vision are needed to transcend the ignorance, fear, and vested interests that sustain it.

POSTSCRIPT

Can the Global Community "Win" the Drug War?

The October 2003 Lisbon International Symposium on Global Drug Policy provided a forum for leading drug policymakers from national governments, senior representatives from various UN agencies, and other experts to address new ideas and innovative solutions. Speakers addressed such varied topics as an international framework for combating drugs, better public health policy, new approaches to the war on drugs, and the variety of new challenges facing the international community. Four key areas of division were spelled out by Martin Jelsma: (1) repression vs. protection; (2) zero tolerance vs. harm reduction; (3) the North–South or donors vs. recipients divide; and (4) demand vs. supply. The failure of nations of the world to reach agreement on these four major areas of contention has resulted, in the judgment of many, in the inability of the global community to address the drug problem successfully. Not enough funds are made available to international agencies like the United Nations, and money that is given is likely to have strings attached to it.

The conference was particularly timely because for the first time in the global war on drugs, policymakers did not debate the issue of whether the current policy was working. Instead, conference participants focused on how to organize a better drug control system. Honorary Secretary-General of Interpol, Raymond Kendall, echoed this view in his closing speech. While Kendall was pleased that debate had shifted to what he called "new levels," the conference did not develop a new plan of action. The issues outlined above were too great to overcome. Nonetheless, progress was made as national examples of successful alternative public policy programs were presented to the delegates.

The United Nations continued the theme of alternative approaches in its "2004 World Drug Report." Acknowledging that effective strategies are discovered through trial and error, the United Nations alluded to a number of recent developments that appear to have potential for helping the global war on drugs. Four major ideas were discussed under the rubric of a "holistic approach." The first is "Addressing the drug problem in a broader sustainable development context." On the one hand, the drug problem hinders development in poor countries and compromises peacemaking efforts in countries torn by civil strife. On the other hand, "poverty, strife and feeble governance are fertile ground for drug production, trafficking and abuse." These situations are interconnected and can only be addressed by a comprehensive approach that recognizes the causes as well as the symptoms of the drug problem.

The second idea is "Providing an integrated response to the drugs and crime nexus." The connections between drug trafficking, organized crime, and even the financing of terrorism has meant that those responsible for addressing each of these scourges must work within the same multilateral system rather than in isolation.

The third development is "Addressing the drugs and crime nexus under the new paradigm of human security." Growing out of the 2000 UN Millennium Summit, the Commission on Human Security is developing a new approach to security that combines human development and human rights. The UN Report suggests that this could provide a critical link between drugs/crime control and sustainable development.

The fourth development is termed "A more synergistic approach." This simply means that not only must there be an integrated and balanced approach to the war on drugs, but that much more needs to be learned. For example, the structure and dynamics of drug markets at the national, regional, and global levels are a mystery beyond the simple belief that normal supply and demand principles are at work.

The 2004 UN report also called for deeper understanding of and a focus on controlling drug epidemics. The report summed it up this way: "The powerful dynamics created by the combination of the incentives and behavior of a ruthless market with the contagious characteristics of an epidemic explain why drug use can expand so rapidly and become so difficult to stem."

For Federico Mayor (in collaboration with Jérôme Bindé, *The World Ahead: Our Future in the Making,* UNESCO, 2001), the basic question of eliminating the supply or drying up the demand is raised. Mayor believes it critical that a major emphasis be placed on both sides of the equation. His motivation is based on the dual points that eliminating the supply is difficult but that the health issues associated with illegal drug use demand that we educate existing and potential users about the evils of such behavior. Addicts must be treated as patients, not criminals. At the same time, Mayor argues that the most effective way to fight the drug war is to destroy the financial power of organized crime. Both strategies are critically important.

Harry G. Levine argues that the emphasis on drug prohibition should be replaced by a focus on "harm reduction," creating mechanisms to address tolerance, regulation, and public health. He suggests that global drug prohibition and a focus on both punishing the supplier and the user have not worked very well. Instead, these approaches must be reexamined with a view toward addressing the plight of the drug user in a much different way.

A number of publications provide insight into the war on drugs. Twenty-eight speeches from the aforementioned 2003 Lisbon Conference are reproduced in *Global Drug Policy: Building a New Framework* (The Senlis Council, February 2004). A study prepared for the U.S. Congress by the Congressional Research Service describes U.S. international drug policy (Raphael Perl, "Drug Control: International Policy and Approaches," September 8, 2003). A balanced assessment of drug policies is found in David R. Mares' *Drug Wars and Coffeehouses: The Political Economy of the International Drug Trade* (CQ Press, 2005). A description of international enforcement operations is found in Gregory D. Lee's *Global Drug Enforcement: Practical Investigative Techniques* (CRC, 2003). A book that examines the global war on drugs from a number of perspectives is Jurg Gerber's *Drug War American Style* (Routledge, 2000).

Criticism of the U.S.-dominated global approach can be found in a number of sources. The reading for this issue suggests a series of short rebuttals to some rather fundamental statements relating to the war on drugs. In response to the statement that "The Global War Can Be Won," Ethan Nadelmann responds: "No, it can't." Six other responses preceded by statements include: "We Can Reduce the Demand for Drugs" (Good luck.); "Reducing the Supply of Drugs Is the Answer" (Not if history is any guide.); "U.S. Drug Policy Is the World's Drug Policy" (Sad, but true.); "Afghan Opium Production Must Be Curbed" (Be careful what you wish for.); "Legalization Is the Best Approach" (It might be.); and Legalization Will Never Happen" (Never say never.). Other books critical of U.S. policy include *U.S. Foreign Policy and the War on Drugs: Displacing the Cocaine and Heroin Industry* (Co Friesendorf, Routledge, 2007) and *Fatal Distraction: The War on Drugs in the Age of Islamic Terror* (Unlimited Publishing, 2006). A recent source critical of efforts of international institutions is *Crime, War, and Global Trafficking: Designing International Cooperation* (Christine Jojarth, Cambridge University Press, 2009).

An important work focusing on Latin America is Ted Galen Carpenter's *Bad Neighbor Policy* (Palgrave Macmillan, 2003). Another is *Intelligence and the War on Drugs* (J. F. Holden-Rhodes, Praeger Publishers). An insider's look at Colombia is found in *Beyond Bogota: Diary of a Drug War Journalist in Colombia* (Garry Leech, Beacon Press, 2009). *The Economist* suggested in its subtitle to an article on drugs that it was "Time to think again about the rules of engagement in the war on drugs" ("Breaking Convention," vol. 366, issue 8318, April 5, 2003). An article offering another perspective is Adam Isacson's "Washington's 'New War' in Colombia: The War on Drugs Meets the War on Terror" (*NACLA Report on the Americas,* vol. 36, issue 5, March/April 2003). Thomas C. Rowe's *Federal Narcotics Laws and the War on Drugs: Money Down a Rat Hole* (Haworth Press, 2006) focuses on the domestic situation in the United States.

A recent comprehensive official report is a U.S. Department of State publication, "International Narcotics Control Strategy Report" (March 2006). Its central message is that "international drug control efforts kept the drug trade on the defensive in 2005." Several long-sought drug kingpins were arrested during the year as well.

ISSUE 11

Is the International Community Adequately Prepared to Address Global Health Pandemics?

YES: Global Influenza Programme, from "Responding to the Avian Influenza Pandemic Threat," World Health Organization (2005)

NO: H.T. Goranson, from "A Primer for Pandemics," Global Envision www.globalenvision.org (March 2006)

ISSUE SUMMARY

YES: The document from the World Health Organization lays out a comprehensive program of action for individual countries, the international community, and WHO to address the next influenza pandemic.

NO: H.T. Goranson, a former top national scientist with the U.S. government, describes the grave dangers posed by global pandemics and highlights flaws in the international community's ability to respond.

Hear the words "global pandemics" and one thinks of the bubonic plague or Black Death of the Middle Ages when an estimated 30 percent of Europe's population died, or the influenza epidemic of 1918 that killed between 25 million and 50 million people worldwide. Both seem like stories from a bygone era, when modern medicine was unknown and people were simply at the mercy of the spreading tendencies of the virulent diseases. The world of medicine is different today, which leads many to assume that somewhere on the shelves of the local pharmacy or the Centers for Disease Control in Atlanta lies a counteragent to whatever killer lurks out there. In 2009, however, the world watches in much the same way as it did 750 years ago or 91 years ago. The reason is the culprit H1N1 swine flu. In April 2009, it was reported that a Mexican boy had flu caused by a mosaic of swine/bird/human influenza viruses known as H1N1. On the other side of the ocean in Cairo, the Egyptian government ordered the killing of 300,000 animals as a precaution. Soon, in every corner of the planet officials began to take precautions, and deaths began to mount.

The world is far different from that of the fourteenth century or even 1918. Globalization is with us. The world has shrunk, literally and figuratively, as the human race's ability to move people, money, goods, information, and also unwanted agents across national boundaries has increased exponentially. Viruses, germs, parasites, and other virulent disease agents can and do move much more easily than at any time in recorded history.

An article prepared for Risk Management LLC by Anup Shah of www .globalissues.org suggests that the problem is compounded by a number of other factors. One billion people have no access to health systems. Over 10 million people died in a recent year from infectious diseases, and a similar number of children under age 5 suffer from malnutrition and other diseases. AIDS/HIV has spread rapidly, with 40 million people living with HIV. These conditions help to facilitate the movement of major contagious diseases.

The word "pandemic" is derived from two Greek words for, "all" and "people." Thus, a global pandemic is an epidemic of some infectious disease that can and is spreading at a rapid rate throughout the world. Throughout history, humankind has fallen victim to many such killers. As early as the Peloponnesian War in fifth-century B.C. Greece, typhoid fever was responsible for the deaths of upward of 25 percent of combatants and civilians alike, necessitating major changes in military tactics. Imperial Rome felt the wrath of a plague thought to be smallpox, as did the eastern Mediterranean during its political height several centuries later. In the past 100 years, influenza (1918, 1957, and 1968), typhoid, and cholera were major killers. In recent years, other infectious diseases have made front-page news: HIV, ebola virus, SARS, and, most recently, avian or bird flu. At this moment, the latter flu is striking tremendous fear in the hearts of global travelers and governmental policymakers everywhere.

According to World Health Organization Europe, as many as 175 million to 360 million people could fall victim to bird flu if the outbreak were severe enough. The bird flu is front-page news because more than 150 million birds have died worldwide from one of its strains, H5N1. This strain was first found in humans in 1997, and WHO estimates report that the human fatality rate has been 50 percent, with 69 deaths occurring as of December 2005. One might be prompted to ask: What is the big deal, with only 134 confirmed cases? It is not quite so simple. Unlike previous pandemics that hit suddenly and with little or no warning, the avian flu is giving us a clear warning. The loss in poultry has been enormous; and as it has jumped from birds to humans, with an initial high mortality rate, our senses have been awakened to the potential for global human disaster.

But there is good news as well. There does appear to be time to prepare for the worst-case scenario and diminish its likelihood. The flu has the attention of all relevant world health agencies and most national agencies, and steps have been undertaken and/or are currently underway to find a way to combat this contagious disease. While this global issue addresses pandemics in general, we have selected avian flu as a case study of world pandemics and global responses because of its current notoriety with the media and policymakers alike. In the first selection, the World Health Organization lays out a comprehensive program of action for individual countries, the international community, and WHO to address the next influenza pandemic. In the second selection, H.T. Goranson, a former top national scientist with the U.S. government, cautions us that the task is enormously difficult. He describes the grave dangers posed by global pandemics and highlights flaws in the international community's ability to respond.

YES Global Influenza Programme

Responding to the Avian Influenza Pandemic Threat

Purpose

This document sets out activities that can be undertaken by individual countries, the international community, and WHO to prepare the world for the next influenza pandemic and mitigate its impact once international spread has begun. Recommended activities are specific to the threat posed by the continuing spread of the H5N1 virus. Addressed to policy-makers, the document also describes issues that can guide policy choices in a situation characterized by both urgency and uncertainty. Recommendations are phase-wise in their approach, with levels of alert, and corresponding activities, changing according to epidemiological indicators of increased threat.

In view of the immediacy of the threat, WHO recommends that all countries undertake urgent action to prepare for a pandemic. Advice on doing so is contained in the recently revised *WHO global influenza preparedness plan* and a new *WHO checklist for influenza pandemic preparedness planning*. To further assist in preparedness planning, WHO is developing a model country plan that will give many developing countries a head start in assessing their status of preparedness and identifying priority needs. Support for rehearsing these plans during simulation exercises will also be provided.

Opportunities to Intervene

As the present situation continues to evolve towards a pandemic, countries, the international community, and WHO have several phase-wise opportunities to intervene, moving from a pre-pandemic situation, through emergence of a pandemic virus, to declaration of a pandemic and its subsequent spread. During the present pre-pandemic phase, interventions aim to reduce the risk that a pandemic virus will emerge and gather better disease intelligence, particularly concerning changes in the behaviour of the virus that signal improved transmissibility. The second opportunity to intervene occurs coincident with the first signal that the virus has improved its transmissibility, and aims to change the early history of the pandemic. The final opportunity occurs after

From *Communicable Disease Surveillance and Response,* Global Influenza Programme, 2005, pp. 1–4, 6–7, 9–10, 12, 14–15. Copyright © 2005 by World Health Organization. Reprinted by permission of WHO Press.

a pandemic has begun. Interventions at this point aim to reduce morbidity, mortality, and social disruption.

Objectives

The objectives of the strategic actions correspond to the principal opportunities to intervene and are likewise phase-wise.

Phase: pre-pandemic
1.   Reduce opportunities for human infection
2.   Strengthen the early warning system
Phase: emergence of a pandemic virus
3.   Contain or delay spread at the source
Phase: pandemic declared and spreading internationally
4.   Reduce morbidity, mortality, and social disruption
5.   Conduct research to guide response measures

Strategic Actions

The document describes strategic actions that can be undertaken to capitalize on each opportunity to intervene. Given the many uncertainties about the evolution of the pandemic threat, including the amount of time left to prepare, a wise approach involves a mix of measures that immediately address critical problems with longer-term measures that sustainably improve the world's capacity to protect itself against the recurring pandemic threat.

Background

Influenza pandemics have historically taken the world by surprise, giving health services little time to prepare for the abrupt increases in cases and deaths that characterize these events and make them so disruptive. Vaccines—the most important intervention for reducing morbidity and mortality—were available for the 1957 and 1968 pandemic viruses, but arrived too late to have an impact. As a result, great social and economic disruption, as well as loss of life, accompanied the three pandemics of the previous century.

The present situation is markedly different for several reasons. First, the world has been warned in advance. For more than a year, conditions favouring another pandemic have been unfolding in parts of Asia. Warnings that a pandemic may be imminent have come from both changes in the epidemiology of human and animal disease and an expanding geographical presence of the virus, creating further opportunities for human exposure. While neither the timing nor the severity of the next pandemic can be predicted, evidence that the virus is now endemic in bird populations means that the present level of risk will not be easily diminished.

Second, this advance warning has brought an unprecedented opportunity to prepare for a pandemic and develop ways to mitigate its effects. To date, the main preparedness activities undertaken by countries have concentrated on preparing and rehearsing response plans, developing a pandemic vaccine, and securing supplies of antiviral drugs. Because these activities are costly, wealthy countries are presently the best prepared; countries where H5N1 is endemic—and where a pandemic virus is most likely to emerge—lag far behind. More countries now have pandemic preparedness plans: around one-fifth of the world's countries have some form of a response plan, but these vary greatly in comprehensiveness and stage of completion. Access to antiviral drugs and, more importantly, to vaccines remains a major problem because of finite manufacturing capacity as well as costs. Some 23 countries have ordered antiviral drugs for national stockpiles, but the principal manufacturer will not be able to fill all orders for at least another year. Fewer than 10 countries have domestic vaccine companies engaged in work on a pandemic vaccine. A November 2004 WHO consultation reached the stark conclusion that, on present trends, the majority of developing countries would have no access to a vaccine during the first wave of a pandemic and possibly throughout its duration.

Apart from stimulating national preparedness activities, the present situation has opened an unprecedented opportunity for international intervention aimed at delaying the emergence of a pandemic virus or forestalling its international spread. Doing so is in the self-interest of all nations, as such a strategy could gain time to augment vaccine supplies. At present capacity, each day of manufacturing gained can mean an additional 5 million doses of vaccine. International support can also strengthen the early warning system in endemic countries, again benefiting preparedness planning and priority setting in all nations. Finally, international support is needed to ensure that large parts of the world do not experience a pandemic without the protection of a vaccine.

Pandemics are remarkable events in that they affect all parts of the world, regardless of socioeconomic status or standards of health care, hygiene and sanitation. Once international spread begins, each government will understandably make protection of its own population the first priority. The best opportunity for international collaboration—in the interest of all countries—is now, before a pandemic begins.

Situation Assessment

1. The risk of a pandemic is great.

Since late 2003, the world has moved closer to a pandemic than at any time since 1968, when the last of the previous century's three pandemics occurred. All prerequisites for the start of a pandemic have now been met save one: the establishment of efficient human-to-human transmission. During 2005, ominous changes have been observed in the epidemiology of the disease in animals. Human cases are continuing to occur, and the virus has expanded its geographical range to include new countries, thus increasing the size of the population at risk. Each new human case gives the virus an opportunity to evolve towards a fully transmissible pandemic strain.

2. The risk will persist.

Evidence shows that the H5N1 virus is now endemic in parts of Asia, having established an ecological niche in poultry. The risk of further human cases will persist, as will opportunities for a pandemic virus to emerge. Outbreaks have recurred despite aggressive control measures, including the culling of more than 140 million poultry. Wild migratory birds—historically the host reservoir of all influenza A viruses—are now dying in large numbers from highly pathogenic H5N1. Domestic ducks can excrete large quantities of highly pathogenic virus without showing signs of illness. Their silent role in maintaining transmission further complicates control in poultry and makes human avoidance of risky behaviours more difficult.

3. Evolution of the threat cannot be predicted.

Given the constantly changing nature of influenza viruses, the timing and severity of the next pandemic cannot be predicted. The final step—improved transmissibility among humans—can take place via two principal mechanisms: a reassortment event, in which genetic material is exchanged between human and avian viruses during co-infection of a human or pig, and a more gradual process of adaptive mutation, whereby the capability of these viruses to bind to human cells would increase during subsequent infections of humans. Reassortment could result in a fully transmissible pandemic virus, announced by a sudden surge of cases with explosive spread. Adaptive mutation, expressed initially as small clusters of human cases with evidence of limited transmission, will probably give the world some time to take defensive action. Again, whether such a "grace period" will be granted is unknown.

4. The early warning system is weak.

As the evolution of the threat cannot be predicted, a sensitive early warning system is needed to detect the first sign of changes in the behaviour of the virus. In risk-prone countries, disease information systems and health, veterinary, and laboratory capacities are weak. Most affected countries cannot adequately compensate farmers for culled poultry, thus discouraging the reporting of outbreaks in the rural areas where the vast majority of human cases have occurred. Veterinary extension services frequently fail to reach these areas. Rural poverty perpetuates high-risk behaviours, including the traditional home-slaughter and consumption of diseased birds. Detection of human cases is impeded by patchy surveillance in these areas. Diagnosis of human cases is impeded by weak laboratory support and the complexity and high costs of testing. Few affected countries have the staff and resources needed to thoroughly investigate human cases and, most importantly, to detect and investigate clusters of cases—an essential warning signal. In virtually all affected countries, antiviral drugs are in very short supply.

The dilemma of preparing for a potentially catastrophic but unpredictable event is great for all countries, but most especially so for countries affected by H5N1 outbreaks in animals and humans. These countries, in which rural subsistence farming is a backbone of economic life, have experienced direct and enormous agricultural losses, presently estimated at more than US$10 billion. They are being asked to sustain—if not intensify—resource-intensive activities needed to safeguard international public health while struggling to cope with many other competing health and infectious disease priorities.

5. Preventive intervention is possible, but untested.

Should a pandemic virus begin to emerge through the more gradual process of adaptive mutation, early intervention with antiviral drugs, supported by other public health measures, could theoretically prevent the virus from further improving its transmissibility, thus either preventing a pandemic or delaying its international spread. While this strategy has been proposed by many influenza experts, it remains untested; no effort has ever been made to alter the natural course of a pandemic at its source.

6. Reduction of morbidity and mortality during a pandemic will be impeded by inadequate medical supplies.

Vaccination and the use of antiviral drugs are two of the most important response measures for reducing morbidity and mortality during a pandemic. On present trends, neither of these interventions will be available in adequate quantities or equitably distributed at the start of a pandemic and for many months thereafter.

1. Reduce Opportunities for Human Infection
Strategic Actions

- **Support the FAO/OIE control strategy**

  The FAO/OIE technical recommendations describe specific control measures and explain how they should be implemented. The global strategy, developed in collaboration with WHO, takes its urgency from the risk to human health, including that arising from a pandemic, posed by the continuing circulation of the virus in animals. The strategy adopts a progressive approach, with different control options presented in line with different disease profiles, including such factors as poultry densities, farming systems, and whether infections have occurred in commercial farms or small rural holdings. The proposed initial focus is on Viet Nam, Thailand, Cambodia, and Indonesia, the four countries where human cases of infection with H5N1 avian influenza have been detected.

Clear and workable measures are proposed for different countries and situations within countries. Vaccination is being recommended as an appropriate control measure in some, but not all, epidemiological situations. Other measures set out in the strategy include strict biosecurity at commercial farms, use of compartmentalization and zoning concepts, control of animal and product movements, and a restructuring of the poultry industry in some countries. The strategy notes strong political will to tackle the problem. Nonetheless, time-frames for reaching control objectives are now being measured in years.

In July 2005, OIE member countries approved new standards, recognized by the World Trade Organization, specific to avian influenza and aimed at improving the safety of international trade of poultry and poultry products. The new standards cover methods of surveillance, compulsory international notification of low- and highly-pathogenic strains of avian influenza, the use of vaccination, and food safety of poultry products. Compliance with these standards should be given priority in efforts to strengthen early detection, reporting, and response in countries currently affected by outbreaks of H5N1 avian influenza.

- **Intensify collaboration between the animal and public health sectors**

WHO will appoint dedicated staff to increase the present exchange of information between agricultural and health sectors at the international level. Increased collaboration between the two sectors serves three main purposes: to pinpoint areas of disease activity in animals where vigilance for human cases should be intensified, to ensure that measures for controlling the disease in animals are compatible with reduced opportunities for human exposure, and to ensure that advice to rural communities on protective measures remains in line with the evolving nature of the disease in animals.

WHO will undertake joint action with FAO and OIE to understand the evolution of H5N1 viruses in Asia. Achieving this objective requires acquisition and sharing of a full inventory of H5N1 viruses, from humans, poultry, wild birds, and other animals, and sequences.

WHO will stress the importance of controlling the disease in rural areas. Measures to control the disease in animals of necessity consider how best to regain agricultural productivity and international trade, and this objective is reflected in the FAO/OIE strategy. While elimination of the virus from the commercial poultry sector alone will aid agricultural recovery, it may not significantly reduce opportunities for human exposure, as the vast majority of cases to date have been associated with exposure to small rural flocks. No case has yet been detected among workers in the commercial poultry sector. The FAO/OIE strategy fully recognizes that control of disease in rural "backyard" flocks will be the most difficult challenge; strong support from the health sector, as expressed by WHO, helps gather the political will to meet this challenge. In addition, it is imperative that measures for controlling disease in rural flocks are accompanied by risk communication to farmers and their families.

A joint FAO/OIE/WHO meeting, held in Malaysia in July 2005, addressed the links between animal disease and risks of human exposures and infections, and defined preventive measures that should be jointly introduced by the animal and public health sectors. Priority was given to interventions in the backyard rural farming system and in so-called wet markets where live poultry are sold under crowded and often unsanitary conditions.

WHO, FAO, and OIE have jointly established a Global Early Warning and Response System (GLEWS) for transboundary animal diseases. The new mechanism combines the existing outbreak alert, verification, and response capacities of the three agencies and helps ensure that disease tracking at WHO benefits from the latest information on relevant animal diseases. The system formalizes the sharing of epidemiological information and provides the operational framework for joint field missions to affected areas.

- **Strengthen risk communication to rural residents**

WHO will, through its research networks and in collaboration with FAO and OIE, improve understanding of the links between animal disease, human behaviours, and the risk of acquiring H5N1 infection. This information will be used as the basis for risk communication to rural residents.

Well-known and avoidable behaviours with a high risk of infection continue to occur in rural areas. Ongoing risk communication is needed to alert rural residents to these risks and explain how to avoid them. Better knowledge about the relationship between animal and human disease, obtained by WHO in collaboration with FAO/OIE, can be used to make present risk communication more precise and thus better able to prevent risky behaviours.

- **Improve approaches to environmental detection of the virus**

WHO, FAO, and OIE will facilitate, through their research networks, the rapid development of new methods for detecting the virus in environmental samples. The purpose of these methods is to gain a better understanding of conditions that increase the risk of human infection and therefore favour emergence of a pandemic virus. Such knowledge underpins the success of primary prevention of a pandemic through disease control in animals. It also underpins advice to rural residents on behaviours to avoid. Reliance on routine veterinary surveillance, which is weak in most risk-prone countries, has not produced an adequate understanding of the relationship between animal and human disease. For example, in some cases, outbreaks in poultry are detected only after a human case has been confirmed. In other cases, investigation of human cases has failed to find a link with disease in animals.

2. Strengthen the Early Warning System
Strategic Actions

- ### Improve the detection of human cases

WHO will provide the training, diagnostic reagents, and administrative support for external verification needed to improve the speed and reliability of case detection. To date, the vast majority of cases have been detected following hospitalization for respiratory illness. Hospitals in affected countries need support in case detection, laboratory confirmation, and reporting. Apart from its role in an early warning system, rapid laboratory confirmation signals the need to isolate patients and manage them according to strict procedures of infection control, and can thus help prevent further cases.

Diagnostic support continues to be provided by laboratories in the WHO network. However, because the initial symptoms of H5N1 infection mimic those of many diseases common in these countries, accurate case detection requires the testing of large numbers of samples. Improved local capacity is therefore a more rational solution.

Because of its high pathogenicity, H5N1 can be handled safely only by specially trained staff working in specially equipped laboratories operating at a high level of biosecurity. These facilities do not presently exist in the majority of affected countries. As an alternative, laboratory capacity can be enhanced by strengthening the existing system of national influenza centres or by providing mobile high-containment laboratories. Supportive activities include training in laboratory methods needed for H5N1 diagnosis, distribution of up-to-date diagnostic reagents, and coordination of work between national laboratories and epidemiological institutions.

An infrastructure needs to be developed to complement national testing with rapid international verification in WHO certified laboratories, especially as each confirmed human case yields information essential to risk assessment. The capacity to do so already exists. WHO offers countries rapid administrative support to ship samples outside affected countries. Such forms of assistance become especially critical when clusters of cases occur and require investigation.

- **Combine detection of new outbreaks in animals with active searches for human cases**

Using epidemiologists in its country offices and, when necessary, external partners, WHO will ensure that detection of new outbreaks of highly pathogenic H5N1 in poultry is accompanied by active searches for human cases. Surveillance in several countries where H5N1 is considered endemic in birds is inadequate and suspicions are strong that human cases have been missed. Cambodia's four human cases were detected only after patients sought treatment in neighbouring Viet Nam, where physicians are on high alert for cases and familiar with the clinical presentation.

- **Support epidemiological investigation**

Reliable risk assessment depends on thorough investigation of sporadic human cases and clusters of cases. Guidelines for outbreak investigation, specific to H5N1 and to the epidemiological situation in different countries, are being developed on an urgent basis for use in training national teams. These guidelines give particular emphasis to the investigation of clusters of cases and determination of whether human-to-human transmission has occurred. Teams assembled from institutions in the WHO Global Outbreak Alert and Response Network (GOARN) can be deployed for rapid on-site investigative support.

- **Coordinate clinical research in Asia**

Clinical data on human cases need to be compiled and compared in order to elucidate modes of transmission, identify groups at risk, and find better treatments. Work has begun to establish a network of hospitals, modelled on the WHO global influenza surveillance network, engaged in clinical research on human disease. The network will link together the principal hospitals in Asia that are treating H5N1 patients and conducting clinical research. Technical support will allow rapid exchange of information and sharing of specimens and research results, and encourage the use of standardized protocols for treatment and standardized sampling procedures for investigation.

Identification of risk groups guides preventive measures and early interventions. Provision of high-quality data on clinical course, outcome, and treatment efficacy meets an obvious and immediate need in countries with human cases. Answers to some key questions—the efficacy of antiviral drugs, optimum dose, and prescribing schedules—could benefit health services elsewhere once a pandemic is under way.

- **Strengthen risk assessment**

WHO's daily operations need to be strengthened to ensure constant collection and verification of epidemiological and virological information essential for risk assessment. Ministries of health and research institutions in affected countries need to be more fully engaged in the collection and verification of data. Ministries and institutions in non-affected countries should help assess the significance of these data, and the results should be issued rapidly. These activities, currently coordinated by WHO, need to escalate; influenza viruses can evolve rapidly and in unexpected ways that alter risk assessment, as evidenced by the recent detection of highly pathogenic H5N1 viruses in migratory birds. Functions of the WHO network of laboratories with expertise in the analysis of H5N1 viruses can be improved through tools, such as a genetic database, and a strong collaboration with veterinary laboratory networks to ensure that animal as well as human viruses are kept under constant surveillance.

- **Strengthen existing national influenza centres throughout the risk-prone region**

Many existing national influenza centres, designated by WHO, already possess considerable infrastructure in the form of equipment and trained personnel. Additional support, particularly in the form of diagnostic reagents, could help strengthen the early warning system in risk-prone countries and their neighbours.

- **Give risk-prone countries an incentive to collaborate internationally**

The promise of assistance is a strong motivation to report cases and share clinical specimens internationally. A high-level meeting should be convened so that heads of state in industrialized countries and in risk-prone countries can seek solutions and reach agreement on the kinds of support considered most desirable by individual countries.

3. Contain or Delay Spread at the Source

Strategic Actions

- **Establish an international stockpile of antiviral drugs**

WHO will establish an international stockpile of antiviral drugs for rapid response at the start of a pandemic. The stockpile is a strategic option that serves the interests of the international community as well as those of the initially affected populations. Issues that need to be addressed include logistics associated with deployment and administration, and licensing for use in individual countries. Mechanisms for using an international stockpile need to be defined more precisely in terms of epidemiological triggers for deploying the stockpile and time-frames for emergency delivery and administration. WHO is working closely with groups engaged in mathematical modelling and others to guide the development of early containment strategies.

While pursuit of this option thus has no guarantee of success, it nonetheless needs to be undertaken as it represents one of the few preventive options for an event with predictably severe consequences for every country in the world. It is also the best guarantee that populations initially affected will have access to drugs for treatment. Should early containment fail to completely halt spread of the virus, a delay in wide international spread would gain time to intensify preparedness. It can be expected that most governments will begin introducing emergency measures only when the threat of a pandemic is certain and immediate. A lead time for doing so of one month or more could allow many health services to build surge capacity and make the necessary conversion from routine to emergency services.

- **Develop mass delivery mechanisms for antiviral drugs**

Several WHO programmes, such as those for the emergency response to outbreaks of poliomyelitis, measles, epidemic-prone meningitis, and yellow fever, have acquired considerable experience in the urgent mass delivery of vaccines in developing countries. Less experience exists for the mass delivery of antiviral drugs, where administration is complicated by the need for drugs to be taken over several days and the need for different dosing schedules according to therapeutic or prophylactic use. WHO will develop and pilot test delivery mechanisms for antiviral drugs in collaboration with national health authorities and industry. Studies will assess coverage rates that could be achieved, taking into account compliance rates, and ways to support this intervention with other measures, such as area quarantine.

- **Conduct surveillance of antiviral susceptibility**

  Using its existing network of influenza laboratories, WHO will establish a surveillance programme for antiviral susceptibility testing, modelled on a similar programme for anti-tuberculosis drugs. Use of an international stockpile to attempt to halt an outbreak will involve administration of drugs to large numbers of people for several weeks. A mechanism must be in place to monitor any resulting changes in virus susceptibility to these drugs. The development of drug resistance would threaten the effectiveness of national stockpiles of antiviral drugs established for domestic use. The work of WHO collaborating centres for influenza and reference laboratories for H5N1 analysis can be coordinated to include anti-viral susceptibility testing.

4. Reduce Morbidity, Mortality, and Social Disruption

Strategic Actions

- **Monitor the evolving pandemic in real time**

  Many characteristics of a pandemic that will guide the selection of response measures will become apparent only after the new virus has emerged and begun to cause large numbers of cases. WHO, assisted by virtual networks of experts, will monitor the unfolding epidemiological and clinical behaviour of the new virus in real time. This monitoring will give health authorities answers to key questions about age groups at greatest risk, infectivity of the virus, severity of the disease, attack rates, risk to health care workers, and mortality rates. Such monitoring can also help determine whether severe illness and deaths are caused by primary viral pneumonia or secondary bacterial pneumonia, which responds to antibiotics, and thus guide the emergency provision of supplies. Experts in mathematical modelling will be included in the earliest field assessment teams to make the forecasting of trends as reliable as possible.

- **Introduce non-pharmaceutical interventions**

  Answers to these questions will help officials select measures—closing of schools, quarantine, a ban on mass gatherings, travel restrictions—that match the behaviour of the virus and thus have the greatest chance of reducing the number of cases and delaying geographical spread. WHO has produced guidance on the use of such measures at different stages at the start of a pandemic and after its international spread.

- **Use antiviral drugs to protect priority groups**

  WHO recommends that countries with sufficient resources invest in a stockpile of antiviral drugs for domestic use, particularly at the start of a pandemic when mass vaccination is not an option and priority groups, such as frontline workers, need to be protected.

- **Augment vaccine supplies**

WHO, in collaboration with industry and regulatory authorities, has introduced fast-track procedures for the development and licensing of a pandemic vaccine. Strategies have also been developed that make the most of scarce vaccine antigen and thus allow more quantities of vaccine to be produced despite the limits of existing plant capacity. Once a pandemic is declared, all manufacturers will switch from production of seasonal vaccines to production of a pandemic vaccine. Countries need to address liability issues that could arise following mass administration of a pandemic vaccine and ensure adequate warehousing, logistics, and complementary supplies, such as syringes.

- **Ensure equitable access to vaccines**

The present strong interdependence of commerce and trade means that the international community cannot afford to allow large parts of the world to experience a pandemic unprotected by a vaccine. The humanitarian and ethical arguments for providing such protection are readily apparent. As a matter of urgency, WHO must build a political process aimed at finding ways to further augment production capacity dramatically and make vaccines affordable and accessible in the developing world. WHO will also work with donor agencies on the latter issue.

- **Communicate risks to the public**

As soon as a pandemic is declared, health authorities will need to start a continuous process of risk communication to the public. Many difficult issues—the inevitable spread to all countries, the shortage of vaccines and antiviral drugs, justification for the selection of priority groups for protection—will need to be addressed. Effective risk communication, supported by confidence in government authorities and the reliability of their information, may help mitigate some of the social and economic disruption attributed to an anxious public. Countries are advised to plan in advance. A communication strategy for a pandemic situation should include training in outbreak communication and integration of communicators in senior management teams.

5. Conduct Research to Guide Response Measures
Strategic Actions

- **Assess the epidemiological characteristics of an emerging pandemic**

At the start of a pandemic, policy-makers will face an immediate need for epidemiological data on the principal age groups affected, modes of transmission, and pathogenicity. Such data will support urgent decisions about target groups for vaccination and receipt of antiviral drugs. They can also be used to support forecasts on local and global patterns of spread as an early warning that helps national authorities intensify preparedness measures. WHO will identify epidemiological centres for collecting these data and establish standardized research protocols.

- **Monitor the effectiveness of health interventions**

  Several non-pharmaceutical interventions have been recommended to reduce local and international spread of a pandemic and lower the rate of transmission. While many of these interventions have proved useful in the prevention and control of other infectious diseases, their effectiveness during a pandemic has never been comprehensively evaluated. More information is needed on their feasibility, effectiveness, and acceptability to populations. WHO will establish study sites and develop study protocols to evaluate these interventions at local, national, and international levels. Comparative data on the effectiveness of different interventions are also important, as several measures are associated with very high levels of social disruption.

- **Evaluate the medical and economic consequences**

  WHO will establish study sites and develop protocols for prospective evaluation of the medical and economic consequences of the pandemic so that future health interventions can be adjusted accordingly. In the past, such evaluations have been conducted only after a pandemic had ended. Their value as a policy guide for the allocation of resources has been flawed because of inadequate data.

A Primer for Pandemics

A few times each year, the world is reminded that a pandemic threat is imminent. What can we do to prepare for the next one?

> According to Dr. Tim Evans, Assistant Director-General for Evidence and Information for Policy, World Health Organization: "There is a chronic global shortage of health workers, as a result of decades of underinvestment in their education, training, salaries, working environment and management. This has led to a severe lack of key skills, rising levels of career switching and early retirement, as well as national and international migration. In sub-Saharan Africa, where all the issues mentioned above are combined with the HIV/AIDS pandemic, there are an estimated 750,000 health workers in a region that is home to 682 million people. By comparison, the ratio is ten to 15 times higher in OECD countries, whose ageing population is putting a growing strain on an over-stretched workforce. Solutions to this crisis must be worked out at local, national and international levels, and must involve governments, the United Nations, health professionals, non-governmental organizations and community leaders."

> "There is no single solution to such a complex problem, but ways forward do exist and must now be implemented. For example, some developed countries have put policies in place to stop active recruitment of health workers from severely understaffed countries. Some developing countries have revised their pay scales and introduced non-monetary incentives to retain their workforce and deploy them in rural areas. Education and training procedures have been tailored to countries' specific needs. Community health workers are helping their communities to prevent and treat key diseases. Action must be taken now for results to show in the coming years."

This article takes a look at global pandemics, and how medical professionals worldwide trained as "detectors" would be the best way to halt the spread of a disease before it became a global threat.

~⊙~

A few times each year, the world is reminded that a pandemic threat is imminent. In 2003, it was SARS. Today, it is a potential avian virus similar to the one that killed 30 million people after 1914.

From ProjectSyndicate.org, March 2006. Copyright © 2006 by Project Syndicate. Reprinted by permission. www.project-syndicate.org

"Bird flu" has already shown that it can jump from fowl to humans, and now even to cats, which indicates that it might be the next global killer. But there are many other potential pandemics, and many are not even viruses. Bacteria, prions, parasites, and even environmental factors could suddenly change in a way that slays us. It is widely predicted that when this happens, the economic and human losses will exceed that of any previous war.

Indeed, it is humbling to remember that some of history's most deadly invasions were carried out by single-cell organisms, such as cholera, bubonic plague, and tuberculosis. Countries with the resources to do so are making resistance plans against pandemics—limited strategies that would protect their own citizens. Most governments are hoping that early detection will make containment possible.

Containment depends heavily on vaccines, but vaccines are only part of the answer. While they are a good defense against many viruses, each vaccine is highly specific to the threat. Viruses are parasites to cells, and each virus attacks a particular type of cell. The virus is shaped so that it can drill into a particular feature of that cell and inject parts of itself inside, confusing the cell into making more viruses and destroying itself in the process. With their very specific forms, the most effective anti-viral vaccines must be designed for a narrow range of factors.

Sometimes the tailored nature of viruses works in our favor. For example, they usually find it difficult to jump between species, because they would have to change their structure. But if large numbers of a host—say, birds—encounter a great number of people, eventually the virus will find a way to prosper in a new type of cell.

Birds are the greatest concern today only because the spread is easy to see. But AIDS jumped from monkeys and several types of flu jumped from swine. Deadly mutations of any kind need to be identified urgently, so that an effective vaccine can be designed before the strain becomes comfortable in the human body. Unfortunately our present methods of detection are not sensitive enough.

This is even more worrying when you realize that scientists should also be monitoring bacteria, prions, and parasites. There are more bacteria than any other life form. Many live harmlessly in our bodies and perform useful functions. They evolve and adapt easily, which means that they learn to sidestep our drugs over time. Bacteria should be checked for two types of mutation: adaptation by a hostile form that enables it to become super-immune to drugs, or a deadly mutant strain that appears in one of the multitude of "safe" bacteria.

Prions are a relatively new discovery. They are made from proteins similar to those that the body uses during healthy operations, which means that they are able to fool the body's tools into making more prions. They have only recently been recognized as the cause of several infectious diseases, including mad cow disease and Creutzfeldt-Jakob Disease, which kill by crowding out healthy brain cells. Many nerve, respiratory and muscle diseases might also be caused by prions.

Finally, parasites, simple animals that infect us, are already classified as pandemics. Malaria afflicts 300 million people and is the world's biggest killer of children. Many parasites are worms: hookworm (800 million people infected), roundworm (1.5 billion), schistosomes (200 million), and the worm that causes Elephantiasis (150 million).

There are also antagonists that are currently ignored. Environmental chemicals and particulates might warrant their own categories. Or consider combinations of problems, such as these chemical infectors mixing with airborne pollens, and apparently pushing up incidences of asthma. New fungal infections are even scarier and might be harder to treat.

The bottom line is that we can't predict where the threat will emerge, so we need a distributed, intelligent detection system. In practical terms, how should it be built?

"Detectors" would have to be expert enough to know when an ordinary-looking symptom is actually an emergency. They would be located everywhere, with an emphasis on vulnerable regions. Initial warning signs of a pandemic are most likely to appear in the developing world, but detection nodes should be positioned in every country, with the least possible expense. This is not as difficult as it sounds. The key is to harness existing infrastructure.

Medical infrastructure exists everywhere, in some form. It also tends to be the least corrupt of institutions in regions where that is a problem. Medical centers and clinics would be expected to investigate the cause of ailments in a large number of their patients, even in cases where the symptoms seem common. A small amount of additional scientific expertise and lab equipment would need to be added to a public health system that serves ordinary needs.

Enhancing existing resources would be effective for two reasons. First, illness is more likely to be reported in a city hospital than at a specialist institute. Second, the investment would boost latent public health in that region. For poor regions, investment in equipment and training would have to come from wealthier counterparts. Rich countries could justify the expense in terms of the savings that would result from early detection of a major threat. Tropical climates and urban slums are humanity's front line against pandemics, and they should be equipped properly.

Public health is an important asset for any nation. With so much at stake, it makes sense to place sentinels near every swamp, city, public market, and farmyard on earth.

POSTSCRIPT

Is the International Community Adequately Prepared to Address Global Health Pandemics?

It is far too easy to adopt one of two extreme positions regarding the potential for a global pandemic such as influenza. The first assumes that because these outbreaks begin somewhere in the poorer regions of the globe far removed geographically from the United States, we in the developed world, particularly in the United States, are not at great risk. One should immediately pause, however, as each winter many Americans find themselves suffering from a much less virulent strain of the flu, which typically has its roots in the same poor regions of the globe. The second position with respect to the future potential for a global pandemic suggests that modern medical science will always find a way to counteract such diseases. As the world's experience with HIV/AIDS has taught us, however, modern viruses and other diseases are increasingly more complicated to address successfully, either in treating the symptoms of the problem or the actual problem itself.

Edwin D. Kilbourne addresses this issue in his analysis of twentieth-century pandemics and lessons learned there from ("Influenza Pandemics of the 20th Century," *Emerging Infectious Diseases,* vol. 12, no. 1, January 2006). Says Kilbourne, "Yes, we can prepare, but with the realization that no amount of hand washing, hand wringing, public education, or gauze masks will do the trick. The keystone of influenza prevention is vaccination." This raises a number of questions, Kilbourne continues. Primary among these are who shall be given the vaccine, the risks of mass administration, and the availability of sufficient quantities of a vaccine of "adequate antigenic potency."

Kilbourne suggests that an appropriate strategy was suggested by the World Health Organization as early as 1969 and endorsed repeatedly since then. The approach assumes that a new influenza outbreak will emerge from 1 of 16 known subtypes HA in avian or mammalian species. This assumption has not yet resulted in a genetic vaccine that can address these subtypes. As the first reading reveals, however, WHO has developed a comprehensive set of strategic actions for the three phases of a pandemic: the pre-pandemic phase, the emergence of a pandemic virus, and the pandemic declared and spreading internationally. As the second reading suggests, however, national governments in the developing world, the likely place of origin of the next global pandemic, suffer from a shortage of skilled medical personnel that would serve as front-line defenders against such infectious diseases.

One piece of good news is that, unlike previous pandemics, the developed world has taken notice of a potential future threat. The U.S. government has pledged close to $4 billion for the current fiscal year, three times its expenditures of five years ago. Private philanthropists led by the Bill and Melinda Gates Foundation have also been active in global health programs.

Literature from both the medical and more general fields has also been more cognizant of the problem and has dramatically focused attention to the potential future problem. One place to begin is a major report from the World Health Organization called *Avian Influenza: Assessing the Pandemic Threat* (2005). It traces the evolution of the outbreaks of the H5N1 avian influenza, lessons from past pandemics, its origins in poultry, and future actions "in the face of an uncertain threat." A second WHO report spells out in greater detail that organization's plan of action, *WHO Global Influenza Preparedness Plan* (2005). One study cautions us about this report, however (Martin Enserink, "New Study Casts Doubt on Plans for Pandemic Containment," *Science,* vol. 311, no. 5764, February 24, 2006).

Several books are useful in understanding global health and pandemics. A primer for how the current global flu pandemic might affect humans is found in *Global Time Bomb: Surviving the H1N1 Swine Flu Pandemic and Other Global Health Threats* (John M. Dorrance, ed., Madrona Books, 2009). A most recent work is Barry Youngerman's *Pandemics and Global Issues* (Facts on File, 2008). Two books that focus on broader global health issues include *Understanding Global Health,* by William Markle et al. (McGraw-Hill, 2007) and *Critical Issues in Global Health* (C. Everett Koop et al., eds., Jossey-Bass, 2002). Two books that address the link between globalization and health include *Globalization and Health: An Introduction* (Kelley Lee, Palgrave Macmillan, 2004) and *Health Impacts of Globalization: Towards Global Governance* (Kelley Lee, Palgrave Macmillan, 2003).

A historical overview of pandemics is R.S. Bray's *Armies of Pestilence: The Effects of Pandemics on History* (Lutterworth Press, 1998). Another general source is "Preparing for Pandemic: High Probability of a Flu Pandemic Prompts WHO to Offer Strategies" (*The Futurist,* vol. 40, no. 1, January/February 2006). A source that focuses on the value of global structures in the fight against pandemics is "Global Network Could Avert Pandemics" (J.P. Chretien, J.C. Gaydos, J.L. Malone, and D.L. Blazes, *Nature,* vol. 440, 2006). A historical overview of the HIV pandemic is found in *The HIV Pandemic: Local and Global Implications* (Eduard J. Beck, Nicholas Mays, and Alan W. Whiteside, eds., Oxford University Press, 2008). Two recent books that focus on the impact of HIV/AIDS are *Global Lessons from the AIDS Pandemic: Economic, Financial, Legal and Political Implications* (Bradly J. Condon and Tapen Sinha, Springer, 2008); and *AIDS and Governance* (Nana K. Poku, Alan Whiteside, and Bjorg Sandkjaer, eds., Ashgate Publishing Company, 2007).

An excellent Internet Web site is www.bmj.com, a comprehensive source of resources by the medical field on global pandemics. One example is "An Iatrogenic Pandemic of Panic," by Luc Bonneux and Wim Van Damme (April 1, 2006).

Finally, a current report on the problem of HIV/AIDS is "The Global Challenge of HIV and AIDS" (Peter R. Lamptey, Jami L. Johnson, and Marya Khan, *Population Reference Bureau,* vol. 61, no. 1, March 2006).

ISSUE 12

Do Adequate Strategies Exist to Combat Human Trafficking?

YES: Janie Chuang, from "Beyond a Snapshot: Preventing Human Trafficking in the Global Economy," *Indiana Journal of Global Legal Studies* (Winter 2006)

NO: Dina Francesca Haynes, from "Used, Abused, Arrested, and Deported: Extending Immigration Benefits to Protect the Victims of Trafficking and to Secure the Prosecution of Traffickers," *Human Rights Quarterly* (vol. 26, no. 2, 2004)

ISSUE SUMMARY

YES: Janie Chuang, practitioner-in-residence at the America University Washington College of Law, suggests that governments have been finally motivated to take action against human traffickers as a consequence of the concern over national security implications of forced human labor movement and the involvement of transnational criminal syndicates.

NO: Dina Francesca Haynes, associate professor of law at the New England School of Law, argues that none of the models underlying domestic legislation to deal with human traffickers is "terribly effective" in addressing the issue effectively.

Human trafficking is defined by the United Nations as "the recruitment, transportation, transfer, harbouring or receipt of persons, by means of the threat or use of force or other forms of coercion, of abduction, of fraud, of deception, of the abuse of power or of a position of vulnerability or of the giving or receiving of payments or benefits to achieve the consent of a person having control over another person, for the purpose of exploitation" ("Trafficking in Persons—Global Patterns," United Nations, Office on Drug and Crime, April 2006). Exploitation may take any one of several forms: prostitution, forced labor, slavery, or other forms of servitude. Although slavery has been with us since ancient times, the existence of human trafficking across national borders, particularly involving major distances, is a relatively new escalation of a problem that in the past was addressed as a domestic issue, if addressed at all.

Its modern manifestation is eerily similar, as reported by the United Nations in the previous source. People are abducted or "recruited" in the country of origin, transferred through a standard network to another region of the globe, and then exploited in the destination country. If at any point exploitation is interrupted or ceases, victims can be rescued and might receive support from the country of destination. Victims might be repatriated to their country of origin or, less likely, relocated to a third country. Too often, victims are treated as illegal migrants and treated accordingly. The United Nations estimates that 127 countries act as countries of origin while 137 countries serve as countries of destination. Profits are estimated by the United Nations to be $7 billion per year, with between 70,000 and 4 million new victims annually.

When one hears of human trafficking, one usually thinks of sexual exploitation rather than of forced labor. This is not surprising as not only are individual victim's stories more compelling, but the former type of exploitation represents the more frequent topic of dialogue among policymakers and is also the more frequent occurrence as reported to the United Nations, by a three-to-one margin. With respect to victims, 77 percent are woman, 33 percent children, 48 percent girls, 12 percent boys, and 9 percent males (the sum of percentages is over 100 because one source can indicate more than one victim profile). It is not surprising that most women and female children are exploited sexually, while most male adults and children are subjected to forced labor. Sexual exploitation is more typically found in Central and Southeastern Europe. Former Soviet republics serve as a huge source of origin. Africa ranks high as a region of victim origin as well, although most end up in forced labor rather than in sexual exploitation. Asia is a region of both origin and destination. Countries at the top of the list include Thailand, Japan, India, Taiwan, and Pakistan.

The same UN study found that nationals of Asia and Europe represent the bulk of traffickers. And most traffickers who are arrested are nationals of the country where the arrest occurred. Two principal types of groups characterize the traffickers: The first group is highly structured and organized, following a disciplined hierarchical pattern of control. In addition to trafficking, this group is involved in transnational movement of a variety of illegal goods such as drugs and firearms. Violence is the norm in this group. The second type is a smaller group that is strictly profit-oriented and opportunistic, and appears to operate under a loose network of associates.

In the first selection, Janie Chuang suggests that governments have adopted a three-pronged approach focusing on prosecuting traffickers, protecting trafficked persons, and preventing trafficking. She argues that there has been greater success with the first two foci, but that the current legal response appears to be having an effect or shows great promise in addressing all three areas. In the second selection, Dina Francesca Haynes suggests that while much rhetoric has occurred, the models underlying domestic legislation are not effective for a variety of reasons.

YES

Janie Chuang

Beyond a Snapshot: Preventing Human Trafficking in the Global Economy

Introduction

Within the last decade, governments have hastened to develop international, regional, and national laws to combat the problem of human trafficking, i.e., the recruitment or movement of persons for forced labor or slavery-like practices. Legal responses to the problem typically adopt a three-prong framework focused on prosecuting traffickers, protecting trafficked persons, and preventing trafficking. In practice, however, these responses emphasize the prosecution of traffickers and, to a lesser extent, the protection of their victims. Most legal frameworks address trafficking as an act (or a series of acts) of violence, with the perpetrators to be punished and the victims to be protected and reintegrated into society. While such responses might account for the consequences of trafficking, they tend to overlook its causes—that is, the broader socioeconomic conditions that feed the problem. Oft-repeated pledges to prevent trafficking by addressing its root causes seldom evolve from rhetoric into reality.

More often than not, trafficking is labor migration gone horribly wrong in our globalized economy. Notwithstanding its general economic benefits, globalization has bred an ever-widening wealth gap between countries, and between rich and poor communities within countries.[1] This dynamic has created a spate of "survival migrants"[2] who seek employment opportunities abroad as a means of survival as jobs disappear in their countries of origin. The desperate need to migrate for work, combined with destination countries tightening their border controls (despite a growing demand for migrant workers), render these migrants highly vulnerable to trafficking. For women in particular, this vulnerability is exacerbated by well-entrenched discriminatory practices that relegate women to employment in informal economic sectors and further limit their avenues for legal migration.

Governments have been deeply reluctant, however, to view trafficking in this broader frame—that is, as a problem of migration, poverty, discrimination, and gender-based violence. They have tended to view trafficking as a "law and order" problem requiring an aggressive criminal justice response. Emerging studies reveal the drawbacks of this myopia. Notwithstanding the hundreds

From *Indiana Journal of Global Legal Studies*, vol. 13, no. 1, Winter 2006, pp. 137–138, 147–157. Copyright © 2006 by Indiana University Press. Reprinted by permission.

215

of millions of dollars already invested in the criminal justice response to the problem, we have yet to see an appreciable reduction in the absolute numbers of people trafficked worldwide.[3] And even in the rare cases where trafficked persons have received rights, protective treatment, and aftercare, they nonetheless are left facing the socioeconomic conditions that rendered them vulnerable to abuse in the first instance.

This article explores governments' reluctance to address trafficking in its broader socioeconomic context, and offers both a plea and a proposal for more comprehensive approaches to trafficking. Because close examination of these issues is beyond the scope of this short symposium piece, this article aims only to lay a foundation for further thought and discussion in this area. This article problematizes current approaches to trafficking by reframing the problem of trafficking as a global migratory response to current globalizing socioeconomic trends. It argues that, to be effective, counter-trafficking strategies must also target the underlying conditions that impel people to accept dangerous labor migration assignments in the first place. The article then examines how the international legal response to the problem is, as yet, inadequate to the task of fostering longterm solutions. Moreover, by failing to assess the long-term implications of existing counter-trafficking strategies, these responses risk being not only ineffective, but counterproductive. Observing the need for more focused inquiry into prevention strategies, the article advocates strategic use of the nondiscrimination principle to give more meaningful application to basic economic, social, and cultural rights, the violation of which sustains the trafficking phenomenon.[4]

Given the enduring nature of socioeconomic deprivation in many parts of the world, it is easy to dismiss calls for substantive prevention strategies as too lofty or impracticable. But the reality that millions of lives remain at risk for trafficking demands that we embrace this challenge.

I. Globalization, Migration, and Trafficking

While the problem of human trafficking has captured widespread public attention in recent years, it has mostly been in response to narrow portrayals of impoverished women and girls trafficked into the sex industry by shady figures connected to organized crime.[5] Considerably less attention has been devoted to the widespread practice of the trafficking of women, men, and children into exploitative agricultural work, construction work, domestic work, or other nonsexual labor.[6] Most portrayals—particularly of sex trafficking—depict trafficking as an act (or series of acts) of exploitation and violence, perpetrated by traffickers and suffered by desperate and poverty-stricken victims. While accurate in some respects, such depictions are incomplete. The problem of trafficking begins not with the traffickers themselves, but with the conditions that caused their victims to migrate under circumstances rendering them vulnerable to exploitation. Human trafficking is but "an opportunistic response" to the tension between the economic necessity to migrate, on the one hand, and the politically motivated restrictions on migration, on the other.[7] This section offers a broader view of trafficking as a product of the larger socioeconomic forces that feed the "emigration push" and "immigration pull" toward risky labor migration practices in our globalized economy.

A. Emigration "Push" Factors

Globalization and the opening of national borders have led not only to greater international exchange of capital and goods, but also to increasing labor migration.[8] The wealth disparities created by our globalized economy have fed increased intra- and transnational labor migration as livelihood options disappear in less wealthy countries and communities.[9] As Anne Gallagher explains, trafficking lies at one extreme end of the emigration continuum,[10] where the migration is for survival—that is, escape from economic, political, or social distress—as opposed to opportunity-seeking migration—that is, merely a search for better job opportunities. Contrary to the popular, sensationalized image of trafficked persons as either kidnapped or coerced into leaving their homes, more often than not the initial decision to migrate is a conscious one.[11] Yet, the decision to uproot oneself, leave one's home, and migrate elsewhere cannot be explained as a straightforward "rational choice by persons who assess the costs and benefits of relocating"; rather, an understanding of this decision must account for "macro factors that encourage, induce, or often compel migration."[12] "Push" factors are not created by the traffickers so much as this broader context, i.e., the economic impact of globalization.[13] Traffickers, being opportunity-seeking by nature, simply take advantage of the resulting vulnerabilities to make a profit.

Because women are over-represented among survival migrants, it is not surprising that women comprise the vast majority of trafficked persons. Recent estimates from the U.S. State Department place the figure at 80 percent.[14] This gender disparity is often attributed to the "feminization of poverty" arising from the failure of existing social structures to provide equal and just educational and employment opportunities for women.[15] While women migrate in response to economic hardship, they also migrate to flee gender-based repression.[16] Women will accept dangerous migration arrangements in order to escape the consequences of entrenched discrimination against women, including unjust or unequal employment, gender-based violence, and the lack of access to basic resources for women.[17]

As the former U.N. Special Rapporteur on Violence against Women, Radhika Coomaraswamy, explains, gender discrimination underlying these migratory flows is maintained through the collusion of factors at the market, state, community, and family levels.[18] Women's role in the market tends to be derived from traditional sex roles and division of labor, e.g., housekeeping, childcare, and other unpaid/underpaid subsistence labor. At the community level, women face discrimination through "uneven division of wage labour and salaries, citizenship rights and inheritance rights,"[19] as well as certain religious and customary practices, which, reinforced by state policies, further entrench and validate the discrimination and perpetuate the cycle of oppression of women. At the family level, gender discrimination manifests, for example, in "the preference for male children and [a] culture of male privilege [that] deprives girls and women of access to basic and higher education."[20]

Women's lack of rights and freedoms is further exacerbated by certain (macro-level) globalizing trends that have produced an environment conducive to trafficking. Professor Jean Pyle has identified these trends to include: (1) the shift to "export-oriented" approaches, where the production of essential goods is targeted for external trade rather than countries' own internal markets; (2) the entry of multinational corporations (MNCs) into developing countries and the MNCs' extensive networks of subcontractors; (3) structural adjustment policies (SAPs) mandated by the International Monetary Fund (IMF) or the World Bank (WB) as a condition for loans, requiring governments to open their markets to further financial and trade flows and to undertake austerity measures which fall heavily on the poor, particularly women; and (4) the shift in the structure of power at the international level—that is, the rise in the power of international institutions focused on markets (such as MNCs, the IMF, the WB, and the World Trade Organization [WTO] relative to those that are more people-centered and concerned with sustainable human development (such as the ILO, many U.N. agencies, and nongovernmental organizations [NGOs]).[21]

These global restructuring trends can have harsh effects on women in developing countries—either fostering exploitative conditions for women working in the formal sector, or pushing women directly into work in the informal sector. To the (limited) extent that women are even permitted to work in the formal economy—such as in small businesses or in agriculture—they are often forced out of business by the cheaper imports that trade liberalization brings.[22] As the manufacturing and service industries have entered developing economies, workers in these countries have joined the "global assembly line"; indeed, many MNCs prefer female workers due to their lower cost and lesser likelihood of resisting adverse working conditions.[23] While MNCs provide a source of jobs, they also create "a pool of low-skilled wage labour exposed to standards of western consumption and representing a potential source of emigration."[24]

Structural adjustment policies add to the pressure on women to migrate in search of work. These policies, which require governments to cut programs and reduce expenditures on social services, cause women to take on additional income-earning activities in order to maintain their families' standards of living, as governments decrease benefits in housing, health care, education, food, and fuel subsidies.[25] This often pushes women to work in the unregulated, informal sectors, thus contributing to the rise of gendered-labor networks—prostitution or sex work, domestic work, and low-wage production work.[26] Women often migrate in search of jobs in these largely unregulated sectors, rendering them all the more vulnerable to traffickers.

Compelled to leave their homes in search of viable economic options, previously invisible, low-wage-earning, migrant women are now playing a critical role in the global economy. Through this dynamic—which Professor Saskia Sassen terms the "feminization of survival"—entire households, communities, and even some governments are increasingly dependent on these women for their economic survival.[27] The changes to the international political economy have caused a number of states in the global south, especially in Asia, which is grappling with foreign debt and rising unemployment, to play a "courtesan's role" to global capital in ways that either directly or indirectly foster these gendered-labor networks.[28] Favored growth strategies include attracting direct foreign investment from MNCs and their subcontracting networks—often sacrificing labor standards to do so—or investing in tourism industries widely associated with recruitment of trafficked females for the entertainment of foreign tourists.[29] Moreover, in an effort to ease their unemployment problems and accumulate foreign currency earnings, deeply indebted countries make use of their comparative advantage in the form of women's surplus labor and encourage their labor force to seek employment in wealthier countries.[30] Through their work and remittances, women enhance the government revenue of deeply indebted countries,[31] helping to "narrow the trade gap, increase foreign currency reserves, facilitate debt servicing, reduce poverty and inequalities in wealth and support sustainable development."[32]

B. Immigration "Pull" Factors

The growth in trafficking reflects not just an increase of "push" factors in the globalized economy, but also the strong "pull" of unmet labor demands in the wealthier destination countries. Most have an aging population, with "[t]he proportion of adults over 60 in high income countries . . . expected to increase from eight percent to 19 percent by 2050, while the number of children will drop by one third" due to low fertility rates.[33] The resulting "labour shortages, skills shortages, and increased tax burdens on the working population . . . to support and provide social benefits to the wider population"[34] means these economies will become increasingly dependent on migrant populations to fill the labor gaps.[35] A number of other factors strengthen the immigration "pull," including, for example, fewer constraints on travel (for example, less restrictions on freedom of movement and cheaper and faster travel opportunities); established migration routes and communities in destination countries plus the active presence of recruiters willing to facilitate jobs or travel; and the promise of higher salaries and standards of living abroad.[36] Advances in information technology, global media, and internet access provide the means to broadcast to even the most isolated communities the promise of better opportunities abroad.[37] This fosters high hopes and expectations of women from poor, unskilled backgrounds who are desperate for employment.[38] The prospect of any job is a strong "pull" factor for survival migrants.

Labor shortages in the informal sector are often filled by migrant workers, who are willing to take the "3-D jobs"—i.e., jobs that are dirty, dangerous, and difficult—rejected by the domestic labor force.[39] The employers' profit potential, particularly in the case of trafficked persons, is much higher than would be the case if local labor were employed. If trafficked persons are paid at all, it is invariably at a lower rate than local workers would require, and the trafficked persons do not receive the costly benefits required in many Western states.[40]

In addition to the cost differential, migrants' "foreignness" appears to be a factor in the demand for migrant workers in the domestic work and commercial sex sectors. As Professors Anderson and O'Connell Davidson report in a recent study of the "demand side" of trafficking, employers favor migrant domestic workers over local domestic workers because of the vulnerability and lack of choice that results from their foreign status.[41] Employers perceive them as more "flexible" and "cooperative" with respect to longer working hours, more vulnerable to "molding" to the requirements of individual households, and less likely to leave their jobs. Moreover, their racial "otherness" makes the hierarchy between employer and employee less socially awkward—it is easier to dress up an exploitative relationship as one of paternalism/maternalism toward the impoverished "other."[42]

Rather than publicly recognize their dependence on migrant labor (skilled and unskilled), destination countries have sought instead to promote increasingly restrictive immigration policies, particularly in the wake of the September 11, 2001, terrorist attacks in the United States. There remains considerable public and political resistance to liberalizing the migration policies of these countries,[43] despite strong demographic and economic evidence that migrants produce more benefit than burden for their host countries.[44] This resistance is linked to popular—yet mistaken—concerns about the negative impact of immigration flows on employment, national security, welfare systems, and national identity.[45] Rather than confront xenophobic reactions to issues of migration, many governments instead have sought electoral or political advantage by promoting increasingly restrictive immigration policies.[46] The tension between economic reality and political expedience thus fosters conditions that enable and promote human trafficking. In reducing the opportunities for regular migration, these policies provide greater opportunities for traffickers, who are "fishing in the stream of migration," to take advantage of the confluence of survival migrants' need for jobs, on the one hand, and the unrelenting market demand for cheap labor, on the other.[47] Indeed, as borders close and migration routes become more dangerous, smuggling costs increase to the point that smugglers turn to trafficking to make a profit.[48]

Situating the trafficking phenomenon in this broader context spotlights how deeply rooted trafficking is in the underlying socioeconomic forces that impel workers to migrate. It also demonstrates how the focus on the back end of the trafficking process—that is, entry of the trafficker and the abuses committed in the course of the trafficking—is but a narrow snapshot of the broader problem of trafficking. Solutions that fail to account for the broader picture can only hope to ameliorate the symptoms, rather than address the cause of the problem.

II. The International Legal Response

Throughout the 1980s and 1990s, human rights advocates worked diligently to draw attention to the problem of trafficking in its broader socioeconomic context.[49] But it was concern over the national security implications of increased labor migration and the involvement of transnational criminal syndicates in the clandestine movement of people that ultimately motivated governments to take action. Viewing trafficking as a border and crime control issue, governments seized the opportunity to develop a new international counter-trafficking law in the form of a trafficking-specific protocol to a new international cooperation treaty to combat transnational crime—the U.N. Convention Against Transnational Organized Crime (Crime Convention).[50] States' eagerness to combat the problem resulted in the conclusion of the U.N. Protocol to Prevent, Suppress and Punish Trafficking in Persons, Especially Women and Children (Palermo Protocol or Protocol) within two years and its entry into force three years later, on December 25, 2003.[51]

The development of the Protocol set the stage for a rapid proliferation of counter-trafficking laws in the past five years. The issue of human trafficking is now high on the agenda; the international community has devoted hundreds of millions of dollars in trafficking interventions.[52] Efforts to combat trafficking have proceeded from a narrow view of trafficking as a criminal justice problem, with a clear focus on targeting the traffickers and, to a lesser extent, protecting their victims. Addressing the socioeconomic factors at the root of the problem, by contrast, has largely fallen outside the purview of government action.

A. The Palermo Protocol

The Palermo Protocol is, at base, an international crime control cooperation treaty designed to promote and facilitate States Parties' cooperation in combating trafficking in persons. Together with the Crime Convention, the Protocol establishes concrete measures to improve communication and cooperation between national law enforcement authorities, engage in mutual legal assistance, facilitate extradition proceedings, and establish bilateral and multilateral joint investigative bodies and techniques.[53] While the criminal justice aspects of this framework are a clear priority, the Palermo Protocol also contains measures to protect trafficked persons and to prevent trafficking. Unlike the criminal justice measures, which are couched as hard obligations, these provisions are mostly framed in programmatic, aspirational terms. Thus, "in appropriate cases and to the extent possible under its domestic law," the Protocol requires states to consider implementing measures providing for trafficked persons' physical and psychological recovery and endeavor to provide for their physical safety, among other goals.[54] With respect to "prevention" efforts, states are to endeavor to undertake measures such as information campaigns and social and economic initiatives to prevent trafficking,[55] as well as "to alleviate the factors that make persons . . . vulnerable to trafficking, such as poverty, underdevelopment and lack of equal opportunity," and to discourage demand for trafficking.[56]

Just as the text of the Protocol reflects states' clear prioritization of the criminal justice response, so does that which was excluded from the Protocol. Human rights advocates lobbied to include a provision in the Protocol granting trafficked persons protections against prosecution for status-related offenses, such as illegal migration, undocumented work, and prostitution,[57] citing the well-documented reality that trafficked persons were frequently deported or jailed rather than afforded protection.[58] But states refused to include such a provision for fear that it would lead to the "unwarranted use of the 'trafficking defense' and a resulting weakening of states' ability to control both prostitution and migration flows through the application of criminal sanctions."[59]

States' concern over maintaining strong border controls was also reflected in their efforts to draw a legal distinction between trafficking and migrant smuggling,[60] despite the difficulty in distinguishing between the two in practice. Defined as the illegal movement of persons across borders for profit, "migrant smuggling" technically applies to any trafficked person who begins his/her journey as a smuggled migrant but is ultimately forced into an exploitative labor situation.[61] Consequently, a victim of incomplete trafficking—for example, a victim who is stopped at the border before the end purpose of the movement is realized—could be treated as a smuggled migrant and thus denied the victim status and protections afforded to trafficked persons.[62] As Anne Gallagher concludes, the Protocol drafters' failure to address this issue was "clear evidence of [states'] unwillingness . . . to relinquish any measure of control over the migrant identification process."[63]

States' refusal to adjust their migration control policies is perhaps symptomatic of states' deep reluctance to expand the rights afforded to migrant workers. Tellingly, it took thirteen years for the International Convention on the Protection of the Rights of All Migrant Workers and Members of their Families (the Migrant Workers Convention) to receive enough ratifications to enter into force on July 1, 2003. By contrast, the Palermo Protocol entered into force three years after its adoption. Despite well-documented abuses of migrant workers' rights in countries of destination, these countries discouraged ratification of the instrument on grounds that its provisions—which address the treatment, welfare, and human rights of migrant workers (documented and undocumented) and their families—are too ambitious and detailed to be practicable and realizable.[64] That states would maintain such a restrictive stance even when the violations are egregious enough to constitute trafficking reveals the strong priority placed on the crime and border control aspects of trafficking over concern for the welfare of trafficked persons.

B. Counter-Trafficking Efforts in Practice

In practice, the priorities set forth in the Palermo Protocol are mirrored in counter-trafficking law and policy initiatives undertaken across the globe. As the U.S. State Department's yearly Trafficking in Persons Report (TIP Report) reveals, most countries' counter-trafficking efforts focus on effectuating a strong criminal justice response to the problem.[65] Although there is a growing awareness of a need for stronger protection of trafficked persons' human rights,[66] current models of protection continue "to prioritise the needs of law enforcement over the rights of trafficked persons."[67] Most governments adopt restrictive immigration policies, which, at times, fail to distinguish between smuggling and trafficking and can lead to summary deportation or incarceration of trafficked persons.[68] This not only exposes trafficked persons to further harm, including possible retrafficking, but it deprives them of access to justice and undermines government efforts to prosecute the traffickers.[69] To the extent trafficked persons are afforded an opportunity to remain in the destination countries, their residency status is often conditioned on their willingness to assist in the prosecution of their traffickers, potentially exposing them to further trauma and reprisals from the traffickers.

Even well-intentioned efforts to adopt a more "victim-centered approach"[70] to the problem can promote a narrow conception of trafficking that diverts attention from its broader labor and migration causes and implications. A review of country practices reveals two trends, in particular, that foster this dynamic: (1) the deliberate de-emphasizing of the movement or recruitment element of the trafficking definition; and (2) an over-emphasis on sex trafficking, to the neglect or exclusion of labor trafficking.

Regarding the first trend, the United States, for example, has adopted an interpretation of the trafficking definition that shifts focus away from the movement or recruitment element to the "end purpose" of the trafficking:

> The means by which people are subjected to servitude—their recruitment and the deception and coercion that may cause movement—are important factors but factors that are secondary to their compelled service. It is the state of servitude that is key to defining trafficking. . . . The movement of [a] person to [a] new location is not what constitutes trafficking; the force, fraud or coercion exercised on that person by another to perform or remain in service to the master is the defining element of trafficking in modern usage.[71]

Granted, de-emphasizing the recruitment or movement aspect of the definition perhaps helps draw much-needed attention to the broader problem of forced labor. But it also has the detrimental effect of diverting attention from the fact that trafficking is a crime committed during migration and against migrants. It also departs from the international legal definition of trafficking, of which movement or recruitment of the person is a defining element:

> [Trafficking is defined as] (a) . . . the recruitment, transportation, transfer, harbouring or receipt of persons, by means of the threat or use of force or other forms of coercion, of abduction, of fraud, of deception, of the abuse of power or of a position of vulnerability or of the giving or receiving of payments or benefits to achieve the consent of a person having control over another person, for the purpose of exploitation. Exploitation shall include, at a minimum, the exploitation of the prostitution of others or other forms of sexual exploitation, forced labour or services, slavery or practices similar to slavery, servitude or the removal of organs; (b) the consent of a victim of trafficking to the intended exploitation set forth in subparagraph (a) shall be irrelevant where any of the means set forth in subparagraph (a) have been used.[72]

The migration element of the definition speaks to the particular vulnerability that migrants face as a result of living and working in an unfamiliar milieu, where language and cultural barriers can prevent the migrant from accessing assistance.[73] De-emphasizing the migration aspect of trafficking thus overlooks a substantial source of vulnerability. It also narrows the focus of state responsibility to the confines of that which has taken place within its borders—that is, the explorative end purpose of the facilitated movement. Moreover, it conveniently sets to the side thorny questions regarding how to address a victim's (often undocumented) immigration status—an issue of immediate and pressing concern to trafficked persons, who often fear return to their home communities. In sum, this formulation glosses over any responsibility on the part of the state for fostering emigration push or immigration pull factors discussed in Part I, above.

As for the second trend, despite the fact that the international legal definition of trafficking encompasses trafficking for nonsexual as well as sexual purposes, many states—including, until recently, the United States[74]—have focused their efforts on trafficking for sexual purposes.[75] Significantly less attention has been devoted to "labor trafficking" or trafficking for nonsexual purposes, despite recent estimates that this practice accounts for at least one-third of all trafficking cases.[76] The moral outrage that images of women trapped in "sexual slavery" so easily provoke has been a galvanizing force behind global efforts to combat trafficking. Sex trafficking and its associated sex crimes also fall neatly within the purview of a criminal justice response. By contrast, labor trafficking, though hardly benign, is perhaps less likely to engender a criminal justice response given our arguably greater moral tolerance for explorative labor conditions. An over-emphasis on sex trafficking thus not only risks overlooking a significant portion of the trafficked population, but it diverts attention away from states' responsibility to promote safe labor conditions.

If protection of the victims is of secondary concern to states, then prevention of trafficking (at least, in the long term) is practically an afterthought. Despite the Protocol's requirement that states should take measures to alleviate the root causes of trafficking, such as "poverty, underdevelopment and lack of equal opportunity,"[77] in practice, "prevention" efforts focus on short-term strategies such as public awareness campaigns regarding the risks of migration. For instance, in her ground-breaking study assessing prevention efforts in southeastern Europe (SEE),[78] Barbara Limanowska found a tendency to adopt "repressive" prevention strategies that "focus on suppressing the negative (or perceived as negative) phenomena related to trafficking, such as [undocumented migration] . . . illegal and forced labor, prostitution, child labor or organized crime."[79] Common strategies include bar raids, computerized border checks, and databases that register the names of undocumented migrants, and public awareness campaigns that broadcast to the general public the risks of trafficking.[80] While efforts to prevent re-trafficking of victims are more victim-focused—providing housing, social services, and legal and medical assistance to victims to assist in reintegration into their home communities—these are only provided on a short-term basis.[81] As Limanowska has concluded with respect to SEE, "[t]here is no comprehensive long-term prevention strategy for the region, nor any clear understanding of what such a strategy should include."[82] Although prevention strategies from other regions of the world have yet to be assessed in as comprehensive a fashion,[83] a review of the country practices in other regions of the world reveals a similar focus on repressive approaches to prevention.[84]

Preliminary evaluation of these strategies indicates that they are ineffective, if not counterproductive. Rather than deterring risky migration, large-scale public awareness campaigns have been dismissed by their target audiences as anti-migration measures resulting from "the manipulation of the anti-trafficking agenda by rich countries that want to keep the poor away from their territory."[85] Efforts to "reintegrate" trafficked persons into their home communities cannot overcome the grim reality that the underlying social conditions that led to their trafficking—such as poverty and unemployment—still exist. Indeed, the myopic failure to recognize, much less address, the root causes of trafficking can actually increase vulnerability to trafficking. For example, as Limanowska reports with respect to SEE, the failure to link domestic violence to trafficking at the policy level has led to the creation of separate shelters for trafficked persons and victims of domestic violence, with the former underutilized and the latter underfunded and overcrowded.[86] Rather than recognizing domestic violence as a possible early warning sign of trafficking, the closing of domestic violence shelters has gone unaddressed, thus increasing the vulnerability to trafficking of an already at-risk population.

States' resistance to addressing the broader social problems that feed human trafficking is, in some respects, unsurprising. Treating trafficking as a criminal justice issue is far less resource-intensive and politically risky than developing long-term strategies to address the labor migration aspects of the problem. Moreover, addressing the socioeconomic root causes of trafficking means confronting vexing questions concerning the measure and content of states' obligations to achieve "progressive realization" of the social, economic, and cultural rights half of the human rights corpus.[87] A long-term strategy would thus require attention to deeper, systemic problems that states have proven highly reluctant to confront—for example, the economic need to migrate and the politically motivated restrictions against doing so, not to mention the cycle of poverty, discrimination, and violence that causes these migratory flows. As discussed below, however, such a strategy is critical to the success of global efforts to eliminate trafficking.

III. Prevention as Necessary Core of Counter-Trafficking Strategy

There is no doubt that a strong criminal justice response is a critical component of any effective global counter-trafficking strategy. Absent meaningful victim protection and long-term prevention measures, however, it is, at best, a temporary solution to a chronic and potentially growing problem.[88] Stopping the vicious cycle of trafficking demands a strategy that frames the problem within its broader socioeconomic context and takes seriously the project of targeting the root causes of this complex problem. As with any call to confront the world's ubiquitous social problems, it is an ambitious task, but one for which a few modest steps could help transform the rhetorical commitment to prevention into a substantive one. Two such measures are proposed and briefly described here.

The first proposed step is to undertake rigorous and independent assessment of the potential long-term effects of existing counter-trafficking strategies. This speaks to the need to ensure that existing counter-trafficking measures do not operate at cross-purposes with the goal of long-term prevention. In their haste to adopt counter-trafficking policies and legislation, governments have largely taken on faith that these strategies are effective with little or no basis in objective evaluations of their outcomes.[89] The sobering results of the few assessments that have been conducted—such as Limanowska's SEE study and even the United States' self-assessment[90]—illustrate the critical need for further evaluation. With data from at least five years of state practice since the adoption of the Protocol by the U.N. General Assembly, there is now a basis for some preliminary evaluations.

The second is to use international human rights law to provide a conceptual framework for addressing the root causes of trafficking. Framing the project of alleviating the root causes of trafficking as a human rights issue would encourage more proactive efforts to address these problems rather than the traditional assumption that such issues are solely within the province of broader development policy. The Palermo Protocol obliges states to "take or strengthen measures . . . to alleviate the factors that make persons . . . vulnerable to trafficking, such as poverty, underdevelopment and lack of equal opportunity."[91] While development policy can provide detailed prescriptions for action on the ground, international human rights law offers an important normative framework within which these strategies can be constructed. Most significantly, a human rights framework offers legal and political space for the disenfranchised to begin to claim these needs as rights, and thereby bring the scope of state responsibility into sharper focus.

A. Assessment of Existing Counter-Trafficking Strategies

A 2003 expert report to the U.N. Commission on the Status of Women concluded that, despite ten years of counter-trafficking laws and policies in the Balkans region, there was no evidence of a significant decrease in trafficking or increase in the number of assisted victims or number of traffickers punished.[92] Considering the hundreds of millions of dollars spent on counter-trafficking programs around the world—the United States contributed $96 million in 2004 alone[93]—and the vast numbers of lives affected by trafficking, this conclusion should give us pause. Regrettably, however, as the International Organization for Migration (IOM) recently reported, "there has been relatively little independent evaluation of counter-trafficking policies and programmes to assess the real impact and effectiveness of different interventions."[94]

The few assessments that have been conducted thus far demonstrate why further evaluation of state practices is vital. Studies such as those conducted by Limanowska not only provide critical, pragmatic insight into best (and worst) practices, but they also expose weaknesses and inaccuracies in the ways in which the problem is conceptualized. For instance, Limanowska's findings concerning the ineffectiveness of large-scale public awareness campaigns in the SEE region underscore how these efforts fail to appreciate fully the migrant perspective. That the target audiences of some of these campaigns so readily dismiss them as rich countries' anti-migration propaganda[95]—despite recognizing the accuracy of the risks portrayed—illustrates the depths of the migrants' need to migrate and the great risks they are willing to assume to do so. This is similarly demonstrated in the fact that the vast majority of calls to helplines created to reach victims of trafficking were "preventive and informative"—that is, to seek information regarding migration for work abroad.[96] Limanowska's evaluation of these and other counter-trafficking initiatives thus underscores governments' chronic failure to appreciate fully the power of the socioeconomic forces underlying migratory flows.

Another area where preliminary studies of programs have called into question the wisdom of existing counter-trafficking strategies relates to efforts to target the demand side of trafficking. Most of these programs are punitive in nature—that is, designed to clamp down on consumer demand, particularly with respect to the commercial sex industry. But as Anderson and O'Connell Davidson demonstrated in their pioneering study of the demand side of trafficking,[97] there are no easy solutions to reducing demand for trafficked labor—sexual or nonsexual. On the one hand, clamping down on demand for street prostitution may actually strengthen demand on other segments of the sex industry where trafficked labor can be an issue, such as pornography, escort agency prostitution, lap- and table-dance clubs, etc.[98] On the other hand, regulating the sex or domestic work sectors "does nothing, in itself, to counteract racism, xenophobia and prejudice against migrants and ethnic minority groups" who tend to comprise the trafficked end of these labor markets and could actually reinforce existing racial, ethnic, and national hierarchies in these sectors.[99] Accordingly, Anderson and O'Connell Davidson suggest that policy makers "pay much closer attention to the unintended and negative consequences of legislating prostitution . . . or of regulating . . . domestic work."[100] Policy makers instead ought to consider concentrating efforts on educational and preventive work targeting the social construction of demand—that is, the social norms that permit exploitation of vulnerable labor.

In addition to evaluating specific counter-trafficking programs and policies, governments should endeavor to assess their overall priorities vis-a-vis the types of programs they pursue—that is, whether oriented toward short-term or long-term results. The SEE experience reveals that funding for programs tends to be channeled toward anti-migration projects reflecting the interests of countries of destination, or in the alternative, "charity work" focused on direct assistance to victims.[101] This has had the unfortunate effect of diverting money away from programs focused on development, equality, and human rights, which hold greater promise of long-lasting change.[102] Trafficking research suffers from the same shortsightedness. Most of the research in the trafficking field is "action-oriented" or designed to prepare for specific counter-trafficking interventions on the ground, typically conducted within a six- to nine-month time frame. "There has been less funding for long-term research [into] the causes of trafficking and the best ways to prevent and combat it, or [into] the impacts of different interventions and policy responses."[103]

The importance of rigorous and independent assessment of existing counter-trafficking programs and research cannot be underestimated. Obtaining meaningful results requires a deeper understanding of the problem and the operational value of the proposed solutions than currently exists today.

B. Addressing Root Causes through a Human Rights Lens

Although there is a general understanding that trafficking has its root causes in poverty, unemployment, discrimination, and violence against women, no large-scale counter-trafficking program has been implemented to address these underlying problems.[104] Even at the level of legal analysis, there is a persistent failure to analyze how international human rights law could be used to address the root causes of the problem. While resource limitations might necessarily slow the implementation of programs targeting root causes on the ground, no such barrier exists to articulating a legal framework to address root causes. Emerging norms and analysis in the field of women's human rights, specifically, and economic, social, and cultural rights, generally, provide a basis upon which such a framework might be developed. Utilizing the principle of nondiscrimination is one potential avenue, as described briefly below.

When one considers trafficking in its broader socioeconomic context, it is not difficult to connect the root causes of trafficking to violations of economic, social, and cultural rights. These include violations of such rights as the right of opportunity to gain a living by work one freely chooses or accepts, the right to just and favorable conditions of work, the right to an adequate standard of living, and the right to education.[105] Race- and gender-based discrimination in the recognition and application of these rights are also critical factors rendering women particularly vulnerable to trafficking.[106] Many of the rights implicated in the root causes of trafficking are the subject of states' obligations under the International Covenant on Economic, Social, and Cultural Rights (ICESCR). With women arguably encountering the most severe deprivations in the area of economic, social, and cultural life,[107] the Convention on the Elimination of All Forms of Discrimination against Women (CEDAW) also plays a critical role in safeguarding these rights vis-a-vis women.

As readily identifiable as these rights violations are, however, legal analyses of trafficking have persistently neglected the economic, social, and cultural rights implications of trafficking. This likely has to do with the fact that, despite being touted as indivisible, interdependent, interrelated, and of equal importance for human dignity,[108] the norm development, monitoring, and implementation of economic, social, and cultural rights—half of the human rights corpus—has fallen far behind that of civil and political rights. The traditional view of economic, social, and cultural rights as merely "programmatic" or "aspirational" in nature—in contrast to the apparently immediately realizable civil and political rights—has fed their marginalization in human rights discourse. Vexing questions and enduring debates over the justiciability of economic, social, and cultural rights—or their capacity to be subject to formal third-party adjudication with remedies for noncompliance[109]—are another likely cause of this relative neglect.

Evolving jurisprudence regarding economic, social, and cultural rights, generally, and their application to women, specifically, nonetheless provides a basis for at least conceptualizing a legal framework to address the root causes of trafficking. The traditional assumption that economic, social, and cultural rights are inherently aspirational, necessarily resource-intensive, and therefore not immediately realizable, has now been cast into doubt.[110] By distinguishing between the types or levels of obligations human rights impose on States Parties—to respect, to protect, and to fulfill—commentators have demonstrated how certain aspects of economic, social, and cultural rights can be of immediate effect.[111] Many of these rights can be safeguarded by virtue of states' noninterference with the freedom and use of resources possessed by individuals. Accordingly, the Committee on Economic, Social and Cultural Rights (the treaty body charged with monitoring state compliance with the ICESCR) has made clear that states have an immediate obligation to ensure that ICESCR rights be exercised without discrimination.[112] Thus, states are obliged to abolish any laws, policies, or practices that affect enjoyment of these rights and, moreover, to take action to prevent discrimination by private persons and bodies in any field of public life.

Interpreted to have broad application under international human rights law, the nondiscrimination principle is particularly well-suited to a human rights analysis of the broad range of root causes of trafficking—poverty, unequal educational and employment opportunities, and violence against women, among others. Under the International Covenant for Civil and Political Rights, states are obliged not only to refrain from discriminatory practices, but also to adopt punitive measures to make equality and nondiscrimination a concrete reality.[113] As General Comment 18, issued by the Human Rights Committee, makes clear, the prohibition on discrimination in law or in fact applies "in any field regulated and protected by public authorities," and thus encompasses economic, social, and cultural rights.[114] In practice, the nondiscrimination principle has been applied to prohibit gender-based differential treatment in the allocation of social benefits, such as unemployment benefits.[115] It has also provided a framework for addressing gender-based violence, "or violence that is directed against a woman because she is a woman or that affects women disproportionately."[116] Poverty is another root cause of trafficking to which the nondiscrimination principle can be applied, as "poverty not only arises from a lack of resources—it may also arise from a lack of access to resources, information, opportunities, power, and mobility. . . . [D]iscrimination may cause poverty, just as poverty may cause discrimination."[117]

As discussed above in Part I, discrimination against women with respect to educational and employment opportunities, the disproportionate burden economic restructuring places on women, the feminization of migration due to violence against women, and the feminization of poverty, among other factors, render women particularly vulnerable to trafficking. "Gender-based discrimination [often] intersects with discriminations based on other forms of 'otherness,' such as race, ethnicity, [and] religion," among others.[118] The nondiscrimination principle, particularly as articulated, interpreted, and applied by treaty bodies such as the Committee on the Elimination of Discrimination against Women (Women's Committee) and the Committee on the Elimination of Racial Discrimination, thus offers a useful framework for addressing the root causes of trafficking.

Moreover, the recent entry into force of the CEDAW Optional Protocol contributes to the practical appeal of a nondiscrimination approach to root causes. The Optional Protocol provides individuals alleging violations of their CEDAW rights the opportunity to pursue complaints against States Parties to the Optional Protocol, and for the Women's Committee to conduct inquiries into allegations of systematic and gross violations of those rights.[119] Using the discrimination framework thus affords rare access to an enforcement mechanism otherwise unavailable for violations of economic, social, and cultural rights.

Conclusion

Situated within its broader frame, the problem of human trafficking demands that efforts to combat this international crime and human rights violation take seriously the need to address its root causes. Over a decade of global counter-trafficking initiatives adopting a "law and order" approach to the problem has yielded questionable, if not disappointing, results. The international community is coming to the growing realization that treating trafficking predominantly, if not solely, as a border and crime control issue is but to respond only to a snapshot view of a much larger problem. There is no question that confronting the poverty, unemployment, discrimination, and gender-based violence, among other factors, that increase an individual's vulnerability to trafficking is a tremendous task that demands creative and long-term strategic thinking. This article has provided a cursory view of two possible approaches by which we might begin to undertake this project. Far more analysis and deeper understanding of the trafficking problem are necessary prerequisites of the project, as is dispossessing ourselves of the traditional view that realization of economic, social, and cultural rights can wait. As daunting of a task as this may be, it is a necessary one if global efforts to eliminate trafficking are to succeed.

Notes

1. See United Nations High Commissioner for Human Rights, Report of the United Nations High Commissioner, [paragraph] 6, delivered to the Economic and Social Council, U.N. Doc. E/1999/96 (July 29, 1999) (noting that while globalization has had its benefits, there is a "clear trend towards a smaller percentage of the population receiving a greater share of wealth, while the poorest simultaneously lose ground"); see generally Executive Summary to U.N. Econ. & Soc. Council [ECOSOC], Comm'n on Human Rights, Integration of the Human Rights of Women and the Gender Perspective: Violence Against Women, at 4 U.N. Doc. E/CN.4/2000/68 (Feb. 29, 2000) (prepared by Radhika Coomaraswamy) [hereinafter Coomaraswamy Report].

2. BIMAL GHOSH, HUDDLED MASSES AND UNCERTAIN SHORES: INSIGHTS INTO IRREGULAR MIGRATION 35 (1998).

3. The number of people trafficked remains staggering. The International Labour Organization (ILO) estimates that 2.5 million people are trafficked at any point in time, generating $32 billion in profits for organized crime. INTERNATIONAL LABOUR OFFICE, A GLOBAL ALLIANCE AGAINST FORCED LABOUR: GLOBAL REPORT UNDER THE FOLLOW-UP TO THE ILO DECLARATION ON FUNDAMENTAL PRINCIPLES AND RIGHTS AT WORK 46, 55 (2005) [hereinafter ILO GLOBAL REPORT].

4. Michael J. Dennis & David P. Stewart, Justiciability of Economic, Social, and Cultural Rights: Should There Be an International Complaints Mechanism to Adjudicate the Rights to Food, Water, Housing, and Health?, 98 AM. J. INT'L L. 462, 464 (2004).

5. See, e.g., Peter Landesman, The Girls Next Door, N.Y. TIMES MAG., Jan. 25, 2004, at 30; Nicholas D. Kristof, Girls for Sale, N.Y. TIMES, Jan. 17, 2004, at A15; Nicholas D. Kristof, Bargaining for Freedom, N.Y. TIMES, Jan. 21, 2004, at A27; Nicholas D. Kristof, Loss of Innocence, N.Y. TIMES, Jan. 28, 2004, at A25; Nicholas D. Kristof, Stopping the Traffickers, N.Y. TIMES, Jan. 31, 2004, at A17.

6. David A. Feingold, Think Again: Human Trafficking, FOREIGN POL'Y, Sept.–Oct. 2005, at 26.

7. ILO GLOBAL REPORT, supra note 3, at 46.

8. COMM. ON FEMINISM AND INT'L LAW, INT'L LAW ASS'N, WOMEN AND MIGRATION: INTERIM REPORT ON TRAFFICKING IN WOMEN 2 (2004). . . .

9. See generally GHOSH, SUpm note 2 (distinguishing between survival migration and opportunity seeking migration); MIKE KAYE, ANTI-SLAVERY INT'L, THE MIGRATION-TRAFFICKING NEXUS: COMBATING TRAFFICKING THROUGH THE PROTECTION OF MIGRANTS' HUMAN RIGHTS 13 (2003). . . .

10. ANNE GALLAGHER ET AL., CONSIDERATION OF THE ISSUE OF TRAFFICKING: BACKGROUND PAPER 16-17 (2002) (citing GHOSH, supra note 2, at 35). . . .

11. Feingold, supra note 6, at 28.

12. Patrick A. Taran, Human Rights of Migrants: Challenges of the New Decade, INT'L MIGRATION, Vol. 38, No. 6 (Special Issue 2), Feb. 2001, at 12.

13. See Saskia Sassen, Women's Burden: Counter-Geographies of Globalization and the Feminization of Survival, 71 NORDIC J. INT'L L. 255, 257 (2002).

14. U.S. DEP'T OF STATE, TRAFFICKING IN PERSONS REPORT 6 (2005) [hereinafter 2005 TIP REPORT]. . . .

15. Coomaraswamy Report, supra note 1, [paragraph] 58.

16. Id. [paragraph][paragraph] 54–60.

17. See id. [paragraph] 60.

18. Id. [paragraph] 57.

19. Id.

20. Id.

21. See Jean L. Pyle, How Globalization Fosters Gendered Labor Networks and Trafficking 23 (Nov 13–15, 2002) (unpublished manuscript). . . .

22. Id. at 5.

23. Id.

24. CHRISTINA BOSWELL & JEFF CRISP, POVERTY, INTERNATIONAL MIGRA-TION AND ASYLUM 6 (United Nations Univ., World Inst. for Dev. Econ. Research, Policy Brief No. 8, 2003).

25. See Sassen, supra note 13, at 263.

26. See U.N. Dip. for the Advancement of Women, The New Borderlanders: Enabling Mobile Women and Girls for Safe Migration and Citizenship Rights, at 5–6, U.N. Doc. CM/MMW/2003/ CRE3 (Jan. 14, 2004) (prepared by Jyoti Sanghera).

27. Sassen, supra note 13, at 258.

28. Vidyamali Samarasinghe, Confronting Globalization in Anti-Trafficking Strategies in Asia, BROWN J. WORLD AFF., Summer–Fall 2003, at 91, 94 (citing JIM MITTLEMAN, THE GLOBALIZATION SYNDROME: TRANSFOR-MATION AND RESISTANCE 15 (2000)).

29. Id. at 92, 94.

30. Id. at 95.

31. Sassen, supra note 13, at 258. Thus, according to Professor Sassen, "[t]he growing immiseration of governments and whole economies in the global south has promoted and enabled the proliferation of survival and profit-making activities that involve migration and trafficking of women." Id. at 255 (from the Abstract). According to the International Organization for Migration, remittances through official channels totaled $93 billion in 2003, INTERNATIONAL ORGANIZATION FOR MIGRATION, WORLD MIGRATION 2005: COSTS AND BENEFITS OF INTERNATIONAL MIGRATION 491 (2005), approached $100 billion in 2004, id. at 124, and now seriously rival devel-opment aid in many countries; unofficial remittances are likely to be two to three times that figure. For example, in El Salvador, "remittances accounted for more than 80 per cent of the total financial inflows in 2000, with over-seas development assistance and foreign direct investment accounting for less than 20 per cent." Kaye, supra note 9, at 14.

32. KAYE, supra note 9, at 14 (spending remittances on locally produced goods and services can have a multiplier effect by simulating demand).

33. Id. at 13.

34. Id.

35. "In order to stabilise the size of the working population in the 15 EU member states, there needs to be a net inflow of some 68 million foreign workers and professionals between 2003 and 2050." Id. (citing INT'L ORG. FOR MIGRATION) WORLD MIGRATION 2003, at 245 (2003)).

36. Id. at 11; accord BOSWELL & CRISP, supra note 24, at 10.

37. Samarasinghe, supra note 28, at 96–97.

38. See BOSWELL & CRISP, supra note 24, at 6.

39. See ILO GLOBAL REPORT, supra note 3, at 46.

40. See Taran, supra note 12, at 15–16.

41. BRIDGET ANDERSON & JULIA O'CONNELL DAVIDSON, IS TRAFFICK-ING IN HUMAN BEINGS DEMAND DRIVEN?: A MULTI-COUNTRY PILOT

STUDY 29–32 (Int'l Org. for Migration, IOM Migration Research Series No. 15, 2003).

42. Id. at 32.

43. BOSWELL & CRISP, supra note 24, at 1.

44. INT'L ORG. FOR MIGRATION, supra note 31, at 170, 188–89 (noting that a recent U.K. study calculated that in 1999–2000, migrants contributed $4 billion more in taxes than they received in benefits, and a U.S. study estimated that national income had expanded $8 billion in 1997 because of immigration).

45. BOSWELL & CRISP, supra note 24, at 21–22.

46. KAYE, SUPRA note 9, at 13.

47. Helen Thomas, Fishing in the Stream of Migration, ADB REV. (ASIAN DEV. BANK, MANILA, PHIL.), February 2004. . . .

48. Migrant smuggling entails payment by a third party to facilitate the movement of the migrant. See Protocol Against the Smuggling of Migrants by Land, Sea and Air, Supplementing the United Nations Convention Against Transnational Organized Crime, G.A. Res. 55/25, annex III, pmbl. & art. 3, U.N. Doc. A/RES/55/25 (Nov. 2, 2000) [hereinafter Migrant Smuggling Protocol]. In addition to whatever profit is to be made from the facilitated migration, traffickers can also profit from the revenue generated from the exploitative end purpose of the movement—e.g., the forced labor or slavery-like practice.

49. See generally HUMAN RIGHTS WATCH, A MODERN FORM of SLAVERY: TRAFFICKING OF BURMESE WOMEN AND GIRLS INTO BROTHELS IN THAILAND (1993). . . ; HUMAN RIGHTS WATCH, RAPE FOR PROFIT: TRAFFICKING OF NEPALI GIRLS AND WOMEN TO INDIAN BROTHELS (1995). . . (report by Human Rights Watch demonstrating that unequal access to education and employment opportunities, among other factors, fed the feminization of poverty and migration and increased women's vulnerability to traffickers).

50. United Nations Convention Against Transnational Organized Crime, G.A. Res. 55/25, annex I, U.N. Doc. A/RES/55/25 (Nov. 2, 2000) [hereinafter Crime Convention].

51. Protocol to Prevent, Suppress and Punish Trafficking in Persons, Especially Women and Children, G.A. Res. 55/25, annex II, U.N. Doc. A/RES/55/25 (Nov. 2, 2000) [hereinafter Palermo Protocol].

52. See 2005 TIP REPORT, supra note 14, at 245 (reporting that the United States alone has invested $295 million in counter-trafficking efforts over the last four fiscal years).

53. Crime Convention, supra note 50, arts. 16, 18, 19, 27, 28.

54. Palermo Protocol, supra note 51, arts. 6–8.

55. Id. art. 9, [paragraph] 2.

56. Id. art. 9, [paragraph][paragraph] 4–5.

57. See Position Paper on the Draft Protocol to Prevent, Suppress and Punish Trafficking in Women and Children, submitted by the Special Rapporteur on Violence Against Women, Report of the Ad Hoc Committee on the Elaboration of a Convention Against Transnational Organized Crime

on its Fourth Session, Held in Vienna June 28 to July 9, 1999, U.N. Doc. A/AC.254/CRP.13 (May 20, 1999) [hereinafter "Coomaraswamy Position Paper"].

58. See, e.g., Coomaraswamy Report, supra note 1, [paragraph] 44.

59. See Anne Gallagher, Human Rights and the New UN Protocols on Trafficking and Migrant Smuggling: A Preliminary Analysis, 23 HuM. RTs. Q. 975, 991 (2001).

60. See Migrant Smuggling Protocol, supra note 48 (migrant smuggling is the subject of one of the other two protocols to the Crime Convention).

61. Smuggling is defined as "the procurement, in order to obtain, directly or indirectly, a financial or other material benefit, of the illegal entry of a person into a State Party of which the person is not a national or a permanent resident." Id. art. 3.

62. "Smuggled migrants are assumed to be acting voluntarily," and are thus afforded less protection under international law. Anne Gallagher, Trafficking, Smuggling and Human Rights: Tricks and Treaties, 12 FORCED MIGRATION REV. 25, 26 (2002).

63. Gallagher, supra note 59, at 1001.

64. Taran, supra note 12, at 18–22.

65. 2005 TIP REPORT, SUPRA note 14, at 34.

66. The United States, for example, is increasingly recognizing how the failure to protect trafficked persons' human rights compromises efforts to prosecute traffickers. For example, noting the significant disparity between the numbers of people trafficked to the United States (14,500–17,500 each year) and the numbers of those who have reported the abuse to law enforcement (757 as of November 2003), the U.S. Department of Justice has made concerted efforts to collaborate more effectively with NGOs and consider more victim-centered approaches to prosecution. DEP'T OF JUSTICE, ASSESSMENT OF U.S. ACTIVITIES TO COMBAT TRAFFICKING IN PERSONS 5, 22, 26–27 (2004).

67. ELAINE PEARSON, ANTI-SLAVERY INT'L, HUMAN TRAFFIC, HUMAN RIGHTS: REDEFINING VICTIM PROTECTION 4 (2002).

68. See, e.g., U.S. DEP'T OF STATE, TRAFFICKING IN PERSONS REPORT 148, 165, 185 (2004) (citing the Italian, Portuguese, and British governments' failure to distinguish between trafficking and smuggling). The 2004 Trafficking in Persons Report also described how trafficked persons in the Czech Republic "were treated as illegal immigrants and expressed fear of testifying due to safety concerns," id. at 134, and in Morocco, were "jailed and/or detained for violating immigration or other laws [and were] not provided adequate legal representation." Id. at 199. In the 2005 Trafficking in Persons Report, Italy, the United Kingdom, and Portugal persisted in their failure to distinguish between trafficking and smuggling or illegal immigration. 2005 TIP REPORT, supra note 14, at 130, 181, 221. France has apparently adopted a practice of "arresting, jailing, and fining trafficking victims as a means of discouraging the operation of trafficking networks and to gain information to pursue cases against traffickers," which, as the U.S. State Department notes, "harms trafficking victims and allows for [their] deportation . . . regardless of possible threats [in their country of origin]." Id. at 106.

69. PEARSON, supra note 69, at 2.

70. See 2005 TIP RETORT, supra note 14, at 5 (referring to the "three P's" of prosecution, protection, and prevention, noting that "a victim-centered approach to trafficking requires us equally to address the 'three R's'— rescue, rehabilitation and reintegration').

71. Id. at 9–10.

72. Palermo Protocol, supra note 51, art. 3.

73. See Coomaraswamy Position Paper, supra note 57, at 3.

74. In the 2005 TIP REPORT, the United States expanded its coverage of trafficking for nonsexual purposes. 2005 TIP REPORT, supra note 14, at 1. This expansion was undoubtedly in response to years of NGO protests over the United States' focus on sex trafficking.

75. Frank Laczko, Introduction, INT'L MIGRATION, Jan. 2005, at 5, 9 (introduction to a special issue entitled "Data and Research on Human Trafficking: A Global Survey," noting that research on trafficking has focused on the sex trafficking of women and children, neglecting other forms of trafficking). Liz Kelly, "You Can Find Anything You Want": A Critical Reflection on Research on Trafficking in Persons Within and into Europe, INT'L MIGRATION, Jan. 2005, at 235, 239 (article in a special issue entitled "Data and Research on Human Trafficking: A Global Survey," noting how most of the content and data in the TIP Reports issued by the U.S. State Department for years 2002–2004 was "confined to sexual exploitation").

76. ILO GLOBAL REPORT, Supra note 3, at 46.

77. Palermo Protocol, supra note 51, art. 9, [paragraph] 4.

78. BARBARA LIMANOWSKA, TRAFFICKING IN HUMAN BEINGS IN SOUTH EASTERN EUROPE xiii (2005) [hereinafter SEE REPORT] (assessing prevention strategies in Albania, Bosnia and Herzegovina, Bulgaria, Croatia, the former Yugoslav Republic of Macedonia, Moldova, Romania, Servia and Montenegro, and Kosovo).

79. Id. at 2.

80. See generally SEE REPORT, Supra note 80.

81. Id. at 36–37.

82. Id. at xiii.

83. The SEE REPORT is one of the few to undertake an assessment of prevention programs. As the IOM found in its survey of data and research on trafficking, there is a lack of information regarding trafficking programs in many regions of the world, including the Middle East, the Americas, and Africa. See Laczko, supra note 77, at 7.

84. See generally 2005 TIP REPORT, Supra note 14.

85. SEE REPORT, supra note 80, at 22.

86. Id. at 20–21.

87. International Covenant on Economic, Social and Cultural Rights, G.A. Res. 2200, U.N. GAOR, 21st Sess., Supp. No. 16, at 49, U.N. Doc. A/6316 (Dec. 16, 1966) [hereinafter ICESCR].

88. The current reality is that the number of traffickers arrested is low compared to the efforts expended to capture them, and of those who are tried,

few are convicted and even fewer serve sentences. Am. Soc'y of Int'l Law, Trafficking in Humans: Proceedings of the 99th Annual Meeting (forthcoming 2006) [hereinafter 2005 ASIL Human Trafficking Panel] (noting that "virtually no kingpins are brought to justice, and criminal networks remain largely undisturbed," and that sentences are relatively minor and often not served) (draft on file with author). It appears to be a socioeconomic reality that there will be others to take advantage of the substantial profit-making potential to be had wherever there is both economic necessity to migrate, yet shrinking avenues for legal migration. See Sassen, supra note 13, at 266–70.

89. See Laczko, supra note 77, at 9.

90. See generally SEE REPORT, supra note 80; DEP'T OF JUSTICE, ASSESSMENT of U.S. ACTIVITIES TO COMBAT TRAFFICKING IN PERSONS (2004).

91. Palermo Protocol, supra note 51, art. 9, [paragraph] 4.

92. U.N. Comm'n on the Status of Women, Women's Human Rights and Elimination of All Forms of Violence Against Women and Girls as Defined in the Beijing Platform of Action and the Outcome Documents of the Twenty-third Special Session of the General Assembly, at 47, U.N. Doc. E/ CN.6/ 2003/12 (Mar. 13, 2003) (prepared by Barbara Limanowska). This report was based on information from the Balkans region. Id. at 1 n.2. See also 2005 ASIL Human Trafficking Panel, supra note 90, at 2–3 (noting the disparity between the proliferation of new counter-trafficking legal and institutional mechanisms, on the one hand, and the achievement of meaningful results, on the other).

93. 2005 TIP REPORT, supra note 14, at 1.

94. Laczko, supra note 77, at 9.

95. See supra text accompanying note 87.

96. SEE REPORT, Supra note 80, at 32–33. On a positive note, however, this experience also suggests the potential preventive role that helplines can play.

97. See generally ANDERSON & O'CONNELL DAVIDSON, supra note 41.

98. Id. at 43. Reports of the Swedish experience illustrate this point. "[W]hen Sweden introduced laws in 1999 to criminalize men who purchase sex, while decriminalizing [the prostitutes/sex workers], the incidence of female sex trafficking dropped. . . . [W]hile the demand for prostitution decreased in Sweden, it increased in neighboring countries. The male clients simply went [elsewhere to satisfy their desires]." Samarasinghe, supra note 28, at 102.

99. ANDERSON & O'CONNELL DAVIDSON, supra note 41, at 44.

100. Id. at 46, 47.

101. SEE REPORT, supra note 80, at 54.

102. Id.

103. Laczko, supra note 77, at 9.

104. See 2005 ASIL Human Trafficking Panel, supra note 90, at 3.

105. ICESCR, supra note 89, arts. 6, 7, 11, 13.

106. See generally Convention on the Elimination of All Forms of Discrimination Against Women, G.A. Res. 34/180, U.N. Doc. A/RES/34/180 (Dec. 18, 1979), reprinted in 19 I.L.M. 33 (1980).

107. Katarina Frostell & Martin Scheinin, Women, in ECONOMIC, SOCIAL AND CULTURAL RIGHTS 331,331 (Asbjorn Eide et al. eds., 2d. rev. ed. 2001).

108. World Conference on Human Rights, June 14–25, 1993, Vienna Declaration and Programme of Action, art. 1, [paragraph] 5, U.N. Doc. A/CONE.157/23 (July 12, 1993), reprinted in 32 I.L.M. 1663 (1993).

109. See Martin Scheinin, Economic and Social Rights as Legal Rights, in ECONOMIC, SOCIAL AND CULTURAL RIGHTS, Supra note 109, at 29, Dennis & Stewart, supra note 4, at 463.

110. See, e.g., Asbjorn Eide, Economic, Social and Cultural Rights as Human Rights, in ECONOMIC, SOCIAL AND CULTURAL RIGHTS, supra note 109, at 9, 23–25.

111. See U.N. Comm'n on Econ., Soc. and Cultural Rights, General Comment 3, annex III, [paragraph] 10, U.N. Doc. E/1991/23 (Dec. 14, 1990) [hereinafter General Comment 3]. "Progressive realization" cannot be used as a "pretext for non-compliance." The Maostricht Guidelines on Violations of Economic, Social and Cultural Rights, reprinted in 20 HUM. RTS. Q. 691, 694 (1998).

112. General Comment 3, supra note 113, [paragraph] 1.

113. See International Covenant on Civil and Political Rights, G.A. Res. 2200, art. 26, U.N. GAOR, 21st Sess., Supp. No. 16, at 52, U.N. Doc. A/6316 (Dec. 16, 1966).

114. See Frostell & Scheinin, supra note 109, at 334 (citing General Comment 18).

115. Id. at 334 & n. 15.

116. U.N. Comm. on the Elimination of All Foms of Discrimination Against Women, General Recommendation 19, U.N. Doc. HRI/GEN/Rev. 3 (noting that "[p]overty and unemployment increase opportunities for trafficking in women").

117. UNITED NATIONS, OFFICE OF THE HIGH COMM'R FOR HUMAN RIGHTS, HUMAN RIGHTS AND POVERTY REDUCTION: A CONCEPTUAL FRAMEWORK 17 (2004).

118. Coomaraswamy Report, supra note 1, [paragraph] 55.

119. See Optional Protocol to the Convention on the Elimination of All Forms of Discrimination Against Women, G.A. Res. 54/4, annex, U.N. Doc. A/54/49 (Oct. 6, 1999).

Dina Francesca Haynes  **NO**

Used, Abused, Arrested, and Deported: Extending Immigration Benefits to Protect the Victims of Trafficking and to Secure the Prosecution of Traffickers

Prologue

Madeleina was a slight, delicate-looking sixteen-year-old girl from Moldova. She left Moldova in 1998, when her sister's husband convinced her and another girl to go with his friend who promised to find them hostess jobs in Italy. She was given a fake passport, and after about a week of traveling, found herself locked in a brothel in what she later discovered was the Republika Srpska, Bosnia and Herzegovina (Bosnia).[1] A woman interpreting for the brothel owner told her that she had been sold to him to be his "wife." The brothel owner forced Madeleina to have sex with him and his friends and told her that she could begin working off her debt to him immediately. He told her that she already owed him more than $2000 for her purchase price and working papers.

Madeleina had no money and no friends. She could not speak the local language and the owner threatened her regularly, beating her and telling her that police would arrest her if she tried to leave. There were at least eleven other girls and women at this brothel, all foreigners. Most of them were from Moldova or Romania, and the brothel owner tried to keep them separated as much as possible to prevent their collusion and escape. The owner sometimes forced them to take drugs to keep them more compliant, the cost of which was added to their debt. The brothel owner kept Madeleina for about five months, forcing her to have sex with as many as twenty men a day. She thought that some of the customers at the brothel were local police. She also knew that Russian and either American, Canadian, or British men, and she thinks Italian, had visited her and had sex with her, in addition to local men.

When police raided that brothel, she was taken by car to Arizona Market, near Brcko, where cars, goods, and women are sold. Two foreign men purchased her; she thinks they were Swiss and American peacekeepers. These two men put her in a car and took her to an apartment in Tuzla where they kept her locked up and came to visit her every day or two, often with friends, and

From *Human Rights Quarterly*, 26:2 (2004), 222–237. Copyright © The John Hopkins University Press. Reprinted with permission of the John Hopkins University Press.

forced her to have sex with them. Over the course of these months, Madeleina had begun to teach herself some of the Serbian language.

One day, after no one had visited her for several days and she was running out of food, the landlord of the apartment opened the door and told her to get out. It was winter, and with no warm clothes Madeleina went out to find the local police, not because she believed the police would help her, but because she knew she would freeze to death with no place to go.

The local police promptly jailed her for prostitution. A Human Rights Officer with the Organization for Security and Co-operation in Europe (OSCE) intervened, and Madeleina was transported to a makeshift shelter in Sarajevo.[2] International and local nongovernmental organizations were then just establishing the shelter.

I. Introduction

Trafficking in human beings is an extremely lucrative business, with profits estimated at $7 billion per year[3] and a seemingly endless supply of persons to traffic, estimated at between 700,000 and four million new victims per year.[4] Trafficked persons, typically women and children, can be sold and resold, and even forced to pay back their purchasers for the costs incurred in their transport and purchase.[5] In fact, the United States Central Intelligence Agency estimates that traffickers earn $250,000 for each trafficked woman.[6] Economic instability, social dislocation, and gender inequality in transitioning countries foster conditions ripe for trafficking.

Trafficking in human beings involves moving persons for any type of forced or coerced labor, for the profit of the trafficker.[7] Several countries are finally adopting domestic legislation to criminalize trafficking in human beings, although many continue to punish the victims of trafficking, charging them with prostitution, possession of fraudulent documents, or working without authorization.[8] Many international organizations and consortiums of grassroots anti-trafficking organizations have also put forward models for combating trafficking.

None of these models is yet terribly effective, for a variety of reasons. At the forefront of these reasons is the fact that several countries have yet to adopt anti-trafficking laws.[9] Second, of those that have, many completely fail to implement those laws even after undertaking domestic and international obligations.[10] A third major reason is that some governments have failed to incorporate the advice of grassroots and international anti-trafficking organizations that have worked for years drafting recommended legislation based upon their observations in the field.[11]

A particular contemporary problem is trafficking for the sexual exploitation of women[12] in and from Central and Southeastern Europe.[13] Currently, Central and Southeastern Europe are the primary sources from which women are drawn into global sex traffic through Europe,[14] and some countries in this region are actively engaged in developing anti-trafficking initiatives pursuant to their obligations as signatories to the 2000 Protocols to the UN Convention on Transnational Organized Crime.[15] In addition, some countries in the

Balkans have the added presence of international peacekeepers and humanitarian workers, which in many respects exacerbates the problem.[16]

This paper will, in Part II, discuss the recent increase in trafficking. Part II will explore how and why governments have failed to effectively address the problem, despite being aware of its existence for decades. Part IV illustrates that two dominant anti-trafficking models have emerged in recent years, one of which is oriented toward prosecution of traffickers while the other emphasizes victim protection. Part V proposes a specific combination of the best of the two models, recommending several additional elements to create a new model that will more effectively combat trafficking, highlighting immigration benefits, and responds to anticipated arguments against such an expansion.

The principal recommendation of this article is that the best of the "jail the offender" and "protect the victim" models should be combined. The new model should incorporate advice from grassroots organizations that work directly with trafficked persons, in order to craft anti-trafficking programs that promote protection of victims. This new model should include immigration protection, should hit traffickers where it hurts, and should prioritize full implementation.

II. The Recent Rise of Trafficking in Human Beings

The horrific practice of trafficking in human beings has long been a serious problem throughout the world, but in the last fifteen years trafficking from European countries has been on the rise. Trafficking in Europe has been fueled by the social dislocations, increasing pockets of poverty, gender imbalance, bureaucratic chaos, and legislative vacuums resulting from the collapse of communism.[17]

Women already disenfranchised within their communities are most often those who fall prey to traffickers: ostracized minorities, women without employment or future economic prospects, and girls without family members to look out for them or who have fallen outside of the educational system.[18] These girls and women are lured by traffickers into leaving their countries, believing that they will work in the West as dancers, hostesses, or nannies, and instead find themselves forced to have sex for the profit of the men and women who purchased them.[19]

In order to secure their silence and compliance, traffickers threaten, beat, rape, drug, and deprive their victims of legitimate immigration or work documents. Women are forced to sell themselves in brothels, often receiving several clients per day.[20] They rarely see any wages for their work; in fact, most victims are kept in indentured servitude and told that they owe their traffickers or the brothel owners for their own purchase price and for the price of procuring working papers and travel documents.[21]

The rings of traffickers are often vast, extremely well connected to police and government officials, well hidden, and reach across borders and continents.[22] Traffickers in human beings are also known to traffic in weapons and drugs, and to use trafficking in human beings to bring in initial cash flow to support the riskier traffic in drugs and arms.[23] Human beings, being reusable commodities that can be sold and resold, are both more lucrative[24] and less risky to traffic than drugs and arms, in that traffickers of human beings are rarely prosecuted for this particular offense.[25]

While between 700,000 and four million women are trafficked each year,[26] only a fraction of those are known to have received assistance in order to escape trafficking.[27] Many are re-victimized by being deported from the countries in which they are found,[28] sanctioned by law when attempting to return to their countries of origin,[29] and ostracized within their communities and families.[30]

Governments appear to have recognized the importance of the issue, many having ratified international instruments established to eradicate trafficking in human beings. Nevertheless, trafficking is neither slowing, nor is the prosecution of traffickers or the protection of their victims becoming any more certain.

III. Governmental Failures to Confront the Issue

As early as 1904, concern over "white slavery," in which European women were exported to the colonies, prompted the adoption of the International Agreement for the Suppression of White Slave Traffic, addressing the fraudulent or abusive recruitment of women for prostitution in another country.[31] The issue was addressed again in 1933 with the International Convention on the Suppression of the Traffic in Women of Full Age, by which parties agreed to punish those who procured prostitutes or ran brothels.[32] In 1949, the United Nations adopted the Convention for the Suppression of the Traffic in Persons and of the Exploitation of the Prostitution of Others.[33] Until 2000, the only other international treaty to address trafficking was the 1979 UN Convention on the Elimination of All Forms of Discrimination Against Women (CEDAW), which required states to take all measures to suppress both trafficking and "exploitation of prostitution," meaning forced prostitution.[34]

Beginning in the late 1980s, the European Union and the United Nations began addressing the issue repeatedly, yet little progress was made and the collapse of communism flooded trafficked persons throughout Europe. With trafficking recognized as a distinct problem since 1903, with the ratification of four treaties by many nations, and with trafficking recently and dramatically on the rise, why has so little progress been made?

A. Some Politicians Use Trafficking to Direct Attention to Unrelated Political Agendas

Trafficking is a low priority for many governments who pay lip service to solving the problem only to harness more support for other political objectives. Because of the visceral reaction trafficking elicits with the public, it has recently been used by politicians and governments to bolster other political agendas, such as curtailing illegal migration, fighting prostitution, and even combating terrorism.

Some governments pretend to care about trafficking when the real objective is controlling unwanted migration.[35] Trafficking in human beings is a very serious topic in its own right, but the gravity and emotional impact of the topic unfortunately render it vulnerable to political manipulation. With illegal migration, smuggling, terrorism, and prostitution now on many political agendas, the pledge to combat trafficking is misused as justification for "clamping down" on these other threats that also have immigration implications.[36] Authorities have remained cynical and hardened to the plight of victims who are easier to treat as prostitutes or illegal immigrants.[37]

In fact, some countries seem to view the existence of trafficked women within their sovereign borders as evidence of a breach of security or the failure of their domestic immigration mechanisms, and accordingly attempt to address trafficking through simple reconfiguration of their border control mechanisms.[38] Traffickers are often extremely savvy transnational organized criminals, while their victims are most often women and children already victimized by economic, political, or social conditions in their home countries. Viewing trafficking as an immigration issue overly simplifies the complexity of preparing effective anti-trafficking measures.

As this section will demonstrate, politicians and governments have blurred the distinctions between illegal migration, trafficking, and smuggling, taking advantage of the current world fear of terrorism committed by legal and illegal immigrants, to restrict immigration and freedom of movement further. They have purposely co-mingled anti-trafficking initiatives with anti-prostitution initiatives. They have tried to further curtail migration by blurring the distinction between trafficking and smuggling. Finally, it is my opinion that some governments are motivated not by a keen belief in the necessity of curtailing trafficking, but by a desire to secure international financial assistance or enter the European Union.

1. Prostitution

Prostitution and trafficking are not one and the same, yet some would treat them as such.[39] Prostitution involves persons willingly engaging in sex work. Although there may be a gray area involving different degrees of consent, choice, and free will, trafficking goes well outside of this gray area. While a valid argument could be made that gender imbalances in economic or social factors drive a woman to consent to such labor as her chosen profession, thus effectively removing her "will,"[40] trafficking involves clear deprivation of choice at some stage, either through fraud, deception, force, coercion, or threats.

Whether a trafficked woman was initially willing or unwilling when she entered into sex work should make no legal difference when the outcome is enslavement or forced servitude; a person cannot consent to enslavement or forced labor of any kind.[41] While some trafficked persons may be willing to work in the sex industry, they do not anticipate being forced to pay off large forcibly imposed debts, being kept against their will, having their travel documents taken from them, or being raped, beaten, and sold like chattel.[42]

Nevertheless, within the community of NGOs, international organizations, governments, and working groups laboring to define and combat trafficking, the issue of prostitution regularly enters the deliberation. As recently as 2001, for example, some persons working for the United Nations Mission in Bosnia and Herzegovina (UNMIBH) and partner organizations tasked with assisting the Bosnian government to eradicate trafficking refused to provide trafficking protection assistance to women who at any point willingly engaged in prostitution.[43]

The Organized Crime Convention has encouraged countries to focus on coercion and use of force in identifying whether a woman is a victim of trafficking, rather than on whether she has ever engaged in prostitution. Nevertheless, the US government agency tasked with distributing funding to international trafficking initiatives recently determined that it would refuse to fight trafficking where doing so might appear to treat prostitution as a legitimate activity.[44] Thus, trafficking is politicized, a volatile topic easily used to affix other political agendas. Even while most experts working in anti-trafficking initiatives agree that trafficking and prostitution are separate issues, to be handled separately as a matter of law, the United States took a step backwards in attempting to tackle prostitution under the guise of combating trafficking.

2. Smuggling

Politicians have also attempted to link smuggling and trafficking in order to achieve tightened border controls. While most governments acknowledge that smuggling and trafficking are two distinct crimes, they nonetheless use trafficking statistics and horrific trafficking stories to justify tightened border controls when the primary goal is not the elimination of trafficking, but the reduction of illegal migration, some of which occurs via smugglers, and perhaps preventing terrorism.

The United States Department of State, for instance, opened the Migrant Smuggling and Trafficking in Persons Coordination Center in December 2000, even while acknowledging, "at their core . . . these related problems are distinct."[45] The US government nevertheless justified combining the two issues by pointing out that "these related problems result in massive human tragedy and affect our national security, primarily with respect to crime, health and welfare, and border control."[46] By way of another example, the Canadian government supported a study jointly reviewing both smuggling and trafficking, even while pointing out the legal distinctions between the two.[47] The study was justified under the premise that "as human smuggling and trafficking are increasing, the tightening of border controls has taken on a new urgency from the fear of terrorism in the West, as well as restrictive measures placed on irregular migratory movements."[48]

Smuggling involves delivering persons to the country they wish to enter, initiated by the potential migrant. Smuggling often takes place under horrible and possibly life threatening conditions, but smuggled persons are left to their own devices upon delivery. Smuggling is not as lucrative for the perpetrators, as smugglers usually make only a short-term profit on the act of moving a person, while traffickers regard people as highly profitable, reusable, re-sellable, and expendable commodities.[49]

In order for anti-trafficking initiatives to be effective, politicians must make the eradication of trafficking and the protection of trafficked persons into a prioritized goal, distinct from the elimination of smuggling or the tightening of border controls.

3. Some Governments are Motivated by a Desire to Meet EU Entrance Requirements or to Obtain Financial Assistance

Not surprisingly, the European Union and the United States, among other institutions and governments, are conditioning financial assistance[50] and entry into the European Union on the country's willingness to develop legislation curtailing trafficking within and across its borders.[51] Countries set to enter the European Union in 2004[52] are eager to pass legislation recommended by the European Union and the Council of Europe (CoE), and join working groups that address stemming the flow of trafficking and smuggling.[53]

Passing recommended legislation and making real efforts to stem the flow of trafficking, however, are often two different things. When countries simply adopt legislation in order to secure entry into the European Union or to meet financial assistance requirements, there is no real ownership or commitment to eradicating trafficking. The legislation, no matter how meticulously in conformity with international standards, will not be fully or adequately implemented at the local level without serious political will.

B. Governments Ignore Obvious Problems with Anti-Trafficking Initiatives

Many countries have now finally adopted some domestic legislation addressing trafficking, and most have eradicated earlier laws that punished trafficked persons for immigration or prostitution offenses.[54] This section points out reasons no current laws are very effective in the fight to eradicate trafficking.

By no means, however, have all countries adopted laws to specifically target trafficking.[55]

1. Governments Fail to Prioritize the Implementation of Anti-Trafficking Laws

A piece of legislation is useful to trafficked persons and threatening to violators only if it is implemented and known by the traffickers to be fully in force. No matter how great the economic or political pressure applied by the European Union or the United States to encourage countries to introduce legislation to prosecute traffickers, no incentive can create the political will to *implement* legislation if such will or ability does not exist or is not prioritized.[56]

In Bosnia, for example, UNMIBH reported that of sixty-three cases brought against traffickers in 2000, only three were successfully prosecuted.[57] Of those three, the defendants were *all* tried on charges related to prostitution, not trafficking. According to the HRW Report, all of the thirty-six cases brought involved charges related to prostitution and not trafficking—not just the three successful ones.[58] In one of the three cases, three trafficked women and two brothel owners were arrested in a raid. Although the defendants admitted that they had purchased the women for prices ranging between $592 and $1162, the court convicted the three women for prostitution and dropped the charges against the male defendants.[59]

Coordination among responsible agencies to implement the law is often flawed in the best of circumstances, further obstructing implementation.[60] Meetings are held at the highest levels and those in attendance come away full of self-congratulations that plans are being made and laws adopted. Yet out in the community, brothels are raided and no screening is done for victims of trafficking; victims identify themselves to police and face prosecution;[61] traffickers supply false passports to border police,[62] and the girls and traffickers are waived through.

For example, during the author's tenure in Belgrade, Serbia, and Montenegro, a brothel was raided and trafficked women were placed in jail, rather than the new shelter for trafficked persons, on the very same day that a high-level regional meeting took place in Belgrade between ministries and Stability Pact, UN, and OSCE officials to discuss follow up victim protection mechanisms for the new shelter. There seemed to be no communication between those making the decisions to adopt new laws and practices and those carrying them out in the field, and there was an inability or unwillingness to train these low-level government employees.

2. Governments Fail to Penalize or Even Acknowledge the Complicity of Peacekeepers and International Workers in Trafficking

Despite a growing awareness that peacekeeping forces and humanitarian workers regularly and knowingly obtain the services of trafficked women and sometimes even engage in or aid and abet trafficking, governments have failed to publicly address this issue. Trafficked women in Bosnia, for instance, report that approximately 30 per cent of their clients are internationals.[63] Countries that had never before been countries of destination began receiving trafficked women when peacekeepers and international aid workers moved into Bosnia, Croatia, and Kosovo.[64] Neighboring countries quickly became countries of transit and origin. While the use of trafficked women by international workers might constitute only a fraction of the total number of trafficked women and the fraction of those trafficked by international workers is even less, the participation of international humanitarian workers and peacekeeping forces in trafficking conveys a powerful symbolic message to local authorities and traffickers. The message is this: governments working to "democratize" developing countries do not really care about eradicating trafficking.

For years international organizations operating in the Balkans have been unwilling to determine how they can best prevent their employees from frequenting brothels known to harbor trafficked women. In recent years, when it has become clear that most brothels in the Balkans, for instance, do contain trafficked women,[65] these international organizations have still failed to enforce internal rules or laws against frequenting brothels.[66]

Ninety per cent of foreign sex workers in the Balkans are estimated to be trafficked, although less than 35 per cent are identified and deemed eligible to receive protection assistance, and less than 7 per cent actually do receive long-term support.[67] It is therefore well known among those charged with teaching Bosnians how to better enforce their laws, e.g. peacekeepers, the International Police Task Force [IPTF][68], and international humanitarian workers, that by visiting a prostitute, one stands a good chance of visiting a trafficked woman.[69] One would think, therefore, that workers paid by the foreign ministries whose goals are combating trafficking and promoting safety and democracy would be strictly forbidden to visit brothels, but they are not. In fact, sometimes they receive no punishment whatsoever even when caught engaging in such activity.[70] How can a victim of trafficking be expected to escape her captor and seek safety with the very men paying her captors for her services?

Some international organizations such as the OSCE and some branches of the United Nations have recently developed "Codes of Conduct" which implicitly forbid their personnel from seeing prostitutes by exhorting that they not "engage in any activity unbecoming of a mission member," subsequent to widely-publicized scandals involving international troops engaged in trafficking.[71] Nevertheless, several recent articles indicate that local police, international peacekeepers, and humanitarian aid workers continue to be major users of brothels in the Balkans in particular.[72] Developing and enforcing prohibitions against this practice are crucial, because the international police, peacekeepers, and humanitarian workers are the very persons whose duty it is to work with local authorities to eradicate trafficking in this part of the world, and the victims are supposed to be looking to international police and peacekeepers for protection.[73]

Notes

1. Bosnia is currently divided into two entities and a district: the Republika Srpska, the Federation, and Brcko District.

2. As related to the author during her work with the OSCE in Bosnia. For similar stories, see Human Rights Watch, Hopes Betrayed: Trafficking of Women and Girls to Post-Conflict Bosnia and Herzegovina for Forced Prostitution (2002) [hereinafter HRW Report]; John McGhie, *Bosnia—Arizona Market: Women for Sale* (UK Channel 4 News television broadcast, 8 June 2000). . . ; William J. Kole & Aida Cerkez-Robinson, *U.N. Police Accused of Involvement in Prostitution in Bosnia, Assoc. Press, 28 June 2001;* Colum Lynch, *U.N. Halted Probe of Officers' Alleged Role in Sex Trafficking,* Wash. Post, 27 Dec. 2001, at A17. . . .

3. United Nations Children's Fund (UNICEF) et al., Trafficking in Human Beings in Southeastern Europe xiii (2002) [hereinafter Joint Report on Trafficking] (stating that trafficking in human beings is the third most lucrative organized crime activity after, and often conjoined with, trafficking in arms and drugs). *See also* Gillian Caldwell et al., Crime and Servitude: An Exposé of the Traffic in Women for Prostitution from the Newly Independent States 14 (1997). . . (citing 1988 German police estimates that "traffickers earned US \$35–50 million annually in interest on loans to foreign women and girls entering Germany to work as prostitutes").

4. U.S. Dep't of State Office to Monitor and Combat Trafficking in Persons, Trafficking in Persons Report 1 (2002).

5. *The Sex Trade: Trafficking of Women and Children in Europe and the United States: Hearing before the Commission on Security and Cooperation in Europe,* 106th Cong., 1st Sess. 22 (1999) (testimony of Laura Lederer) [hereinafter,

The Lederer Report] (stating that women trafficked into North America are sold for as much as $16,000 to each new brothel owner, and have to pay or work off a debt of $20,000 to $40,000); *see also,* Jennifer Lord, *EU Expansion Could Fuel Human Trafficking,* United Press Int'l, 9 Nov. 2002. . . .

6. Caldwell, *supra* note 3, at 10.

7. While there are a multitude of definitions of trafficking, the most widely used definition derives from the current legal standard bearer, the Protocol to Prevent, Suppress and Punish Trafficking in Persons, Especially Women and Children, Supplementing the United Nations Convention Against Transnational Organized Crime, *adopted* 15 Nov. 2000, G.A. Res. A/55/25, Annex II, 55 U.N. GAOR Supp. (No. 49), at 60, U.N. Doc. A/45/49 (Vol. I) (2001) (*entered into force* 25 Dec. 2003) [hereinafter Trafficking Protocol]. Article 3 of The Protocol defines trafficking as:

> the recruitment, transportation, transfer, harbouring or receipt of persons, by means of the threat or use of force or other forms of coercion, of abduction, of fraud, of deception, of the abuse of power or of a position of vulnerability or of the giving or receiving of payments or benefits to achieve the consent of a person having control over another person, for the purpose of exploitation.

See United Nations, Office of Drugs and Crime. . . . Solely for the purposes of narrowing discussion, this article will emphasize trafficking for sex work. This narrow focus should not be viewed as support for a definition of trafficking that bifurcates trafficking that results in sex work from other forms of trafficking (such as indentured domestic service, forced labor, forced marriage, subjugation in making pornography, etc.). All trafficking in human beings is a violation of human rights in that it involves affronts to human dignity and arguably constitutes a form of slavery.

8. *See infra* text and accompanying notes pt. IV(A).

9. In South Eastern Europe, for instance, Croatia, Serbia, and Montenegro, have no distinct criminal offense for trafficking, despite being known countries of origin, transit, or destination, although a law is under consideration in Serbia. For review of laws related to trafficking in these countries, *see* Kristi Severance, ABA: Central European an Eurasian Law Initiative Survey of Legislative Frameworks for Combating Trafficking in Persons (2003) [hereinafter ABA CEELI Report]. . . . *See infra* note 109. In March 2003, the Office of the High Representative imposed a law criminalizing trafficking as a distinct offense, as the Bosnian authorities had failed to do. As yet, however, no traffickers have been charged under this new law.

10. *See infra* text pt. III(B)(1).

11. *See infra* text pt. IV(B)(1)(b).

12. For the purposes of simplicity, the paper will refer to women in particular, and use the feminine pronouns when referring to victims of trafficking, as the majority of victims of trafficking for sexual exploitation are women and girls.

13. Since the early 1990s countries in political and economic transition in Central, Eastern, and South Eastern Europe and the Former Soviet Union

have not only become main countries of origin for trafficked persons, but also of transit and destination. See Office for Democratic Institutions and Human Rights, Organization for Security and Co-operation in Europe, Reference Guide for Anti-Trafficking Legislative Review 20 (2001) [hereinafter OSCE Reference Guide]. South Eastern European countries offer the unique combination of being countries deeply mired in trafficking, and simultaneously interested in entering the European Union (EU). As such, they are in the process of bringing their legislation and administrative bodies into compliance with European standards, and are particularly useful for viewing the process of developing anti-trafficking initiatives. Cyprus, the Czech Republic, Estonia, Hungary, Latvia, Lithuania, Malta, Poland, the Slovak Republic, and Slovenia, and are set to join the EU in 2004, while Romania, Bulgaria, and Turkey all have active applications for EU membership. . . .

14. Central and Eastern Europe have surpassed Asia and Latin America as countries of origin since the breakdown of the Soviet Union in 1989. See OSCE Reference Guide, *supra* note 13, at 7.

15. U.N. Convention Against Transnational Organized Crime, G.A. Res. 55/25, Annex I, U.N. GAOR 55th Sess., Supp. No. 49, at 44, U.N. Doc. A/45/49 (Vol. 1) (2000), *entered into force* 29 Sept. 2003 [hereinafter Organized Crime Convention]. Serbia, Montenegro, and Bosnia have ratified the Organized Crime Convention, and its Protocols. All other South Eastern European countries are parties and it remains unclear as to how they will implement their commitments.

16. *See infra* text pt. III(B)(2). International Administration is still in effect in Kosovo (through the U.N. Mission in Kosovo, pursuant to U.N. Resolution 1244 (S.C. Res 1244, U.N. SCOR, 4011th mtg., S/RES/1244 (1999)), and partially in Bosnia and Herzegovina.

17. *See* Jenna Shearer Demir, the Trafficking of Women for Sexual Exploitation: A Gender-Based and Well-founded Fear of Persecution? 4–5 (2003) . . . (arguing that women disproportionately suffer the effects of an economic upheaval); Sergei Blagov, *Equal Opportunities Remain a Pipe-dream,* Asia Times Online, 10 Mar. 2000, . . . (stating that "[s]ome 70 per cent of Russian unemployed with college degrees are women. In some regions, women make up almost 90 per cent of the unemployed.")

18. Based on the author's discussion with anti-trafficking NGOs and UN officials in Bosnia and Serbia, and on direct discussion with trafficking victims.

19. *Id.*

20. HRW Report, *supra* note 2, at 18.

21. *Id.* at 4, 11.

22. *Report of the Special Rapporteur on Violence Against Women, its Causes and Consequences, Ms. Radhika Coomaraswamy,* U.N. ESCOR, Comm'n on Hum. Rts., 53rd Sess., U.N. Doc. E/CN.4/1997/47 (1997) § IV (expressing concern about government complicity in trafficking).

23. *See* Amy O'Neill Richard, U.S. Dep't of State Center for the Study of Intelligence: International Trafficking in Women to the United States: A Contemporary Manifestation of Slavery and Organized Crime 1 (1999) . . .

[hereinafter CSI Report]. *See also* IOM, Applied Research and Data Collection on a Study of Trafficking in Women and Children for Sexual Exploitation to through and from the Balkan Region 7 (2001) [hereinafter IOM Report].

24. *See* CSI Report, *supra* note 23, at 19–20.

25. *See infra* text pt. IV (C)(2)(a).

26. U.S. Dep't of State, Office to Monitor and Combat Trafficking in Persons, Trafficking in Persons Report 1, *supra* note 4, at 1. The numbers for South Eastern Europe in particular are difficult to specify. For example, one Swedish NGO estimates that "500,000 women . . . are trafficked each year into Western Europe alone. A large proportion of these come from the former Soviet Union countries." Joint Report on Trafficking, *supra* note 3, at 4. IOM estimates that in 1997, "175,000 women and girls were trafficked from Central and Eastern Europe and the Newly Independent States." *Id.* As of 2002, IOM estimates that 120,000 women and children are trafficked into the EU each year, mostly through the Balkans, and that 10,000 are working in Bosnia alone, mostly from Moldova, Romania and the Ukraine. *Id.*

27. Joint Report on Trafficking, *supra* note 3, at xv (only 7 per cent of the foreign migrant sex workers known to be victims of trafficking receive any long term assistance and support).

28. HRW Report, *supra* note 2, at 38.

29. Global Alliance Against Traffic in Women et al., Human Rights Standards for the Treatment of Trafficked Persons 13, 15 (1999). . . . Countries from which trafficked persons originate are referred to as countries of origin. Countries through which victims are trafficked are called countries of transit, and destination countries are those in which victims ultimately find themselves engaged in sex work.

30. *Id.* at 13.

31. International Agreement for the Suppression of White Slave Traffic, 1 U.N.T.S. 83 (*signed* 18 May 1904) (*entered into force* 18 July 1905) (amended by the Protocol signed at Lake Success, New York, 4 May 1949). The Agreement was ratified by Belgium, Denmark, France, Germany, Italy, the Netherlands, Portugal Russia, Spain, Sweden, and Norway, Switzerland, and the United Kingdom and consented to by their respective colonies, and dealt with European women being exported to the colonies for prostitution, sometimes forcibly.

32. International Convention for the Suppression of the Traffic in Women of Full Age, Concluded at Geneva 11 Oct. 1933, as amended by the Protocol signed at Lake Success, New York, on 12 Nov. 1947, *registered* 24 Apr. 1950, No. 772.

33. Convention for the Suppression of the Traffic in Persons and of the Exploitation of the Prostitution of Others, *opened for signature* 21 Mar. 1950, 96 U.N.T.S. 271 (*entered into force* 25 July 1951). Parties agreed to "punish any person who, to gratify the passions of another: (1) Procures, entices or leads away, for purposes of prostitution, another person, even with the consent of that person; (2) Exploits the prostitution of another person, even with the consent of that person." *Id.* art. 1.

34. Convention on the Elimination of All Forms of Discrimination Against Women, *adopted* 18 Dec. 1979, G.A. Res. 34/180, U.N. GAOR, 34th Sess.,

Supp. No. 46, U.N. Doc. A/34/46 (1980) (*entered into force* 3 Sept. 1981), 1249 U.N.T.S. 13, *reprinted* in 19 I.L.M. 33 (1980).

35. *See* CSI Report, *supra* note 23, at 31 (stating that "[d]efinitional difficulties still persist regarding trafficking in women. . . . Distinctions regarding trafficking in women, alien smuggling, and irregular migration are sometimes blurred with INS [former US immigration department] predisposed to jump to the conclusion that most cases involving illegal workers are alien smuggling instead of trafficking cases").

36. *See,* e.g., Richard Monk, Organization for Security and Co-operation in Europe Mission to the Fry: Study on Policing in the Federal Republic of Yugoslavia 21 (2001) . . . [hereinafter Monk Report] (Commenting: "Additionally, these statistics [on successful anti-trafficking ventures] are used for various political purposes—for example, prevention of trafficking is used as an argument for refusing young women entry to a country or for refusing to issue them a visa, and then, in the police statistics, these cases are relabeled as successful cases of rescuing 'victims of trafficking.'").

37. *See,* e.g., CSI Report, *supra* note 23, at 35 (US government officials cited as holding the opinion that trafficking victims are part of the conspiracy and therefore view them as accomplices).

38. "More often than not, anti-trafficking laws, be it domestic or international, tend to be conceived and are employed as border-control and immigration mechanisms," Agnes Khoo, *Trafficking and Human Rights: Some Observations and Questions,* 12 Asia Pacific-Forum on Law, Women and Development 3 (Dec. 1999). . . .

39. In explaining its priorities for 2003, the Stability Pact of South-Eastern Europe stated: "Attention will be drawn to maintain the differentiation between victims of human trafficking and prostitutes, which is currently becoming blurred, to the detriment of effective and targeted victim protection." Special Co-ordinator of the Stability Pact for South Eastern Europe Task Force on Trafficking in Human Beings, Anti-Trafficking Policy-Outline for 2003 [hereinafter SP Trafficking Task Force Priorities]. . . . For more discussion on the Stability Pact, see discussion *infra* pt. IV(D)(3).

40. NGO Consultation with the UN/IGO's on Trafficking in Persons, Prostitution and the Global Sex Industry, Trafficking and the Global Sex Industry: The Need for a Human Rights Framework, 21–22 (1999), Room XII Palais des Nations, Geneva, Switzerland [Panel A and Panel B] (some IGO's arguing that all prostitution is forced prostitution and calling for its abolition, with others arguing for a distinction between voluntary and forced prostitution in order to focus on preventing the worst forms of exploitation of prostitutes).

41. *See,* e.g., CSI Report, *supra* note 23, at vi ("The Thirteenth Amendment outlawing slavery prohibits an individual from selling himself or herself into bondage, and Western legal tradition prohibits contracts consenting in advance to assaults and other criminal wrongs."). This argument is further developed in pt. V(A)(1).

42. *See* HRW Report, *supra* note 2, at 15–20 (detailing common treatment and expectations of trafficked women).

43. *Id.* at 13. This practice of excluding prostitutes from victim protection results from criteria set by donor agencies rather than international law; *see e.g., infra* note 44 and accompanying text.

44. In its report entitled "Trafficking in Persons, The USAID Strategy for Response," designed to implement several provisions within the Trafficking Victim's Protection Act (TVPA), the US Agency for International Development (USAID) states that it will only work with [e.g. fund] local NGOs "committed . . . to combat trafficking *and prostitution,*" [emphasis added], explaining that: "organizations advocating prostitution as an employment choice or which advocate or support the legalization of prostitution are not appropriate partners," US Agency for International Development, Trafficking in Persons: The USAID Strategy for Response (Feb. 2003). . . .

45. U.S. Dep't of State International Information Programs, Fact Sheet: Migrant Smuggling and Trafficking in Persons (2000). . . .

46. *Id.*

47. *See* Jacqueline Oxman-Martinez, Human Smuggling and Traficking: Achieving the Goals of the UN Protocols? 1 (2003). . . .

48. *Id.* at 1.

49. In the last decade, Southeast Asia alone has produced nearly three times as many victims of trafficking than produced during the entire history of slavery from Africa. Melanie Nezer, *Trafficking in Women and Children: "A Contemporary Manifestation of Slavery,"* 21 Refugee Reports 1, 3 (2000) (400 years of slavery from Africa produced 11.5 million victims; victims of trafficking in the 1990s within and from Southeast Asia are estimated to be more than 30 million).

50. The United States Trafficking Victims Protection Act of 2000, Pub. L. No. 106-386, 114 Stat. 1464 (2000) [hereinafter TVPA], for instance, requires an annual submission to Congress by the Department of State on the status of trafficking in each country. Financial assistance is tied directly to the level of each country's compliance with US directives. U.S. Dep't of State Office to Monitor and Combat Trafficking in Persons, Trafficking in Persons Report 10 (2002). (Beginning in 2003, those countries ranked lowest in this report "will be subject to certain sanctions, principally termination of non-humanitarian, non-trade-related assistance. Consistent with the Act, such countries also would face U.S. opposition to assistance . . . from international financial institutions.")

51. In the case of the European Union, entry into the Union is conditioned upon compliance with general respect for human rights and compliance with human rights standards.

52. For list of applicant countries to the European, *see supra* note 13.

53. In the author's experience working with ministries of justice, interior, and human rights in Bosnia, Croatia, and Serbia and Montenegro, high level government authorities were typically keen to attend high level working groups addressing the drafting of trafficking legislation, but were much harder to pin down when it came to establishing work plans to train field level government authorities.

54. *See infra* text pt. IV(A). For example, in Israel as recently as 1998, a victim's best hope was to have the brothel or massage parlor she worked in raided by police. She would then be taken to prison, not a shelter or detention center, and offered two options: be deported and have criminal prostitution charges dropped, or file a complaint against her trafficker or

those holding her in involuntary servitude. If she chose to file charges, however, she would remain in prison until a trial was held. Not surprisingly, no women between 1994 and 1998 chose to testify against their traffickers in Israel. Most traffickers were well aware that the laws favored them, if only because the women they trafficked were illegally in the country and were engaging in criminal activity. Michael Specter, *Traffickers' New Cargo: Naïve Slavic Women*, N.Y. Times, 11 Jan. 1998, at A1.

55. Serbia, Montenegro, and Croatia, for example, have no distinct criminal offense for trafficking. *See* generally ABA CEELI Report, *supra* note 9, for updates on domestic trafficking legislation. Although Bosnia's law criminalizing trafficking was imposed in March 2003, it has yet to yield a prosecution. *See infra* note 109.

56. One way to encourage implementation of anti-trafficking laws is for the European Union and United States to condition their assistance on implementation, rather than on simple passage of anti-trafficking laws, a recommendation made in this paper, and finally acknowledged in the 2003 Trafficking in Persons Report, U.S. Dep't of State Office to Monitor and Combat Trafficking in Persons, Trafficking in Persons Report 2 (2003) [hereinafter 2003 Trafficking in Persons Report]. . . .

57. HRW Report, *supra* note 2, at 36.

58. *Id.*

59. *Id.*

60. CSI Report, *supra* note 23, at 31. Questions about whether the United States can be considered an example of the "best of circumstances" aside, the CSI Report states that at least in 1999, prior to passage of the TVPA, "information sharing among the various entities remain[ed] imperfect. Several Department of Justice [DOJ] offices look at the trafficking issue through the prism of their particular offices' interest, be it eliminating civil rights violations, tackling organized crime, or protecting minors. Even within the [DOJ], information is not always shared." *See also* Monk Report, *supra* note 36, at 76. Although Serbia and Montenegro are actively participating in high level working groups to combat trafficking, including suggesting progressive programs for victim protection, the police force is incapable of coping with the scale of the phenomenon:

> Apart from within the border police departments, there is poor awareness and interest generally on the part of police and the public about the subject [of trafficking], and the prevailing disregard for gender equality contributes to indifference about the plight of victims. . . . Because of the lack of reciprocal agreements with neighboring States, the incompatibility of laws, the absence of [domestic] laws which enable successful prosecutions to be brought against the traffickers and pimps and the lack of [domestic] legal authority to produce evidence obtained by the internal use of technical and surveillance aids, victim's cases are generally viewed as time and energy consuming and inevitably unproductive. The very fact that victim's statements, both verbal and written, will be in a foreign language further reduces responsiveness.

61. HRW Report, *supra* note 2, at 61.

62. *See id.* at 16.

63. Id. at 11. *See also,* 2003 Trafficking in Persons Report, *supra* note 56, at 35 (acknowledging that the international civilian and military personnel have contributed to trafficking in Bosnia).

64. *See, e.g.,* HRW Report, *supra* note 2, at 4, 11. ("According to [IGOs and NGOs] trafficking first began to appear [in Bosnia] in 1995," and "[l]ocal NGOs believe that the presence of thousands of expatriate civilians and soldiers has been a significant motivating factor for traffickers to Bosnia and Herzegovina.")

65. *See id.* at 4 (227 of the nightclubs in Bosnia are suspected of harboring trafficked women).

66. *Id.* at 46–60.

67. *See* Joint Report on Trafficking, *supra* note 3, at xv.

68. In January 2003, the duties of the IPTF were assumed by the European Union, and are now referred to as "European Union Police Mission."

69. In Serbia for example, of 600 women questioned by police during brothel raids between January 2000 and July 2001, 300 were determined to be victims of trafficking. *See id.,* at 78.

70. HRW Report, *supra* note 2, at 62–67.

71. The author, a member of the OSCE Mission to Bosnia, signed such a Code of Conduct.

72. *See, e.g.,* McGhie, *supra* note 2; Kole, *supra* note 2; Lynch, *supra* note 2; Daniel McGrory, *Woman Sacked for Revealing UN Links with Sex Trade,* The Times Online (London), 7 Aug. 2002; Robert Capps, *Crime Without Punishment,* SALON.COM, 27 Jun. 2002 . . . Robert Capps, Outside the Law, SALON.COM, 26 June. 2002 . . . *US Scandal, Prostitution, Pimping and Trafficking,* Bosnia Daily, Daily e-newspaper, 25 Jul. 2001, No. 42, at 1 (on file with author).

73. UNHCHR recently addressed this issue openly in its guideline covering "Obligations of peacekeepers, civilian police and humanitarian and diplomatic personnel," asking states to consider "[e]nsuring that staff employed in the context of peacekeeping, peace-building, civilian policing, humanitarian and diplomatic missions do not engage in trafficking and related exploitation or use the services of persons in relation to which there are reasonable grounds to suspect that they may have been trafficked." *Recommended Principles and Guidelines on Human Rights and Human Trafficking, U.N. High Commissioner for Human Rights,* E/2002/68/Add.1, Guideline 10, ¶ 3 [hereinafter *Recommended Principles and Guidelines*]. *See infra* text pt. IV(C)(2).

POSTSCRIPT

Do Adequate Strategies Exist to Combat Human Trafficking?

Human trafficking has been part of the global landscape for centuries. What is different today are the magnitude and scope of the trafficking and the extent to which organized crime is involved in facilitating such nefarious activity. And yet the global community is still only in the position of trying to identify the nature and extent of the problem and has not yet ascertained how to deal with it. In April 2006, the UN Office on Drugs and Crime released its most recent report on the human trafficking problem. Titled *Trafficking in Persons: Global Patterns* (United Nations Office on Drugs and Crime, April 2006), its message was clear. The starting point for addressing the problem is the implementation of the Protocol to Prevent, Suppress and Punish Trafficking in Persons, especially Women and Children. National governments are called upon to take a leading role in (1) the prevention of trafficking, (2) the prosecution of violators, and (3) the protection of victims.

Consider the task of prevention. Nations are expected to establish comprehensive policies and programs to prevent and combat trafficking, including research, information, and media campaigns. Nations must attempt to alleviate the vulnerability of people, especially women and children. They must create steps to discourage demand for victims. Nations must also prevent transportation opportunities for traffickers. Finally, they must exchange information and increase cooperation among border control agencies.

The UN report also suggests several steps with respect to prosecution. The first step is to "ensure the integrity and security of travel and identity documents" and thus prevent their misuse. Domestic laws must be enacted making human trafficking a criminal offense, and these laws must apply to victims of both genders and all ages. Penalties must be adequate to the crime. Finally, victims must be protected and possibly compensated.

The third role outlined in the UN report focuses on protection of victims. Specifically, victims must be able to achieve "physical, psychological and social recovery." The physical safety of victims is also paramount. The final step relates to the future home of victims, whether they want to remain in the location where found or whether they wish to return home.

The essence of the report suggests the changing character of global issues in this age of globalization. No longer can nation-states solve problems alone. Moreover, no longer can they simply create a new international organization to address the problem. The issue is simply too complex. An array of interlocking structures, agreements, international law, and national initiatives (what was termed an international regime earlier) is needed and is well on the way to being created. As with other issues in this volume, modern technology combined with the process of globalization demands such a strategy if the international community is going to successfully address the evils of human trafficking.

On February 1, 2008, European nations signed an historic treaty termed the Council of Europe Convention on Action against Trafficking in Human Beings. For the first time, these countries will have a comprehensive treaty that addresses both efforts to prevent trafficking and steps to prosecute traffickers.

The UN report cited above represents an excellent starting point for additional readings about human trafficking. A second comprehensive source is "Victims of Trafficking for Forced Prostitution: Protection Mechanisms and the Right to Remain in the Destination Countries" (*Global Migration Perspectives*, Global Commission on International Migration, no. 2, July 2004).

A 2005 book edited by Kamala Kempadoo, *Trafficking and Prostitution Reconsidered: New Perspectives on Migration, Sex Work, and Human Rights* (Paradigm Publishers) examines the contemporary situation in Asia. Other useful books include *Data and Research on Human Trafficking: A Global Survey* (Frank Laczko, United Nations, 2005); *Global Trafficking in Women and Children* (Obi N.I. Ebbe and Dilip K. Das, eds., CRC, 2007); *Human Trafficking, Human Security, and the Balkans* (H. Richard Friman and Simon Reich, eds., University of Pittsburgh Press, 2007); *Not for Sale: The Return of the Global Slave Trade—and How We Can Fight It* (David Batstone, HarperOne, 2007); and *Unspeakable: The Hidden Truth Behind the World's Fastest Growing Crime* (Raymond Bechard, 2006); *Selling Olga: Stories of Human Trafficking* (Louisa Waugh, Phoenix, 2008); and *A Crime So Monstrous: Face-to-Face with Modern-Day Slavery* (E. Benjamin Skinner, Free Press, 2009). Three recent books apply solid empirical research and scholarship to an analysis of the problem: *Human Trafficking* (Maggy Lee, ed., Willan Publishing, 2007); *Smuggling and Trafficking in Human Beings: All Roads Lead to America* (Sheldon X. Zhang, Praeger, 2007); and *Human Trafficking, Human Misery: The Global Trade in Human Beings* (Alexis A. Aronowitz, Praeger, 2009).

Four recent books focus on efforts to combat human trafficking. They are *Not for Sale: The Return of the Global Slave Trade and How We Can Fight It* (David Batstone, HarperOne, 2007); *Sex Trafficking: Inside the Business of Modern Slavery* (Columbia University Press, 2008); *The War on Human Trafficking: U.S. Policy Assessed* (Anthony M. DeStefano, Rutgers University Press, 2008); and *Trafficking in Humans: Social, Cultural and Political Dimensions* (Sally Cameron and Edward Newman, eds., UNU Press. 2008).

A number of articles provide useful insights into aspects of the problem. Ilana Kramer's "Modern-Day Sex Slavery" (*Lilith*, vol. 31, no. 1, Spring 2006) describes the problem as it relates to Israel. John R. Miller's " Modern-Day Slavery" (*Sheriff*, vol. 58, no. 2, March/April 2006) describes trafficking problems within the United States. Gail Kligman and Stephanie Limoncelli address the trafficking of women in post-Communist Eastern Europe in "Trafficking Women after Socialism: To, Through, and From Eastern Europe" (*Social Politics: International Studies in Gender, State and Society*, Spring 2005). Amy Fraley provides information about national anti-trafficking legislation in "Child Sex

Tourism Legislation Under the Protect Act: Does It Really Protect?" (St. John's Law Review Association, 2005). An assessment of UN progress as of 2003 can be found in "Global Trafficking in Human Beings: Assessing the Success of the United Nations Protocol to Prevent Trafficking in Persons" (LeRoy G. Potts, Jr., *The George Washington International Law Review,* 2003). See also the work of Professor Cynthia Messer, University of Minnesota, at http://www.tourism.umn.edu/about/staff/messer.html. Two official reports provide comprehensive information about the problem of human trafficking: *2007 Trafficking in Persons Report* (U.S. Department of State) and *Combating Child Trafficking* (UNICEF, 2005). A comprehensive look at the new agreements can be found in Anne Gallagher, "Human Rights and the New UN Protocols on Trafficking and Migrant Smuggling: A Preliminary Analysis" (*Human Rights Quarterly,* vol. 23, 2001). The UN Web site for its Office on Drugs and Crime is http://www.unodc.org/unodc/multimedia.html. For information about the Council of Europe's efforts, see http//:www.coe.int?T/E/human_rights/trafficking. "Federal Government Efforts to Combat Human Trafficking" provides links to multiple U.S. Government sites on human trafficking.

A number of other Web sites are also useful. Among these are http://www.wnhcr.ch (the UN High Commissioner for Refugees); http://www.unicef.org (International Child Development Center); http://www.unifem.org (United Nations Development Fund for Women); http://www.ecre.org/research/smuggle.shtml (European Council on Refugees and Exiles); http://www.bayswan.org?FoundTraf.html (Foundation against Trafficking in Women); http://www. trafficked-women.org (Coalition to Abolish Slavery and Trafficking); http://www.uri.edu/artsci/wms/hughes/pubvio.htm (Coalition Against Trafficking in Women); http://www.gaatw.org (Global Alliance against Traffic in Women); http://www.ecpatw.org (End Child Prostitution and Trafficking); and http://www.antislavery.org (Antislavery International). Additional sites include http://www.endhumantrafickingnow.com (End Human Trafficking Now); http://www.sharedhope.org (Shared Hope International); http://www.freetheslaves.net (Free the Slaves); and http://humantrafficking.org.

ISSUE 13

Is Globalization a Positive Development for the World Community?

YES: Robyn Meredith and **Suzanne Hoppough**, from "Why Globalization Is Good," *Forbes* (April 16, 2007)

NO: Steven Weber, Naazneen Barma, Matthew Kroenig, and **Ely Ratner**, from "How Globalization Went Bad," *Foreign Policy* (January/February 2007)

ISSUE SUMMARY

YES: Meredith and Hoppough argue that the data supports the conclusion that globalization works for both rich and poor. They particularly point to the growing middle class in many countries throughout Asia, Africa, and Latin America, to support this conclusion.

NO: Weber et al. argue that globalization and the American predominance that drives it amplify a myriad of evils, including terrorism, global warming, and interethnic conflict, creating a less stable and less just world community.

Globalization is a phenomenon and a revolution. It is sweeping the world with increasing speed and changing the global landscape into something new and different. Yet, like all such trends, its meaning, development, and impact puzzle many. We talk about globalization and experience its effects, but few of us really understand the forces that are at work in the global political economy.

When people use their cell phones, log onto the Internet, view events from around the world on live television, and experience varying cultures in their own backyards, they begin to believe that this process of globalization is a good thing that will bring a variety of new and sophisticated changes to people's lives. Many aspects of this technological revolution bring fun, ease, and sophistication to people's daily lives. Yet the anti–World Trade Organization (WTO) protests in Seattle, Washington, in 1999 and Washington, DC, in 2000 are graphic illustrations of the fact that not everyone believes that globalization is a good thing. Many Americans who have felt left out of the global economic boom, as well as Latin Americans, Africans, and Asians who feel that their job skills and abilities are being exploited by multinational corporations (MNCs) in a global division of labor, believe that this system does not meet their needs. Local cultures who believe that Wal-Mart and McDonald's bring cultural change and harm rather than inexpensive products and convenience criticize the process. In this way, globalization, like all revolutionary forces, polarizes people, alters the fabric of their lives, and creates rifts within and between people.

Many in the West, along with the prominent and elite—among MNCs, educators, and policymakers—seem to have embraced globalization. They argue that it helps to streamline economic systems, disciplines, labor and management, brings forth new technologies and ideas, and fuels economic growth. They point to the relative prosperity of many Western countries and argue that this is proof of globalization's positive effects. They see little of the problems that critics identify. In fact, those who recognize some structural problems in the system argue that despite these issues, globalization is like an inevitable tide of history, unfortunate for some but unyielding and impossible to change. Any problems that are created by this trend, they say, can be solved.

Many poor and middle-class workers, as well as hundreds of millions of people across the developing world, view globalization as an economic and cultural wave that tears at the fabric of centuries-old societies. They see jobs emerging and disappearing in a matter of months, people moving across the landscape in record numbers, elites amassing huge fortunes while local cultures and traditions are swept away, and local youth being seduced by promises of American material wealth and distanced from their own cultural roots. These critics look past the allure of globalization and focus on the disquieting impact of rapid and system-wide change.

The irony of such a far-ranging and rapid historical process such as globalization is that both proponents and critics may be right. The realities of globalization are both intriguing and alarming. As technology and the global infrastructure expand, ideas, methods, and services are developed and disseminated to greater and greater numbers of people. As a result, societies and values are altered, some for the better and others for the worse.

In the selections that follow, the authors explore the positive and negative impacts of globalization and reach different conclusions. Meredith and Hoppough argue that the facts of globalization show that it works for rich and poor alike. They point to the elevation into middle class of literally hundreds of millions of people across Asia, Latin America, and Africa as a proof, along with the realization that by lifting bans and restrictions, people around the globe can elevate their own economic condition and have done so. Weber et al. contend that globalization combined with America's predominance has created a kind of warping of globalization that accentuates the bad aspects (terrorism, global warming, cultural conflict) while mitigating its more positive effects.

YES ⤶

Robyn Meredith and
Suzanne Hoppough

Why Globalization Is Good

A ragtag army of save-the-world crusaders has spent years decrying multi-national corporations as villains in the wave of globalization overwhelming the Third World. This ominous trend would fatten the rich, further impoverish and oppress the poor and crush local economies.

The business-bashing group Public Citizen argued as much in a proclamation signed by almost 1,500 organizations in 89 countries in 1999. Whereupon hundreds of protesters rioted outside a conference of the World Trade Organization in Seattle, shattering windows, blocking traffic and confronting cops armed with tear gas and pepper spray. Six hundred people were arrested.

Cut to 2007, and the numbers are in: The protesters and do-gooders are just plain wrong. It turns out globalization is good—and not just for the rich, but *especially* for the poor. The booming economies of India and China—the Elephant and the Dragon—have lifted 200 million people out of abject poverty in the 1990s as globalization took off, the International Monetary Fund says. Tens of millions more have catapulted themselves far ahead into the middle class.

It's remarkable what a few container ships can do to make poor people better off. Certainly more than $2 trillion of foreign aid, which is roughly the amount (with an inflation adjustment) that the U.S. and Europe have poured into Africa and Asia over the past half-century.

In the next eight years almost 1 billion people across Asia will take a Great Leap Forward into a new middle class. In China middle-class incomes are set to rise threefold, to $5,000, predicts Dominic Barton, a Shanghai managing partner for McKinsey & Co.

As the Chindia revolution spreads, the ranks of the poor get smaller, not larger. In the 1990s, as Vietnam's economy grew 6% a year, the number of people living in poverty (42 million) fell 7% annually; in Uganda, when GDP growth passed 3%, the number fell 6% per year, says the World Bank.

China unleashed its economy in 1978, seeding capitalism first among farmers newly freed to sell the fruits of their fields instead of handing the produce over to Communist Party collectives. Other reforms let the Chinese create 22 million new businesses that now employ 135 million people who otherwise would have remained peasants like the generations before them.

As seen in *Forbes Magazine*, April 16, 2007. Adapted from *The Elephant and the Dragon: The Rise of India and China, and What It Means for All of Us*, by Robyn Meredith (W.W. Norton & Co., 2007). Copyright © 2007 by Robin Meredith. Reprinted by permission of W.W. Norton & Co, Inc.

Foreign direct investment, the very force so virulently opposed by the do-gooders, has helped drive China's gross domestic product to a more than tenfold increase since 1978. Since the reforms started, $600 billion has flooded into the country, $70 billion of it in the past year. Foreigners built hundreds of thousands of new factories as the Chinese government built the coal mines, power grid, airports and highways to supply them.

As China built infrastructure, it created Special Economic Zones where foreign companies willing to build modern factories could hire cheap labor, go years without paying any taxes and leave it to government to build the roads and other infrastructure they needed. All of that, in turn, drove China's exports from $970 million to $974 billion in three decades. Those container loads make Americans better off, too. You can get a Chinese DVD player at Wal-Mart for $28, and after you do you will buy some $15 movies made in the U.S.A.

Per-person income in China has climbed from $16 a year in 1978 to $2,000 now. Wages in factory boomtowns in southern China can run $4 a day—scandalously low in the eyes of the protesters, yet up from pennies a day a generation ago and far ahead of increases in living costs.

Middle-class Chinese families now own TVs, live in new apartments and send their children to private schools. Millions of Chinese have traded in their bicycles for motorcycles or cars. McDonald's has signed a deal with Sinopec, the huge Chinese gasoline retailer, to build drive-through restaurants attached to gas stations on China's new roads.

Today 254 Starbucks stores serve coffee in the land of tea, including one at the Great Wall and another at the Forbidden Palace. (The latter is the target of protesters.) In Beijing 54 Starbucks shops thrive, peddling luxury lattes that cost up to $2.85 a cup and paying servers $6 for an 8-hour day. That looks exploitative until you peek inside a nearby Chinese-owned teahouse where the staff works a 12-hour day for $3.75.

Says one woman, 23, who works for an international cargo shipper in Beijing: "My parents were both teachers when they were my age, and they earned 30 yuan [$3.70] a month. I earn 4,000 yuan ($500) a month, live comfortably and feel I have better opportunities than my parents did."

Tony Ma, age 51, was an unwilling foot soldier in Mao's Cultural Revolution. During that dark period from 1966 to 1976 universities were closed, and he was sent at age 16 to work in a steel mill for $2 a month. He cut metal all day long for seven years and feared he might never escape.

When colleges reopened, he landed a spot to study chemistry, transferred to the U.S., got a Ph.D. in biochemistry and signed on with Johnson & Johnson at $45,000 a year. Later he returned to the land he fled and now works for B.F. Goodrich in Hong Kong.

The young college grads in China today wouldn't bother immigrating to the U.S. for a job that pays $45,000, he says—because now they have better opportunities at home.

Capitalism alone, however, isn't enough to remake Third World economies—globalism is the key. A big reason India trails behind its bigger neighbor to the northeast in lifting the lower classes is that, even after embracing capitalism, it kept barriers to the flow of capital from abroad.

Thus 77% of Indians live on $2 a day or less, the Asian Development Bank says, down only nine percentage points from 1990. A third of the population is illiterate. In 1980 India had more of its population in urban centers than China did (23% versus 20% for China). But by 2005 China had 41% in cities, where wages are higher; India's urbanites had grown to only 29%.

Freed of British colonial rule in 1947 and scarred by its paternalistic effects, India initially combined capitalism with economic isolationism. It thwarted foreign companies intent on investing there and hampered Indian firms trying to sell abroad. This hurt Indian consumers and local biz: A $100 Microsoft operating system got slapped with duties that brought the price to $250 in India, putting imported software and computers further from reach for most people and businesses. Meanwhile, the government granted workers lavish job protections and imposed heavy taxes and regulations on employers. Government jobs usually were by rote and paid poorly, but they guaranteed lifetime employment. They also ensured economic stagnation.

Financial crisis struck in 1991. Desperate for cash, India flew a planeload of gold reserves to London and began, grudgingly, to open its economy. Import duties were lowered or eliminated, so India's consumers and companies could buy modern, foreign-made goods and gear. Overseas firms in many industries were allowed to own their subsidiaries in India for the first time since 1977. India all but banned foreign investment until 1991. Since then foreign companies have come back, but not yet on the scale seen in China. Foreign companies have invested $48 billion in India since 1991—$7.5 billion of that just in the last fiscal year—the same amount dumped into China every six weeks. By the mid-1990s the economy boomed and created millions of jobs.

By the late 1990s U.S. tech companies began turning to India for software design, particularly in the Y2K crunch. The Indians proved capable and cheap, and the much-maligned offshoring boom began. Suddenly Indian software engineers were programming corporate America's computers. New college graduates were answering America's customer service phone calls. Builders hired construction workers to erect new high-rise buildings suddenly in demand as American and European firms rushed to hire Indian workers.

The new college hires, whose older siblings had graduated without finding a job, tell of surpassing their parents' salaries within five years and of buying cell phones, then motorcycles, then cars and even houses by the time they were 30. All of that would have been impossible had India failed to add globalization to capitalism.

Today, despite its still dilapidated airports and pothole-riddled highways, the lumbering Elephant now is in a trot, growing more than 7% annually for the last decade. In 2005, borrowing from the Chinese, India began a five-year, $150 billion plan to update its roads, airports, ports and electric plants. India is creating free trade zones, like those in China, to encourage exports of software, apparel, auto parts and more.

S.B. Kutwal manages the assembly line where Tata Motors builds Safari SUVs. He remembers how, in the 1980s, people waited five years to buy a scooter and cars were only for the rich. "Since we've liberated the economy, lots of companies have started coming into India," says Kutwal. "People couldn't afford cars then. Now the buying power is coming."

In Mumbai (formerly Bombay), Delhi, Bangalore and other big cities, shopping malls have sprung up, selling everything from Levi's jeans to Versace. India still has raggedy street touts, but when they tap on car windows at stoplights, instead of peddling cheap plastic toys, they sell to the new India: copies of *Vogue* and *House & Garden* magazines. Western restaurants are moving in, too: Domino's Pizza and Ruby Tuesday's have come to India, and 107 McDonald's have sprung up, serving veggie burgers in the land where cattle are sacred.

None of this gives pause to an entity called International Forum on Globalization. The group declares that globalism's aim is to "benefit transnational corporations over workers; foreign investors over local businesses; and wealthy countries over developing nations. While promoters . . . proclaim that this model is the rising tide that will lift all boats, citizen movements find that it is instead lifting only yachts."

"The majority of people in rich and poor countries aren't better off" since the World Trade Organization formed in 1995 to promote global trade, asserts Christopher Slevin, deputy director of Global Trade Watch, an arm of Ralph Nader's Public Citizen. "The breadth of the opposition has grown. It's not just industrial and steel workers and people who care about animal rights. It includes high-tech workers and the offshoring of jobs, also the faith-based community."

While well-off American techies may be worried, it seems doubtful that an engineer in Bangalore who now earns $40,000 a year, and who has just bought his parents' house, wants to ban foreign investment.

Slevin's further complaint is that globalism is a creature of WTO, the World Bank and other unelected bodies.

But no, the people do have a voice in the process, and it is one that is equivocal on the matter of free market capitalism. The Western World's huge agriculture subsidies—$85 billion or more annually, between the U.S., Japan and the European Union—are decreed by democratically elected legislatures. The EU pays ranchers $2 per cow in daily subsidies, more than most Indians earn. If these farmers weren't getting handouts, and if trade in farm products were free, then poor farmers in the Third World could sell more of their output, and could begin to lift themselves out of poverty.

Steven Weber et al.

NO

How Globalization Went Bad

From terrorism to global warming, the evils of globalization are more dangerous than ever before. What went wrong? The world became dependent on a single superpower. Only by correcting this imbalance can the world become a safer place.

The world today is more dangerous and less orderly than it was supposed to be. Ten or 15 years ago, the naive expectations were that the "end of history" was near. The reality has been the opposite. The world has more international terrorism and more nuclear proliferation today than it did in 1990. International institutions are weaker. The threats of pandemic disease and climate change are stronger. Cleavages of religious and cultural ideology are more intense. The global financial system is more unbalanced and precarious.

It wasn't supposed to be like this. The end of the Cold War was supposed to make global politics and economics easier to manage, not harder. What went wrong? The bad news of the 21st century is that globalization has a significant dark side. The container ships that carry manufactured Chinese goods to and from the United States also carry drugs. The airplanes that fly passengers nonstop from New York to Singapore also transport infectious diseases. And the Internet has proved just as adept at spreading deadly, extremist ideologies as it has e-commerce.

The conventional belief is that the single greatest challenge of geopolitics today is managing this dark side of globalization, chipping away at the illegitimate co-travelers that exploit openness, mobility, and freedom, without putting too much sand in the gears. The current U.S. strategy is to push for more trade, more connectivity, more markets, and more openness. America does so for a good reason—it benefits from globalization more than any other country in the world. The United States acknowledges globalization's dark side but attributes it merely to exploitative behavior by criminals, religious extremists, and other anachronistic elements that can be eliminated. The dark side of globalization, America says, with very little subtlety, can be mitigated by the expansion of American power, sometimes unilaterally and sometimes through multilateral institutions, depending on how the United States likes it. In other

Reprinted in entirety by McGraw-Hill with permission from *FOREIGN POLICY,* January/February 2007, pp. 48+. www.foreignpolicy.com. © 2007 Washingtonpost.Newsweek Interactive, LLC.

words, America is aiming for a "flat," globalized world coordinated by a single superpower.

That's nice work if you can get it. But the United States almost certainly cannot. Not only because other countries won't let it, but, more profoundly, because that line of thinking is faulty. The predominance of American power has many benefits, but the management of globalization is not one of them. The mobility of ideas, capital, technology, and people is hardly new. But the rapid advance of globalization's evils is. Most of that advance has taken place since 1990. Why? Because what changed profoundly in the 1990s was the polarity of the international system. For the first time in modern history, globalization was superimposed onto a world with a single superpower. What we have discovered in the past 15 years is that it is a dangerous mixture. The negative effects of globalization since 1990 are not the result of globalization itself. They are the dark side of American predominance.

The Dangers of Unipolarity

A straightforward piece of logic from market economics helps explain why unipolarity and globalization don't mix. Monopolies, regardless of who holds them, are almost always bad for both the market and the monopolist. We propose three simple axioms of "globalization under unipolarity" that reveal these dangers.

Axiom 1: Above a certain threshold of power, the rate at which new global problems are generated will exceed the rate at which old problems are fixed.

Power does two things in international politics: It enhances the capability of a state to do things, but it also increases the number of things that a state must worry about. At a certain point, the latter starts to overtake the former. It's the familiar law of diminishing returns. Because powerful states have large spheres of influence and their security and economic interests touch every region of the world, they are threatened by the risk of things going wrong—anywhere. That is particularly true for the United States, which leverages its ability to go anywhere and do anything through massive debt. No one knows exactly when the law of diminishing returns will kick in. But, historically, it starts to happen long before a single great power dominates the entire globe, which is why large empires from Byzantium to Rome have always reached a point of unsustainability.

That may already be happening to the United States today, on issues ranging from oil dependency and nuclear proliferation to pandemics and global warming. What Axiom 1 tells you is that more U.S. power is not the answer; it's actually part of the problem. A multipolar world would almost certainly manage the globe's pressing problems more effectively. The larger the number of great powers in the global system, the greater the chance that at least one of them would exercise some control over a given combination of space, other actors, and problems. Such reasoning doesn't rest on hopeful notions that the great powers will work together. They might do so. But even if they don't, the result is distributed governance, where some great power is interested in most every part of the world through productive competition.

Axiom 2: In an increasingly networked world, places that fall between the networks are very dangerous places—and there will be more ungoverned zones when there is only one network to join.

The second axiom acknowledges that highly connected networks can be efficient, robust, and resilient to shocks. But in a highly connected world, the pieces that fall between the networks are increasingly shut off from the benefits of connectivity. These problems fester in the form of failed states, mutate like pathogenic bacteria, and, in some cases, reconnect in subterranean networks such as al Qaeda. The truly dangerous places are the points where the subterranean networks touch the mainstream of global politics and economics. What made Afghanistan so dangerous under the Taliban was not that it was a failed state. It wasn't. It was a partially failed and partially connected state that worked the interstices of globalization through the drug trade, counterfeiting, and terrorism.

Can any single superpower monitor all the seams and back alleys of globalization? Hardly. In fact, a lone hegemon is unlikely to look closely at these problems, because more pressing issues are happening elsewhere, in places where trade and technology are growing. By contrast, a world of several great powers is a more interest-rich environment in which nations must look in less obvious places to find new sources of advantage. In such a system, it's harder for troublemakers to spring up, because the cracks and seams of globalization are held together by stronger ties.

Axiom 3: Without a real chance to find useful allies to counter a superpower, opponents will try to neutralize power, by going underground, going nuclear, or going "bad."

Axiom 3 is a story about the preferred strategies of the weak. It's a basic insight of international relations that states try to balance power. They protect themselves by joining groups that can hold a hegemonic threat at bay. But what if there is no viable group to join? In today's unipolar world, every nation from Venezuela to North Korea is looking for a way to constrain American power. But in the unipolar world, it's harder for states to join together to do that. So they turn to other means. They play a different game. Hamas, Iran, Somalia, North Korea, and Venezuela are not going to become allies anytime soon. Each is better off finding other ways to make life more difficult for Washington. Going nuclear is one way. Counterfeiting U.S. currency is another. Raising uncertainty about oil supplies is perhaps the most obvious method of all.

Here's the important downside of unipolar globalization. In a world with multiple great powers, many of these threats would be less troublesome. The relatively weak states would have a choice among potential partners with which to ally, enhancing their influence. Without that more attractive choice, facilitating the dark side of globalization becomes the most effective means of constraining American power.

Sharing Globalization's Burden

The world is paying a heavy price for the instability created by the combination of globalization and unipolarity, and the United States is bearing most of the burden. Consider the case of nuclear proliferation. There's effectively a market out there for proliferation, with its own supply (states willing to share nuclear technology) and demand (states that badly want a nuclear weapon). The overlap of unipolarity with globalization ratchets up both the supply and demand, to the detriment of U.S. national security.

It has become fashionable, in the wake of the Iraq war, to comment on the limits of conventional military force. But much of this analysis is overblown. The United States may not be able to stabilize and rebuild Iraq. But that doesn't matter much from the perspective of a government that thinks the Pentagon has it in its sights. In Tehran, Pyongyang, and many other capitals, including Beijing, the bottom line is simple: The U.S. military could, with conventional force, end those regimes tomorrow if it chose to do so. No country in the world can dream of challenging U.S. conventional military power. But they can certainly hope to deter America from using it. And the best deterrent yet invented is the threat of nuclear retaliation. Before 1989, states that felt threatened by the United States could turn to the Soviet Union's nuclear umbrella for protection. Now, they turn to people like A.Q. Khan. Having your own nuclear weapon used to be a luxury. Today, it is fast becoming a necessity.

North Korea is the clearest example. Few countries had it worse during the Cold War. North Korea was surrounded by feuding, nuclear-armed communist neighbors, it was officially at war with its southern neighbor, and it stared continuously at tens of thousands of U.S. troops on its border. But, for 40 years, North Korea didn't seek nuclear weapons. It didn't need to, because it had the Soviet nuclear umbrella. Within five years of the Soviet collapse, however, Pyongyang was pushing ahead full steam on plutonium reprocessing facilities. North Korea's founder, Kim Il Sung, barely flinched when former U.S. President Bill Clinton's administration readied war plans to strike his nuclear installations preemptively. That brinkmanship paid off. Today North Korea is likely a nuclear power, and Kim's son rules the country with an iron fist. America's conventional military strength means a lot less to a nuclear North Korea. Saddam Hussein's great strategic blunder was that he took too long to get to the same place.

How would things be different in a multipolar world? For starters, great powers could split the job of policing proliferation, and even collaborate on some particularly hard cases. It's often forgotten now that, during the Cold War, the only state with a tougher nonproliferation policy than the United States was the Soviet Union. Not a single country that had a formal alliance with Moscow ever became a nuclear power. The Eastern bloc was full of countries with advanced technological capabilities in every area except one—nuclear weapons. Moscow simply wouldn't permit it. But today we see the uneven and inadequate level of effort that non-superpowers devote to stopping proliferation. The Europeans dangle carrots at Iran, but they are unwilling to consider serious sticks.

The Chinese refuse to admit that there is a problem. And the Russians are aiding Iran's nuclear ambitions. When push comes to shove, nonproliferation today is almost entirely America's burden.

The same is true for global public health. Globalization is turning the world into an enormous petri dish for the incubation of infectious disease. Humans cannot outsmart disease, because it just evolves too quickly. Bacteria can reproduce a new generation in less than 30 minutes, while it takes us decades to come up with a new generation of antibiotics. Solutions are only possible when and where we get the upper hand. Poor countries where humans live in close proximity to farm animals are the best place to breed extremely dangerous zoonotic disease. These are often the same countries, perhaps not entirely coincidentally, that feel threatened by American power. Establishing an early warning system for these diseases—exactly what we lacked in the case of SARS a few years ago and exactly what we lack for avian flu today—will require a significant level of intervention into the very places that don't want it. That will be true as long as international intervention means American interference.

The most likely sources of the next ebola or HIV-like pandemic are the countries that simply won't let U.S. or other Western agencies in, including the World Health Organization. Yet the threat is too arcane and not immediate enough for the West to force the issue. What's needed is another great power to take over a piece of the work, a power that has more immediate interests in the countries where diseases incubate and one that is seen as less of a threat. As long as the United States remains the world's lone superpower, we're not likely to get any help. Even after HIV, SARS, and several years of mounting hysteria about avian flu, the world is still not ready for a viral pandemic in Southeast Asia or sub-Saharan Africa. America can't change that alone.

If there were rival great powers with different cultural and ideological leanings, globalization's darkest problem of all—terrorism—would also likely look quite different. The pundits are partly right: Today's international terrorism owes something to globalization. Al Qaeda uses the Internet to transmit messages, it uses credit cards and modern banking to move money, and it uses cell phones and laptops to plot attacks. But it's not globalization that turned Osama bin Laden from a small-time Saudi dissident into the symbolic head of a radical global movement. What created Osama bin Laden was the predominance of American power.

A terrorist organization needs a story to attract resources and recruits. Oftentimes, mere frustration over political, economic, or religious conditions is not enough. Al Qaeda understands that, and, for that reason, it weaves a narrative of global jihad against a "modernization," "Westernization," and a "Judeo-Christian" threat. There is really just one country that both spearheads and represents that threat: the United States. And so the most efficient way for a terrorist to gain a reputation is to attack the United States. The logic is the same for all monopolies. A few years ago, every computer hacker in the world wanted to bring down Microsoft, just as every aspiring terrorist wants to create a spectacle of destruction akin to the September 11 attacks inside the United States.

Al Qaeda cells have gone after alternate targets such as Britain, Egypt, and Spain. But these are not the acts that increase recruitment and fundraising, or mobilize the energy of otherwise disparate groups around the world. Nothing enhances the profile of a terrorist like killing an American, something Abu Musab al-Zarqawi understood well in Iraq. Even if al Qaeda's deepest aspirations lie with the demise of the Saudi regime, the predominance of U.S. power and its role supporting the house of Saud makes America the only enemy really worth fighting. A multipolar world would surely confuse this kind of clear framing that pits Islamism against the West. What would be al Qaeda's message if the Chinese were equally involved in propping up authoritarian regimes in the Islamic, oil-rich Gulf states? Does the al Qaeda story work if half its enemy is neither Western nor Christian?

Restoring the Balance

The consensus today in the U.S. foreign-policy community is that more American power is always better. Across the board. For both the United States and the rest of the globe. The National Security Strategy documents of 2002 and 2006 enshrine this consensus in phrases such as "a balance of power that favors freedom." The strategy explicitly defines the "balance" as a continued imbalance, as the United States continues "dissuading potential competitors . . . from challenging the United States, its allies, and its partners."

In no way is U.S. power inherently a bad thing. Nor is it true that no good comes from unipolarity. But there are significant downsides to the imbalance of power. That view is hardly revolutionary. It has a long pedigree in U.S. foreign policy thought. It was the perspective, for instance, that George Kennan brought to the table in the late 1940s when he talked about the desirability of a European superpower to restrain the United States. Although the issues today are different than they were in Kennan's time, it's still the case that too much power may, as Kennan believed, lead to overreach. It may lead to arrogance. It may lead to insensitivity to the concerns of others. Though Kennan may have been prescient to voice these concerns, he couldn't have predicted the degree to which American unipolarity would lead to such an unstable overlap with modern-day globalization.

America has experienced this dangerous burden for 15 years, but it still refuses to see it for what it really is. Antiglobalization sentiment is coming today from both the right and the left. But by blaming globalization for what ails the world, the U.S. foreign-policy community is missing a very big part of what is undermining one of the most hopeful trends in modern history—the reconnection of societies, economies, and minds that political borders have kept apart for far too long.

America cannot indefinitely stave off the rise of another superpower. But, in today's networked and interdependent world, such an event is not entirely a cause for mourning. A shift in the global balance of power would, in fact, help the United States manage some of the most costly and dangerous consequences of globalization. As the international playing field levels, the scope of these problems and the threat they pose to America will only decrease. When that happens, the United States will find globalization is a far easier burden to bear.

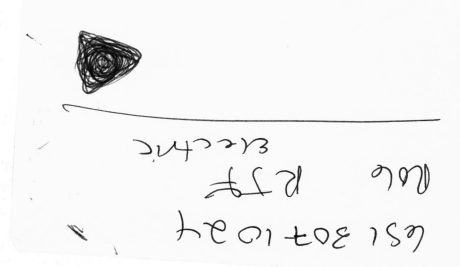

POSTSCRIPT

Is Globalization a Positive Development for the World Community?

It is hard to argue that this kind of revolution is all positive or all negative. Many will find the allure of technological growth and expansion too much to resist. They will adopt values and ethics that seem compatible with a materialistic Western culture. And they will embrace speed over substance, technical expertise over knowledge, and wealth over fulfillment.

Others will reject this revolution. They will find its promotion of materialism and Western cultural values abhorrent and against their own sense of humanity and being. They will seek enrichment in tradition and values rooted in their cultural pasts. This resistance will take many forms. It will be political and social, and it will involve actions ranging from protests and voting to division and violence.

Trying to determine whether a force as dominant and all-encompassing as globalization is positive or negative is like determining whether the environment is harsh or beautiful. It is both. One can say that in the short term, globalization will be destabilizing for many millions of people because the changes that it brings will cause some fundamental shifts in beliefs, values, and ideas. Once that period is past, it is conceivable that a more stable environment will result as people come to grips with globalization and either learn to embrace it, cope with it, or keep it at bay.

The literature on globalization is growing rapidly, much of it centering on defining its parameters and evaluating its impact. Any analysis of globalization should begin with Thomas Friedman's work, which helps shape the boundaries of globalization while arguing strongly for its promotion and inherent strengths. Friedman's work *The Lexus and the Olive Tree* (Farrar, Straus and Giroux, 1999), *The World Is Flat* (Farrar, Straus and Giroux, 2005), and *Hot, Flat and Crowded*, (Farrar, Straus and Giroux, 2008) map the terrain and discuss globalization's revolutionary impact. Some counter-perspectives have emerged, and they cover a range of thought and depth of analysis. Two interesting and accessible efforts include William Grieder's *One World Ready or Not: The Manic Logic of Global Capitalism* (Simon & Schuster, 1997) and David Korten's *When Corporations Rule the World* (Kumarian Press, 1996). Also, see Anthony Gidden's work *Runaway World* and John Micklethwait and Adrian Wooldridge's *A Future Perfect: The Challenge and Hidden Promise of Globalization*.

The literature that will help us to understand the full scope of globalization has not yet been written. Also, the determination of globalization's positive or negative impact on the international system has yet to be decided. For certain, globalization will bring profound changes that will cause people from America to Zimbabwe to rethink assumptions and beliefs about how the world works. And equally certain is the realization that globalization will empower some people but that it will also leave others out, helping to maintain and perhaps exacerbate the divisions that already exist in global society.

ISSUE 14

Is the World a Victim of American Cultural Imperialism?

YES: Allan Brian Ssenyonga, from "Americanization or Globalization," *Global Envision* (October 2, 2006)

NO: Tyler Cowen, from "Some Countries Remain Resistant to American Culture Exports," *The New York Times* (February 22, 2007)

ISSUE SUMMARY

YES: Allan Brian Ssenyonga, a Ugandan freelance writer for *The New York Times,* suggests that America is now selling its culture to the rest of the world "as a new and improved product of what we (the world) have as a culture." He decries the negative effects of the global spread of many things American.

NO: Tyler Cowen, a George Mason University professor of economics, argues that the "complaint of '(American) cultural imperialism' is looking increasingly implausible" as the evidence suggests that (1) local culture commands loyalty, and (2) cultural influences come from many external cultures, not just from America.

In 1989, the Berlin Wall collapsed. Two years later the Soviet Union ceased to exist. With this relatively peaceful and monumental series of events, the cold war ended, and with it one of the most contentious and conflict-ridden periods in global history. It is easy to argue that in the wake of those events the United States is in ascendancy. The United States and its Western allies won the cold war, defeating communism politically and philosophically. Since 1990, democracies have emerged and largely flourished as never before across the world stage. According to a recent study, over 120 of the world's 190 nations now have a functioning form of democracy. Western companies, values, and ideas now sweep across the globe via airwaves, computer networks, and fiber-optic cables that bring symbols of U.S. culture and values (such as Michael Jordan and McDonald's) into villages, schools, and cities around the world.

If American culture is embodied in the products sold by many multinational corporations (MNCs), such as McDonald's, Ford, IBM, The Gap, and others, then the American cultural values and ideas that are embedded in these products are being bought and sold in record numbers around the world. Globalization largely driven by MNCs and their control of technology brings with it values and ideas that are largely American in origin and expression. Values such as speed and ease of use, a strong emphasis on leisure time over work time, and a desire for increasing material wealth and comfort dominate the advertising practices of these companies. For citizens of the United States, this seems a natural part of the landscape. They do not question it; in fact, many Americans enjoy seeing signs of "home" on street corners abroad: a McDonald's in Tokyo, a Sylvester Stallone movie in Djakarta, or a Gap shirt on a student in Nairobi, for example.

Although comforting to Westerners, this trend is disquieting to the hundreds of millions of people around the world who wish to partake of the globalizing system without abandoning their own cultural values. Many people around the globe wish to engage in economic exchange and develop politically but do not want to abandon their own cultures amidst the wave of values embedded in Western products. This tension is most pronounced in its effect on the youth around the world. Millions of impressionable young people in the cities and villages of the developing world wish to emulate the American icons that they see on soft drink cans or in movie theaters. They attempt to adopt U.S. manners, language, and modes of dress, often in opposition to their parents and local culture. These young people are becoming Americanized and, in the process, creating huge generational rifts within their own societies. Some of the seeds of these rifts and cultural schisms can be seen in the actions of the young Arab men who joined Al Qaeda and participated in the terrorist attacks of September 11, 2001.

In this section, the authors offer two competing conceptions of whether there is American cultural imperialism. Ssenyonga views the influx of foods, music, movies, language, and dress as decidedly imperialistic. He sees these things as elements in the washing away of local culture and as part and parcel of a globalizing economic world system. Cowen believes that this is grossly overstated because it misses the complexity of multiple cultures living side by side with each other and also misses people's ability to embrace multiple customs simultaneously.

YES    Allan Brian Ssenyonga

Americanization or Globalization?

A Ugandan writer explores the meaning of globalization and the growing influence of American culture around the world. Global socio-political issues never cease to fascinate any interested soul. From the times of civilization came the era of colonialism then independence. This was followed by the cold war era where the Soviets were slowly but surely out-smarted by the more versatile capitalists of the day.

The post cold war era led to the increasing influence of what some people these days call quasi-governments (such as the International Monetary Fund and the World Bank).

The IMF and World Bank consequently took on the role of the world's economic 'police,' telling particularly poorer nations how to spend their money. In order to receive more aid, these Bretton Woods institutions demanded that countries open up their economies to liberalization under Structural Adjustment Programmes that encouraged governments to fund privatization programmes, ahead of welfare and public services. Concurrently we had the influence of multinational organisations like the United Nations Organisation also greatly formatting global issues.

Fast-forward to the new millennium—things took a different path. All of a sudden we were being pumped with rhetoric titled globalization. Globalization is an umbrella term for a complex series of economic, social, technological, and political changes seen as increasing interdependence and interaction between people and companies in disparate locations. In general use within the field of economics and political economy, it refers to the increasing integration of economies around the world, particularly through trade and financial flows. The term sometimes also refers to the movement of people (labour) and knowledge (technology) across international borders. There are also broader cultural, political and environmental dimensions of globalization. For the common man it was always argued that the world had become like a global village of sorts.

At its most basic, there is nothing mysterious about globalization. But not so fast; some people are now arguing that globalization has mainly benefited the already strong economies of the world and it has given them leverage to not only trade with the rest of the world but to also influence their general lifestyles and politics. Proponents of the school of thought contend that countries like U.S.A. are using globalization as an engine of "corporate imperialism"; one

Originally from *The New Times*, by Allan Brian Ssenyonga, October, 2006. Copyright © 2006 by Allan Brian Ssenyonga. Reprinted by permission of the author.

which tramples over the human rights of developing societies, claims to bring prosperity, yet often simply amounts to plundering and profiteering.

Another negative effect of globalization has been cultural assimilation via cultural imperialism. This can be further explained as a situation of exporting of artificial wants, and the destruction or inhibition of authentic local cultures. This brings me to the gist of my submission. At a closer look, globalization is slowly shifting towards Americanization. Have you heard the word "Americanization"? Well in the early 1900's Americanization meant taking new immigrants and turning them into Americans . . . whether they wanted to give up their traditional ways or not. This process often involved learning English and adjusting to American culture, customs, and dress.

Critics now say globalization is nothing more than the imposition of American culture on the entire world. In fact, the most visible sign of globalization seems to be the spread of American hamburgers and cola (Pepsi and Coca Cola products) to nearly every country on earth. The song "Amerika" by the German rock band Rammstein is often seen as a satire of Americanization. It has received mixed reviews: some perceive it as anti-American, others as being opposed to globalization. The band views it as a satirical commentary on "cocacolonization".

According to information from Globalisation.about.com, even globalization champions like Thomas Friedman see it. In a recent column describing why terrorists hate the United States, Friedman wrote: ". . . globalization is in so many ways Americanization: globalization wears Mickey Mouse ears, it drinks Pepsi and Coke, eats Big Macs, does its computing on an IBM laptop with Windows 98. Many societies around the world can't get enough of it, but others see it as a fundamental threat."

The rest of the world seems to be following Uncle Sam (U.S.A.) and leaving behind its authentic ways of life. This has not spared even the 'air tight' Chinese society. Americanization is the contemporary term used for the influence the United States of America has on the culture of other countries, substituting their culture with American culture. When encountered unwillingly, it has a negative connotation; when sought voluntarily, it has a positive connotation.

How Are We Being Americanized?

U.S.A, which has the world's biggest economy and strongest known army, has taken gigantic steps in persuading the rest of the world to think and act like them. Many people, especially the Europeans, have often despised Americans, saying they have no culture. But as any sociologist will tell you, even having no culture is a culture in itself. So for many years, the land of immigrants has been on a process of creating an identity and hence a culture. Now they seem to be selling their culture to the rest of the world as a new and improved product of what we all have as culture.

As far as fashion is concerned, the casual 'American' style of wearing jeans, T-shirts and sports shoes is now common and acceptable in many places. For the office it is not rare to see someone wearing tight jeans with a long-sleeved shirt plus a tie. His defence is, of course, that it is the American style (read modern). Cowboy hats, boots and large silver belt buckles are also a common imitation of the dress style of Americans, especially those from Texas and Arizona. The American music industry has also gone a long way in influencing the dress culture of other people around the world. What about the example youths have picked up from famous American rap artists like 50-cent, Eminem, Tupac Shakur (R.I.P) and Snoop Dogg with their flashy fashions characterized by what is commonly known as "bling bling" (expensive shiny jewellery and watches). Look at the music played in the Nyamirambo-bound taxis and you will be amazed at how it matches with the dress style of the passengers!

Around the world the United States is perhaps best known for it's numerous and successful fast food franchises. Such chains, including McDonald's, Burger King, and Kentucky Fried Chicken, are known for selling simple, pre-prepared meals of foods such as hamburgers, French fries (chips), soft drinks, fried chicken, and ice cream. Though undeniably popular, such food, with its emphasis on deep-frying, has been criticized by dietitians in recent decades for being unhealthy and a cause of obesity. It has thus become somewhat of a stereotype to associate American cuisine with obesity and junk food. The whole world now is full of similar eating joints. In Africa many are referred to as take-aways.

Popular Culture

This transmission of American culture has been mainly through several conduits, with the number one medium being the electronic media. Television in particular has done a lot in Americanizing those who view images especially from Hollywood. The guys in Hollywood have made us adore the tough cigar-smoking guys in the Casinos, the thin shapely long-legged women, and to dream about rags-to-riches stories that are a common tag line of the movies. We now adore jazz, hip-hop, rap music, [and] country music as well as gospel music, all of which were pioneered by the United States.

And trust us in following Uncle Sam; many countries now have equivalents of the American awards of Oscars for the movies and Grammy's for the music. Just check out the PAM awards in Uganda or the Kisima awards in Kenya, not forgetting the continental Kora awards held annually in South Africa. Many countries have also gone ahead to construct theme parks based on the American Disney World model. Americanization has also led to the popularity and acceptability of what is known as American English. I have seen many posters here in Rwanda of schools claiming to teach American English. Many youths are now using this type of English, considering it 'modern'.

We ought not to ignore the heavy influence that the United States has demonstrated in the development of the Internet and it's subsequent control. Remember the conference that was held at the beginning of this year in Tunisia where nations were complaining about the control the US has over the Internet? They were proposing that instead an international body should take over, but the conference ended in defeat of this line of argument. The iPod, the most popular gadget for portable digital music, is also [an] American invention.

American sports, especially basketball, have now become famous world-wide, especially among college students. However other games like baseball and American football have not been easily adopted by other people in the world, as has been the case with basketball. Soccer, which is known to be the world's most popular sport, is not so popular in the US. However the US women's soccer team is one the of the world's premier women's sides.

War on Terrorism

Americans have also been known to spearhead the spread of the Pentecostal, Charismatic, Evangelical or born-again religious movements worldwide. American preachers are always globetrotting all in the name of spreading the word of 'God'. We should not ignore the fact that the United States Constitution enshrined individual freedom of religious practice, which courts have since interpreted to mean that the government is a secular institution, an idea called "separation of church and state". This notion of separating religion from the state is one of the controversial aspects of exporting American culture. This is embedded in the Bush administration's "War on Terror" which some have gone ahead to read as a war on Islam. This controversial American policy is what inspired Prof. Mamdani to write a book titled, *Good Muslim, Bad Muslim*.

America, which has thousands of military servicemen around the world, has of late been preoccupied with fighting terror in Afghanistan, Iraq, and it is getting ready to deal with the Iran problem soon. Actually some people are already speculating that the current crisis between Israel and Hezbollah is a precursor to America's war with Iran—that [the] US is supporting the Olmert government to keep bombing Lebanon until Iran, which is said to be the Godfather of Hezbollah, gets angry enough to join the war. At this point it is argued that the US will join hands with Israel and fight the Iran government because "they have weapons of mass destruction". At the end of the war, as usual [the] US will be expected by many viewers to have conquered another oil-producing country.

Many see the War on Terror as a veil for acquiring cheap oil to run the US economy. Returning to the Israeli conflict with Hezbollah, one cannot fail to see an American tone in the whole conflict. Do you remember the first people to use the words "collateral damage"? This was what Americans first used to describe the death of innocent civilians and destruction of infrastructure by 'precision' missiles during the Afghan war after 9/11. This was an excuse used for having bombed the Chinese Embassy and a Red Cross facility during the war. Now compare it with the death of thousands of Lebanese civilians and the destruction of hundreds of buildings. The death of UN officers and the recent Qana massacre can be accurately referred to as collateral damage by the Israeli government.

This notion of separating religion from the state is one of the controversial aspects of exporting American culture. This is embedded in the Bush administration's "War on Terror" which some have gone ahead to read as a war on Islam.

The apparent determination by the US to appoint itself "Mr. Fix it all" is a somewhat naive but optimistic belief among Americans that all problems can be fixed with enough commitment and effort. This sometimes leads America into problematic situations such as Vietnam and Iraq. In some cases though, [the] American fix-it-all attitude has positively led to [a] large outpouring of humanitarianism. This is clearly evidenced by the enormous aid that Americans, especially at the individual level, are sending to poor nations. Americans like Bill Gates and CNN's Ted Turner are some of the world's biggest donors.

In conclusion, therefore, the global stage is at a period of American conquest in many [more] different ways than you can imagine. Globalization seems to be hijacked by the Americans. The world also seems to be clamouring for more of the Yankee lifestyle. However simply dismissing—or demonizing— globalization as mere Americanization is misleading. Globalization has the ability to alter much more than just the movies or food consumed by a society. And the results can be powerfully positive, devastatingly negative, or (more often) something in between.

 **NO**

Some Countries Remain Resistant to American Cultural Exports

American movies and music have done very well in some countries like Sweden and less well in others like *India*. This may sound like a simple difference in human tastes, but decisions to consume culture have an economic aspect.

Loyalties to cultural goods and services—be it heavy metal music or the opera—are about social networking and choosing an identity and an aspiration. That is, we use culture to connect with other people and to define ourselves; both are, to some extent, economic decisions. The continuing and indeed growing relevance of local economic connections suggests that cultural imperialism will not prove to be the dominant trend.

Local culture commands loyalty when people are involved in networks of status and caste, and they pursue religious and communal markers of identity. Those individuals use local cultural products to signal their place in hierarchies.

An Indian Muslim might listen to religious Qawwali music to set himself apart from local Hindus, or a native of Calcutta might favor songs from Bengali cinema. The Indian music market is 96 percent domestic in origin, in part because India is such a large and multifaceted society. Omar Lizardo, an assistant professor of sociology at the *University of Notre Dame,* explains this logic in his recent paper *"Globalization and Culture: A Sociological Perspective."*

Today, economic growth is booming in countries where American popular culture does not dominate, namely India and China. Population growth is strong in many Islamic countries, which typically prefer local music and get their news from sources like the satellite broadcaster *Al Jazeera*.

The combination of these trends means that American entertainment, for largely economic reasons, will lose relative standing in the global marketplace. In fact, Western culture often creates its own rivals by bringing creative technologies like the recording studio or the printing press to foreign lands.

American popular culture tends to be popular when people interact with others from around the world and seek markers of global identity. My stepdaughter spent last summer studying French in Nice, with students from many other countries. They ate and hung out at *McDonald's*, a name and symbol they all share, even though it was not everyone's favorite meal.

From *The New York Times,* February 22, 2007. Copyright © 2007 by The New York Times Company. Reprinted by permission via PARS International.

Globalization is most likely to damage local culture in regions like Scandinavia that are lightly populated, not very hierarchical and looking for new global cultural symbols. But the rest of the world's population is in countries—China and India, of course, but also Brazil, Mexico, Egypt and Indonesia—that do not fit that description.

"American" cultural products rely increasing on non-American talent and international symbols and settings. "Babel," which won this year's Golden Globe for best drama, has a Mexican director, and is set in Morocco, Japan and Mexico, mostly with non-English dialogue.

Hollywood movies are popular in Europe in part because of the successes of European welfare states and of European economic integration. Western Europe has become more equal in its treatment of citizens, it has moved away from an aristocratic class society, and it has strong global connections. All those factors favor an interest in American and global popular culture; Hollywood movies often capture 70 percent or more of a typical European cinematic market. Social democracy, which the Europeans often hold up in opposition to the American model, in fact aided this cultural invasion by making Europe more egalitarian.

Many smaller countries have been less welcoming of cultural imports. It is common in Central America for domestically produced music to command up to 70 percent of market share. In Ghana, domestic music has captured 71 percent of the market, according to *Unesco* figures. Critics of cultural imperialism charge that rich cultures dominate poor ones. But the data supplied by Professor Lizardo show that the poorer a country, the more likely it will buy and listen to its own domestic music. This makes sense given that music is a form of social networking and the relevant networks are primarily local.

That said, the poorest countries don't produce many of the films they watch. Making a movie costs much more than cutting an album. So as the world becomes richer, the relative market share of Hollywood movies will probably fall more than the relative market share of American popular music. Furthermore, moviegoers are starting to look to Bollywood films, or other Asian productions, rather than Hollywood, for their markers of global identity.

The complaint of "cultural imperialism" is looking increasingly implausible. As I argued in *"Creative Destruction: How Globalization Is Changing the World's Cultures,"* the funk of *James Brown* helped shape the music of West Africa; Indian authors draw upon Charles Dickens; and Arabic pop is centered in France and Belgium. Western cultural exports are as likely to refresh foreign art forms as to destroy them. Western technologies—from the metal carving knife to acrylic paint to digital filmmaking—have spurred creativity worldwide.

Culture is not a zero-sum game, so the greater reach of one culture does not necessarily mean diminished stature for others. In the broad sweep of history, many different traditions have grown together and flourished. American popular culture will continue to make money, but the 21st century will bring a broad mélange of influences, with no clear world cultural leader.

POSTSCRIPT

Is the World a Victim of American Cultural Imperialism?

Globalization is a process of technological change and economic expansion under largely capitalist principles. The key actors driving the globalization process are multinational corporations like McDonald's, Coca-Cola, Nike, and Exxon Mobil. These companies are rooted in the American–Western cultural experience, and their premise is based on a materialistic world culture that is striving for greater and greater wealth. That value system is Western and American in origin and evolution. It is therefore logical to assume that as globalization goes, so goes American culture.

Evidence of "American" culture can be seen across the planet: kids in Djakarta or Lagos wearing Michael Jordan jerseys and Nike shoes, for example, and millions of young men and women from Cairo to Lima listening to Michael Jackson records. Symbols of American culture abound in almost every corner of the world, and most of that is associated with economics and the presence of multinational corporations.

As the youth of the world are seduced into an American cultural form and way of life, other cultures are often eclipsed. They lose traction and fade with generational change. Many would argue that this loss is unfortunate, but others would counter that it is part of the historical sweep of life. Social historians suggest that the cultures of Rome, Carthage, Phoenicia, and the Aztecs, while still influential, were eclipsed by a variety of forces that were dominant and historically rooted. Although tragic, it was inevitable in the eyes of some social historians.

Regardless of whether this eclipse is positive or negative, the issue of cultural imperialism remains. Larger and more intrusive networks of communication, trade, and economic exchange bring values. In this world of value collision comes choices and change. Unfortunately, millions will find themselves drawn toward a lifestyle of materialism that carries with it a host of value choices. The losers in this clash are local cultures and traditions that, as so often is the case among the young, are easily jettisoned and discarded. It remains to be seen whether or not they will survive the onslaught.

Works on this subject include Edward Said's classic *Culture and Imperialism* (First Vintage Books, 1994); Gerald R. Gems, *The Athletic Crusade, Sport and American Cultural Imperialism* (The University of Nebraska Press, 2006); Benjamin Barber, "Democracy at Risk: American Culture in a Global Culture," *World Policy Journal* (Summer 1998); "Globalism's Discontents," *The American Prospect* (January 1, 2002); Seymour Martin Lipset, *American Exceptionalism: A Double-Edged Sword* (W. W. Norton, 1996); and Richard Barnet and John Cavanagh, *Global Dreams: Imperial Corporations and the New World Order* (Simon & Schuster, 1995).

ISSUE 15

Is the Global Economic Crisis a Failure of Capitalism?

YES: Katsuhito Iwai, from "Global Financial Crisis Shows Inherent Instability of Capitalism," *The Tokyo Foundation,* (December 8, 2008)

NO: Dani Rodrik, from "Coming Soon: Capitalism 3.0," *The Taipei Times* (February 11, 2009)

ISSUE SUMMARY

YES: Katsuhito Iwai, professor of economics at the University of Tokyo, argues that the current economic collapse is a sign of the inherent instability of global capitalism. He argues that capitalism's failure in this crisis is inherent because capitalism is based on speculation and therefore belief or faith in the strength of the system and its various parts.

NO: Dani Rodrik, professor of international political economy at Harvard University's John F. Kennedy School of Government, contends that the current economic downturn is not a sign of capitalism's failure but rather its need for reinvention and adaptation. Rodrik argues that this is precisely why capitalism will survive and thrive because it is so changeable based on new trends and conditions.

The past year has seen one of the most monumental economic shifts in modern times. In the world economy, tens of trillions of dollars of value have been lost and entire fortunes have disappeared in a shrinking stock market. Currencies plummeted, land values around the globe have fallen, and major economic giants seemingly collapsed overnight (Lehman Brothers, AIG, GM, Chrysler). The sheer shock of the collapse and the magnitude of the crisis have left millions around the world wondering not only what happened but also what comes next.

This is not the first such collapse, nor is it necessarily the worst; witness the economic shocks of 1873 and 1929 as examples. But the speed of the collapse (facilitated by technology among other things) and the recognition by most of us that seemingly no "expert" knew how or why this occurred has added to a sense of shock and fear.

Amidst the tumult, the analysis of this economic collapse has begun, and many point to an inflated housing market, deregulation, excess greed, and a failure of economic leadership, or all of the above, as reasons for the collapse. Mostly this analysis comes from those who see the system as fixable. They argue that the fundamentals are still there, but mechanisms need adjustment and government intervention is required. This view is probably shared by most of the political parties in most of the democracies of the world today.

Others are arguing that this collapse is a more fundamental shift in economics, away from capitalism. They argue that the collapse represents basic flaws in capitalism tied to credit, speculation, regulations, and the like, ultimately requiring a complete overhaul, if not scrapping, of the capitalist system.

In this section, two authors address the issue of what this collapse means for capitalism as a system. Iwai contends that this crisis illuminates fundamental issues with capitalism that reflect its inherent instability. He argues that if these issues aren't addressed, then capitalism as we know it will not, and probably cannot, survive. Rodrik takes a more optimistic view. He sees capitalism as a highly flexible system able to adapt to waves of technological and social changes to meet current and future demands, and thus views this crisis as part of a longer line of such events and not, as some might argue, the death knell of capitalism.

YES

Katsuhito Iwai

Global Financial Crisis Shows Inherent Instability of Capitalism

The Great Depression set off by the US stock market crash in 1929 dragged on through the 1930s. I doubt anyone will deny that the current financial crisis is the biggest in scale that the world has experienced since then. Unlike at the time of the Great Depression, when governments were slow to take countermeasures, the financial authorities of Japan, the United States, and Europe have been coordinating their response to provide financial institutions with infusions of public funds. This seems to have worked for now, causing the situation to become somewhat calmer. The chances of another 1930s-style Great Depression are small. But stock prices continue to move up and down violently, and the world is at the brink of falling into a "lost decade" if matters are mishandled in the period lying ahead.

I am surprised that such a major financial panic has occurred during my own lifetime. Timing aside, however, the occurrence itself does not surprise me. I have always maintained that capitalism is inherently unstable, and so this development was theoretically predictable.

John Maynard Keynes believed that the market economy was unstable and that it was necessary to use monetary and fiscal policy to tame its instability. This thinking became the pillar of government policy after the Great Depression, particularly in the United States, and it proved successful. But this successful approach ended up being carried too far, with the result that the institutions of the state for countercyclical economic policy measures became overgrown and highly wasteful.

From the 1960s on, the neoclassical economics propounded by Milton Friedman and others came to the fore in Britain, the United States, and elsewhere. According to this theory, the market economy should be kept as free as possible of government intervention and regulation; the purer it is allowed to be, the more efficient and stable it will become. Neoclassical economics provided the theoretical underpinnings of the policies adopted by the Thatcher administration in Britain and the Reagan administration in the United States during the 1980s, and it has established itself as the orthodox form of economic thinking.[1]

As seen on www.tokyofoundation.org, December 8, 2008. Originally appeared in *Asahi Shimbun*, October 17, 2008. Copyright © 2008 by Asahi Shimbun Publishing Co. Reprinted by permission.

This thinking has been carried to the extreme by the current Bush administration, which has sought to do away with regulations, allow the securitization of debts and everything else imaginable, and spread the workings of the market to every corner of the world.

It is fair to consider what we have been witnessing in recent years to have been a grand experiment of global scale aimed at the creation of the laissez-faire utopia conceived by the neoclassical school. The experiment's success came under test from around the time of the East Asian currency crisis in the late 1990s, and it had begun to show signs of unraveling, but the current crisis has brought its collapse. An inconvenient truth about capitalism is that efficiency and stability cannot be achieved simultaneously.

Even Money Is Purely Speculative

Why is capitalism unstable? Because it is fundamentally based on speculation. Consider carmakers, for example. They build automobiles not for themselves but in the expectation that others will buy them to ride in. There is an element of speculation in this process.

Milton Friedman and his followers in mainstream economics, however, claim that speculation leads to stability. Those investors who buy high and sell low, they argue, are irrational and will promptly fall by the wayside. Only the rational investors who buy low and sell high will survive; this will cause markets to be stable.

What they assert may apply to an idyllic market where investors mediate between producers and consumers. But, the activity in financial markets, including markets for stocks, bonds, foreign currency and their derivatives, is of entirely different nature. It is professional investors and investment funds that dominate the markets and compete with each other. They buy and sell based not on their forecasts of long-term demand/supply conditions but on their observations of each other's movements and readings of each other's intentions. When a price is expected to rise or fall, it is not irrational to buy or sell more and move the price further up or down, leading to speculative bubbles and panics.

The more fundamental reason I believe that capitalism as a whole is speculative and inherently unstable is that the money on which it is based is itself speculative. Money has made the economy much more efficient by making it possible to conduct transactions without the trouble of exchanging on a barter basis. But money has no intrinsic value. People are willing to hold it only because they expect other people to accept it in exchange for something else, with the people who accept it expecting that yet other people will accept it in turn.

To hold money is, in other words, the purest form of speculation, and trust in it is based on circular, bootstrap logic: Everybody uses money as money merely because everybody believes everybody else uses it as money.

In this light, we can see that money has two faces: It brings greater efficiency, but at the same time it has the potential of causing great instability. In a capitalist economy supported by money, it is impossible for efficiency and stability to coexist as claimed by the neoclassical economists.

This bootstrap logic of money also underlies the present financial crisis. The subprime loans that set off the crisis are extremely risky loans to people with low creditworthiness. Because the risk of default on such loans is so high, a single subprime loan by itself is unattractive as a financial product. But bundling many such loans together and securitizing them made the risks seem diluted, and as a result of further bundling with numerous other financial instruments into big packages that were then dispersed around the globe, the risks became invisible from the surface.

As the financial products created in this way were traded more and more steadily among numerous parties, they began to be considered readily convertible to cash and other safe assets. They came to be seen as being like the money in which people place supreme trust. Here again we see the workings of bootstrap logic: Everybody trusted the products as safe merely because everybody believed everybody else trusted them as safe. But when the subprime loans whose risks were concealed therein went bad, trust in all financial products toppled like a row of dominoes. This is the essence of the current financial crisis.

A major difference between this and the Asian currency crisis and other financial crises that preceded it is that the value of the US dollar, the key currency of the international monetary system, may be severely shaken. The instability of money as a purely speculative construct—a problem that has been concealed up to now—may come to the surface henceforth in the form of the crisis in the key currency. I do not have space to discuss this problem here, however.

Aim for Second Best

What should we do next? The capitalist world is inherently unstable. So, contrary to the assertions of the neoclassical school, there is no ideal state that we can seek to achieve; all we can do is aim for second best. Capitalism has to be freed from the capitalistic ideology of laissez-faire, and we have to reassert the old-fashioned idea of the necessity of governmental controls on financial institutions to curb their high leverage and excessive speculation. And whenever a crisis strikes, we just have to deal with it using a patchwork of rescue measures, such as buying up of bad loans and infusions of public funds.

This outlook may seem bleak, but if we look back over history, we see that economies have repeatedly experienced the formation of bubbles followed by their collapse, but meanwhile, they have steadily grown more efficient over the course of time. Our only option is eternal pragmatism in search of a better second best.

Like Adam and Eve, we have tasted the forbidden fruit. In our case it is the freedom that capitalism has given us. The sweet fruit of freedom carries its own "original sin," namely the knowledge that capitalism is inherently unstable. But this freedom is not something we should—or can—give up.

Note

1. In Japan's case, neoclassical economic thinking informed the structural reform program of Prime Minister Jun'ichiro Koizumi's administration (2001–6), which sought to achieve an economic recovery led by the private sector, eschewing the previous reliance on fiscal pump priming. . . .

Coming Soon: Capitalism 3.0

Capitalism is in the throes of its most severe crisis in many decades. A combination of deep recession, global economic dislocations and effective nationalisation of large swathes of the financial sector in the world's advanced economies has deeply unsettled the balance between markets and states. Where the new balance will be struck is anybody's guess.

Those who predict capitalism's demise have to contend with one important historical fact: capitalism has an almost unlimited capacity to reinvent itself. Indeed, its malleability is the reason it has overcome periodic crises over the centuries and outlived critics from Karl Marx on. The real question is not whether capitalism can survive—it can—but whether world leaders will demonstrate the leadership needed to take it to its next phase as we emerge from our current predicament.

Capitalism has no equal when it comes to unleashing the collective economic energies of human societies. That is why all prosperous societies are capitalistic in the broad sense of the term: they are organized around private property and allow markets to play a large role in allocating resources and determining economic rewards. The catch is that neither property rights nor markets can function on their own. They require other social institutions to support them.

So property rights rely on courts and legal enforcement, and markets depend on regulators to rein in abuse and fix market failures. At the political level, capitalism requires compensation and transfer mechanisms to render its outcomes acceptable. As the current crisis has demonstrated yet again, capitalism needs stabilising arrangements such as a lender of last resort and a counter-cyclical fiscal policy. In other words, capitalism is not self-creating, self-sustaining, self-regulating or self-stabilising.

The history of capitalism has been a process of learning and re-learning these lessons. Adam Smith's idealised market society required little more than a 'night-watchman state.' All that governments needed to do to ensure the division of labour was to enforce property rights, keep the peace and collect a few taxes to pay for a limited range of public goods.

Through the early part of the twentieth century, capitalism was governed by a narrow vision of the public institutions needed to uphold it. In practice, the state's reach often went beyond this conception (as, say, in the case of Bismarck's introduction of old-age pensions in Germany in 1889). But governments continued to see their economic roles in restricted terms.

From *Taipei Times*, February 11, 2009, p. 9. Copyright © 2009 by Project Syndicate. Reprinted by permission. www.project-syndicate.org.

This began to change as societies became more democratic and labour unions and other groups mobilised against capitalism's perceived abuses. Anti-trust policies were spearheaded in the Unites States. The usefulness of activist monetary and fiscal policies became widely accepted in the aftermath of the Great Depression.

The share of public spending in national income rose rapidly in today's industrialised countries, from below 10 per cent on average at the end of the nineteenth century to more than 20 per cent just before World War II. And, in the wake of WWII, most countries erected elaborate social-welfare states in which the public sector expanded to more than 40 per cent of national income on average.

This 'mixed-economy' model was the crowning achievement of the twentieth century. The new balance that it established between state and market set the stage for an unprecedented period of social cohesion, stability and prosperity in the advanced economies that lasted until the mid-1970s.

This model became frayed from the 1980s on, and now appears to have broken down. The reason can be expressed in one word: globalization.

The postwar mixed economy was built for and operated at the level of nation-states and required keeping the international economy at bay. The Bretton Woods-GATT regime entailed a 'shallow' form of international economic integration that implied controls on international capital flows, which Keynes and his contemporaries had viewed as crucial for domestic economic management. Countries were required to undertake only limited trade liberalisation, with plenty of exceptions for socially sensitive sectors (agriculture, textiles, services). This left them free to build their own versions of national capitalism, as long as they obeyed a few simple international rules.

The current crisis shows how far we have come from that model. Financial globalisation, in particular, played havoc with the old rules. When Chinese-style capitalism met American-style capitalism, with few safety valves in place, it gave rise to an explosive mix. There were no protective mechanisms to prevent a global liquidity glut from developing and then, in combination with US regulatory failings, from producing a spectacular housing boom and crash. Nor were there any international roadblocks to prevent the crisis from spreading from its epicentre.

The lesson is not that capitalism is dead. It is that we need to reinvent it for a new century in which the forces of economic globalisation are much more powerful than before. Just as Smith's minimal capitalism was transformed into Keynes' mixed economy, we need to contemplate a transition from the national version of the mixed economy to its global counterpart.

This means imagining a better balance between markets and their supporting institutions at the global level. Sometimes, this will require extending institutions outward from nation-states and strengthening global governance. At other times, it will mean preventing markets from expanding beyond the reach of institutions that must remain national. The right approach will differ across country groupings and among issue areas.

Designing the next capitalism will not be easy. But we do have history on our side: capitalism's saving grace is that it is almost infinitely malleable.

POSTSCRIPT

Is the Global Economic Crisis a Failure of Capitalism?

We are still reeling amidst the economic crisis of 2008–2009. President Obama, G20 leaders, and businesses and organizations around the world are still grappling with the depth, magnitude, scope, and scale of the problems. No economist seems to have a total handle on this issue and it might be foolish to expect that anyone would. What we do know is that the world economy is in an economic downturn. The diminution of wealth and capital reserves is staggering in its scope and complexity. The root causes and how to undo the damage have yet to be illuminated, and certainly there is no consensus on the best approaches moving forward.

Whether one is a laissez-faire capitalist, a Keynesian, a socialist, or even a Marxist, the future is unclear. Capitalism may be in a period of readjustment and "rebooting," as some would argue, or in the midst of a fast decline and elimination. Both authors and many others will be writing about this question for years to come, and as a global issue, the economic crisis is not going away but rather will be with us in its aftermath for years, if not decades.

Some basic conclusions can be made at this early juncture. First, the system clearly operated in a highly deregulated fashion and as such spun out of control. The collapse of corporate giants on the speculative housing and derivatives markets is evidence of this problem. Second, some kind of government intervention as has occurred in the United States, across Europe, and in Asia was necessary if for nothing else, then to restore some semblance of confidence in the markets. Third, no one seems to have an answer as to how the crisis developed and accelerated and what comes next. There is no consensus on what follows, nor is there a common frame of reference on how to disentangle these huge and complex markets.

The Obama administration, the G20 nations, and indeed the entire global economic system, are grappling with the hows, whys, and what comes next. Your own personal situation and the analysis that flows from that experience will shape your own answer to the question at hand. If history tells us anything, however, it is to not count out capitalism. It is a highly adaptable and resilient economic system that has suffered several major challenges and overcome them all while maintaining its basic precepts through 200 years of evolution.

There is not a great deal of work yet available on this crisis save recent articles and early analyses. Some of these include, Amatyra Sen, "Capitalism Beyond the Crisis" (*New York Times Review of Books,* March, 2009); Louis R.

Woodhill, "Sorry but Capitalism Did Not Fail" (*Real Clear Markets*, March 2009); "Capitalism on Trial" (SocialistWorkers.org, September 2008); and Charles R. Morris, *The Trillion Dollar Meltdown: High Rollers, easy Money and the Great credit Crash* (Public Affairs, 2009).

Internet References . . .

Nuclear Terrorism: How to Prevent It

This site of the Nuclear Control Institute discusses nuclear terrorism, such as the possibility of another nuclear 9/11 and how best to prevent it. Topics include terrorists' ability to build nuclear weapons, the threat of "dirty bombs," and whether nuclear reactors are adequately protected against attack. This site features numerous links to key nuclear terrorism documents and Web sites as well as to recent developments and related news items.

http://www.nci.org/nuketerror.htm

Center for Defense Information

The Center provides expert analysis on 48 different topic areas in the U.S. national and international security.

http://www.cdi.org

Public Broadcasting System (PBS)

On the PBS website, use the key phrase "religious extremism" to locate a variety of sources relating to religious and cultural extremism and their contemporary consequences.

http://www.pbs.org

Exploring Global Conflict: An Internet Guide to the Study of Conflict

Exploring Global Conflict: An Internet Guide to the Study of Conflict is an Internet resource designed to provide understanding of global conflict. Information related to specific conflicts in areas such as Northern Ireland, the Middle East, the Great Lakes region in Africa, and the former Yugoslavia is included on this site. Current news and educational resource sites are listed as well.

http://www.uwm.edu/Dept/CIS/conflict/congeneral.html

Central Intelligence Agency

The U.S. government agency provides substantial information on its Web site regarding U.S. issues abroad.

http://www.cia.gov/terrorism/

The Cato Institute

This U.S. public organization conducts research on a wide range of public policy issues. It subscribes to what it terms "basic American principles."

http://cato.org/current/civil-liberties/

Center for Strategic and International Studies (CSIS)

CSIS is a Washington-based organization that now provides substantial information on terrorism in the aftermath of 9/11, and the threats from Iran and China. The URL noted here leads directly to its thinking on the issue of homeland defense.

http://www.csis.org/homeland

The New Global Security Dilemma

*W*ith the end of the Cold War, the concept of security was freed *from the constraints of bipolar power politics. No longer were issues framed simply in terms of U.S.–Soviet conflict (Vietnam, Afghanistan, the Middle East) but rather seen in more complex terms related to issues of ethnicity, fundamentalism and cultural division, nuclear proliferation, and new forms of conflict. These concerns were always there but were always muted by the apparent "larger" issues of superpower rivalry. Whether this was largely a Soviet and U.S. construct is for historians to decide. What is clear is that these issues have taken center stage in terms of security threats to the stability of the global community.*

These include concerns over nuclear proliferation, religious and cultural extremism, terrorism, and the reemergence of great power politics in the form of Russian–Chinese and American rivalries. This section examines some of the key issues shaping the security dilemma of the twenty-first century.

- Are We in a New Cold War?
- Are We Headed Toward a Nuclear 9/11?
- Is Religious and Cultural Extremism a Global Security Threat?
- Is a Nuclear Iran a Global Security Threat?
- Will China Be the Next Superpower?

ISSUE 16

Are We in a New Cold War?

YES: Stephen F. Cohen, from "The New American Cold War," *The Nation* (June 8, 2007)

NO: Stephen Kotkin, from "The Myth of the New Cold War," *Prospect Magazine* (April, 2008)

ISSUE SUMMARY

YES: Stephen F. Cohen, professor of Russian studies at New York University, suggests that U.S.–Russian relations have "deteriorated so badly they should now be understood as a new cold war—or possibly a continuation of the old one." He argues that the origins of this circumstance can be found in the attitudes and policies of both the Clinton and Bush administrations.

NO: Stephen Kotkin, professor of history and director of the Program in Russian Studies at Princeton University, argues that Russia has not reverted to totalitarianism under Putin and his successor. Rather, it is a combination of a closed unstable political system and a growing economic power that poses a threat to the West for that reason, not because its poses a military threat.

The collapse of the Soviet Union was one of the cataclysmic events of the twentieth century. One of the two superpowers imploded and with it, an entire ideology, political, economic, social, and military system. The Western reaction was shock, joy, and uncertainty as to what comes next. The result has been not unexpected. Russia and the states of the old Soviet Union have grappled with their new status with varying levels of triumph, failure, and upheaval. Political, social, and cultural movements have emerged, rivalries resurfaced or new ones created, and revisionism as to Russia's status in Europe and the world has become of primary consequence in the post-Yeltsin era.

In the United States and the West, efforts at reconciliation, partnership, engagement, and negotiation have been both successful (the Persian Gulf War, G20) and contentious (Georgia, expansion of NATO, nonproliferation). The emergence of both the Bush and Putin regimes has heightened the differences in policy and attitudes between the United States and Russia around traditional notions of respect and security.

Today, with the Obama presidency promising a new era of dialogue with Russia, the issues remain potent and potentially destabilizing. How far east should NATO be extended? Should Russia support the West's efforts at limiting nuclear technology to such states as Iran? How dependent should Western Europe be on Russian natural gas and oil? How much influence should Russia or the United States have on Soviet successor states like Georgia, the Baltic republics or Ukraine? Can Russia and the United States agree on further nuclear reductions of their arsenals?

These issues and many others, and how each state approaches them, determine the tenor of that relationship. Is it more cooperative and conciliatory or hawkish and cold war in its tone and scope?

The two authors explore this relationship and come to differing conclusions. Long-time Soviet analyst Stephen Cohen contends that the two sides are in a new cold war in terms of rhetoric and approach and that this dynamic is potentially dangerous for both sides, Europe, and beyond. Kotkin maintains that the rhetoric and issues are important but overblown. He argues that the relationship is not nearly approaching cold war status as in the past and that there are real areas of cooperation and mutual interest.

YES

Stephen F. Cohen

The New American Cold War

Two reactions to this article were particularly noteworthy when it first appeared in *The Nation* almost exactly one year ago. Judging by activity on the magazine's website and by responses sent to me personally, it was very widely read and discussed both in the United States and in Russia, where it was quickly translated on a Russian-language site. And, unlike most Russian commentators, almost every American specialist who reacted to the article, directly or indirectly adamantly disputed my thesis that US-Russian relations had deteriorated so badly they should now be understood as a new cold war— or possibly as a continuation of the old one.

Developments during the last year have amply confirmed that thesis. Several examples could be cited, but two should be enough. The increasingly belligerent charges and counter-charges by officials and in the media on both sides, "Cold-War-style rhetoric and threats," as the Associated Press recently reported, read like a replay of the American-Soviet discourse of the 1970s and early 1980s. And the unfolding conflict over US plans to build missile defense components near post-Soviet Russia, in Poland and the Czech Republic, threatens to reintroduce a dangerous military feature of that cold-war era in Europe.

Nonetheless, most American officials, journalists and academics, unwilling perhaps to confront their unwise policies and mistaken analyses since the Soviet Union ended in 1991, continue to deny the cold-war nature of today's relationship with Russia. A resident expert at the Council on Foreign Relations tells us, for example, that "the situation today is nothing like the Cold War times," while another think-tank specialist, testifying to Congress, can "see no prospect of a new Cold War."

Indeed, many commentators even insist that cold war is no longer possible because today's US-Russian conflicts are not global, ideological or clashes between two different systems; because post-Soviet Russia is too weak to wage such a struggle; and because of the avowed personal "friendship" between Presidents Bush and Putin. They seem unaware that the last cold war began regionally, in Central and Eastern Europe; that present-day antagonisms between Washington's "democracy-promotion" policies and Moscow's self-described "sovereign democracy" have become intensely ideological; that Russia's new, non-Communist system is scarcely like the American one; that Russia is well situated, as I explained in the article, to compete in a new cold war whose front lines run through the former Soviet territories, from Ukraine and Georgia to Central Asia; and that there was also, back in the cold-war 1970s, a Nixon-Brezhnev "friendship."

Reprinted by permission from the June 8, 2007, (originally published July 10, 2006) issue of *The Nation*. Copyright © 2007 by The Nation. For subscription information, call 1-800-333-8536. Portions of each week's Nation magazine can be accessed at www.thenation.com.

Nor is this merely an academic dispute. Unless US policy-makers and opinion-makers recognize how bad the relationship has become, we risk losing not only the historic opportunity for an American-Russian partnership created in the late 1980s by Gorbachev, Reagan and the first President Bush, and which is even more essential for our real national security today; we also risk a prolonged cold war even more dangerous than was the last one, for reasons spelled out in my article.

Still worse, the overwhelming majority of US officials and opinion-makers who do acknowledge the serious deterioration in relations between Washington and Moscow blame the development solely on Putin's domestic and foreign policies. Not surprisingly, the most heretical part of my article—that the origins of the new cold war are to be found instead in attitudes and policies toward post-Soviet Russia adopted by the Clinton administration back in the 1990s and largely continued by this Bush administration—has found even less support. But unless it too is fully acknowledged, we are left only with the astonishing admission of a leading academic specialist with longstanding ties in Washington. Lamenting the state of US-Russian relations, he informs us, "Nobody has a good idea of what is to be done."

What must be done, however, is clear enough. Because the new cold war began in Washington, steps toward ending it also have to begin in Washington. Two are especially urgent, for reasons also explained in the article: A US recognition that post-Soviet Russia is not a defeated supplicant or American client state, as seems to have been the prevailing view since 1991, but a fully sovereign nation at home with legitimate national interests abroad equal to our own; and an immediate end to the reckless expansion of NATO around Russia's borders.

According to principles of American democracy, the best time to fight for such a change in policy is in the course of campaigns for the presidency. That is why I am pleased my article is reappearing at this time. On the other hand, the hour is late, and it is hard to be optimistic.

—**Stephen F. Cohen**
June, 8, 2007

·⚙·

Contrary to established opinion, the gravest threats to America's national security are still in Russia. They derive from an unprecedented development that most US policy-makers have recklessly disregarded, as evidenced by the undeclared cold war Washington has waged, under both parties, against post-Communist Russia during the past fifteen years.

As a result of the Soviet breakup in 1991, Russia, a state bearing every nuclear and other device of mass destruction, virtually collapsed. During the 1990s its essential infrastructures—political, economic and social—disintegrated. Moscow's hold on its vast territories was weakened by separatism, official corruption and Mafia-like crime. The worst peacetime depression in modern history brought economic losses more than twice those suffered in World War II. GDP plummeted by nearly half and capital investment by 80 percent. Most Russians were thrown into poverty. Death rates soared and the population shrank. And in August 1998, the financial system imploded.

No one in authority anywhere had ever foreseen that one of the twentieth century's two superpowers would plunge, along with its arsenals of destruction, into such catastrophic circumstances. Even today, we cannot be sure what Russia's collapse might mean for the rest of the world.

Outwardly, the nation may now seem to have recovered. Its economy has grown on average by 6 to 7 percent annually since 1999, its stock-market index increased last year by 83 percent and its gold and foreign currency reserves are the world's fifth largest. Moscow is booming with new construction, frenzied consumption of Western luxury goods and fifty-six large casinos. Some of this wealth has trickled down to the provinces and middle and lower classes, whose income has been rising. But these advances, loudly touted by the Russian government and Western investment-fund promoters, are due largely to high world prices for the country's oil and gas and stand out only in comparison with the wasteland of 1998.

More fundamental realities indicate that Russia remains in an unprecedented state of peacetime demodernization and depopulation. Investment in the economy and other basic infrastructures remains barely a third of the 1990 level. Some two-thirds of Russians still live below or very near the poverty line, including 80 percent of families with two or more children, 60 percent of rural citizens and large segments of the educated and professional classes, among them teachers, doctors and military officers. The gap between the poor and the rich, Russian experts tell us, is becoming "explosive."

Most tragic and telling, the nation continues to suffer wartime death and birth rates, its population declining by 700,000 or more every year. Male life expectancy is barely 59 years and, at the other end of the life cycle, 2 to 3 million children are homeless. Old and new diseases, from tuberculosis to HIV infections, have grown into epidemics. Nationalists may exaggerate in charging that "the Motherland is dying," but even the head of Moscow's most pro-Western university warns that Russia remains in "extremely deep crisis."

The stability of the political regime atop this bleak post-Soviet landscape rests heavily, if not entirely, on the personal popularity and authority of one man, President Vladimir Putin, who admits the state "is not yet completely stable." While Putin's ratings are an extraordinary 70 to 75 percent positive, political institutions and would-be leaders below him have almost no public support.

The top business and administrative elites, having rapaciously "privatized" the Soviet state's richest assets in the 1990s, are particularly despised. Indeed, their possession of that property, because it lacks popular legitimacy, remains a time bomb embedded in the political and economic system. The huge military is equally unstable, its ranks torn by a lack of funds, abuses of authority and discontent. No wonder serious analysts worry that one or more sudden developments—a sharp fall in world oil prices, more major episodes of ethnic violence or terrorism, or Putin's disappearance—might plunge Russia into an even worse crisis. Pointing to the disorder spreading from Chechnya through the country's southern rim, for example, the eminent scholar Peter Reddaway even asks "whether Russia is stable enough to hold together."

As long as catastrophic possibilities exist in that nation, so do the unprecedented threats to US and international security. Experts differ as to which danger is the gravest—proliferation of Russia's enormous stockpile of nuclear, chemical and biological materials; ill-maintained nuclear reactors on land and on decommissioned submarines; an impaired early-warning system controlling missiles on hair-trigger alert; or the first-ever civil war in a shattered superpower, the terror-ridden Chechen conflict. But no one should doubt that together they constitute a much greater constant threat than any the United States faced during the Soviet era.

Nor is a catastrophe involving weapons of mass destruction the only danger in what remains the world's largest territorial country. Nearly a quarter of the planet's people live on Russia's borders, among them conflicting ethnic and religious groups. Any instability in Russia could easily spread to a crucial and exceedingly volatile part of the world.

There is another, perhaps more likely, possibility. Petrodollars may bring Russia long-term stability, but on the basis of growing authoritarianism and xenophobic nationalism. Those ominous factors derive primarily not from Russia's lost superpower status (or Putin's KGB background), as the US press regularly misinforms readers, but from so many lost and damaged lives at home since 1991. Often called the "Weimar scenario," this outcome probably would not be truly fascist, but it would be a Russia possessing weapons of mass destruction and large proportions of the world's oil and natural gas, even more hostile to the West than was its Soviet predecessor.

How has the US government responded to these unprecedented perils? It doesn't require a degree in international relations or media punditry to understand that the first principle of policy toward post-Communist Russia must follow the Hippocratic injunction: Do no harm! Do nothing to undermine its fragile stability, nothing to dissuade the Kremlin from giving first priority to repairing the nation's crumbling infrastructures, nothing to cause it to rely more heavily on its stockpiles of superpower weapons instead of reducing them, nothing to make Moscow uncooperative with the West in those joint pursuits. Everything else in that savaged country is of far less consequence.

Since the early 1990s Washington has simultaneously conducted, under Democrats and Republicans, two fundamentally different policies toward post-Soviet Russia—one decorative and outwardly reassuring, the other real and exceedingly reckless. The decorative policy, which has been taken at face value in the United States, at least until recently, professes to have replaced America's previous cold war intentions with a generous relationship of "strategic partnership and friendship." The public image of this approach has featured happy-talk meetings between American and Russian presidents, first "Bill and Boris" (Clinton and Yeltsin), then "George and Vladimir."

The real US policy has been very different—a relentless, winner-take-all exploitation of Russia's post-1991 weakness. Accompanied by broken American promises, condescending lectures and demands for unilateral concessions, it has been even more aggressive and uncompromising than was Washington's approach to Soviet Communist Russia. Consider its defining elements as they have unfolded—with fulsome support in both American political parties, influential newspapers and policy think tanks—since the early 1990s:

§□A growing military encirclement of Russia, on and near its borders, by US and NATO bases, which are already ensconced or being planned in at least half the fourteen other former Soviet republics, from the Baltics and Ukraine to Georgia, Azerbaijan and the new states of Central Asia. The result is a US-built reverse iron curtain and the remilitarization of American-Russian relations.

§□A tacit (and closely related) US denial that Russia has any legitimate national interests outside its own territory, even in ethnically akin or contiguous former republics such as Ukraine, Belarus and Georgia. How else to explain, to take a bellwether example, the thinking of Richard Holbrooke, Democratic would-be Secretary of State? While roundly condemning the Kremlin for promoting a pro-Moscow government in neighboring Ukraine, where Russia has centuries of shared linguistic, marital, religious, economic and security ties, Holbrooke declares that far-away Slav nation part of "our core zone of security."

§□Even more, a presumption that Russia does not have full sovereignty within its own borders, as expressed by constant US interventions in Moscow's internal affairs since 1992. They have included an on-site crusade by swarms of American "advisers," particularly during the 1990s, to direct Russia's "transition" from Communism; endless missionary sermons from afar, often couched in threats, on how that nation should and should not organize its political and economic systems; and active support for Russian anti-Kremlin groups, some associated with hated Yeltsinera oligarchs.

That interventionary impulse has now grown even into suggestions that Putin be overthrown by the kind of US-backed "color revolutions" carried out since 2003 in Georgia, Ukraine and Kyrgyzstan, and attempted this year in Belarus. Thus, while mainstream editorial pages increasingly call the Russian president "thug," "fascist" and "Saddam Hussein," one of the Carnegie Endowment's several Washington crusaders assures us of "Putin's weakness" and vulnerability to "regime change." (Do proponents of "democratic regime change" in Russia care that it might mean destabilizing a nuclear state?)

§□Underpinning these components of the real US policy are familiar cold war double standards condemning Moscow for doing what Washington does—such as seeking allies and military bases in former Soviet republics, using its assets (oil and gas in Russia's case) as aid to friendly governments and regulating foreign money in its political life.

More broadly, when NATO expands to Russia's front and back doorsteps, gobbling up former Soviet-bloc members and republics, it is "fighting terrorism" and "protecting new states"; when Moscow protests, it is engaging in "cold war thinking." When Washington meddles in the politics of Georgia and

Ukraine, it is "promoting democracy"; when the Kremlin does so, it is "neoimperialism." And not to forget the historical background: When in the 1990s the US-supported Yeltsin overthrew Russia's elected Parliament and Constitutional Court by force, gave its national wealth and television networks to Kremlin insiders, imposed a constitution without real constraints on executive power and rigged elections, it was "democratic reform"; when Putin continues that process, it is "authoritarianism."

§☐Finally, the United States is attempting, by exploiting Russia's weakness, to acquire the nuclear superiority it could not achieve during the Soviet era. That is the essential meaning of two major steps taken by the Bush Administration in 2002, both against Moscow's strong wishes. One was the Administration's unilateral withdrawal from the 1972 Anti-Ballistic Missile Treaty, freeing it to try to create a system capable of destroying incoming missiles and thereby the capacity to launch a nuclear first strike without fear of retaliation. The other was pressuring the Kremlin to sign an ultimately empty nuclear weapons reduction agreement requiring no actual destruction of weapons and indeed allowing development of new ones; providing for no verification; and permitting unilateral withdrawal before the specified reductions are required.

The extraordinarily anti-Russian nature of these policies casts serious doubt on two American official and media axioms: that the recent "chill" in US-Russian relations has been caused by Putin's behavior at home and abroad, and that the cold war ended fifteen years ago. The first axiom is false, the second only half true: The cold war ended in Moscow, but not in Washington, as is clear from a brief look back.

The last Soviet leader, Mikhail Gorbachev, came to power in 1985 with heretical "New Thinking" that proposed not merely to ease but to actually abolish the decades-long cold war. His proposals triggered a fateful struggle in Washington (and Moscow) between policy-makers who wanted to seize the historic opportunity and those who did not. President Ronald Reagan decided to meet Gorbachev at least part of the way, as did his successor, the first President George Bush. As a result, in December 1989, at a historic summit meeting at Malta, Gorbachev and Bush declared the cold war over. (That extraordinary agreement evidently has been forgotten; thus we have *The New York Times* recently asserting that the US-Russian relationship today "is far better than it was 15 years ago.")

Declarations alone, however, could not terminate decades of warfare attitudes. Even when Bush was agreeing to end the cold war in 1989-91, many of his top advisers, like many members of the US political elite and media, strongly resisted. (I witnessed that rift on the eve of Malta, when I was asked to debate the issue in front of Bush and his divided foreign policy team.) Proof came with the Soviet breakup in December 1991: US officials and the media immediately presented the purported "end of the cold war" not as a mutual Soviet-American decision, which it certainly was, but as a great American victory and Russian defeat.

That (now standard) triumphalist narrative is the primary reason the cold war was quickly revived—not in Moscow a decade later by Putin but in

Washington in the early 1990s, when the Clinton Administration made two epically unwise decisions. One was to treat post-Communist Russia as a defeated nation that was expected to replicate America's domestic practices and bow to its foreign policies. It required, behind the facade of the Clinton-Yeltsin "partnership and friendship" (as Clinton's top "Russia hand," Strobe Talbott, later confirmed), telling Yeltsin "here's some more shit for your face" and Moscow's "submissiveness." From that triumphalism grew the still-ongoing interventions in Moscow's internal affairs and the abiding notion that Russia has no autonomous rights at home or abroad.

Clinton's other unwise decision was to break the Bush Administration's promise to Soviet Russia in 1990-91 not to expand NATO "one inch to the east" and instead begin its expansion to Russia's borders. From that profound act of bad faith, followed by others, came the dangerously provocative military encirclement of Russia and growing Russian suspicions of US intentions. Thus, while American journalists and even scholars insist that "the cold war has indeed vanished" and that concerns about a new one are "silly," Russians across the political spectrum now believe that in Washington "the cold war did not end" and, still more, that "the US is imposing a new cold war on Russia."

That ominous view is being greatly exacerbated by Washington's ever-growing "anti-Russian fatwa," as a former Reagan appointee terms it. This year it includes a torrent of official and media statements denouncing Russia's domestic and foreign policies, vowing to bring more of its neighbors into NATO and urging Bush to boycott the G-8 summit to be chaired by Putin in St. Petersburg in July; a call by would-be Republican presidential nominee Senator John McCain for "very harsh" measures against Moscow; Congress's pointed refusal to repeal a Soviet-era restriction on trade with Russia; the Pentagon's revival of old rumors that Russian intelligence gave Saddam Hussein information endangering US troops; and comments by Secretary of State Condoleezza Rice, echoing the regime-changers, urging Russians, "if necessary, to change their government."

For its part, the White House deleted from its 2006 National Security Strategy the long-professed US-Russian partnership, backtracked on agreements to help Moscow join the World Trade Organization and adopted sanctions against Belarus, the Slav former republic most culturally akin to Russia and with whom the Kremlin is negotiating a new union state. Most significant, in May it dispatched Vice President Cheney to an anti-Russian conference in former Soviet Lithuania, now a NATO member, to denounce the Kremlin and make clear it is not "a strategic partner and a trusted friend," thereby ending fifteen years of official pretense.

More astonishing is a Council on Foreign Relations "task force report" on Russia, co-chaired by Democratic presidential aspirant John Edwards, issued in March. The "nonpartisan" council's reputed moderation and balance are nowhere in evidence. An unrelenting exercise in double standards, the report blames all the "disappointments" in US-Russian relations solely on "Russia's wrong direction" under Putin—from meddling in the former Soviet republics and backing Iran to conflicts over NATO, energy politics and the "rollback of Russian democracy."

Strongly implying that Bush has been too soft on Putin, the council report flatly rejects partnership with Moscow as "not a realistic prospect." It calls instead for "selective cooperation" and "selective opposition," depending on which suits US interests, and, in effect, Soviet-era containment. Urging more Western intervention in Moscow's political affairs, the report even reserves for Washington the right to reject Russia's future elections and leaders as "illegitimate." An article in the council's influential journal *Foreign Affairs* menacingly adds that the United States is quickly "attaining nuclear primacy" and the ability "to destroy the long-range nuclear arsenals of Russia or China with a first strike."

Every consequence of this bipartisan American cold war against post-Communist Russia has exacerbated the dangers inherent in the Soviet breakup mentioned above. The crusade to transform Russia during the 1990s, with its disastrous "shock therapy" economic measures and resulting antidemocratic acts, further destabilized the country, fostering an oligarchical system that plundered the state's wealth, deprived essential infrastructures of investment, impoverished the people and nurtured dangerous corruption. In the process, it discredited Western-style reform, generated mass anti-Americanism where there had been almost none—only 5 percent of Russians surveyed in May thought the United States was a "friend"—and eviscerated the once-influential pro-American faction in Kremlin and electoral politics.

Military encirclement, the Bush Administration's striving for nuclear supremacy and today's renewed US intrusions into Russian politics are having even worse consequences. They have provoked the Kremlin into undertaking its own conventional and nuclear buildup, relying more rather than less on compromised mechanisms of control and maintenance, while continuing to invest miserly sums in the country's decaying economic base and human resources. The same American policies have also caused Moscow to cooperate less rather than more in existing US-funded programs to reduce the multiple risks represented by Russia's materials of mass destruction and to prevent accidental nuclear war. More generally, they have inspired a new Kremlin ideology of "emphasizing our sovereignty" that is increasingly nationalistic, intolerant of foreign-funded NGOs as "fifth columns" and reliant on anti-Western views of the "patriotic" Russian intelligentsia and the Orthodox Church.

Moscow's responses abroad have also been the opposite of what Washington policy-makers should want. Interpreting US-backed "color revolutions" as a quest for military outposts on Russia's borders, the Kremlin now opposes pro-democracy movements in former Soviet republics more than ever, while supporting the most authoritarian regimes in the region, from Belarus to Uzbekistan. Meanwhile, Moscow is forming a political, economic and military "strategic partnership" with China, lending support to Iran and other anti-American governments in the Middle East and already putting surface-to-air missiles back in Belarus, in effect Russia's western border with NATO.

If American policy and Russia's predictable countermeasures continue to develop into a full-scale cold war, several new factors could make it even more dangerous than was its predecessor. Above all, the growing presence of Western bases and US-backed governments in the former Soviet republics has moved the "front lines" of the conflict, in the alarmed words of a Moscow newspaper, from Germany to Russia's "near abroad." As a "hostile ring tightens around the Motherland," in the view of former Prime Minister Evgeny Primakov, many different Russians see a mortal threat. Putin's chief political deputy, Vladislav Surkov, for example, sees the "enemy . . . at the gates," and the novelist and Soviet-era dissident Aleksandr Solzhenitsyn sees the "complete encirclement of Russia and then the loss of its sovereignty." The risks of direct military conflict could therefore be greater than ever. Protesting overflights by NATO aircraft, a Russian general has already warned, "If they violate our borders, they should be shot down."

Worsening the geopolitical factor are radically different American and Russian self-perceptions. By the mid-1960s the US-Soviet cold war relationship had acquired a significant degree of stability because the two superpowers, perceiving a stalemate, began to settle for political and military "parity." Today, however, the United States, the self-proclaimed "only superpower," has a far more expansive view of its international entitlements and possibilities. Moscow, on the other hand, feels weaker and more vulnerable than it did before 1991. And in that asymmetry lies the potential for a less predictable cold war relationship between the two still fully armed nuclear states.

There is also a new psychological factor. Because the unfolding cold war is undeclared, it is already laden with feelings of betrayal and mistrust on both sides. Having welcomed Putin as Yeltsin's chosen successor and offered him its conception of "partnership and friendship," Washington now feels deceived by Putin's policies. According to two characteristic commentaries in the *Washington Post*, Bush had a "well-intentioned Russian policy," but "a Russian autocraft . . . betrayed the American's faith." Putin's Kremlin, however, has been reacting largely to a decade of broken US promises and Yeltsin's boozy compliance. Thus Putin's declaration four years ago, paraphrased on Russian radio: "The era of Russian geopolitical concessions [is] coming to an end." (Looking back, he remarked bitterly that Russia has been "constantly deceived.")

Still worse, the emerging cold war lacks the substantive negotiations and cooperation, known as détente, that constrained the previous one. Behind the lingering facade, a well-informed Russian tells us, "dialogue is almost nonexistent." It is especially true in regard to nuclear weapons. The Bush Administration's abandonment of the ABM treaty and real reductions, its decision to build an antimissile shield, and talk of pre-emptive war and nuclear strikes have all but abolished long-established US-Soviet agreements that have kept the nuclear peace for nearly fifty years. Indeed, according to a report, Bush's National Security Council is contemptuous of arms control as "baggage from the cold war." In short, as dangers posed by nuclear weapons have grown and a new arms race unfolds, efforts to curtail or even discuss them have ended.

Finally, anti-cold war forces that once played an important role in the United States no longer exist. Cold war lobbies, old and new ones, therefore operate virtually unopposed, some of them funded by anti-Kremlin Russian oligarchs in exile. At high political levels, the new American cold war has been, and remains, fully bipartisan, from Clinton to Bush, Madeleine Albright to Rice, Edwards to McCain. At lower levels, once robust pro-détente public groups, particularly anti-arms-race movements, have been largely demobilized by official, media and academic myths that "the cold war is over" and we have been "liberated" from nuclear and other dangers in Russia.

Also absent (or silent) are the kinds of American scholars who protested cold war excesses in the past. Meanwhile, a legion of new intellectual cold warriors has emerged, particularly in Washington, media favorites whose crusading anti-Putin zeal goes largely unchallenged. (Typically, one inveterate missionary constantly charges Moscow with "not delivering" on US interests, while another now calls for a surreal crusade, "backed by international donors," to correct young Russians' thinking about Stalin.) There are a few notable exceptions—also bipartisan, from former Reaganites to *Nation* contributors—but "anathematizing Russia," as Gorbachev recently put it, is so consensual that even an outspoken critic of US policy inexplicably ends an article, "Of course, Russia has been largely to blame."

Making these political factors worse has been the "pluralist" US mainstream media. In the past, opinion page editors and television producers regularly solicited voices to challenge cold war zealots, but today such dissenters, and thus the vigorous public debate of the past, are almost entirely missing. Instead, influential editorial pages are dominated by resurgent cold war orthodoxies, led by the *Post,* whose incessant demonization of Putin's "autocracy" and "crude neoimperialism" reads like a bygone Pravda on the Potomac. On the conservative *New York Sun's* front page, US-Russian relations today are presented as "a duel to the death—perhaps literally."

The Kremlin's strong preference "not to return to the cold war era," as Putin stated May 13 in response to Cheney's inflammatory charges, has been mainly responsible for preventing such fantasies from becoming reality. "Someone is still fighting the cold war," a British academic recently wrote, "but it isn't Russia." A fateful struggle over this issue, however, is now under way in Moscow, with the "pro-Western" Putin resisting demands for a "more hard line" course and, closely related, favoring larger FDR-style investments in the people (and the country's stability). Unless US policy, which is abetting the hard-liners in that struggle, changes fundamentally, the symbiotic axis between American and Russian cold warriors that drove the last conflict will reemerge. If so, the Kremlin, whether under Putin or a successor, will fight the new one—with all the unprecedented dangers that would entail.

Given different principles and determined leadership, it is still not too late for a new US policy toward post-Soviet Russia. Its components would include full cooperation in securing Moscow's materials of mass destruction; radically reducing nuclear weapons on both sides while banning the development of new ones and taking all warheads off hair-trigger alert; dissuading other states from acquiring those weapons; countering terrorist activities and drug-trafficking near Russia; and augmenting energy supplies to the West.

None of those programs are possible without abandoning the warped priorities and fallacies that have shaped US policy since 1991. National security requires identifying and pursuing essential priorities, but US policy-makers have done neither consistently. The only truly vital American interest in Russia today is preventing its stockpiles of mass destruction from endangering the world, whether through Russia's destabilization or hostility to the West.

All of the dangerous fallacies underlying US policy are expressions of unbridled triumphalism. The decision to treat post-Soviet Russia as a vanquished nation, analogous to postwar Germany and Japan (but without the funding), squandered a historic opportunity for a real partnership and established the bipartisan premise that Moscow's "direction" at home and abroad should be determined by the United States. Applied to a country with Russia's size and long history as a world power, and that had not been militarily defeated, the premise was inherently self-defeating and certain to provoke a resentful backlash.

That folly produced two others. One was the assumption that the United States had the right, wisdom and power to remake post-Communist Russia into a political and economic replica of America. A conceit as vast as its ignorance of Russia's historical traditions and contemporary realities, it led to the counterproductive crusade of the 1990s, which continues in various ways today. The other was the presumption that Russia should be America's junior partner in foreign policy with no interests except those of the United States. By disregarding Russia's history, different geopolitical realities and vital interests, this presumption has also been senseless.

As a Eurasian state with 20-25 million Muslim citizens of its own and with Iran one of its few neighbors not being recruited by NATO, for example, Russia can ill afford to be drawn into Washington's expanding conflict with the Islamic world, whether in Iran or Iraq. Similarly, by demanding that Moscow vacate its traditional political and military positions in former Soviet republics so the United States and NATO can occupy them—and even subsidize Ukraine's defection with cheap gas—Washington is saying that Russia not only has no Monroe Doctrine-like rights in its own neighborhood but no legitimate security rights at all. Not surprisingly, such flagrant double standards have convinced the Kremlin that Washington has become more belligerent since Yeltsin's departure simply "because Russian policy has become more pro-Russian."

Nor was American triumphalism a fleeting reaction to 1991. A decade later, the tragedy of September 11 gave Washington a second chance for a real partnership with Russia. At a meeting on June 16, 2001, President Bush sensed in Putin's "soul" a partner for America. And so it seemed after September 11, when Putin's Kremlin did more than any NATO government to assist the US war effort in Afghanistan, giving it valuable intelligence, a Moscow-trained Afghan combat force and easy access to crucial air bases in former Soviet Central Asia.

The Kremlin understandably believed that in return Washington would give it an equitable relationship. Instead, it got US withdrawal from the ABM treaty, Washington's claim to permanent bases in Central Asia (as well as Georgia) and independent access to Caspian oil and gas, a second round of NATO expansion taking in several former Soviet republics and bloc members, and a still-growing indictment of its domestic and foreign conduct. Astonishingly, not even September 11 was enough to end Washington's winner-take-all principles.

Why have Democratic and Republican administrations believed they could act in such relentlessly anti-Russian ways without endangering US national security? The answer is another fallacy—the belief that Russia, diminished and weakened by its loss of the Soviet Union, had no choice but to bend to America's will. Even apart from the continued presence of Soviet-era weapons in Russia, it was a grave misconception. Because of its extraordinary material and human attributes, Russia, as its intellectuals say, has always been "destined to be a great power." This was still true after 1991.

Even before world energy prices refilled its coffers, the Kremlin had ready alternatives to the humiliating role scripted by Washington. Above all, Russia could forge strategic alliances with eager anti-US and non-NATO governments in the East and elsewhere, becoming an arsenal of conventional weapons and nuclear knowledge for states from China and India to Iran and Venezuela. Moscow has already begun that turning away from the West, and it could move much further in that direction.

Still more, even today's diminished Russia can fight, perhaps win, a cold war on its new front lines across the vast former Soviet territories. It has the advantages of geographic proximity, essential markets, energy pipelines and corporate ownership, along with kinship and language and common experiences. They give Moscow an array of soft and hard power to use, if it chooses, against neighboring governments considering a new patron in faraway Washington.

Economically, the Kremlin could cripple nearly destitute Georgia and Moldova by banning their products and otherwise unemployed migrant workers from Russia and by charging Georgia and Ukraine full "free-market" prices for essential energy. Politically, Moscow could truncate tiny Georgia and Moldova, and big Ukraine, by welcoming their large, pro-Russian territories into the Russian Federation or supporting their demands for independent statehood (as the West has been doing for Kosovo and Montenegro in Serbia). Militarily Moscow could take further steps toward turning the Shanghai Cooperation Organization—now composed of Russia, China and four Central Asian states, with Iran and India possible members—into an anti-NATO defensive alliance, an "OPEC with nuclear weapons," a Western analyst warned.

That is not all. In the US-Russian struggle in Central Asia over Caspian oil and gas, Washington, as even the triumphalist Thomas Friedman admits, "is at a severe disadvantage." The United States has already lost its military base in Uzbekistan and may soon lose the only remaining one in the region, in Kyrgyzstan; the new pipeline it backed to bypass Russia runs through Georgia, whose stability depends considerably on Moscow; Washington's new friend in oil-rich Azerbaijan is an anachronistic dynastic ruler; and Kazakhstan, whose enormous energy reserves make it a particular US target, has its own large Russian population and is moving back toward Moscow.

Nor is the Kremlin powerless in direct dealings with the West. It can mount more than enough warheads to defeat any missile shield and illusion of "nuclear primacy." It can shut US businesses out of multibillion-dollar deals in Russia and, as it recently reminded the European Union, which gets 25 percent of its gas from Russia, "redirect supplies" to hungry markets in the East.

And Moscow could deploy its resources, connections and UN Security Council veto against US interests involving, for instance, nuclear proliferation, Iran, Afghanistan and possibly even Iraq.

Contrary to exaggerated US accusations, the Kremlin has not yet resorted to such retaliatory measures in any significant way. But unless Washington stops abasing and encroaching on Russia, there is no "sovereign" reason why it should not do so. Certainly, nothing Moscow has gotten from Washington since 1992, a Western security specialist emphasizes, "compensates for the geopolitical harm the United States is doing to Russia."

American crusaders insist it is worth the risk in order to democratize Russia and other former Soviet republics. In reality, their campaigns since 1992 have only discredited that cause in Russia. Praising the despised Yeltsin and endorsing other unpopular figures as Russia's "democrats," while denouncing the popular Putin, has associated democracy with the social pain, chaos and humiliation of the 1990s. Ostracizing Belarus President Aleksandr Lukashenko while embracing tyrants in Azerbaijan and Kazakhstan has related it to the thirst for oil. Linking "democratic revolutions" in Ukraine and Georgia to NATO membership has equated them with US expansionism. Focusing on the victimization of billionaire Mikhail Khodorkhovsky and not on Russian poverty or ongoing mass protests against social injustices has suggested democracy is only for oligarchs. And by insisting on their indispensable role, US crusaders have all but said (wrongly) that Russians are incapable of democracy or resisting abuses of power on their own.

The result is dark Russian suspicions of American intentions ignored by US policy-makers and media alike. They include the belief that Washington's real purpose is to take control of the country's energy resources and nuclear weapons and use encircling NATO satellite states to "de-sovereignize" Russia, turning it into a "vassal of the West." More generally, US policy has fostered the belief that the American cold war was never really aimed at Soviet Communism but always at Russia, a suspicion given credence by *Post* and *Times* columnists who characterize Russia even after Communism as an inherently "autocratic state" with "brutish instincts."

To overcome those towering obstacles to a new relationship, Washington has to abandon the triumphalist conceits primarily responsible for the revived cold war and its growing dangers. It means respecting Russia's sovereign right to determine its course at home (including disposal of its energy resources). As the record plainly shows, interfering in Moscow's internal affairs, whether on-site or from afar, only harms the chances for political liberties and economic prosperity that still exist in that tormented nation.

It also means acknowledging Russia's legitimate security interests, especially in its own "near abroad." In particular, the planned third expansion of NATO, intended to include Ukraine, must not take place. Extending NATO to Russia's doorsteps has already brought relations near the breaking point (without actually benefiting any nation's security); absorbing Ukraine, which Moscow regards as essential to its Slavic identity and its military defense, may be the point of no return, as even pro-US Russians anxiously warn. Nor would it be democratic, since nearly two-thirds of Ukrainians are opposed. The explosive possibilities were adumbrated in late May and early June when local citizens in ethnic Russian Crimea blockaded a port and roads where a US naval ship and contingent of Marines suddenly appeared, provoking resolutions declaring the region "anti-NATO territory" and threats of "a new Vietnam."

Time for a new US policy is running out, but there is no hint of one in official or unofficial circles. Denouncing the Kremlin in May, Cheney spoke "like a triumphant cold warrior," a *Times* correspondent reported. A top State Department official has already announced the "next great mission" in and around Russia. In the same unreconstructed spirit, Rice has demanded Russians "recognize that we have legitimate interest . . . in their neighborhood," without a word about Moscow's interests; and a former Clinton official has held the Kremlin "accountable for the ominous security threats . . . developing between NATO's eastern border and Russia." Meanwhile, the Bush Administration is playing Russian roulette with Moscow's control of its nuclear weapons. Its missile shield project having already provoked a destabilizing Russian buildup, the Administration now proposes to further confuse Moscow's early-warning system, risking an accidental launch, by putting conventional warheads on long-range missiles for the first time.

In a democracy we might expect alternative policy proposals from would-be leaders. But there are none in either party, only demands for a more anti-Russian course, or silence. We should not be surprised. Acquiescence in Bush's monstrous war in Iraq has amply demonstrated the political elite's limited capacity for introspection, independent thought and civic courage. (It prefers to falsely blame the American people, as the managing editor of *Foreign Affairs* recently did, for craving "ideological red meat.") It may also be intimidated by another revived cold war practice—personal defamation. The *Post* and *The New Yorker* have already labeled critics of their Russia policy "Putin apologists" and charged them with "appeasement" and "again taking the Russian side of the Cold War."

The vision and courage of heresy will therefore be needed to escape today's new cold war orthodoxies and dangers, but it is hard to imagine a US politician answering the call. There is, however, a not-too-distant precedent. Twenty years ago, when the world faced exceedingly grave cold war perils, Gorbachev unexpectedly emerged from the orthodox and repressive Soviet political class to offer a heretical way out. Is there an American leader today ready to retrieve that missed opportunity?

Stephen Kotkin

 **NO**

Myth of the New Cold War

What is it about Russia that drives the Anglo-American world mad? Soviet communism collapses, the empire is relinquished. Then come the wild hopes and failures of the 1990s—including the 1993 half-coup and the tank assault on Russia's legislature, the results-adjusted referendum on a new constitution (still in force), the dubious privatisations, the war in Chechnya and the financial default in 1998. But after all that, in December 1999 Boris Yeltsin apologises, steps down early—and names his prime minister and former secret police chief Vladimir Putin as acting president. To widespread consternation, Yeltsin predicts that the obscure spy is the man to "unite around himself those who will revive Great Russia." Incredibly, this is exactly what transpires.

And this is a grand disappointment, even a frightening prospect? The elevation of Putin—a secret deal promoted by Yeltsin's personal and political family, motivated less by patriotism than self-preservation—will go down as one of the most enduring aspects of Yeltsin's shaky legacy. Now, Putin, just like his benefactor, has selected his successor, Russia's new president Dmitri Medvedev. Sure, Putin has no plans to retire to a hospital-dacha, where Yeltsin had spent much of his presidency. Still, in his crafty way Putin has abided by the constitutional limit of two presidential terms. In May, Medvedev will acquire the immense powers of the Russian presidency (a gift of Yeltsin) in circumstances whereby the Russian state is no longer incoherent (a gift of Putin). And this is grounds for near universal dismissal in the west?

Two clashing myths have opened a gulf of misunderstanding towards Russia. First is the myth in the west that the chaos and impoverishment under Yeltsin amounted to a rough democracy, which Putin went on to destroy. When something comes undone that easily, it was probably never what it was cracked up to be. Still, the myth of Russia's overturned democracy unites cold war nostalgists, who miss the enemy, with a new generation of Russia-watchers, many of whom participated earnestly in the illusory 1990s democracy-building project in Russia and are now disillusioned (and tenured).

Second is the myth, on the Russian side, that the KGB was the one Soviet-era institution that was uncorrupted, patriotic and able to restore order. This credits Putin's stooge entourage for the economic liberalisation that was actually pushed through by the non-KGB personnel around him.

Each of these myths deeply rankles the other side. When a big majority of Russians accept or even applaud Putin's concentration of power, Anglo-American observers suspect not just ignorance but a love of authoritarianism.

From *Prospect Magazine*, Issue 145, April 2008. Copyright © 2008 by Prospect Publishing. Reprinted by permission of New York Times Syndicate.

(Unfortunately, Russians have never been offered genuine democracy and the rule of law alongside soaring living standards.) When foreign-based commentators and academics celebrate Yeltsin's Russia, which was worth a paltry $200bn and suffered international humiliation, while denouncing Putin's Russia, which has a GDP of $1.3 trillion and has regained global stature, most Russians detect not just incomprehension but ill-will.

Let's take a deep breath. To recognise that Putin inherited a dysfunctional situation derived from rampant insider theft and regional misrule is not to condone his KGB-style rule, which has often been nasty and sometimes self-defeating. Even though many Russian officials are conscientious and competent, the state remains too corrupt, as in most places around the world. At the top, privileged functionaries have grabbed (and are still grabbing) prime business holdings. At all levels, officialdom now seeks its rewards by mimicking the Kremlin's repression and manipulation. But Russia is also increasingly prosperous, with a new consumer-driven market economy and a burgeoning middle-class society full of pride. This combination of a relatively closed, unstable political system and a relatively open, stable society may seem incompatible—but there it is.

What happens when a large, important country turns out to have a dynamic, open market economy integrated into the global system, yet a political system that is undemocratic and not democratising? A lot of head-scratching by experts. It may be comforting in the corridors of punditry and social science to write about how economic growth without the rule of law is doomed to fail (China?) or how economic growth eventually brings political liberalisation. But many countries, not just Russia, have more or less manipulated elections while lacking the rule of law, and yet still have dynamic market economies. In Russia private property is not guaranteed—and property ownership is widespread.

A conceptual adjustment to Russia's seemingly impossible reality is now under way, but the process is painful and slow, "When I worked in Moscow in 1994 and 1995 for the National Democratic Institute, an American NGO, I could not have imagined the present situation," confessed Sarah Mendelson, a senior fellow in Russian affairs at the Centre for Strategic and International Studies, in the American Scholar recently. "We thought we were on the frontier of a democratic revolution. We weren't. We were witnessing a market revolution." This basic understanding, so long in coming, is not yet widespread. For the most part, pathetic cries about how "the west," whatever that is, has (again) "lost" Russia, and how the west must somehow "resist" Putin, persist.

Edward Lucas, by his telling, was once deported by the KGB. This happened in 1990, when Lucas, a British passport-holder, entered Lithuania on a Lithuanian visa after it declared its independence but before the Soviet Union had been formally dissolved. As far as this reviewer is aware, Lucas has never been imprisoned for his convictions. Still, though not technically a dissident, he argues like one. That is how a very perspicacious journalist like Lucas, the central and eastern Europe correspondent of the Economist, could end up writing a not very persuasive polemic called The New Cold War: How the Kremlin Menaces Both Russia and the West. Russia, he argues, is aggressively waging a global war for influence with its vast natural resources and piles of cash, and although the US and Britain are trying to stand up to the mighty bear, Germany is colluding, and China is, possibly, "co-operating."

Refutation of the idea that the cold war has returned is in fact provided by Lucas himself. He notes that eastern Europe is now free. Russians can go abroad. Russia's consumerist economy booms. Russia is not a military menace (its defence budget is at least 12 times smaller than that of the US). In Lucas's words, "the old cold war is indeed over." As for what Lucas calls "the new ideology" in Russia, which has led him to claim a new cold war, he writes that its "main ingredients are unexceptional: an edgy sense of national destiny, a preference for stability over freedom and a strong dislike of western hypocrisy and shallowness." He adds that "similar views are held in many countries outside Russia." And yet, he insists, "it is the combination and intensity [of these views in Russia] that are unusual." Not in the least. It is the circumstance that Russia can do something about such globally shared views that appears to be the rub. Unlike Germany and Japan, which were defeated in the second world war, Lucas writes, Russia is "unrepentant" and "petulant."

Imagine that. And imagine this: "The Kremlin's representatives throw habitual tantrums in international organisations. They block programmes in countries they don't like." And this: Russia is bullying small states. And this: Russia is cosying up to despotisms. Russia is using its leverage to acquire prime assets abroad. Russia is hiring lobbyists and agents of influence in western countries. Power politics is not pretty, but is Russia's muscle-flexing that unusual, or at all effective? "Slice by slice" Lucas warns, "the Kremlin is adding to its sphere of influence." Is that true? Here's his new domino theory: if Russia is allowed to get its bullying way in the Caucasus and the Balkans, then comes the turn of central Europe, even western Europe, and the Arctic. Once again, however, the reader can turn to Lucas for relief. The Kremlin, he writes, "has systematically overplayed its hand." Huffing and puffing over the Kremlin's various pipeline projects, Lucas has to conclude that "the biggest question for Europe in the coming decade is likely to be how to deal with a Russia that is short of gas." So much for the energy weapon. Russia is "stuck," Lucas writes. "It settles for being noticed." Further: "it compensates for real weakness by showing pretend strengths."

Lucas bores right through Russia's posturing, and still insists on a call to arms. "Eastern Europe," he warns several times, "sits on the front line of the new cold war." Incredibly, he invokes Chamberlain and Munich in 1938. The same countries, the same lessons, he claims. Lucas is, in fact, uncommonly lucid on today's eastern European states. "The paradox," he writes, "is that these ill-governed, tetchy and intolerant countries are the front line that the west is trying to defend." In other words, Lucas is crying wolf about some new cold war while the very countries he insists lie in grave danger are inside the EU and Nato. Has he read the Nato charter? He goes so far as to demand "a confrontation now" because "if we don't win the new cold war on terms of our choosing, we will fight at a time and place chosen by our adversary." Lucas works himself into a lather over how the Kremlin conceals its "lawless, brutal and greedy reality" behind the trappings of elections. Is this really "clever manoeuvring"? Ed—we are not fooled! Russia is an authoritarian regime. Its elites' actions are frequently reprehensible, and sometimes criminal even by Russian standards.

This could be the smartest incoherent book this reviewer has ever read. Lucas writes divinely and offers a sharp-eyed foray through the thicket of post-Soviet misinterpretations—up to a point. Take his sober attitude toward the Yeltsin years. "Some sort of clean-up was certainly overdue," he writes. He calls the 1990s muddle "perfect . . . for a quiet putsch by the heirs of the KGB." He further notes that "the oligarchs were certainly a deserving target," even if the selectivity of those attacks bothers him. Even more pointedly, Lucas writes that post-Yeltsin Russia "is a country in which it is possible for a private citizen to dream about personal fulfilment through brains and hard work." And this: "Never in Russian history have so many Russians lived so well and so freely." All the same, Lucas asserts that compared with Putinism, "the Yeltsin years now look less bad" and that Putin "betrayed" Yeltsin's commitment to "friendship" with the west. Back and forth Lucas goes, alternately incisive and unconvincing.

Unlike his employer, the *Economist,* Lucas does not undersell Russia's economic achievements in order to diminish Putin. Rather, he likens the new Russia to today's Brazil, or to India. He also notes Russia's huge positive significance for Europe. "Russia is one of the most lucrative markets in the world, bigger than all the other central and east European countries combined," Lucas says. At the same time, confoundingly, he suggests both that "western businessmen show no shame in following their wallets" and that "it is hard to fault German companies for acting in the interests of their shareholders." Which is it? His purple passages read like the inverse of the Kremlin's election-year propaganda: "We are facing people who want to harm us, frustrate us and weaken us," he asserts. But if, as he writes, Russia's authoritarian version of capitalism "is not a new civilisation but a dead end," what exactly is the problem?

The problem seems to be twofold. First, when Lucas urges European countries to overcome their differences with each other and with the US, he inadvertently shows that "the west" may no longer exist in the unified sense usually invoked. Second, Russia's authoritarian capitalism might not be a dead end at all. The rest of the world might have to live with an authoritarian, increasingly rich Russia (and again—not just Russia). Lucas has reconfirmed that the long, torturous era of civilising missions has passed. White men's burdens, new world orders, grandiose development schemes, huge foreign aid boondoggles, civil society building—goodbye to all that. Like it or not, effective geopolitics in the 21st century can no longer be about forcing others to be like you, but must involve accommodating new rising countries. Lucas knows this, but he doesn't seem to know what to do about it. His advice for handling the supposed new cold war involves a mere two steps. The first is to throw off "our" illusions and acknowledge Russian reality. The next is to give up the naive idea that the west can influence Russia's domestic politics.

"We are," Lucas himself concludes, "back in the era of great-power politics." Welcome to the 18th century. Still, there's one very important exception here. The political friars in London, Berlin and even Brussels will manage a modus vivendi with Russia as well as China, while holding at home to their liberal and democratic values. But can Washington, the capital of a country that has only been around since the era of the civilising mission and ultimately owes its existence to Puritans, survive a world without self-assigned crusades? In the US, Russia's very make-up, let alone its conduct, is treated as nothing less than an issue of American identity.

Just how many times can America "lose" Russia? A limitless number, it seems. But there may be hope: someone has finally traced in compelling detail the long-standing, religiously inspired American movement to remake Russia. In The American Mission and the "Evil Empire": The Crusade for a "Free Russia" since 1881, David S Foglesong, a professor at Rutgers University, shows that the missionaries, economic advisers and activists promoting God, capitalism and freedom in Russia stretch back in time to America's former slave abolitionists. American fascination with Russia took off with the terrorists' assassination of Czar Alexander II in St Petersburg in 1881, after which, James William Buel, a Missouri journalist and author of a popular account of the outlaws Jesse and Frank James, dashed across the tsarist empire to gather material for a book. "Civilisation is spreading rapidly eastward; it cannot stop or go around Russia," Buel wrote, "and whether with bayonet or psalm-book the march will be made through every part of the czar's dominions."

Foglesong demonstrates that powerful Americans have again and again seen the possibility, even necessity, of spreading the word to Russia, and then, when Russia fails to transform itself into something resembling the US, have recoiled and condemned Russia's perfidious national character or its leaders—most recently Putin. The author's singular achievement is to show that well before the cold war, Russia served as America's dark double, an object of wishful thinking, condescension and self-righteousness in a quest for American purpose-without much to show for such efforts inside Russia. The author thereby places in context the cold war, when pamphleteers like William F Buckley Jr and politicians like Ronald Reagan pushed a crusade to revitalise the American spirit. Russia then was a threat but also a means to America's end (some fixed on a rollback of the alleged Soviet "spawn" inside the US—the welfare state—while others, after the Vietnam debacle, wanted to restore "faith in the United States as a virtuous nation with a unique historical mission"). Foglesong's exposé of Americans' "heady sense of their country's unique blessings" helps make sense of the giddiness, followed by rank disillusionment, vis-à-vis the post-Soviet Russia of the 1990s and 2000s.

In today's downer phase of the recurrent cycle that Foglesong identifies, however, the mission endures. Consider that, in 2006, Stephen Sestanovich of the US Council on Foreign Relations spearheaded a high-profile report sensationally entitled "Russia's Wrong Direction: What the United States Can and Should Do" (put out under the names of the politicians John Edwards and Jack Kemp). The document acknowledges that Washington's efforts to make Moscow into a (junior) partner for America's global agenda have failed. So the report recommends "selective co-operation" on issues for which Moscow could supposedly still be coaxed into doing the US bidding. At the same time, the report admits that the US faces a difficult task in the ancient mission of trying to rescue Russia from authoritarianism. And yet, despite how vital Russia seems to the US—in the report's illogic, precisely because of that very need—the democratisation of Russia must remain a US foreign policy goal. "To go beyond mere expressions about the rollback of Russian democracy," the report advises, "the US should increase—not cut—Freedom Support Act funds, focusing in particular on organisations committed to free and fair parliamentary and presidential elections in 2007–08."

Still more influential has been an essay published earlier this year in Foreign Affairs, "The Myth of the Authoritarian Model: How Putin's Crackdown Holds Russia Back" by Michael McFaul and Kathryn Stoner-Weiss. It is a rallying cry for America's besieged democracy-promoters, who are eager to regain the ground they lost after Iraq. The two authors are at pains to show that Putin's Russia is autocratic compared with Boris Yeltsin's "electoral" democracy (a telling modifier), and that Putin's autocracy has had nothing to do with Russia's economic success. This argument is a red herring. The point is not autocracy but the many vital economic liberalisation measures that were passed during Putin's first term (radical tax revision, red tape reduction, private property in land) as well as the maintenance of tough fiscal discipline and macroeconomic stability. The authors downplay these breakthroughs (while also failing to note that second-term presidencies the world over are rarely known for continued bold policy achievements). McFaul, the lead author, seems unaware that his unsolicited concern for Russia continues more than a century of failed evangelism, as outlined by Foglesong. Indeed, McFaul and his co-author, both at Stanford, cannot be accused of excessive self-reflection: they condemn as "paranoid nationalism" Putin's straightforward observations regarding the "growing influx of cash used directly to meddle in our domestic affairs"—a policy that McFaul has taken part in and continues to advocate.

That McFaul and Stoner-Weiss must fight their democracy-promotion battle on economic grounds does not help their cause. When they assert that increased state ownership in the last few years has slowed Russia's economic performance, they underestimate the degree to which until very recently, Russian growth was helped by squeezing the last drops of blood from Soviet-era investments, a tactic that has stopped working. Moreover, excluding the two energy giants Rosneft and Gazprom, the increase in state ownership of companies in Russia is not dramatic. And many Russian state-owned firms, including the energy giants, are either at or set to reduce the state share in themselves to 51 per cent. (In 2007, Russian companies sold $33bn in stock flotations, mostly on international markets.) Russia's state-owned companies, too, whatever their dubious methods, have not been resting on their bureaucratic laurels but rather acquiring assets for the money (and ego). Of course, high debt accumulation to underwrite M&A may not be a smart growth strategy (it sure looks stupid in the US). But as David Woodruff of the LSE has pointed out, Russia's state-owned companies can redeem international capital market obligations only by increased market share and profits. They may turn out not to be up to the challenge. But hey, that's capitalism.

As their supposedly clinching argument, McFaul and Stoner-Weiss cite the circumstance that growth rates in Russia's neighbours have often been slightly better than Russia's—to wit, they write that from 1999 to 2006 Russia occupied ninth place among the 15 former Soviet republics in ranking of growth rates. The differences in growth and hence rankings are not that large, but let's accept them. The larger point, which the authors miss, is that these economies are all linked, so the authors need to take into account the impact of the large Russian economy's growth on these far smaller ones. In 2007, a half dozen or more of the former Soviet republics were utterly dependent on Russia as a source of remittances. More than 30 per cent of Tajikistan's GDP in 2007 consisted of remittances from Tajiks labouring in Russia. The estimate for remittances from Russia to Moldova was close to 30 per cent of GDP, for Kyrgyzstan more than 20 per cent, and for Georgia and Armenia probably between 10 and 20 per cent. And so on. Consider the possible effects if the millions of Ukrainians who have found work in Russia suddenly had to go home, unemployed. Comparable numbers for economic dependency are perhaps found only in the many countries receiving remittances from their nationals working in the US. There are many reasons to be critical of Russian economic performance and policies, but the super-high growth rate of Kazakhstan is not one of them.

In reality, though, McFaul and Stoner-Weiss are driven not by any interest in economics, but by the alleged urgency of democratisation for US foreign policy. In this regard, Robert Legvold, editor of the collection Russian Foreign Policy in the Twenty-first Century and the Shadow of the Past, published last year, provides an echo. His introduction is a defence of a long overdue recourse to some history in analysing contemporary Russia. But even as he urges analysts to study Russia's past, he urges Russia "to escape its past," by which Legvold means its authoritarianism. Above all, he insists that the US and the EU have "legitimate" interests in Russia's domestic political arrangements because of their impact on Russia's neighbours. (He might also have mentioned the impact on Russia's inhabitants, through international human rights policy.) In other words, Russian foreign policy, in Legvold's mind, flows not from the maw of Russian national interests but from the nature of its political system. Voilà. Here, projected outwards, we have hit upon one of those quintessentially American beliefs about itself: namely, that the US conducts itself in the world not on the basis of its national interests but on the basis of its democracy.

Not all the authors in the volume agree with Legvold that Russia's absolutism is unsuited to an era of globalisation. David McDonald portrays absolutism in Russia as a capacious toolbox, and one that today, too, can advance the country economically and culturally, even if such an approach carries the danger of overreach. Still, the general tenor of the volume falls in line with what Foglesong has shown to be an American-identity crusade projected on to Russia since 1881. Foglesong quotes David Lawrence, founder of US News and World Report, expressing the American establishment's underlying credo back in 1958: "There can be no safety in the world as long as we have autocratic regimes." This belief opens the widest possible field for a missionary foreign policy (and for the inevitable hypocrisy). It succeeded in uniting liberal internationalists, like McFaul and Stoner-Weiss, with neocons over Iraq, and like all fundamentalist beliefs, it survived that debacle. What it may not survive is the conversion of the American dollar into the Mexican peso.

The unsolved murders of Russian journalists and the arrests of political activists make many observers want at a minimum to chalk up Putin's boom to dumb luck—floating on highly priced reservoirs of oil and gas left by nature hundreds of millions of years ago—and to predict a come-uppance. Maybe Russia is set for a fall. In terms of quotidian state functions, Russia is badly governed, which makes it vulnerable in a crisis. In a global world where everything is connected, if China's boom loses air, Russia too will feel the enormous downdraught. And Wall Street's financial engineering may yet annihilate everyone, good and bad alike. Whatever the future holds, it is clear that the world has not seen such large authoritarian market economies like Russia's or China's since, well, Nazi Germany and its ally Japan. But today's authoritarian Russia and China are not militarily aggressive. And Edward Lucas notwithstanding, these countries are also not likely to be defeated in war and occupied so that the likes of Michael McFaul and Kathryn Stoner-Weiss can have another go at the democracy crusade so well chronicled by David Foglesong.

The power of the Kremlin can seem all-encompassing. Across the 20th century, the average time in office for leaders in the democratic US has been about six years. In autocratic Russia, it has been around ten. Remove Stalin's long despotism, and the figure falls to eight. Still, authoritarian successions are always difficult from a regime's point of view. (Perhaps the most remarkable fact about China is not its market transformation but its two smooth, albeit opaque, political transitions after Deng Xiaoping stepped down, first to Jiang Zemin and then to Hu Jintao.) One of the many weak points of authoritarianism is that it makes bad options appear attractive—like hoping, as many do, that Putin remains Russia's real ruler. But whatever the fate of the latest succession, the Kremlin's China-like strategy will likely continue: suppressing many of the politically liberalising aspects of globalisation while pursuing its economic aspects to the ends of the earth.

Just like the Chinese and the Arab autocracies, the Russians are coming— and for real this time. When Russian capital, already highly visible in Europe and Britain, comes with ever greater force to Wall Street and to Main Street America, will Americans understand the value of Russia having a substantial stake in US success? Will Americans appreciate that having Russian-owned assets on American soil that could be seized provides a huge source of leverage over the Kremlin that is today lacking? As for the EU, it may be crucial for north Africa and the Levant, but it is far less so for Russia (or China). The EU seems likely to be bedevilled for some time over the status of Turkey, while Russia, just like China, continues to pursue bilateral relations with individual European countries. Russia's trade with EU countries is huge—three times its trade with the former Soviet republics—and Germany is easily Russia's biggest single partner (in 2007 their bilateral trade hit $52.8bn). Still, right now no place matters more to Russia than London as a commercial hub of globalisation. London's importance is one reason Russia has tried—with episodes like the British Council harassment—to send forceful diplomatic messages over anything related to its sovereignty, just as China does, without undermining real interests.

We should not, however, exaggerate Russia's global power. In future the US, the EU and China will each account for no less than one fifth of global

GDP. Even if Russia does become the world's fifth largest economy, it would still constitute no more than 3 or so per cent of global GDP. The Kremlin will use its seat on the UN security council and presence at the G8 to defend its interests globally, while also seeking good relations with China in various forums. But Russia is not an EU country, not a US ally and not a China ally. It is perceived as a possible partner, but also as a potential enemy, by all three. Above all, if Russian companies, whether state-owned or private, are not able to go toe-to-toe with the best companies in the world, you can forget the whole game. "Even with the economic situation in our favour at the moment, we are still only making fragmentary attempts to modernise our economy," Putin said in a speech this year on Russia's long-term development strategy to 2020. "This inevitably increases our dependence on imported goods and technology, and reinforces our role as a commodities base for the world economy." He added that "the Russian economy's biggest problem today is that it is extremely ineffective. Labour productivity in Russia remains very low. We have the same labour costs as in the most developed countries, but the return is several times lower. This situation is all the more dangerous when global competition is increasing."

In short, President Medvedev and, if so named, Prime Minister Putin have their work cut out.

POSTSCRIPT

Are We in a New Cold War?

The Cold War that pitted the United States against the Soviet Union was one that covered almost every aspect of geopolitics. The conflict extended into military competition, proxy wars in which hundreds of thousands of people were killed, the nuclear arms race, economic competition, ideological rivalry, sports competition, and the like. It was clear, demonstrative, and at times dangerous. The Cuban Missile crisis is but one example of when that Cold War could easily have led to global nuclear Armageddon.

Today, many elements of that old rivalry are not germane. The ideological component is all but gone. Whatever ideology the Putin regime articulates has no weight in Russian policy. It is clear that Russia is interested in satisfying its geopolitical national interests exclusively and not interested in promoting an overarching ideology. Second, Russia's geopolitical calculations around the world are less about thwarting American or Chinese interests and more about promoting its own. Therefore the likelihood that proxy wars of the type that we saw during the Cold War will reemerge is slim. Third, it is clear that at least for the time being, neither side sees the other as a proximate threat to its very survival.

However, there are some ominous signs. Russia continues to reassert primary position vis-à-vis its former republics, and Georgia is the latest example of its willingness to use force to maintain that primacy. Second, the Putin regime has clearly turned its back on a true democratic system, instead forging a kind of corporatist authoritarian regime, with Putin managing the polity from various positions. Third, Russia's policy toward Iran indicates a clear desire to chart a course apart from U.S. influence or policy, and a potentially conflictual one given Iran's nuclear ambitions and their impact on the volatile Middle East.

The Cold War between the United States and the Soviet Union was a complex, multilayered rivalry that spanned a variety of arenas. It is rooted in a fundamentally different view of geopolitics, economics, and political participation. It grew out of decades of mistrust and secrecy and exploded in a series of "battles" throughout the world.

Today's U.S.-Russian relationship is less complex and more direct. One superpower with preeminent influence engaging with a failed great power who is just now (over the last 10 years) determining its future course out of revolution and engaging in a reassertion of prominence, if not prestige and national self interest. Although it is clear that the relationship is rocky and there are many areas of disagreement, it is certainly premature to state that a new cold war exists, if for no other reason than that a cold war has a deeper and more complex meaning than simply two states with competing interests. Although

Cohen may be right, it appears that several more years of events and analysis will be needed before such a conclusion can be made on its face without significant evidence for rebuttal.

Some recent scholarship in this area includes Edward Lucas, *The New Cold War: Putin's Russia and the Threat to the West* (St Martin's Press, 2003); Mark McKinnon, *The New Cold War: Revolutions, Rigged Elections and Pipelines* (Random House, 2007); Nancy Soderberg, *The Superpower Myth* (John Wiley & Sons, 2005); and Katrina Vanden Hauvel, "Joe Biden and the Myth of Foreign Policy Experience," *The Nation* (August 24, 2008).

ISSUE 17

Are We Headed Toward a Nuclear 9/11?

YES: Brian Michael Jenkins, from "Terrorists Can Think Strategically: Lessons Learned from the Mumbai Attacks," Rand Corporation (January 2009)

NO: Graham Allison, from "Time to Bury a Dangerous Legacy—Part I," *Yale Global Online* (March 14, 2008)

ISSUE SUMMARY

YES: Brian Michael Jenkins, senior advisor to the President of the Rand Corporation, in testimony before the U.S. Senate Committee on Homeland Security and Governmental Affairs, posited that a team of terrorists could be inserted into the United States and carry out a Mumbai-style attack as terrorism has "increasingly become an effective strategic weapon."

NO: Graham Allison, Harvard professor and director of the Belfer Center for Science and International Affairs, affirms that we are not likely to experience a nuclear 9/11 because "nuclear terrorism is preventable by a feasible, affordable agenda of actions that . . . would shrink the risk of nuclear terrorism to nearly zero."

Since the terrorist attacks of September 11, 2001, much has been written about the specter of nuclear terrorism and the releasing of a dirty bomb (one loaded with radioactive material) in an urban/civilian setting. The events of September 11 have all but ensured the world's preoccupation with such an event for the foreseeable future. Indeed, the arrest of a U.S. man with dirty bomb materials indicates that such plans may indeed be in the works between Al Qaeda and other terrorist cells. When this horror is combined with the availability of elements of nuclear-related material in places like the states of the former Soviet Union, Pakistan, India, Iraq, Iran, North Korea, and many other states, one can envision a variety of sobering scenarios.

Hollywood feeds these views with such films as *The Sum of All Fears* and *The Peacemaker*, in which nuclear terrorism is portrayed as all too easy to carry out and likely to occur. It is difficult in such environments to separate fact from fiction and to ascertain objectively the probabilities of such events. So many factors go into a successful initiative in this area. One must find a committed cadre of terrorists, sufficient financial backing, technological know-how, intense security and secrecy, the means of delivery, and many other variables, including luck. In truth, such acts may have already been advanced and thwarted by governments, security services, or terrorist mistakes and incompetence. We do not know, and we may never know.

Regional and ethnic conflicts of a particularly savage nature in places like Chechnya, Kashmir, Colombia, and Afghanistan help to fuel fears that adequately financed zealots will see in nuclear weapons a swift and catastrophic answer to their demands and angers. Osama bin Laden's contribution to worldwide terrorism has been the success of money over security and the realization that particularly destructive acts with high levels of coordination can be "successful." This will undoubtedly encourage others with similar ambitions against real or perceived enemies.

Conversely, many argue that fear of the terrorist threat has left us imagining that which is not likely. They point to a myriad of roadblocks to terrorist groups' obtaining all of the elements necessary for a nuclear or dirty bomb. They cite technological impediments, monetary issues, lack of sophistication, and inability to deliver. They also cite governments' universal desire to prevent such actions. Even critics of [former] Iraqi leader Saddam Hussein have argued that were he to develop such weapons, he would not deliver them to terrorist groups nor would he use them except in the most dire of circumstances, such as his own regime's survival. They argue that the threat is overblown and, in some cases, merely used to justify increased security and the restriction of civil liberties.

The following selections reflect the debate about a nuclear 9/11. Jenkins focuses on the ability and resourcefulness of the terrorists and argues that recent events indicate a real ability to carry out such an attack. Allison focuses on the targets, the United States and the West, and insists that a coordinated strategy can stop such an event.

YES

Brian Michael Jenkins

Terrorists Can Think Strategically

Lessons Learned From the Mumbai Attacks

Mr. Chairman and Members of the Committee, it is an honor to appear before you today. The Mumbai attack was still ongoing when RAND initiated an analysis to determine what lessons might be learned from it. This analysis, part of RAND's continuing research on terrorism and homeland security, was documented in a report I co-authored along with other RAND analysts. Specifically, I contributed the sections on the terrorists' strategic motives and the execution of the attack.

We relied on both informed official sources and media reporting. My analysis benefited greatly from the detailed descriptions of the attack provided by officers from the New York Police Department, who were on the scene and whose reports were shared with law enforcement and others in the United States.

Copies of our report have been made available to members of the Committee. Additional copies are available here, and the report is also on RAND's website. For convenience, I have appended the key findings to my testimony. The following observations derive from this report and other relevant research.

Terrorism has increasingly become an effective strategic weapon. Earlier generations of terrorists seldom thought beyond the barrels of their guns. In contrast, the masterminds of the Mumbai terrorist attacks displayed sophisticated strategic thinking in their choice of targets and their efforts to achieve multiple objectives. They were able to capture and hold international attention. They sought to exacerbate communal tensions in India and provoke a crisis between India and Pakistan, thereby persuading Pakistan to redeploy troops to its frontier with India, which in turn would take pressure off of the Taliban, al Qaeda, and other groups operating along the Afghan frontier. All terrorist attacks are recruiting posters. The Mumbai attackers established their terrorist credentials and now rival al Qaeda in reputation.

Al Qaeda is not the only galaxy in the jihadist universe—new contenders that have signed on to al Qaeda's ideology of global terror. Even as we have degraded al Qaeda's operational capabilities, the idea of a violent global jihad has spread from North Africa to South Asia. The Mumbai attack foreshadows

From *Testimony Series*, January 2009, pp. 1–4. Copyright © 2009 by Rand Corporation. Reprinted by permission.

a continuing terrorist campaign in India. More broadly, it suggests that the global struggle against the jihadists is far from over.

Terrorists can innovate tactically to obviate existing security measures and confuse authorities. Authorities are obliged to prevent the recurrence of the most recent attack, while knowing that other terrorists will analyze the security in place, devise new tactics, and do the unexpected. The Mumbai attackers did not plant bombs in crowded train coaches, as in the 2006 Mumbai terrorist attack. Instead, gunmen attacked the train station. They did not detonate car bombs as in the 1993 Mumbai attacks or the more recent terrorist attacks on hotels in Indonesia, Egypt, Jordan and Pakistan. They seized control of hotels where they started fires. Multiple attacks at different locations prevented authorities from developing an overall assessment of the situation.

Once again, terrorists have demonstrated that with simple tactics and low-tech weapons, they can produce vastly disproportionate results. The Mumbai attack was sequential, highly mobile, and a departure from the now common suicide bombings, but the tactics were simple—armed assaults, carjackings, drive-by shootings, building takeovers, barricade and hostage situations. The attack was carried out by ten men armed with easily obtained assault weapons, semi-automatic pistols, hand grenades, and simple improvised explosive devices—little more than the arsenal of an infantryman in the 1940s—along with 21st century cell phones, BlackBerries, and GPS locators.

Terrorists will continue to focus on soft targets that offer high body counts and that have iconic value. Nationally and internationally recognized venues that offer ease of access, certainty of tactical success, and the opportunity to kill in quantity will guide target selection. Public spaces are inherently difficult to protect. Major investments in target hardening make sense for government only when these provide a net security benefit, that is, when they do not merely displace the risk to another equally lucrative and accessible target.

Terrorists view public surface transportation as a killing field. One of the two-man terrorist teams went to Mumbai's main train station and opened fire on commuters. While the attacks on the other targets were theoretically aimed at killing foreigners, the attack at the train station was aimed solely at slaughter. It accounted for more than a third of the total deaths.

This underscores a trend that should be a priority issue in the United States. Public surface transportation offers terrorists easily accessible, dense populations in confined environments—ideal killing zones for gunmen or improvised explosive devices, which remain the most common form of attack. According to analysis by the Mineta Transportation Institute's National Transportation Security Center, two-thirds of all terrorist attacks on surface transportation were intended to kill; 37 percent resulted in fatalities (compared with between 20 and 25 percent of terrorist attacks overall); 75 percent of the fatal attacks involved multiple fatalities; and 28 percent of those involved 10 or more fatalities.

Terrorist attacks on flagship hotels are increasing in number, in total casualties, and in casualties per incident.   This trend places increasing demands on hotel security. However, while terrorist attacks are spectacular, they are statistically rare in comparison to ordinary violent crime. In the past forty years, fewer than five hundred hotel guests in the entire world have been killed by terrorists, out of a total global hotel guest population at any time of nearly ten million.

Pakistan's principal defense against external pressure is not its nuclear arsenal, but its own political fragility—its government's less-than-full cooperation is preferable to the country's collapse and descent into chaos.   Pakistan continues to play a prominent and problematic role in the overlapping armed conflicts and terrorist campaigns in India, Afghanistan, and Pakistan itself. Al Qaeda, the Taliban, Lashkar-e-Taiba and other insurgent and terrorist groups find sanctuary in Pakistan's turbulent tribal areas. Historically, some of them have drawn on support from the Pakistan government itself. While the Government of Pakistan has been helpful in capturing some key terrorist operatives, Pakistan is accused of protecting others. And it has been understandably reluctant to use military force against its own citizens in the remote tribal areas where these groups reside. When it has used military force, government forces have not fared well. Public sentiment imposes further constraints. Many Pakistanis regard India and the United States, not al Qaeda or the Taliban, as greater threats to Pakistan's national security. This was perceived as an obstacle to U.S. counterterrorist efforts even before 9/11.

The success of the Mumbai attackers in paralyzing a large city and commanding the attention of the world's news media for nearly three days will encourage similar operations in the future.   Terrorists will continue to effectively embed themselves among civilians, taking hostages and using them as human shields to impede responders and maximize collateral casualties. We should expect to see more of this tactic.

Could a Mumbai-style attack happen in the United States?   It could. The difference lies in planning and scale. Assembling and training a ten-man team of suicidal attackers seems far beyond the capabilities of the conspirators identified in any of the local terrorist plots discovered in this country since 9/11. We have no evidence of that level of dedication or planning skills.

However, we have seen lone gunmen and pairs of shooters, motivated by mental illness or political cause, run amok, determined to kill in quantity. The Long Island Railroad, Empire State Building, LAX, Virginia Tech, and Columbine cases come to mind. In 1955, four Puerto Rican separatists opened fire in a then unguarded Capitol Building, wounding five members of Congress. Firearms are readily available in the United States. And some of the perpetrators of the attacks mentioned above planned for their attacks for months, while building their arsenals. Therefore, an attack on the ground, carried out by a small number of self-radicalized, homegrown terrorists armed with readily available weapons, perhaps causing scores of casualties, while still far beyond what we have seen in the terrorist plots uncovered thus far, is not inconceivable.

Could a team of terrorists, recruited and trained abroad as the Mumbai attackers were, be inserted into the United States, perhaps on a U.S.-registered fishing vessel or pleasure boat, to carry out a Mumbai-style attack? Although our intelligence has greatly improved, the answer again must be a qualified yes. It could conceivably happen here, although I would expect our police response to be much swifter and more effective than we saw in Mumbai.

Time to Bury a Dangerous Legacy–Part I

One month after the terrorist assault on the World Trade Center and the Pentagon, on October 11, 2001, President George W. Bush faced a more terrifying prospect. At that morning's presidential daily intelligence briefing, George Tenet, the director of central intelligence, informed the president that a CIA agent codenamed "Dragonfire" had reported that Al Qaeda terrorists possessed a 10-kiloton nuclear bomb, evidently stolen from the Russian arsenal. According to Dragonfire, this nuclear weapon was in New York City.

The government dispatched a top-secret nuclear emergency support team to the city. Under a cloak of secrecy that excluded even Mayor Rudolph Giuliani, these nuclear ninjas searched for the bomb. On a normal workday, half a million people crowd the area within a half-mile radius of Times Square. A noon detonation in Midtown Manhattan would kill them all instantly. Hundreds of thousands of others would die from collapsing buildings, fire and fallout in the hours thereafter. The electromagnetic pulse generated by the blast would fry cell phones and other electronic communication. The wounded would overwhelm hospitals and emergency services. Firemen would fight an uncontrolled ring of fires for days afterward.

In the hours that followed, Condoleezza Rice, then national security adviser, analyzed what strategists call the "problem from hell." Unlike the Cold War, when the US and the Soviet Union knew that an attack against the other would elicit a retaliatory strike or greater measure, Al Qaeda—with no return address—had no such fear of reprisal. Even if the president were prepared to negotiate, Al Qaeda has no phone number to call.

Concerned that Al Qaeda could have smuggled a nuclear weapon into Washington as well, the president ordered Vice President Dick Cheney to leave the capital for an "undisclosed location," where he would remain for weeks to follow—standard procedure to ensure "continuity of government" in case of a decapitation strike against US political leadership. Several hundred federal employees from more than a dozen government agencies joined the vice president at this secret site, the core of an alternative government that would seek to cope in the aftermath of a nuclear explosion that destroyed Washington.

Six months earlier the CIA's Counterterrorism Center had picked up chatter in Al Qaeda channels about an "American Hiroshima." The CIA knew that Osama bin Laden's fascination with nuclear weapons went back at least to

From *YaleGlobal Online*, March 14, 2008. Copyright © 2008 by Yale Center for the Study of Globalization. Reprinted by permission of YaleGlobal Online. www.yaleglobal.yale.edu

1992, when he attempted to buy highly enriched uranium from South Africa. Al Qaeda operatives were alleged to have negotiated with Chechen separatists in Russia to buy a nuclear warhead, which the Chechen warlord Shamil Basayev claimed to have acquired from Russian arsenals. The CIA's special task force on Al Qaeda had noted the terrorist group's emphasis on thorough planning, intensive training and repetition of successful tactics. The task force highlighted Al Qaeda's preference for symbolic targets and spectacular attacks.

As CIA analysts examined Dragonfire's report and compared it with other bits of information, they noted that the September attack on the World Trade Center had set the bar higher for future terrorist attacks. Psychologically, a nuclear attack would stagger the world's imagination. New York was, in the jargon of national-security experts, "target rich."

As it turned out, Dragonfire's report proved to be a false alarm. But the central takeaway from the case is this: The US government had no grounds in science or logic to dismiss this possibility, nor could it do so today.

There's no established methodology for assessing the probability of an unprecedented event that could have such catastrophic consequences. Nonetheless, in "Nuclear Terrorism" I state my considered judgment that if the US and other governments just keep doing what they are doing today, a nuclear terrorist attack in a major city is more likely than not by 2014.

Richard Garwin, a designer of the hydrogen bomb whom Enrico Fermi once called, "the only true genius I had ever met," told Congress in March 2007 that he estimated a "20 percent per year probability of a nuclear explosion with American cities and European cities included." My Harvard colleague Matthew Bunn has created a model that estimates the probability of a nuclear terrorist attack over a 10-year period to be 29 percent—identical to the average estimate from a poll of security experts commissioned by Senator Richard Lugar in 2005.

Former Secretary of Defense William Perry has expressed his own view that my work may underestimate the risk. Warren Buffet, the world's most successful investor and legendary odds-maker in pricing insurance policies for unlikely but catastrophic events, concluded that nuclear terrorism is "inevitable." As he has stated: "I don't see any way that it won't happen."

The good news is that nuclear terrorism is preventable by a feasible, affordable agenda of actions that, if taken, would shrink the risk of nuclear terrorism to nearly zero. A global strategy to prevent this ultimate catastrophe can be organized under a Doctrine of Three No's: No loose nukes, no new nascent nukes, no new nuclear weapons. The first requires securing all nuclear weapons and weapons-usable material, on the fastest possible timetable, to a new "gold standard." The second does not allow for any new national capabilities to enrich uranium or reprocess plutonium. The third draws a line under the current eight and a half nuclear powers—the five members of the Security Council and India, Israel, Pakistan and North Korea—and says unambiguously: "Stop. No More."

The US cannot unilaterally sustain a successful strategy to prevent nuclear terrorism. Nor can the necessary actions simply be commanded, compelled or coerced. Instead, they require deep and steady international cooperation rooted in the recognition that nations share a common threat that requires a common strategy. A Global Alliance Against Nuclear Terrorism is therefore in order. The mission of this alliance should be to minimize the risk of nuclear terrorism by taking every action physically, technically and diplomatically possible to prevent nuclear weapons or materials from falling into the hands of terrorists.

Constructing such an alliance will require the US and other nuclear-weapons states to confront the question of a "fourth no": no nuclear weapons. While US or Russian possession of nuclear arsenals is not a major driver of Iran's nuclear ambitions, and while Osama bin Laden would not be less interested in acquiring a nuclear weapon if the US eliminated its current arsenals, the proposition that nuclear weapons are necessary for the security of US and Russia but intolerably dangerous if acquired by Iran or South Africa is difficult to sell to nuclear have-nots.

The question of a categorical "fourth no" has come to the fore with the January 2007 opinion piece in the *Wall Street Journal* by George P. Shultz, William J. Perry, Henry A. Kissinger and Sam Nunn, calling upon the US and other states to act to realize their Non-Proliferation Treaty commitment and President Reagan's vision of "a world free of nuclear weapons." Towards that goal, the immediate agenda should be to devalue nuclear weapons and minimize their role in international affairs. This should begin with nuclear-weapons states pledging to the following principles: no new national enrichment, no nuclear tests, no first use of a nuclear bomb and no new nuclear weapons.

Faced with the possibility of an American Hiroshima, many are paralyzed by a combination of denial and fatalism. This is unwarranted. Through a combination of imagination, a clear agenda for action and fierce determination to pursue it, the countdown to a nuclear 9/11 can be stopped.

POSTSCRIPT

Are We Headed Toward a Nuclear 9/11?

There are many arguments to support the contention that nuclear and dirty bombs are hard to obtain, difficult to move and assemble, and even harder to deliver. There is also ample evidence to suggest that most, if not all, of the U.S. government's work is in one way or another designed to thwart such actions because of the enormous consequences were such acts to be carried out. These facts should make Americans rest easier and allay fears if only for reasons of probability.

However, Allison's contention that failure to assume the worst may prevent the thwarting of such terrorist designs is persuasive. Since September 11, it is clear that the world has entered a new phase of terrorist action and a new level of funding, sophistication, and motivation. The attitude that because something is difficult it is unlikely to take place may be too dangerous to possess. The collapse of the USSR has unleashed a variety of forces, some positive and some more sinister and secretive. The enormous prices that radioactive material and nuclear devices can command on the black market make the likelihood of temptation strong and possibly irresistible.

If states are to err, perhaps they should err on the side of caution and preventive action rather than on reliance on the statistical probability that nuclear terrorism is unlikely. We may never see a nuclear terrorist act in this century, but it is statistically likely that the reason for this will not be for lack of effort on the part of motivated terrorist groups.

Some important research and commentary on nuclear terrorism can be found in Elaine Landau, *Osama bin Laden: A War Against the West* (Twenty-First Century Books, 2002); Jan Lodal, *The Price of Dominance: The New Weapons of Mass Destruction and Their Challenge to American Leadership* (Council on Foreign Relations Press, 2001); Jessica Stern, *The Ultimate Terrorists* (Harvard University Press, 1999); Graham Allison, *Nuclear Terrorism: The Ultimate Preventable Catastrophe* (Times Books, 2004); and Zbigniew Brzezinski, *The Choice: Global Domination or Global Leadership* (Basic Books, 2005).

ISSUE 18

Is Religious and Cultural Extremism a Global Security Threat?

YES: Hussein Solomon, from "Global Security in the Age of Religious Extremism," *PRISM* (August 2006)

NO: Shibley Telhami, from "Testimony Before the House Armed Services Committee: Between Terrorism and Religious Extremism" (November 3, 2005)

ISSUE SUMMARY

YES: Solomon argues that when religious extremism, which is a security threat in and of itself, is merged with state power, the threat to global security is potentially catastrophic and must be met with clear and uncompromising policies. He contends that this is present across all religions, and he uses both a born-again George Bush and a fundamentalist Mahmoud Ahmadinejad as his examples.

NO: Telhami, on the other hand, does not argue that religious extremism is the threat, but rather that global security threats are from political groups with political agendas and not extremism as such.

Religious and cultural extremism has been a part of the global landscape for millennia. Since the dawn of civilization, groups of people have defined themselves by their language, religious beliefs, race, and other factors distinguishing their culture from "the other." Once this occurred, conflicts over resources, land, and allegiances began and have continued to varying degrees. Religion as a catalyst for this conflict has always been present, particularly in Europe, the Middle East, and Asia throughout the Greek–Roman period and the Middle Ages.

Although religious and cultural extremism is not a new force, the methods of idea dissemination and the speed with which groups can connect certainly are. Today in the age of globalization, religious extremism has a variety of mediums through which it can transmit its messages and, as such, appears at least to be a very potent force. This is certainly true in the Islamic world. Fundamentalist Islam has seized the mantle of religious extremism even though there are such extremists among all major religious groups. The increasing radicalism of the Palestinian movement combined with the high-profile acts of al-Qaeda has underscored this perception. The concept of martyrdom has now permeated the extremist culture such that suicide attacks, be they in a Jerusalem school or at the World Trade Center, are offered as pure manifestations of allegiance to one's faith. Although it is often difficult to extract the political and economic motivations of these groups from their religious zealotry, one dimension is clear. Whatever the real politick motives of the leaders of these groups may be, the rank and file truly believe that they are martyrs in a cause ordained and blessed by their God.

The globalization of media in all of its forms has transformed more localized fundamentalist extremism into global movements with reach through every computer terminal and into the home of every disgruntled believer. As such, extremist cells have emerged throughout the world, with a small, but highly motivated, minority of believers committed to violence as their only means of political and social expression. Although the highest profile acts appear to be committed by Islamic fundamentalists, all faiths possess such zealotry and have examples of violence in the name of "pure belief."

With this reality comes the prevalence and proliferation of weaponry, be it biological, chemical, or nuclear, that can transform an extremist act from local to global in seconds.

In the following section, two noted scholars argue whether it is religious extremism or simply political goals that are the security threat. Dr. Soloman contends that when religious extremism is combined with state power in any system, violence, conflict, and death will follow. He makes the controversial argument that a George Bush with his fundamentalist Christian beliefs and Mahmoud Ahmadinejad with his Islamic fundamentalism present global security threats. He contends that their fundamentalism, when merged with instruments of state power, leads to abuses, conflict, and death for their own citizens and innocents in arenas of conflict.

Shibley Telhami presents the case that states and interests compete, and extremism, in and of itself, is not the culprit. He argues that the extremism of the Iranian regime or al-Qaeda is not what makes them a threat, but rather the anti-western sentiment that they have tapped into. Their goals and interests combined with a willingness to engage in violent terrorism constitutes the security threat, and not the fact that they have a religious base.

YES

Hussein Solomon

Global Security in the Age of Religious Extremism

A World Caught between Hope and Despair

We live in a world fecund with both hope and despair. Images of hope are aplenty. From Ireland, comes the story of the Irish Republican Army (IRA) formally giving up its armed struggle. From the Gaza strip, we see Israel's evacuation of Jewish settlers from occupied Palestinian land; and from Kashmir we witness rapprochement and reconciliation overcoming the enmity and quest for vengeance of the past. At the same time there is despair; which emanates from the fact that religion, which brings meaning to one's life and preaches peace, love and generosity has morphed into something ugly and violent. In Japan, we have seen Aum Shinrikyo (the Supreme Truth) cult release sarin gas in Tokyo's subways. From India's Gujarat State, we saw Hindu fundamentalists kill hundreds of their fellow Muslim citizens. In northern Uganda, Joseph Kony and his Christian fundamentalist Lord's Resistance Army aim to overthrow the secular government of Yoweri Museveni and to replace it with a government observant of the biblical Ten Commandments. In the process, the commandment "Thou Shall Not Kill" has been violated thousands of times. From the United States, we see people motivated by strong Christian principles bombing abortion clinics or federal buildings as in the case of Timothy McVeigh—the infamous Oklahoma bomber. The world has also witnessed Jewish fundamentalism in the form of Yigal Amir's assassination of former Israeli Prime Minister Yitzhak Rabin after he signed the Oslo Peace Accords. The rise of a violent Islamic fundamentalism was vividly illustrated by the tragic events of 9/11 in New York and Washington and by the atrocities committed more recently in Amman, Jordan.

While the violent religious fundamentalism of these non-state actors constitute a grave threat to national, regional and international security—this article will focus rather on the threat posed by state-sanctioned religious fundamentalism. The underlying premise here is that when religious extremists capture state power, the threat posed to international security is infinitely worse than that posed by non-state actors given the control that they can now exercise over the resources of the state. Two cases illustrate the point well: the United States under George W. Bush and Iran under Mahmoud Ahmadinejad.

From *PRISM* (www.e-prism.org), August 2006. Copyright © 2006 by Hussein Solomon. Reprinted by permission of the author.

George W. Bush Finds God

In 1985 George W. Bush found God by way of a Bible study group and studied the scriptures intensely for the next two years. In the process he developed an ideology, which dovetailed neatly with the mentality of the conservative evangelicals in the US. Later when he decided to run for public office, his political strategist Karl Rove drew the link between Bush's Christian beliefs and the evangelical sector. This proved to be an immensely successful strategy given the evangelical voting bloc—one in three American Christians call themselves evangelical. To put it another way, there are 80 million born-again Christians of voting age in the United States—George W. Bush is one of them. As he prepared for elections first as Governor and later for the presidency, whilst others candidates spoke about their political platform, Bush spoke about his faith. Thus when a reporter asked him who his favourite philosopher was, Bush replied: *"Christ, because he changed my heart."* Using religion to get elected, however, was one thing; acting on those strong Christian beliefs as president is quite another. Yet this is exactly what the Christian right sought to achieve—after all, their man occupied the White House. Their efforts ranged across the social spectrum from the issue of euthanasia to same sex marriage to the teaching of intelligent design (another term for creationism) as opposed to evolution in school textbooks.

However, it is perhaps in the realm of foreign policy that the religious views of George Bush hold the greatest menace. For one thing, he subscribes to Manichaeism that divides reality into Absolute Good and Absolute Evil. Juan Stam notes that the Christian Church rejected this as heretical many centuries ago. Yet, time and time again George W. Bush uses this rather simple dichotomy of good versus evil. The U.S. and its allies are good and have been "called" by God to serve as his instrument against the evildoers. On the other hand—the other side is described as the "Axis of Evil." Such a simplistic dichotomy is extremely problematic. First, do Iran and North Korea really have so much in common with one another that one lumps them together? Second, using phrases like "Axis of Evil" suggest that a regime, a country, or a set of countries are merely evil but does not point to the level of factionalism occurring inside a country or how one might capitalise on it to serve one's own national interest. To sum up then, "Axis of Evil" is a primitive and simple term for a complex world that is characterised less by black and white and more by shades of grey.

Beyond the terminology, however, there are even more serious problems with George W. Bush occupying the Oval Office and these relate to the idea that God speaks to him. Arnon Regular writing in Israel's *Haaretz* newspaper reported that when George Bush met with then Palestinian Prime Minister Abbas in Aqaba he said: *"God told me to strike at Al-Qaeda and I struck them and then He instructed me to strike at Saddam, which I did, and now I am determined to solve the problem in the Middle East."* Such statements do irreparable harm to US policy in the Middle East. How does one promote secular democracies in the Middle East when the President of the United States is himself undermining the First Amendment as it relates to the separation of Church and State?

Meanwhile Ira Chernus raised other objections against such a statement: *"If he truly believes that he hears the voice of God, there is no telling what God might say tomorrow. This is a man who can launch the world's biggest arsenal of weapons of mass destruction—biological, chemical, and nuclear at any moment. . . . When the President lets God tell him what to do, it violates the spirit of democracy. In a democracy, it is the people, not God, who make the decisions. The president is supposed to represent the will of the people. Yes, he must seek the best advice he can get and use his own best judgment. That means relying on facts, intelligent analysis, and rational thought—not divine inspiration. Once the President lets God's voice replace the human mind, we are back in the Middle Ages, back in the very situation our revolution was supposed to get us out of."*

Professor Ira Chernus' perspective was echoed almost fifty years previously by that formidable First Lady, Eleanor Roosevelt: *"Anyone who knows history, particularly the history of Europe, will, I think, recognize that the domination of education or of government by any one particular religious faith is never a good arrangement for the people."*

Throughout the Afghan and Iraqi wars, President Bush did not shy away from identifying God with his own project. Thus when he appeared in his flight suit on the aircraft carrier Abraham Lincoln, he said to US troops: *"And wherever you go, you carry a message of hope—a message that is ancient and ever new. In the words of the prophet Isaiah, 'To the captives, come out! To those who are in darkness, be free!'"* It should be noted that Bush's use of God and the Bible is unprecedented in US political history and stands in sharp contrast to, for instance, President Abraham Lincoln. During the American Civil War, Lincoln did not claim that God was on his side. Indeed in his famous second inaugural address, he said that the war was a curse on both armies.

Mahmoud Ahmadinejad and the Mahdi

June 2005 witnessed the election of Mahmoud Ahmadinejad as President of the Islamic Republic of Iran. Amongst the people voting for him some cited his anti-corruption stance, others his desire to better the lot of the common Iranian man and woman, and still others his piety. Few could have guessed where this piety was to lead him and Iran as soon as he assumed the presidency. For one thing, the delicate balance between conservatives and reformists that the regime sought to preserve has been destroyed with Ahmadinejad's election. Before the June elections, Iran's supreme leader Ayatollah Ali Khamenei, stated that *". . . the existence of two factions [conservative and reformist] serves the regime, like the two wings of a bird."* But Ahmadinejad has been removing reformists as well as those conservatives allied to his political rivals from positions of power and has been replacing them with incompetent cronies who share his ideological vision. The political establishment in Tehran is bound to experience further shocks following the announcement by Ahmadinejad's spiritual advisor, the extremist Ayatollah Mohammed Taqi Mesbah-Yazdi, that *". . . with a true Islamic government at hand, Iran has no need for future elections."* The delicate balance that Ayatollah Khamenei has sought to preserve has been utterly destroyed.

At this point it might be useful to ask what this pious ideological vision that Ahmadinejad subscribes to is. Much of his vision relates to his devotion to the 12th Imam, also known as the Mahdi, who vanished in 941. According to Shiite Muslims this Imam will return at the end of time to lead an era of Islamic justice. The fact that Ahmadinejad fervently believes in this should not be viewed as a problem. The fact that President Ahmadinejad is prepared to act out on this belief as Iranian President should be cause for alarm. As mayor of Tehran, Ahmadinejad refurbished a major boulevard on the grounds that the Mahdi was to travel along it upon his return. Similarly, soon after winning the presidency, Ahmadinejad allocated the equivalent of 12 million British pounds of government funds to enlarge the shrine and mosque of the Mahdi. Diverting public funds in this manner, from pressing social needs towards the "imminent" return of an Imam who has not made his appearance in eleven centuries, borders on either the criminal or the insane.

However, it is not only at the level of social expenditure that the Mahdi intrudes on Ahmadinejad's thoughts. Indeed, Ahmadinejad believes in reorienting the country's economic, cultural and political policies based on the Mahdi's return and judgment day. Moreover, the urgency to reorient the country's policies emanates from Ahmadinejad's belief that the Hidden Imam will appear in two years. How he knows that the Mahdi will appear in two years, time is anyone's guess, though some supporters of the Iranian President suggest that he must have heard it from the Mahdi himself. Ahmadinejad was also quite prepared to share his penetrating insights with the world when he addressed the United Nations in September, calling for the reappearance of the Imam.

Nevertheless, Ahmadinejad's address to the UN General Assembly was memorable for other reasons as well. When recounting his address to Ayatollah Javadi Amoli, one of Iran's leading clerics, Ahmadinejad stated that he felt that there was a light around him during his entire address at the podium *"during which time the world leaders did not blink. They were astonished as if a hand held them there and made them sit. It had opened their eyes and ears for the message of the Islamic Republic."* Some commentators have taken this mysticism of the Iranian President seriously and wonder if his saying these things serves a political purpose—transforming Ahmadinejad into the instrument of the Mahdi, thereby placing him above political reproach. In that case, the comment by Ayatollah Mesbah-Yazdi on there not being a need for future elections does fit into this broader political strategy.

Ahmadinejad's strong belief in the imminent return of the Mahdi does hold grave foreign policy implications. The fact that the Mahdi will only return at the End Times—a period characterised by intense international turmoil, is in itself instructive and may help to explain Ahmadinejad's foreign policy. Some analysts commented on how unfazed he was following the tremendous international outcry after he stated that Israel should be wiped off the map. However, from his ideological position both his statement and the reaction to it only contributed to the intense international turmoil that is a necessary precondition for the reappearance of the Mahdi. In that sense any punitive measures embarked upon by the international community would, rather than prompting a moderation of Tehran's current bellicose foreign policy, prompt the hawks around Ahmadinejad to congratulate themselves on a job well done. Moreover, such punitive measures may also serve to push moderates in Iran into the camp of Ahmadinejad, not because they share his ideology, but in order to provide a united front in defence of the national interest.

The Response

So how does one defeat the religious fundamentalists occupying high office? The first thing to realise is that, whilst both Bush and Ahmadinejad need to be neutralised in that as presidents of their respective countries they have tremendous power in order to engage in their religious fantasies, we should not personalise the issue either. Both Bush and Ahmadinejad head up powerful constituencies who share the beliefs of their president. The Reverend Pat Robertson's calling for the removal of Venezuelan President Hugo Chavez illustrates the point well. Thus the ideology of the movement that has brought them into high office needs to be delegitimised by their co-religionists. This is already happening in both the US and Iran.

In the US, clerics like Fritz Ritsch, Presbyterian minister in Bethesda, Maryland are deeply offended by Bush's simple dichotomy of good and evil and the characterisation that the US is on the side of angels. As he stated: *"It is by no means certain that we are as pure as the driven snow or that our international policy is so pure."* Indeed nearly all the mainstream churches, including Bush's own United Methodists are opposed to the war in Iraq. Meanwhile, academics, journalists, and various civil society groupings in the US have started opposing various aspects of the agenda of the Christian right. Amongst the most prominent of these has been former US President Jimmy Carter. In his latest book entitled *Our Endangered Values: America's Moral Crisis*, Carter, a devout Southern Baptist, raised serious concerns about the religious right's openly political agenda. He also argues that their open hostility to a range of sinners from homosexuals to the federal judiciary run counter to America's democratic freedom. Finally he calls for a clear separation of Church and State.

In Iran, too, the religious, academic, and political establishments have taken on Ahmadinejad in a dramatic way. Akbar Alami, an Iranian legislator, has questioned the President's claims of being surrounded by an aura of light, noting that not even Islam's holiest figures have made such claims. Ayatollah Mohammed Ali Abtahi, a former vice president, expressed his concern with the use of religious slogans and Ayatollah Yusuf Saanei urged: *"We should rule the country according to Islamic law, but we should not use religious ideas in politics. Even Ayatollah Khomeini did not believe we should do this."* Professor Hamid Reza Jalaipour at Tehran University also casts doubt on the broader politico-religious project of the President: *"The question is, can his reliance on Imam Mahdi be turned into a political ideology? I don't think so. Even the leading theologians in Qum do not take these allusions seriously."*

The second aspect of a response relates to neutralising the incumbent politically. In the US, this process is well advanced and George W. Bush has been transformed into a lame-duck president. What is interesting is that Republicans have also turned against their president as they vote with the Democrats. From Plamegate and Scooter Libby to the spiralling deficit, to the war in Iraq, and to the issue of illegal wiretaps, the Bush Administration is under extreme pressure. In recent weeks, the Administration suffered two humiliating setbacks. The first relates to it accepting the anti-torture amendment proposed by Republican Senator John McCain after initially making clear its objection to it. This underscores the weakness of the Bush Administration at this moment. Second, Bush and his fellow hawks had to fight tooth and nail to get the Patriot Act renewed. In the process major concessions were made on the part of the Administration.

In Iran, too, the process of vigorously neutralising President Ahmadinejad has begun. Inside the country, Ahmadinejad has been criticised for his seeming lack of tact and his confrontational style. For instance, shortly after Ahmadinejad's statement that Israel should be wiped off the map, Ali Akbar Rafsanjani, a former Iranian President and currently a major ally of Ayatollah Khamenei, stated at Friday prayers in Tehran: "*We have no problems with the Jews and highly respect Judaism as a holy religion.*" Those opposed to Ahmadinejad's bellicose foreign policy have also established discreet back-channel contacts with the Americans over Iran's nuclear programme.

The Iranian Parliament has also moved to politically neutralise Ahmadinejad in two ways, firstly, by undermining his populist political programme. In this regard it has already dismantled the centrepiece of Ahmadinejad's populist programme—the Imam Reza Care Fund that sought to provide interest-free loans for young people to marry as well as various employment programmes. Second, parliament has sought to weaken the President and strengthen the hand of Ayatollah Khamenei. For instance, the Speaker of Parliament, Gholamali Haddad-Adel, urged support for the concept of *Velayat-e-Faqih* (leadership of the supreme jurisprudent), introduced by Ayatollah Khomeini. However Ayatollah Khamenei is also taking active measures to weaken Ahmadinejad. Recently he gave the Expediency Council, a 32-member non-elected political arbitration body, sweeping new powers to supervise parliament, the judiciary, and the executive. This body is headed up by Rafsanjani. More ominously for Ahmadinejad, the Expediency Council's secretary, Mohsen Razaie, announced: "*The adjudication of the Expediency Council is the final word. And even if other state actors do not agree with it, it is still the final word and they have to accept that.*" Here it is interesting to note that Razaie used to be the commander of the Islamic Revolutionary Guard Corps (IRGC). This has led some commentators to believe that the senior echelons of the Revolutionary Guards may still be loyal to Ayatollah Khamenei as opposed to Ahmadinejad.

The third response has been to capitalise on the failure of the incumbent, thereby neutralising him further. Iraq has been such a failure for the Bush Administration. According to US statistics, 2,071 US soldiers have lost their lives and 16,000 others were wounded. Moreover, 39 percent of soldiers returning from Iraq are suffering from psychological trauma. In addition to the human costs, the Iraq and Afghanistan wars have already cost the American taxpayer $300 billion. Seen in the light of the US budget deficit, these economic costs are staggering. Opponents of the Bush Administration—Republican and Democrat—have been quick to attack and they have pressed Bush for a timetable for the withdrawal of US troops from Iraq. The senior military echelons have also voiced their concern on the sustainability of current troop levels in Iraq vis-à-vis securing other US interests. Failure in Iraq has certainly tempered the messianic zeal of Bush's foreign policy hawks. Thus their approach to the nuclear programme of Tehran and the already nuclear-armed Pyongyang regime has been radically different from that of Baghdad under Saddam Hussein when they refused to give Hans Blix and his nuclear weapons inspectors more time.

Whilst it is still early days for the Ahmadinejad administration, it is equally clear that a strategy of setting the incumbent up for failure that would then be used against him is being pursued. Consider the way the Iranian parliament has been dismantling aspects of Ahmadinejad's populist programme as described above. Whilst Ayatollah Khamenei's supporters may hope that this might undermine Ahmadinejad in the eyes of his supporters in that he will be unable to make good on his promises, it is equally clear that such a strategy is a high risk one. Ahmadinejad might well fail in his social programme and this might well anger his support base. However, Ahmadinejad could also direct this popular anger towards parliament, towards Ayatollah Khamenei and Rafsanjani. In the process, he could become stronger.

We also need to realise that Ahmadinejad is not simply passively allowing these machinations against him to take place. He has also gone on the offensive against his political rivals. For instance, he has recently purged the upper echelons of Iran's diplomatic corps. According to some reports, these may number as many as 40 of Iran's senior diplomats. These were inevitably allies of Rafsanjani or others who were appointed by the reformist Ayatollah Mohammed Khatami, Ahmadinejad's predecessor. Even more disconcerting is the fact that amongst those purged were Iran's ambassadors to London, Paris, Geneva, Berlin and Kuala Lumpur. This has resulted in Ed Blanche speculating on whether the purge of these particular diplomats was also an attempt on the part of Ahmadinejad to close the back-channel contacts existing between Tehran and Washington.

Conclusion

As this titanic power struggle continues in Tehran, there are deeper questions that need to be posed in the short-to-medium term. In the medium term, we do believe that the political power of the religious right-wing in the US will weaken as developments deteriorate in Iraq, Afghanistan and elsewhere, such as Latin America where we have seen the roll-back of American influence most dramatically in Evo Morales' Bolivia and Hugo Chavez's Venezuela. Indeed some pollsters are comparing George Bush's low popularity ratings with those of President Nixon at the time of the Watergate scandal. More importantly, the United States was established as a secular state and increasingly we see prominent individuals like President Carter as well as a plethora of civil society groups fighting back for the secular state promised in the US Constitution and the Bill of Rights. They seem to be winning the battle.

It is a very different situation in Iran. The 1979 Iranian revolution established a theocratic state that, in its current composition, cannot be secular. Nor, indeed can it be democratic. To understand this, we need to understand the fundamental split between Shiites and Sunnis in Islam. The democratic tradition is strong in Islam. Concepts such as freedom (*hurriyyah*), equality (*musawat*) and justice (*'adl*) are all intrinsic to the Qur'an. The fact that the first caliph after Prophet Muhammad's death in 632 C.E. was elected by majority consensus by a council of various Muslim tribes is ample proof of the democratic credentials of Islam. But this very election of the first Caliph saw the split between Sunnis and Shiites. Shiites broke away from mainstream Muslims after the election of the first Caliph since they wanted Imam Ali who was the cousin and son-in-law of Prophet Muhammad to succeed as Caliph. The majority (Sunnis) did not vote for Ali on the basis of his youth and inexperience. Thus the very origins of Shi'ism as a political doctrine lay in its anti-democratic foundations.

These anti-democratic foundations have been built upon by Ayatollah Khomeini, the founder of the Islamic Republic in 1979 when he established such concepts as the *Velayat-e-Faqih* or Leadership of the Supreme Jurisprudent. This concept has more in common with Plato's Philosopher-King and the Divine Right of Kings in the Middle Ages than with Islamic political thought and serves no other purpose than to consolidate the power of the ruling mullahs over a hapless population. It is important to understand this structure of the Iranian state in order to understand the limitation of reform of the state itself. This limitation was patently obvious during the presidency of Ahmadinejad's predecessor, Ayatollah Khatami. Despite him stressing moderation and a dialogue of civilizations as opposed to clash of civilizations, the reform movement foundered on the bedrock of a totalitarian theocratic state. One should also bear in mind that even without Ahmadinejad, the Iranian state will continue to be a source of insecurity to its own people as well as to the region—notice here Tehran's support for Hamas and Hezbollah.

In the short-term the most troubling aspect relates to Iran's nuclear programme. Whilst the Iranian regime stresses that their nuclear programme is for civilian purposes, as Mohammed El-Khawas notes the problem is that much of the technology used for civilian power generation could also be used for weapons as well. However, the problem goes beyond merely dual use technology in that the Iranian government did conceal its nuclear programme for eighteen years. It should be noted here that failure to notify the International Atomic Energy Agency (IAEA) is a clear breach of Iran's nuclear obligations under the Nuclear Non-Proliferation Treaty (NPT). Iran also failed to disclose to the IAEA all its uranium enrichment facilities. Other worrying indicators that Tehran may not be interested in nuclear energy for purely civilian purposes are the fact that "*. . . IAEA inspectors discovered traces of highly enriched uranium far above the levels needed for civilian use.*" Moreover, El-Khawas also notes that Iran is building the infrastructure for nuclear weapons production like the heavy-water reactor at Arak that can produce plutonium.

Still another reason to hold a somewhat sceptical stance towards the Iranian regime lies in the cat-and-mouse game it has been playing with the IAEA. In November 2004, for instance, Tehran agreed in Paris to freeze its entire uranium enrichment programme until a long-term agreement was reached. Some weeks later, however, when UN inspectors tried to confirm

Iran's compliance with the suspension, they were not permitted to put UN seals on some enrichment equipment at Natanz. These developments clearly do not inspire confidence in the regime. In the final instance, the international community cannot allow President Ahmadinejad's bellicose regime to possess nuclear weapons. More so, the international community cannot allow a man who believes in the return of the Mahdi and with him the End Times in two years time. The international community cannot allow a man who believes that a halo of light surrounds him to have his finger on a nuclear button.

Testimony Before the House Armed Services Committee Between Terrorism and Religious Extremism

Let me say at the outset that the gravest threat to the United States today is neither Islamic groups nor Islamic fundamentalism as such. The central threat facing the United States of America is the threat of catastrophic terror by al-Qaeda and its allies. The nature of this threat justifies the allocation of significant resources to counter the threat and defeat al-Qaeda and its allies. But we must be very careful in identifying who the core enemy is and not waste resources and energies on strategies that do not confront the primary threat, and worse yet, could backfire.

First, while we must oppose all terrorism, and we have many local enemies in various parts of the world, most such enemies do not pose the kind of catastrophic threat that al-Qaeda does, and thus do not warrant the kind of resources that could take away from our effort to directly confront the primary threat.

Second, although religious extremism is something most of us would oppose, we have to be very careful not to jump to the conclusion that the threat to the United States stems from religious extremism as such. We have extremists all over the world, as we do in our own country, but most of them do not seek to cause catastrophic harm to us and most do not have the capacity or the support to do so even if they wanted to.

Third, al-Qaeda presents such a high threat to the United States primarily for three reasons: Unlike most local extremist groups around the world, it has a demonstrated capacity to organize on a global scale and a demonstrated global reach. As a non-state actor, it is not sensitive to deterrence and thus is capable of being maximally reckless in its operations and thus poses the potential for catastrophic attacks that are limited only by its capabilities. And while it may care about local issues in the Muslim world, in the end its agenda is broader and more dangerous and could thus not be realistically satisfied by political means. In the end, it is reasonable to conclude that al-Qaeda does aim to overthrow the existing political order in the Muslim world and replace it with a Taliban-like fanatical order, and it sees the United States as the anchor of the existing order.

U.S. House of Representatives, November 3, 2005.

But it is wrong and even dangerous to assume that this aim of al-Qaeda is their primary strength, or that it is the primary reason some in the Muslim countries have expressed sympathy with it. It is also wrong to assume that most Muslim groups, including local extremist groups, share its objectives. We must differentiate above all what we see as pervasive unfavorable views in the Muslim world from the views of al-Qaeda and like-minded groups. We must also differentiate between the causes of anti-Americanism and the causes of al-Qaeda terrorism. If we don't, we risk helping push vastly diverse groups together in a way that undermines our effort to defeat al-Qaeda.

It is no secret that the United States has faced significant resentment in the past few years in Muslim countries. Is this a consequence of a rising clash of values that plays into the strengths of al-Qaeda? Most public opinion surveys in Arab and Muslim countries indicate otherwise. In my most recent survey completed October 24th, 2005, (with Zogby International) among 3900 Arabs in Saudi Arabia, Egypt, the United Arab Emirates, Jordan, Lebanon, and Morocco, 78 percent say that they base their views on American policies and only 12 percent say they base them on values. When given a number of Western, Muslim, and other non-Western countries to choose from as possible places to live or send family members to study, most of them name Western European countries or the US and those who name the other countries, including Muslim Pakistan, are in the single digit.

More importantly the cause of the sympathy that some have for al-Qaeda is vastly different from al-Qaeda's own aims: When asked what aspects of al-Qaeda, if any, they sympathize with most, only six percent said they sympathize with the aim of establishing a Taliban-like state, and only seven percent sympathized with al-Qaeda's methods. On the other hand, 35 percent said they sympathize with its standing up to the US and another 19 percent said they sympathize with its stand on behalf of Muslim causes such as the issue of Palestine. Twenty-six percent said "none."

These results are bolstered by other findings. Contrary to the Taliban world view, the vast majority of Arabs (88 percent), including in Saudi Arabia, want women to have the right to work outside the home either always or when economically necessary. That is precisely why al-Qaeda primarily highlights issues that resonate with the public in its recruitment tapes and strategies, such as Iraq, Palestine, and authoritarianism. Even those who oppose the US presence in Iraq and want to see the US defeated do not wish to have Abu Musaab al-Zarqawi as their ruler. That is not what they wish for their own children.

It is dangerous to have a high level of resentment of the United States, whatever its sources, not only because it may increase the ability of al-Qaeda and its allies to recruit, but also because people's incentives to help the United States to effectively combat the threat of al-Qaeda diminishes. If they resent us more than they fear al-Qaeda, our challenge increases dramatically. If they start believing, as most have, that one of our real aims is to weaken the Muslim world, not just to defeat al-Qaeda, al-Qaeda gains by default.

What are the issues for most Muslims in their attitudes toward the U.S.? What makes a difference in bridging the gap? Before I make some ending remarks on this issue, allow me to note that the Muslim world is not the only place where resentment of the United States runs high today, so some of the answers are not particular to the Muslim world and may have to do with the role of the United States in the current international system. But in the Arab and Muslim world there are some specific issues that we can identify.

From the public opinion surveys that I have conducted in the Middle East, the single most important demographic variable in the Arab world explaining unfavorable views of the United States was income. It speaks volumes about the rampant poverty and unemployment, linked to poor education, which must be confronted.

Second, regional issues are paramount. Iraq is certainly central, but the Palestinian-Israeli conflict remains the "prism of pain" through which Arabs see the United States. This speaks to the need for active American diplomacy to resolve regional conflict.

Third, Zogby International polls have shown clearly that those who have visited the United States or studied here, and those who have had other encounters with Americans in the region, were far more disposed to having a favorable opinion of the United States than those who didn't. This speaks to the need for major public diplomacy programs to encourage interactions.

In the end, we must define the central enemy correctly. It is primarily al-Qaeda and its allies as organizations that must be defeated. It is not terrorism broadly and it is not Islamism broadly. Terrorism is not an ideology, and al-Qaeda's ideology of seeking a Taliban-like world order is its source of weakness in the Muslim world, not its source of strength. Our strategy must isolate it by addressing the issues that most Muslims care about—not blur the distinction between the vast majorities with whom we have no principled quarrel and those few whose aims can never be reconciled with America's.

Allow me to end on a cautionary note. In broadly defining the threat as "Islamic extremism" without specifying what we mean exactly, we risk much. In fighting serious threats like that posed by al-Qaeda there is certainly a need to rely in part on significant covert operations as well as overt ones. But, there have recently been reports of the possible broadening of such operations to include extremist groups, leaders, and clergy. My worry is that we do not have, and probably never will, the kind of expertise that allows us to determine who's a friend and who's an enemy simply on the basis of utterances. One could end up targeting as suspects millions of people in a world of 1.2 billion Muslims. Given the deficient expertise in our bureaucracies in the languages, religions, and cultures of the Muslim world, we risk the chance of mistakes that could backfire, relying on locals who have their own agendas, and wasting precious resources. The strategy in the first place must remain focused on the operational and the logistical, not on what people say.

POSTSCRIPT

Is Religious and Cultural Extremism a Global Security Threat?

The events of 9/11 did not happen in a vacuum. They are merely one of several thousand acts of terrorism and violence perpetrated by groups bent on destroying their perceived enemy for professed reasons of faith. Clearly, anyone who is a victim of such attacks identifies the attacker as a threat to his or her security and, of course, global security. The central issues or questions arising from this are as follow:

- Is it religious and cultural extremism that fuels these attacks on security or merely geopolitical interests couched as faith?
- Do the organizers of these actions, like Osama bin Laden and others, really believe their rhetoric?
- Is this violence any more or less pronounced than it has been in the past and thus is it truly an emerging global security threat, or is it merely a continuing historical threat from the global fringe?

Scholars have been researching cultural and religious extremism for decades. The work is usually cyclical and results from the ebbs and flows of violence perpetrated by such groups. Whether it is Christian, Hindu, Muslim, or Jewish extremism fueling attacks on "non-believers," the focus is always on whether this behavior is growing, whether it is in response to external threats, and whether it is state sanctioned. Solomon argues with some persuasiveness that when political leaders develop devout fundamentalist views, they tend to be willing to engage in "extreme," that is, violent behavior to promote their perceived righteousness. They do this with all of the instruments of state power and, of course, are able to couch their policies as consistent with the national interest. His argument that Bush and Ahmadinejad share these dimensions and thus lead their countries to extremist policies bears further objective analysis. Yet it is still difficult to disentangle belief systems from policy decisions. We may believe that a Bush or Ahmadinejad used his spiritual fundamentalism as the central gyroscope on which all decisions are based; but in the final analysis we may never know.

Telhami tends to take a more real politic perspective when he contends that we must objectively analyze Islamic extremism for what it is and who it represents or, more importantly, the vast majority that it does not represent. It is al-Qaeda as a political organization that is the enemy, not Islam or fundamentalism per se. The rhetoric that we use and the tools that we employ must realize this fact and be consistent with it, lest we fuel religious "holy wars" that are frankly neither.

Ultimately, the question of whether religious or cultural extremism is a global security threat rests not with how we define such extremism or who believes what. It may simply be a function of two objective dimensions of a globalizing society. One is the ability of extremist groups to have global projection through technology and thus activate like-minded souls and second is the prevalence of weapons of mass destruction that, if allowed to fall into extremist hands, will most definitely pose a grave threat to global security.

The experience of the cold war tells us that rational, national interest usually wins out over mass destruction; the Cuban Missile Crisis is the quintessential example. But can anyone argue that rational self-interest will guide al-Qaeda zealots or anti-abortion activists or Jewish extremists when they confront their perceived enemies possessing nuclear or biological weapons? The likelihood of that catastrophe clarifies the question of extremism as a security threat: that it is merely a function of weapons possession.

Some interesting work in this area includes Sam Harris' controversial argument regarding religion and terror, *The End of Faith: Religion, Terror and the Future of Reason* (W.W. Norton & Company, 2004) and Christopher Hutchins' *God is Not Great: How Religion Poisons Everything* (Warner Books, 2007). In addition, take a look at Mark Juergensmeyer's *Terror in the Mind of God: The Global Rise of Religious Violence* (University of California Press, 2003) and J.P. Larsson's, *Understanding Religious Violence: Thinking Outside the Box on Terrorism* (Ashgate Publishing, 2004).

ISSUE 19

Is a Nuclear Iran a Global Security Threat?

YES: U.S. House of Representatives Permanent Select Committee on Intelligence, Subcommittee on Intelligence Policy, from "Recognizing Iran as a Strategic Threat: An Intelligence Challenge for the United States" (August 23, 2006)

NO: Office of Director of National Intelligence, from "Iran: Nuclear Intentions and Capabilities," *National Intelligence Estimate* (November 2007)

ISSUE SUMMARY

YES: The House Select Committee concludes that Iran's weapons program and missile development technology combined with the nature of fundamentalist regimes pose a grave security threat and thus must be addressed.

NO: The National Intelligence Estimate contends that Iran is not a global security threat because they have decided to suspend their nuclear weapons program and would not be able to develop the capacity for such weapons until at least 2015.

$\mathbf{T}$he issue of nuclear proliferation has been a global concern since the first atomic explosion at Alamogordo, New Mexico, in 1945. That event ushered in a new era in weaponry, war, strategy, and tactics that still resonates today. Each successive nuclear power and the proclaimed nuclear club of states (the United States, Russia, China, Great Britain, France, India, Pakistan) and unproclaimed countries (Israel, South Africa) have been deeply aware of the issue of proliferation. In fact, all of these states, to one degree or another, have largely agreed on the need to maintain the smallness of the nuclear club.

The fall of the Soviet Union did much to change the dynamics of nuclear proliferation policy. Essentially, many regional states with interests opposed to the United States now saw no countervailing superpower to protect their interests and thus faced a bandwagon or balancing dilemma. Do we move toward the United States as the preeminent power to satisfy our interests or balance against it by developing our own regional weapon deterrent to U.S.

hegemony? States across the globe chose either of these approaches and acted accordingly. Iran in rhetoric and actions has chosen the path of balancing against U.S. policy interests in a myriad of ways. They have supported groups opposed to U.S. policy interests, funded terrorism against Israel and the United States, and of course to some degree, pursued nuclear technology with the assistance of the French, Russians, and others.

In the following section, the U.S. government through two separate branches articulates the dichotomy of views regarding Iran as a global security threat. The House Select Committee report argues that Iran may indeed be the gravest threat to global security should they achieve nuclear status, which the report clearly argues they are committed to doing. They piece together Iranian rhetoric, policy positions, intelligence, and supposition to contend that Iran poses the gravest of threats to U.S. interests and thus to global security. The National Intelligence Estimate, which was released earlier this year, argues that Iran has suspended its nuclear program and as such does not pose a grave security threat and will not do so for the foreseeable future should they maintain their current course.

While both analyses agree that Iran pursues interests antithetical to the U.S. policy, they have different conclusions regarding Iran's current level of security threat and future scenarios.

YES

Recognizing Iran as a Strategic Threat: An Intelligence Challenge for the United States

"The annihilation of the Zionist regime will come . . . Israel must be wiped off the map . . . And God willing, with the force of God behind it, we shall soon experience a world without the United States and Zionism."[1]

"They have invented a myth that Jews were massacred and place this above God, religions and the prophets."[2]

"I officially announce that Iran has joined countries with nuclear technology."[3]

—Iranian President Mahmoud Ahmadinejad

Summary

Threats against the United States and Israel by Iranian President Ahmadinejad—coupled with advances in the Iranian nuclear weapons program, support for terror, and resistance to international negotiations on its nuclear program—demonstrate that Iran is a security threat to our nation that requires high caliber intelligence support. The seriousness of the Iranian threat has been amplified by the recent rocket attacks against Israel by the Iranian-backed Lebanese terrorist group Hezbollah, which, according to press accounts, has received as many as 10,000 rockets from Iran.[4]

Director of National Intelligence John Negroponte provided his assessment in his 2006 Annual Threat Report that Iran is seeking nuclear weapons.[5] America's intelligence agencies have also assessed the following about the Iranian threat:

- Iran has conducted a clandestine uranium enrichment program for nearly two decades in violation of its International Atomic Energy Agency (IAEA) safeguards agreement, and despite its claims to the contrary, Iran is seeking nuclear weapons. The U.S. Intelligence

U.S. House of Representatives, August 23, 2006.

Community believes that Tehran probably has not yet produced or acquired the fissile material (weapons-grade nuclear fuel) needed to produce a nuclear weapon; Director of National Intelligence John Negroponte has stated that Iran will not be "in a position to have a nuclear weapon" until "sometime between the beginning of the next decade and the middle of the next decade".[6]

- Iran likely has an offensive chemical weapons research and development capability.[7]
- Iran probably has an offensive biological weapons program.[8]
- Iran has the largest inventory of ballistic missiles in the Middle East. The U.S. Intelligence Community has raised the concern that Tehran may integrate nuclear weapons into its ballistic missiles.[9]
- Iran provides funding, training, weapons, rockets, and other material support to terrorist groups in Lebanon, the Palestinian Territories, and elsewhere.
- Elements of the Iranian national security apparatus are actively supporting the insurgency in Iraq.

Iran's August 22, 2006 letter expressing its willingness to enter into "serious negotiations" on its nuclear program presents significant challenges for U.S. policymakers who must assess Iranian intentions, the likelihood that it would abide by a new diplomatic agreement, and whether Iran would exploit a new agreement to advance its nuclear weapons program. The U.S. Intelligence Community will play an important role in helping policymakers evaluate these questions. U.S. intelligence agencies will have to devote resources to verify adherence to whatever result negotiations might produce—Iran's compliance with any agreement that may be reached, or the international community's compliance with any new trade sanctions the international community may place on Iran should efforts to use negotiations to resolve the crisis fail.

Intelligence Gaps and Why They Are Critical

Accurate and comprehensive intelligence is critical for the development of good policy. There is a great deal about Iran that we do not know. It would be irresponsible to list the specific intelligence gaps in an unclassified paper, as identifying our specific shortcomings would provide critical insights to the Iranian government. Suffice it to say, however, that the United States lacks critical information needed for analysts to make many of their judgments with confidence about Iran and there are many significant information gaps. A special concern is major gaps in our knowledge of Iranian nuclear, biological, and chemical programs. U.S. policymakers and intelligence officials believe, without exception, that the United States must collect more and better intelligence on a wide range of Iranian issues—its political dynamics, economic health, support for terrorism, the nature of its involvement in Iraq, the status of its nuclear, biological, and chemical weapons efforts, and many more topics of interest. The national security community must dedicate the personnel and resources necessary to better assess Iran's plans, capabilities, and intentions, and the Director of National Intelligence (DNI) must identify, establish, and report on intelligence goals and performance metrics to measure progress on critical fronts.

This report provides an unclassified assessment of the Iran question to help the American public understand the seriousness of the Iranian threat and to discuss ways U.S. intelligence collection and analysis against Iran must be improved.

The Nature of the Threat

Iran poses a threat to the United States and its allies due to its sponsorship of terror, probable pursuit of weapons of mass destruction, and support for the insurgency in Iraq. The profile of the Iranian threat has increased over the last year due to the election of President Mahmoud Ahmadinejad, who has made public threats against the United States and Israel, the continuation of Iranian nuclear weapons research, and the recent attacks by Hezbollah, an Iranian terrorist proxy, against Israel. Iran has provided Hezbollah with financial support and weapons, including the thousands of rockets Hezbollah fired against Israel in July and August 2006. Iran thus bears significant responsibility for the recent violence in Israel and Lebanon.

Iran's efforts since December 2005 to resume enrichment of uranium, in defiance of the international community, Tehran's willingness to endure international condemnation, isolation, and economic disruptions in order to carry out nuclear activities covertly indicate Iran is developing nuclear weapons. It is worth noting, however, that some outside experts hold another view and believe that senior Iranian leaders are divided on whether to proceed with a nuclear weapons program, and contend that some Iranian officials argue that Iran should pursue nuclear research within the guidelines of the Nuclear Non-Proliferation Treaty (NPT) so Iran can maintain international trade links.[10] These outside experts hold that until the leadership's intentions and decisions are known, it is difficult to assert with confidence that Iran is actually pursuing nuclear weapons.

A nuclear-armed Iran would pose a serious strategic threat to the United States and its allies because:

- A nuclear-armed Iran would likely embolden the leadership in Tehran to advance its aggressive ambitions in and outside of the region, both directly and through the terrorists it supports—ambitions that gravely threaten stability and the security of U.S. friends and allies.
- An Iranian leadership which believes a nuclear arsenal protects it from retaliation may be more likely to use force against U.S. forces and allies in the region, the greater Middle East, Europe, and Asia. Nuclear weapons could thus lower the threshold for Iran's use of conventional force.

The principal method Iran is pursuing at this time to produce fissile material for nuclear weapons is a process known as uranium enrichment. This method involves spinning gaseous uranium hexafluoride (UF6) in large numbers of centrifuge machines to increase the fraction of uranium-235 (U-235), the uranium isotope that can be used as weapons fuel. Naturally occurring uranium contains only a very small fraction of this isotope (0.71%), thus the need for enrichment process. Weapons-grade uranium contains about 90% U-235.

The IAEA has also uncovered evidence that Iran has pursued another route for nuclear weapons by producing plutonium. Plutonium can be separated from irradiated nuclear material such as "spent" fuel rods from a nuclear power reactor. North Korea is believed to have produced plutonium for nuclear weapons by separating plutonium from spent fuel rods.

- A nuclear-armed Iran would likely exacerbate regional tensions. Israel would find it hard to live with a nuclear armed Iran and could take military action against Iranian nuclear facilities. A deliberate or miscalculated attack by one state on the other could result in retaliation, regional unrest, and an increase in terrorist attacks.

Iran's Nuclear Weapons Program

Two decades ago, Iran embarked on a secret program to acquire the capability to produce weapons-grade nuclear material. Iran has developed an extensive infrastructure, from laboratories to industrial facilities, to support its research for nuclear weapons. Producing fissile material is a complicated process and Tehran faces several key obstacles to acquiring a nuclear capability: its inability to produce or purchase fissile material, the challenges of marrying a nuclear warhead to a missile, and the difficulty of adjusting its existing missiles to carry a nuclear payload.

Since 2002, the IAEA has issued a series of reports detailing how Iran has covertly engaged in dozens of nuclear-related activities that violate its treaty obligations to openly cooperate with the IAEA. These activities included false statements to IAEA inspectors, carrying out certain nuclear activities and experiments without notifying the IAEA, and numerous steps to deceive and mislead the IAEA.[11]

Recent Diplomatic Developments

From late 2003 until early 2006, the United Kingdom, France, and Germany (the "EU-3") attempted to find a diplomatic solution to the Iranian nuclear program that addressed unanswered questions about Tehran's nuclear activities and its lack of cooperation with the IAEA. Despite some signs of progress in 2004 and 2005, a major turning point occurred on September 24, 2005 when the IAEA Board of Governors passed a resolution concluding that Iran's "many failures and breaches" to comply with its obligations under the Nuclear Non-proliferation Treaty constituted noncompliance with the IAEA statute.[12] The resolution also expressed an "absence of confidence that Iran's nuclear program is exclusively for peaceful purposes" and called for Iran to reestablish a full and sustained suspension of uranium enrichment and reprocessing. The EU-3 effort collapsed in early 2006 when Iran defied the September 2005 IAEA resolution by announcing it would break IAEA seals placed on uranium enrichment facilities and end its moratorium on enriching uranium. As a result, on February 4, 2006, the IAEA Board of Governors reported Iran's failure to allay concerns about the nature of its nuclear program to the United Nations Security Council.[13] The Security Council met to discuss the Iranian nuclear program in March 2006 but was only able to pass a mild statement urging Iran to abide by its IAEA obligations due to opposition to tougher action by China and Russia.[14]

On June 6, 2006, Iran was presented with an incentives package backed by the United States, Russia, UK, France, and China to convince it to suspend its uranium enrichment program and begin negotiations with the EU-3 and the United States. After Iran refused to provide a clear answer as to whether or when it would respond to the offer, the UN Security Council passed Resolution 1696 on July 31, 2006 giving Iran until August 31, 2006 to fully implement a suspension of its uranium enrichment program as mandated by the IAEA Board of Governors resolution of February 4, 2006. If Iran does not comply by this date, Resolution 1696 states the Security Council's intention to take "additional measures" to compel Iran to comply. The United States is prepared to propose trade sanctions against Iran as the "additional measures."[15] Iranian President Ahmadinejad rejected Resolution 1696 on August 1, 2006, indicating that his country would not be pressured into stopping its nuclear program and stating "if some think they can still speak with threatening language to the Iranian nation, they must know that they are badly mistaken." Iran responded to the incentives package on August 22, 2006, claiming it had provided a "new formula" to resolve the dispute and was ready to enter into "serious negotiations." The details of this response were not available when this report went to press.

The recent attempt by the United States, the United Kingdom, France, and Germany to begin a new round of negotiations with Iran on ending its nuclear weapons program raises a number of difficult issues. U.S. policymakers must carefully evaluate Iran's August 22, 2006 response to the incentives package, Iranian intentions, and past behavior to make a judgment as to whether Tehran would abide by a new agreement curtailing its nuclear weapons program or would attempt to exploit a new agreement to advance its weapons program, such as by harvesting plutonium from new light water reactors an agreement might provide to Iran or continuing nuclear weapons research using the small uranium enrichment capability that EU-3 states are proposing to permit Iran to retain as part of an agreement. This evaluation will determine our participation in any negotiations and whether America could ultimately agree to be a party to a diplomatic agreement with Iran. A determination also needs to be made as to whether Iran's August 22, 2006 response addresses the requirements of UN Security Council Resolution 1696—which requires Iran to suspend its uranium enrichment program—and whether additional action by the Council, such as trade sanctions against Iran, are warranted. We expect the U.S. Intelligence Community would play an important role in assisting U.S. policymakers with these questions—including whether Iran can be trusted to abide by a diplomatic agreement—and to assess the effectiveness and implementation of trade sanctions against Iran that could be employed if diplomatic efforts fail.

Evidence for an Iranian Nuclear Weapons Program

The WMD Commission (officially known as the Commission on the Intelligence of the United States Regarding Weapons of Mass Destruction) concluded in its March 2005 unclassified report that "across the board, the Intelligence Community knows disturbingly little about the nuclear programs of many of the world's most dangerous actors."[16] American intelligence agencies do not know nearly enough about Iran's nuclear weapons program. However, based on what is known about Iranian behavior and Iranian deception efforts, the U.S. Intelligence Community assesses that Iran is intent on developing a nuclear weapons capability. Publicly available information also leads to the conclusion that Iran has a nuclear weapons program, especially taking into account the following facts:

- Iran has covertly pursued two parallel enrichment programs—a laser process based on Russian technology and a centrifuge process. The Russian government terminated cooperation with Iran on laser enrichment in 2001, following extensive consultations with the United States, and it appears to be no longer active.[17]
- In February 2004, Iran admitted to obtaining uranium centrifuge technology on the black market shortly after Dr. A.Q. Khan, the father of Pakistan's nuclear weapons program, confessed to secretly providing this technology to Iran, Libya, and North Korea.[18] Khan also sold nuclear bomb plans to Libya.[19] It is not known whether Khan sold nuclear weapon plans to Iran.
- The IAEA reported on February 27, 2006 that Iran has produced approximately 85 tons of uranium hexafluoride ($UF6$).[20] If enriched through centrifuges to weapons-grade material—a capability Iran is working hard to master—this would be enough for 12 nuclear bombs.[21]
- To produce plutonium, Iran has built a heavy water production plant and is constructing a large, heavy water-moderated reactor whose technical characteristics are well-suited for the production of weapons-grade plutonium. In support of this effort, Iran admitted in October 2003 to secretly producing small quantities of plutonium without notifying the IAEA, a violation of its treaty obligations.[22]
- The IAEA has discovered documentation in Iran for casting and machining enriched uranium hemispheres, which are directly relevant to production of nuclear weapons components.[23] The IAEA is also pursuing information on nuclear-related high-explosive tests[24] and the

design of a delivery system,[25] both of which point to a military rather than peaceful purpose of the Iranian nuclear program.

- The IAEA discovered evidence in September 2003 that Iran had covertly produced the short-lived radioactive element polonium 210 (Po-210), a substance with two known uses: a neutron source for a nuclear weapon and satellite batteries. Iran told the IAEA that the polonium 210 was produced for satellite batteries but could not produce evidence for this explanation.[26] The IAEA found Iran's explanation about its polonium experiments difficult to believe, stating in a September 2004 report that "it remains, however, somewhat uncertain regarding the plausibility of the stated purpose of the experiments given the very limited applications of short lived Po-210 sources."[27] . . .

Dubious Claims and Explanations for Iran's Nuclear Activities

Iran has engaged in an extensive campaign to conceal from the IAEA and the world the true nature of its nuclear program.

- Iran claims that its nuclear program is peaceful and for civilian electricity. While there are differences among some experts as to whether Iran may have an interest in a civilian nuclear program in addition to a weapons program, recent findings by the Department of Energy make a convincing case that the Iranian nuclear program is inconsistent with the Iranian Government's stated purpose of developing civil nuclear power in order to achieve energy independence.[28] Iran's claims that its nuclear program is peaceful also is belied by its record of non-cooperation with the IAEA, its decision to pursue nuclear technology covertly, and the fact that Iran does not have enough indigenous uranium resources to fuel even one power-generating reactor over its lifetime,[29] although it does have enough uranium to make several nuclear bombs.
- Aside from Iran's lack of uranium deposits, Iran's claim that its nuclear program is for electricity production appears doubtful in light of its large oil and natural gas reserves. Iran's natural gas reserves are the second largest in the world and the energy industry estimates that Iran flares enough natural gas annually to generate electricity equivalent to the output of four Bushehr reactors. Iran's energy reserves are compared in Figure 1.
- Furthermore, there is no rational reason for Iran to pursue a peaceful nuclear program in secret and risk international sanctions when the International Atomic Energy Agency encourages and assists peaceful nuclear programs. If Iran sincerely wanted a peaceful nuclear program, the IAEA would have helped it develop one provided that Tehran agreed to IAEA supervision and monitoring.

In an October 1, 2003 agreement with the EU-3, Iran pledged "to engage in full cooperation with the IAEA to address and resolve through full transparency all requirements and outstanding issues of the Agency." In spite of this, Iran has admitted to conducting certain nuclear activities

Figure 1

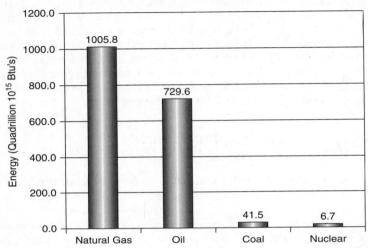

Iranian Energy Reserves by Type U.S. Department of Energy Chart, April 2006 [30]

Energy equivalence used = 1070 Btu/ft^3 natural gas, 5.8e6 Btu/barrel oil, 11,000 Btu/lb coal, 4.41e11 Btu/mton U-235. Source Nuclear Engineering: Theory and Technology of Commercial Nuclear Power–Knief. Energy data from March 2005 U.S. EIA Iran Country Analysis Brief.

to IAEA inspectors only after the IAEA presented it with clear evidence or asked Tehran to correct prior explanations that were inaccurate, implausible, or fraught with contradictions. Iran's admissions have been grudging and piecemeal, and its cooperation with IAEA inspectors has been accompanied by protests, accusations, and threats. Iran's recalcitrant behavior toward IAEA inspections drove IAEA Director Mohammed ElBaradei to declare in a November 2003 report:

> "The recent disclosures by Iran about its nuclear program clearly show that, in the past, Iran had concealed many aspects of its nuclear activities, with resultant breaches of its obligation to comply with the provisions of the Safeguards Agreement. Iran's policy of concealment continued until last month, with co-operation being limited and reactive, and information being slow in coming, changing and contradictory."[31]

Although it is likely that Iran is pursuing nuclear weapons, there is the possibility that Iran could be engaged in a denial and deception campaign to exaggerate progress on its nuclear program such as Saddam Hussein apparently did concerning his WMD programs. U.S. leaders need more definitive intelligence to judge the status of the Iranian nuclear program and whether there have been any related deception efforts.

While not an instance of Iranian perfidy, the spring 2006 decision by IAEA Director General ElBaradei to remove Mr. Christopher Charlier, the chief IAEA Iran inspector, for allegedly raising concerns about Iranian deception regarding its nuclear program and concluding that the purpose of Iran's nuclear program is to construct weapons, should give U.S. policymakers great pause. The United States has entrusted the IAEA with providing a truly objective assessment of Iran's nuclear program. IAEA officials should not hesitate to conclude that the purpose of Iranian nuclear program is to produce weapons if that is where the evidence leads. If Mr. Charlier was removed for not adhering to an unstated IAEA policy barring IAEA officials from telling the whole truth about the Iranian nuclear program, the United States and the international community have a serious problem on their hands.[32] . . .

The Threat from the Iranian Ballistic Missile Program

One of the most disturbing aspects of the Iranian WMD program is its determined effort to construct ballistic missiles that will enable Tehran to deliver conventional or, potentially, chemical, biological, or nuclear warheads against its neighbors in the region and beyond. Iran claimed last fall that its Shahab-3 missile can currently strike targets at distances up to 2,000 km (1,200 miles), including Israel, Egypt, Turkey, Saudi Arabia, Afghanistan, India, Pakistan, and southeastern Europe.[33] It is believed that Iran's Shahab-4 will have a range of 4,000 km (2,400 miles), enabling Iran to strike Germany, Italy, and Moscow. The below map by the Congressional Research Service[34] illustrates the estimated ranges of the ballistic missiles Iran is developing.

The U.S. Intelligence Community concluded in its November 2004 *721 Report:*

> "Iran's ballistic missile inventory is among the largest in the Middle East and includes some 1,300-km-range Shahab-3 medium-range ballistic missiles (MRBMs) and a few hundred short-range ballistic missiles (SRBMs)—including the Shahab-1 (Scud-B), Shahab-2 (Scud C), and Tondar-69 (CSS-8)—as well as a variety of large unguided rockets. Already producing Scud SRBMs, Iran announced that it had begun production of the Shahab-3 MRBM and a new solid-propellant SRBM, the Fateh-110. In addition, Iran publicly acknowledged the development of follow-on versions of the Shahab-3. It originally said that another version, the Shahab-4, was a more capable ballistic missile than its predecessor but later characterized it as solely a space launch vehicle with no military applications. Iran is also pursuing longer-range ballistic missiles."[35]

DNI Negroponte stated a similar finding in February 2006, adding his concern that Iran may weaponize missiles to deliver nuclear warheads:

> ". . . the danger that it [Iran] will acquire a nuclear weapon and the ability to integrate it with the ballistic missiles Iran already possesses is a

reason for immediate concern. Iran already has the largest inventory of ballistic missiles in the Middle East, and Tehran views its ballistic missiles as an integral part of its strategy to deter—and if necessary retaliate against—forces in the region, including US forces."[36]

IAEA Director General ElBaradei also raised the specter of Iran adapting its missiles to transport nuclear warheads when he wrote in a February 2006 report that the IAEA had asked Iran to meet to discuss "tests related to high explosives and the design of a missile re-entry vehicle, all of which could involve nuclear material." ElBaradei reported that Iran refused to discuss its alleged missile re-entry vehicle with the IAEA.[37] These and other recent reported developments about Iran's ballistic missile program are alarming and pose a serious threat to America's allies, especially in the Middle East.

Figure 2

Ranges of Iran's Missiles

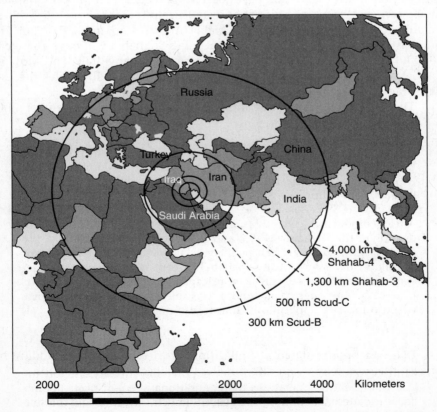

Iran's WMD and Missile Programs: What Policymakers Need from U.S. Intelligence Agencies

Although Iran, being a denied area with active denial and deception efforts, is a difficult target for intelligence analysis and collection, it is imperative that the U.S. Intelligence Community devote significant resources against this vital threat. Detection and prevention are the two most important intelligence challenges concerning Iran's WMD and ballistic missile programs.

The U.S. Intelligence Community needs to improve its analysis and collection on the problem of detecting and characterizing Iran's WMD programs. This is particularly important regarding Iran's nuclear program, where U.S. efforts to reach a diplomatic agreement are at a critical and sensitive point. The IC's ability to provide accurate and timely intelligence on a number of facets of Iran's program will be equally critical whether there is a negotiated solution to the current nuclear impasse or if sanctions are imposed.

Improving intelligence collection and analysis to better understand and counter Iranian influence and intentions is vital to our national security. The Intelligence Community lacks the ability to acquire essential information necessary to make judgments on these essential topics, which have been recognized as essential to U.S. national security for many, many years.

An important dimension of the detection of Iran's WMD program is how intelligence analysts use intelligence to characterize these programs in their analysis. Intelligence Community managers and analysts must provide their best analytic judgments about Iranian WMD programs and not shy away from provocative conclusions or bury disagreements in consensus assessments.

It is vital that the Intelligence Community also provide intelligence the United States can use to prevent Iran from acquiring WMD technology and materials. This is a global challenge and the U.S. Intelligence Community must be prepared to play an important role as the Administration seeks the cooperation of like-minded government officials in efforts to prevent Iran from acquiring WMD or discouraging the Iranian regime and people from continuing to pursue such programs.

How Iran Is Destabilizing Iraq

Iranian involvement in Iraq is extensive, and poses a serious threat to U.S. national interests and U.S. troops. It is enabling Shia militant groups to attack Coalition forces and is actively interfering in Iraqi politics. General John Abizaid told the Senate Armed Service Committee on March 14, 2006:

> "Iran is pursuing a multi-track policy in Iraq, consisting of overtly supporting the formation of a stable, Shia Islamist-led central government while covertly working to diminish popular and military support for U.S. and Coalition operations there. Additionally, sophisticated bomb making material from Iran has been found in improvised explosive devices (IEDs) in Iraq."[38]

DNI Negroponte stated in February 2006 that Iran has demonstrated a degree of restraint in its support of violent attacks against Coalition forces in Iraq:

> "Tehran's intentions to inflict pain on the United States in Iraq has been constrained by its caution to avoid giving Washington an excuse to attack it, the clerical leadership's general satisfaction with trends in Iraq, and Iran's desire to avoid chaos on its borders."[39]

Some Iranian assistance to Iraqi insurgents already has been provided. However, through its terrorist proxies, intelligence service, Revolutionary Guard Corps (IRGC), and other tools of power projection and influence, Iran could at any time significantly ramp up its sponsorship of violent attacks against U.S. forces in Iraq and elsewhere in the Middle East if it believed doing so would keep the United States distracted or would otherwise be in Iran's national interest. Iran's support of the June 25, 1996 truck bombing of the Khobar Towers in Saudi Arabia, a terrorist act that killed 19 U.S. Servicemen and wounded 500, demonstrated that Tehran is willing to organize attacks on U.S. personnel.[40]

Iranian Involvement in Iraq's Political Process

In February 2005, then-Defense Intelligence Agency (DIA) Director Lowell E. ("Jake") Jacoby testified to the Senate Select Committee on Intelligence that Iran seeks a "weakened and Shia-dominated Iraq that is incapable of posing a threat to Iran."[41] Iran has long supported Iraqi Shia political parties, both in Iraq and in exile, and it continues to work through these groups to affect the political process. Non-government observers believe that Tehran consciously works to gain leverage with multiple political leaders, parties and organizations in the current Iraqi political system—even those who are no fans of Iran, such as Shia cleric and Mahdi Army leader Muqtada al-Sadr—to ensure it has options for influencing events no matter which group gains prominence in the Iraqi polity.[42]

On March 16, 2006, Ali Larijani, Secretary of Iran's Supreme National Security Council, indicated Iran was prepared to begin direct talks with the U.S. on Iraq, stating that, "the important thing for us is an established government in Iraq and that security is restored." Larijani was responding to Secretary of State Condoleezza Rice's authorization for U.S. Ambassador to Iraq Zalmay Khalilzad to hold bilateral talks limited to the situation in Iraq. Secretary Rice responded on March 24th that such talks would place "at the appropriate time." National Security Adviser Hadley expressed skepticism about the sincerity of Iran's offer to engage in talks with the U.S., noting that "Iran waited months to agree to a U.S. proposal to take up the issue, and did so only after its atomic program was referred to the UN Security Council for possible sanctions.[43]

Some have raised concerns about opening a dialogue with Iran while it is backing death squads in Iraq and insurgent attacks on U.S. forces. Ambassador Khalilzad said during a March 23, 2006 *Washington Post* interview that he believed Iran was publicly professing its support for Iraq's stalemated political process while its military and intelligence services back outlawed militias and insurgent groups. *The Washington Post* quoted Khalilzad stating that

> "Our judgment is that training and supplying, direct or indirect, takes place, and that there is also provision of financial resources to people, to militias, and that there is presence of people associated with Revolutionary Guard and with MOIS [Ministry of Intelligence and Security]."[44]

Iranian Support to Iraqi Militias

The U.S. Intelligence Community, the Department of State, and the Department of Defense have reported that Iran provides training, funds, and weapons to a variety of Shia militias in Iraq which have been linked to assassinations, human rights abuses, and the planting of improvised explosive devices (IEDs) designed to maim and kill U.S. troops.[45] The full extent of Iranian support to these militias is unknown, but three groups in particular have received Iranian support.

- Badr Brigade: The 20,000 strong Badr Brigade (recently renamed the Badr Organization to symbolize a transformation to a political organization) is widely believed by experts inside and outside of the U.S. Government to be controlled by the Iranian-supported Supreme Council for the Islamic Revolution in Iraq (SCIRI). It has been accused of running "death squads" that kidnap, torture, and kill Sunnis, including the 173 Sunnis found in a secret prison in a Ministry of Interior building in Jadriyah in November 2005.[46] General George Casey, the U.S. military commander in Iraq, said on December 12, 2005 that the Badr Brigade openly placed its personnel in security units in the Iraqi internal security forces, and that the loyalty of these forces remains primarily to the militia, not the national security forces.[47] Given the degree of Iranian influence over the group, the Badr Organization is widely seen as a means through which Iran has "taken over many of the Iraqi Interior Ministry's intelligence activities and infiltrated its elite commando units," to the point that "the Interior Ministry had become what amounted to an Iranian fifth column inside the U.S.-backed Iraqi government."[48] The organization is also believed to help Iran move agents, weapons, and materiel into Iraq.[49] If Iran indeed has such influence inside the Ministry of Interior, it will have great insights into the Iraqi police force's strategies, plans and possibly even operations, thus giving Iran opportunities to defeat Iraqi efforts to undermine Shia extremists in Iraq.
- Wolf Brigade: The 2,000-member "Wolf Brigade," a Badr offshoot, is led by SCIRI member Abu Walid and reported to be under the control of Iranian-influenced officials at the Interior Ministry.[50] It is reputed to have targeted Iraqi Sunnis for kidnapping, torture, and murder.[51]

Iranian Involvement in Attacks on U.S. and Coalition Forces

Evidence has mounted that Iran has facilitated IED attacks on U.S. forces. In a March 13 speech, President Bush stated that "coalition forces have seized IEDs and components that were clearly produced in Iran" and that "some of the most powerful IED's we're seeing in Iraq today include components that came from Iran."[52] DNI Negroponte echoed the president's remarks when he told Congress in February 2006 that:

> "Iran provides guidance and training to select Iraqi Shia political groups and weapons and training to Shia militant groups to enable anti-Coalition attacks. Tehran has been responsible for at least some of the increasing lethality of anti-Coalition attacks by providing Shia militants with the capability to build IEDs with explosively formed projectiles similar to those developed by Iran and Lebanese Hezbollah."[53]

While there appears to be clear evidence that Iraqi insurgent groups receive assistance from entities in Iran, however, Joint Chiefs Chairman General Peter Pace asserted that he has seen no evidence Iran's *government* is the driving force behind such activity.[54] Better intelligence collection and analysis is needed to determine the nature and extent of Iranian ties to Iraqi insurgent groups.

Iran's Role in Iraq: What Policymakers Need from U.S. Intelligence Agencies

The United States needs a range of information to adequately assess Iran's intentions and activities in Iraq. The U.S. needs to understand better Tehran's ongoing support to Shia militants conducting lethal attacks in Iraq in order to save Coalition lives and ensure the future of a stable, democratic Iraqi government. Insights into Tehran's efforts to exert long-term influence over Iraqi institutions will be important as well.

Iranian Support for Terrorism Outside Iraq

The July 2006 Hezbollah attacks on Israel likely is the latest use of terrorism by Iran to advance its regional policy goals. Iran has used terrorism over the years as a means of projecting power, mostly against Israel but also against internal dissidents and other adversaries in Europe. The State Department's annual *Country Reports on Terrorism 2004* (issued April 2005) calls Iran "the most active state sponsor of terrorism," stating that the MOIS and the IRGC both "provided Lebanese Hezbollah and Palestinian terrorist groups—notably HAMAS, the Palestinian Islamic Jihad, the al-Aqsa Martyrs' Brigade, and the Popular Front for the Liberation of Palestine-General Command—with funding, safe haven, training and weapons."[55] Secretary of State Condoleezza Rice has referred to Iran as the "central banker for terrorism."[56]

Iran's links are strongest to Lebanese Hezbollah and Palestinian rejectionist groups, both of which have been designated by the United States as foreign terrorist organizations. Tehran is reported to have links to al-Qaeda, though U.S. intelligence information is insufficient to make a conclusive judgment on this relationship.

Hezbollah

Iran's influence over Hezbollah gives it a role in the Israeli-Palestinian peace process, making Tehran a player on an issue of global importance. Its ties to Hezbollah also provide Iran with a power projection tool—"an extension of their state," according to State Department Counterterrorism Coordinator Henry Crumpton—allowing it to authorize (or prevent) terror attacks as a way to exercise influence in the region or beyond.[57] Iran also employs the threat of stepped-up terror attacks as a deterrent against hostile powers; the possibility that Iran might unleash its terrorist proxies against the United States and its allies undoubtedly gives pause to those who might call for aggressive action against Iran.

The extent to which Iran directed the July/August 2006 Hezbollah attacks against Israel is unknown, as are possible Iranian objectives for provoking hostilities with Israel at this point in time. Certainly, Iran could benefit if the international community's attention was diverted away from Iran's nuclear program. It is urgent that the U.S. Intelligence Community redouble its efforts to uncover any Iranian agenda behind the attacks and learn how Iran may be directing them.

Iranian assistance to Hezbollah consists of funds, training, equipment, and intelligence.[58] Hezbollah leader Hassan Nasarallah stated in a May 2005 speech that Hezbollah had more than 12,000 rockets with ranges of 25–45 miles.[59] The IRGC reportedly has a strong presence in Lebanon to coordinate aid to Hezbollah, including Stinger surface-to-air missiles, Katyusha rockets, mortars, and other weaponry.[60] The State Department *Country Reports on Terrorism* stated that Iran provided Hezbollah an unmanned aerial vehicle that it flew in November 2004 into Israeli airspace, providing target reconnaissance regarding northern Israeli cities.[61] There were several unconfirmed news accounts in August 2006 of Hezbollah UAVs crashing or being shot down by Israeli forces. The press accounts claimed the UAVs may have been packed with explosives.[62]

Hezbollah has also served as a conduit for Iranian provision of weapons to Palestinian groups inside Israel. The ship *Karine-A,* seized by Israel in the Red Sea in January 2002, was filled with weapons destined for the Palestinian Authority; Hezbollah reportedly provided the funds for purchasing the weapons and hiring the ship, which was loaded in Iran.[63]

Palestinian Groups

The State Department *2004 Country Reports on Terrorism* stated that "Iran provided Palestinian terrorist groups—notably HAMAS, the Palestinian Islamic Jihad, the al-Aqsa Martyr's Brigades, and the Popular Front for the Liberation of Palestine-General Command—with funding, safe haven, training, and weapons."[64]

- <u>HAMAS:</u> While Iran has provided funding to HAMAS in the past, Tehran has increased its promise of support since the beginning of 2006. After HAMAS won Palestinian legislative elections in January, leading Western governments to cut off aid to the PA government, Iran has pledged to provide $250 million in financial support and urged other Muslim countries to do so as well.[65] It is not clear, however, whether Iran (or other countries) will actually provide such funding.
- <u>Palestinian Islamic Jihad (PIJ):</u> As early as 1993, PIJ founder Fathi Shiqaqi publicly acknowledged receiving funding from Iran, which it then provided to operatives in the West Bank and Gaza.[66] Israeli intelligence agencies assert that Iran continues to influence the group and that Tehran has urged PIJ to launch attacks ahead of the March 2006 Knesset elections.[67]
- <u>Popular Front for the Liberation of Palestine-General Command (PFLP-GC):</u> The PFLP-GC was the first Palestinian group to receive funding from Iran, in 1989. Its guerrillas launched numerous attacks against Israel in the 1980s and 1990s and has served in recent years as a leading conduit through which Iran provided weapons and materiel to HAMAS and PIJ.

Al-Qaeda

It is unclear whether and to what extent Iran may have ties to al-Qaeda. The primarily Sunni Arab terrorist group is an unlikely partner for the overwhelmingly Shia Persian nation; its leader, Osama bin Laden, recently referred to Shia in Iraq as "rejectionist," "traitors" and "agents of the Americans."[68] Bin Laden's primary lieutenant in Iraq, the recently killed Abu Musab al-Zarqawi, declared a Sunni jihad against Iraqi Shia, targeting the community that hosts Iran's primary allies and proxies in Iraq.

That said, some observers believe that Iran is actively supporting al-Qaeda operatives; others suggest that Iran may passively tolerate the group's activities in the country. In November 2005, Under Secretary of State for Political Affairs R. Nicholas Burns said the U.S. believed "that some Al Qaeda members and those from like-minded extremist groups continue to use Iran as a safe haven and as a hub to facilitate their operations," without stating whether the Iranian government is actively complicit in these activities.[69] Similarly, without claiming that the Iranian regime actively provides assistance, Secretary of Defense Rumsfeld stated as early as April 2002 that "there is no question but that al-Qaeda have moved into and found sanctuary in Iran. And there is no question but that al-Qaeda has moved into Iran and out of Iran to the south and dispersed to some other countries."[70]

Iran has had a number of senior al-Qaeda operatives in custody since 2003, and the United States has repeatedly called for Iran to bring these individuals to justice. The Iranian government appears to have little willingness to do so, though it is not clear whether its reasons stem from sympathy for al-Qaeda's shared hostility toward the United States or simply a desire to use the terrorists as a future bargaining chip with Washington.[71] The nature of Iran's relationship with al-Qaeda, if any, is unclear, and U.S. intelligence must enhance its insights into this critical dynamic.[72]

WMD Terrorism

The Department of State provided a persuasive assessment of Iran and WMD terrorism in its *2005 Country Reports on Terrorism:*

> "State sponsors of terrorism pose a grave WMD threat. A WMD program in a state sponsor of terrorism could enable a terrorist organization to acquire a sophisticated WMD. State sponsors of terrorism and nations that fail to live up to their international obligations deserve special attention as potential facilitators of WMD terrorism. Iran presents a particular concern, given its active sponsorship of terrorism and continued development of a nuclear program. Iran is also capable of producing biological and chemical agents or weapons. Like other state sponsors of terrorism with WMD programs, Iran could support terrorist organizations seeking to acquire WMD."[73]

Several outside experts have asserted that while it is possible Iran could give WMD to terrorists, they believe this is highly unlikely. For example, Anthony Cordesman and Khalid Al-Radhan believe that, "plausible deniability is doubtful, and an opponent simply may not care if it can prove Iran is responsible."[74] Middle East expert Kenneth Pollack put it more bluntly: "The use of proxies or cutouts would not shield Iran from retaliation," and neither the United States nor any other victim would hesitate to respond with full force."[75]

Iran's Support of Terrorism: What Policymakers Need from U.S. Intelligence Agencies

The United States needs a range of information to adequately assess Iran's sponsorship of terror. Current events in Lebanon highlight the danger Iranian support for terrorist proxies, such as Hezbollah, poses for peace in the region and underscores the need for timely and accurate intelligence on a wide range of issues related to Iran, Hezbollah, and other groups that enjoy Iranian support. Iran's relationship with its proxies give it a global reach, which would be even more alarming should Tehran divert WMD to these groups.

Conclusion: Iran Is a Serious Security Threat on Which the United States Needs Better Intelligence

This report attempts to explain to the American people that, although intelligence is inadequate to develop a thorough understanding of the threat posed by Iranian activities, there is sufficient information available to conclude that Iran poses a serious threat to U.S. national security and to the security of our friends and allies. Based only on unclassified material, it is reasonable to assume that Iran has a program to produce nuclear weapons. The United States needs better intelligence to assess the status of Iran's nuclear program and how soon it will have an operational nuclear weapon. Iran's misleading reports to the IAEA about its nuclear research activities, many of which violate its treaty agreements, suggest hostile intentions. Iran's missile programs provide Tehran with the ability to strike targets far beyond its borders, as do its support of terrorism and meddling in Iraq. Moreover, the IAEA's belief that the Iranians may be testing missile reentry vehicles with nuclear applications poses the real possibility that Iran could spark a major regional war.

The July/August 2006 Hezbollah attacks against Israel sparked an outbreak of violence with major ramifications for peace in the Middle East. These attacks may be fully backed by Tehran and could mark the beginning of a new and more dangerous policy by Iran to use a terrorist proxy to inflict pain on Israel and the West. The U.S. Intelligence Community will play an important role in assisting American policymakers in ascertaining the extent and objectives of any Iranian role in the Hezbollah attacks.

The worst-case scenario is that Iran is run by a government into which we have little insight, and that this government is determined to acquire nuclear, chemical and biological weapons, support terrorism, and undermine political stability in Iraq. However, before we can conclude that this worst-case scenario is the reality faced by the United States, the Intelligence Community must provide policymakers with better insights into developments inside Iran.

The U.S. Intelligence Community will play a pivotal role before, during, and after any negotiations with Iran. Iran's August 22, 2006 response to the nuclear incentives package will need a thorough and complete evaluation. Policymakers will need high quality intelligence to assess Iranian intentions to prepare for any new round of negotiations on its nuclear program and for possible future discussions about the situation in Iraq. U.S. negotiators will need as complete an understanding as possible about the Iranian nuclear program, including its research facilities and its leaders' intentions. U.S. intelligence agencies will need to assess the likelihood of activities at undeclared nuclear facilities and how to verify Iranian compliance with a possible agreement on its nuclear program. If negotiations with Iran fail and a new set of trade sanctions are placed on Iran, the Intelligence Community will need to provide analysis and collection to verify international compliance with the sanctions. These and many other tasks will require a substantial commitment of collection and analytical resources by U.S. intelligence agencies.

Recommendations for the Intelligence Community

U.S. intelligence agencies need to take a wide range of steps to fill intelligence gaps and improve their collection and analysis of information on Iran, including:

1. <u>Improve analysis.</u> The IC's analysis on vital national security issues like Iran must be thorough and timely. Analysts must evaluate all contingencies and consider out-of-the box assessments that challenge conventional wisdom. Iran WMD analysis could improve once the DNI Iran and Counterproliferation mission managers integrate analysts more thoroughly with collectors and with their colleagues in other agencies. Iran analysts must also make greater use of open source intelligence on Iran, the availability of which is augmented by Iran's prolific (if persecuted) press.

2. <u>Improve coordination on Iran-specific issues.</u> To make effective use of the full range of tools and capabilities at its disposal, the Intelligence Community must ensure that each agency's efforts are fully coordinated and deconflicted. On the recommendation of the WMD Commission, the Director of National Intelligence established a Mission Manager for Iran to develop and implement a coordinated IC-wide strategy for Iran. This function, while still new, needs committed leadership and interagency cooperation to succeed. At a more operational level, individual agencies must ensure that their staffs—operators, analysts, targeters, and others—share information with each other and with their counterparts in other agencies to ensure that resources are allocated effectively and efforts are not duplicated by multiple agencies. The Mission Manager must focus in particular on filling the many intelligence gaps that prevent a thorough understanding and assessment of critical issues.

3. <u>Improve coordination on counterproliferation issues.</u> The DNI has directed that the National Counterproliferation Center (NCPC), created by the Intelligence Reform and Terrorism Prevention Act of 2004, serve as the IC's Mission Manager for Counterproliferation. The NCPC can potentially play an important advisory role in improving proliferation analysis and collection. The NCPC and Iran Mission Manager must coordinate closely to ensure that they pursue consistent and complementary strategies on issues related to Iran's potential WMD programs. Furthermore, all IC experts should be called upon to bring their knowledge to bear on the problem. WMD experts at the Department of Energy National Labs, for example, should be more thoroughly integrated into the debates that take place inside the Beltway so others in the Intelligence Community can benefit from their in-depth expertise.

4. <u>Enhance HUMINT capabilities.</u> The DNI has recognized that the Intelligence Community needs to improve its human intelligence (HUMINT) capabilities writ large, both on foreign intelligence and counterintelligence matters. Certainly, the nature of the Iranian target poses unique HUMINT challenges; since American officials have so little physical access to Iran, it is difficult to collect information there.

5. <u>Augment linguistic capabilities.</u> Without question, the IC needs more staff who speak Farsi at a native or professionally proficient level.[76] HUMINT collectors need such language skills to operate effectively in Iranian communities around the world; signals intelligence (SIGINT) analysts need language fluency to understand intercepted communications; and analysts need language skills to read original documents

and develop a feel for Iran's political system and culture. The Intelligence Community and the Defense Department should devote more resources to Farsi language training, but they should also work with other parts of the U.S. government to promote the teaching of Farsi and other critical foreign languages in civilian schools and universities. The country needs more high school and college graduates with critical language skills than the U.S. Government alone can train.

The Intelligence Community must also employ creative means of working around the shortage of skilled linguists. The National Virtual Translation Center (NVTC), created by the Intelligence Authorization Act for Fiscal Year 2003, has the potential to fill many of the Community's language shortfalls. The NVTC's use of contract linguists, many of whom have security clearances, gives it the flexibility to respond immediately to urgent taskings, augment capabilities provided by full-time IC staff, and provide real-time support to intelligence missions around the world. It is a unique and invaluable asset. The Director of National Intelligence must ensure that the Center receives the personnel and funding it requires to serve its IC customers in the coming fiscal years.

6. <u>Strengthen counterintelligence efforts.</u> We must assume that Iran attempts to collect intelligence on U.S. Government plans, strategies, and capabilities, as well as on sensitive technologies. The Intelligence Community must ensure that comprehensive counterintelligence training is given to professionals throughout the national security and scientific communities, both inside government and out, who are likely to be targeted by Iranian intelligence collectors.

7. <u>Define goals and develop metrics.</u> The DNI must clearly identify his goals for improving Iran-related collection and analysis so members of the Community know what they are supposed to achieve. He must also promulgate detailed performance metrics so Community managers can assess, on an ongoing basis, whether they are improving capabilities and making progress toward their critical intelligence objectives. The DNI should share these objectives and metrics with it so the legislative branch can conduct meaningful, continuous oversight of its activities regarding this critical national security challenge.

Notes

1. Remarks by Iranian President Mahmoud Ahmadinejad during a meeting with protesting students at the Iranian Interior Ministry, October 25, 2005.

2. Iranian President Mahmoud Ahmadinejad in a speech given in southeastern Iran, December 14, 2005.

3. Comments by Iranian President Mahmoud Ahmadinejad during a nationally televised ceremony, April 11, 2006.

4. Neil MacFaquhar and Hassan Fattah, "At crossroads, Hezbollah goes on the attack," *International Herald Tribune,* July 16, 2006 . . .; Michael Gordon, "Militants Are Said to Amass Missiles in South Lebanon," *New York Times,* July 16, 2006. . . .

5. Director of National Intelligence John D. Negroponte, "Annual Threat Assessment of the Director of National Intelligence," Testimony to the Senate Select Committee on Intelligence, February 2, 2006.

6. Interview of Director of National Intelligence John D. Negroponte with James Naughtie of the BBC, June 2, 2006. . . .

7. U.S. Department of State, Adherence and Compliance with Arms Control, Nonproliferation, and Disarmament Agreements, August 2005, pp. 55–56.

8. U.S. Department of State, Adherence and Compliance with Arms Control, Nonproliferation, and Disarmament Agreements, August 2005, pp. 20–21.

9. Director of National Intelligence John D. Negroponte, "Annual Threat Assessment of the Director of National Intelligence," Testimony to the Senate Select Committee on Intelligence, February 2, 2006.

10. Cited in Ray Takeyh, testimony before the Senate Committee on Foreign Relations, March 2, 2006.

11. A complete set of IAEA documentation on the Iranian nuclear program is available on the IAEA website. . . .

12. IAEA Board of Governors Resolution, September 24, 2005, GOV/2005/ 77. . . .

13. IAEA Board of Governors document GOV/2006/14, February 4, 2006.

14. UN Security Council Presidential Statement, March 29, 2006, S/PRST/ 2006/15.

15. "Iran Reported Ready for Serious Talks on Nuclear Program," CNN.com, August 22, 2006. . . .

16. Commission on the Intelligence Capabilities of the United States Regarding Weapons of Mass Destruction ("The WMD Commission"), *Report to the President of the United States,* March 31, 2005, p. 4.

17. U.S. Department of State, Adherence and Compliance with Arms Control, Nonproliferation, and Disarmament Agreements, August 2005, p. 77.

18. "Implementation of the NPT Safeguards Agreement in the Islamic Republic of Iran: Report by the Director General." International Atomic Energy Agency, Vienna, Austria, GOV/2004/11, February 24, 2004, p. 8; CNN.com, March 10, 2005. . . .

19. Michael Laufer, "A.Q. Khan Chronology, Proliferation Brief, Volume 8, Number 8, Carnegie Endowment, 2006. . . .

20. "Implementation of the NPT Safeguards Agreement in the Islamic Republic of Iran: Report by the Director General." International Atomic Energy Agency, Vienna, Austria, GOV/2006/15, February 27, 2006, p. 15.

21. Reuters via DefenseNews.com, April 11, 2006. . . .

22. "Implementation of the NPT Safeguards Agreement in the Islamic Republic of Iran: Report by the Director General." International Atomic Energy Agency, Vienna, Austria, GOV/2003/75, November 10, 2003, p. 5.

23. "Implementation of the NPT Safeguards Agreement in the Islamic Republic of Iran: Report by the Director General." International Atomic Energy Agency, Vienna, Austria, GOV/2005/87, November 18, 2005, p. 2.

24. "Implementation of the NPT Safeguards Agreement in the Islamic Republic of Iran: Report by the Director General." International Atomic Energy Agency, Vienna, Austria, GOV/2006/15, February 27, 2006, p. 8.

25. Ibid.

26. "Implementation of the NPT Safeguards Agreement in the Islamic Republic of Iran: Report by the Director General." International Atomic Energy Agency, Vienna, Austria, GOV/2004/11, February 24, 2004, pp. 4–6.

27. "Implementation of the NPT Safeguards Agreement in the Islamic Republic of Iran: Report by the Director General." International Atomic Energy Agency, Vienna, Austria, GOV/2004/83, November 15, 2004, p. 19.

28. Thomas Wood, Matthew Milazzo, Barbara Reichmuth, and Jeff Bewdell, *The Economics of Energy Independence for Iran,* Los Alamos National Laboratory and Pacific Northwest National Laboratory, U.S. Department of Energy, March 2006.

29. Ibid.

30. Ibid.

31. "Implementation of the NPT Safeguards Agreement in the Islamic Republic of Iran: Report by the Director General." International Atomic Energy Agency, Vienna, Austria, GOV/2003/75, November 10, 2003, p. 10.

32. Bruno Schirra, "Atomic Secrets: The Man Who Knew Too Much." *Die Welt,* July 8, 2006 . . .; George Jahn, "Iran Asks IAEA to Remove Chief Inspector," *Washington Post,* July 9, 2006. . . .

33. FoxNews.com, October 5, 2004. . . .

34. "Missile Survey: Ballistic and Cruise Missiles of Foreign Countries." Congressional Research Service Report RL30427, March 5, 2004, p. 17.

35. Unclassified Report to Congress on the Acquisition of Technology Relating to Weapons of Mass Destruction and Advanced Conventional Munitions, July 1 Through December 31, 2003, November 2004.

36. Director of National Intelligence John D. Negroponte, "Annual Threat Assessment of the Director of National Intelligence," Testimony to the Senate Select Committee on Intelligence, February 2, 2006.

37. "Implementation of the NPT Safeguards Agreement in the Islamic Republic of Iran: Report by the Director General." International Atomic Energy Agency, Vienna, Austria, GOV/2006/15, February 27, 2006, p. 8.

38. General John Abizaid, Commander, U.S. Central Command, "2006 Posture of the United States Central Command," Testimony before the Senate Armed Services Committee, March 14, 2006.

39. Ibid.

40. See FBI Indictment on Khobar Towers bombing, June 21, 2001. . . .

41. Vice Admiral Lowell E. Jacoby, USN, Director, Defense Intelligence Agency, "Current and Projected National Security Threats to the United States," Testimony to the Senate Select Committee on Intelligence, February 16, 2005.

42. Daniel Byman, "Iran, Terrorism, and Weapons of Mass Destruction," Testimony before the House Homeland Security Committee, Subcommittee on the Prevention of Nuclear and Biological Attacks, September 8, 2005.

43. BBC News website, Friday, March 17, 2006.

44. Jonathan Finer and Ellen Knickmeyer, "Envoy Accuses Iran of Duplicity on Iraq," *Washington Post*, March 24, 2006, page A12.

45. Director of National Intelligence John D. Negroponte, "Annual Threat Assessment of the Director of National Intelligence," Testimony to the Senate Select Committee on Intelligence, February 2, 2006; Nicholas Burns, Under Secretary of State for Political Affairs, "United States Policy Toward Iran," Testimony before the House International Relations Committee, March 8, 2006; Scarborough, Rowan. "Rumsfeld Says Iran 'Allowing' Weapons Into Iraq." *Washington Times,* August 10, 2005.

46. Lionel Beehner, "Background Q&A: Iraq Militia Groups," Council on Foreign Relations. . . .

47. General George Casey, quoted in Tom Lasseter, "Iran Gaining Influence, Power in Iraq Through Militia," Knight-Ridder Newspapers, December 12, 2005.

48. Tom Lasseter, "Iran Gaining Influence, Power in Iraq Through Militia," Knight-Ridder Newspapers, December 12, 2005.

49. Edward T. Pound, "Special Report: The Iran Connection," *U.S. News & World Report,* November 22, 2004.

50. Kenneth Katzman, "Iran's Influence in Iraq," Congressional Research Service Report RS22323, November 30, 2005.

51. Lionel Beehner, "Background Q&A: Iraq Militia Groups," Council on Foreign Relations. . . .

52. President George W. Bush, speech to the Foundation for the Defense of Democracies, George Washington University, Washington DC, March 13, 2006.

53. John Negroponte, *Annual Threat Assessment of the Director of National Intelligence for the Senate Select Committee on Intelligence,* February 2, 2006, p. 13.

54. Department of Defense News Briefing with Secretary Rumsfeld and Gen. Pace, 14 March 2006. . . .

55. U.S. Department of State, *Country Reports on Terrorism 2004,* April 2005, pp. 88–89.

56. Secretary of State Condoleezza Rice, Roundtable With Australian, Indonesian and Latin American Journalists, March 9, 2006. . . .

57. State Department Coordinator for Counterterrorism Henry Crumpton, quoted in Dana Priest, "Attacking Iran May Trigger Terrorism," *Washington Post,* April 2, 2006, p. A1.

58. Paula DeSutter, Assistant Secretary of State for Verification and Compliance, Testimony before the U.S.-Israel Joint Parliamentary Committee, September 17, 2003.

59. Neil MacFaquhar and Hassan Fattah, "At crossroads, Hezbollah goes on the attack," *International Herald Tribune,* July 16, 2006. . . .

60. Robin Wright, "Most of Iran's Troops in Lebanon Are Out, Western Officials Say," *Washington Post,* April 13, 2005, page A10. *Also* Kenneth Katzman, "Iran: U.S. Concerns and Policy Responses," Congressional Research Service Report RL32048, March 20, 2006, p. 21.

61. U.S. Department of State, *Country Reports on Terrorism 2004*, April 2005, pp. 89.

62. *Jerusalem Post,* August 13, 2006 . . . ; STRAFOR.com, August 14, 2006. . . .

63. U.S. Department of State, *Patterns of Global Terrorism 2002*, April 30, 2003. Also Ari Fleischer, White House Press Briefing, March 25, 2002. Also, regarding Hezbollah as a source of funding for the Karine-A shipment, see "Iran and Syria as Strategic Support for Palestinian Terrorism," Israel Ministry of Foreign Affairs, September 30, 2002. . . .

64. U.S. Department of State, *Country Reports on Terrorism 2004*, April 2005, pp. 89.

65. Associated Press, "Iran Promises Hamas $250 Million in Aid," *Ha'aretz,* 28 February 2006.

66. Matthew A. Levitt, "Sponsoring Terrorism: Syria and Islamic Jihad," Middle East Intelligence Bulletin, November–December 2002. . . .

67. Amos Harel, "Iran urging Islamic Jihad to attack Israel ahead of election," *Ha'aretz,* March 13, 2006.

68. Octavia Nasr, "Tape: Bin Laden Tells Sunnis to Fight Shiites in Iraq," CNN.com, July 1, 2006.

69. R. Nicholas Burns, "U.S. Policy Toward Iran," Speech at Johns Hopkins University, Paul H. Nitze School of Advanced International Studies, Washington, DC, November 30, 2005.

70. Secretary of Defense Donald Rumsfeld, quoted in Associated Press, "US: Iran Gives Al-Qaeda Safe Passage," April 3, 2002.

71. Nicholas Burns, Under Secretary of State for Political Affairs, "United States Policy Toward Iran," Testimony before the House International Relations Committee, March 8, 2006.

72. Ibid.

73. *Country Reports on Terrorism 2005,* U.S Department of State, Publication 11324, April 2006, p. 173.

74. Anthony Cordesman and Khalid Al-Rodhan, *Iranian Nuclear Weapons? The Threats from Iran's WMD and Missile Programs* (Working Draft) (Washington: Center for Strategic and International Studies, February 21, 2006), p. 44.

75. Daniel Byman, "Iran, Terrorism, and Weapons of Mass Destruction," Testimony to the House Homeland Security Committee, Subcommittee on the Prevention of Nuclear and Biological Attacks, 8 September 2005, citing Kenneth Pollack, *The Persian Puzzle* (New York: Random House, 2004), pp. 420–421.

76. General John Abizaid, Commander, U.S. Central Command, "2006 Posture of the United States Central Command," Testimony before the Senate Armed Services Committee, March 14, 2006.

Iran: Nuclear Intentions
and Capabilities

Office of the Director of National Intelligence

The Director of National Intelligence serves as the head of the Intelligence Community (IC), overseeing and directing the implementation of the National Intelligence Program and acting as the principal advisor to the President, the National Security Council, and the Homeland Security Council for intelligence matters.

The Office of the Director of National Intelligence is charged with:

- Integrating the domestic and foreign dimensions of US intelligence so that there are no gaps in our understanding of threats to our national security;
- Bringing more depth and accuracy to intelligence analysis; and
- Ensuring that US intelligence resources generate future capabilities as well as present results.

National Intelligence Council

Since its formation in 1973, the National Intelligence Council (NIC) has served as a bridge between the intelligence and policy communities, a source of deep substantive expertise on critical national security issues, and as a focal point for Intelligence Community collaboration. The NIC's key goal is to provide policymakers with the best, unvarnished, and unbiased information—regardless of whether analytic judgments conform to US policy. Its primary functions are to:

- Support the DNI in his role as Principal Intelligence Advisor to the President and other senior policymakers.
- Lead the Intelligence Community's effort to produce National Intelligence Estimates (NIEs) and other NIC products that address key national security concerns.

From *National Intelligence Estimate,* November 2007, published by Office of the Director, National Intelligence Council. http://www.dni.gov/press_releases/20071203_release.pdf

- Provide a focal point for policymakers, warfighters, and Congressional leaders to task the Intelligence Community for answers to important questions.
- Reach out to nongovernment experts in academia and the private sector—and use alternative analyses and new analytic tools—to broaden and deepen the Intelligence Community's perspective.

National Intelligence Estimates and the NIE Process

National Intelligence Estimates (NIEs) are the Intelligence Community's (IC) most authoritative written judgments on national security issues and designed to help US civilian and military leaders develop policies to protect US national security interests. NIEs usually provide information on the current state of play but are primarily "estimative"—that is, they make judgments about the likely course of future events and identify the implications for US policy.

The NIEs are typically requested by senior civilian and military poli-cymakers, Congressional leaders and at times are initiated by the National Intelligence Council (NIC). Before a NIE is drafted, the relevant NIO is respon-sible for producing a concept paper or terms of reference (TOR) and circulates it throughout the Intelligence Community for comment. The TOR defines the key estimative questions, determines drafting responsibilities, and sets the drafting and publication schedule. One or more IC analysts are usually assigned to produce the initial text. The NIC then meets to critique the draft before it is circulated to the broader IC. Representatives from the relevant IC agencies meet to hone and coordinate line-by-line the full text of the NIE. Working with their Agencies, reps also assign the level of confidence they have in each key judgment. IC reps discuss the quality of sources with col-lectors, and the National Clandestine Service vets the sources used to ensure the draft does not include any that have been recalled or otherwise seriously questioned.

All NIEs are reviewed by National Intelligence Board, which is chaired by the DNI and is composed of the heads of relevant IC agencies. Once approved by the NIB, NIEs are briefed to the President and senior policymakers. The whole process of producing NIEs normally takes at least several months.

The NIC has undertaken a number of steps to improve the NIE process under the DNI. These steps are in accordance with the goals and recommenda-tions set out in the SSCI and WMD Commission reports and the 2004 Intel-ligence Reform and Prevention of Terrorism Act. Most notably, over the last year and a half, the IC has:

- *Created new procedures to integrate formal reviews of source reporting and technical judgments*. The Directors of the National Clandestine Service, NSA, NGA, and DIA and the Assistant Secretary/INR are now required to submit formal assessments that highlight the strengths, weaknesses, and overall credibility of their sources used in developing the critical judgments of the NIE.

- *Applied more rigorous standards.* A textbox is incorporated into all NIEs that explains what we mean by such terms as "we judge" and that clarifies the difference between judgments of likelihood and confidence levels. We have made a concerted effort to not only highlight differences among agencies but to explain the reasons for such differences and to prominently display them in the Key Judgments.

Scope Note

This National Intelligence Estimate (NIE) assesses the status of Iran's nuclear program, and the program's outlook over the next 10 years. This time frame is more appropriate for estimating capabilities than intentions and foreign reactions, which are more difficult to estimate over a decade. In presenting the Intelligence Community's assessment of Iranian nuclear intentions and capabilities, the NIE thoroughly reviews all available information on these questions, examines the range of reasonable scenarios consistent with this information, and describes the key factors we judge would drive or impede nuclear progress in Iran. This NIE is an extensive reexamination of the issues in the May 2005 assessment.

This Estimate focuses on the following key questions:

- What are Iran's intentions toward developing nuclear weapons?
- What domestic factors affect Iran's decision making on whether to develop nuclear weapons?
- What external factors affect Iran's decision making on whether to develop nuclear weapons?
- What is the range of potential Iranian actions concerning the development of nuclear weapons, and the decisive factors that would lead Iran to choose one course of action over another?
- What is Iran's current and projected capability to develop nuclear weapons? What are our key assumptions, and Iran's key choke points/ vulnerabilities?

This NIE does *not* assume that Iran intends to acquire nuclear weapons. Rather, it examines the intelligence to assess Iran's capability and intent (or lack thereof) to acquire nuclear weapons, taking full account of Iran's dual-use uranium fuel cycle and those nuclear activities that are at least partly civil in nature.

This Estimate does assume that the strategic goals and basic structure of Iran's senior leadership and government will remain similar to those that have endured since the death of Ayatollah Khomeini in 1989. We acknowledge the potential for these to change during the time frame of the Estimate, but are unable to confidently predict such changes or their implications. This Estimate does not assess how Iran may conduct future negotiations with the West on the nuclear issue.

This Estimate incorporates intelligence reporting available as of 31 October 2007.

WHAT WE MEAN WHEN WE SAY: AN EXPLANATION OF ESTIMATIVE LANGUAGE

We use phrases such as *we judge, we assess*, and *we estimate*—and probabilistic terms such as *probably* and *likely*—to convey analytical assessments and judgments. Such statements are not facts, proof, or knowledge. These assessments and judgments generally are based on collected information, which often is incomplete or fragmentary. Some assessments are built on previous judgments. In all cases, assessments and judgments are not intended to imply that we have "proof" that shows something to be a fact or that definitively links two items or issues.

In addition to conveying judgments rather than certainty, our estimative language also often conveys 1) our assessed likelihood or probability of an event; and 2) the level of confidence we ascribe to the judgment.

Estimates of Likelihood. Because analytical judgments are not certain, we use probabilistic language to reflect the Community's estimates of the likelihood of developments or events. Terms such as *probably, likely, very likely*, or *almost certainly* indicate a greater than even chance. The terms *unlikely* and *remote* indicate a less then even chance that an event will occur; they do not imply that an event will not occur. Terms such as *might* or *may* reflect situations in which we are unable to assess the likelihood, generally because relevant information is unavailable, sketchy, or fragmented. Terms such as *we cannot dismiss, we cannot rule out*, or *we cannot discount* reflect an unlikely, improbable, or remote event whose consequences are such that it warrants mentioning. The chart provides a rough idea of the relationship of some of these terms to each other.

Remote	Very unlikely	Unlikely	Even chance	Probably/ Likely	Very likely	Almost certainly

Confidence in Assessments. Our assessments and estimates are supported by information that varies in scope, quality and sourcing. Consequently, we ascribe *high, moderate*, or *low* levels of confidence to our assessments, as follows:

- *High confidence* generally indicates that our judgments are based on high-quality information, and/or that the nature of the issue makes it possible to render a solid judgment. A "high confidence" judgment is not a fact or a certainty, however, and such judgments still carry a risk of being wrong.
- *Moderate confidence* generally means that the information is credibly sourced and plausible but not of sufficient quality or corroborated sufficiently to warrant a higher level of confidence.
- *Low confidence* generally means that the information's credibility and/or plausibility is questionable, or that the information is too fragmented or poorly corroborated to make solid analytic inferences, or that we have significant concerns or problems with the sources.

Key Judgements

A.   We judge with high confidence that in fall 2003, Tehran halted its nuclear weapons program; we also assess with moderate-to-high confidence that Tehran at a minimum is keeping open the option to develop nuclear weapons. We judge with high confidence that the halt, and Tehran's announcement of its decision to suspend its declared uranium enrichment program and sign an Additional Protocol to its Nuclear Non-Proliferation Treaty Safeguards Agreement, was directed primarily in response to increasing international scrutiny and pressure resulting from exposure of Iran's previously undeclared nuclear work.

- We assess with high confidence that until fall 2003, Iranian military entities were working under government direction to develop nuclear weapons.
- We judge with high confidence that the halt lasted at least several years. (Because of intelligence gaps discussed elsewhere in this Estimate, however, DOE and the NIC assess with only moderate confidence that the halt to those activities represents a halt to Iran's entire nuclear weapons program.)
- We assess with moderate confidence Tehran had not restarted its nuclear weapons program as of mid-2007, but we do not know whether it currently intends to develop nuclear weapons.
- We continue to assess with moderate-to-high confidence that Iran does not currently have a nuclear weapon.
- Tehran's decision to halt its nuclear weapons program suggests it is less determined to develop nuclear weapons than we have been judging since 2005. Our assessment that the program probably was halted primarily in response to international pressure suggests Iran may be more vulnerable to influence on the issue than we judged previously.

B.   We continue to assess with low confidence that Iran probably has imported at least some weapons-usable fissile material, but still judge with moderate-to-high confidence it has not obtained enough for a nuclear weapon. We cannot rule out that Iran has acquired from abroad—or will acquire in the future—a nuclear weapon or enough fissile material for a weapon. Barring such acquisitions, if Iran wants to have nuclear weapons it would need to produce sufficient amounts of fissile material indigenously—which we judge with high confidence it has not yet done.

C.   We assess centrifuge enrichment is how Iran probably could first produce enough fissile material for a weapon, if it decides to do so. Iran resumed its declared centrifuge enrichment activities in January 2006, despite the continued halt in the nuclear weapons program. Iran made significant progress in 2007 installing centrifuges at Natanz, but we judge with moderate confidence it still faces significant technical problems operating them.

- We judge with moderate confidence that the earliest possible date Iran would be technically capable of producing enough HEU for a weapon is late 2009, but that this is very unlikely.

- We judge with moderate confidence Iran probably would be technically capable of producing enough HEU for a weapon sometime during the 2010–2015 time frame. (INR judges Iran is unlikely to achieve this capability before 2013 because of foreseeable technical and programmatic problems.) All agencies recognize the possibility that this capability may not be attained until *after* 2015.

D.   Iranian entities are continuing to develop a range of technical capabilities that could be applied to producing nuclear weapons, if a decision is made to do so. For example, Iran's civilian uranium enrichment program is continuing. We also assess with high confidence that since fall 2003, Iran has been conducting research and development projects with commercial and conventional military applications—some of which would also be of limited use for nuclear weapons.

E.   We do not have sufficient intelligence to judge confidently whether Tehran is willing to maintain the halt of its nuclear weapons program indefinitely while it weighs its options, or whether it will or already has set specific deadlines or criteria that will prompt it to restart the program.

- Our assessment that Iran halted the program in 2003 primarily in response to international pressure indicates Tehran's decisions are guided by a cost-benefit approach rather than a rush to a weapon irrespective of the political, economic, and military costs. This, in turn, suggests that some combination of threats of intensified international scrutiny and pressures, along with opportunities for Iran to achieve its security, prestige, and goals for regional influence in other ways, might—if perceived by Iran's leaders as credible—prompt Tehran to extend the current halt to its nuclear weapons program. It is difficult to specify what such a combination might be.
- We assess with moderate confidence that convincing the Iranian leadership to forgo the eventual development of nuclear weapons will be difficult given the linkage many within the leadership probably see between nuclear weapons development and Iran's key national security and foreign policy objectives, and given Iran's considerable effort from at least the late 1980s to 2003 to develop such weapons. In our judgment, only an Iranian political decision to abandon a nuclear weapons objective would plausibly keep Iran from eventually producing nuclear weapons—and such a decision is inherently reversible.

F.   We assess with moderate confidence that Iran probably would use covert facilities—rather than its declared nuclear sites—for the production of highly enriched uranium for a weapon. A growing amount of intelligence indicates Iran was engaged in covert uranium conversion and uranium enrichment activity, but we judge that these efforts probably were halted in response to the fall 2003 halt, and that these efforts probably had not been restarted through at least mid-2007.

G. We judge with high confidence that Iran will not be technically capable of producing and reprocessing enough plutonium for a weapon before about 2015.

H. We assess with high confidence that Iran has the scientific, technical and industrial capacity eventually to produce nuclear weapons if it decides to do so.

Table

Key Differences Between the Key Judgments of This Estimate on Iran's Nuclear Program and the May 2005 Assessment

2005 IC Estimate	2007 National Intelligence Estimate
Assess with high confidence that Iran currently is determined to develop nuclear weapons despite its international obligations and international pressure, but we do not assess that Iran is immovable.	Judge with high confidence that in fall 2003, Tehran halted its nuclear weapons program. Judge with high confidence that the halt lasted at least several years. (DOE and the NIC have moderate confidence that the halt to those activities represents a halt to Iran's entire nuclear weapons program.) Assess with moderate confidence that Tehran had not restarted its nuclear weapons program as of mid-2007, but we do not know whether it currently intends to develop nuclear weapons. Judge with high confidence that the halt was directed primarily in response to increasing international scrutiny and pressure resulting from exposure of Iran's previously undeclared nuclear work. Assess with moderate-to-high confidence that Tehran at a minimum is keeping open the option to develop nuclear weapons.
We have moderate confidence in projecting when Iran is likely to make a nuclear weapon; we assess that it is unlikely before early-to-mid next decade.	We judge with moderate confidence that the earliest possible date Iran would be technically capable of producing enough highly enriched uranium (HEU) for a weapon is late 2009, but that this is very unlikely. We judge with moderate confidence that Iran probably would be technically capable of producing enough HEU for a weapon sometime during the 2010–2015 time frame. (INR judges that Iran is unlikely to achieve this capability before 2013 because of foreseeable technical and programmatic problems.)
Iran could produce enough fissile material for a weapon by the end of this decade if it were to make more rapid and successful progress than we have seen to date.	We judge with moderate confidence that the earliest possible date Iran would be technically capable of producing enough highly enriched uranium (HEU) for a weapon is late 2009, but that this is very unlikely.

POSTSCRIPT

Is a Nuclear Iran a Global Security Threat?

The nuclear proliferation issue is a constant source of anxiety for nuclear and non-nuclear states alike. Who will join the club next? Are they a stable regime? What are their interests and goals, and would they be predisposed to using nuclear weapons to achieve their regional interests? Views about these issues are divergent and reflect the differences that exist in the global community. Most people believe that more nuclear powers mean a greater chance for a nuclear exchange. Most also believe that the control of nuclear weaponry by a few means that those states possess the upper hand on the adjudication of global issues and interests.

In the Middle East and the Persian Gulf, the stakes are even higher. Global oil supplies, the Israeli–Palestinian enmity, terrorism, Islamic fundamentalism, and U.S. geopolitical interests combine to make for a volatile and unstable mix. The only nuclear powers in the region are Israel, India, and Pakistan. If we exclude India and Pakistan for a moment, we see that a nuclear fundamentalist Iran forces the world community to examine several important questions. Would a nuclear Iran change the balance of power between Israel and its Arab neighbors? Would Israel allow such a development or pre-empt as they did in Osirak, Iraq, in 1979? Would Iran be predisposed to distributing nuclear technology to terrorist groups they support, like the Hezbollah of Lebanon?

Essentially, one must decide whether Iran would use nuclear weapons if they possessed them or would the weapons simply be a signal of pride and status for Iran in the regional and global communities. One school of thought, argued by many states that do not possess nuclear weapons, is that in over 60 years only one state has used nuclear weapons in war, the United States, and that despite the growth of the nuclear club, no weapons have been launched. Thus, to assume that a nuclear Iran would be a global security threat is to ignore the fact that no evidence suggests they would use them in anger. Further, the argument is presented that painting Iran as a global security threat serves U.S. foreign policy but does not reflect Iranian regional or global interests.

The other school of thought contends that a nuclear Iran will bring nuclear weapons into the hands of religious extremists bent on obliterating Israel and spreading fundamentalism. Thus, regional states, U.S. military forces, and others are at risk of Iranian pre-emption to achieve their aims. Additionally, the "unstable" nature of a fundamentalist regime makes the use of nuclear weapons more likely and thus the possibility of a catalytic nuclear war a real threat. This view is certainly predicated on the assumption that a fundamentalist religious regime such as Iran's would have less restraints on using said weapons to achieve their aims.

Whatever one's perspective, one fact is certainly clear. States like Iran, Saudi Arabia, North Korea, Syria, and others will get closer to having the ability to produce nuclear technology and weaponry. The current proliferation regime can mitigate these developments but probably cannot stop them. Thus, the world community will have to deal with nuclear proliferation and the real or perceived "threats" that these weapons create. The result will be a greater probability of a regional nuclear war.

Some interesting work here includes Michael Evans and Jerome Corsi's *Showdown with Nuclear Iran: Radical Islam's Messianic Mission to Destroy Israel and Cripple the United States* (Thomas Nelson, 2006), A. J. Venter's *Iran's Nuclear Option* (Casemate, 2005), and Scott Ritter's *Target Iran: The Truth about the White Houses Plans for Regime Change* (Nation Books, 2006).

ISSUE 20

Will China Be the Next Superpower?

YES: Shujie Yao, from "Can China Really Become the Next Superpower?" *China Policy Institute* (April 2007)

NO: Pranab Bardhan, from "China, India Superpower? Not So Fast!" *YaleGlobal Online* (October 25, 2005)

ISSUE SUMMARY

YES: Yao analyzes the current state of the Chinese economy and policy and postulates several possible scenarios for development. Ultimately, Yao surmises that China will develop as the next superpower by the mid-twenty-first century.

NO: Bardhan argues that there are many variables and factors that can and will hinder China's development into a superpower, including vast poverty, weak infrastructure, and China's authoritarian government.

In 1979, after the death of Mao and the reign of the Gang of Four, Deng Sho Ping emerged as the supreme leader of the Chinese Communist party. At that moment, he set China on a course of economic growth and expansion, military modernization and reform, and profound social and political change. The impact of this sea change in Chinese communist policy has been monumental. China now is one of the fastest growing economies on earth, producing goods and services at a rate of sustained growth unseen in the global economy. Its share of the export/import market has grown exponentially such that little is consumed or used that does not have a China link.

With this growth have come infrastructure development, urban expansion, monetary wealth creation, and profound societal change. While the Chinese Communist party maintains tight control, the society and economy continue to revolutionize themselves. Scholars and policymakers marvel at this change while trying to analyze its short- and long-term impact. Opinions vary as to how sustainable this growth is and whether it can be managed and controlled by an authoritarian regime. Further, there is wide disagreement as to whether China's resurgence is creating a superpower or a paper tiger, and as to how strong is the educational, social, and political foundation on which this growth is based.

In the following section, two authors will explore a question that will be of primary focus for global scholars for the next decade. Will China be the next superpower? Yao summarizes his analysis by determining that the probability of China's emergence as a superpower is great, given the presence of certain key variables. These include prudent and careful management of a mixed economy, available labor pool, access to resources, and, of course, the capacity to innovate. Bardhan points to structural defects in the Chinese (and Indian) economies and systems that preclude superpower status. These include income inequality, infrastructure obstacles, bureaucratic inefficiencies, and a less-than-sophisticated notion of capital accumulation and reinvestment.

Fundamentally, both analyses agree that the potential is there, yet both see different scenarios as to how and in what form that potential will be realized.

YES

Shujie Yao

Can China Really Become the Next Superpower?

This paper aims to answer the question whether China can really become the next superpower through assessing China's economic performance in the past three decades and evaluating the key constraints on China's future development. It presents a few possible scenarios to sketch how likely it is that China will become the next superpower towards the middle of the 21st century.

Introduction

China has been successful in the last three decades under economic reform and a policy of openness. The economic miracle has been due to Deng Xiaoping's gradualism and pragmatism in economic reforms and social changes, the smooth transformation to a mixed economy and the shift of development strategy from closed-door to openness.

China's fast growth has been accompanied by many difficult social, political and environmental problems. Rising inequality, persistence of absolute poverty, environmental degradation, corruption, and declining standards of traditional Chinese moral and social values are key constraints and challenges to China's further growth. China's future depends on its ability to solve these problems.

The most pessimistic scenario is that China is unable to face up to those challenges and constraints, rendering the country vulnerable to polarisation, corruption and financial/material crises with little hope of becoming a real superpower. The most optimistic scenario is that China is able to maintain high economic growth, to reduce inequality and poverty, to improve the natural environment, and to overcome the potential problems of energy and material shortage. In this scenario, China will overtake Japan by 2017 and the US by 2037. China will also become a world leader of science and technology, possessing the world's most advanced space, nuclear, computer, biological, medical, energy and military technologies.

From *China Policy Institute*, April 2007. Copyright © 2007 by Shujie Yao, China Policy Institute, School of Contemporary Chinese Studies/University of Nottingham. Reprinted by permission of the author. http://www.nottingham.ac.uk/china-policy-institute/

What Constitutes a Superpower

The US and the former USSR are two examples of superpowers. The US has been the most powerful country in all aspects: the size of its economy, per capita gross domestic product (GDP), military strength, science and technologies, and international influence. The former USSR used to have huge military capability and influence over the world order. It was the only country able to challenge the US before the end of the cold war. Its economic strength was by no means comparable to that of the US. The key question is whether there will be another superpower in the next few decades, and if yes, which country? Russia, India, Japan or Germany is unlikely to become the next superpower for various reasons. Hence, one likely candidate must be China.

However, even if China can become the world's largest economy, it does not mean that China will automatically become a superpower. There are some other conditions for China to be a real superpower. Such conditions should include the level of per capita income, social justice and income equality, the ability to become a world leader of science and technology, and the ability to influence regional and global peace and order.

China's Rise and Its Significance in the World Economy

China's economic reform is the largest project in human history because it has affected a population 16 times that of the four Asian Tigers (South Korea, Taiwan, Singapore and Hong Kong) combined, and more than 10 times that of Japan.

During 1978–2006, China achieved an average annual growth of 9.6% in real GDP. Two different ways are currently used to measure GDP: in nominal dollars using official exchange rates and in [the purchasing power in American dollars of other currencies—in this case, the Chinese currency] dollars using the actual buying power of currencies. Measured in PPP dollars, China's GDP in 2006 was $10.5 trillion, compared with $12.9 trillion for the US, $13.0 trillion for the EU, $4.1 trillion for Japan, $3.9 trillion for India, $2.6 trillion for Germany and $1.9 trillion for the UK. China is the third largest economic bloc after the EU and the US and the second largest economy after the US. PPP dollars tend to overstate the level of GDP for poor countries like China and India. Measured in nominal dollars, China was the fourth largest economy after the US, Japan, and Germany, with a total GDP of $2.72 trillion (20.94 trillion [the official Chinese currency]) in 2006. China will overtake Germany to become the third largest economy in 2007 or 2008.

In the last thirty years, China's real GDP increased 13 fold, real per capita GDP over nine fold, and real per capita consumption more than six fold. Many consumer goods and services that were virtually unknown in 1978 have become daily necessities in Chinese households today, including colour TVs, telephones, motor cycles and computers. In 1978, China ranked number 23 in world trade. By 2006, China was the third largest trading nation in both imports and exports, with a total trade volume of $1.8 trillion, generating a surplus of $177.8 billion. China had little foreign direct investment (FDI) before 1992 but has been competing with the US in recent years as the world's largest host of foreign capital.

China is the world's largest producer and consumer of many key industrial and agricultural products, including steel, cement, coal, fertilizers, colour TVs, cloth, cereals, meat, fish, vegetables, fruits, cotton and rapeseeds. By 2006, China had constructed 3.48 million km of highways and 45,460 km of motorways, or five times the total length of motorways in the UK. China is currently constructing the same length of the entire UK motorway system every two years. In 1978, China had only 598 universities recruiting 0.4 million students; by 2006, it had 1,800 universities recruiting over 5 million students and sending another 120,000 students abroad.

High and sustained economic growth has led to rapid industrialisation and urbanization. During 1978–2006, agriculture's share in national GDP declined from 28% to 11%, agricultural employment in national employment from 71% to 45%, rural population in national population from 82% to 57%.

Why China Succeeds

China's economic miracle can be attributed to its institutional reforms, transforming the former plan system to a mixed plan and market system. The approach of reform is gradual, guided by Deng's theory of 'Crossing the River by Feeling the Stones'. The reform was carefully managed with appropriate experimentation, accurate timing, correct sequence and manageable scale. Reforms progressed from agriculture and the countryside to the urban economy and state-owned enterprises, from the real economic sectors to the banking and other financial sectors, and from prices to the labour and capital markets, etc.

Adopting appropriate development strategies is another reason for China's success. Development strategies are shifted from import substitution to export-push and from closed-door to openness and globalisation.

China's reforms have been guided by some important development theories unavailable from existing economics text books. One such theory is 'Spots to Lead Areas' development, which is featured with some growing centres propelling the growth in the surrounding areas and then remote regions through the transmission of growth momentum incubated in the growth centres. In the early 1980s, China established the special economic zones and open coastal cities to be the country's growth centres.

Another theory is 'Walking with Two Legs' development to improve China's capability in science, technology and innovation. China has relied heavily on foreign technologies through direct purchase or indirectly through FDI to improve productivity. It has also invested heavily to improve its ability in technological innovation and knowledge creation at home.

Constraints and Challenges

Although China has made tremendous progress in the last thirty years, it is now faced with many challenges and constraints. The most important problems include high and rising inequality, corruption and persistency of poverty, environmental pollution, and over-dependency on non-renewable resources. All these problems could loom so large that China may become vulnerable to various crises. China's GDP is about 5% (14% in PPP terms) of the world total but it consumes more than one-third of the world's out-puts of coal, steel and cement. China's past pattern of industrial growth is unlikely to be sustainable in the future.

Rising inequality and corruption are two major social and political issues which can render China vulnerable to social and political unrest, causing unwanted disruption to its economic progress.

Current Policies and Possible Scenarios

The government is aware of China's development constraints and challenges. Some policies have been implemented to resolve these problems through building a harmonious society and reducing income inequality. In agriculture, more land will be converted into forest and grass. Agricultural production will become more efficient and less dependent on chemical fertilisers and pesticides. More investments will be made in the rural areas to improve farm incomes and reduce urban-rural and inter-regional inequality. More effective measures are being adopted to combat corruption and strengthen the leadership of the Communist Party. Huge investments have been planned for the next 30 years to greatly improve the country's human capital, research and innovation capability in the strategic areas of space, energy, environment, computer and internet, biology and medicine, military affairs and defence, transportation and telecommunications, etc.

If the current policies are ineffective, China's growth can slow down, leading to higher unemployment and more poverty. In this scenario, the chance of China becoming a superpower will be small. If all policies are effectively implemented, China will be able to maintain high growth, to reduce inequality, poverty, and corruption, to improve production efficiency and the environment. In this scenario, China will overtake Japan to become the second largest economy by 2017 and the US by 2037, and will become another superpower. This prediction is based on the assumption that all countries continue to grow in the next 30 years following their own growth trends in the past three decades and that GDP is measured in nominal dollars, not in PPP dollars. By 2037, China will also become a world leader of science and technology and have sufficient military and/or diplomatic capability to compete with the US in maintaining regional and global peace and order.

Further Readings

Hu, Angang (2007), *'Five Major Scale Effects of China's Rise on the World'*, paper presented to the 18th Annual Conference of Chinese Economic Association (UK), April, University of Nottingham.

Hu, Angang (2007), 'National Life Cycle and the Rise of China', paper presented to the 18th Annual Conference of Chinese Economic Association (UK), April, University of Nottingham.

Yao, Shujie (2005), *Economic Growth, Income Distribution and Poverty Reduction in China under Economic Reforms*, RoutledgeCurzon, ISBN 0-415-33196-X.

Yao, Shujie and Kailei, Wei (2007), 'Economic Growth in the Present of FDI from a Newly Industrializing Economy's Perspective', *Journal of Comparative Economics,* 35(1), 211–234.

Yao, Shujie, L. Hanmer, and Zhongyi, Zhang (2004), 'The Implications of Growing Inequality on Poverty Peduction in China', *China Economic Review,* 15, 145–163.

Pranab Bardhan

NO

China, India Superpower?
Not So Fast!

Despite Impressive Growth, the Rising Asian Giants Have Feet of Clay

The media, particularly the financial press, are all agog over the rise of China and India in the international economy. After a long period of relative stagnation, these two countries, nearly two-fifths of the world population, have seen their incomes grow at remarkably high rates over the last two decades. Journalists have referred to their economic reforms and integration into the world economy in all kinds of colorful metaphors: giants shaking off their "socialist slumber," "caged tigers" unshackled, and so on. Columnists have sent breathless reports from Beijing and Bangalore about the inexorable competition from these two new whiz kids in our complacent neighborhood in a "flattened," globalized playing field. Others have warned about the momentous implications of "three billion new capitalists," largely from China and India, redefining the next phase of globalization.

While there is no doubt about the great potential of these two economies in the rest of this century, severe structural and institutional problems will hobble them for years to come. At this point, the hype about the Indian economy seems patently premature, and the risks on the horizon for the Chinese polity—and hence for economic stability—highly underestimated.

Both China and India are still desperately poor countries. Of the total of 2.3 billion people in these two countries, nearly 1.5 billion earn less than US$2 a day, according to World Bank calculations. Of course, the lifting of hundreds of millions of people above poverty in China has been historic. Thanks to repeated assertions in the international financial press, conventional wisdom now suggests that globalization is responsible for this feat. Yet a substantial part of China's decline in poverty since 1980 already happened by mid-1980s (largely as a result of agricultural growth), before the big strides in foreign trade and investment in the 1990s. Assertions about Indian poverty reduction primarily through trade liberalization are even shakier. In

From *YaleGlobal Online*, October 25, 2005. Copyright © 2005 by Yale Center for the Study of Globalization. Reprinted by permission of YaleGlobal Online. www.yaleglobal.yale.edu

the nineties, the decade of major trade liberalization, the rate of decline in poverty by some aggregative estimates has, if anything, slowed down. In any case, India is as yet a minor player in world trade, contributing less than one percent of world exports. (China's share is about 6 percent.)

What about the hordes of Indian software engineers, call-center operators, and back-room programmers supposedly hollowing out white-collar jobs in rich countries? The total number of workers in all possible forms of IT-related jobs in India comes to less than a million workers—one-quarter of one percent of the Indian labor force. For all its Nobel Prizes and brilliant scholars and professionals, India is the largest single-country contributor to the pool of illiterate people in the world. Lifting them out of poverty and dead-end menial jobs will remain a Herculean task for decades to come.

Even in China, now considered the manufacturing workshop of the world (though China's share in the worldwide manufacturing value-added is below 9 percent, less than half that of Japan or the United States), less than one-fifth of its labor force is employed in manufacturing, mining, and construction combined. In fact, China has lost tens of millions of manufacturing jobs since the mid-1990s. Nearly half of the country's labor force remains in agriculture (about 60 percent in India). As per acre productivity growth has stagnated, reabsorbing the hundreds of millions of peasants will remain a challenge in the foreseeable future for both countries. Domestic private enterprise in China, while active and growing, is relatively weak, and Chinese banks are burdened with "bad" loans. By most aggregative measures, capital is used much less efficiently in China than in India, even though in terms of physical infrastructure and progress in education and health, China is better poised for further economic growth. Commercial regulatory structures in both countries are still slow and heavy-handed. According to the World Bank, to start a business requires in India 71 days, in China 48 days (compared to 6 days in Singapore); enforcing debt contracts requires 425 days in India, 241 days in China (69 days in Singapore).

China's authoritarian system of government will likely be a major economic liability in the long run, regardless of its immediate implications for short-run policy decisions. In the economic reform process, the Chinese leadership has often made bold decisions and implemented them relatively quickly and decisively, whereas in India, reform has been halting and hesitant. This is usually attributed to the inevitably slow processes of democracy in India. And though this may be the case, other factors are involved. For example, the major disruptions and hardships of restructuring in the Chinese economy were rendered somewhat tolerable by a minimum rural safety net—made possible to a large extent by land reforms in 1978. In most parts of India, no similar rural safety net exists for the poor; and the more severe educational inequality in India makes the absorption of shocks in the industrial labor market more difficult. So the resistance to the competitive process of market reform is that much stiffer.

But inequalities (particularly rural-urban) have been increasing in China, and those left behind are getting restive. With massive layoffs in the rust-belt provinces, arbitrary local levies on farmers, pervasive official corruption, and toxic industrial dumping, many in the countryside are highly agitated. Chinese police records indicate a sevenfold increase in the number of incidents of social unrest in the last decade.

China is far behind India in the ability to politically manage conflicts, and this may prove to be China's Achilles' Heel. Over the last fifty years, India's extremely heterogeneous society has been riddled with various kinds of conflicts, but the system has by and large managed these conflicts and kept them within moderate bounds. For many centuries, the homogenizing tradition of Chinese high culture, language, and bureaucracy has not given much scope to pluralism and diversity, and a centralizing, authoritarian Communist Party has carried on with this tradition. There is a certain pre-occupation with order and stability in China (not just in the Party), a tendency to over-react to difficult situations, and a quickness to brand dissenting movements and local autonomy efforts as seditious, and it is in this context that one sees dark clouds on the horizon for China's polity and therefore the economy.

We should not lose our sense of proportion in thinking about the rise of China and India. While adjusting its economies to the new reality and utilizing the new opportunities, the West should not overlook the enormity of the economic gap that exists between it and those two countries (particularly India). There are many severe pitfalls and roadblocks which they have to overcome in the near future, before they can become significant players in the international economic scene on a sustained basis.

POSTSCRIPT

Will China Be the Next Superpower?

Over the past 30 years, China has overcome its Maoist experiment and earlier colonial history to emerge as a vibrant growing economy. GDP growth rates alone have been between 8 and 15 percent per year for several years. The ingenuity, hard work, and vast resources of China have been unleashed in a mixed economic set of policies, and the result has been vast increases in production, huge amounts of foreign investment, and vast wealth creation that is transforming China. On these points, all scholars agree.

China's 1.3 billion people are also subjected to immense poverty in the countryside and in selected urban areas. They have significant infrastructure issues left over from the Communist era, and the political system leaves little room for expression and community empowerment for literally billions. China is in many ways the best global example of a dramatic play with important and broadly defined characters acting out on a global stage, and it is unclear as to where the story will go.

Several key variables will determine China's ultimate direction. First, China is in the midst of a strong growth and investment phase that is directly tied to this era of globalization. In fact, it would have been impossible for China to have grown so quickly in the last 15 years without the presence of globalization. This means that many factors outside of China's control will impact its development, including the direction of the U.S., European, and other economies and the ability of China to embrace technological changes.

Second, the enormous growth of a strong middle class in China raises questions as to the political expression for these tens of millions and what values this middle class will embrace. Will they be content with an authoritarian model, or will they demand greater forms of expressions that tear at the foundational fabric of the political system.

Third, can the current labor supply and costs in China be maintained amidst a growing and interdependent global economy? Already there are signs of breaks in the China advantage in this area as other regions of the world compete for manufacturing jobs based on cheap labor costs.

Fourth, will China be able to translate economic growth into political influence and power in places like the Middle East, Africa, and Latin America? Superpower status is in part a function of global influence and reach, and China has yet to show the will to exercise that reach and influence. Can China develop the military force structure for such power projection, and what drain will this place on the civilian economy? It remains an open question as to whether they aspire for such a role.

Certainly, China has the potential to be the next superpower, and it also has a well-thought-out plan for growth and modernization. Can China pull it off? Even the most generous analysis of the U.S. rise to superpower status admits that it was a process that took generations to come to fruition. The explosion of the atomic bomb was merely the culmination of a long path of industrialization, military expansion, and developing internationalism among the political elite. China seems to be on the path, but whether they can sustain it and continue to embrace it remains an open question.

Some works that are illustrative include Susan Shirk's *China: Fragile Superpower: How China's Internal Politics Could Derail Its Peaceful Rise* (Oxford University Press, 2007); C. Fred Bergsten et al.'s *China the Balance Sheet: What the World Needs to Know About the Emerging Superpower* (Public Affairs, 2006), and Ted C. Fishman's *China Inc: How the Rise of the Next Superpower Challenges America and the World* (Scribner, 2006).

ISSUE 21

Is the International Community Making Progress in Addressing Natural Disasters?

YES: United Nations, from "Risk and Poverty in a Changing Climate: Invest Today for a Safer Tomorrow," *Summary and Recommendations: 2009 Global Assessment Report on Disaster Risk Reduction* (2009)

NO: David Rothkopf, from "Averting Disaster: Calamities Like the Haiti Quake Aren't Just Predictable—They're Preventable," *Newsweek* (January 25, 2010)

ISSUE SUMMARY

YES: The International Strategy for Disaster Reduction Secretariat, a unit within the United Nations, suggests that countries are making "significant progress" in strengthening their capacities to address past deficiencies and gaps in their disaster preparedness and response. At the center of progress is the plan, *Hyogo Framework for Action 2005–2015,* which is aimed at reducing human and nonhuman disaster losses.

NO: David Rothkopf, president of Garten Rothkopf (an international consulting agency) and a member of former president Bill Clinton's international trade team, argues that the efforts of international organizations to prevent natural disasters from escalating into megadisasters "have fallen short of what is required."

In the first two months of 2010, the world witnessed two high-impact, earthquakes, when Haiti and Chile were dramatically victimized by the changing forces of nature. The death toll in impoverished Haiti reached a quarter of a million people and the level of property damage was unparalleled in recent memory. While Chile sustained far less loss of human life, the devastation was also far-reaching despite the government's prolonged attempts to earthquake-proof its major cities.

While these two traumatic events captured the attention of newsmakers and the public the world over, there is an enormous number of smaller disasters in a given year, that together produce a significant amount of human and nonhuman loss. And the number of natural disasters and the level of damages caused therein have been growing for decades. Thirty-five years ago, the global costs of weather-related disasters, for example, totaled about $9 billion, 15 years ago, the amount had risen to about $45 billion, and costs continue to soar each passing year. The United Nations (UN) has estimated that while 2009 had fewer natural disasters than usual, there were still 245 events that affected 58 million people worldwide. Others have suggested that over the past two decades, an average of 200,000 individuals have been affected by such events each year. The International Federation of Red Cross and Red Crescent Societies has estimated that if present trends continue, global natural disaster costs will reach $300 billion annually by mid-century.

While natural disasters are random phenomena, it is clear, that the consequences per calamity continue to magnify because of human action. This is not surprising, as the International Federation of Red Cross and Red Crescent Societies has suggested. For this organization, earlier disasters that were more locally confined with fewer people affected, are now more likely to yield consequences that ignore national boundaries in their increasing geographical scope or impact far greater numbers of more heavily concentrated populations. The organization suggests that the increased risk is due to "population growth, unplanned urbanization, environmental degradation, technological and socio-economic conditions, climate change, disease epidemics, poverty and pressure from development within high risk zones."

In December 1989, the UN designated the 1990s as the International Decade for Natural Disaster Reduction (IDNDR) with the objective of using cooperative global efforts to reduce loss and disruption of life brought on by natural disasters. This, in turn, led to the first World Conference on Disaster Reduction, held in Yokohama, Japan in 1994. The plan of action focused on recommendations for addressing the prevention, preparedness, and mitigation of disaster risk.

The international community reconvened in Kobe, Japan in early 2005 for the purpose of "taking stock" of the previous decade's efforts to address natural disasters. The conference acknowledged that disaster loss was on the rise with increasingly global consequences. Additionally, it stated that accelerated cooperative steps must be undertaken to build the necessary capacities to "manage and reduce risk." Its action plan, the *Hyogo Framework for Action 2005–2015: Building the Resilience of Nations and Communities to Disasters,* emphasized five major priorities for action: (1) "Ensure that disaster risk reduction is a national and a local priority with a strong institutional basis for implementation;" (2) "Identify, assess and monitor disaster risks and enhance early warning;" (3) "Use knowledge, innovation and education to build a culture of safety and resilience at all levels;" (4) "Reduce the underlying risk factors;" and (5) "Strengthen disaster preparedness for effective response at all levels."

The important role played by early warning systems, whether with respect to tsunamis, volcanoes, or every kind of disaster in between, has been particularly emphasized in virtually every meeting and every document relating to natural disasters since then.

In the first selection, the "2009 Global Assessment Report" concludes that countries are "making significant progress" in overcoming deficiencies in the area of disaster preparedness and response, despite increases in disaster risk. Enhanced early warning capabilities have appeared throughout the globe. David Rothkopf argues that the most shocking part of the Haiti disaster was that the "damage was so predictable." He suggests that the number of megadisasters such as Haiti will only increase unless the international community commits the billions of dollars necessary to really address disaster prevention and risk reduction.

Risk and Poverty in a Changing Climate: Invest Today for a Safer Tomorrow

Summary and Recommendations: 2009 Global Assessment Report on Disaster Risk Reduction

Key Findings and Recommendations

- Global disaster risk is highly concentrated in poorer countries with weaker governance. Particularly in low and low-middle income countries with rapid economic growth, the exposure of people and assets to natural hazards is growing at a faster rate than risk-reducing capacities are being strengthened, leading to increasing disaster risk.
- Countries with small and vulnerable economies, such as many small-island developing states (SIDS) and land-locked developing countries (LLDCs), have the highest economic vulnerability to natural hazards. Many also have extreme trade limitations.
- Most disaster mortality and asset destruction is intensively concentrated in very small areas exposed to infrequent but extreme hazards. However, low-intensity damage to housing, local infrastructure, crops and livestock, which interrupts and erodes livelihoods, is extensively spread within many countries and occurs very frequently. Such damage represents a significant and largely unaccounted for facet of disaster impacts.
- Poorer communities suffer a disproportionate share of disaster loss. Poor households are usually less resilient to loss and are rarely covered by insurance or social protection. Disaster impacts lead to income and consumption shortfalls and negatively affect welfare and human development, often over the long term.
- Weather-related disaster risk is expanding rapidly both in terms of the territories affected, the losses reported and the frequency of events. This expansive tendency cannot be explained by improved disaster reporting alone. In countries with weaker risk-reducing capacities, underlying risk drivers such as poor urban governance, vulnerable rural livelihoods and ecosystem decline underpin this rapid expansion of weather-related disaster risk.

From *2009 Global Assessment Report on Disaster Risk Reduction*, 2009, pp. 3–4, 6–9, 12–14, 15–20 (excerpts). Copyright © 2009 by United Nations Publications. Reprinted by permission.

- Climate change is already changing the geographic distribution, frequency and intensity of weather-related hazards and threatens to undermine the resilience of poorer countries and their citizens to absorb loss and recover from disaster impacts. This combination of increasing hazard and decreasing resilience makes climate change a global driver of disaster risk. Climate change will magnify the uneven distribution of risk skewing disaster impacts even further towards poor communities in developing countries.

- Progress towards reducing disaster risk is still mixed. In general terms, countries are making significant progress in strengthening capacities, institutional systems and legislation to address deficiencies in disaster preparedness and response. Good progress is also being made in other areas, such as the enhancement of early warning. In contrast, countries report little progress in mainstreaming disaster risk reduction considerations into social, economic, urban, environmental and infrastructural planning and development.

- The governance arrangements for disaster risk reduction in many countries do not facilitate the integration of risk considerations into development. In general, the institutional and legislative arrangements for disaster risk reduction are weakly connected to development sectors.

- The policy and institutional frameworks for climate change adaptation and poverty reduction are only weakly connected to those for disaster risk reduction, at both the national and international levels. Countries have difficulty addressing underlying risk drivers such as poor urban and local governance, vulnerable rural livelihoods and ecosystem decline in a way that leads to a reduction in the risk of damages and economic loss.

- Documented experience in upgrading squatter settlements, providing access to land and infrastructure for the urban poor, strengthening rural livelihoods, protecting ecosystems, and using microfinance, microinsurance and index-based insurance to strengthen resilience shows that it is possible to address the underlying drivers of disaster risk. However, in most countries these experiences are not integrated into the policy mainstream.

- A failure to address the underlying risk drivers will result in dramatic increases in disaster risk and associated poverty outcomes. In contrast, if addressing these drivers is given priority, risk can be reduced, human development protected and adaptation to climate change facilitated. Rather than a cost, this should be seen as an investment in building a more secure, stable, sustainable and equitable future. Given the urgency posed by climate change, decisive action needs to be taken now. . . .

Global Disaster Risk: The Challenge

Risk Is Intensively Concentrated

The risk of both mortality and economic loss in disasters is highly concentrated in a very small portion of the Earth's surface. Countries with large populations exposed to severe natural hazards account for a very large proportion of global disaster risk. For example, 75% of global flood mortality risk is concentrated in only three countries: Bangladesh, China and India.

Similarly mortality and economic loss are concentrated in a very small number of disasters. Between 1975 and 2008, EMDAT[1] recorded 8,866 disasters killing 2,283,767 people. Of these 23 megadisasters killed 1,786,084 people, meaning that 0.26% of the events accounted for 78.2% of the mortality[2]. In the same period internationally recorded economic losses were US$ 1,527.6 billion. Just 25 megadisasters, representing 0.28% of the events, accounted for 40% of the loss.

However, small island developing states (SIDS) and other small countries have far higher levels of relative risk with respect to the size of their populations and economies. For example, in the case of tropical cyclones, Vanuatu has the highest mortality risk per million inhabitants in the world, with St. Kitts and Nevis in third place.

Risk Is Unevenly Distributed

Disaster risk is not evenly distributed. Developing countries concentrate a hugely disproportionate share of the risk. For example, both Japan and the Philippines are exposed to frequent tropical cyclones. In Japan, approximately 22.5 million people are exposed annually, compared to 16 million people in the Philippines. However, the estimated annual death toll from cyclones in the Philippines is almost 17 times greater than that of Japan.

This uneven distribution of risk is also true for groups of countries. For the same number of people exposed to tropical cyclones, mortality risk in low-income countries is approximately 200 times higher than in OECD countries.

Poorer countries also experience higher economic losses in relation to the size of their economies. OECD countries, including Australia, Japan and the United States of America, account for almost 70% of estimated global annual economic losses to tropical cyclones—approximately 90 times more than the losses in exposed countries in sub-Saharan Africa. However, when looked at in terms of economic loss relative to exposed GDP, sub-Saharan African countries experience almost three and a half times more economic loss; Latin America and the Caribbean over six times more; and in the case of floods South Asia experiences approximately 15 times more economic loss than OECD countries.

These examples show that disaster risk is not just a consequence of hazard severity and exposure. Risk is configured by a range of other drivers related to a country's economic and social development. These include not only income and economic strength but also governance factors such as the quality of institutions, transparency and accountability. Wealthier countries tend to have better institutions, more effective early warning, disaster preparedness and response systems, and more open government that tends to be more supportive of disaster risk reduction. Well-governed countries with higher human development indicators generally have lower levels of risk than countries with weaker governance.

Risk Is Increasing

While wealthier countries are usually less risk prone than poorer countries, economic development must be accompanied by the strengthening of governance capacities if disaster risk is to be reduced. Rapid economic and urban development can lead to a growing concentration of people and economic assets in hazard prone cities, fertile river valleys and coastal areas. Disaster risk increases if the exposure of people and assets to natural hazards increases faster than countries can strengthen their risk-reducing capacities by putting policy, institutions, legislation, planning and regulatory frameworks in place.

In absolute terms, and assuming constant hazard levels, global disaster risk increased between 1990 and 2007. In the case of floods, mortality risk increased by 13% from 1990 to 2007. Over the same period flood economic loss risk increased by 35%. These increases in disaster risk are primarily driven by the growing exposure of people and economic assets. The number of people exposed to floods increased by 28% over the same period, while exposed GDP increased by 98%. Most flood risk is concentrated in Asian countries, such as China and India. While global GDP increased by 64%, China and India increased their GDP by 420% and 185%, respectively. Over the same period, vulnerability declined; in the case of flood mortality risk by 11%, and flood economic loss risk by 32%. But this reduction in vulnerability was insufficient to compensate for the increase in exposure.

This suggests that disaster risk is increasing fastest in low- and lower-middle income countries with rapidly growing economies. These countries have rapidly increasing exposure but relatively weak institutions. While they are making improvements in risk-reducing capacities these have yet to catch up with rising exposure. In contrast, most high-income countries experience more moderate increases in exposure and have already reduced a significant part of their vulnerability.

Relative to the size of the global population and GDP, risk may actually be falling. For example, when recorded economic losses are adjusted for inflation and expressed as a proportion of global GDP they are fairly stable.

Small and Vulnerable Economies Are Least Resilient

Countries with small and vulnerable economies, such as many SIDS and landlocked developing countries (LLDCs), have seen their economic development set back decades by disaster impacts. The countries with the highest ratio of economic losses in disasters, with respect to their capital stock are all SIDS and LLDCs, such as Samoa and St. Lucia. Madagascar shows a different pattern but a clear impact of disaster loss on cumulative net capital formation.

In contrast, the impact of major disasters on high-income countries such as the United States of America is imperceptible, even though that country has experienced huge economic losses, for example the US$ 125 billion associated with Hurricane Katrina in 2005. Similarly, there is no marked effect in large low-income countries such as India or middle-income countries such as Colombia. The implications are that disasters do not have a significant impact on capital accumulation in countries with large economies, but a devastating impact on those with small economies.

The countries with the highest economic vulnerability are those with the highest ratio of economic losses to capital stock and the lowest economic resilience to shocks, indicated by very low national savings. Many of these countries also have extreme limitations to their ability to benefit from international trade, characterized by a very low participation in world export markets (less than 0.1%) and low export diversification. SIDS and LLDCs together constitute 60% of the countries with high, and 67% with very high, economic vulnerability to disasters, as measured by the above variables, and comprise about two thirds of all countries affected by extreme trade limitations in the same groups. . . .

The Underlying Risk Drivers

Poor Urban Governance

By 2008, over half the world's population was living in urban areas and by 2010 it is projected that 73% of the world's urban population and most of its largest cities will be in developing countries. . . .

Evidence from cities in Africa, Asia and Latin America, shows that the expansion of informal settlements is closely associated with the rapid increase in weather-related disaster reports in urban areas. . . . The centrifugal expansion of reported floods has mirrored the expansion of informal settlements in the city.

Urbanization per se tends to increase the intensity of run-off during storms and heavy rains. Instead of being absorbed into the ground, greater volumes of rainwater are channelled into drains, culverts and streams. Informal settlements typically occupy land deemed unsuitable for residential or commercial use, located in low lying flood prone areas, on landslide prone hillsides or in ravines, exposing people to hazard. Houses are built and modified without reference to hazard resistant building standards. In many cities there has been an underinvestment in building drains and in maintaining those that exist, particularly in informal settlements. Many floods are caused as much by deficient or non-existent drainage as by the intensity of rainfall.

Vulnerable Rural Livelihoods

Livelihood vulnerability is an underlying driver of disaster risk and poverty in many areas. Approximately 75% of the people living below the international poverty line (US$ 1.25 per day) live and work in rural areas:[3] 268 million in sub-Saharan Africa; 223 million in East Asia and the Pacific; and 394 million in South Asia. Even in countries experiencing rapid economic development, such as China, there are 175 million rural dwellers below this poverty line. Disaster losses affect huge numbers in poor rural areas. In sub-Saharan Africa, during the 2001–2003 drought, an estimated 206 million people, or 32% of the region's population, were undernourished, a number only slightly less than the total 268 million rural poor[4]. . . .

The high structural vulnerability of housing, schools, infrastructure and other assets in poor rural areas exposed to floods, tropical cyclones and earthquakes also leads to major mortality in disasters. Rural housing is usually built with local materials and labour and without hazard resistant building techniques. The collapse of heavy earth walls led to the destruction of 329,579 houses in the 2005 Kashmir earthquake. The lack of protection offered by wattle and daub, and thatch houses in Myanmar contributed to the deaths of 140,000 people in the 2008 cyclone. The isolation of many poor rural areas, combined with under investment by government in infrastructure and in disaster preparedness and response capacities, further increases asset and mortality risk.

Declining Ecosystems

People receive substantial benefits or services from ecosystems. These include provisioning services which provide energy, water, food and fibre for both urban and rural households, as well as regulating services, such as the mitigation of floods and storm surges. Most ecosystems have been intentionally or unintentionally modified to increase the supply of certain categories of services and institutions have been developed to govern access and use of these services. However, because ecosystems produce many services simultaneously, an increase in the supply of one service, such as food, can frequently lead to declines in other services, such as flood regulation.

The Millennium Assessment found that the supply of approximately 60% of the ecosystem services evaluated (15 of 24) were in decline.[5] At the same time, consumption of more than 80% of the services was found to be increasing. In other words, the flow of most ecosystem services is increasing at the same time as the total stock is decreasing. In particular, the Millennium Assessment identified that while people have modified ecosystems to increase provisioning services, these modifications have led to the decline of regulating ecosystem services, including those responsible for mitigating hazards, such as fires and floods. . . .

Global Climate Change

Changes in Means and Extremes Lead to Increasing Hazard and Declining Resilience

Climate change is probably the greatest global outcome of environmental inequity. It is driven by greenhouse gas emissions that have brought benefits to affluent societies and individuals, yet most of the burdens fall on developing countries and their poorest citizens. . . .

There is already evidence that some kinds of weather-related hazard are increasing. . . . The average annual number of cyclones has been fairly stable, (between 54.9 and 58.1 per year) since 1976, regardless of sea surface temperature (SST). However, in warmer years there are more Category 3 and 4 (i.e. more intense) cyclones and fewer in Categories 1 and 2. In particular, compared to the period between 1976 and 1984, when there were no data on SST, there are now significantly more category 4 and 5 cyclones. This is in line with the findings of the IPCC Fourth Assessment Report and recent research that has estimated that a 1°C increase in SST would lead to a 31% increase in the global frequency of Category 4 and 5 cyclones per year.

Climate Change Magnifies the Uneven Distribution of Disaster Risk

By increasing hazard at the same time as it erodes resilience, climate change has a magnifying effect on disaster risk. In particular, climate change will magnify the uneven distribution of risk, skewing disaster impacts even further towards poor communities in developing countries. . . .

. . . Ninety-seven percent of the documented local-level loss reports are weather-related. This means that a very significant part of emerging disaster risk in developing countries is highly sensitive to any increase in hazard intensity and frequency due to climate change. It is likely that climate change is already contributing to the rapid increase in the number of weather-related loss reports since 1980, although at present it is not possible to calculate by how much. . . .

Progress in Addressing Disaster Risk

The Hyogo Framework for Action

In 2005, 168 countries adopted the Hyogo Framework of Action (HFA), a comprehensive set of five priorities that aim to achieve a substantial reduction in disaster losses, in terms of lives and social, economic and environmental assets of communities and countries by 2015.

A recent review by 62 countries[6] indicates that progress towards this objective is still mixed. In general terms, countries are making significant progress in strengthening capacities, institutional systems and legislation to address deficiencies in disaster preparedness and response. Good progress is also being made in other areas, such as the enhancement of early warning. As a result, some lower-income countries, such as Bangladesh and Cuba, have already made dramatic strides in reducing mortality risk in the face of hazards such as tropical cyclones and floods, which are sensitive to improvements in early warning, preparedness and response. For example, despite being hit by five successive hurricanes in 2008, only 7 deaths were reported in Cuba.

In contrast, countries report little progress in mainstreaming disaster risk reduction considerations into social, economic, urban, environmental and infrastructural planning and development. Early warning and preparedness can help to evacuate people in the case of a cyclone. But housing, schools and infrastructure cannot be evacuated and, if not structurally resistant, they are damaged or destroyed.

Across all five HFA Priorities for Action, high-income countries outperform low- and middle-income countries. In these high-income countries, the adoption of hazard resistant building standards, planning and environmental regulations as well as a web of institutions and systems that protect citizens when disasters occur, have enabled a substantial reduction in vulnerability.

In the case of the least-developed countries, some lack the basic technical, human, institutional and financial capacities to address even the most basic aspects of disaster risk reduction.

Between these two poles, many middle- and low-income countries have made major strides towards developing national policies, institutional systems and legislation for disaster risk reduction. Unfortunately this has not been translated into reductions in disaster risk in the principal development sectors. It would appear that countries have difficulty addressing underlying risk drivers such as poor urban and local governance, vulnerable rural livelihoods and ecosystem decline in a way that leads to a reduction in the risk of damage and economic loss. At the same time, the governance arrangements for disaster risk reduction in many countries do not facilitate the integration of risk considerations into development. In general, the institutional and legislative arrangements for disaster risk reduction are weakly connected to development sectors. Mainstreaming is challenged by a range of factors that include difficulties in compiling comprehensive information on disaster risks, weak engagement by the development sectors and major difficulties in ensuring implementation, enforcement and accountability.

Climate Change Adaptation

Many countries are also developing plans and strategies to adapt to climate change, for example through National Adaptation Programmes of Action (NAPAs). In principle, given that increased risk from weather-related hazards is a manifestation of climate change, adaptation could and should reinforce disaster risk reduction efforts. The Report has not comprehensively reviewed progress in adaptation. However, there is evidence to show that progress in implementation is still slow and adaptation policy and institutional frameworks are largely disconnected from those created to reduce disaster risk, at both the national and international levels. Adaptation faces similar challenges to disaster risk reduction, in particular a governance framework that can allow risk in the development sectors to be addressed.

Poverty Reduction

Large numbers of Poverty Reduction Strategy Papers (PRSPs) explicitly recognize the poverty outcomes associated with disaster impacts and some include sections on disaster risk reduction. In principle, poverty reduction efforts in both rural and urban areas have a considerable potential to address the underlying risk drivers if they are clearly focused. In most countries, however, poverty reduction has only weak functional connections to the policy and institutional frameworks for disaster risk reduction. Unless disaster risk considerations are factored into poverty-reducing development, the result may be increased risk, as the collapse of schools in earthquakes so poignantly illustrates. At the same time, the inclusion of disaster risk reduction in PRSPs is often limited to disaster preparedness and response aspects. Therefore, the potential of PRSPs to address the underlying risk drivers is still not fully exploited.

Conclusions

The Imperative for Urgent Action

Current progress under the HFA and in related areas of poverty reduction and climate change adaptation is not leading to a reduction in disaster risk. The Report highlights that risk is continuing to increase, even assuming constant hazard levels, and that any further increase will disproportionately affect poor communities in developing countries. Climate change magnifies the uneven distribution of risk, increasing both disaster risk and poverty outcomes in these communities. Unless this trend is reversed it will be impossible to achieve the HFA and progress towards the Millennium Development Goals (MDGs) will be compromised.

The evidence provided in the Report underlines the urgency of avoiding dangerous climate change. Greater urgency in efforts to reduce global green-house gas emissions and reduce energy consumption are required if a potentially catastrophic increase in disaster risk is to be avoided, the impacts of which will be largely concentrated in developing countries.

Action in other policy areas is also required. The countries with the highest relative risk and the lowest resilience to disaster impacts are those with small and vulnerable economies, such as many SIDS and LLDCs. The low resilience of these countries is associated with extreme limitations in their ability to participate in global trade. Efforts are therefore required to coordinate policies on trade and productive sector development in these countries.

Unfortunately, the world is committed to significant climate change, even if rapid progress is achieved towards a low-carbon economy. Therefore, disaster prone countries will only be able to avoid further increases in disaster impacts and poverty outcomes by taking decisive action to address the under-lying drivers that are responsible for the concentration and expansion of risk. The Report highlights the need to strengthen capacities to address three key drivers: poor urban governance, vulnerable rural livelihoods and ecosystem decline. Weak social protection is a fourth driver, which, while not examined in depth in the Report, is also important.

A failure to address these drivers will result in dramatic increases in disaster risk and associated poverty outcomes. In contrast, if addressing these drivers is given priority, risk can be reduced, human development protected and adaptation to climate change facilitated. Rather than a cost, this should be seen as an investment in building a more secure, stable, sustainable and equitable future. Given the urgency posed by climate change, decisive action needs to be taken now.

A Policy Framework for Risk-Reducing Development

It is possible to address the underlying drivers of disaster risk. In all regions of the world, documented experience in upgrading squatter settlements, providing access to land and infrastructure for the urban poor, strengthening rural livelihoods, protecting ecosystems, and using microfinance, microinsurance and index-based insurance to strengthen resilience show that it can be done.

The most successful of these experiences have emerged in the context of innovative partnerships between national and local governments and civil society and are leading to a sustainable reduction in risks.

These experiences demonstrate that the underlying risk drivers can be addressed, and that the tools, methods and approaches necessary to do so already exist. However, they must still be integrated into the policy mainstream. Most countries still lack a determined and focused high-level development policy framework that addresses these drivers and is supportive of such innovative approaches. Without such central support, ongoing efforts in disaster risk reduction and climate change adaptation cannot gain traction.

The need to strengthen capacities to develop and implement such a policy framework is particularly urgent in those low- and middle-income countries where hazard exposure is growing most rapidly, where risks are concentrated, and where the magnifying effects of climate change will be most felt. Risk-reducing development is essential if disaster risk reduction is to be mainstreamed into development and if development is to be adapted to climate change.

The adoption of such an overarching policy framework would allow the different plans, programmes and projects in poverty reduction, climate change adaptation and disaster risk reduction—as well as in sustainable development in general—to become better aligned in order to address the underlying drivers of disaster risk. These plans and programmes include PRSPs, NAPAs, United Nations Development Assistance Frameworks and nationally specific programming instruments. To be relevant and successful such a policy framework must be at the centre of the political agenda, backed by dedicated resources in the national budget, and should have leadership at the highest levels of government.

If a policy framework for risk-reducing development is to be actionable a different culture of implementation will be required, one that builds on government-civil society partnerships and cooperation. Such partnerships can dramatically reduce the costs of risk reduction, ensure local acceptance, and help to build social capital, which reduces long-term vulnerability.

Effective Risk Reduction Governance

In addition to a policy framework that prioritizes risk-reducing development, a set of governance arrangements is needed for disaster risk reduction, poverty reduction and climate change adaptation that is capable of ensuring that risk considerations are factored into all development investments. Improvements to risk reduction governance are critical, in order to provide a vehicle for policy and a systematic approach to planning, financing and monitoring investment in all sectors.

In particular, the existing institutional and governance arrangements for disaster risk reduction and climate change adaptation need to be harmonized, building on existing systems of public administration. The development of a single governance framework for risk reduction would seem to offer opportunities for more effective policy implementation and for avoiding duplication and lack of coordination. The harmonization of international frameworks and requirements for planning and reporting would be supportive of better integration at the country level.

The institutional and administrative responsibility for risk reduction has to be vested at the highest possible level in government, in order to have the necessary political authority and resources to influence development policy. If risk reduction can be included explicitly in national development plans and budgets, all parts of government are then able to programme risk reduction actions and investments.

Fortunately, many countries are already putting into place innovative mechanisms that enable this mainstreaming and harmonization to occur. These include factoring disaster risk reduction into national development plans and budgets; development of new institutional structures for hazard monitoring and risk assessment that integrate existing scientific and technical institutions; the inclusion of cost–benefit analysis into public investment systems; the involvement of the national audit or controller's office in supporting implementation, enforcement and accountability in all sectors and at all levels of government; improvements in early warning systems; and the application of innovative mechanisms for risk transfer.

Disaster Risk Reduction Is an Investment Not a Cost

To seriously address the underlying risk factors on the scale necessary requires major investment. It is difficult to provide an accurate global estimate of this cost but the calculations developed by the Millennium Project serve to give an idea of the magnitude. These costs can be significantly reduced through adopting participatory approaches, but it is clear that several hundred billion dollars are required. This figure is coherent with estimates regarding the cost of climate change adaptation. An increase in the resources available for climate change adaptation will be required, as well as those pledged for the MDGs. In the context of the global economic crisis, investments in infrastructure and employment creation can provide opportunities to address the underlying risk drivers, for example through investments to improve drainage in flood prone areas.

Disaster risk reduction is usually conceptualized as an additional cost. In fact one of the principal arguments used to justify a lack of progress in disaster risk reduction is that developing countries have other priorities, such as reducing poverty, and cannot afford the additional costs of disaster risk reduction. The Report puts forward a contrasting view. Investment in disaster risk reduction generally represents a large saving in terms of avoided losses and reconstruction costs and is thus a way of lowering the costs of poverty reduction and of addressing the underlying risk factors. This means that the real cost of addressing the underlying risk drivers is actually lower if disaster risk reduction is included.

In conclusion, the key requirements are to help countries strengthen governance arrangements and improve management of investments for addressing the underlying risk factors, and to ensure disaster risk reduction is incorporated into those investments. Without strengthening these arrangements and capacities, even large investments in development may have little tangible effect or be counter-productive. If governance arrangements and capacities for risk reduction can be strengthened, small investments can produce huge benefits. Investing today to strengthen capacities is essential if future generations are to enjoy a safer tomorrow.

Endnotes

1. The Office for US Foreign Disaster Assistance/Centre for Research on the Epidemiology of Disasters (OFDA/CRED) International Disaster Database: . . .

2. EMDAT does not register reports of small-scale disasters below its threshold of 10 deaths, 100 people affected or a call for international assistance.

3. Ravaillon, C. (2008) *The Developing World Is Poorer Than We Thought but No Less Successful in the Fight Against Poverty.* Washington DC. World Bank.

4. FAO (Food and Agriculture Organization of the United Nations) (2006) *The State of Food Insecurity in the World.* Rome. FAO.

5. Millennium Ecosystem Assessment (2005) *Ecosystems and Human Well-Being: Current State and Trends: Findings of the Condition and Trends Working Group.* Washington DC. Island Press.

6. The number of countries that had prepared interim HFA progress reports by the end of February, 2009.

David Rothkopf  **NO**

Averting Disaster: Calamities Like the Haiti Quake Aren't Just Predictable—They're Preventable

The most shocking thing about the disaster in Haiti was not that it was so sudden, violent, and horrific in its human toll. It's that the damage was so predictable. Seismologists warned that the country was at risk as recently as two years ago. Haiti is also the latest in a string of nearly annual megadisasters extending back through the past decade, calamities claiming tens of thousands of lives more because poverty and the forces of nature met with foreseeably tragic consequences.

During the Clinton administration, I helped lead an interagency effort to assist the country after our intervention there in 1994. Our reasons for wanting to help were not, of course, entirely or even primarily charitable. While we acted out of a sincere commitment on the part of a president who is now the U.N. special envoy to that battered country, we naturally also worried that further social disintegration would result in waves of unwanted immigrants arriving on our shores. Viewing tiny Haiti primarily as a source of problems for America has been—after neglect—the single most important driver of U.S. policies toward that country since its independence.

Traveling regularly to Port-au-Prince, I could not help but be struck by Haiti's vibrancy or its largely untapped promise. Nor, sadly, could I ignore the deprivation or the petty infighting among the island's elites that blocked Haitians from the few opportunities at progress that ever wafted across their shores. We tried to help, to organize business missions, to mobilize funding of local projects, to apply comparatively low-voltage policy paddles to the heart of a nearly lifeless economic victim. But given the island's manifold, often heartbreaking, problems—weak governance, feeble infrastructure, illiteracy— it was clear that our efforts would likely be only palliative.

And it was also clear that America's interest would wane and Haiti would remain on life support. Year to year, such countries receive just enough aid for them to fade from our consciousness and consciences. Development dollars seem to have two purposes: buying friends we may need to advance specific national interests and renting a little peace of mind by postponing calamity. But inevitably the money is too little, and countries like Haiti come crashing

From *Newsweek*, January 25, 2010. Copyright © 2010 by Newsweek, Inc. All rights reserved. Used by permission and protected by the Copyright Laws of the United States. The printing, copying, redistribution, or retransmission of the Material without express written permission via PARS International Corp. is prohibited.

into our lives with the next crisis—almost invariably a crisis that is more costly in human and financial terms than the steps we might have taken to prevent or mitigate it in the first place.

Weep as one might at the pictures now streaming out of Port-au-Prince, what is sadder still is that it is just the latest example of a blight to which the international community has devoted too little attention and too few resources. Take every terror attack in the past 20 years. Add every airline crash. Add SARS or H1N1. Add many of the diseases whose causes are championed by high-profile telethons and gala fundraisers. The total death toll pales when compared with what might be called the world's megadisasters. Before Haiti, an estimated 70,000 people perished in 2008's earthquake in Sichuan, China. Before that almost 150,000 died when the cyclone Nargis struck Burma. In 2005, the death toll from an earthquake in the mountains of Kashmir approached 90,000. The year before, in the greatest such recent disaster, the Indian Ocean tsunami killed perhaps 230,000.

While the events seem disparate, in each case telltale traits recur. Fragile communities of the world's most vulnerable people were forced by circumstance to root themselves in treacherous soil—near shorelines but below or too near sea level, on mountainsides, and in cities along fault lines. As in the case of Haiti, scientists warned that the situations were precarious. As in the case of Haiti, local governments failed—often due to lack of resources—to establish or enforce minimum building codes or to put in place the infrastructure that could make warning, escape, or rescue likely.

These stunning calamities are almost inevitably reported as "out of the blue" events, "acts of God," proof of fate's fickleness. But in fact they are a class of global threat as real and as manageable as pandemics or many of the other problems with which the international community grapples. We could take several more meaningful steps to prevent natural disasters from becoming megadisasters: establishing and effectively promoting best practices for building, safety inspection, and remedial construction that can work in impoverished settings; sharing technical know-how; providing early-warning technologies; better training societies and preparing the international community to respond; providing essential infrastructure; and where necessary relocating communities or providing needed sea walls, retaining walls, structural supports, survivable power, water systems, and first-response capacity.

Organizations like the United Nations have made earnest and periodic efforts to address these concerns. But the results have clearly fallen far short of what is required. Would it be expensive to promote these changes more fully? By what measure? Tens of billions? Yes. Hundreds of billions? Perhaps. But compared to the cost of the war in Iraq or the Wall Street bailout? Just a fraction. To the human cost of the disasters themselves? Incalculably less.

Current trends—from rising seas and the changing severe weather patterns associated with global warming to the rapid, often poorly planned urbanization of the developing world—mean megadisasters will only become more likely. Wouldn't it be fitting—and a sign that we appreciated the true costs of what has happened in tragic Haiti—if the rebuilding there became a case study in how the international community can work together to develop new standards, new designs, and a genuine commitment to reducing the risk of such calamities in the future? A reborn Port-au-Prince could be a showcase for ideas about affordable, durable housing, for enhanced regional cooperation—and for how we can apply lessons that have been learned at an unfathomably great cost.

POSTSCRIPT

Is the International Community Making Progress in Addressing Natural Disasters?

It is certainly true that the challenges associated with global disasters have increased significantly in recent times, as suggested in the "2009 Global Assessment Report." And the risk of substantial loss of property and life is concentrated in a very small portion of the Earth's surfaces as well as in a very small number of disasters. Data in the report show that between 1975 and 2008, 8,866 disasters resulted in 2,283,767 deaths. Of these, 23 megadisasters were responsible for 1,786,084 deaths, or to put it another way, 0.26 percent of the calamities resulted in 78.2 percent of the mortality. And just 25 megadisasters (0.28 percent) accounted for 40 percent of the economic losses.

Risk is also not evenly divided, as poorer countries appear to have a disproportionately high share of the risk and also experience greater economic losses. Of equal concern is the fact that global disaster risk is increasing, particularly in those countries below the median income levels. And these latter countries are precisely the ones least resilient, in the words of the report.

As mentioned earlier, underlying risk drivers affect both the incidence and the severity of natural disasters. Poor urban governance, vulnerable rural livelihoods, declining ecosystems, and global climate change are all pinpointed as culprits in the ongoing disaster sagas.

It is not surprising, therefore, that particularly after a megadisaster such as the two experienced in early 2010, cries of inadequate global preparedness and response along the lines of the article by David Rothkopf are heard in many quarters. Watching the gut-wrenching television images of the death and destruction following these disasters was not for the faint of heart.

But a careful survey of the literature reveals considerable systematic and organized global attention to the variety of problems inherent in addressing natural disasters. The number of international governmental and nongovernmental organizations addressing some aspect of the problem is truly impressive. Twenty-one specialized UN agencies and other related organizations are involved in the assault on natural disasters, and numerous other UN agencies also play a role. As a consequence, it is evident that there has been major attention paid to natural disasters by both international organizations and national governments over the past 30 years, and this attention is increasing, not diminishing. The basic problem is, though, that the potential for greater and greater levels of human and nonhuman damage is also increasing as a consequence of how humans organize their lives, mentioned earlier. The result is that significant breakthroughs in addressing the consequences of natural disasters, including preventing them from becoming megadisasters, await both a dramatic increase in funding from the international community and moving well beyond focusing on early warning systems to dealing with the underlying risk drivers.

There are a number of reports that describe the evolution of the global community's interest in natural disasters. The first one is *Report of the World Conference on Natural Disaster Reduction, Yokohama, May 23–27, 1994* (International Decade for Natural Disaster Reduction, United Nations, 1994). This comprehensive report includes the strategic plan and all related conference documents. Another major report, *Hyogo Framework for Action 2005–2015: Building the Resilience of Nations and Communities to Disasters* (International Strategy for Disaster Reduction [ISDR], 2006), provides comprehensive information about the World Conference on Disaster Reduction in Kobe, Japan in early 2005. The report spells out lessons learned and gaps identified in the Yokohama strategy and describes the priorities for 2005–2015. Another ISDR publication is *Implementing the Hyogo Framework for Action in Europe: Advances and Challenges* (2009). Another UN report describes an important gathering, the Global Platform for Disaster Risk Reduction in Geneva in 2009 (*Creating Linkages for a Safer Tomorrow*—Proceedings). The ISDR Scientific and Technical Committee published a major document, *Reducing Disaster Risks through Science: Issues and Actions* (United Nations, 2009), which examines the potential role of science in selected disaster situations. A study that focuses on early warning systems for tsunamis and other ocean hazards is *Five Years After the Tsunami in the Indian Ocean* (United Nations, 2009). An important nongovernmental organization publication is *World Disasters Report 2009—Focus on Early Warning, Early Action* (International Federation of Red Cross and Red Crescent Societies, 2009). The latter organization has also produced a report on its work in combating national disasters (*The Global Alliance for Disaster Risk Reduction: Building Safer, Resilient Communities*).

There are also a number of relevant publications written outside the international organizational community. Some of these publications are *Natural Disaster Hotspots: A Global Risk Analysis* (Maxx Dilley et al., World Bank Publications, 2005); *Natural Disaster Reduction: Global Perspectives, South East Asian Realities and Global Strategies* (Dilip Kumar Sinha, Anthem Press, 2007); *Natural Disasters, Cultural Responses: Case Studies toward a Global Environmental History* (Lexington Books, 2009); *Global Catastrophic Risks* (Nick Bostrom and Milan M. Cirkovic, eds., Oxford University Press, 2008); *Mitigation of Natural Hazards and Disasters: International Perspectives* (C. Emdad Haque, ed., Springer, 2005); and *Surviving the Century: Facing Climate Chaos and Other Global Challenges* (Herbert Girardet, ed., Earthscan Publications, 2008).

ISSUE 22

Has Al-Qaeda and Its Jihad against the United States Been Defeated?

YES: Fareed Zakaria, from "The Jihad against the Jihadis: How Moderate Muslim Leaders Waged War on Extremists—and Won," *Newsweek* (February 22, 2010)

NO: Scott Stewart, from "Jihadism in 2010: The Threat Continues," *STRATFOR* (January 6, 2010)

ISSUE SUMMARY

YES: Fareed Zakaria argues through the acts of moderate Muslims across the Islamic world, "We have turned the corner on the war between extremism and the West and . . . now we are in a new phase of clean up and rebuilding of relationships." His argument rests on the actions of Muslim regimes in Saudi Arabia, Pakistan, and Indonesia who are fighting back against jihadism, engaging in military and political policies that are marginalizing extremists and consequently winning the war.

NO: Scott Stewart contends that despite Western victories against al-Qaeda based in the Afghan–Pakistan border region, regional groups and cells have taken up the slack and the threat of extremism and jihad is still strong and ominous. He focuses on the work of these groups in Somalia, Yemen, and North Africa to illustrate this continued fight.

September 11, 2001 was not the beginning of the enmity between Islamic fundamentalism and the United States and her allies, but it certainly was the explosion that turned the conflict into a full-fledged war. For close to 10 years, the United States has been at war with fundamentalist terrorist groups and in particular al-Qaeda led by Osama bin Laden. The U.S. invasion of Afghanistan, its later invasion of Iraq, and its support for regimes from Pakistan to Indonesia to Saudi Arabia and Morocco are predicated in part on our shared opposition to al-Qaeda.

Al-Qaeda and its allies around the Muslim world have identified the United States as one of several threats to the purity of Islam and the primacy of

Muslims in what they consider Muslim lands. Along with secular and/or corrupt Arab regimes and of course Israel, al-Qaeda has launched a jihad against these forces and is using terrorism as its main weapon.

The tenor of the conflicts around the world has grown increasingly bitter and the casualties continue to mount. There are ebbs and flows to this conflict in the various theatres of battle. For example, since 9/11 several efforts at like-minded attacks have been thwarted, most recently the "underwear bomber" over Detroit. However, other bombings from Bali to London to Moscow have been successful. In Afghanistan and the border regions of Pakistan the battle rages with renewed U.S. troop levels, allied assistance, and increasing attacks from al-Qaeda and its Taliban allies.

Amid the military struggle, there is a political, philosophical battle ensuing between these sides for essentially the hearts and minds of the Muslim world. That battle is waged over the airwaves and through the Internet. Al-Qaeda is a tiny minority to be sure but they, along with the United States and others, are waging a propaganda battle for the sympathy, support, and active involvement of the so-called Muslim street, those hundreds of millions of Muslims who watch and evaluate their position in the struggle.

Lately, there has been much talk and writing about victory or at least turning the corner in the struggle. Analysts have speculated about whether al-Qaeda is on the run, on its last legs, or near collapse. Others have argued that this is a long struggle and while there will be victories and defeats, one cannot defeat this enemy until other changes occur in the Muslim world that are more socioeconomic and thus systemic.

Our authors represent two perspectives on this issue. Fareed Zakaria contends that through a series of events and actions, moderate Muslims have made their choice and are actively fighting al-Qaeda and such extremism and thus are winning the conflict. In fact, Zakaria argues that the battle is essentially over and now all that is left is to mop up the remaining zealots and holdouts.

Scott Stewart of *STRATFOR* argues that the al-Qaeda threat and jihad remain but it is just changing character and tactics to adapt to the changing force structure. He argues that it is becoming more decentralized and localized and thus represents a strong threat. The battle is not over; it is just entering a new phase.

YES

Fareed Zakaria

The Jihad against the Jihadis: How Moderate Muslim Leaders Waged War on Extremists—and Won

September 11, 2001, was gruesome enough on its own terms, but for many of us, the real fear was of what might follow. Not only had al-Qaeda shown it was capable of sophisticated and ruthless attacks, but a far greater concern was that the group had or could establish a powerful hold on the hearts and minds of Muslims. And if Muslims sympathized with al-Qaeda's cause, we were in for a herculean struggle. There are more than 1.5 billion Muslims living in more than 150 countries across the world. If jihadist ideology became attractive to a significant part of this population, the West faced a clash of civilizations without end, one marked by blood and tears.

These fears were well founded. The 9/11 attacks opened the curtain on a world of radical and violent Islam that had been festering in the Arab lands and had been exported across the globe, from London to Jakarta. Polls all over the Muslim world revealed deep anger against America and the West and a surprising degree of support for Osama bin Laden. Governments in most of these countries were ambivalent about this phenomenon, assuming that the Islamists' wrath would focus on the United States and not themselves. Large, important countries like Saudi Arabia and Indonesia seemed vulnerable.

More than eight eventful years have passed, but in some ways it still feels like 2001. Republicans have clearly decided that fanning the public's fears of rampant jihadism continues to be a winning strategy. Commentators furnish examples of backwardness and brutality from various parts of the Muslim world—and there are many—to highlight the grave threat we face.

But, in fact, the entire terrain of the war on terror has evolved dramatically. Put simply, the moderates are fighting back and the tide is turning. We no longer fear the possibility of a major country succumbing to jihadist ideology. In most Muslim nations, mainstream rulers have stabilized their regimes and their societies, and extremists have been isolated. This has not led to the flowering of Jeffersonian democracy or liberalism. But modern, somewhat secular forces are clearly in control and widely supported across the Muslim world. Polls, elections, and in-depth studies all confirm this trend.

From *Newsweek*, February 22, 2010. Copyright © 2010 by Newsweek, Inc. All rights reserved. Used by permission and protected by the Copyright Laws of the United States. The printing, copying, redistribution, or retransmission of the Material without express written permission via PARS International Corp. is prohibited.

The focus of our concern now is not a broad political movement but a handful of fanatics scattered across the globe. Yet Washington's vast nation-building machinery continues to spend tens of billions of dollars in Iraq and Afghanistan, and there are calls to do more in Yemen and Somalia. What we have to ask ourselves is whether any of that really will deter these small bands of extremists. Some of them come out of the established democracies of the West, hardly places where nation building will help. We have to understand the changes in the landscape of Islam if we are going to effectively fight the enemy on the ground, rather than the enemy in our minds.

Once, no country was more worrying than bin Laden's homeland. The Kingdom of Saudi Arabia, steward of the holy cities of Mecca and Medina, had surpassed Egypt as the de facto leader of the Arab world because of the vast sums of money it doled out to Islamic causes—usually those consonant with its puritanical Wahhabi doctrines. Since 1979 the Saudi regime had openly appeased its home-grown Islamists, handing over key ministries and funds to reactionary mullahs. Visitors to Saudi Arabia after 9/11 were shocked by what they heard there. Educated Saudis—including senior members of the government—publicly endorsed wild conspiracy theories and denied that any Saudis had been involved in the 9/11 attacks. Even those who accepted reality argued that the fury of some Arabs was inevitable, given America's one-sided foreign policy on the Arab–Israeli issue.

America's initial reaction to 9/11 was to focus on al-Qaeda. The group was driven out of its base in Afghanistan and was pursued wherever it went. Its money was tracked and blocked, its fighters arrested and killed. Many other nations joined in, from France to Malaysia. After all, no government wanted to let terrorists run loose in its land.

But a broader conversation also began, one that asked, "Why is this happening, and what can we do about it?" The most influential statement on Islam to come out of the post-9/11 era was not a presidential speech or an intellectual's essay. It was, believe it or not, a United Nations report. In 2002 the U.N. Development Program published a detailed study of the Arab world. The paper made plain that in an era of globalization, openness, diversity, and tolerance, the Arabs were the world's great laggards. Using hard data, the report painted a picture of political, social, and intellectual stagnation in countries from the Maghreb to the Gulf. And it was written by a team of Arab scholars. This was not paternalism or imperialism. It was truth.

The report, and many essays and speeches by political figures and intellectuals in the West, launched a process of reflection in the Arab world. The debate did not take the form that many in the West wanted—no one said, "You're right, we are backward." But still, leaders in Arab countries were forced to advocate modernity and moderation openly rather than hoping that they could quietly reap its fruits by day while palling around with the mullahs at night. The Bush administration launched a series of programs across the Muslim world to strengthen moderates, shore up civil society, and build forces of tolerance and pluralism. All this has had an effect. From Dubai to Amman to Cairo, in some form or another, authorities have begun opening up economic and political systems that had been tightly closed. The changes have sometimes been small, but the arrows are finally moving in the right direction.

Ultimately, the catalyst for change was something more lethal than a report. After 9/11, al-Qaeda was full of bluster: recall the videotapes of bin Laden and his deputy, Ayman al-Zawahiri, boasting of their plans. Yet they confronted a far less permissive environment. Moving money, people, and materials had all become much more difficult. So they, and local groups inspired by them, began attacking where they could—striking local targets rather than global ones, including a nightclub and hotel in Indonesia, a wedding party in Jordan, cafés in Casablanca and Istanbul, and resorts in Egypt. They threatened the regimes that, either by accident or design, had allowed them to live and breathe.

Over the course of 2003 and 2004, Saudi Arabia was rocked by a series of such terrorist attacks, some directed against foreigners, but others at the heart of the Saudi regime—the Ministry of the Interior and compounds within the oil industry. The monarchy recognized that it had spawned dark forces that were now endangering its very existence. In 2005 a man of wisdom and moderation, King Abdullah, formally ascended to the throne and inaugurated a large-scale political and intellectual effort aimed at discrediting the ideology of jihadism. Mullahs were ordered to denounce suicide bombings and violence more generally. Education was pried out of the hands of the clerics. Terrorists and terror suspects were "rehabilitated" through extensive programs of education, job training, and counseling. Central Command chief Gen. David Petraeus said to me, "The Saudi role in taking on al-Qaeda, both by force but also using political, social, religious, and educational tools, is one of the most important, least reported positive developments in the war on terror."

Perhaps the most successful country to combat jihadism has been the world's most populous Muslim nation, Indonesia. In 2002 that country seemed destined for a long and painful struggle with the forces of radical Islam. The nation was rocked by terror attacks, and a local Qaeda affiliate, Jemaah Islamiah, appeared to be gaining strength. But eight years later, JI has been marginalized and mainstream political parties have gained ground, all while a young democracy has flowered after the collapse of the Suharto dictatorship.

Magnus Ranstorp of Stockholm's Center for Asymmetric Threat Studies recently published a careful study examining Indonesia's success in beating back extremism. The main lesson, he writes, is to involve not just government but civil society as a whole, including media and cultural figures who can act as counterforces to terrorism. (That approach obviously has greater potential in regions and countries with open and vibrant political systems—Southeast Asia, Turkey, and India—than in the Arab world.)

Iraq occupies an odd place in this narrative. While the invasion of Iraq inflamed the Muslim world and the series of blunders during the initial occupation period created dangerous chaos at the heart of the Middle East, Iraq also became a stage on which al-Qaeda played a deadly hand, and lost. As al-Qaeda in Iraq gained militarily, it began losing politically. It turned from its broader global ideology to focus on a narrow sectarian agenda, killing Shias and fueling a Sunni–Shia civil war. In doing so, the group also employed a level of brutality and violence that shocked most Iraqis. Where the group gained control, even pious people were repulsed by its reactionary behavior. In Anbar province, the heart of the Sunni insurgency, al-Qaeda in Iraq would routinely cut off the fingers of smokers. Even those Sunnis who feared the new Iraq began to prefer Shia rule to such medievalism.

Since 9/11, Western commentators have been calling on moderate Muslim leaders to condemn jihadist ideology, issue *fatwas* against suicide bombing, and denounce al-Qaeda. Since about 2006, they've begun to do so in significant numbers. In 2007 one of bin Laden's most prominent Saudi mentors, the preacher and scholar Salman al-Odah, wrote an open letter criticizing him for "fostering a culture of suicide bombings that has caused bloodshed and suffering, and brought ruin to entire Muslim communities and families." That same year Abdulaziz al ash-Sheikh, the grand mufti of Saudi Arabia, issued a *fatwa* prohibiting Saudis from engaging in jihad abroad and accused both bin Laden and Arab regimes of "transforming our youth into walking bombs to accomplish their own political and military aims." One of al-Qaeda's own top theorists, Abdul-Aziz el-Sherif, renounced its extremism, including the killing of civilians and the choosing of targets based on religion and nationality. Sherif—a longtime associate of Zawahiri who crafted what became known as al-Qaeda's guide to jihad—has called on militants to desist from terrorism, and authored a rebuttal of his former cohorts.

Al-Azhar University in Cairo, the oldest and most prestigious school of Islamic learning, now routinely condemns jihadism. The Darul Uloom Deoband movement in India, home to the original radicalism that influenced al-Qaeda, has inveighed against suicide bombing since 2008. None of these groups or people have become pro-American or liberal, but they have become anti-jihadist.

This might seem like an esoteric debate. But consider: the most important moderates to denounce militants have been the families of radicals. In the case of both the five young American Muslims from Virginia arrested in Pakistan last year and Christmas bomber Umar Farouk Abdulmutallab, parents were the ones to report their worries about their own children to the U.S. government—an act so stunning that it requires far more examination, and praise, than it has gotten. This is where soft power becomes critical. Were the fathers of these boys convinced that the United States would torture, maim, and execute their children without any sense of justice, they would not have come forward. I doubt that any Chechen father has turned his child over to Vladimir Putin's regime.

The data on public opinion in the Muslim world are now overwhelming. London School of Economics professor Fawaz Gerges has analyzed polls from dozens of Muslim countries over the past few years. He notes that in a range of places—Jordan, Pakistan, Indonesia, Lebanon, and Bangladesh—there have been substantial declines in the number of people who say suicide bombing and other forms of violence against civilian targets can be justified to defend Islam. Wide majorities say such attacks are, at most, rarely acceptable.

The shift has been especially dramatic in Jordan, where only 12 percent of Jordanians view suicide attacks as "often or sometimes justified" (down from 57 percent in 2005). In Indonesia, 85 percent of respondents agree that terrorist attacks are "rarely/never justified" (in 2002, by contrast, only 70 percent opposed such attacks). In Pakistan, that figure is 90 percent, up from 43 percent in 2002.

Gerges points out that, by comparison, only 46 percent of Americans say that "bombing and other attacks intentionally aimed at civilians" are "never justified," while 24 percent believe these attacks are "often or sometimes justified."

This shift does not reflect a turn away from religiosity or even from a backward conception of Islam. That ideological struggle persists and will take decades, not years, to resolve itself. But the battle against jihadism has fared much better, much sooner, than anyone could have imagined.

The exceptions to this picture readily spring to mind—Afghanistan, Pakistan, Yemen. But consider the conditions in those countries. In Afghanistan, jihadist ideology has wrapped itself around a genuine ethnic struggle in which Pashtuns feel that they are being dispossessed by rival groups. In Pakistan, the regime is still where Saudi Arabia was in 2003 and 2004: slowly coming to realize that the extremism it had fostered has now become a threat to its own survival. In Yemen, the state simply lacks the basic capacity to fight back. So the rule might simply be that in those places where a government lacks the desire, will, or capacity to fight jihadism, al-Qaeda can continue to thrive.

But the nature of the enemy is now quite different. It is not a movement capable of winning over the Arab street. Its political appeal does not make rulers tremble. The video messages of bin Laden and Zawahiri once unsettled moderate regimes. Now they are mostly dismissed as almost comical attempts to find popular causes to latch onto. (After the financial crash, bin Laden tried his hand at bashing greedy bankers.)

This is not an argument to relax our efforts to hunt down militants. Al-Qaeda remains a group of relentless, ruthless killers who are trying to recruit other fanatics to carry out hideous attacks that would do terrible damage to civilized society. But the group's aura is gone, its political influence limited. Its few remaining fighters are spread thinly throughout the world and face hostile environments almost everywhere.

America is no longer engaged in a civilizational struggle throughout the Muslim world, but a military and intelligence campaign in a set of discrete places. Now, that latter struggle might well require politics, diplomacy, and development assistance—in the manner that good foreign policy always does (Petraeus calls this a "whole-of-government strategy"). We have allies; we need to support them. But the target is only a handful of extremist organizations that have found a small group of fanatics to carry out their plans. To put it another way, even if the United States pursues a broad and successful effort at nation building in Afghanistan and Yemen, does anyone really think that will deter the next Nigerian misfit—or fanatic from Detroit—from getting on a plane with chemicals in his underwear? Such people cannot be won over. They cannot be reasoned with; they can only be captured or killed.

The enemy is not vast; the swamp is being drained. Al-Qaeda has already lost in the realm of ideology. What remains is the battle to defeat it in the nooks, crannies, and crevices of the real world.

Jihadism in 2010: The Threat Continues

For the past several years, STRATFOR has published an annual forecast on al-Qaeda and the jihadist movement. Since our first jihadist forecast in January 2006, we have focused heavily on the devolution of jihadism from a phenomenon primarily involving the core al-Qaeda group to one based mainly on the wider jihadist movement and the devolving, decentralized threat it poses.

The central theme of last year's forecast was that al-Qaeda was an important force on the ideological battlefield, but that the efforts of the United States and its allies had marginalized the group on the physical battlefield and kept it bottled up in a limited geographic area. Because of this, we forecast that the most significant threat in terms of physical attacks stemmed from regional jihadist franchises and grassroots operatives and not the al-Qaeda core. We also wrote that we believed the threat posed by such attacks would remain tactical and not rise to the level of a strategic threat. To reflect this reality, we even dropped al-Qaeda from the title of our annual forecast and simply named it jihadism in 2009: The Trends Continue.

The past year proved to be very busy in terms of attacks and thwarted plots emanating from jihadist actors. But, as forecast, the primary militants involved in carrying out these terrorist plots were almost exclusively from regional jihadist groups and grassroots operatives, and not militants dispatched by the al-Qaeda core. We anticipate that this dynamic will continue, and if anything, the trend will be for some regional franchise groups to become even more involved in transnational attacks, thus further usurping the position of al-Qaeda prime at the vanguard of jihadism on the physical battlefield.

A Note on "Al-Qaeda"

As a quick reminder, STRATFOR views what most people refer to as "al-Qaeda" as a global jihadist network rather than a monolithic entity. This network consists of three distinct entities. The first is a core vanguard organization, which we frequently refer to as al-Qaeda prime or the al-Qaeda core. The al-Qaeda core is comprised of Osama bin Laden and his small circle of close, trusted associates, such as Ayman al-Zawahiri. Due to intense pressure by the U.S.

From *STRATFOR Weekly Terrorism Intelligence Report*, January 6, 2010. Copyright © 2010 by STRATFOR. Reprinted by permission.

government and its allies, this core group has been reduced in size since 9/11 and remains relatively small because of operational security concerns. This insular group is laying low in Pakistan near the Afghan border and comprises only a small portion of the larger jihadist universe.

The second layer of the network is composed of local or regional terrorist or insurgent groups that have adopted jihadist ideology. Some of these groups have publicly claimed allegiance to bin Laden and the al-Qaeda core and become what we refer to as franchise groups, like al-Qaeda in the Islamic Maghreb (AQIM) or al-Qaeda in the Arabian Peninsula (AQAP). Other groups may adopt some or all of al-Qaeda's jihadist ideology and cooperate with the core group, but they will maintain their independence for a variety of reasons. Such groups include the Tehrik-i-Taliban Pakistan (TTP), Lashkar-e-Taiba (LeT) and Harkat-ul-Jihad e-Islami (HUJI). Indeed, in the case of some larger organizations such as LeT, some of the group's factions may actually oppose close cooperation with al-Qaeda.

The third and broadest layer of the network is the grassroots jihadist movement, that is, people inspired by the al-Qaeda core and the franchise groups but who may have little or no actual connection to these groups.

As we move down this hierarchy, we also move down in operational capability and expertise in what we call terrorist tradecraft—the set of skills required to conduct a terrorist attack. The operatives belonging to the al-Qaeda core are generally better trained than their regional counterparts, and both of these layers tend to be far better trained than the grassroots operatives. Indeed, many grassroots operatives travel to places like Pakistan and Yemen in order to seek training from these other groups.

The Internet has long proved to be an important tool for these groups to reach out to potential grassroots operatives. Jihadist chat rooms and Web sites provide indoctrination in jihadist ideology and also serve as a means for aspiring jihadists to make contact with like-minded individuals and even the jihadist groups themselves.

2009 Forecast Review

Overall, our 2009 forecast was fairly accurate. As noted above, we wrote that the United States would continue its operations to decapitate the al-Qaeda core and that this would cause the group to be marginalized from the physical jihad, and that has happened.

While we missed forecasting the resurgence of jihadist militant groups in Yemen and Somalia in 2008, in our 2009 forecast we covered these two countries carefully. We wrote that the al-Qaeda franchises in Yemen had taken a hit in 2008 but that they could recover in 2009 given the opportunity. Indeed, the groups received a significant boost when they merged into a single group that also incorporated the remnants of al-Qaeda in Saudi Arabia, which had been forced by Saudi security to flee the country. We closely followed this new group, which named itself al-Qaeda in the Arabian Peninsula (AQAP), and STRATFOR was the first organization we know of to discuss the threat AQAP posed to civil aviation when we raised this subject on Sept. 2 and elaborated on it Sept. 16, in an analysis titled Convergence: The Challenge of Aviation Security. That threat manifested itself in the attempt to destroy an airliner traveling from Amsterdam to Detroit on Christmas Day 2009—an operation that very nearly succeeded.

Regarding Somalia, we have also been closely following al Shabaab and the other jihadist groups there, such as Hizbul Islam. Al Shabaab publicly pledged allegiance to Osama bin Laden in September 2009 and therefore has formally joined the ranks of al-Qaeda's regional franchise groups. However, as we forecast last January, while the instability present in Somalia provides al Shabaab the opportunity to flourish, the factionalization of the country (including the jihadist groups operating there) has also served to keep al Shabaab from dominating the other actors and assuming control of the country.

We also forecast that, while Iraq had been relatively quiet in 2008, the level of violence there could surge in 2009 due to the Awakening Councils being taken off the U.S. payroll and having their control transferred to the Shiite-dominated Iraqi government, which might not pay them and integrate them into the armed forces. Indeed, since August, we have seen three waves of major coordinated attacks against Iraqi ministry buildings in Baghdad linked to the al-Qaeda affiliate in Iraq, the Islamic State of Iraq. Since this violence is tied to the political situation in Iraq, and there is a clear correlation between the funds being cut to the Awakening Councils and these attacks, we anticipate that this violence will continue through the parliamentary elections in March. The attacks could even continue after that, if the Sunni powers in Iraq deem that their interests are not being addressed appropriately.

As in 2008, we paid close attention in 2009 to the situation in Pakistan. This not only was because Pakistan is the home of the al-Qaeda core's leadership but also because of the threat that the TTP and the other jihadist groups in the country posed to the stability of the nuclear-armed state. As we watched Pakistan for signs that it was becoming a failed state, we noted that the government was actually making considerable headway in its fight against its jihadist insurgency. Indeed, by late in the year, the Pakistanis had launched not only a successful offensive in Swat and the adjacent districts but also an offensive into South Waziristan, the heart of the TTP's territory.

We also forecast that the bulk of the attacks worldwide in 2009 would be conducted by regional jihadist franchise groups and, to a lesser extent, grassroots jihadists, rather than the al-Qaeda core, which was correct.

In relation to attacks against the United States, we wrote that we did not see a strategic threat to the United States from the jihadists, but that the threat of simple attacks against soft targets remained in 2009. We said we had been surprised that there were no such attacks in 2008 but that, given the vulnerabilities that existed and the ease with which such attacks could be conducted, we believed they were certainly possible. During 2009, we did see simple attacks by grassroots operatives in Little Rock, Arkansas, and at Fort Hood, Texas, along with several other grassroots plots thwarted by authorities.

Forecast for 2010

In the coming year we believe that, globally, we will see many of the trends continue from last year. We believe that the al-Qaeda core will continue to be marginalized on the physical battlefield and struggle to remain relevant on the ideological battlefield. The regional jihadist franchise groups will continue to be at the vanguard of the physical battle, and the grassroots operatives will remain a persistent, though lower-level, threat.

One thing we noticed in recent months was that the regional groups were becoming more transnational in their attacks, with AQAP involved in the attack on Saudi Deputy Interior Minister Prince Mohammed bin Nayef in Saudi Arabia as well as the trans-Atlantic airliner bombing plot on Christmas Day. Additionally, we saw HUJI planning an attack against the Jyllands-Posten newspaper and cartoonist Kurt Westergaard in Denmark, and on Jan. 1, 2010, a Somali man reportedly associated with al Shabaab broke into Westergaard's home armed with an axe and knife and allegedly tried to kill him. We believe that in 2010 we will see more examples of regional groups like al Shabaab and AQAP reaching out to become more transnational, perhaps even conducting attacks in the United States and Europe.

We also believe that, due to the open nature of the U.S. and European societies and the ease of conducting attacks against them, we will see more grassroots plots, if not successful attacks, in the United States and Europe in the coming year. The concept behind AQAP leader Nasir al-Wahayshi's article calling for jihadists to conduct simple attacks against a variety of targets may be gaining popularity among grassroots jihadists. Certainly, the above-mentioned attack in Denmark involving an axe and knife was simple in nature. It could also have been deadly had the cartoonist not had a panic room within his residence. We will be watching for more simple attacks.

As far as targets, we believe that they will remain largely the same for 2010. Soft targets such as hotels will continue to be popular, since most jihadists lack the ability to attack hard targets outside of conflict zones. However, jihadists have demonstrated a continuing fixation on attacking commercial aviation targets, and we can anticipate additional plots and attacks focusing on aircraft.

Regionally, we will be watching for the following:

- **Pakistan:** Can the United States find and kill the al-Qaeda core's leadership? A Pakistani official told the Chinese Xinhua news agency on Jan. 4 that terrorism will come to an end in Pakistan in 2010, but we are not nearly so optimistic. Even though the military has made good progress in its South Waziristan offensive, most of the militants moved to other areas of Pakistan rather than engage in frontal combat with Pakistan's army. The area along the border with Pakistan is rugged and has proved hard to pacify for hundreds of years. We don't think the Pakistanis will be able to bring the area under control in only one year. Clearly, the Pakistanis have made progress, but they are not out of the woods. The TTP has launched a number of attacks in the Punjabi core of Pakistan (and in Karachi) and we see no end to this violence in 2010.

- **Afghanistan:** We will continue to closely monitor jihadist actors in this war-torn country. Our forecast for this conflict is included in our Annual Forecast 2010, published on Jan. 4.
- **Yemen:** We will be watching closely to see if AQAP will follow the normal jihadist group lifespan of making a big splash, coming to the notice of the world and then being hit heavily by the host government with U.S. support. This pattern was exhibited a few years back by AQAP's Saudi al-Qaeda brethren, and judging by the operations in Yemen over the past month, it looks like 2010 might be a tough year for the group. It is important to note that the strikes against the group on Dec. 17 and Dec. 24 predated the Christmas bombing attempt, and the pressure on them will undoubtedly be ratcheted up considerably in the wake of that attack. Even as the memory of the Christmas Day attack begins to fade in the media and political circles, the focus on Yemen will continue in the counterterrorism community.
- **Indonesia:** Can Tanzim Qaedat al-Jihad find an effective leader to guide it back from the edge of destruction after the death of Noordin Mohammad Top and the deaths or captures of several of his top lieutenants? Or will the Indonesians be able to enjoy further success against the group's surviving members?
- **North Africa:** Will AQIM continue to shy away from the al-Qaeda core's targeting philosophy and essentially function as the Salafist Group for Preaching and Combat with a different name in Algeria? Or will AQIM shift back toward al-Qaeda's philosophy of attacking the far enemy and using suicide bombers and large vehicle bombs? In Mauritania, Niger and Mali, will the AQIM-affiliated cells there be able to progress beyond amateurish attacks and petty banditry to become a credible militant organization?
- **Somalia:** We believe the factionalism in Somalia and within the jihadist community there will continue to hamper al Shabaab. The questions we will be looking to answer are: Will al Shabaab be able to gain significant control of areas of the country that can be used to harbor and train foreign militants? And, will the group decide to use its contacts within the Somali diaspora to conduct attacks in East Africa, South Africa, Australia, Europe and the United States? We believe that al Shabaab is on its way to becoming a transnational player and that 2010 may well be the year that it breaks out and then draws international attention like AQAP has done in recent months.
- **India:** We anticipate that Kashmiri jihadist groups will continue to plan attacks against India in an effort to stir-up communal violence in that country and stoke tensions between India and Pakistan—and provide a breather to the jihadist groups being pressured by the government of Pakistan.

As long as the ideology of jihadism survives, the jihadists will be able to recruit new militants and their war against the world will continue. The battle will oscillate between periods of high and low intensity as regional groups rise in power and are taken down. We don't believe jihadists pose a strategic geopolitical threat on a global, or even regional, scale, but they will certainly continue to launch attacks and kill people in 2010.

POSTSCRIPT

Has Al-Qaeda and Its Jihad against the United States Been Defeated?

There is a revolution in the Muslim world. It has been developing and evolving throughout most of the twentieth century. In the wake of World War I and British and French colonialism, Islamic fundamentalist thought grew in Egypt among what would become the Muslim Brotherhood and it spread throughout the Arab world and then into non-Arab Islam. The genesis of this thought was the need for the Islamic world to rediscover its roots, reject much of the influences of non-Muslim peoples and places, and develop conceptions of governance fused with Islam and not separate from it.

The forms that this movement has taken among both Shiite and Sunni Muslims have been numerous. The most dramatic examples of its success are of course in Iran, Afghanistan under the Taliban, Algeria, and in other places. As this movement has encountered resistance from secular Muslim regimes, kingdoms, and authoritarian dictatorships, and from the West, it has increasingly seen itself as downtrodden, thwarted, and under attack. These feelings and beliefs have led to its further radicalization and the growing adoption of terrorism as its weapon of resistance.

Thus, the war between the United States and al-Qaeda, between the West and fundamentalist Islam, has a long genesis. Its most recent phase in the post-9/11 period has been marked by violence and war across several states in south Asia and the Middle East, Europe, and here in the United States.

Consequently, it is difficult to divorce the rise of extreme fundamentalist thought in the Muslim world from violence against those that it believes opposes it. The fundamentalist revolution in the Muslim world must run its course principally among Muslims. In that sense Zakaria is right. Only Muslims can defeat Muslims in the greater battle for the hearts and minds of Muslim thought. Whether that battle is military, political, socioeconomic, or philosophical, that is where the ultimate success of al-Qaeda will be determined.

Whether jihad has been defeated by the United States and the West is more than likely an open question. Ups and downs in that battle will likely continue as long as extreme fundamentalism has a voice and converts those who see the United States as the primary enemy to their interests and ambitions. Religious extremism and zealotry are and have been parts of every great faith. How they are dealt with is usually determined not by those who believe in something different but by those who believe in the same things.

Overall, issues of economic development, political enfranchisement, and the Israeli–Palestinian relations will determine the long-term prospects of jihadism and radical fundamentalism in the Muslim world.

Contributors to This Volume

EDITORS

JAMES E. HARF currently serves as professor of political science as well as associate vice president and director of the Center for Global Education at Maryville University in St. Louis. He spent most of his career at The Ohio State University, where he holds the title of professor emeritus. He is coeditor of *The Unfolding Legacy of 9/11* (University Press of America, 2004) and coauthor of *World Politics and You: A Student Companion to International Politics on the World Stage, 5th ed.* (Brown & Benchmark, 1995) and *The Politics of Global Resources* (Duke University Press, 1986). His first novel, *Memories of Ivy* (Ivy House Publishing Group, 2005), about life as a university professor, was published in 2005. He also coedited a four-book series on the global issues of population, food, energy, and environment, as well as three other book series on national security education, international studies, and international business. His current research interests include tools for addressing international conflict and student strategies for maximizing study abroad experiences. As a staff member on the Presidential Commission on Foreign Language and International Studies in the late 1970s, he was responsible for undergraduate education recommendations. He also served 15 years as executive director of the Consortium for International Studies Education. He is a frequent radio commentator on international issues.

MARK OWEN LOMBARDI is the president and chief executive officer of Maryville University in St. Louis, Missouri. He is the coeditor and author of *The Unfolding Legacy of 9/11* (University Press of America, 2004) and the coeditor of *Perspectives of Third-World Sovereignty: The Postmodern Paradox* (Macmillan, 1996). Dr. Lombardi has authored numerous articles and book chapters on such topics as U.S. foreign policy, African political economy, the politics of the Cold War, and curriculum reform at colleges and universities. Dr. Lombardi is a member of numerous civic organizations and boards locally and nationally, and he has given over 200 speeches to local and national groups on topics ranging from higher education reform to U.S. Politics, international affairs, and U.S. foreign policy. He is also a frequent contributor to local news programs speaking on national and international issues.

AUTHORS

DIVYA ABHAT is a science and environment reporter, specializing in wildlife issues in North America and the rest of the world. Originally from Mumbai, India, Abhat came to the United States for a graduate degree in journalism from the University of Missouri-Columbia and focused on international reporting and science, health, and environmental journalism.

GRAHAM ALLISON is Douglas Dillon Professor of Government at the John F. Kennedy School of Government at Harvard University and director of the Belfer Center for Science and International Affairs.

RONALD BAILEY is science correspondent for *Reason* magazine and author of *ECOSCAM: The False Prophets of Ecological Apocalypse.*

PRANAB BARDHAN is a professor of economics at the University of California, Berkeley.

NAAZNEEN BARMA, MATTHEW KROENIG, AND ELY RATNER are Ph.D. candidates at the University of California, Berkeley.

DAVID BIELLO is associate editor for *Scientific American.*

LESTER R. BROWN is founder and president of Earth Policy Institute. He is described by *The Washington Post* as "one of the most influential thinkers" and is the author of numerous books on environmental issues.

JANIE CHUANG is an international legal expert, is a practitioner-in-residence in the International Human Rights Clinic and serves as assistant professor of law at American University Washington College of Law.

MARK CLAYTON is a staff writer for *The Christian Science Monitor.*

STEPHEN F. COHEN is a professor of Russian studies at New York University.

TYLER COWEN is a professor of economics at George Mason University and is associated with the Center for the Study of Public Choice.

SHAUNA DINEEN is Foster Care Coordinator and Animal Care and Adoption Counselor at MSPCA. Formerly, she served as Administrative and Programs Assistant at The New England Antivivisection Society and was Editorial and Public Relations Intern at E/The Environmental Magazine.

PETE ENGARDIO is a senior writer for *BusinessWeek* and coauthor of *Meltdown: Asia's Boom, Bust, and Beyond* in 2004. He joined *BusinessWeek* in 1985.

H.T. GORANSON is the lead scientist for Earl Research and was senior scientist with the United States Defense Advanced Research Projects Agency.

DINA FRANCESCA HAYNES is an associate professor of law at the New England School of Law. She has published in the areas of international law, immigration law, human rights law, and human trafficking.

SUZANNE HOPPOUGH was until recently a reporter for *Forbes* magazine.

KATSUHITO IWAI is professor of economics at the University of Tokyo.

BRIAN MICHAEL JENKINS is senior advisor to the President of the Rand Corporation and Director of the Mineta Transportation Institute's Transportation Center.

TAMSYN JONES is a multi-talented writer and reporter and with experience and interest in agriculture, environment, science and explanatory writing. Her writing range from magazine and hard news stories to fact sheets and PR pieces.

STEPHEN KOTKIN is professor of history and director of the Program in Russian Studies at Princeton University.

STEPHEN LENDMAN is a research associate of the Centre for Research on Globalization, based in Montreal, Canada.

RICHARD S. LINDZEN is the Alfred P. Sloan professor of meteorology in the Department of Earth, Atmosphere, and Planetary Sciences at MIT.

BJØRN LOMBORG author of *The Skeptical Environmentalist,* director of the Copenhagen Consensus Center, and adjunct professor at the Copenhagen Business School.

MIA MacDONALD is a senior fellow at the Worldwatch Institute.

CAROL MATLACK is *BusinessWeek's* Paris bureau chief, after serving previously as Paris correspondent. Prior to Paris, she worked as a freelancer for *BusinessWeek* in Moscow.

ROBYN MEREDITH is the senior editor for *Forbes* magazine in Asia.

MICHAEL MEYER formerly of *Newsweek International,* is director of Communications and Speechwriting for the United Nations Secretary-General, Ban Ki-Moon.

STEVEN W. MOSHER is president of the Population Research Institute.

JIM MOTAVILLI is a freelance journalist, book author, and radio personality on environmental issues. He previously spent 14 years as editor of *E/The Environmental Magazine.*

ETHAN NADELMANN is founder and executive director of the Drug Policy Alliance, the leading U.S. organization promoting alternatives to the war on drugs.

DANIELLE NIERENBERG is senior fellow at the Worldwatch Institute.

DAVID PIMENTEL is professor emeritus of entomology, ecology, and systematics at Cornell University. He is author of almost 500 scientific papers and 20 books.

TERRY M. REDDING is a communications consultant.

DANI RODRIK is professor of international political economy at the John F. Kennedy School of Government, Harvard University.

DAVID ROTHKOPF is president and CEO of Garten Rothkopf, an international advisory firm specializing in emerging markets investing and risk management related services. Previously, he served as deputy under secretary of commerce for international trade in the Clinton Administration.

NANSEN G. SALERI is president and CEO of Quantum Reservoir Input, and the oil industry's preeminent authority on reservoir management and upstream technologies.

HUSSEIN SOLOMON is a lecturer at the University of Pretoria and the director of the Centre of International Political Studies.

ALLAN BRIAN SSENYONGA is a Ugandan freelance writer based in Rwanda.

SCOTT STEWART is affiliated with STRATFOR, an organization that delivers intelligence and perspective to the public through situation reports, analysis, and multimedia. Stewart provides reports that assess world events and their significance.

SHIBLEY TELHAMI is the Anwar Sadat Professor for peace and development, University of Maryland, and nonresident senior fellow at Saban Center, Brookings Institute.

STEVEN WEBER is a professor of political science and the director of the Institute of International Studies at the University of California, Berkeley.

BEN WILSON writes as a critic for *The New Yorker.*

SHUJIE YAO is a professor of economics and Chinese sustainable development at the China Policy Institute, University of Nottingham.

FAREED ZAKARIA is editor of Newsweek International, a Newsweek and Washington Post columnist, weekly host for CNN, and a New York Times bestselling author. He was described in 1999 by Esquire Magazine as "the most influential foreign policy adviser of his generation" and in 2007, Foreign Policy and Prospect magazines named him one of the 100 leading public intellectuals in the world.